THE BIG BOOK OF
BAKING

THE BIG BOOK OF BAKING was conceived, edited, and designed
by McRae Books, Florence, Italy
Borgo Santa Croce, 8 - 50122 Florence (Italy)
Publishers: Anne McRae and Marco Nardi
info@mcraebooks.com

Project editor: Anne McRae
Text: Carla Bardi
Editing: Helen Farrow
Photography: Walter Mericchi, Keeho Casati, Stefano Pratesi, Stefania Talini,
Leonardo Pasquinelli
Home Economist: Benedetto Rillo
Art Buying: Arianna Capellini, Francesco Piccardi
Graphic Design: Marco Nardi
Layout: Marco Nardi

The publishers would like to thank Bellini Più, Montespertoli (Florence), Ceramiche
il Pozzo, Montespertoli (Florence), Ceramiche Virginia, Montespertoli (Florence),
Cive Vetreria in Toscana.Coop S.r.l, Empoli (Florence), Il Nodo Ceramiche
Montelupo f.no (Florence), Ceramiche Toscane, Montelupo f.no (Florence),
Vetreria Lux, Montelupo f.no (Florence), Ceramiche Nicola Fasano, Grottaglie
(Puglia), Decortex Tessuti, Calenzano (Prato), Ceramiche d'Arte, Milan

Color separations: Fotolito RAF, Florence and Studio Leonardo, Florence

ISBN 88-89272-53-8

Printed and bound in China

THE BIG BOOK OF
BAKING

Carla Bardi

McRae Books

Contents

Introduction

Easy citrus cake, p. 96

Successful home baking is one of life's simple pleasures. With a minimum of effort and skill you can fill your home with the delectable aromas of freshly baked cakes, cookies, and breads and delight your friends and family with mouth-watering gifts while you bask in their pleasure and praise. With more than 700 classic recipes, The Big Book of Baking *is unique both for the huge number and range of recipes offered as well as for the clarity and ease with which they are explained. With every recipe rated either 1 (simple), 2 (fairly simple), or 3 (complicated), home bakers at every level will find recipes they can be sure of alongside others that will challenge their culinary skills. To help novice bakers, the book begins with a section featuring hints and tips for successful baking and a very visual look at basic ingredients and utensils. This is followed by a large section on cakes with recipes for everything from simple tea cakes to healthy fruit and vegetable cakes, to elaborate sponges, gateaux, and meringues, to fabulous tarts and pies. The next section features small cakes, muffins, cookies, bars, and brownies. The final section focuses on breads and savory baking, with superb recipes for snacks, pizza, focaccia, quiches, and bread. A cornerstone in your cooking library, this is the only book of baking you will ever need—Enjoy!*

Black forest cherry cake, p. 218

Jamaican coconut crisps, p. 604

Braided herb loaf, p. 738

The Secrets of Successful Baking

All the recipes in this book have been graded into three categories: 1 (Simple), 2 (Medium), and 3 (Complicated). Most recipes fall into the first or second categories, with just a few complicated ones for when you feel like a challenge. So, before you begin any of the recipes, take a look at the *"Serves"* line at the top of the method, which not only tells you how difficult the recipe will be, but also provides information on yield and cooking and preparation times. Then read the entire recipe through to make sure you have all the ingredients and equipment required to complete the dish with success.

INGREDIENTS

FLOUR: Generally speaking, cakes, cookies, and pastries are best made with soft wheat flour, which is lower in protein-forming gluten, while breads, focaccia, and pizza—or any baked product that requires extensive kneading—are better made with hard wheat flour which has a much richer store of gluten. That said, almost all the recipes in this book can be made with all-purpose (plain) flour, which is a mixture of hard and soft wheat flour. Where another flour is required it has been specified in the ingredients list.

CORNSTARCH (CORNFLOUR): This fine powdery flour is made from corn and is used to lighten and improve texture in baked goods.

EGGS: Eggs add flavor, color, texture, and nutritional value to baked goods. The recipes in this book have been tested using large eggs, which means each one should weigh about 2 ounces (60 g) in the shell. Always allow your eggs to come to room temperature before using them to bake. If you wish to bake something quickly, place refrigerator-cold eggs in a bowl of warm water for about 15 minutes before use. Many recipes called for stiffly beaten egg whites to help leaven the baked goods. Always use eggs that are more than 3–4 days old for whipping, as they will beat to the greatest volume and leaven your cake more effectively.

SUGAR: Not only does sugar add sweetness to cakes and cookies, it also contributes smooth texture (when beaten) and good color. Where not otherwise stated, all the recipes in this book can be made using ordinary white granulated sugar.

CONFECTIONERS' (ICING) SUGAR: This is very finely ground granulated sugar which is mainly used to make frostings and glazes. It can also be added to cake or cookie batters that need to be dense and silky.

BROWN SUGAR: Brown sugar comes in various shades, from dark to light brown, depending on how much of the molasses has been removed during the refinement process. Brown sugar can be heavy so it is not suitable for light or foam cakes. However, it does have much more flavor than refined white sugar and adds a lovely nutty taste to more substantial cakes and cookies. Generally speaking, the darker the color of the sugar, the richer it will be in flavor. Brown sugar is ideal as a topping, and is the basic ingredient in most streusels. It is no less sweet than white sugar, but when measuring by volume (into spoons or cups), always make sure it is firmly packed.

SALT: Adding small quantities of salt to sweet baked goods such as cakes and cookies heightens the flavor of the finished product. For this reason we have added tiny amounts to many of the recipes; if preferred, the salt can be left out. It may also depend on whether you are using salted or unsalted butter.

FAT: This is a generic term for butter, margarine, shortening, and vegetable oils. We have used butter almost exclusively because we believe that, all things considered, it is a healthier and better-tasting choice than many of the industrially prepared products available today. Once again, this is a matter of personal preference and the recipes will work equally well using the same quantities of margarine or solid vegetable shortenings. Unless otherwise stated in the recipe, always use butter or other solid fats at room temperature. When using vegetable oils for sweet baked goods, in most cases it is best to choose an oil that is neutral in flavor, such as safflower, sunflower, or peanut oil.

BAKING POWDER: This is a chemical raising agent added to many cake and cookie batters. Adding too much baking powder to cake batters will make them rise very quickly in the oven only to collapse soon afterward. Stick to the quantities given in the recipes for best results.

BAKING SODA (BICARBONATE OF SODA): This is another common raising agent. Because it is an alkaline substance, it is often added to cake or cookie batters that have acid ingredients such as sour cream or yogurt. baking soda can also help to deepen the color of baked goods.

YEAST: For the recipes in the breads, focaccia, and pizza section of this book we have generally recommended either fresh yeast (sold in compressed cakes) or active dry yeast (sold in envelopes weighing a quarter ounce (7 g), or about 1 tablespoon).

EQUIPMENT

ELECTRIC MIXERS: Nowadays most home kitchens are equipped with a mixer of some sort with which to prepare cake and cookie batters. Many also have attachments that can be used to "knead" bread or pizza dough.

FOOD PROCESSORS AND BLENDERS: These machines have a wide range of uses and we have assumed that your kitchen will contain one or the other.

CAKE PANS: All of the recipes in this book have been tested in a specific pan. The pan size is included in all recipes; for perfect results you should use the suggested pan size, or something very close to it. Springform pans are ideal for cheesecakes or other cakes that have to be unmolded.

MIXING BOWLS: You will need a range of different sized bowls, from small to large. Stainless-steel or ceramic bowls are a better choice than plastic, which can retain flavors from previous uses—you wouldn't want your delicate sponge cake to pick up traces of garlic, for example, if you have used the same bowl on other occasions to prepare a tasty herb omelet.

MEASURING CUPS AND SPOONS: You will need one cup for measuring liquids, and a set of cups and spoons for measuring volume.

COOLING RACKS: You will need wire racks for your baked goods to cool on after they are removed from the oven.

SPATULAS: You will need both rubber and metal spatulas, for mixing, folding, and spreading tasks.

TESTING DEVICES: throughout the cake section of this book we have suggested that you insert a toothpick into the center of a cake. If it comes out dry, the cake is done. You can also use the special metal cake testing needles sold in baking stores.

SIFTERS: Flour should be sifted before use. For volume measurements in this book we have assumed that you will measure the flour first and then sift it into a bowl.

OVENS: Ovens can be either electric or gas; both are equally good. The most important thing when baking is that the oven heats evenly throughout. Convection ovens, which blow hot air around inside, are good for baking. However, if using a convection oven remember that it will be slightly hotter than an ordinary oven so reduce the temperature by about 50°F (25°C). It will reduce the baking time by about 20 percent. Whatever the oven you are using, always turn it on about 15 minutes before you intend to place the baked goods inside.

Basic Ingredients

Most baked products are based on various combinations of flour, fat, a liquid, and, in the case of cakes and cookies, sugar and usually eggs. Many also include some kind of raising agent, whether of the quick-acting type, such as baking powder or baking soda, or the slower types of yeast which require time to rise or "proof."

FLOUR
Almost all the recipes in this book can be made using all-purpose (plain) flour. Some recipes call for whole-wheat (wholemeal), rye, rice, or polenta (finely ground maize/corn) flours. Rice flour is often a good substitute for those with wheat or gluten intolerance.

ALL-PURPOSE FLOUR

CORNSTARCH

CORNSTARCH (CORNFLOUR)
Silky cornstarch is often used as a thickener for soups, stews, and sauces. When added to baked goods it adds lightness and smoothness to the finished products.

BUTTER

VEGETABLE OIL

LARD

MILK

FATS
Most baked goods are made using butter or another fat such as margarine, vegetable oil, shortening, or lard. Butter provides the best flavor and texture. Margarine has less flavor although it usually contains no cholesterol and may be chosen for that reason. Lard, or rendered pork fat, is not as common in baking as it used to be but is still perhaps the best fat to make the perfect flaky pie crust.

CREAM

LIQUIDS
Milk and cream are among the most common liquids used in baking. All recipes calling for milk or cream in this book should be made with homogenized milk or heavy (double) cream unless otherwise stated.

EGGS
Eggs are an important ingredient in most cookie and cake recipes. They are less common in savory baked dishes, such as pizza or bread. All the recipes in this book should be made using large (2 oz/60g) eggs.

BROWN SUGAR

CONFECTIONERS'
(ICING) SUGAR

SUGAR

Sugar adds sweetness to cakes and cookies as well as improving texture and color. Unless otherwise stated, the recipes in this book make use of ordinary granulated sugar. Many recipes also call for brown sugar, confectioners' sugar, honey, molasses, or maple syrup.

GRANULATED SUGAR

ACTIVE DRY
YEAST

HONEY

RAISING AGENTS

Baking powder and baking soda (also known as bicarbonate of soda) are both finely ground powders that are added to cakes and cookies along with the flour. Fresh compressed or active dry yeasts are mainly used to make bread products, including pizza and focaccia. They act more slowly and required extended periods to rise or leaven before baking.

FRESH COMPRESSED YEAST

YOGURT / SOUR CREAM

Yogurt and sour cream add acidity to cake batter. They also add their own distinctive flavors to fillings and frostings.

YOGURT

CREAM CHEESE

Cream cheese is the basic ingredient in most cheesecakes. For perfect results always use top quality cream cheese an bring it to room temperature before use.

RICOTTA CHEESE

CREAM CHEESE

RICOTTA CHEESE

Fresh Ricotta cheese is often used in cheesecakes. It lends them a delicious soft and slightly granular texture.

Dried Fruit, Nuts, Spices, and Aromas

These are the ingredients that add special flavor and texture to cakes, cookies, tarts, pies, muffins, and many types of bread. They include well-known spices such as nutmeg, cloves, ginger, and cinnamon, and all the various types of dried fruit and nuts, from raisins and dried figs to walnuts, hazelnuts, pecans, and almonds. The most commonly used aromas are coffee, chocolate, cocoa, liqueur, and extracts, such as vanilla and almond.

CANDIED PINEAPPLE

CANDIED FRUIT

GOLDEN RAISINS
(SULTANAS)

DRIED AND CANDIED FRUIT
Traditional cakes and cookies are often flavored with mixed candied fruit, dried apricots, raisins, and golden raisins. Nowadays exotic dried and/or candied fruit, such as pineapple, mango, and papaya, as well as candied ginger root are common and easily obtainable ingredients.

CANDIED PAPAYA

CANDIED GINGER

DRIED APRICOTS

CANDIED MANGO

SPICES
Most spices are derived from the roots, seeds, bark, flowers, or fruit of plants. They can be fairly potent when fresh and in baking are usually used in small amounts to add zing and flavor. Many spices come from tropical zones; take care when buying them to ensure that they are fresh and store them in sealed containers. Always try to acquire them as whole as possible and grind or crush them just before use.

NUTMEG

FENNEL SEEDS

CLOVES

CINNAMON STICKS

GROUND GINGER

WALNUTS

HAZELNUTS

ALMONDS

NUTS

Nuts add texture and smooth, rich flavor to cakes and cookies. They are best in season, and should always be bought whole, in their shells. Some nuts, such as almonds, have fine inner skins which should be removed before use. To remove these, blanch the shelled nuts in boiling water for 5 minutes, then drain and rub dry in a clean cloth. The skins will come away easily. Where recipes called for ground nuts, place them in a food processor with 2 tablespoons of sugar (this will absorb the oil). Do not over process or they will turn into an oily paste.

BRAZIL NUTS

PINE NUTS

ROOT GINGER

CHESTNUTS

COCONUT

COCOA

VANILLA EXTRACT

CHOCOLATE

COFFEE

LIQUEUR

Fresh Fruit and Vegetables

Eye-catching fresh fruit is often used to decorate cakes and desserts. But fruit and vegetables can also be basic ingredients in a whole range of cakes, cookies, muffins, quiches, pizzas, and bread. In this book we have included some delicious recipes for cakes based on carrots, zucchinis, potatoes, and even beets. We have a savory cheesecake made with cherry tomatoes, and a good selection of focaccia, pizza, and breads that feature tomatoes, zucchini flowers and a host of other fresh fruits and vegetables.

ZUCCHINI (COURGETTES)

ZUCCHINI (COURGETTE) FLOWERS

CARROTS

PUMPKIN

TOMATOES

POTATOES

PEARS

APPLES

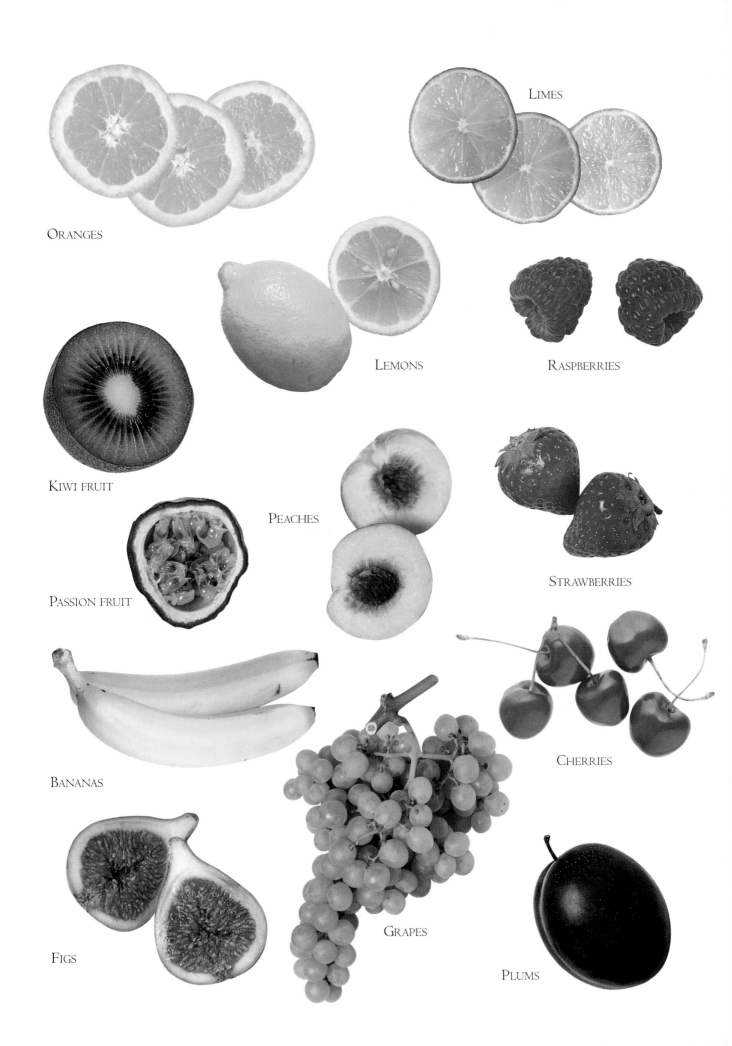

ORANGES

LIMES

LEMONS

RASPBERRIES

KIWI FRUIT

PASSION FRUIT

PEACHES

STRAWBERRIES

BANANAS

CHERRIES

FIGS

GRAPES

PLUMS

Baking Equipment

The sheer range of high quality cooking equipment now available has made home baking both easier and more fun. Well-stocked kitchen supply stores can be found in towns and cities across the country, and mail order catalogs can supply more remote areas. To create the dishes in this book you won't need a lot of expensive or complicated equipment; most recipes call for very basic utensils, such as mixing bowls, spoons, scales, measuring spoons and cups, beating or mixing equipment (electric or manual, as preferred), baking pans or sheets, and, of course, an oven. Throughout the book we have given baking temperatures in fahrenheit, celsius, and for gas ovens. Always remember to turn your oven on 15 to 20 minutes before you intend to start baking.

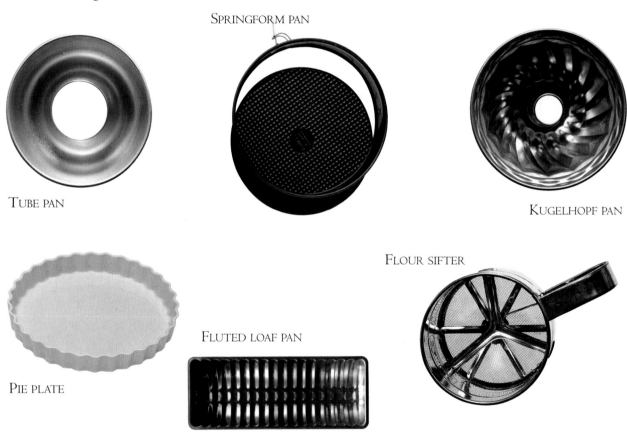

SPRINGFORM PAN

TUBE PAN

KUGELHOPF PAN

FLOUR SIFTER

PIE PLATE

FLUTED LOAF PAN

PIZZA AND
FOCACCIA PANS

BAKING SHEET

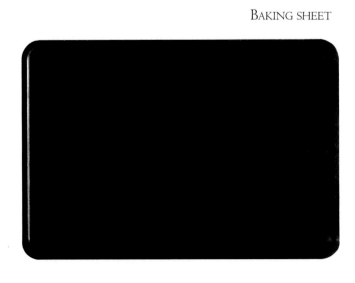

CAKE SLICE

APPLE CORER

ICE CREAM SCOOP

CANNOLI MOLDS

PASTRY BRUSH

WHISK

WOODEN SPOON

BABÀ MOLDS

SAUCEPAN

RUBBER SPATULA

SCALES

COOKIE CUTTERS

FOOD PROCESSOR

ICE CREAM MAKER

PASTRY BAG

PARCHMENT PAPER

BAKING STONE

HAND BEATER

ROLLING PIN

PIZZA CUTTER

HANDHELD ELECTRIC MIXER

Shortcrust pastry

Shortcrust pastry is not hard to make, although inexperienced bakers should take care not to knead the dough for too long.

Makes: pastry for a 10-12-inch (25-30-cm) pie pan; Preparation: 10 minutes + 15 minutes to chill; Level of difficulty: 1

Hand Method: Sift the flour and salt into a large bowl. • Make a well in the center and add the butter, egg, egg yolk, and 1 tablespoon of water. Cut with a pastry blender until well mixed. The dough should be coarse and granular, but moist enough to stick together. Add the remaining water if it is too dry. • Place the dough on a lightly floured work surface and sprinkle with a little flour. Knead briefly by pushing the dough away from you using the heel of your hand. Fold back and repeat three or four times, or until the dough is smooth and does not stick to the work surface. Do not knead the dough too long or it will become tough and shrink during baking. • Shape into a disk, wrap in plastic wrap (cling film), and refrigerate for 15 minutes. Food Processor Method: Place the flour, salt, butter, egg, egg yolk, and 1 tablespoon of water in a food processor and pulse with a metal blade for about 25 seconds, or until just amalgamated. • Shape into a flat disk, wrap in plastic wrap (cling film), and refrigerate for 15 minutes.

■ INGREDIENTS

- 2 cups (300 g) all-purpose (plain) flour
- ¼ teaspoon salt
- ½ cup (125 g) butter, cut up
- 1 large egg + 1 large egg yolk
- about 2 tablespoons cold water

Sweet shortcrust pastry

The method for Sweet shortcrust pastry is the same as the recipe above.

Makes: pastry for a 10-12-inch (25-30-cm) pie pan; Preparation: 10 minutes + 15 minutes to chill; Level of difficulty: 1

Hand Method and Food Processor Method: Proceed as in the recipe above for both versions; just add the sugar along with the flour.

■ INGREDIENTS

- 2 cups (300 g) all-purpose (plain) flour
- ¼ teaspoon salt
- ¼ cup (50 g) sugar
- ½ cup (125 g) butter, cut up
- 1 large egg + 1 large egg yolk
- about 2 tablespoons cold water

Never-fail quiche crust

Makes: pastry for a 10-12-inch (25-30-cm) pie pan; Preparation: 10 minutes + 30 minutes to chill; Level of difficulty: 1

Sift the flour and salt into the bowl of a food processor with a metal blade. Add the butter and 2 tablespoons of water. Pulse until just amalgamated, adding more water if too crumbly. • Remove from the processor and press into a ball. • Wrap in plastic wrap (cling film) and refrigerate for 30 minutes.

■ INGREDIENTS

- 1⅔ cups (250 g) all-purpose (plain) flour
- ¼ teaspoon salt
- ½ cup (125 g) butter, cut up
- 2–4 tablespoons cold water

Right: *Shortcrust pastry*

Puff pastry

Puff pastry can be bought in easy-to-use frozen sheets and thawed before use for all the recipes in this book. However, it can also be fun to make your own.

Makes: about 2 lb (1 kg) pastry; Preparation: 30 minutes + 1 hour to rest; Level of difficulty: 3

Sift the flour and salt into a large bowl. Make a well in the center and pour half the water into it. Use your hands to mix the ingredients until the dough is about the same consistency as the softened butter. Adjust the dough to achieve the required consistency by adding flour or water. • Roll the dough into a ball, wrap in plastic wrap (cling film) and set aside for 30 minutes. • Use a rolling pin to roll the dough out on a floured work surface into a square shape until about ½ inch (1 cm) thick. • Cut the softened butter in pieces and place them at the center of the square. Fold the 4 sides of the square so that the butter is completely sealed in, and roll the dough out in a rectangular shape about ½ inch (1 cm) thick. • Fold the rectangle in 3, turn the folded dough, and roll it out again. Fold it again and let stand for about 10 minutes. • Repeat this operation 3 times, letting the dough rest each time for 10 minutes. • Roll out to ½ inch (1 cm) thickness and use as indicated.

■ INGREDIENTS

- 3 cups (450 g) all-purpose (plain) flour
- ½ teaspoon salt
- about 1 cup (250 ml) water
- 1 cup (250 g) butter

Choux pastry

Makes: about 1½ lb (750 g); Preparation: 15 minutes; Level of difficulty: 3

Line a baking sheet with parchment paper. • Place the water, butter, sugar, and salt in a large pan over medium-low heat. When the mixture boils, remove from the heat and add the flour all at once. Use a wooden spoon to stir vigorously until a smooth paste forms. • Return to medium heat and stir constantly until the mixture pulls away from the pan sides. Remove from the heat and let cool for 5 minutes. • Add five eggs, beating one at a time, until just blended after each addition. The batter should be shiny and stiff enough to hold its shape if dropped onto a baking sheet. Add another egg if required.

■ INGREDIENTS

- 2 cups (500 ml) water
- ⅔ cup (180 g) butter, cut up
- 1 tablespoon sugar
- ¼ teaspoon salt
- 1⅔ cups (250 g) all-purpose (plain) flour
- 5–6 large eggs

Right: Puff pastry

Strudel pastry

Makes: dough for one strudel; Preparation: 20 minutes + 25 minutes to rest; Level of difficulty: 1
Melt the butter in the water in a saucepan over medium heat. • Sift the flour and salt into a large bowl and make a well in the center. Mix in the egg and the butter mixture. The dough should be soft enough to knead, but not sticky. Add more flour or water as needed. • Knead the dough on a lightly floured surface until smooth and elastic, about 5–7 minutes. • Shape into a ball, wrap in plastic wrap (cling film), and let rest in a warm place for 25 minutes.

■ INGREDIENTS

• 4 tablespoons butter
• ½ cup (125 ml) warm water + more as needed
• 1⅔ cups (250 g) all-purpose (plain) flour + more as needed
• ⅛ teaspoon salt
• 1 large egg, lightly beaten

Basic bread dough

*The method for making dough for pizza, focaccia, or bread is basically the same.
For the recipes in this book, use the quantities given here.*

Makes: enough dough for a 12-inch (30-cm) pizza or focaccia, or about 1 lb (500 g) of bread dough; Preparation: 30 minutes; Rising time: 1 hour 30 minutes; Level of difficulty: 1
Place the yeast in a small bowl. Add the sugar and half the warm water and stir until dissolved. • Set aside for 15 minutes. It will look creamy when ready. Stir well. • Place the flour in a large bowl and sprinkle with the salt. • Make a hollow in the center and pour in the yeast mixture and remaining water. Stir until the flour has been absorbed. • Kneading: Sprinkle a work surface, preferably made of wood, with a little flour. • Place the dough on the work surface. Curl your fingers around it and press together to form a compact ball. • Press down on the dough with your knuckles to spread it a little. Take the far end of the dough, fold it a short distance toward you, then push it away again with the heel of your palm. Flexing your wrist, fold it toward you again, give it a quarter turn, then push it away. Repeat, gently and with the lightest possible touch, for 8–10 minutes. When the dough is firm and no longer sticks to your hands or the work surface, lift it up and bang it down hard against the work surface a couple of times. This will develop the gluten. The dough should be smooth and elastic, show definite air bubbles beneath the surface, and spring back if you flatten it with your palm. • Place in a large, lightly oiled bowl and cover with a cloth. Set aside to rise. The dough should double in volume. This will take about 1 hour 30 minutes. • To test if ready, poke your finger gently into the dough; if the impression remains, then it is ready. Remember that yeast is a living ingredient, affected by temperature and humidity, among other things. Some days it will take longer to rise than others.

■ INGREDIENTS

BASIC PIZZA OR FOCACCIA
• 1 oz (25 g) fresh yeast or 2 (¼-oz/7-g) packages active dry yeast
• 1 teaspoon sugar
• about ¾ cup (200 ml) warm water
• 3⅓ cups (500 g) all-purpose (plain) flour + ½ cup (75 g) to sprinkle work surface
• ¾ teaspoon salt

BASIC BREAD
• 1 oz (25 g) fresh yeast or 2 (¼-oz/7-g) packages active dry yeast
• 1 teaspoon sugar
• about 1½ cups (350 ml) warm water
• 5 cups (750 g) all-purpose (plain) flour + ½ cup (75 g) to sprinkle work surface
• 1 teaspoon salt

Right: *Strudel pastry*

Basic sponge cake

Serves: 8-10; Preparation: 25 minutes; Cooking: 15 minutes; Level of difficulty: 2

Preheat the oven to 350°F/180°C/gas 4. • Butter two 9-inch (23-cm) or 10-inch (25-cm) round cake pans. Line with waxed paper. • Beat the egg yolks and sugar in a large bowl with an electric mixer at high speed until pale and thick. • Use a large rubber spatula to fold in the dry ingredients. • With mixer at high speed, beat the egg whites in a large bowl until stiff peaks form. Fold them into the batter. • Bake for about 15 minutes, or until a toothpick inserted into the center comes out clean. • Turn out onto racks and carefully remove the paper. Let cool completely.

■ INGREDIENTS

- 4 large eggs, separated
- ¾ cup (150 g) sugar
- ¾ cup (125 g) cornstarch (cornflour)
- 2 tablespoons all-purpose (plain) flour
- 1 teaspoon cream of tartar
- ½ teaspoon baking soda

Basic chocolate sponge cake

Serves: 8-10; Preparation: 25 minutes; Cooking: 15 minutes; Level of difficulty: 2

Preheat the oven to 350°F/180°C/gas 4. • Butter two 9-inch (23-cm) or 10-inch (25-cm) round cake pans. Line with parchment paper. • Sift the cornstarch, flour, cocoa, cream of tartar, and baking soda into a large bowl. • Beat the egg yolks and sugar in a large bowl with an electric mixer at high speed until pale and thick. • Use a large rubber spatula to fold in the dry ingredients. • With mixer at high speed, beat the egg whites in a large bowl until stiff peaks form. Fold them into the batter. • Bake for about 15 minutes, or until a toothpick inserted into the center comes out clean. • Cool the cakes in the pans for 15 minutes. Turn out onto racks and carefully remove the paper. Let cool completely.

■ INGREDIENTS

- ¾ cup (125 g) cornstarch (cornflour)
- 2 tablespoons all-purpose (plain) flour
- 2 tablespoons unsweetened cocoa powder
- 1 teaspoon cream of tartar
- ½ teaspoon baking soda
- 4 large eggs, separated
- ¾ cup (150 g) sugar

Basic cheesecake crust

Makes: crust for a 9-10-inch (23-25-cm pan); Preparation: 15 minutes; Cooking: 10 minutes; Level of difficulty: 1

Preheat the oven to 350°F/180°C/gas 4. • Butter a 9-inch (23-cm) or 10-inch (25-cm) springform pan. • Melt the butter and mix with the crumbs, sugar, cinnamon, and ginger in a medium bowl. • Press into the bottom and partway up the sides of the prepared pan. • Bake for about 10 minutes, or until lightly browned. • Cool the crust completely in the pan on a rack.

■ INGREDIENTS

- 4 tablespoons butter
- 1½ cups (225 g) graham cracker crumbs (digestive biscuits)
- 2 tablespoons raw sugar
- 1 teaspoon each ground cinnamon and ginger

Right: *Basic chocolate sponge cake*

Italian sponge cake

Serves: 8-10; Preparation: 25 minutes; Cooking: 40 minutes; Level of difficulty: 2

Preheat the oven to 350°F/180°C/gas 4. • Butter a deep 10-inch (25-cm) springform pan. Line with parchment paper. • Sift the flour and salt into a medium bowl. • Beat the egg yolks, sugar, and lemon zest in a large bowl with an electric mixer at high speed until pale and creamy. • Beat the egg whites in a large bowl until stiff peaks form. • Use a large rubber spatula to fold the dry ingredients into the egg yolk mixture. Carefully fold in the beaten whites. • Working quickly, spoon the batter into the prepared pan. • Bake for about 40 minutes, or until springy to the touch and the cake shrinks from the pan sides. • Cool the cake in the pan for 5 minutes. Loosen and remove the pan sides. Invert the cake onto a rack. Loosen and remove the pan bottom. Carefully remove the paper. Turn the cake top-side up and let cool completely.

■ INGREDIENTS

- 1 cup (150 g) cake flour
- ¼ teaspoon salt
- 6 large eggs, separated
- 1¼ cups (250 g) sugar
- ½ tablespoon grated lemon zest

Génoise

Despite its name, a Génoise is a classic French sponge cake and the basis for many spectacular gâteaux.

Serves: 8-10; Preparation: 25 minutes; Cooking: 35 minutes; Level of difficulty: 2

Preheat the oven to 375°F/190°C/gas 5. • Butter a deep 10-inch (25-cm) springform pan. Line with parchment paper. • Sift the flour and cornstarch into a medium bowl. • Beat the eggs and superfine sugar in a large heatproof bowl. Fit the bowl into a large wide saucepan of barely simmering water over low heat. (Bottom of bowl should not touch the water.) Beat until the sugar has dissolved and the mixture is hot to the touch. • Remove from the heat. Beat the eggs with an electric mixer at high speed until cooled, tripled in volume, and very thick. • Use a large rubber spatula to gradually fold the dry ingredients into the batter. • Place 2 cups (500 ml) of batter in a small bowl and fold in the melted butter and vanilla. Fold this mixture into the batter. • Working quickly, spoon the batter into the prepared pan. • Bake for about 35 minutes, or until a toothpick inserted into the center comes out clean. • Cool the cake in the pan for 5 minutes. • Loosen and remove the pan sides. Invert the cake onto a rack. Loosen and remove the pan bottom. Carefully remove the paper. Turn the cake top-side up and let cool completely.

■ INGREDIENTS

- ⅔ cup (100 g) cake flour
- ⅔ cup (100 g) cornstarch (cornflour)
- 6 large eggs
- ¾ cup (150 g) superfine (caster) sugar
- 6 tablespoons butter, melted and cooled slightly
- 1 teaspoon vanilla extract

Right: *Italian sponge cake*

Basic meringues

Serves: 6-8; Preparation: 15 minutes; Cooking: 1 hour 15 minutes for rounds, 25 minutes for rosettes; Level of difficulty: 1

Preheat the oven to 300°F/150°C/gas 2. • Beat the egg whites and salt in a large bowl with an electric mixer at high speed until stiff peaks form. • With mixer at low speed, gradually beat in the water, sugar, and cornstarch. Add the vinegar and vanilla. • Spoon the meringue into a pastry bag fitted with a ½-inch (1-cm) plain tip. • Meringue Round: Cut out a 9-inch (23-cm) round of parchment paper and place on a baking sheet. Pipe the meringue in a spiral to fill the round, leaving a ½-inch (1-cm) border around the edge. • Bake for about 1 hour 15 minutes, or until crisp. • Meringue Rosettes: Line a baking sheet with parchment paper. • Pipe the meringue in 1½-inch (3.5-cm) rosettes on the paper. • Bake for about 25 minutes, or until crisp. • Place on racks and let cool completely.

■ INGREDIENTS

- 3 large egg whites
- ⅛ teaspoon salt
- 3 tablespoons cold water
- 1½ cups (300 g) sugar
- 1 tablespoon cornstarch (cornflour)
- 1 teaspoon vinegar
- ½ teaspoon vanilla extract

Basic dacquoise

Serves: 6-8; Preparation: 30 minutes; Cooking: 1 hour 30 minutes; Level of difficulty: 2

Preheat the oven to 300°F/150°C/gas 2. • Cut out three 9-inch (23-cm) rounds of parchment paper and place on baking sheets. • Beat the egg whites and salt in a large bowl with an electric mixer at medium speed until frothy. With mixer at high speed, gradually add the sugar, beating until stiff, glossy peaks form. • Use a large rubber spatula to fold in the almonds and cornstarch. • Spoon the meringue into a pastry bag fitted with a ½-inch (1-cm) plain tip. Pipe the meringue in a spiral to fill the paper rounds, leaving a ½-inch (1-cm) border around the edge. • Bake for about 1 hour 30 minutes, or until crisp. • Cool for 10 minutes. Invert onto racks. Carefully remove the paper and let cool completely.

■ INGREDIENTS

- 6 large egg whites
- ⅛ teaspoon salt
- 1½ cups (300 g) sugar
- 1½ cups (200 g) almonds, finely ground
- 1 tablespoon cornstarch (cornflour)

Chantilly cream

Chantilly is a simple French cream made by beating heavy (double) cream and sugar until well thickened. It can be used to fill cakes, sponges, and meringue cakes, among other things.

Makes: about 4 cups (1 liter); Preparation: 10 minutes; Level of difficulty: 1

Place the cream and sugar in a large bowl and beat with an electric mixer at high speed until stiff.

■ INGREDIENTS

- 2 cups (500 ml) heavy (double) cream
- ¼ cup (50 g) sugar

Right: Basic meringue cake with chantilly and raspberries

Vanilla custard

Makes: about 2 cups (500 ml); Preparation: 10 minutes; Cooking: 15 minutes; Level of difficulty: 1

Bring the milk and half the sugar to a boil in a saucepan. • Beat the egg yolks and remaining sugar in a large bowl with an electric mixer at high speed until pale and thick. • Stir the milk into the yolks. Return to the saucepan. • Cook over low heat, stirring constantly with a wooden spoon, for about 10 minutes, or until thick. Remove from the heat and add the vanilla. Set aside to cool.

■ INGREDIENTS
- 2 cups (500 ml) milk
- ½ cup (100 g) sugar
- 6 large egg yolks
- 1 teaspoon vanilla extract

Pastry cream

Makes: about 2 cups (500 ml); Preparation: 10 minutes; Cooking: 15 minutes; Level of difficulty: 1

Beat the egg yolks and sugar with an electric mixer at high speed until pale and thick. • Bring the milk to a boil with the salt and vanilla, then stir it into the egg and sugar. • Cook over low heat, stirring constantly with a wooden spoon, for about 10 minutes, or until thick.

VARIATIONS
– To make Chocolate Pastry Cream, melt 7 oz (200 g) bittersweet chocolate in a double boiler over barely simmering water and stir into the cream.
– For Lemon Pastry Cream, add 1 tablespoon finely grated lemon zest.

■ INGREDIENTS
- 5 large egg yolks
- ⅔ cup (140 g) sugar
- ⅓ cup (50 g) all-purpose (plain) flour
- 2 cups (500 ml) whole milk
- ⅛ teaspoon salt
- 1 teaspoon vanilla extract

Sherry frosting

Makes: about 3 cups (750 ml); Preparation: 10 minutes; Level of difficulty: 1

Beat the confectioners' sugar, butter, sherry, and vanilla in a large bowl with an electric mixer at low speed until smooth.

■ INGREDIENTS
- 5 cups (750 g) confectioners' (icing) sugar
- 1 cup (250 g) butter, softened
- 3½ tablespoons dry sherry
- 2 teaspoons vanilla extract

Right: *Vanilla custard*

Basic chocolate frosting

Makes: about 1 cup (250 ml); Preparation: 5 minutes; Level of difficulty: 1

Stir together the confectioners' sugar and cocoa in a double boiler. Add the butter, vanilla, and enough of the water to make a firm paste. Stir over simmering water until smooth, about 3 minutes.

■ INGREDIENTS

- 2 cups (300 g) confectioners' (icing) sugar
- 2 tablespoons unsweetened cocoa powder
- 2 tablespoons butter, softened
- 1 teaspoon vanilla extract
- about 2 tablespoons boiling water

Vanilla frosting

Makes: about 1 cup (250 ml); Preparation: 5 minutes; Level of difficulty: 1

Place the confectioners' sugar in a large bowl. • Stir in the vanilla and enough water to make a thick spreadable frosting.

■ INGREDIENTS

- 2 cups (300 g) confectioners' (icing) sugar
- 2–4 tablespoons boiling water
- 1 teaspoon vanilla extract

Lemon frosting

Makes: about 2 cups (500 ml); Preparation: 10 minutes; Level of difficulty: 1

Beat the confectioners' sugar, butter, lemon zest, and 4 tablespoons of lemon juice in a large bowl with an electric mixer at medium speed until smooth. • Add enough of the remaining lemon juice, a tablespoon at a time, to make a thick spreadable frosting.

■ INGREDIENTS

- 4 cups (600 g) confectioners' (icing) sugar
- ½ cup (125 g) butter, softened
- 1 tablespoon finely grated lemon zest
- 4–6 tablespoons lemon juice

Rich chocolate frosting

Makes: about 2 cups (500 ml); Preparation: 15 minutes; Cooking: 10 minutes; Level of difficulty: 1

Bring the sugar and 1 cup (250 ml) cream to a boil in a saucepan over medium heat. Boil for 1 minute, then remove from the heat. • Stir in the chocolate. • Return the saucepan to medium heat and cook, without stirring, until the mixture reaches 238°F (114°C), or the soft-ball stage. Remove from the heat. • Add the butter and vanilla, without stirring, and place the saucepan in a larger pan of cold water for 5 minutes before stirring. • Beat with a wooden spoon until the frosting begins to lose its sheen, 5–10 minutes. Immediately stir in 1 tablespoon of cream. Do not let the frosting harden too much before adding the cream. • Let stand for 3–4 minutes, then stir until smooth and spreadable.

■ INGREDIENTS

- 2 cups (400 g) sugar
- 1 cup (250 ml) heavy (double) cream + 1–2 tablespoons as needed
- 8 oz (250 g) bittersweet chocolate, coarsely chopped
- 2 tablespoons butter
- 1 teaspoon vanilla extract

Right: Basic chocolate frosting

White chocolate ganache

■ INGREDIENTS

Makes: about 1½ cups (375 ml); Preparation: 15 minutes + 30 minutes to chill; Level of difficulty: 1

Heat the cream almost to a boil in a small saucepan over low heat. • Place the chocolate in a large bowl. Pour the cream over the chocolate and stir until the chocolate is melted and smooth. • Refrigerate until thick and spreadable, about 30 minutes, stirring occasionally.

- ½ cup (125 ml) heavy (double) cream
- 13 oz (375 g) white chocolate, coarsely chopped

Chocolate ganache

■ INGREDIENTS

Makes: about 2 cups (500 ml); Preparation: 20 minutes; Level of difficulty: 1

Bring the cream and corn syrup to a boil in a medium saucepan over medium heat. • Remove from heat. • Stir the chocolate into the pan, then set aside for 2 minutes. • Beat until the chocolate has melted and the cream is thick.

- 1½ cups (375 ml) heavy (double) cream
- 1 tablespoon corn (golden) syrup
- 10 oz (300 g) bittersweet chocolate, coarsely chopped

Chocolate sauce

■ INGREDIENTS

Makes: about 2 cups (500 ml); Preparation: 15 minutes; Cooking: 5 minutes; Level of difficulty: 1

Melt the butter with the water in a saucepan over medium heat. Bring to a boil, stirring constantly. • Stir in the chocolate until melted. • Add the sugar, corn syrup, and salt. Bring to a boil and simmer for 5 minutes. Remove from the heat and add the vanilla. • Serve hot or warm.

- ½ cup (125 g) butter
- ⅔ cup (180 ml) water
- 5 oz (150 g) bittersweet chocolate, coarsely chopped
- 1¼ cups (250 g) sugar
- 4 tablespoons corn (golden) syrup
- ¼ teaspoon salt
- 2 teaspoons vanilla extract

Cream cheese frosting

■ INGREDIENTS

Makes: about 1 cup (250 g); Preparation: 10 minutes; Level of difficulty: 1

Beat the cream cheese, butter, and vanilla in a large bowl with an electric mixer at medium speed until creamy. • With mixer at low speed, beat in the confectioners' sugar until smooth and spreadable.

- 3 oz (90 g) cream cheese, softened
- 4 tablespoons butter, softened
- 1 teaspoon vanilla extract
- 2 cups (300 g) confectioners' (icing) sugar

VARIATION
– To make Chocolate Cream Cheese Frosting, add 4 tablespoons of unsweetened cocoa powder together with the confectioners' sugar.

Right: *White chocolate ganache*

Strawberry coulis

■ INGREDIENTS

- 1 lb (500 g) fresh strawberries, hulled
- ½ cup (100 g) sugar
- 4 tablespoons lemon juice

Makes: about 2 cups (500 ml); Preparation: 15 minutes; Level of difficulty: 1

Purée the strawberries, sugar, and juice in a blender until smooth, about 1 minute.

> VARIATION
> – Replace the strawberries with the same amount of raspberries or blackberries.

Tropical morning coulis

■ INGREDIENTS

- 1 (7 oz/200 g) mango, peeled and coarsely chopped
- 1–2 (7 oz/200 g) papaya, peeled and seeded
- 2 passion fruit, pulped
- ¾ cup (150 g) sugar
- 4 tablespoons dark rum

Makes: about 2 cups (500 ml); Preparation: 15 minutes; Level of difficulty: 1

Purée the mango, papaya, passion fruit, sugar, and rum in a blender until smooth, about 1 minute.

Citrus sauce

■ INGREDIENTS

- 1½ cups (300 g) sugar
- 1 cup (250 ml) orange juice
- ½ cup (125 ml) lemon or lime juice
- 2 tablespoons finely grated orange zest
- 2 tablespoons finely grated lemon zest
- 6 tablespoons orange liqueur

Makes: about 2 cups (500 ml); Preparation: 15 minutes; Level of difficulty: 1

Bring the sugar, orange juice, lemon juice, orange zest, and lemon zest to a boil in a saucepan. Continue cooking over low heat until the sauce becomes syrupy, about 10 minutes. • Remove from the heat and stir in the orange liqueur. • Strain the sauce into a bowl. • Serve hot or cold.

Simple applesauce

■ INGREDIENTS

- 2½ lb (1.25 kg) tart cooking apples (Granny Smiths are ideal), peeled, cored, and chopped
- 1 cup (250 ml) cold water
- 1 cup (200 g) sugar
- 6 tablespoons lemon juice
- 1 teaspoon vanilla extract

Makes: about 2½ cups (625 ml); Preparation: 30 minutes; Cooking: 20 minutes; Level of difficulty: 1

Cook the apples, water, and sugar in a large saucepan over low heat until the apples are mushy, about 20 minutes. • Remove from the heat and stir in the lemon juice and vanilla. • Strain the mixture in a food mill or purée in a food processor or blender.

Right: *Strawberry coulis*

Zabaglione

This wine-flavored custard originally comes from Italy where it is said to have been invented in the Medici court in Florence during the 16th century. Whatever its origins, it makes a wonderful filling for tarts and cakes and is very good served by itself or spooned over fresh fruit.

Makes: about 1 cup (250 ml); Preparation: 5 minutes; Cooking: 15 minutes; Level of difficulty: 1

Beat the egg yolks and sugar in a double boiler with an electric mixer at high speed until pale and thick. • Gradually add the Marsala. • Cook over barely simmering water, stirring constantly, until thick, about 15 minutes.

■ INGREDIENTS

- 4 large egg yolks
- ¼ cup (50 g) sugar
- ½ cup (125 ml) dry Marsala wine or dry sherry

Buttercream

Buttercream is a rich cream that is used to fill or top cakes and cookies. This is the basic recipe and method. See the variations below to create a host of delicious creams to finish every kind of cake and cookie to perfection.

Makes: about 2 cups (500 ml); Preparation: 10 minutes; Cooking: 15 minutes; Level of difficulty: 1

Stir the water and sugar in a saucepan over medium heat until the sugar has dissolved. • With a pastry brush dipped in cold water, wash down the sides of the pan to prevent sugar crystals from forming. Cook, without stirring, until the mixture reaches 238°F (114°C), or the soft-ball stage. • Beat the egg yolks in a double boiler with an electric mixer at high speed until pale. • Gradually beat the syrup into the beaten yolks. • Place over barely simmering water, stirring constantly with a wooden spoon, until the mixture lightly coats a metal spoon or registers 160°F (71°C) on an instant-read thermometer. • Immediately plunge the pan into a bowl of ice water and stir until cooled. • Beat the butter in a large bowl until creamy. Beat into the egg mixture.

■ INGREDIENTS

- ½ cup (125 ml) water
- ¾ cup (150 g) sugar
- 3 large egg yolks
- 1 cup (250 g) butter, softened

VARIATIONS
– To make Vanilla Buttercream, add 1 teaspoon of vanilla extract.
– To make Almond Buttercream, add ½ teaspoon almond extract.
– To make Coffee Buttercream, replace 2 tablespoons of the water with the same amount of very strong black coffee.
– To make Liqueur Buttercream, replace 2 tablespoons of the water with the same amount of liqueur.
– To make Chocolate Buttercream, melt 5 oz (150 g) of bittersweet chocolate in a double boiler and stir into the cream.

Right: *Zabaglione*

Passion fruit curd

Try this curd spread on warm Basic muffins (see page 520).

Makes: about 2 cups (500 ml); Preparation: 15 minutes; Cooking: 5 minutes; Level of difficulty: 1

Beat the passion fruit, sugar, butter, and eggs in a double boiler until well blended. • Place over low heat, stirring constantly, until the mixture lightly coats a metal spoon or registers 160°F (71°C) on an instant-read thermometer. Immediately plunge the pan into a bowl of ice water and stir until cooled.

■ INGREDIENTS

- 10 large passion fruit, pulped
- 2 cups (400 g) sugar
- 2 tablespoons butter
- 4 large eggs, lightly beaten

Almond and vanilla cream

Makes: about 2 cups (500 ml); Preparation: 15 minutes; Level of difficulty: 1

Beat the butter and sugar in a medium bowl with an electric mixer at high speed until pale and creamy. • Stir in the almonds and vanilla.

■ INGREDIENTS

- ¾ cup (180 g) butter, softened
- ¾ cup (150 g) sugar
- 1⅓ cups (200 g) finely ground almonds
- 1 teaspoon vanilla extract

Orange frosting

Substitute lime or lemon juice for the orange to complement the flavor of your cakes or muffins.

Makes: 1 cup (250 ml); Preparation: 5 minutes; Level of difficulty: 1

Sift the confectioners' sugar into a large bowl. • Stir in the orange juice and orange extract until smooth.

■ INGREDIENTS

- 2 cups (300 g) confectioners' (icing) sugar
- 2–4 tablespoons orange juice
- ½ teaspoon vanilla extract

Soft caramel frosting

Makes: about 2¼ cups (360 ml); Preparation: 30 minutes; Cooking: 10 minutes; Level of difficulty: 1

Stir both sugars, cream, and butter in a medium saucepan over low heat until the sugars have dissolved. • Increase heat to medium. Wash down the sides of the pan with a pastry brush dipped in cold water to prevent sugar crystals from forming. Cook, without stirring, until the mixture reaches 238°F (114°C), or the soft-ball stage. Remove from the heat and set aside to cool for 15 minutes. • Transfer to a medium bowl, and beat in the vanilla with an electric mixer at low speed until the frosting loses its sheen and thickens slightly.

■ INGREDIENTS

- 2 cups (400 g) firmly packed brown sugar
- ⅓ cup (70 g) sugar
- 1 cup (250 ml) heavy (double) cream
- 4 tablespoons butter, cut up
- 2 teaspoons vanilla extract

Right: Passionfruit curd

Marzipan fruit

These attractive candies are perfect as petits fours to serve with coffee at the end of a meal.
Or use them to top your favorite cakes to add a professional finish.

Makes: about 50 fruit shapes; Preparation: 1 hour; Level of difficulty: 2

Use your hands to work together the almonds, confectioners' sugar, and rose water to form a firm dough. • Divide the dough in 4. • Add several drops of food coloring to each piece and work in the color. Dust your hands and work surface with confectioners' sugar to prevent the marzipan from becoming too sticky. • Divide the marzipan into small pieces and shape into fruit. • To make oranges and lemons, create the "peel" by rolling the marzipan against a fine grater. • Shape green and red marzipan into apples and strawberries, and yellow marzipan into bananas. Paint brown lines with food coloring down the banana skins. Short pieces of crystallized angelica make good fruit stalks. • Let harden for 24 hours.

■ INGREDIENTS

- 4½ cups (650 g) finely ground almonds
- 3 cups (450 g) confectioners' (icing) sugar + extra for kneading and dusting
- 3 tablespoons rose water or orange-flower water
- red, yellow, green, and orange food coloring

Mock cream

Makes: about 1 cup (250 ml); Preparation: 5 minutes; Level of difficulty: 1

Beat the butter, sugar, water, and vanilla in a large bowl with an electric mixer at high speed until thick and creamy. • The mixture may curdle as you beat; continue beating until smooth.

■ INGREDIENTS

- ½ cup (125 g) butter, softened
- ½ cup (100 g) sugar
- ½ cup (125 ml) boiling water
- 1 teaspoon vanilla extract

Lemon glaze

Makes: about 1 cup (250 ml); Preparation: 5 minutes; Level of difficulty: 1

Place the confectioners' sugar in a medium bowl. • Beat in 4 tablespoons of lemon juice and the zest until smooth, adding the additional tablespoon of lemon juice as needed to make a good spreading consistency.

■ INGREDIENTS

- 2 cups (300 g) confectioners' (icing) sugar
- 4–5 tablespoons lemon juice
- 2 teaspoons finely grated lemon zest

Right: *Homemade marzipan*

Tea and Coffee Cakes

Many of the cakes in this chapter are perfect to serve at breakfast or brunch, or later in the day with a cup of coffee or tea. Most are not too fancy or rich in themselves, but they can all be dressed up with fillings or cream for more special occasions.

Paradise tea cake

Serves: 8-10; Preparation: 25 minutes; Cooking: 50 minutes; Level of difficulty: 1

Preheat the oven to 350°F/180°C/gas 4. • Butter and flour a 10-inch (25-cm) round cake pan. Line with waxed paper. Butter the paper. • Sift the flour, cornstarch, baking powder, and salt into a large bowl. • Beat the butter, sugar, and lemon zest in a large bowl with an electric mixer at medium speed until creamy. • In a separate bowl, beat the eggs and yolks until frothy. Gradually beat the egg mixture into the butter and sugar. • With mixer at low speed, gradually beat in the dry ingredients. • Spoon the batter into the prepared pan. • Bake for about 50 minutes, or until a toothpick inserted into the center comes out clean. • Cool the cake in the pan for 10 minutes. Turn out onto a rack. Carefully remove the waxed paper and let cool completely. • Dust with the confectioners' sugar just before serving.

VARIATIONS
– Replace the lemon zest with the same quantity of orange or lime zest.
– Add 1 teaspoon each of ground cinnamon and nutmeg together with the flour.

INGREDIENTS

- 1 cup (150 g) all-purpose (plain) flour
- 1 cup (150 g) cornstarch (cornflour)
- 2 teaspoons baking powder
- ¼ teaspoon salt
- 1 cup (250 g) butter
- 1¼ cups (250 g) sugar
- 2 tablespoons finely grated lemon zest
- 4 large eggs + 4 large egg yolks
- ⅓ cup (50 g) confectioners' (icing) sugar, to dust

Basic yellow cake

Serves: 6-8; Preparation: 15 minutes; Cooking: 50 minutes; Level of difficulty; 1

Preheat the oven to 350°F/180°C/gas 4. • Butter and flour a 9-inch (23-cm) round cake pan. Line with waxed paper. Butter the paper. • Sift the flour, baking powder, and salt into a large bowl. • Beat the butter, sugar, and vanilla in a large bowl with an electric mixer at medium speed until creamy. • Add the eggs, one at a time, beating until just blended after each addition. • With mixer at low speed, gradually beat in the dry ingredients, alternating with the milk. • Spoon the batter into the prepared pan. • Bake for about 50 minutes, or until a toothpick inserted into the center comes out clean. • Cool the cake in the pan for 10 minutes. Turn out onto a rack. Carefully remove the waxed paper and let cool completely.

INGREDIENTS

- 1½ cups (225 g) all-purpose (plain) flour
- 1½ teaspoons baking powder
- ¼ teaspoon salt
- 1 cup (250 g) butter
- 1 cup (200 g) sugar
- 2 teaspoons vanilla extract
- 4 large eggs
- ¾ cup (200 ml) milk

Right: *Paradise tea cake*

Coconut buttermilk cake

Serves: 6-8; Preparation: 25 minutes; Cooking: 45 minutes; Level of difficulty: 1

Preheat the oven to 350°F/180°C/gas 4. • Butter a deep 8-inch (20-cm) square baking pan. Line with waxed paper. Butter the paper. • Stir together the flour, coconut, sugar, and almonds in a large bowl. Make a well in the center and stir in the buttermilk, eggs, vanilla, and butter. • Spoon the batter into the prepared pan. • Bake for about 45 minutes, or until a toothpick inserted into the center comes out clean. • Cool the cake in the pan for 10 minutes. Turn out onto a rack to cool completely.

■ INGREDIENTS

- 1⅔ cups (250 g) all-purpose (plain) flour
- ⅓ cup (45 g) shredded (desiccated) coconut
- 1 cup (200 g) sugar
- ⅔ cup (100 g) almonds, finely ground
- 1 cup (250 ml) buttermilk
- 3 large eggs, lightly beaten
- 1 teaspoon vanilla extract
- ⅔ cup (150 g) butter, melted

Moist coffee cake with chocolate crunch

Serves: 6-8; Preparation: 20 minutes; Cooking: 50 minutes; Level of difficulty: 1

Preheat the oven to 350°F/180°C/gas 4. • Butter and flour a 13 x 9-inch (33 x 23-cm) baking pan. • Chocolate Crunch: Stir the sugar and flour in a medium bowl. Use a pastry blender to cut in the butter until the mixture resembles fine crumbs. Stir in the chocolate chips and walnuts. • Cake: Sift the flour, baking powder, baking soda, and salt into a large bowl. • Beat the butter, cream cheese, sugar, and vanilla in a large bowl with an electric mixer at medium speed until creamy. • Add the eggs, one at a time, beating until just blended after each addition. • With mixer at low speed, gradually beat in the dry ingredients, alternating with the milk. • Spoon the batter into the prepared pan. Sprinkle with the topping. • Bake for about 50 minutes, or until a toothpick inserted into the center comes out clean. • Cool the cake completely in the pan on a rack.

■ INGREDIENTS

CHOCOLATE CRUNCH

- ½ cup (100 g) firmly packed brown sugar
- ½ cup (75 g) all-purpose (plain) flour
- 4 tablespoons butter
- 1 cup (180 g) semisweet chocolate chips
- ½ cup (50 g) walnuts, coarsely chopped

CAKE

- 2½ cups (375 g) all-purpose (plain) flour
- 2 teaspoons baking powder
- ½ teaspoon baking soda
- ¼ teaspoon salt
- ⅔ cup (180 g) butter
- 1 package (8 oz/250 g) cream cheese
- 1½ cups (300 g) sugar
- 1 teaspoon vanilla extract
- 3 large eggs
- ¾ cup (200 ml) milk

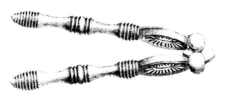

Right: *Coconut buttermilk cake*

Classic marble cake

Serves: 8-10; Preparation: 30 minutes; Cooking: 45 minutes; Level of difficulty: 1

Preheat the oven to 350°F/180°C/gas 4. • Butter and flour a deep 9-inch (23-cm) square pan. • Sift the flour, baking powder, and salt into a large bowl. • Beat the butter, sugar, and vanilla in a large bowl with an electric mixer at high speed until creamy. • With mixer at medium speed, add the eggs, one at a time, beating until just blended after each addition. • With mixer at low speed, gradually beat in the dry ingredients, alternating with the milk. • Divide the batter evenly among three small bowls. Stir the cocoa into one and red food coloring into another. Leave one bowl plain. • Drop alternate spoonfuls of the batters into the prepared pan, swirling them together with a knife to create a marbled effect. • Bake for about 45 minutes, or until a toothpick inserted into the center comes out clean. • Cool the cake in the pan on a rack. • Spread with the frosting.

■ INGREDIENTS

- 2⅓ cups (350 g) all-purpose (plain) flour
- 2½ teaspoons baking powder
- ¼ teaspoon salt
- 1 cup (250 g) butter
- 1 cup (200 g) sugar
- 1 teaspoon vanilla extract
- 3 large eggs
- ¾ cup (200 ml) milk
- ⅓ cup (50 g) unsweetened cocoa powder
- ½ teaspoon red food coloring
- 1 quantity *Basic Chocolate Frosting* (see page 30)

Spiced marble cake with chocolate chips

Serves: 8-10; Preparation: 30 minutes; Cooking: 45 minutes; Level of difficulty: 1

Preheat the oven to 350°F/180°C/gas 4. • Butter and flour a 13 x 9-inch (33 x 23-cm) baking pan. • Sift the flour, baking powder, and salt into a medium bowl. • Mix ½ cup (50 g) of sugar with the cocoa and cinnamon in a small bowl. • Beat the butter and cream cheese in a large bowl with an electric mixer at medium speed until creamy. Gradually beat in the remaining sugar and vanilla until smooth. • Add the eggs, one at a time, beating until just blended after each addition. • With mixer at low speed, gradually beat in the dry ingredients. • Stir in the chocolate chips. • Spoon two-thirds of the batter into the prepared pan. Sprinkle with the cocoa mixture. Spoon the remaining batter on the top and run a knife through the layers to create a marbled effect. • Bake for about 45 minutes, or until a toothpick inserted into the center comes out clean. • Cool the cake completely in the pan on a rack.

■ INGREDIENTS

- 2⅓ cups (350 g) all-purpose flour
- 1½ teaspoons baking powder
- ¼ teaspoon salt
- 2 cups (400 g) sugar
- 2 tablespoons unsweetened cocoa powder
- 2 tablespoons ground cinnamon
- 1 cup (250 g) butter
- 1 package (8 oz/250 g) cream cheese
- 2 teaspoons vanilla extract
- 4 large eggs
- ¾ cup (150 g) semisweet chocolate chips

Right: *Michelangelo's marble cake*

Michelangelo's marble cake

Serves: 6-8; Preparation: 30 minutes; Cooking: 45 minutes; Level of difficulty: 1

INGREDIENTS

- 2 cups (300 g) all-purpose (plain) flour
- 2 teaspoons baking powder
- ¼ teaspoon salt
- ¾ cup (200 g) butter
- ¾ cup (150 g) sugar
- 1 teaspoon vanilla extract
- 3 large eggs
- ½ teaspoon almond extract
- ½ teaspoon red food coloring
- ½ teaspoon green food coloring

Preheat the oven to 350°F/180°C/gas 4. • Butter and flour a 9-inch (23-cm) tube pan. • Sift the flour, baking powder, and salt into a medium bowl. • Beat the butter, sugar, and vanilla in a large bowl with an electric mixer at high speed until creamy. • With mixer at medium speed, add the eggs, one at a time, beating until just blended after each addition. • With mixer at low speed, gradually beat in the dry ingredients. • Divide the batter evenly among three small bowls. Stir the almond extract into one, the red food coloring into another, and the green food coloring into the third. • Drop alternate spoonfuls of the three batters into the prepared pan, swirling them together with a knife to create a marbled effect. • Bake for about 45 minutes, or until a toothpick inserted into the center comes out clean. • Turn out onto the rack to cool completely.

Cinnamon tea cake with lemon frosting

■ INGREDIENTS

- 1½ cups (225 g) all-purpose (plain) flour
- 2 teaspoons ground cinnamon
- 1½ teaspoons baking powder
- ¼ teaspoon salt
- ½ cup (125 g) butter
- 1 cup (200 g) sugar
- 1 teaspoon vanilla extract
- 2 large eggs
- ½ cup (125 ml) milk
- 1 quantity *Lemon Frosting* (see page 30)

Serves: 6-8; Preparation: 30 minutes; Cooking: 40 minutes; Level of difficulty: 1

Preheat the oven to 350°F/180°C/gas 4. • Butter and flour a 9-inch (23-cm) square baking pan. • Sift the flour, cinnamon, baking powder, and salt into a large bowl. • Beat the butter, sugar, and vanilla in a large bowl with an electric mixer at medium speed until creamy. • Add the eggs, one at a time, beating until just blended after each addition. • With mixer at low speed, gradually beat in the dry ingredients, alternating with the milk. • Spoon the batter into the prepared pan. • Bake for about 40 minutes, or until a toothpick inserted into the center comes out clean. • Cool the cake completely in the pan on a rack. • Spread with the frosting.

Cinnamon loaf with spiced topping

■ INGREDIENTS

- 1½ cups (225 g) all-purpose (plain) flour
- 2 teaspoons ground cinnamon
- 1 teaspoon baking powder
- ¼ teaspoon salt
- ½ cup (100 g) sugar
- 6 tablespoons milk
- 4 tablespoons melted butter
- 1 large egg, lightly beaten

SPICED TOPPING

- 4 tablespoons butter, cut up
- 4 tablespoons sugar
- 1 teaspoon ground cinnamon

Serves: 6-8; Preparation: 15 minutes; Cooking: 35 minutes; Level of difficulty: 1

Preheat the oven to 350°F/180°C/gas 4. • Butter and flour a 9 x 5-inch (23 x 13-cm) loaf pan. • Sift the flour, cinnamon, baking powder, and salt into a large bowl. Stir in the sugar. • With an electric mixer at low speed, beat in the milk, butter, and egg. • Spoon the batter into the prepared pan. • Bake for about 35 minutes, or until a toothpick inserted into the center comes out clean. • Spiced Topping: Dot the butter over the cake. Sprinkle with the sugar and cinnamon. • Cool the loaf completely in the pan on a rack.

Left: *Cinnamon tea cake with lemon frosting*

Frosted ginger loaf

This is a classic, never-fail gingerbread recipe. Make it without the frosting and serve it thinly sliced with just a smear of salted butter, or go the whole hog and serve with this delicious tangy lime frosting. You may vary the citrus flavoring in the frosting to lemon or orange with excellent results.

Serves: 6-8; Preparation: 30 minutes; Cooking: 50 minutes; Level of difficulty: 1

Preheat the oven to 350°F/180°C/gas 4. • Butter a 9 x 5-inch (23 x 13-cm) loaf pan. Line with waxed paper. Butter the paper. • Stir the molasses and butter in a small saucepan over low heat until the butter has melted. Keep warm. • Stir together the flour, sugar, baking powder, baking soda, ginger, cinnamon, cloves, mace, and salt in a large bowl. • With an electric mixer at low speed, gradually beat in the milk and egg. • By hand, stir the hot molasses mixture into the batter. • Spoon the batter into the prepared pan. • Bake for about 50 minutes, or until a toothpick inserted into the center comes out clean. • Cool the loaf in the pan for 15 minutes. Turn out onto a rack. Carefully remove the paper and let cool completely. • Lime Frosting: With mixer at medium speed, beat the butter and lime zest in a medium bowl until creamy. • With mixer at low speed, gradually beat in the confectioners' sugar and enough of the lime juice to make a thick, spreadable frosting. • Spread the frosting over the top and sides of the loaf.

INGREDIENTS

- ½ cup (125 ml) dark molasses
- 4 tablespoons butter
- 1 cup (150 g) all-purpose (plain) flour
- ¾ cup (150 g) sugar
- 1 teaspoon baking powder
- ½ teaspoon baking soda
- 1 teaspoon ground ginger
- 1 teaspoon ground cinnamon
- ¼ teaspoon each ground cloves, mace, and salt
- ½ cup (125 ml) milk
- 1 large egg, lightly beaten

LIME FROSTING

- ½ cup (125 g) butter
- 1 tablespoon finely grated lime zest
- 2 cups (300 g) confectioners' (icing) sugar
- 1 tablespoon lime juice

Frosted butter cake

Serves: 6-8; Preparation: 30 minutes; Cooking: 45 minutes; Level of difficulty: 1

Preheat the oven to 350°F/180°C/gas 4. • Butter a 9-inch (23-cm) square cake pan. Line with waxed paper. Butter the paper. • Sift the flour, cornstarch, baking powder, and salt into a medium bowl. • Beat the butter and sugar in a large bowl with an electric mixer at medium speed until creamy. • Add the egg yolks, one at a time, beating until just blended after each addition. • With mixer at low speed, gradually beat in the dry ingredients. • With mixer at high speed, beat the egg whites in a medium bowl until stiff peaks form. Use a large rubber spatula to fold them into the batter. • Spoon the batter into the prepared pan. • Bake for about 45 minutes, or until a toothpick inserted into the center comes out clean. • Cool the cake completely in the pan on a rack. • Spread with the frosting.

INGREDIENTS

- 1 cup (150 g) all-purpose (plain) flour
- 1 cup (150 g) cornstarch (cornflour)
- 1 teaspoon baking powder
- ¼ teaspoon salt
- 1¼ cups (310 g) butter
- 1½ cups (300 g) sugar
- 3 large eggs, separated
- 1 quantity *Vanilla Frosting* or ½ quantity *Lemon Frosting* (see page 30)

Right: Frosted ginger loaf

Simple pound cake

*This cake is excellent served with tea or coffee. It is plain enough to serve at breakfast
for those with a sweet tooth and tasty enough to serve throughout the day.
You may also use it as a basic cake for trifles and charlottes.*

Serves: 10-12; Preparation: 30 minutes; Cooking: 1 hour; Level of difficulty: 1

Preheat the oven to 350°F/180°C/gas 4. • Butter and flour a 10-inch (25-cm)
tube pan. • Sift the flour, baking powder, baking soda, and salt into a
large bowl. • Beat the butter, sugar, and vanilla and almond extracts in a
large bowl with an electric mixer at medium speed until creamy. • Add
the eggs, one at a time, beating until just blended after each addition. •
With mixer at low speed, gradually beat in the dry ingredients,
alternating with the milk. • Spoon the batter into the prepared pan. •
Bake for about 1 hour, or until a toothpick inserted into the center
comes out clean. • Run a knife around the edges of the pan to loosen
the cake. Cool the cake in the pan for 15 minutes. Turn the cake out onto
a rack to cool completely.

■ INGREDIENTS

- 3 cups (450 g) all-purpose (plain) flour
- 1 teaspoon baking powder
- ½ teaspoon baking soda
- ½ teaspoon salt
- 1 cup (250 g) butter
- 2 cups (400 g) sugar
- 2 teaspoons vanilla extract
- 1 teaspoon almond extract
- 5 large eggs
- 1 cup (250 ml) milk

Peach and vodka pound cake

Serves: 10-12; Preparation: 30 minutes; Cooking: 1 hour; Level of difficulty: 1

Preheat the oven to 325°F/170°C/gas 3. • Butter and flour a 10-inch (25-cm)
tube pan. • Sift the flour, salt, and baking soda into a large bowl. • Beat
the butter, sugar, and orange zest in a large bowl with an electric mixer
at medium speed until creamy. • Add the eggs, one at a time, beating
until just blended after each addition. • With mixer at low speed,
gradually beat in the dry ingredients, alternating with the yogurt and
peach vodka. • Spoon the batter into the prepared pan. • Bake for about
1 hour, or until a toothpick inserted into the center comes out clean. •
Run a knife around the edges of the pan to loosen the cake. Cool the
cake in the pan for 15 minutes. Turn out onto a rack to cool completely.
• Glaze: Mix the peach preserves, vodka, and lemon zest in a saucepan
and bring to a boil over medium heat. Let boil for 1 minute. Drizzle the
glaze over the cake.

■ INGREDIENTS

- 3 cups (450 g) all-purpose (plain) flour
- ½ teaspoon salt
- ¼ teaspoon baking soda
- 1 cup (250 g) butter
- 2 cups (200 g) sugar
- 1 tablespoon finely grated orange zest
- 6 large eggs
- 1 cup (250 ml) yogurt
- 4 tablespoons peach vodka

GLAZE

- 1 cup (250 g) peach preserves
- ½ cup (125 ml) peach vodka
- 1 teaspoon finely grated lemon zest

Right: *Peach and vodka pound cake*

Classic pound cake

INGREDIENTS

- 2 cups (300 g) all-purpose (plain) flour
- ½ teaspoon baking powder
- ¼ teaspoon salt
- 1½ cups (375 g) butter
- 1½ cups (300 g) sugar
- 1 teaspoon vanilla extract
- 5 large eggs, separated
- 6 tablespoons milk

Serves: 8-10; Preparation: 30 minutes; Cooking: 1 hour; Level of difficulty: 1

Preheat the oven to 350°F/180°C/gas 4. • Butter and flour a 9-inch (23-cm) tube pan. • Sift the flour, baking powder, and salt into a large bowl. • Beat the butter, sugar, and vanilla in a large bowl with an electric mixer at medium speed until creamy. • Add the egg yolks, one at a time, beating until just blended after each addition. • With mixer at low speed, gradually beat in the dry ingredients, alternating with the milk. • With mixer at high speed, beat the egg whites in a large bowl until stiff peaks form. • Use a large rubber spatula to fold them into the batter. • Spoon the batter into the prepared pan. • Bake for about 1 hour, or until a toothpick inserted into the center comes out clean. • Run a knife around the edges of the pan to loosen the cake. Cool the cake in the pan for 15 minutes. Turn out onto a rack to cool completely.

Pound cake with coconut-almond syrup

Serves: 8-10; Preparation: 15 minutes; Cooking: 1 hour; Level of difficulty: 1

Preheat the oven to 350°F/180°C/gas 4. • Butter and flour a 10-inch (25-cm) tube pan. • Sift the flour, baking powder, baking soda, and salt into a large bowl. • Beat the butter, sugar, and rum and coconut extracts in a large bowl with an electric mixer at medium speed until creamy. • Add the eggs, one at a time, beating until just blended after each addition. • With mixer at low speed, gradually beat in the dry ingredients, alternating with the milk and cream. • Spoon the batter into the prepared pan. • Bake for about 1 hour, or until a toothpick inserted into the center comes out clean. • Run a knife around the edges of the pan to loosen the cake. Cool the cake in the pan for 15 minutes. Turn out onto a rack to cool until warm. • Coconut-Almond Syrup: Bring the sugar, water, and extracts to a boil in a saucepan over low heat, stirring constantly. • Place the cake on a rack in a jelly-roll pan. Poke holes all over the cake. Spoon the syrup over the cake. Scoop up any syrup from the pan and drizzle over the cake.

■ INGREDIENTS

- 2 cups (300 g) all-purpose (plain) flour
- 1 teaspoon baking powder
- ½ teaspoon baking soda
- ¼ teaspoon salt
- 1 cup (250 g) butter
- 2 cups (400 g) sugar
- 2 teaspoons rum extract
- 1 teaspoon coconut extract
- 4 large eggs
- 6 tablespoons milk
- 6 tablespoons cream

COCONUT-ALMOND SYRUP

- ½ cup (100 g) sugar
- ½ cup (125 ml) water
- 1 teaspoon almond extract
- 1 teaspoon coconut extract

Frosted coconut pound cake

Serves: 8-10; Preparation: 20 minutes; Cooking: 1 hour; Level of difficulty: 1

Preheat the oven to 350°F/180°C/gas 4. • Butter and flour a 10-inch (25-cm) tube pan. • Sift the flour, baking powder, and salt into a large bowl. Add the coconut. • Beat the butter and sugar in a large bowl with an electric mixer at medium speed until creamy. • Add the eggs, one at a time, until just blended after each addition. • With mixer at low speed, gradually beat in the dry ingredients, alternating with the milk and coconut extract. • Spoon the batter into the prepared pan. • Bake for about 1 hour, or until the cake shrinks from the pan sides and a toothpick inserted into the center comes out clean. • Run a knife around the edges of the pan to loosen the cake. Cool the cake in the pan for 15 minutes. Turn out onto a rack to cool completely. • Spread with the frosting.

■ INGREDIENTS

- 1½ cups (225 g) all-purpose (plain) flour
- 1 teaspoon baking powder
- ½ teaspoon salt
- 1¼ cups (200 g) shredded (desiccated) coconut
- ¾ cup (200 g) butter
- 1½ cups (300 g) sugar
- 4 large eggs
- 6 tablespoons milk
- 1½ teaspoons coconut extract
- 1 quantity *Vanilla Frosting* (see page 30)

Right: *Pound cake with coconut-almond syrup*

Crunchy coconut cake

Serves: 6-8; Preparation: 30 minutes; Cooking: 45 minutes; Level of difficulty: 1

Preheat the oven to 350°F/180°C/gas 4. • Butter and flour a 9-inch (23-cm) springform pan. • Sift the flour, baking powder, and salt into a medium bowl. • Beat the egg yolks, sugar, and vanilla in a large bowl with an electric mixer at high speed until pale and thick. • With mixer at low speed, gradually beat in the dry ingredients, alternating with the coconut milk. • With mixer at high speed, beat the egg whites in a medium bowl until stiff peaks form. Use a rubber spatula to fold them into the batter. • Spoon the batter into prepared pan. • Bake for about 45 minutes, or until springy to the touch and a toothpick inserted into the center comes out clean. • Crunchy Topping: Mix the coconut, brown sugar, and butter in a small bowl. • Turn on the broiler. Spread the topping over the cake as soon as it comes out of the oven. Broil the cake 6–8 inches (15–18 cm) from the heat source for 2–3 minutes, or until the topping is bubbly and lightly browned. • Cool the cake completely in the pan on a rack. Loosen and remove the pan sides to serve.

■ INGREDIENTS

- 1½ cups (225 g) all-purpose (plain) flour
- 1½ teaspoons baking powder
- ¼ teaspoon salt
- 2 large eggs, separated
- 1 cup (200 g) sugar
- 1 teaspoon vanilla extract
- ¾ cup (200 ml) unsweetened coconut milk

CRUNCHY TOPPING

- 1 cup (125 g) coarsely grated coconut flesh
- ⅓ cup (70 g) firmly packed brown sugar
- 3 tablespoons butter, melted

Frosted lemon loaf

Serves: 6-8; Preparation: 30 minutes; Cooking: 55 minutes; Level of difficulty: 1

Preheat the oven to 350°F/180°C/gas 4. • Butter and flour a 9 x 5-inch (23 x 13-cm) loaf pan. • Sift the flours and baking powder into a large bowl. • Beat the butter and sugar in a large bowl with an electric mixer at medium speed until creamy. Add the lemon zest and eggs, beating until just blended. • With mixer at low speed, gradually add the dry ingredients. • Pour the batter into the prepared pan. • Bake for about 55 minutes, or until a toothpick inserted into the center comes out clean. • Cool the cake in the pan for 15 minutes. • Turn out onto a rack and let cool completely. • Frosting: Beat the confectioners' sugar with enough lemon juice to make a thick frosting. • Spread over the top of the cake and serve.

■ INGREDIENTS

- 1¼ cups (180 g) potato flour
- 2 cups (300 g) all-purpose (plain) flour
- 2 teaspoons baking powder
- 1 cup (250 g) butter
- 1¼ cups (250 g) sugar
- finely grated zest of 1 lemon
- 4 eggs
- 1½ cups (225 g) confectioners' (icing) sugar
- juice of 1 lemon

Right: Crunchy coconut cake

Pacific coconut cake

Serves: 6-8; Preparation: 30 minutes + 1 hour to stand; Cooking: 45 minutes; Level of difficulty: 1

Mix the milk, coconut, and orange juice in a medium bowl. Cover and let stand at room temperature for 1 hour. • Preheat the oven to 325°F/170°C/gas 3. • Butter a 9-inch (23-cm) round cake pan. Line with waxed paper. • Beat the butter, sugar, and orange zest in a large bowl with an electric mixer at medium speed until creamy. • Add the eggs, one at a time, beating until just blended after each addition. • With mixer at low speed, gradually beat in the flour, baking powder, and salt, alternating with the coconut mixture. • Spoon the batter into the prepared pan. • Bake for about 45 minutes, or until a toothpick inserted into the center comes out clean. • Cool the cake in the pan for 10 minutes. Turn out onto a rack. Carefully remove the paper and let cool completely. • Frosting: Mix the confectioners' sugar and butter in a medium bowl. Add enough orange juice to make a thick, spreadable frosting. • Spread over the top of the cake.

■ INGREDIENTS

- 1 cup (250 ml) milk
- ¾ cup (90 g) shredded (desiccated) coconut
- 4 tablespoons orange juice
- ½ cup (125 g) butter
- 1 cup (200 g) sugar
- 2 tablespoons finely grated orange zest
- 2 large eggs
- 2 cups (300 g) all-purpose (plain) flour
- 2 teaspoons baking powder
- ½ teaspoon salt

FROSTING

- 2 cups (300 g) confectioners' (icing) sugar
- 2 tablespoons butter, melted
- 3 tablespoons orange juice

Frosted lemon sour cream cake

Serves: 6-8; Preparation: 30 minutes; Cooking: 40 minutes; Level of difficulty: 1

Preheat the oven to 325°F/170°C/gas 3. • Butter and flour a 9-inch (23-cm) tube pan. • Sift the flour, baking powder, baking soda, and salt into a medium bowl. • Beat the butter, sugar, and lemon zest in a large bowl with an electric mixer at medium speed until creamy. • Add the eggs, one at a time, beating until just blended after each addition. • With mixer at low speed, gradually beat in the dry ingredients, alternating with the sour cream. • Spoon the batter into the prepared pan. • Bake for about 40 minutes, or until golden and a toothpick inserted into the center comes out clean. • Cool the cake in the pan for 5 minutes. Turn out onto a rack to cool completely. • Lemon Frosting: With a mixer at high speed, beat the butter and lemon zest in a medium bowl until creamy. Gradually beat in the confectioners' sugar and enough lemon juice to make a spreadable frosting. • Spread the top and sides of the cake with the frosting.

■ INGREDIENTS

- 1⅓ cups (200 g) all-purpose (plain) flour
- 1 teaspoon baking powder
- ½ teaspoon baking soda
- ¼ teaspoon salt
- ½ cup (125 g) butter
- 1 cup (200 g) sugar
- 1 tablespoon finely grated lemon zest
- 2 large eggs
- 6 tablespoons sour cream

LEMON FROSTING

- 4 tablespoons butter
- 1 tablespoon finely grated lemon zest
- 1½ cups (225 g) confectioners' (icing) sugar
- 2-3 tablespoons lemon juice

Right: Pacific coconut cake

Crisp coconut ring

■ INGREDIENTS

- 1½ cups (225 g) all-purpose (plain) flour
- 2 teaspoons baking powder
- ¼ teaspoon salt
- ½ cup (125 g) butter
- ½ cup (100 g) sugar
- 3 large egg yolks
- 1 teaspoon vanilla extract
- ½ cup (125 ml) milk
- ½ cup (100 g) raspberry preserves (jam)

TOPPING

- 3 large egg whites
- ¼ cup (50 g) sugar
- ½ cup shredded (desiccated) coconut
- ½ teaspoon almond extract

Serves: 6-8; Preparation: 30 minutes; Cooking: 45 minutes; Level of difficulty: 1

Preheat the oven to 350°F/180°C/gas 4. • Butter and flour a 9-inch (23-cm) tube pan. • Sift the flour, baking powder, and salt into a large bowl. • Melt the butter in a saucepan over low heat. Remove from the heat. Beat in the sugar, egg yolks, and vanilla. • Stir in the dry ingredients, alternating with the milk. • Spoon the batter into the prepared pan. • Spoon dollops of jam over the batter. • Topping: Beat the egg whites in a large bowl with an electric mixer at medium speed until frothy. With mixer at high speed, gradually beat in the sugar until stiff, glossy peaks form. • Use a large rubber spatula to fold in the coconut and almond extract. • Spread the topping over the batter. • Bake for about 45 minutes, or until a toothpick inserted into the center comes out clean. • Cool the cake in the pan for 15 minutes. Turn out onto a rack. Turn top-side up and let cool completely.

■ INGREDIENTS

- 1⅓ cups (200 g) all-purpose (plain) flour
- 1 teaspoon baking powder
- ¼ teaspoon salt
- 6 tablespoons butter
- 1 cup (200 g) sugar
- 2 tablespoons finely grated lemon zest
- 1 large egg
- 6 tablespoons milk

CINNAMON CRUNCH

- ½ cup (100 g) brown sugar
- 2 teaspoons ground cinnamon
- 2 tablespoons butter, melted

■ INGREDIENTS

WALNUT CRUNCH

- ¾ cup (150 g) firmly packed brown sugar
- ⅓ cup (50 g) all-purpose (plain) flour
- 4 tablespoons butter, cut up
- ¾ cup (100 g) walnuts, coarsely chopped

CAKE

- 2 cups (300 g) all-purpose (plain) flour
- 2 teaspoons baking powder
- 1 teaspoon nutmeg
- ¼ teaspoon salt
- ½ cup (125 g) butter
- ¾ cup (150 g) firmly packed brown sugar
- 1 teaspoon vanilla extract
- 4 large eggs
- ¾ cup (200 ml) buttermilk

Cinnamon crunch tea cake

Serves: 6-8; Preparation: 30 minutes; Cooking: 30 minutes; Level of difficulty: 1

Preheat the oven to 350°F/180°C/gas 4. • Butter a 9-inch (23-cm) round cake pan. Line with waxed paper. Butter the paper. • Sift the flour, baking powder, and salt into a medium bowl. • Beat the butter, sugar, and lemon zest in a large bowl with an electric mixer at medium speed until creamy. Add the egg, beating until just blended. • With mixer at low speed, gradually beat in the dry ingredients, alternating with the milk. • Spoon the batter into the prepared pan. • Bake for about 30 minutes, or until a toothpick inserted into the center comes out clean. • Turn out onto a rack. Carefully remove the paper, then turn top-side up. • Cinnamon Crunch: Stir together the brown sugar and cinnamon. Brush the cake with the butter and sprinkle with the cinnamon-sugar.

Emily's favorite walnut cake

Serves: 8-10; Preparation: 30 minutes; Cooking: 55 minutes; Level of difficulty: 1

Preheat the oven to 350°F/180°C/gas 4. • Butter a 9-inch (23-cm) tube pan. • Walnut Crunch: Stir the brown sugar and flour in a medium bowl. Use a pastry blender to cut in the butter until the mixture resembles fine crumbs. Stir in the walnuts. • Cake: Sift the flour, baking powder, nutmeg, and salt into a medium bowl. • Beat the butter, brown sugar, and vanilla in a large bowl with an electric mixer at medium speed until creamy. • Add the eggs, one at a time, beating until just blended after each addition. • With mixer at low speed, gradually beat in the dry ingredients, alternating with the buttermilk. • Spoon half the batter into the prepared pan. Sprinkle with half the walnut crunch. Spoon the remaining batter over the top and sprinkle with the remaining walnut crunch. • Bake for about 55 minutes, or until the topping is golden brown. • Cool the cake in the pan on a rack. Carefully turn out, turn topping-side up, and serve warm.

Left: *Cinnamon crunch tea cake*

Filled ginger cake

Serves: 8–10; Preparation: 30 minutes; Cooking: 30 minutes; Level of difficulty: 1

Preheat the oven to 350°F/180°C/gas 4. • Butter and flour two 8-inch (20-cm) round cake pans. Line with waxed paper. Butter the paper. • Sift the flour, baking powder, ginger, and salt into a large bowl. • Beat the butter, brown sugar, and vanilla in a large bowl with an electric mixer at high speed until creamy. • With mixer at medium speed, add the eggs, one at a time, beating until just blended after each addition. • With mixer at low speed, gradually beat in the dry ingredients. • Spoon half the batter into each of the prepared pans. • Bake for about 30 minutes, or until a toothpick inserted into the center comes out clean. • Cool the cakes in the pans for 10 minutes. Turn out onto a rack. Carefully remove the paper and let cool completely. • Ginger Filling: With mixer at high speed, beat the cream, confectioners' sugar, and ginger in a large bowl until stiff. • Place one cake on a serving plate and spread with the filling. Top with the remaining cake.

■ INGREDIENTS

- 2 cups (300 g) all-purpose (plain) flour
- 2 teaspoons baking powder
- 2 teaspoons ground ginger
- ¼ teaspoon salt
- ¾ cup (200 g) butter
- ¾ cup (150 g) firmly packed brown sugar
- 1 teaspoon vanilla extract
- 3 large eggs

GINGER FILLING

- ¾ cup (200 ml) heavy (double) cream
- 2 tablespoons confectioners' (icing) sugar
- 1 teaspoon ground ginger

Queen Anne butter cake

Serves: 8–10; Preparation: 30 minutes; Cooking: 45 minutes; Level of difficulty: 1

Preheat the oven to 350°F/180°C/gas 4. • Butter a 9-inch (23-cm) round cake pan. Line with waxed paper. Butter the paper. • Sift the flour, baking powder, and salt into a large bowl. • Beat the butter and sugar in a large bowl with an electric mixer at medium speed until creamy. • Add the eggs, one at a time, beating until just blended after each addition. • With mixer at low speed, gradually beat in the dry ingredients, alternating with the sherry. • Spoon the batter into the prepared pan. • Bake for about 45 minutes, or until golden and a toothpick inserted into the center comes out clean. • Cool the cake in the pan for 10 minutes. Turn out onto a rack. Carefully remove the paper and let cool completely. • Dust with the confectioners' sugar.

■ INGREDIENTS

- 2 cups (300 g) all-purpose (plain) flour
- 2 teaspoons baking powder
- ¼ teaspoon salt
- ¾ cup (200 g) butter
- 1 cup (100 g) sugar
- 3 large eggs
- 2 tablespoons sweet sherry
- 6 tablespoons confectioners' (icing) sugar, to dust

Right: *Filled ginger cake*

Five-flavored cake

Serves: 10-12; Preparation: 30 minutes; Cooking: 1 hour 30 minutes; Level of difficulty: 1

Preheat the oven to 325°F/170°C/gas 3. • Butter and flour a 10-inch (25-cm) tube pan. • Pour the milk into a small bowl with the four extracts. • Sift the flour, baking powder, and salt into a large bowl. • Beat the butter, oil, sugar, and peanut butter in a large bowl with an electric mixer at medium speed until creamy. • Add the eggs, one at a time, beating until just blended after each addition. • With mixer at low speed, gradually beat in the dry ingredients, alternating with the milk mixture. • Spoon the batter into the prepared pan. • Bake for about 1 hour and 30 minutes, or until a toothpick inserted into the center comes out clean. • Run a knife around the edges of the pan to loosen the cake. Cool the cake in the pan for 15 minutes. Turn out onto a rack to cool completely. • Glaze: Beat the sugar, water, peanut butter, and the four extracts in a saucepan and bring to a boil over low heat. Cook, stirring constantly, until the sugar has dissolved. Set aside to cool. • Drizzle over the cake.

■ INGREDIENTS

- ¾ cup (200 ml) milk
- 1 teaspoon each almond, coconut, rum, and vanilla extracts
- 2½ cups (375 g) all-purpose (plain) flour
- 1 teaspoon baking powder
- ¼ teaspoon salt
- ¾ cup (200 g) butter
- 6 tablespoons vegetable oil
- 2½ cups (500 g) sugar
- 2 tablespoons peanut butter
- 4 large eggs

GLAZE
- ½ cup (100 g) sugar
- ½ cup (125 ml) water
- 1 tablespoon peanut butter
- ½ teaspoon each almond, coconut, vanilla, and rum extracts

Seville pound cake

Serves: 10-12; Preparation: 30 minutes; Cooking: 1 hour 15 minutes; Level of difficulty: 1

Preheat the oven to 350°F/180°C/gas 4. • Butter and flour a 10-inch (25-cm) tube pan. • Sift the flour, baking powder, and salt into a large bowl. • Beat the butter, sugar, and orange zest in a large bowl with an electric mixer at medium speed until creamy. • Add the eggs, one at a time, beating until just blended after each addition. • With mixer at low speed, gradually beat in the dry ingredients, alternating with the milk. • Spoon the batter into the prepared pan. • Bake for about 1 hour 15 minutes, or until a toothpick inserted into the center comes out clean. • Run the knife around the edges of the pan to loosen the cake. Cool the cake in the pan for 15 minutes. Turn out onto a rack to cool completely. • Glaze: Beat the confectioners' sugar and butter in a medium bowl. Beat in enough of the water to make a smooth glaze. Drizzle the cake with the glaze. Sprinkle the cake with the orange zest.

■ INGREDIENTS

- 3 cups (450 g) all-purpose (plain) flour
- 1 teaspoon baking powder
- ½ teaspoon salt
- 1½ cups (375 g) butter
- 3 cups (600 g) sugar
- 1 tablespoon finely grated orange zest
- 5 large eggs
- 1 cup (250 ml) milk

GLAZE
- 2 cups (300 g) confectioners' (icing) sugar
- 4 tablespoons butter
- 1–2 tablespoons hot water
- 1 tablespoon finely grated orange zest

Right: *Five-flavored cake*

Tangy lemon syrup cake

Serves: 10-12; Preparation: 30 minutes; Cooking: 55 minutes; Level of difficulty: 1

Preheat the oven to 350°F/180°C/gas 4. • Butter and flour a 9-inch (23-cm) tube pan. • Sift the flour, baking powder, and salt into a large bowl. • Beat the butter, sugar, and lemon zest in a large bowl with an electric mixer at medium speed until creamy. • Add the egg yolks, one at a time, beating until just blended after each addition. • With mixer at low speed, gradually beat in the dry ingredients, alternating with the buttermilk. • With mixer at high speed, beat the egg whites in a medium bowl until stiff peaks form. Use a large rubber spatula to fold them into the batter. • Spoon the batter into the prepared pan. • Bake for about 55 minutes, or until a toothpick inserted into the center comes out clean. • Cool the cake in the pan for 10 minutes. Turn out onto a rack and place the rack in a jelly-roll pan. • Lemon Syrup: Bring the sugar, lemon juice, and water to a boil in a saucepan over low heat. Pour the syrup over the hot cake. Scoop up any syrup from the pan and drizzle over the cake.

■ INGREDIENTS

- 2⅓ cups (350 g) all-purpose (plain) flour
- 2 teaspoons baking powder
- ¼ teaspoon salt
- 1 cup (250 g) butter
- 1¼ cups (250 g) sugar
- 2 tablespoons finely grated lemon zest
- 3 large eggs, separated
- 1 cup (250 ml) buttermilk

LEMON SYRUP

- ¾ cup (150 g) sugar
- 6 tablespoons lemon juice
- 4 tablespoons water

Lemon honey syrup cake

Serves: 10-12; Preparation: 30 minutes; Cooking: 50 minutes; Level of difficulty: 2

Preheat the oven to 350°F/180°C/gas 4. • Butter and flour a 10-inch (25-cm) tube pan. • Stir the flour, coconut, baking powder, and salt in a large bowl. • Beat the butter, sugar, and lemon zest in a large bowl with an electric mixer at medium speed until creamy. • Add the eggs, one at a time, beating until just blended after each addition. • With mixer at low speed, gradually beat in the dry ingredients, alternating with the yogurt and lemon juice. • Spoon the batter into the prepared pan. • Bake for about 50 minutes, or until a toothpick inserted into the center comes out clean. • Cool in the pan for 10 minutes. Turn out onto a rack. Place the cake on the rack in a jelly-roll pan. • Syrup: Bring the lemon juice, water, and honey to a boil in a saucepan over low heat. • Pour the syrup over the hot cake. Scoop up any syrup from the pan and drizzle over the cake.

■ INGREDIENTS

- 3 cups (450 g) all-purpose (plain) flour
- ¾ cup (100 g) shredded (desiccated) coconut
- 2 teaspoons baking powder
- ¼ teaspoon salt
- 1 cup (250 g) butter
- 1 cup (200 g) sugar
- 1 tablespoon finely grated lemon zest
- 3 large eggs
- ¾ cup (200 ml) plain yogurt
- 2 tablespoons lemon juice

SYRUP

- 6 tablespoons lemon juice
- 6 tablespoons water
- 4 tablespoons honey

VARIATIONS
– For a different flavor, replace the lemon zest and juice with the same quantity of lime zest and juice.

Left: *Tangy lemon syrup cake*

Coffee cake with coffee liqueur cream

Serves: 6-8; Preparation: 30 minutes; Cooking: 30 minutes; Level of difficulty: 1

Preheat the oven to 350°F/180°C/gas 4. • Butter and flour a 9-inch (23-cm) springform pan. • Sift the flour, baking powder, and salt into a medium bowl. • Beat the butter and sugar in a large bowl with an electric mixer at medium speed until creamy. • Add the eggs, one at a time, beating until just blended after each addition. • With mixer at low speed, beat in the dry ingredients. • Spoon the batter into the prepared pan. • Bake for about 30 minutes, or until golden brown and a toothpick inserted into the center comes out clean. • Cool the cake in the pan for 5 minutes. Loosen and remove the pan sides. Invert the cake onto a rack and turn the cake top-side up. Let cool until warm. Transfer to a serving plate. • Poke holes in the cake with a skewer. Drizzle with the coffee. • Cream: With mixer at high speed, beat the cream, confectioners' sugar, liqueur, and vanilla in a large bowl until stiff. Spread the cake with the cream.

■ INGREDIENTS

- 1⅓ cups (200 g) all-purpose (plain) flour
- 2 teaspoons baking powder
- ¼ teaspoon salt
- ½ cup (125 g) butter
- ¾ cup (150 g) sugar
- 3 large eggs
- ½ cup (125 ml) cold strong black coffee

CREAM

- 1½ cups (375 ml) heavy (double) cream
- 2 tablespoons confectioners' (icing) sugar
- 3 tablespoons coffee liqueur
- 1 teaspoon vanilla extract

Frosted vanilla coffee cake

Serves: 8-10; Preparation: 30 minutes; Cooking: 1 hour; Level of difficulty: 1

Preheat the oven to 350°F/180°C/gas 4. • Butter and flour a 9-inch (23-cm) tube pan. • Sift the flour, baking powder, baking soda, and salt into a large bowl. • Beat the butter, sugar, and vanilla in a large bowl with an electric mixer at medium speed until pale and creamy. • Add the eggs, one at a time, beating until just blended after each addition. • With mixer at low speed, gradually beat in the dry ingredients, alternating with the sour cream. • Transfer one-third of the batter to a small bowl and stir in the coffee. • Spoon half the plain batter into the prepared pan. Spoon the coffee-flavored batter over the top. Spread the remaining batter on top. • Bake for about 1 hour, or until golden brown and a toothpick inserted into the center comes out clean. • Cool the cake in the pan for 15 minutes. Turn out onto a rack to cool until warm. • Frosting: Stir the coffee mixture into the confectioners' sugar in a small bowl. • Spread over the cake.

■ INGREDIENTS

- 2 cups (300 g) all-purpose (plain) flour
- 1 teaspoon baking powder
- ½ teaspoon baking soda
- ¼ teaspoon salt
- ¾ cup (200 g) butter
- 1 cup (200 g) sugar
- 2 teaspoons vanilla extract
- 2 large eggs
- 1 cup (250 ml) sour cream
- 2 tablespoons freeze-dried coffee granules dissolved in 1 tablespoon boiling water

FROSTING

- 2 teaspoons freeze-dried coffee granules dissolved in 4 tablespoons cold strong coffee
- 1½ cups (225 g) confectioners' (icing) sugar

Right: Frosted vanilla coffee cake

Brown sugar breakfast cake

Serves: 8-10; Preparation: 30 minutes; Cooking: 40 minutes; Level of difficulty: 1

Preheat the oven to 350°F/180°C/gas 4. • Butter a 13 x 9-inch (33 x 23-cm) baking pan. • Topping: Stir the brown sugar, flour, and orange extract in a medium bowl. Use a pastry blender to cut in the butter until the mixture resembles fine crumbs. Stir in the almonds. • Cake: Sift the flour, baking powder, ginger, and salt in a large bowl. Stir in the ground almonds. • Beat the butter, sugar, and almond extract in a large bowl with an electric mixer at medium speed until creamy. • Add the eggs, one at a time, beating until just blended after each addition. • With mixer at low speed, gradually beat in the dry ingredients, alternating with the sour cream and milk. • Spoon the batter into the prepared pan. Sprinkle with the topping. • Bake for about 40 minutes, or until golden brown and a toothpick inserted into the center comes out clean. • Cool the cake completely in the pan on a rack.

■ INGREDIENTS

TOPPING
- ½ cup (100 g) firmly packed brown sugar
- ⅓ cup (50 g) all-purpose (plain) flour
- 1 teaspoon orange extract
- 4 tablespoon cold butter
- ½ cup (75 g) almonds, coarsely chopped

CAKE
- 1½ cups (225 g) all-purpose (plain) flour
- 2 teaspoons baking powder
- 1 teaspoon ground ginger
- ¼ teaspoon salt
- ½ cup (60 g) almonds, finely ground
- ½ cup (125 g) butter
- ½ cup (100 g) sugar
- ½ teaspoon almond extract
- 3 large eggs
- ¾ cup (200 ml) sour cream
- 4 tablespoons milk

Sour cream layer cake

Serves: 10-12; Preparation: 30 minutes; Cooking: 30 minutes; Level of difficulty: 2

Preheat the oven to 350°F/180°C/gas 4. • Butter and flour three 9-inch (23-cm) round cake pans. • Sift the flour, baking soda, and salt into a large bowl. • Beat the butter, sugar, and vanilla in a large bowl with an electric mixer at medium speed until creamy. • Beat in the eggs one at a time. • With mixer at low speed, gradually beat in the dry ingredients, alternating with the sour cream. • Spoon one-third of the batter into each of the prepared pans. • Bake for about 30 minutes, or until a toothpick inserted into the center comes out clean. • Cool the cakes in the pans for 15 minutes. Turn out onto racks to cool completely. • Frosting: Melt the butter in a large saucepan over low heat. Stir in the brown sugar and milk and simmer for 5 minutes, stirring constantly. Remove from the heat and stir in the vanilla. • Beat in the confectioners' sugar. • Place one cake on a serving plate and spread with frosting. Top with another cake and spread with frosting. Top with the remaining cake. Spread the top and sides of the cake with the remaining frosting.

■ INGREDIENTS

- 2⅔ cups (400 g) all-purpose (plain) flour
- 1 teaspoon baking soda
- ¼ teaspoon salt
- 1 cup (250 g) butter
- 2 cups (400 g) sugar
- 1 tablespoon vanilla extract
- 6 large eggs
- 1 cup (250 ml) sour cream

FROSTING
- 6 tablespoons butter
- 1 cup (200 g) firmly packed brown sugar
- ¾ cup (200 ml) milk
- 1 tablespoon vanilla extract
- 2 cups (300 g) confectioners' (icing) sugar

Right: Brown sugar breakfast cake

Sherry syrup butter cake

■ INGREDIENTS

- 1½ cups (225 g) all-purpose (plain) flour
- 1½ teaspoons baking powder
- ¼ teaspoon salt
- ½ cup (125 g) butter
- ¾ cup (150 g) sugar
- 1 teaspoon vanilla extract
- 4 large eggs

SHERRY SYRUP

- 1 cup (250 ml) water
- 1 cup (200 g) sugar
- 4 tablespoons dry sherry

Serves: 6-8; Preparation: 40 minutes; Cooking: 30 minutes; Level of difficulty: 1

Preheat the oven to 350°F/180°C/gas 4. • Butter and flour a 9-inch (23-cm) round cake pan. • Sift the flour, baking powder, and salt into a medium bowl. • Beat the butter, sugar, and vanilla in a large bowl with an electric mixer at medium speed until creamy. • Add the eggs, one at a time, beating until just blended after each addition. • With mixer at low speed, gradually beat in the dry ingredients. • Spoon the batter into the prepared pan. • Bake for about 30 minutes, or until golden and a toothpick inserted into the center comes out clean. • Cool the cake in the pan for 10 minutes. Turn out onto a rack and let cool completely. • Sherry Syrup: Bring the water and sugar to a boil in a small saucepan over medium heat, stirring constantly. Cook, without stirring, until the mixture reaches 238°F (114°C), or the soft-ball stage. Remove from heat and let cool for 15 minutes. • Stir in the sherry. • Place the cake on a rack in a jelly-roll pan. Poke holes in the cake with a skewer. Spoon the syrup over the cake. Scoop up any syrup from the pan and drizzle over the cake.

Rainbow cake

■ INGREDIENTS

- 2 cups (300 g) all-purpose (plain) flour
- 2 teaspoons baking powder
- ¼ teaspoon salt
- 4 large eggs
- 1 cup (200 g) sugar
- 2 tablespoons butter
- 1 cup (250 ml) + 2 tablespoons milk, warmed
- 1 teaspoon vanilla extract
- 3 tablespoons cocoa powder
- 2 teaspoons red food coloring
- 1½ cups (375 ml) heavy (double) cream

GLAZE

- 1½ cups (225 g) confectioners' (icing) sugar
- ½ teaspoon vanilla extract
- 2–4 tablespoons boiling water

Left: *Sherry syrup butter cake*

Serves: 8-10; Preparation: 40 minutes; Cooking: 25 minutes; Level of difficulty: 1

Preheat the oven to 350°F/180°C/gas 4. • Butter three 8-inch (20-cm) round baking pans. Line with waxed paper. Butter the paper. • Sift the flour, baking powder, and salt into a large bowl. • Beat the eggs and sugar in a large bowl with an electric mixer at medium speed until pale and thick. • Melt the butter with the milk in a medium saucepan over medium heat. Stir in the vanilla. • With mixer at low speed, gradually beat in the dry ingredients, alternating with the milk. • Divide the batter evenly among three small bowls. Stir the cocoa into one and the food coloring into another. Leave one bowl plain. • Spoon each type of batter into a separate prepared pan. • Bake for about 25 minutes, or until a toothpick inserted into the center comes out clean. • Cool the cakes in the pans for 5 minutes. Turn out onto racks. Carefully remove the paper and let cool completely. • Beat the cream in a large bowl until stiff. • Place the plain layer of cake on a serving plate. Spread with half the cream. Cover with the pink cake and spread with the remaining cream. Top with the chocolate layer. • Glaze: Beat the confectioners' sugar and vanilla with enough water to make a liquid glaze. Drizzle over the cake.

Lemon-frosted almond cake

Serves: 8-10; Preparation: 30 minutes; Cooking: 45 minutes; Level of difficulty: 1

Preheat the oven to 350°F/180°C/gas 4. • Butter and flour an 11 x 7-inch (28 x 18-cm) baking pan. Line with waxed paper. Butter and flour the paper. • Stir together the flour, almonds, baking powder, ground ginger, baking soda, and salt in a large bowl. • Beat the butter, sugar, and almond extract in a large bowl with an electric mixer at medium speed until creamy. • Add the eggs, one at a time, beating until just blended after each addition. • With mixer at low speed, gradually beat in the dry ingredients and chopped ginger, alternating with the milk. • Spoon the batter into the prepared pan. • Bake for about 45 minutes, or until a toothpick inserted into the center comes out clean. • Cool the cake completely in the pan on a rack. • Spread with the frosting.

■ INGREDIENTS

- 1 cup (150 g) all-purpose (plain) flour
- 1 cup (150 g) finely ground almonds
- 2 teaspoons baking powder
- 2 teaspoons ground ginger
- ½ teaspoon baking soda
- ¼ teaspoon salt
- 1 cup (250 g) butter
- 1 cup (200 g) sugar
- ½ teaspoon almond extract
- 4 large eggs
- ¼ cup (50 g) chopped candied ginger
- 6 tablespoons milk
- ½ quantity (250 ml) *Lemon Frosting* (see page 30)

Orange-frosted butter cake

Serves: 8-10; Preparation: 40 minutes; Cooking: 55 minutes; Level of difficulty: 1

Preheat the oven to 350°F/180°C/gas 4. • Butter and flour a 10-inch (25-cm) springform pan. • Sift the flour, cornstarch, baking powder, and salt into a large bowl. • Beat the butter, sugar, orange zest, and vanilla in a large bowl with an electric mixer at medium speed until creamy. • Add the eggs, one at a time, beating until just blended after each addition. • With mixer at low speed, gradually beat in the dry ingredients, alternating with the milk. • Spoon the batter into the prepared pan. • Bake for about 55 minutes, or until a toothpick inserted into the center comes out clean. • Cool the cake in the pan on a rack for 15 minutes. Loosen and remove the pan sides. Invert the cake onto the rack. Remove the pan bottom and let cool completely. • Frosting: With mixer at medium speed, beat the cream cheese and sugar in a large bowl until smooth. • Beat in the candied orange and vanilla. • With mixer at high speed, beat the cream in a medium bowl until thick. Use a large rubber spatula to fold it into the cream cheese mixture. • Spread the top and sides of the cake with the frosting.

■ INGREDIENTS

- 2⅓ cups (350 g) all-purpose (plain) flour
- 1 cup (150 g) cornstarch (cornflour)
- 2 teaspoons baking powder
- ¼ teaspoon salt
- 1 cup (250 g) butter
- 1 cup (200 g) sugar
- 1 tablespoon finely grated orange zest
- 1 teaspoon vanilla extract
- 5 large eggs
- ½ cup (125 ml) milk

FROSTING
- 1 package (8 oz/250 g) cream cheese
- ½ cup (100 g) sugar
- 2 tablespoons finely chopped candied orange
- 1 teaspoon vanilla extract
- 1 cup (250 ml) heavy (double) cream

Right: Orange-frosted butter cake

Yellow cake with lemon liqueur cream

Serves: 6-8; Preparation: 30 minutes + 30 minutes to chill; Cooking: 35 minutes; Level of difficulty: 1

Preheat the oven to 350°F/180°C/gas 4. • Butter two 9-inch (23-cm) round cake pans. Line with waxed paper. Butter the paper. • Sift both flours, baking powder, and salt into a medium bowl. • Beat the butter, sugar, lemon zest, and vanilla and lemon extracts in a large bowl with an electric mixer at medium speed until creamy. • Add the eggs, one at a time, beating until just blended after each addition. • With mixer at low speed, gradually beat in the dry ingredients and liqueur. • Spoon half the batter into each of the prepared pans. Sprinkle one cake with the almonds. • Bake for about 35 minutes, or until a toothpick inserted into the center comes out clean. • Cool the cakes in the pans for 5 minutes. Turn out onto racks to cool completely. Carefully remove the paper. • Place the cake without the almonds on a serving plate and spread with the lemon pastry cream. Place the remaining cake almond-side up on top. • Refrigerate for 30 minutes before serving.

■ INGREDIENTS

- 1½ cups (225 g) all-purpose (plain) flour
- ¾ cup (125 g) rice flour
- 2 teaspoons baking powder
- ¼ teaspoon salt
- 1 cup (250 g) butter
- 1 cup (200 g) sugar
- 1 tablespoon finely grated lemon zest
- 1 teaspoon vanilla extract
- 1 teaspoon lemon extract
- 4 large eggs
- 2 tablespoons lemon liqueur
- ½ cup (50 g) coarsely chopped almonds
- 1 quantity *Pastry Cream* (see page 28), flavored with 2 tablespoons lemon liqueur

Caraway almond cake

Serves: 6-8; Preparation: 20 minutes; Cooking: 50 minutes; Level of difficulty: 1

Preheat the oven to 350°F/180°C/gas 4. • Butter a 9-inch (23-cm) square baking pan. Line with waxed paper. Butter the paper. • Sift the flour, baking powder, and salt into a medium bowl. Stir in the caraway seeds. • Beat the butter, sugar, and lemon zest in a large bowl with an electric mixer at medium speed until creamy. • Add the eggs, one at a time, beating until just blended after each addition. • With mixer at low speed, gradually beat in the dry ingredients, alternating with the milk. • Spoon the batter into the prepared pan. Sprinkle with the slivered almonds. • Bake for about 50 minutes, or until a toothpick inserted into the center comes out clean. • Cool the cake in the pan for 5 minutes. Turn out onto a rack. Carefully remove the paper and let cool completely.

■ INGREDIENTS

- 1½ cups (225 g) all-purpose (plain) flour
- 1½ teaspoons baking powder
- ¼ teaspoon salt
- 2 tablespoons caraway seeds
- ½ cup (125 g) butter
- ½ cup (100 g) sugar
- 1 tablespoon finely grated lemon zest
- 2 large eggs
- ½ cup (125 ml) milk
- 4 tablespoons slivered almonds

Right: *Yellow cake with lemon liqueur cream*

Almond tube cake

Serves: 10-12; Preparation: 30 minutes; Cooking: 1 hour 15 minutes; Level of difficulty: 1

INGREDIENTS

- 2 cups (300 g) all-purpose (plain) flour
- 1 teaspoon baking powder
- ¼ teaspoon salt
- 1 cup (150 g) almonds, finely ground
- 1½ cups (375 g) butter
- 3 cups (600 g) sugar
- 2 teaspoons almond extract
- 1 teaspoon vanilla extract
- 6 large eggs
- 1 cup (250 ml) milk
- ¾ cup (125 g) slivered almonds

Preheat the oven to 350°F/180°C/gas 4. • Butter and flour a 10-inch (25-cm) tube pan. • Sift the flour, baking powder, and salt into a large bowl. Stir in the almonds. • Beat the butter, sugar, and almond and vanilla extracts in a large bowl with an electric mixer at medium speed until creamy. • Add the eggs, one at a time, beating until just blended after each addition. • With mixer at low speed, gradually beat in the dry ingredients, alternating with the milk. • Spoon the batter into the prepared pan. • Sprinkle with the slivered almonds. • Bake for about 1 hour 15 minutes, or until golden brown and a toothpick inserted into the center comes out clean. • Run a knife around the edges of the pan to loosen the cake. Cool the cake in the pan for 15 minutes. Turn out onto a rack to cool completely.

Sweet polenta cake

Serves: 10-12; Preparation: 30 minutes; Cooking: 35 minutes; Level of difficulty: 1

Preheat the oven to 375°F/190°C/gas 5. • Butter and flour a 9-inch (23-cm) round baking pan. • Beat 3 egg yolks and 2 cups (300 g) confectioners' sugar in a large bowl with an electric mixer at medium speed until pale and thick. • Add the remaining egg yolks, one at a time, beating until just blended after each addition. • With mixer at low speed, gradually beat in the polenta, cornstarch, and lemon zest. • With mixer at high speed, beat the egg whites and salt in a medium bowl until stiff peaks form. Use a large rubber spatula to fold them into the mixture. • Spoon the batter into the prepared mold and smooth the top. • Bake for about 35 minutes, or until lightly browned and a toothpick inserted into the center comes out clean. • Cool the cake in the pan for 10 minutes. Turn out onto a rack to cool completely. • Dust with the remaining confectioners' sugar.

■ INGREDIENTS

- 6 large eggs, separated
- 2¼ cups (330 g) confectioners' (icing) sugar
- 1 cup (150 g) polenta (finely ground yellow cornmeal)
- 1 cup (150 g) cornstarch (cornflour)
- 2 tablespoons finely grated lemon zest
- ¼ teaspoon salt

Big butterscotch cake

This delicious big cake is perfect for breakfast or brunch and also good later in the day.
You can vary the flavor easily by changing the extracts.
Try a mixture of vanilla and almond, or lemon and almond.

Serves: 10-12; Preparation: 20 minutes; Cooking: 1 hour; Level of difficulty: 1

Preheat the oven to 325°F/170°C/gas 3. • Butter and flour a 10-inch (25-cm) tube pan. • Sift the flour, baking powder, baking soda, and salt into a large bowl. Stir in the sugar. • With an electric mixer at high speed, beat in the buttermilk, butter, eggs, and vanilla and butterscotch extracts. • Spoon the batter into the prepared pan. • Bake for about 1 hour, or until a toothpick inserted into the center comes out clean. • Cool the cake in the pan for 15 minutes. Run a knife around the edges of the pan to loosen the cake. Turn out onto a rack to cool completely.

■ INGREDIENTS

- 3 cups (450 g) all-purpose (plain) flour
- 2 teaspoons baking powder
- ½ teaspoon baking soda
- ½ teaspoon salt
- 2 cups (400 g) sugar
- 1 cup (250 ml) buttermilk
- 1 cup (250 g) butter, melted and slightly cooled
- 4 large eggs
- 2 teaspoons vanilla extract
- 1 teaspoon butterscotch extract

Right: Sweet polenta cake

Frosted lemon yogurt cake

Serves: 8-10; Preparation: 30 minutes; Cooking: 40 minutes; Level of difficulty: 1

Preheat the oven to 325°F/170°C/gas 3. • Butter a 9-inch (23-cm) round cake pan. Line with waxed paper. Butter the paper. • Sift the flour, baking powder, and salt into a medium bowl. • Beat the butter, sugar, and lemon zest in a large bowl with an electric mixer at medium speed until creamy. • Add the egg yolks, one at a time, beating until just blended after each addition. • With mixer at low speed, gradually beat in the dry ingredients, alternating with the yogurt. • With mixer at high speed, beat the egg whites in a medium bowl until stiff peaks form. Use a large rubber spatula to fold them into the batter. • Spoon the batter into the prepared pan. • Bake for about 40 minutes, or until a toothpick inserted into the center comes out clean. • Cool the cake in the pan for 5 minutes. Turn out onto a rack. Carefully remove the paper and let cool completely. • Frosting: Mix the confectioners' sugar and butter in a medium bowl. Beat in enough of the lemon juice to make a thick, spreadable frosting. Stir in the candied lemon peel. • Spread the top and sides of the cake with the frosting.

■ INGREDIENTS

- 2 cups (300 g) all-purpose (plain) flour
- 2 teaspoons baking powder
- ¼ teaspoon salt
- ½ cup (125 g) butter
- 1 cup (200 g) sugar
- 1 tablespoon grated lemon zest
- 3 large eggs, separated
- 1 cup (250 ml) yogurt

FROSTING

- 2 cups (300 g) confectioners' (icing) sugar
- 3 tablespoons butter, melted
- 2–3 tablespoons lemon juice
- 2 tablespoons candied lemon peel, coarsely chopped

Glazed citrus pound cake

Serves: 10-12; Preparation: 30 minutes; Cooking: 1 hour 15 minutes; Level of difficulty: 1

Preheat the oven to 325°F/170°C/gas 3. • Butter and flour a 10-inch (25-cm) ring pan. • Sift the flour, baking powder, baking soda, and salt into a large bowl. • Beat the butter, sugar, and orange zest in a large bowl with an electric mixer at medium speed until creamy. • Add the eggs, one at a time, beating until just blended after each addition. • With mixer at low speed, gradually beat in the dry ingredients, alternating with the milk and lemon juice. • Spoon the batter into the prepared pan. • Bake for about 1 hour 15 minutes, or until a toothpick inserted into the center comes out clean. • Run a knife around the edges of the pan to loosen the cake. Cool the cake in the pan for 15 minutes. Turn out onto a rack to cool completely. • Glaze: Beat the confectioners' sugar, milk, and orange juice in a medium bowl until smooth. Drizzle over the cake.

■ INGREDIENTS

- 3 cups (450 g) all-purpose (plain) flour
- ½ teaspoon baking powder
- ½ teaspoon baking soda
- ½ teaspoon salt
- 1 cup (250 g) butter
- 2 cups (400 g) sugar
- 2 tablespoons finely grated orange zest
- 4 large eggs
- ¾ cup (200 ml) milk
- 1 tablespoon lemon juice

GLAZE

- 2 cups (300 g) confectioners' (icing) sugar
- 1 tablespoon milk
- 1 tablespoon orange juice

Right: *Frosted lemon yogurt cake*

Jane's poppy seed cake

Serves: 8-10; Preparation: 15 minutes + 30 minutes to stand; Cooking: 50 minutes; Level of difficulty: 1

INGREDIENTS

- ¾ cup (200 ml) milk
- ⅓ cup (45 g) poppy seeds
- 2 cups (300 g) all-purpose (plain) flour
- 1 cup (200 g) sugar
- ¾ cup (200 g) butter
- 3 large eggs
- 2 teaspoons almond extract
- 2 teaspoons baking powder
- ¼ teaspoon salt

Place the milk and poppy seeds in a large bowl. Cover and let stand for 30 minutes. • Preheat the oven to 325°F/170°C/gas 3. • Butter a 9-inch (23-cm) round cake pan. Line with waxed paper. Butter the paper. • Beat the flour, sugar, butter, eggs, almond extract, baking powder, and salt into the poppy seed mixture with an electric mixer at low speed until well blended. • Spoon the batter into the prepared pan. • Bake for about 50 minutes, or until a toothpick inserted into the center comes out clean. • Cool the cake in the pan for 5 minutes. Turn out onto a rack. Carefully remove the paper and let cool completely.

Lemon-frosted poppy seed cake

Serves: 8-10; Preparation: 35 minutes; Cooking: 35 minutes; Level of difficulty: 1

INGREDIENTS

- 1 cup (250 ml) milk
- ⅓ cup (45 g) poppy seeds
- 2 cups (300 g) all-purpose (plain) flour
- 2 teaspoons baking powder
- ¼ teaspoon salt
- ¾ cup (200 g) butter
- 1½ cups (300 g) sugar
- 2 teaspoons vanilla extract
- 3 large egg whites
- 1 quantity *Lemon Frosting* (see page 30)

Bring the milk to a boil in a small saucepan over medium-low heat. Remove from the heat. Stir in the poppy seeds and set aside to cool. • Preheat the oven to 350°F/180°C/gas 4. • Butter and flour two 8-inch (20-cm) round cake pans. • Sift the flour, baking powder, and salt into a medium bowl. • Beat the butter, 1¼ cups (250 g) of sugar, and the vanilla in a large bowl with an electric mixer at medium speed until creamy. • With mixer at low speed, gradually beat in the dry ingredients, alternating with the milk and poppy seeds. • With mixer at medium speed, beat the egg whites in a large bowl until frothy. With mixer at high speed, gradually add the remaining sugar, beating until stiff, glossy peaks form. • Use a large rubber spatula to fold the beaten whites into the batter. • Spoon half the batter into each of the prepared pans. • Bake for about 35 minutes, or until a toothpick inserted into the center comes out clean. • Cool the cakes in the pans for 10 minutes. Turn out onto racks and let cool completely. • Place one cake on a serving plate. Spread with one-third of the frosting. Top with the remaining cake and spread the top and sides with the remaining frosting.

Left: Jane's poppy seed cake

Banana and ginger loaf

Serves: 6-8; Preparation: 25 minutes; Cooking: 55 minutes; Level of difficulty: 1

Preheat the oven to 350°F/180°C/gas 4. • Butter a 9 x 5-inch (23 x 13-cm) loaf pan. Line with aluminum foil, letting the edges overhang. • Sprinkle the raisins and ginger with enough flour to cover them lightly, about 1–2 tablespoons. • Sift the remaining flours and baking powder into a large bowl. • Beat the butter and confectioners' sugar in a large bowl with an electric mixer at high speed until creamy. • With mixer at medium speed, add the eggs and egg yolks one at a time, beating until just blended after each addition. • Beat in the rum, vanilla, salt, and lemon zest. • With mixer at low speed, gradually beat in the dry ingredients, followed by the raisins, ginger, and banana. • Spoon the batter into the prepared pan, smoothing the top. • Bake for about 55 minutes, or until a toothpick inserted into the center comes out clean. • Cool the loaf in the pan for 5 minutes. • Using the foil as a lifter, remove the loaf from the pan. Carefully remove the foil. Cool the loaf completely on a rack.

■ INGREDIENTS

- ¾ cup (135 g) golden raisins (sultanas), soaked in warm water for 10 minutes and drained
- ¾ cup (75 g) candied ginger, cut into small cubes
- 1 cup (150 g) all-purpose (plain) flour
- ⅓ cup (50 g) whole-wheat (wholemeal) flour
- ½ teaspoon baking powder
- ⅔ cup (180 g) butter
- 1⅓ cups (200 g) confectioners' (icing) sugar
- 2 large eggs + 4 egg yolks
- 1 tablespoon dark rum
- ½ teaspoon vanilla extract
- ⅛ teaspoon salt
- finely grated zest of 1 lemon
- 1 large ripe banana, mashed with a fork

Simple light orange cake

Serve this light and airy cake with tea or coffee or use as a base for trifles or charlottes. Dress it up with Chantilly cream (see page 26) and segments of seedless mandarins.

Serves: 6-8; Preparation: 30 minutes; Cooking: 35 minutes; Level of difficulty: 1

Preheat the oven to 350°F/180°C/gas 4. • Butter and flour a 9-inch (23-cm) springform pan. • Sift the flour, baking powder, and salt into a large bowl. • Beat the egg yolks, sugar, and orange juice and zest in a large bowl with an electric mixer at medium speed until creamy. • With mixer at low speed, gradually beat in the dry ingredients, alternating with the butter. • With mixer at high speed, beat the egg whites in a separate large bowl until stiff. Fold the egg whites into the mixture. • Spoon the batter into the prepared pan. • Bake for about 35 minutes, or until a toothpick inserted into the center comes out clean. • Cool the cake in the pan for 10 minutes. Loosen the sides and turn out onto a rack to cool completely.

■ INGREDIENTS

- 2 cups (300 g) all-purpose (plain) flour
- 2 teaspoons baking powder
- ¼ teaspoon salt
- ¾ cup (150 g) sugar
- 3 large eggs, separated
- juice and finely grated zest of 2 oranges
- 5 tablespoons butter, melted

Right: Simple light orange cake

Fluted lime and yogurt ring

Serves: 8-10; Preparation: 30 minutes; Cooking: 45 minutes; Level of difficulty: 1

Preheat the oven to 350°F/180°C/gas 4. • Butter and flour a 10-inch (25-cm) fluted tube pan. • Sift the flour, baking powder, and salt into a large bowl. • Beat the butter, sugar, and lime zest in a large bowl with an electric mixer at medium speed until pale and creamy. • With mixer at medium speed, beat in the egg yolks one at a time. • With mixer at low speed, gradually beat in the dry ingredients, alternating with the lime juice and yogurt. • With mixer at high speed, beat the egg whites in a separate large bowl until stiff. Fold the egg whites into the mixture. • Spoon the batter into the prepared pan. • Bake for about 45 minutes, or until a toothpick inserted into the center comes out clean. • Cool the cake in the pan for 10 minutes. Turn out onto a rack to cool completely. • Dust with the confectioners' sugar just before serving.

Wholesome orange syrup cake

■ INGREDIENTS

- 1 large orange
- 1½ cups (225 g) whole-wheat (wholemeal) flour
- 1 teaspoon baking powder
- ½ teaspoon baking soda
- ¼ teaspoon salt
- ½ cup (125 g) butter
- ¾ cup (150 g) sugar
- 2 large eggs
- ½ cup (125 ml) milk

SYRUP

- ½ cup (100 g) sugar
- ½ cup (125 ml) orange juice
- 4 tablespoons butter

Serves: 6-8; Preparation: 30 minutes; Cooking: 35 minutes; Level of difficulty: 1

Preheat the oven to 350°F/180°C/gas 4. • Butter and flour a 9-inch (23-cm) springform pan. • Squeeze the orange, reserving the juice for the syrup. Place the rest of the orange in a food processor and chop finely. • Sift the whole-wheat flour, baking powder, baking soda, and salt into a medium bowl. • Beat the butter and sugar in a large bowl with an electric mixer at medium speed until creamy. • Add the eggs, one at a time, beating until just blended after each addition. • With mixer at low speed, gradually beat in the dry ingredients, alternating with the milk. Stir in the chopped orange. • Spoon the batter into the prepared pan. • Bake for about 35 minutes, or until a toothpick inserted into the center comes out clean. • Cool the cake in the pan for 10 minutes. Turn onto a rack to cool. • Syrup: Stir the sugar, reserved orange juice, and butter in a saucepan over low heat until the sugar is dissolved and the butter is melted. • Place the cake on the rack in a jelly-roll pan. Poke holes in the cake with a skewer. Pour the syrup over the cake. Scoop any syrup from the pan and drizzle on the cake.

Rustic lemon and almond cake

■ INGREDIENTS

- 1⅔ cups (250 g) whole-wheat (wholemeal) flour
- 2 teaspoons baking powder
- ¼ teaspoon salt
- ⅓ cup (50 g) almonds, finely ground
- ½ cup (125 g) butter
- ¾ cup (150 g) firmly packed brown sugar
- 3 tablespoons finely grated lemon zest
- 3 large eggs
- ¾ cup (200 ml) milk
- 4 tablespoons lemon juice

Serves: 6-8; Preparation: 20 minutes; Cooking: 35 minutes; Level of difficulty: 1

Preheat the oven to 350°F/180°C/gas 4. • Butter and flour a 9-inch (23-cm) round cake pan. • Sift the flour, baking powder, and salt into a medium bowl. Stir in the almonds. • Beat the butter, brown sugar, and lemon zest in a large bowl with an electric mixer at medium speed until creamy. • Add the eggs, one at a time, beating until just blended after each addition. • With mixer at low speed, gradually beat in the dry ingredients, alternating with the milk and lemon juice. • Spoon the batter into the prepared pan. • Bake for about 35 minutes, or until a toothpick inserted into the center comes out clean. • Cool the cake in the pan for 10 minutes. Turn out onto a rack to cool completely.

Left: Wholesome orange syrup cake

Sweet lime syrup cake

Serves: 8-10; Preparation: 30 minutes; Cooking: 50 minutes; Level of difficulty: 2

Preheat the oven to 350°F/180°C/gas 4. • Butter and flour a 9-inch (23-cm) tube pan. • Stir together the flour, coconut, almonds, baking powder, and salt in a large bowl. • Beat the butter, sugar, and lime zest in a large bowl with an electric mixer at medium speed until creamy. • Add the eggs, one at a time, beating until just blended after each addition. • With mixer at low speed, gradually beat in the dry ingredients, alternating with the yogurt and lime juice. • Spoon the batter into the prepared pan. • Bake for about 50 minutes, or until a toothpick inserted into the center comes out clean. • Cool in the pan for 10 minutes. • Turn out onto a rack. • Syrup: Peel the limes and slice the zest into thin strips. Squeeze the juice from the limes and place in a small saucepan with the zest, water, honey, and cardamom pods. Bring to a boil over low heat and simmer for 5 minutes. • Strain the syrup. • Place the cake on the rack in a jelly-roll pan. • Poke holes in the cake with a skewer. Pour the syrup over the hot cake. Scoop up any syrup from the pan and drizzle over the cake.

■ INGREDIENTS

- 2½ cups (425 g) cake flour
- ¾ cup (90 g) shredded (desiccated) coconut
- ¼ cup (30 g) almonds, finely ground
- 2 teaspoons baking powder
- ¼ teaspoon salt
- 1 cup (250 g) butter
- 1 cup (200 g) sugar
- 1 tablespoon finely grated lime zest
- 3 large eggs
- ¾ cup (200 ml) plain yogurt
- 2 tablespoons lime juice

SYRUP

- 2 limes
- ½ cup (125 ml) cold water
- 4 tablespoons honey
- 4 cardamom pods, smashed with flat side of chef's knife

Sour cream citrus cake

This cake is equally good made with lemon or orange zest, instead of the lime. It can also be frosted (try Cream cheese frosting, see page 32) or Lemon glaze (see page 40).

Serves: 10-12; Preparation: 20 minutes; Cooking: 45 minutes; Level of difficulty: 1

Preheat the oven to 325°F/170°C/gas 3. • Butter a 13 x 9-inch (33 x 23-cm) baking pan. • Sift the flour, baking powder, and salt into a large bowl. • Beat the butter, sugar, and lime zest in a large bowl with an electric mixer at medium speed until creamy. • Add the eggs, one at a time, beating until just blended after each addition. • With mixer at low speed, gradually beat in the dry ingredients, alternating with the sour cream. • Spoon the batter into the prepared pan. • Bake for about 45 minutes, or until a toothpick inserted into the center comes out clean. • Cool the cake completely in the pan on a rack. • Dust with the confectioners' sugar or glaze or frost, as liked.

■ INGREDIENTS

- 2 cups (300 g) all-purpose (plain) flour
- 2 teaspoons baking powder
- ¼ teaspoon salt
- 1 cup (250 g) butter
- 2 cups (400 g) sugar
- 2 tablespoons finely grated lime zest
- 6 large eggs
- ¾ cup (200 ml) sour cream
- confectioners' (icing) sugar, to dust (optional)

Right: Sweet lime syrup cake

Raspberry tea cake

Serves: 6-8; Preparation: 30 minutes; Cooking: 35 minutes; Level of difficulty: 1

Preheat the oven to 350°F/180°C/gas 4. • Butter a 9-inch (23-cm) round cake pan. Line with waxed paper. Butter the paper. • Sift the flour, baking powder, and salt into a large bowl. • Beat the butter, sugar, and almond and vanilla extracts in a large bowl with an electric mixer at medium speed until creamy. • Add the egg yolks, one at a time, beating until just blended after each addition. • With mixer at low speed, gradually beat in the dry ingredients, alternating with the milk. • With mixer at high speed, beat the egg whites in a large bowl until stiff peaks form. • Use a large rubber spatula to fold them into the batter. • Spoon the batter into the prepared pan. • Bake for about 35 minutes, or until a toothpick inserted into the center comes out clean. • Cool the cake in the pan for 10 minutes. Turn out onto a rack. Carefully remove the paper and let cool completely. • Split the cake horizontally. Place one cake layer on a serving plate and spread with the raspberry preserves. Cover with half the buttercream. Top with the remaining layer and spread with the remaining buttercream. • Cut the candied cherries in half and press them into the top of the cake.

■ INGREDIENTS

- 1½ cups (225 g) all-purpose (plain) flour
- 1½ teaspoons baking powder
- ¼ teaspoon salt
- ½ cup (125 g) butter
- ¾ cup (150 g) sugar
- ¼ teaspoon almond extract
- ¼ teaspoon vanilla extract
- 4 large eggs, separated
- 6 tablespoons milk
- ½ cup (125 g) raspberry preserves (jam)
- 1 quantity *Almond and Vanilla Cream* (see page 38)
- candied cherries, to decorate

Fluted apricot brandy cake

Serves: 8-10; Preparation: 25 minutes; Cooking: 50 minutes; Level of difficulty: 1

Preheat the oven to 350°F/180°C/gas 4. • Butter a 9-inch (23-cm) fluted tube pan. • Sift the flour, baking soda, and salt into a large bowl. • Beat the butter, sugar, and vanilla extract in a large bowl with an electric mixer at medium speed until pale and creamy. • Add the eggs, one at a time, beating until just blended after each addition. • With mixer at low speed, gradually beat in the dry ingredients, alternating with the yogurt and brandy. • Spoon the batter into the prepared pan. • Bake for about 50 minutes, or until a toothpick inserted into the center comes out clean. • Cool the cake in the pan for 15 minutes. Turn out onto a rack to cool completely. • Dust with the confectioners' sugar just before serving.

■ INGREDIENTS

- 2 cups (300 g) all-purpose (plain) flour
- ½ teaspoon baking soda
- ½ teaspoon salt
- ⅔ cup (180 ml) butter
- 2 cups (400 g) sugar
- 2 teaspoons vanilla extract
- 4 large eggs
- ⅔ cup (180 ml) apricot yogurt
- 6 tablespoons apricot brandy
- 6 tablespoons confectioners' (icing) sugar, to dust

Right: Raspberry tea cake

Quick Mix Cakes

Wonderfully quick to make, and without any loss of flavor or texture, the cakes in this chapter can be whipped up in just a few minutes, either by hand or using an electric mixer.

Easy citrus cake

Serves: 6-8; Preparation: 10 minutes; Cooking: 40 minutes; Level of difficulty: 1

Preheat the oven to 350°F/180°C/gas 4. • Butter a 9-inch (23-cm) square pan. • Beat the flour, sugar, eggs, butter, milk, orange juice and zest, baking powder, and salt in a large bowl with an electric mixer at low speed until well blended. Increase the mixer speed to medium and beat for 5 minutes more, or until pale and thick. • Spoon the batter into the prepared pan. • Bake for about 40 minutes, or until a toothpick inserted into the center comes out clean. • Cool the cake completely in the pan on a rack. • Lemon Frosting: With a wooden spoon, beat the confectioners' sugar and butter in a medium bowl. Beat in enough lemon juice to make a spreadable frosting. • Spread the cake with the frosting.

- 1½ cups (225 g) all-purpose (plain) flour
- ⅔ cup (140 g) sugar
- 3 large eggs
- ½ cup (125 g) butter
- 4 tablespoons milk
- 2 tablespoons orange juice
- 2 tablespoons finely grated orange zest
- 1½ teaspoons baking powder
- ¼ teaspoon salt

LEMON FROSTING

- 1½ cups (225 g) confectioners' (icing) sugar
- 2 tablespoons butter, melted
- 2–3 tablespoons lemon juice

VARIATIONS
– Replace the orange juice and zest with the same quantity of lemon or lime juice and zest.
– For extra taste, dust the frosting with 2–3 tablespoons of unsweetened shredded (desiccated) coconut.

Easy lemon and vanilla cake

Serves: 6-8; Preparation: 15 minutes; Cooking: 30 minutes; Level of difficulty: 1

Preheat the oven to 325°F/170°C/gas 3. • Butter a 9-inch (23-cm) square pan. • Sift the flour, baking powder, and salt into a large bowl. • Cut in the butter until the mixture resembles coarse bread crumbs. • Add the sugar, lemon zest, and vanilla extract. Gradually beat in the milk using a wooden spoon or electric mixer on low speed until smooth. • Spoon the batter into the prepared pan. • Bake for about 30 minutes, or until a toothpick inserted into the center comes out clean. • Cool the cake completely in the pan on a rack.

- 2 cups (300 g) all-purpose (plain) flour
- 2 teaspoons baking powder
- ¼ teaspoon salt
- ½ cup (125 g) butter
- ½ cup (100 g) sugar
- 1 tablespoon finely grated lemon zest
- 1 teaspoon vanilla extract
- 1 cup (250 ml) milk

Right: *Easy citrus cake*

Filled cherry jam cake

*Vary the flavor of the preserves (jam) and nuts in this cake according to personal preference.
Apricot preserves with pecan nuts is a good combination,
as is raspberry preserves with walnuts.*

Serves: 8-10; Preparation: 20 minutes; Cooking: 30 minutes; Level of difficulty: 1

Preheat the oven to 350°F/180°C/gas 4. • Butter and flour two 9-inch (23-cm) round cake pans. • Stir together the flour, baking powder, baking soda, cinnamon, nutmeg, ginger, cloves, and salt in a large bowl. Stir in the sugar and 1 cup (125 g) nuts. • Add the oil, buttermilk, preserves, eggs, and vanilla and beat with an electric mixer at low speed until well mixed. • Spoon half the batter into each of the prepared pans and sprinkle with the remaining nuts. • Bake for about 30 minutes, or until a toothpick inserted into the center comes out clean. • Cool the cakes in the pans for 10 minutes. Turn out onto racks to cool completely. • Place a cake on a plate and spread with the Mock Cream. Top with the remaining cake.

INGREDIENTS

- 2 cups (300 g) all-purpose (plain) flour
- 1 teaspoon baking powder
- 1 teaspoon baking soda
- 1 teaspoon each ground cinnamon, nutmeg, and ginger
- ¼ teaspoon ground cloves
- ½ teaspoon salt
- 1½ cups (300 g) sugar
- 2 cups (250 g) walnuts or pecans, coarsely chopped
- 1 cup (250 ml) vegetable oil
- 1 cup (250 ml) buttermilk
- 1 cup (325 ml) cherry preserves (jam)
- 3 large eggs, lightly beaten
- 1 teaspoon vanilla extract
- 1 quantity *Mock Cream* (see page 40)

Italian almond cake

*This cake comes from the northern Italian regions of Lombardy and the Veneto. It is very dry
and crumbly and is usually served at the end of a meal accompanied by a sweet dessert wine.*

Serves: 10-12; Preparation: 30 minutes; Cooking: 40 minutes; Level of difficulty: 1

Preheat the oven to 350°F/180°C/gas 4. • Butter and flour a 10-inch (25-cm) springform pan. • Stir together the flour, almonds, sugar, and salt in a large bowl. • Use your fingers to rub the butter and eggs into the dry ingredients, until the dough resembles large crumbs. • Spoon the dough into the prepared pan, pressing it down gently. • Bake for about 40 minutes, or until a toothpick inserted into the center comes out clean. • Cool the cake in the pan for 10 minutes. Loosen the pan sides and let cool completely. • Serve broken into irregular diamond shapes.

INGREDIENTS

- 2 cups (300 g) all-purpose (plain) flour
- 2 cups (300 g) almonds, finely ground
- 1 cup (200 g) sugar
- ¼ teaspoon salt
- ⅔ cup (180 g) cold butter, cut up
- 4 large eggs, lightly beaten

Right: *Filled cherry jam cake*

Mediterranean vanilla cake

Be sure to use only the very best quality extra-virgin olive oil. Make sure too that the oil is fresh; it should not be more than 12 months old. If your oil is not fresh or of an inferior quality, the cake will have a strong, unpleasant taste and odor.

Serves: 10-12; Preparation: 25 minutes; Cooking: 1 hour; Level of difficulty: 1

Preheat the oven to 350°F/180°C/gas 4. • Butter and flour a 10-inch (25-cm) springform pan. Line with waxed paper. Butter the paper. • Sift the flour, baking powder, baking soda, and salt into a large bowl. • Beat the eggs, sugar, and vanilla in a large bowl with an electric mixer at medium speed until pale and thick. • With mixer at low speed, gradually beat in the dry ingredients, alternating with the water and oil. • Spoon the batter into the prepared pan. • Bake for about 1 hour, or until a toothpick inserted into the center comes out clean. • Cool the cake in the pan for 10 minutes. Turn out onto a rack. Carefully remove the paper and let cool completely. • Spread with the frosting.

VARIATION
– Add 4 tablespoons of unsweetened cocoa powder and frost with either *Rich Chocolate Frosting* (see page 30) or *Basic Chocolate Frosting* (see page 30).

■ INGREDIENTS

- 3 cups (450 g) all-purpose (plain) flour
- 2 teaspoons baking powder
- 1 teaspoon baking soda
- ½ teaspoon salt
- 4 large eggs
- ¾ cup (150 g) sugar
- 2 teaspoons vanilla extract
- 2 cups (500 ml) water
- ¾ cup (200 ml) vegetable oil
- 1 quantity *Vanilla Frosting* (see page 30)

Spicy spice cake

Serves: 6-8; Preparation: 25 minutes; Cooking: 45 minutes; Level of difficulty: 1

Preheat the oven to 350°F/180°C/gas 4. • Butter and flour a 9-inch (23-cm) springform pan. • Sift the flour, baking powder, cinnamon, ginger, nutmeg, cloves, and salt into a large bowl. • Beat the eggs and sugar in a large bowl with an electric mixer at medium speed until pale and thick. • With mixer at low speed, gradually beat in the dry ingredients and butter. • Spoon the batter into the prepared pan. • Bake for about 45 minutes, or until a toothpick inserted into the center comes out clean. • Cool the cake in the pan for 10 minutes. Turn out onto a rack. Carefully remove the paper and let cool completely. • Spread the top and sides with the frosting.

■ INGREDIENTS

- 1½ cups (225 g) all-purpose (plain) flour
- 1½ teaspoons baking powder
- 1 teaspoon ground cinnamon
- 1 teaspoon ground ginger
- ½ teaspoon ground nutmeg
- ¼ teaspoon ground cloves
- ¼ teaspoon salt
- 3 large eggs
- ¾ cup (150 g) sugar
- ½ cup (125 g) butter, melted
- 1½ quantities *Cream Cheese Frosting* (see page 32)

Right: *Mediterranean vanilla cake*

Quick banana cake

INGREDIENTS

- 1½ cups (225 g) all-purpose (plain) flour
- ¾ teaspoon baking soda
- ¼ teaspoon salt
- ½ cup (125 g) butter
- ¾ cup (150 g) firmly packed dark brown sugar
- 1 large egg
- 1 medium ripe banana
- 6 tablespoons milk
- ⅓ cup (45 g) coarsely chopped almonds
- 1 quantity *Vanilla Frosting* (see page 30) (optional)

Serves: 6-8; Preparation: 10 minutes; Cooking: 35 minutes; Level of difficulty: 1

Preheat the oven to 350°F/180°C/gas 4. • Butter and flour a 9-inch (23-cm) springform pan. • Sift the flour, baking soda, and salt into a large bowl. • Beat the butter, brown sugar, egg, banana, milk, and dry ingredients in a large bowl with an electric mixer at medium speed until smooth. • Stir in the almonds. • Spoon the batter into the prepared pan. • Bake for about 35 minutes, or until a toothpick inserted into the center comes out clean. • Cool the cake in the pan for 10 minutes. Turn out onto a rack. Let cool completely. • If liked, spread the top with the frosting.

Pineapple pecan cake

■ INGREDIENTS

- 2 cups (300 g) all-purpose (plain) flour
- 1½ cups (300 g) sugar
- 1 teaspoon baking soda
- ¼ teaspoon salt
- 2½ cups (250 g) crushed canned pineapple, with juice
- 2 large eggs
- ¾ cup (150 g) firmly packed brown sugar
- 1½ cups (180 g) pecans, chopped

Serves: 8-10; Preparation: 15 minutes; Cooking: 35 minutes; Level of difficulty: 1

Preheat the oven to 350°F/180°C/gas 4. • Butter and flour a 13 x 9-inch (33 x 23-cm) baking pan. • Stir together the flour, sugar, baking soda, and salt in a large bowl. Beat in the crushed pineapple and juice and eggs with an electric mixer at low speed until smooth. • Spoon the batter into the prepared pan. • Mix together the brown sugar and pecans and sprinkle evenly over the top of the cake. • Bake for about 35 minutes, or until a toothpick inserted into the center comes out clean. • Cool the cake completely in the pan on a rack.

Quick fix brunch cake

■ INGREDIENTS

- 1¼ cups (250 g) firmly packed brown sugar
- 1½ cups (225 g) all-purpose (plain) flour
- 3 large eggs
- 4 tablespoons butter
- 1 teaspoon vanilla extract
- 1 teaspoon each ground cinnamon and nutmeg
- 1 teaspoon baking powder
- ½ teaspoon baking soda
- ¼ teaspoon salt
- 2 medium tart apples, grated
- 1½ cups (180 g) walnuts, coarsely chopped
- 1 cup (180 g) raisins

Serves: 8-10; Preparation: 15 minutes; Cooking: 55 minutes; Level of difficulty: 1

Preheat the oven to 350°F/180°C/gas 4. • Butter a 9-inch (23-cm) square baking pan. • Beat the brown sugar, flour, eggs, butter, vanilla, cinnamon, nutmeg, baking powder, baking soda, and salt in a large bowl with an electric mixer at medium speed until well blended, about 3 minutes. • Stir in the apples, nuts, and raisins. • Spoon the batter into the prepared pan. • Bake for about 55 minutes, or until a toothpick inserted into the center comes out clean. • Cool the cake completely in the pan on a rack.

Left: *Quick fix brunch cake*

Fresh fruit bake

This dessert is really a type of clafoutis—just beat the eggs, sugar, and flour and pour them over the fruit in a pie pan and bake. Vary the fruit with the seasons. Delicious!

Serves: 4-6; Preparation: 10 minutes; Cooking: 20 minutes; Level of difficulty: 1

Preheat the oven to 350°F/180°C/gas 4. • Butter a 10-inch (25-cm) pie pan. • Peel, pit, and slice the fruit thinly. Place in the bottom of the prepared pan. • Beat the eggs, sugar, flour, and salt in a large bowl with an electric mixer at medium speed until thick. • Pour the batter over the fruit in the prepared pan. • Bake for about 20 minutes, or until golden and a toothpick inserted into the center comes out clean. • Serve hot or at room temperature.

INGREDIENTS

- 1 banana
- 1 large apple, peeled and cored
- 1 kiwifruit
- 1 large peach
- 2 apricots
- 5 large eggs
- ½ cup (100 g) firmly packed light brown sugar
- 4 tablespoons all-purpose (plain) flour
- ¼ teaspoon salt

Quick potato and spice fruit cake

This is an excellent way to use up leftover mashed potatoes.

Serves: 8-10; Preparation: 10 minutes + 15 minutes to cool; Cooking: 1 hour; Level of difficulty: 1

Preheat the oven to 325°F/170°C/gas 3. • Butter a 9-inch (23-cm) pie pan. • Sift the flour, baking powder, allspice, cinnamon, ginger, and salt into a large bowl. • Place the dried fruit, butter, and sugar in a large saucepan over low heat until the butter is melted. Remove from heat and let cool for 15 minutes. • Add the mashed potato, eggs, and dry ingredients and stir until well mixed. • Spoon the batter into the prepared pan. • Bake for about 1 hour, or until a toothpick inserted into the center comes out clean. • Cool the cake in the pan.

INGREDIENTS

- 2 cups (300 g) all-purpose (plain) flour
- 2 teaspoons baking powder
- 1 teaspoon each allspice, cinnamon, and ginger
- ½ teaspoon salt
- 1 lb (500 g) mixed dried fruit
- ¾ cup (200 g) butter
- 1¼ cups (250 g) firmly packed dark brown sugar
- 1 cup (250 g) mashed potato
- 2 large eggs

Right: Fresh fruit bake

Rich and tangy chocolate apple cake

Serves: 10-12; Preparation: 15 minutes; Cooking: 55 minutes; Level of difficulty: 1

Preheat the oven to 350°F/180°C/gas 4. • Butter and flour a 13 x 9-inch (33 x 23-cm) baking pan. Line with waxed paper. Butter the paper. • Beat the apples, flour, butter, sugar, eggs, cocoa, water, baking powder, baking soda, and salt in a large bowl with an electric mixer at low speed until just blended. • Spoon the batter into the prepared pan. • Bake for about 55 minutes, or until a toothpick inserted into the center comes out clean. • Cool the cake in the pan for 10 minutes. Turn out onto a rack. Carefully remove the waxed paper and let cool completely. • Spread the top and sides of the cake with the frosting.

INGREDIENTS

- 1 lb (500 g) coarsely grated tart-tasting apples (Granny Smiths are ideal)
- 2 cups (300 g) all-purpose (plain) flour
- 1½ cups (375 g) butter
- 1¼ cups (250 g) sugar
- 3 large eggs
- ⅓ cup (50 g) unsweetened cocoa powder
- 6 tablespoons water
- 2 teaspoons baking powder
- ½ teaspoon baking soda
- ¼ teaspoon salt
- 1 quantity *Rich Chocolate Frosting* (see page 30)

Quick chocolate ginger ring

Serves: 8-10; Preparation: 15 minutes; Cooking: 40 minutes; Level of difficulty: 1

Preheat the oven to 350°F/180°C/gas 4. • Butter and flour a 9-inch (23-cm) tube baking pan. • Sift the flour, cocoa, ginger, baking powder, baking soda, and salt into a large bowl. • Place the butter, corn syrup, and sugar in a large saucepan over low heat and stir until the butter is melted. Do not boil. Let cool for 5 minutes. • Add the milk, eggs, and dry ingredients to the butter mixture and beat with an electric mixer at low speed until smooth and well mixed. • Spoon the batter into the prepared pan. • Bake for about 40 minutes, or until a toothpick inserted into the center comes out clean. • Cool the cake in the pan for 10 minutes. Turn out onto a rack and let cool completely. • Spread with the frosting and sprinkle with the nuts.

INGREDIENTS

- 1⅔ cups (250 g) all-purpose (plain) flour
- ⅓ cup (50 g) unsweetened cocoa powder
- 1 tablespoon ground ginger
- 1½ teaspoons baking powder
- ½ teaspoon baking soda
- ¼ teaspoon salt
- ½ cup (125 g) butter
- ⅔ cup (180 ml) light corn (golden) syrup
- ½ cup (100 g) sugar
- ½ cup (125 ml) milk
- 2 large eggs
- 2 quantities *Basic Chocolate Frosting* (see page 30)
- ⅓ cup (45 g) coarsely chopped walnuts

Right: *Rich and tangy chocolate apple cake*

Nutty whole-wheat honey cake

INGREDIENTS

- ⅔ cup (100 g) all-purpose (plain) flour
- ⅔ cup (100 g) whole-wheat (wholemeal) flour
- 2 teaspoons baking powder
- ¼ teaspoon salt
- ⅔ cup (180 g) butter
- ½ cup (100 g) sugar
- 3 tablespoons honey
- 6 tablespoons milk
- 1 large egg, lightly beaten
- 1½ quantities *Cream Cheese Frosting* (see page 32)

Serves: 6-8; Preparation: 15 minutes; Cooking: 40 minutes; Level of difficulty: 1

Preheat the oven to 350°F/180°C/gas 4. • Butter and flour a deep 8-inch (20-cm) springform pan. • Sift both flours, the baking powder, and salt into a large bowl. • Place the butter, sugar, honey, and milk in a medium saucepan over low heat and stir until the butter is melted. Do not boil. Let cool 5 minutes. • Add the egg and dry ingredients and beat with an electric mixer at low speed until smooth and well mixed. • Spoon the batter into the prepared pan. • Bake for about 40 minutes, or until a toothpick inserted into the center comes out clean. • Cool the cake in the pan for 10 minutes. Turn out onto a rack and let cool completely. • Spread with the frosting.

Boiled pineapple and date loaf

Serves: 8-10; Preparation: 15 minutes + 30 minutes to cool; Cooking: 55 minutes; Level of difficulty: 1

Preheat the oven to 325°F/170°C/gas 3. • Butter a 9 x 5-inch (23 x 13-cm) loaf pan. Line with aluminum foil, letting the edges overhang. Butter the foil. • Sift the flour, baking powder, and salt into a large bowl. • Place the pineapple, dates, butter, and sugar in a large saucepan over medium-low heat. Bring to a boil, stirring constantly. Boil for 3 minutes, then remove from heat. Let cool for 30 minutes. • Add the eggs and dry ingredients and beat until smooth. • Spoon the batter into the prepared pan. • Bake for about 55 minutes, or until a toothpick inserted into the center comes out clean. • Cool the cake in the pan for 10 minutes. Turn out onto a rack to cool completely. • If liked, spread the top and sides of the loaf with frosting.

■ INGREDIENTS

- 2 cups (300 g) all-purpose (plain) flour
- 2 teaspoons baking powder
- ¼ teaspoon salt
- 1 can (14 oz/450 g) crushed pineapple, in heavy syrup
- 1½ cups (250 g) pitted dates, coarsely chopped
- ½ cup (125 g) butter
- ½ cup (100 g) sugar
- 2 large eggs, lightly beaten
- 1½ quantities *Cream Cheese Frosting* (see page 32) (optional)

Sweet and sticky raisin loaf

Serves: 6-8; Preparation: 10 minutes; Cooking: 1 hour 15 minutes; Level of difficulty: 1

Preheat the oven to 300°F/150°C/gas 2. • Butter a 9 x 5-inch (23 x 13-cm) loaf pan. Line with aluminum foil, letting the edges overhang. Butter the foil. • Beat the raisins, flour, brown sugar, butter, eggs, sherry, marmalade, baking powder, and salt in a large bowl with an electric mixer at low speed until well blended. • Spoon the batter into the prepared pan. • Bake for about 1 hour and 15 minutes, or until a toothpick inserted into the center comes out clean. • Cool the cake in the pan for 15 minutes. Turn out onto a rack to cool completely.

VARIATION
– Change the flavor of this more-ish loaf by replacing the sherry with Tequila or dark rum.

■ INGREDIENTS

- 1 lb (500 g) raisins or golden raisins (sultanas)
- 1 cup (150 g) all-purpose (plain) flour
- ¾ cup (150 g) firmly packed brown sugar
- ½ cup (125 g) butter, melted
- 2 large eggs, lightly beaten
- 4 tablespoons sweet sherry
- 2 tablespoons orange marmalade
- 1 teaspoon baking powder
- ¼ teaspoon salt

Right: *Sweet and sticky raisin loaf*

Fresh Fruit Cakes

Packed with vitamins and naturally sweet, fresh fruit makes a wonderful basic ingredient for a range of cakes. This chapter includes recipes for everything from exotic passion fruit sheet cakes to tasty banana cakes and classic apple crumbles.

Apple crumble cake

Serves: 8-10; Preparation: 30 minutes; Cooking: 45 minutes; Level of difficulty: 1

Preheat the oven to 350°F/180°C/gas 4. • Butter a 9-inch (23-cm) square baking pan. • Bring the apples, lemon juice, and brown sugar to a boil in a medium saucepan over medium heat. Cover, reduce the heat, and simmer for about 10 minutes, or until tender. Drain well and set aside to cool. • Beat the butter and sugar in a large bowl with an electric mixer at medium speed until creamy. • Add the eggs, one at a time, beating until just blended after each addition. • With mixer at low speed, gradually beat in the flour, baking powder, and salt, alternating with the milk. • Spoon two-thirds of the batter into the prepared pan. Spoon the apples over the top. Spoon the remaining batter on top. • Crumble: Stir together the flour, brown sugar, and cinnamon in a large bowl. Use a pastry blender to cut in the butter until the mixture resembles coarse crumbs. Stir in the walnuts. • Sprinkle over the cake. • Bake for about 45 minutes, or until a toothpick inserted into the center comes out clean. • Cool the cake completely in the pan on a rack.

INGREDIENTS

- 14 oz (400 g) tart-tasting cooking apples, peeled, cored, and thinly sliced
- 4 tablespoons lemon juice
- 2 tablespoons brown sugar
- ¾ cup (200 g) butter
- ¾ cup (150 g) sugar
- 2 large eggs
- 2⅓ cups (350 g) all-purpose (plain) flour
- 2 teaspoons baking powder
- ¼ teaspoon salt
- ¾ cup (200 ml) milk

CRUMBLE
- 1 cup (150 g) all-purpose (plain) flour
- ½ cup (100 g) firmly packed brown sugar
- 1 tablespoon ground cinnamon
- 6 tablespoons cold butter
- 1 cup (125 g) walnuts, coarsely chopped

Glazed banana loaf

Serves: 6-8; Preparation: 30 minutes; Cooking: 40 minutes; Level of difficulty: 1

Preheat the oven to 350°F/180°C/gas 4. • Butter and flour an 9 x 5-inch (23 x 13-cm) loaf pan. • Stir together the flour, sugar, baking powder, cinnamon, and salt in a large bowl. • Process the bananas and eggs in a food processor until smooth. • Stir the banana mixture and butter into the mixed dry ingredients until well blended. • Spoon the batter into the prepared pan. • Bake for about 40 minutes, or until a toothpick inserted into the center comes out clean. • Cool the loaf in the pan for 10 minutes. Turn out onto a rack to cool completely. • Spread with the frosting.

INGREDIENTS

- 1½ cups (225 g) all-purpose (plain) flour
- ¾ cup (150 g) sugar
- 1½ teaspoons baking powder
- 1 teaspoon ground cinnamon
- ¼ teaspoon salt
- 2 large very ripe bananas
- 2 large eggs
- ⅔ cup (180 g) butter, melted
- 1½ quantities *Vanilla Frosting* (see page 30)

VARIATION
– Omit the frosting and serve thinly sliced with just a scraping of salted butter.

Right: *Apple crumble cake*

INGREDIENTS

- 2 cups (300 g) all-purpose (plain) flour
- ⅔ cup (180 g) sugar
- ½ cup (75 g) toasted wheat germ
- 2 teaspoons baking powder
- ½ teaspoon baking soda
- 1 teaspoon ground cinnamon
- ½ teaspoon ground nutmeg
- ¼ teaspoon ground cloves
- ½ teaspoon salt
- 1 cup (250 g) unsweetened applesauce
- ½ cup (60 g) raisins
- 2 tablespoons grated orange zest
- 1 large egg
- 1 tablespoon extra-virgin olive oil
- ½ cup (125 ml) orange juice

INGREDIENTS

- ⅓ cup (75 g) firmly packed brown sugar
- 2 large apples, peeled and cored
- 1 tablespoon lemon juice
- 2 cups (300 g) all-purpose (plain) flour
- 1½ teaspoons baking powder
- ½ teaspoon baking soda
- 1 teaspoon each ground cardamom and cinnamon
- ¼ teaspoon salt
- ¾ cup (200 g) butter
- ¾ cup (150 g) sugar
- 1 teaspoon vanilla extract
- 2 large eggs
- ½ cup (125 ml) milk

Healthy applesauce cake

Serves: 8-10; Preparation: 15 minutes; Cooking: 40 minutes; Level of difficulty: 1

Preheat the oven to 350°F/180°C/gas 4. • Butter and flour a 9-inch (23-cm) cake pan. • Stir together the flour, sugar, wheat germ, baking powder, baking soda, cinnamon, nutmeg, cloves, and salt in a large bowl. • Beat in the applesauce, raisins, and orange zest with an electric mixer at low speed until well blended. • With a fork, beat the egg and oil into the orange juice. Beat the orange juice mixture into the batter. • Spoon the batter into the prepared pan. • Bake for about 40 minutes, or until a toothpick inserted into the center comes out clean. • Cool the cake completely in the pan on a rack.

French apple cake

Serves: 8-10; Preparation: 30 minutes; Cooking: 50 minutes; Level of difficulty: 1

Preheat the oven to 350°F/180°C/gas 4. • Butter a 9-inch (23-cm) round cake pan. • Sprinkle the pan with half the brown sugar. Slice one apple into thin rings and lay over the brown sugar. Sprinkle with the remaining brown sugar and drizzle with the lemon juice. • Sift the flour, baking powder, baking soda, cardamom, cinnamon, and salt into a medium bowl. • Beat the butter, sugar, and vanilla in a large bowl with an electric mixer at medium speed until creamy. • Add the eggs, one at a time, beating until just blended after each addition. • With mixer at low speed, gradually beat in the dry ingredients, alternating with the milk. • Chop the remaining apple finely and stir into the batter. • Spoon the batter over the sliced apple. • Bake for about 50 minutes, or until a toothpick inserted into the center comes out clean. • Cool the cake in the pan for 15 minutes. Turn out onto a rack. • Serve warm or at room temperature.

Left: *Healthy applesauce cake*

Whole-wheat banana cake

Serves: 8-10; Preparation: 30 minutes; Cooking: 50 minutes; Level of difficulty: 1

Preheat the oven to 350°F/180°C/gas 4. • Butter and flour a 9-inch (23-cm) square cake pan. • Chop the dates in a food processor with the milk. • Add the oil, egg yolks, and applesauce and blend until smooth. • Stir together the flour, milk powder, cinnamon, baking powder, baking soda, cloves, nutmeg, and salt in a large bowl. • With an electric mixer at low speed, gradually beat in the date mixture and bananas. • With mixer at high speed, beat the egg whites in a large bowl until stiff peaks form. Use a large rubber spatula to fold them into the batter. • Spoon the batter into the prepared pan. • Bake for about 50 minutes, or until a toothpick inserted into the center comes out clean. • Cool the cake in the pan on a rack.

VARIATION
– Spread with *Vanilla Frosting* (see page 30) or *Cream Cheese Frosting* (see page 32).

■ INGREDIENTS

- ½ cup (60 g) pitted dates
- ½ cup (125 ml) milk
- 4 tablespoons vegetable oil
- 2 large eggs, separated
- ¾ cup (200 ml) unsweetened applesauce
- 2 cups (300 g) whole-wheat (wholemeal) flour
- 2 tablespoons nonfat dry milk powder
- 2 teaspoons ground cinnamon
- 2 teaspoons baking powder
- 1 teaspoon baking soda
- ½ teaspoon each ground cloves and nutmeg
- ½ teaspoon salt
- 2 large very ripe bananas, mashed with a fork

Chocolate banana bake

Serves: 10-12; Preparation: 30 minutes; Cooking: 1 hour; Level of difficulty: 1

Preheat the oven to 350°F/180°C/gas 4. • Butter and flour a 9-inch (23-cm) tube pan. • Sift the flour, baking powder, baking soda, cinnamon, ginger, allspice, and salt into a large bowl. • Beat the butter, brown sugar, and vanilla in a large bowl with an electric mixer at medium speed until creamy. • Add the egg yolks, one at a time, beating until just blended after each addition. • With mixer at low speed, gradually beat in the bananas, followed by the dry ingredients and chocolate chips. • With mixer at high speed, beat the egg whites in a large bowl until stiff peaks form. Use a large rubber spatula to fold them into the batter. • Spoon the batter into the prepared pan. • Bake for about 1 hour, or until a toothpick inserted into the center comes out clean. • Cool the cake in the pan for 15 minutes. Turn out onto a rack to cool completely. • Spread the top and sides of the cake with the frosting, if desired.

■ INGREDIENTS

- 3 cups (450 g) all-purpose (plain) flour
- 1 teaspoon each baking powder and baking soda
- 1 teaspoon each ground cinnamon and ginger
- ½ teaspoon allspice
- ¼ teaspoon salt
- ½ cup (125 g) butter
- 1½ cups (300 g) firmly packed brown sugar
- 2 teaspoons vanilla extract
- 4 large eggs, separated
- 3 large very ripe bananas, mashed with a fork
- 1 cup (200 g) semisweet chocolate chips
- 1 quantity *Rich Chocolate Frosting* (see page 30) (optional)

Right: *Whole-wheat banana cake*

Apricot ring

- 1 cup (150 g) whole-wheat (wholemeal) flour
- 1 cup (150 g) all-purpose (plain) flour
- 1 teaspoon baking powder
- ½ teaspoon baking soda
- 1 teaspoon each ground cinnamon and ginger
- ¼ teaspoon salt
- ½ cup (125 g) butter
- ¾ cup (150 g) firmly packed brown sugar
- 1 tablespoon finely grated orange zest
- 2 large eggs
- 1 cup (250 ml) plain yogurt
- 1 tablespoon orange juice
- 2 cups (400 g) chopped canned apricots

TOPPING

- ⅓ cup (50 g) all-purpose (plain) flour
- ¼ cup (50 g) firmly packed brown sugar
- 2 tablespoons butter
- 1 tablespoon finely grated orange zest
- 1 teaspoon each ground cinnamon and ginger

Serves: 8-10; Preparation: 30 minutes; Cooking: 55 minutes; Level of difficulty: 2

Preheat the oven to 350°F/180°C/gas 4. • Butter and flour a 10-inch (25-cm) tube pan. • Sift both flours, baking powder, baking soda, cinnamon, ginger, and salt into a large bowl. • Beat the butter, brown sugar, and orange zest in a large bowl with an electric mixer at medium speed until creamy. • Add the eggs, one at a time, beating until just blended after each addition. • With mixer at low speed, gradually beat in the dry ingredients, alternating with the yogurt and orange juice. Stir in the apricots. • Spoon the batter into the prepared pan. • Topping: Stir all the ingredients in a medium bowl until crumbly. Sprinkle over the batter. • Bake for about 55 minutes, or until a toothpick inserted into the center comes out clean. • Cool the cake completely in the pan on a rack. Carefully turn out of the pan and serve topping-side up.

Frosted lemon and raisin loaf

- 1½ cups (225 g) all-purpose (plain) flour
- ½ teaspoon baking soda
- 6 tablespoons butter
- ½ cup (100 g) sugar
- finely grated zest and juice of 1 lemon
- 1 cup (120 g) raisins
- ½ cup (125 ml) milk
- ½ quantity *Lemon Frosting* (see page 30)

Serves: 6-8; Preparation: 30 minutes; Cooking: 45 minutes; Level of difficulty: 1

Preheat the oven to 325°F/170°C/gas 3. • Butter a 9 x 5-inch (23 x 13-cm) loaf pan. Line with aluminum foil, letting the edges overhang. Butter the foil. • Sift the flour and baking soda into a medium bowl. • Use your fingers to rub in the butter until the mixture resembles coarse crumbs. • Stir in the sugar, lemon zest, and raisins. • Mix in the lemon juice and milk until well blended. • Spoon the batter into the prepared pan. • Bake for about 45 minutes, or until a toothpick inserted into the center comes out clean. • Cool the cake in the pan for 15 minutes. Invert onto a rack and carefully remove the paper. Let cool completely. • Spread with the frosting.

Left: Apricot ring

Pear and nut sheet cake

Serves: 8-10; Preparation: 30 minutes; Cooking: 50 minutes; Level of difficulty: 1

Preheat the oven to 350°F/180°C/gas 4. • Butter and flour a 13 x 9-inch (33 x 23-cm) baking pan. • Topping: Stir the brown sugar, flour, and cinnamon in a medium bowl. Use a pastry blender to cut in the butter until the mixture resembles fine crumbs. Stir in the hazelnuts. • Cake: Sift the flour, baking powder, cinnamon, baking soda, and salt into a medium bowl. • Beat the butter, sugar, and lemon extract in a large bowl with an electric mixer at medium speed until creamy. • Add the eggs, one at a time, beating until just blended after each addition. • With mixer at low speed, gradually beat in the dry ingredients, alternating with the sour cream. • Stir in the pears. • Spoon the batter into the prepared pan. • Sprinkle with the topping. • Bake for about 50 minutes, or until a toothpick inserted into the center comes out clean. • Cool the cake completely in the pan on a rack.

VARIATIONS
– Replace the hazelnuts in the topping with the same amount of walnuts.
– Replace the pears with two large, very ripe yellow peaches. Peel and dice before adding to the batter.

INGREDIENTS

TOPPING
- ½ cup (100 g) firmly packed brown sugar
- ⅓ cup (50 g) all-purpose (plain) flour
- 1 teaspoon ground cinnamon
- 4 tablespoons butter
- ¾ cup (100 g) hazelnuts, coarsely chopped

CAKE
- 1½ cups (225 g) all-purpose (plain) flour
- 1 teaspoon baking powder
- 1 teaspoon ground cinnamon
- ½ teaspoon baking soda
- ¼ teaspoon salt
- ½ cup (125 g) butter
- 1 cup (200 g) sugar
- ½ teaspoon lemon extract
- 2 large eggs
- ¾ cup (200 ml) sour cream
- 2 large firm-ripe pears, peeled, cored, and diced

Pear and marsala bake

Serves: 10-12; Preparation: 30 minutes; Cooking: 35 minutes; Level of difficulty: 1

Place the pears in a bowl and drizzle with the lemon juice. • Preheat the oven to 350°F/180°C/gas 4. • Butter a 9-inch (23-cm) springform pan. • Sift the flour, 2 teaspoons cinnamon, baking powder, and salt into a large bowl. • Beat the eggs and ¾ cup (150 g) of sugar in a large bowl with an electric mixer at high speed until pale and thick. • With mixer at low speed, gradually beat in the dry ingredients, alternating with the melted butter and wine. • Spoon half the batter into the prepared pan. Top with the pears. • Dot the pears with the butter and sprinkle with 3 tablespoons sugar and the remaining cinnamon. • Spoon the remaining batter over the top. Don't worry if the pears are not completely covered. Sprinkle with the remaining sugar. • Bake for about 35 minutes, or until a toothpick inserted into the center comes out clean. • Cool the cake completely in the pan on a rack. Loosen and remove the pan sides to serve.

INGREDIENTS

- 2 lb (1 kg) ripe pears, peeled, cored, and sliced
- 3 tablespoons lemon juice
- 1⅓ cups (200 g) all-purpose (plain) flour
- 1 tablespoon ground cinnamon
- 1½ teaspoons baking powder
- ¼ teaspoon salt
- 3 large eggs
- 1½ cups (300 g) sugar
- ½ cup (125 g) butter, melted + 3 tablespoons
- 6 tablespoons dry Marsala wine

Right: Pear and nut sheet cake

Polenta and apple cake

■ INGREDIENTS

- 1 cup (250 g) butter
- 1 cup (200 g) sugar +
  2 tablespoons extra
- 1½ cups (225 g) polenta
  (yellow cornmeal)
- 1½ cups (225 g) all-
  purpose (plain) flour
- 2 teaspoons baking
  powder
- ⅔ cup (180 ml) vegetable
  oil
- ½ cup (125 ml) dry white
  wine
- 1 apple, peeled, cored,
  and thinly sliced
- 2 tablespoons lemon
  juice

Serves: 8-10; Preparation: 20 minutes; Cooking: 50 minutes; Level of difficulty: 1

Preheat the oven to 350°F/180°C/gas 4. • Butter a 9-inch (23-cm) springform pan. • Beat the butter and sugar in a large bowl with an electric mixer at medium speed until pale and creamy. • With mixer at low speed, gradually beat in the polenta, flour, and baking powder, followed by the the oil and wine. • Spoon the batter into the prepared pan. • Arrange the apple over the batter. Drizzle with the lemon juice and sprinkle with the extra sugar. • Bake for about 50 minutes, or until a toothpick inserted into the center comes out clean. • Cool the cake in the pan for 15 minutes. Loosen and remove the pan sides and let cool completely.

Banana passion sheet cake

Serves: 8-10; Preparation: 30 minutes; Cooking: 45 minutes; Level of difficulty: 1

Preheat the oven to 350°F/180°C/gas 4. • Butter a 9-inch (23-cm) square baking pan. • Sift the flour, baking powder, baking soda, ginger, and salt into a medium bowl. • Beat the butter and brown sugar in a large bowl with an electric mixer at medium speed until creamy. • Add the eggs, one at a time, beating until just blended after each addition. • With mixer at low speed, gradually beat in the dry ingredients, alternating with the bananas, sour cream, and milk. • Spoon the batter into the prepared pan. • Bake for about 45 minutes, or until a toothpick inserted into the center comes out clean. • Cool the cake completely in the pan. • Frosting: Stir together the confectioners' sugar, passion fruit pulp, and butter in a double boiler over barely simmering water until thick and spreadable. Add more confectioners' sugar if needed. • Spread the top of the cake with the frosting.

■ INGREDIENTS

- 1⅔ cups (250 g) all-purpose (plain) flour
- 1 teaspoon each baking powder and baking soda
- 1 teaspoon ground ginger
- ¼ teaspoon salt
- ½ cup (125 g) butter
- ¾ cup (150 g) firmly packed dark brown sugar
- 3 large eggs
- 2 large very ripe bananas, mashed with a fork
- ½ cup (125 ml) sour cream
- 4 tablespoons milk

FROSTING

- 2 cups (300 g) confectioners' (icing) sugar
- 3–4 tablespoons fresh passion fruit pulp
- 1 tablespoon butter

Upside-down orange polenta cake

Serves: 10-12; Preparation: 30 minutes; Cooking: 55 minutes; Level of difficulty: 1

Preheat the oven to 350°F/180°C/gas 4. • Butter a 9-inch (23-cm) springform pan. • Heat 1¼ cups (310 ml) of water and ¾ cup (150 g) of sugar in a large saucepan over medium heat. Bring to a boil and cook and stir for 5 minutes. • Add the oranges and simmer for 8 minutes, or until the peel is tender. • Remove the slices from the syrup and press them onto the bottom and sides of the prepared pan. • Return the syrup to heat and stir in the remaining water. Simmer until light gold. Spoon the syrup over the slices in the pan. • Stir the flour, polenta, almonds, baking powder, and salt in a medium bowl. • Beat the butter, remaining sugar, and orange zest in a large bowl until creamy. • Add the eggs, one at a time, beating until just blended after each addition. • Gradually beat in the dry ingredients, alternating with the sour cream and orange juice. • Spoon the batter into the prepared pan. • Bake for about 55 minutes, or until a toothpick inserted into the center comes out clean. • Cool the cake in the pan for 15 minutes. Loosen and remove the pan sides. Invert onto a serving dish. Serve warm.

■ INGREDIENTS

- 1½ cups (375 ml) water
- 1¾ cups (350 g) sugar
- 2 large oranges, thinly sliced
- 1 cup (150 g) all-purpose (plain) flour
- ⅔ cup (100 g) polenta (yellow cornmeal)
- ½ cup (75 g) almonds, finely ground
- 1 teaspoon baking powder
- ¼ teaspoon salt
- ½ cup (125 g) butter
- 1 tablespoon finely grated orange zest
- 3 large eggs
- 6 tablespoons sour cream
- 4 tablespoons orange juice

Right: Banana passion sheet cake

Frosted banana lemon cake

■ INGREDIENTS

- 2 cups (300 g) all-purpose (plain) flour
- 1 teaspoon baking powder
- 1 teaspoon baking soda
- ¼ teaspoon salt
- ¾ cup (200 g) butter
- 1 cup (200 g) sugar
- 2 large eggs
- 1 cup (225 g) mashed banana
- 1 tablespoon finely grated lemon zest
- 4 tablespoons yogurt

FROSTING

- 2 cups (300 g) confectioners' (icing) sugar
- 2 tablespoons plain yogurt
- 1 tablespoon finely grated lemon zest
- 2 tablespoons lemon juice

Serves: 8-10; Preparation: 30 minutes; Cooking: 55 minutes; Level of difficulty: 1

Preheat the oven to 350°F/180°C/gas 4. • Butter a 9-inch (23-cm) square baking pan. Line with waxed paper. • Sift the flour, baking powder, baking soda, and salt into a large bowl. • Beat the butter and sugar in a large bowl with an electric mixer at medium speed until creamy. • Add the eggs, one at a time, beating until just blended after each addition. • With mixer at low speed, gradually beat in the banana, lemon zest, and dry ingredients, alternating with the yogurt. • Spoon the batter into the prepared pan. • Bake for about 55 minutes, or until a toothpick inserted into the center comes out clean. • Cool the cake in the pan for 10 minutes. Turn out onto a rack. Carefully remove the paper and let cool completely. • Frosting: With mixer at low speed, beat the confectioners' sugar, yogurt, lemon zest, and 1 tablespoon lemon juice in a large bowl until smooth and spreadable. Add the remaining lemon juice as required. • Spread over the top and sides of the cake.

Orange and almond loaf

■ INGREDIENTS

- ¾ cup (125 g) raisins
- 1 cup (250 ml) warm water
- 1½ cups (225 g) all-purpose (plain) flour
- 1½ teaspoons baking powder
- ¼ teaspoon salt
- ½ cup (125 ml) milk
- 1 large egg, lightly beaten
- 6 tablespoons butter, melted
- 6 tablespoons orange marmalade
- 2 tablespoons brandy
- 2 tablespoons grated orange zest
- 1 cup (120 g) almonds, coarsely chopped

Serves: 8-10; Preparation: 40 minutes; Cooking: 45 minutes; Level of difficulty: 1

Plump the raisins in the water in a small bowl for 20 minutes. Drain well and pat dry with paper towels. • Preheat the oven to 350°F/180°C/gas 4. • Butter a 9 x 5-inch (23 x 13-cm) loaf pan. Line with aluminum foil, letting the edges overhang. Butter the foil. • Sift the flour, baking powder, and salt into a large bowl. • Beat in the milk, egg, butter, marmalade, brandy, and orange zest with an electric mixer at low speed. • Stir in the almonds and raisins. • Spoon the batter into the prepared pan. • Bake for about 45 minutes, or until a toothpick inserted into the center comes out clean. • Cool the loaf on a rack for 10 minutes. Using the foil as a lifter, remove the loaf from the pan. Carefully remove the foil. Cool the loaf completely on a rack.

VARIATION
– Replace the orange marmalade and grated zest with the same quantities of lemon marmalade and grated lemon zest.

Left: Frosted banana lemon cake

Green glazed coconut cake

The green food coloring in the frosting gives this cake a rather "glamorous" appearance.
You may leave it out, if preferred.

Serves: 10-12; Preparation: 30 minutes; Cooking: 25 minutes; Level of difficulty: 1

Preheat the oven to 350°F/180°C/gas 4. • Butter and flour a 13 x 9-inch (33 x 23-cm) baking pan. • Sift the flour, baking powder, baking soda, and salt into a medium bowl. • Beat the butter, sugar, and lime zest in a large bowl with an electric mixer at medium speed until creamy. • Add the egg yolks, one at a time, beating until just blended after each addition. • With mixer at low speed, gradually beat in the dry ingredients, alternating with the lime juice. • With mixer at high speed, beat the egg whites in a large bowl until stiff peaks form. • Use a large rubber spatula to fold them into the batter. Fold in the coconut. • Spoon the batter into the prepared pan. • Bake for about 25 minutes, or until a toothpick inserted into the center comes out clean. • Cool the cake completely in the pan on a rack. • Frosting: Mix the confectioners' sugar, and butter in a medium bowl. Beat in the food coloring and enough lime juice to make a fairly soft frosting. Spread over the cake.

■ INGREDIENTS

- 2 cups (300 g) all-purpose (plain) flour
- 1 teaspoon baking powder
- ½ teaspoon baking soda
- ¼ teaspoon salt
- 1 cup (250 g) butter
- ¾ cup (150 g) sugar
- 2 tablespoons finely grated lime zest
- 5 large eggs, separated
- 4 tablespoons lime juice
- 1½ cups (225 g) shredded (desiccated) coconut

FROSTING
- 2 cups (300 g) confectioners' (icing) sugar
- 4 tablespoons butter, melted
- ½ teaspoon green food coloring
- 2–3 tablespoons lime juice

Blueberry cake with cinnamon crumble

Serves: 10-12; Preparation: 30 minutes; Cooking: 45 minutes; Level of difficulty: 1

Preheat the oven to 350°F/180°C/gas 4. • Butter and flour a 13 x 9-inch (33 x 23-cm) baking pan. • Crumble: Stir together the flour, sugar, and cinnamon in a medium bowl. Use a pastry blender to cut in the butter until the mixture resembles fine crumbs. • Cake: Sift the flour, baking powder, and salt into a medium bowl. • Beat the butter, sugar, and vanilla in a large bowl with an electric mixer at medium speed until creamy. • Add the eggs, one at a time, beating until just blended after each addition. • With mixer at low speed, gradually beat in the dry ingredients, alternating with the milk. • Stir in the blueberries. • Spoon the batter into the prepared pan. Sprinkle with the crumble. • Bake for about 45 minutes, or until a toothpick inserted into the center comes out clean. • Cool the cake completely in the pan on a rack.

■ INGREDIENTS

CRUMBLE
- ½ cup (75 g) all-purpose (plain) flour
- ½ cup (100 g) sugar
- 1 teaspoon ground cinnamon
- 4 tablespoons cold butter

CAKE
- 2 cups (300 g) all-purpose (plain) flour
- 2 teaspoons baking powder
- ¼ teaspoon salt
- ½ cup (125 g) butter
- ¾ cup (150 g) sugar
- ½ teaspoon vanilla extract
- 2 large eggs
- 6 tablespoons milk
- 2 cups (300 g) fresh or frozen blueberries

Right: *Green glazed coconut cake*

Banana and white chocolate cake

Serves: 10-12; Preparation: 35 minutes; Cooking: 30 minutes; Level of difficulty: 1

Preheat the oven to 350°F/180°C/gas 4. • Butter two 9-inch (23-cm) round cake pans. Line with waxed paper. Butter the paper. • Sift the flour, baking powder, baking soda, ginger, cloves, and salt into a large bowl. • Beat the butter, brown sugar, and vanilla in a large bowl with an electric mixer at medium speed until creamy. • Add the eggs, one at a time, beating until just blended after each addition. • With mixer at low speed, gradually beat in the bananas and dry ingredients, alternating with the yogurt. Stir in the chocolate chips. • Spoon half the batter into each of the prepared pans. • Bake for about 30 minutes, or until a toothpick inserted into the center comes out clean. • Cool the cakes in the pans for 15 minutes. Turn out onto racks. Carefully remove the paper and let cool completely. • Place a cake on a serving plate. Spread with the Chantilly Cream. • Peel and slice the whole banana thinly, and drizzle with the lemon juice so it doesn't discolor. Top the cream with the banana slices and cover with the remaining cake. • Dust with the confectioners' sugar.

■ INGREDIENTS

- 3 cups (450 g) all-purpose (plain) flour
- 1½ teaspoons baking powder
- 1 teaspoon baking soda
- 1 teaspoon ground ginger
- ½ teaspoon cloves
- ½ teaspoon salt
- ⅔ cup (180 g) butter
- 1¼ cups (250 g) brown sugar
- 2 teaspoons vanilla extract
- 3 large eggs
- 3 large very ripe bananas, mashed + 1 extra, whole
- ½ cup (125 g) plain yogurt
- 1 cup (120 g) white chocolate chips
- ½ quantity *Chantilly Cream* (see page 26)
- 1 tablespoon lemon juice
- ⅓ cup (50 g) confectioners' (icing) sugar

Pineapple and macadamia cake

Serves: 10-12; Preparation: 30 minutes; Cooking: 1 hour; Level of difficulty: 1

Preheat the oven to 350°F/180°C/gas 4. • Butter and flour a 10-inch (25-cm) tube pan. • Sift the flour, baking powder, baking soda, and salt into a large bowl. Stir in the coconut. • Beat the butter, sugar, and coconut extract in a large bowl with an electric mixer at medium speed until creamy. • Add the eggs, one at a time, beating until just blended after each addition. • With mixer at low speed, gradually beat in the dry ingredients, alternating with the pineapple. Stir in the nuts. • Spoon the batter into the prepared pan. • Bake for about 1 hour, or until a toothpick inserted into the center comes out clean. • Cool the cake in the pan for 10 minutes. Turn out onto a rack to cool completely.

■ INGREDIENTS

- 2 cups (300 g) all-purpose (plain) flour
- 1 teaspoon baking powder
- 1 teaspoon baking soda
- ¼ teaspoon salt
- ¾ cup (120 g) shredded (desiccated) coconut
- ¾ cup (200 g) butter
- 1½ cups (300 g) sugar
- 1 teaspoon coconut extract
- 3 large eggs
- 1 can (20 oz/625 g) crushed pineapple, drained
- 1 cup (120 g) macadamia nuts, chopped

Right: Banana and white chocolate cake

Layered pineapple and apricot loaf

Serves: 6-8; Preparation: 25 minutes; Cooking: 45 minutes; Level of difficulty: 1

Preheat the oven to 350°F/180°C/gas 4. • Butter a 9 x 5-inch (23 x 13-cm) loaf pan. Line with aluminum foil, letting the edges overhang. Butter the foil. • Stir together the flour, almonds, baking powder, and salt in a large bowl. • Place the butter, sugar, and apricot nectar in a medium saucepan over medium heat and stir until the sugar has dissolved. Remove from heat and let cool slightly. • Beat the butter mixture into the dry ingredients with an electric mixer at low speed. • With mixer at medium speed, add the eggs, one at a time, beating until just blended after each addition. • Spoon the batter into the prepared pan. • Bake for about 45 minutes, or until a toothpick inserted into the center comes out clean. • Cool in the pan for 15 minutes. Using the foil as a lifter, remove the loaf from the pan. Carefully remove the foil and let cool completely on a rack. • Coarsely chop 5 pineapple rings. • With mixer at high speed, beat the cream and confectioners' sugar in a large bowl until stiff. • Split the cake into thirds horizontally. • Place a cake layer on a serving plate. Brush with a little pineapple syrup. Spread with a quarter of the cream and half the chopped pineapple. Repeat with another cake layer. Top with the remaining layer. Brush with pineapple syrup. Spread the top and sides with the remaining cream. • Press the almonds into the sides of the cake and decorate the top with the remaining pineapple rings.

INGREDIENTS

- 1 cup (150 g) all-purpose (plain) flour
- ½ cup (60 g) almonds, finely ground
- 1½ teaspoons baking powder
- ¼ teaspoon salt
- ¾ cup (200 g) butter
- 1 cup (200 g) sugar
- ½ cup (125 ml) apricot nectar
- 2 large eggs, lightly beaten
- 8 canned pineapple rings in heavy syrup, drained and patted dry (reserve 6 tablespoons syrup)
- 2 cups (500 ml) heavy (double) cream
- 2 tablespoons confectioners' (icing) sugar
- ½ cup (60 g) slivered almonds

Elizabeth's lemon cake

Serves: 10-12; Preparation: 30 minutes; Cooking: 35 minutes; Level of difficulty: 1

Filling: Heat the milk with the lemon zest until just boiling. • Beat the egg yolks, sugar, cornstarch, and vanilla in a large bowl with an electric mixer at medium speed until pale in color. • Add the milk, discarding the lemon zest, stirring constantly. • Return the mixture to the pan and cook over low heat, stirring constantly, until thick. Remove from heat. • Cake: Preheat the oven to 400°F/200°C/gas 6. • Butter and flour a 9-inch (23-cm) springform pan. • Mix the flour, sugar, 2 tablespoons lemon zest, baking powder, and salt in a large bowl. • Use a pastry blender to cut in the butter until the mixture resembles crumbs. • Stir in the egg and egg yolks until smooth • Divide the dough into 2 pieces, one slightly larger than the other. Form into rounds. Roll out the larger

INGREDIENTS

FILLING
- 2 cups (500 ml) milk
- zest of 1 large lemon, cut in one spiral piece
- 4 large egg yolks
- ⅓ cup (70 g) sugar
- 3 tablespoons cornstarch (cornflour)
- 1 teaspoon vanilla extract

Right: Pineapple and apricot layered loaf

CAKE

- 2 cups (300 g) all-purpose (plain) flour
- ¾ cup (150 g) sugar
- 4 tablespoons finely grated lemon zest
- 1 teaspoon baking powder
- ¼ teaspoon salt
- ⅔ cup (180 g) cold butter, cut up
- 1 large egg
- 2 large egg yolks

piece on a lightly floured work surface until large enough to line the prepared pan. Prick all over with a fork. Sprinkle with the remaining grated lemon zest. • Spoon the filling into the pastry shell. • Roll the remaining dough out into a 9-inch (23-cm) round and place it over the filling. Press down at the edges to seal. • Bake for about 35 minutes, or until the top is golden brown. • Cool the cake in the pan on a rack. • Loosen and remove the sides of the pan and serve warm.

Orange cake with citrus honey crunch

Serves: 8–10; Preparation: 30 minutes; Cooking: 35 minutes; Level of difficulty: 1

Preheat the oven to 375°F/190°C/gas 5. • Butter a 9-inch (23-cm) square baking pan. • Sift the flour, baking powder, and salt into a large bowl. • Beat the butter, sugar, and orange zest in a large bowl with an electric mixer at medium speed until creamy. • Add the eggs, one at a time, beating until just blended after each addition. • With mixer at low speed, beat in the dry ingredients. • Spoon the batter into the prepared pan. • Bake for about 35 minutes, or until a toothpick inserted into the center comes out clean. • Cool the cake completely in the pan on a rack. • Citrus Honey Crunch: Warm the honey in a medium saucepan over medium heat. Stir in the candied peel, almonds, and ginger. Spread the top of the cake with the topping. Cool before serving.

INGREDIENTS

- 2 cups (300 g) all-purpose (plain) flour
- 2 teaspoons baking powder
- ½ teaspoon salt
- 1 cup (250 g) butter
- ¾ cup (150 g) sugar
- 2 tablespoons finely grated orange zest
- 3 large eggs

CITRUS HONEY CRUNCH

- 6 tablespoons honey
- 1 cup (125 g) chopped mixed candied citrus peel
- ½ cup (120 g) slivered almonds
- 1 teaspoon ground ginger

Lumberjack apple cake

Serves: 8–10; Preparation: 30 minutes; Cooking: 1 hour 30 minutes; Level of difficulty: 1

Preheat the oven to 350°F/180°C/gas 4. • Butter an 11 x 7-inch (28 x 18-cm) baking pan. • Place the apples, dates, and baking soda in a large bowl. Pour in the boiling water and cover with plastic wrap. Set aside for 15 minutes. • Beat the butter, sugar, and vanilla in a large bowl with an electric mixer at medium speed until creamy. • Add the egg, beating until just blended. • With mixer at low speed, gradually beat in the flour and salt, alternating with the apple mixture. • Spoon the batter into the prepared pan. • Bake for 1 hour (do not remove from the oven). • Stir the coconut, brown sugar, milk, and butter in a medium saucepan over low heat until the butter has melted and the sugar has dissolved. • After the cake has baked for 1 hour, spread with the topping. Bake for 15 more minutes. • Turn on the broiler (grill). Broil the cake about 6 inches (15 cm) from the heat source for 5–10 minutes, or until golden and bubbly. • Cool the cake completely in the pan.

INGREDIENTS

- 1 lb (500 g) tart apples peeled, cored, and grated
- 1¾ cups (250 g) pitted dates, finely chopped
- 1 teaspoon baking soda
- 1 cup (250 ml) boiling water
- ½ cup (125 g) butter
- 1 cup (200 g) sugar
- 1 teaspoon vanilla extract
- 1 large egg
- 1½ cups (225 g) all-purpose (plain) flour
- ¼ teaspoon salt
- ⅔ cup (100 g) shredded (desiccated) coconut
- ½ cup (100 g) firmly packed brown sugar
- ½ cup (125 ml) milk
- 4 tablespoons butter

Right: *Orange cake with citrus honey crunch*

Banana cake with chantilly, chocolate, and fruit

Serves: 10-12; Preparation: 35 minutes; Cooking: 25 minutes; Level of difficulty: 2

Preheat the oven to 350°F/180°C/gas 4. • Butter two 9-inch (23-cm) round cake pans. Line with waxed paper. Butter the paper. • Sift the flour, baking powder, baking soda, and salt into a large bowl. Stir in the sugar. • Beat in the banana, yogurt, butter, eggs, and vanilla with an electric mixer at medium speed. • Spoon half the batter into each of the prepared pans. • Bake for about 25 minutes, or until a toothpick inserted into the center comes out clean. • Cool the cakes in the pans for 10 minutes. Turn out onto racks. Carefully remove the paper and let cool completely. • Divide the Chantilly in two equal portions. Fold the raspberries into one half and the pineapple into the other. • Split each cake horizontally. Place one layer on a serving plate. Spread with the raspberry cream. Top with another layer. Spread with some of the frosting. Sprinkle with half the nuts. Top with another layer. Spread with the pineapple cream. Place the remaining layer on top. • Spread with the remaining frosting. Sprinkle with the remaining nuts.

■ INGREDIENTS

- 2 cups (300 g) all-purpose (plain) flour
- 1½ teaspoons baking powder
- ¾ teaspoon baking soda
- ¼ teaspoon salt
- 1½ cups (300 g) sugar
- 1 large very ripe banana, mashed with a fork
- ½ cup (125 ml) banana yogurt
- ½ cup (125 g) butter
- 2 large eggs
- 1 teaspoon vanilla extract
- ½ quantity *Chantilly Cream* (see page 26)
- 1 cup (150 g) raspberries
- ¾ cup (150 g) well-drained crushed canned pineapple
- 1 quantity *Basic Chocolate Frosting* (see page 30)
- 1 cup (125 g) pecans, coarsely chopped

Down-under pineapple cake

Serves: 6-8; Preparation: 20 minutes; Cooking: 45 minutes; Level of difficulty: 1

Preheat the oven to 350°F/180°C/gas 4. • Melt 4 tablespoons of butter and pour it into a 9-inch (23-cm) springform pan. Sprinkle with the walnuts. Arrange the pineapple rings in the pan, cutting to fit. • Beat the sugar, remaining butter, vanilla, and eggs in a medium bowl with an electric mixer at medium speed until just blended. • With mixer at low speed, gradually beat in the flour, baking powder, and salt, alternating with the milk. The batter should be smooth and quite sticky. • Spoon the batter over the pineapple. • Bake for about 45 minutes, or until a toothpick inserted into the center comes out clean. • Cool the cake in the pan for 20 minutes. Loosen the sides and invert onto a serving plate.

■ INGREDIENTS

- ½ cup (125 g) butter
- 12 walnut halves, broken
- 9 rings drained canned pineapple
- ⅔ cup (140 g) sugar
- 1 teaspoon vanilla extract
- 2 large eggs
- 1½ cups (225 g) all-purpose (plain) flour
- 1½ teaspoons baking powder
- ¼ teaspoon salt
- ½ cup (125 ml) milk

Right: Banana cake with chantilly, chocolate, and fruit

Pear ring with white chocolate frosting

Serves: 8-10; Preparation: 30 minutes; Cooking: 50 minutes; Level of difficulty: 1

Preheat the oven to 325°F/170°C/gas 3. • Butter and flour a 9-inch (23-cm) tube pan. • Melt the chocolate in a double boiler over barely simmering water. Set aside to cool. • Sift the flour, baking powder, and salt into a medium bowl. • Beat the butter and sugar in a large bowl with an electric mixer at medium speed until creamy. • Add the egg yolks, one at a time, beating until just blended after each addition. • With mixer at low speed, gradually beat in the chocolate and dry ingredients, alternating with the milk. • With mixer at high speed, beat the egg whites in a large bowl until stiff peaks form. Use a large rubber spatula to fold them into the batter. • Spoon half the batter into the prepared pan. Top with the sliced pears. Spoon the remaining batter over the pears. • Bake for about 50 minutes, or until a toothpick inserted into the center comes out clean. • Cool the cake in the pan for 10 minutes. Turn out onto a rack to cool completely. • Frosting: Mix the confectioners' sugar and butter in a medium bowl. Beat in enough of the reserved pear syrup to make a spreadable frosting. Spread over the top and sides of the cake.

■ INGREDIENTS

- 4 oz (125 g) white chocolate, coarsely chopped
- 1½ cups (225 g) all-purpose (plain) flour
- 1½ teaspoons baking powder
- ¼ teaspoon salt
- ½ cup (125 g) butter
- ½ cup (100 g) sugar
- 3 large eggs, separated
- ½ cup (125 ml) milk
- 1 (15¼ oz/450 g) can pear halves, drained and sliced (syrup reserved)

FROSTING

- 2 cups (300 g) confectioners' (icing) sugar
- 4 tablespoons butter, melted
- reserved pear syrup

Fresh fruit and nut ring

In this recipe we have used raspberries, but you can substitute with the same quantities of any other mashed berry (strawberries, bilberries, etc.) or with peaches, apricots, or nectarines.

Serves: 8-10; Preparation: 15 minutes; Cooking: 55 minutes; Level of difficulty: 1

Preheat the oven to 350°F/180°C/gas 4. • Butter and flour a 9-inch (23-cm) tube pan. • Stir together the flours, brown sugar, baking powder, baking soda, cinnamon, ginger, and nutmeg in a large bowl. Add the nuts. • Mash the bananas and raspberries with a fork and beat together with the oil and eggs with an electric mixer at low speed. • Mix in the dry ingredients until well blended. • Spoon the batter into the prepared pan. • Bake for about 55 minutes, or until a toothpick inserted into the center comes out clean. • Cool the cake in the pan for 10 minutes. Turn out onto a rack to cool completely.

■ INGREDIENTS

- 1 cup (150 g) all-purpose (plain) flour
- ½ cup (75 g) whole-wheat (wholemeal) flour
- 1 cup (200 g) firmly packed brown sugar
- 1 teaspoon baking powder
- 1 teaspoon baking soda
- 1 teaspoon each ground cinnamon, ginger, and nutmeg
- ¾ cup (100 g) chopped walnuts
- 1 large very ripe banana
- 1 cup (225 g) raspberries
- ½ cup (125 ml) vegetable oil
- 2 large eggs, lightly beaten

Right: Pear ring with white chocolate frosting

Frosted apple pound cake

Serves: 12-14; Preparation: 30 minutes; Cooking: 1 hour 30 minutes; Level of difficulty: 1

Preheat the oven to 350°F/180°C/gas 4. • Butter and flour a 12-inch (30-cm) tube pan. • Sift the flour, baking soda, cinnamon, ginger, nutmeg, cloves, and salt into a large bowl. • Beat the butter and brown sugar in a large bowl with an electric mixer at medium speed until creamy. • Add the eggs, one at a time, beating until just blended after each addition. • With mixer at low speed, gradually beat in the dry ingredients, alternating with the applesauce. By hand, stir in the dates and walnuts. • Spoon the batter into the prepared pan. • Bake for about 1 hour and 30 minutes, or until a toothpick inserted into the center comes out clean. • Run a knife around the edges of the pan to loosen the cake. Cool the cake in the pan for 15 minutes. Turn out onto a rack to cool completely. • Frosting: Place the butter and brown sugar in a small saucepan over low heat. Cook, stirring, until the butter melts and the mixture boils. Boil, stirring occasionally, for 2 minutes. • Add the milk, and stir until the mixture returns to a boil. Remove from the heat and let cool for 5 minutes. • Transfer to a large bowl and beat in the confectioners' sugar and vanilla until creamy. • Spread the top and sides of the cake with the frosting.

- 3⅓ cups (500 g) all-purpose (plain) flour
- 2 teaspoons baking soda
- 1 teaspoon each ground cinnamon, ginger, and nutmeg
- ½ teaspoon ground cloves
- ½ teaspoon salt
- ½ cup (125 g) butter
- 2 cups (400 g) firmly packed brown sugar
- 2 large eggs
- 3 cups (600 g) applesauce
- ¾ cup (120 g) pitted dates, coarsely chopped
- 1 cup (125 g) walnuts, coarsely chopped

FROSTING

- ½ cup (125 g) butter
- 1 cup (200 g) firmly packed brown sugar
- 4 tablespoons milk
- 2 cups (300 g) confectioners' (icing) sugar
- 1 teaspoon vanilla extract

Frosted ginger and pineapple cake

Serves: 8-10; Preparation: 30 minutes; Cooking: 40 minutes; Level of difficulty: 1

Preheat the oven to 325°F/170°C/gas 3. • Butter and flour a 9-inch (23-cm) springform pan. • Sift the flour, baking powder, ginger, and salt into a large bowl. Stir in the coconut. • Beat the butter and sugar in a large bowl with an electric mixer at medium speed until creamy. • Add the eggs, one at a time, beating until just blended after each addition. • With mixer at low speed, gradually beat in the dry ingredients, alternating with the pineapple. • Spoon the batter into the

- 2 cups (300 g) all-purpose (plain) flour
- 2 teaspoons baking powder
- 1 teaspoon ground ginger
- ¼ teaspoon salt
- ¾ cup (120 g) shredded (desiccated) coconut
- ½ cup (125 g) butter
- 1 cup (200 g) sugar
- 2 large eggs

Right: Frosted apple pound cake

- ½ cup (125 g) crushed canned pineapple, with some of the juice (reserve the rest for the frosting)

PINEAPPLE FROSTING

- 2 cups (300 g) confectioners' (icing) sugar
- 2 tablespoons butter
- 1 teaspoon ground ginger
- 4 tablespoons pineapple juice
- chopped candied ginger, to decorate (optional)

prepared pan. • Bake for about 40 minutes, or until a toothpick inserted into the center comes out clean. • Cool the cake in the pan for 10 minutes. Loosen and remove the pan sides. Place the cake on a rack and let cool completely. • Pineapple Frosting: Mix the confectioners' sugar, butter, and ginger in a medium bowl. Add enough pineapple juice to make a smooth spreadable frosting. • Spread the top and sides of the cake with the frosting and, if desired, decorate with the candied ginger.

Easy apple bake

Serve this wholesome quick bake piping hot straight from the oven during the winter months. Accompany with vanilla ice cream or freshly whipped cream flavored with sugar, ground cinnamon, and ginger.

Serves: 6-8; Preparation: 20 minutes + 1 hour to soak; Cooking: 50 minutes; Level of difficulty: 1

Preheat the oven to 400°F/200°C/gas 6. • Butter a 10-inch (25-cm) pie pan. • Soak the raisins in the brandy. Drain. • Beat the eggs and sugar in a large bowl with an electric mixer at high speed until pale and creamy. • With mixer at low speed, gradually beat in the flour, milk, lemon zest, salt, and raisins. • Arrange the apples in the prepared pan. • Spoon the batter over the top of the apples. • Bake for about 50 minutes, or until golden brown. • Serve hot.

■ INGREDIENTS

- 6 tablespoons raisins, soaked in 3 tablespoons of brandy for 1 hour, drained
- 4 large eggs
- ½ cup (100 g) sugar
- 1¼ cups (180 g) all-purpose (plain) flour
- ¾ cup (200 ml) milk
- finely grated zest of 1 lemon
- ¼ teaspoon salt
- 4 large apples, peeled, cored, and thickly sliced

Banana and pineapple layer cake

Serves: 6-8; Preparation: 30 minutes; Cooking: 30 minutes; Level of difficulty: 1

Preheat the oven to 350°F/180°C/gas 4. • Butter two 8-inch (20-cm) round cake pans. Line with waxed paper. Butter the paper. • Sift the flour, baking powder, baking soda, and salt into a medium bowl. • Beat the butter, brown sugar, and vanilla in a large bowl with an electric mixer at medium speed until creamy. • Add the egg yolks, one at a time, beating until just blended after each addition. • With mixer at low speed, gradually beat in the dry ingredients, alternating with the bananas and rum. • With mixer at high speed, beat the egg whites in a medium bowl until stiff peaks form. Use a large rubber spatula to fold them into the batter. • Spoon half the batter into each of the prepared pans. • Bake for about 30 minutes, or until a toothpick inserted into the center comes out clean. • Cool the cakes in the pans for 10 minutes. Turn out onto racks. Carefully remove the paper and let cool completely. • Topping: With mixer at high speed, beat the cream and sugar in a large bowl until stiff. • Drizzle the banana with the lemon juice. • Place a cake on a serving plate. Spread with a quarter of the cream and cover with a layer of banana. Top with the remaining cake. Spread with the remaining cream. Press the pineapple into the cream around the sides and on top of the cake. Fill the gaps on the top with the remaining banana slices.

■ INGREDIENTS

- 1⅔ cups (250 g) all-purpose (plain) flour
- 2 teaspoons baking powder
- ½ teaspoon baking soda
- ¼ teaspoon salt
- ½ cup (125 g) butter
- ¾ cup (150 g) firmly packed light brown sugar
- 1 teaspoon vanilla extract
- 2 large eggs, separated
- 2 large very ripe bananas, mashed with a fork
- 2 tablespoons dark rum

TOPPING

- 1½ cups (375 ml) heavy (double) cream
- 1 tablespoon sugar
- 1 medium banana, peeled and thinly sliced
- 2 tablespoons lemon juice
- 6 thin slices cored fresh pineapple, cut into quarters

Right: Easy apple bake

Fresh raspberry cake

Serves: 6-8; Preparation: 25 minutes; Cooking: 25 minutes; Level of difficulty: 1

Preheat the oven to 350°F/180°C/gas 4. • Butter an 8-inch (20-cm) round cake pan. • Mix the raspberries and brown sugar in a small bowl. • Stir together the flour, sugar, baking powder, baking soda, and salt in a large bowl. • Beat the yogurt, egg, butter, and vanilla into the dry ingredients with an electric mixer at medium speed. • Spoon the batter into the prepared pan. Spoon the raspberry mixture over the top, pressing it in slightly. Sprinkle with the almonds. • Bake for about 25 minutes, or until a toothpick inserted into the center comes out clean. • Cool the cake in the pan on a rack. • Serve warm or at room temperature.

■ INGREDIENTS

- 1 cup (150 g) raspberries
- 4 tablespoons firmly packed brown sugar
- 1 cup (150 g) all-purpose (plain) flour
- ⅓ cup (70 g) sugar
- ½ teaspoon baking powder
- ¼ teaspoon baking soda
- ¼ teaspoon salt
- ½ cup (125 g) plain yogurt
- 1 large egg
- 2 tablespoons butter, melted
- 1 teaspoon vanilla extract
- 4 tablespoons unblanched almonds

Banana cinnamon breakfast cake

Serves: 8-10; Preparation: 30 minutes; Cooking: 30 minutes; Level of difficulty: 1

Preheat the oven to 350°F/180°C/gas 4. • Butter and flour a 9-inch (23-cm) tube pan. • Topping: Stir the flour, brown sugar, cinnamon, and nutmeg in a medium bowl. Use a pastry blender to cut in the butter until the mixture resembles fine crumbs. Stir in the almonds. • Cake: Sift the flour, baking soda, baking powder, and salt into a large bowl. • Beat the butter, sugar, orange zest, and vanilla in a large bowl with an electric mixer at medium speed until creamy. • Add the eggs, one at a time, beating until just blended after each addition. • With mixer at low speed, gradually beat in the dry ingredients, alternating with the banana, sour cream, and raisins. • Spoon the batter into the prepared pan. Sprinkle with the topping. • Bake for about 30 minutes, or until the topping is golden brown and a toothpick inserted into the center comes out clean. • Cool the cake completely in the pan on a rack. Serve warm or at room temperature.

INGREDIENTS

TOPPING

- ½ cup (75 g) all-purpose (plain) flour
- ½ cup (100 g) firmly packed brown sugar
- 1 teaspoon cinnamon
- ½ teaspoon nutmeg
- 4 tablespoons cold butter
- ½ cup (50 g) almonds, coarsely chopped

CAKE

- 2 cups (300 g) all-purpose (plain) flour
- 1 teaspoon baking soda
- ½ teaspoon baking powder
- ¼ teaspoon salt
- ½ cup (125 g) butter
- ¾ cup (150 g) sugar
- 1 tablespoon finely grated orange zest
- 1 teaspoon vanilla extract
- 2 large eggs
- 2 large very ripe bananas, mashed with a fork
- 2 tablespoons sour cream
- ½ cup (90 g) raisins

Raspberry and nut cake

Serves: 8-10; Preparation: 25 minutes; Cooking: 55 minutes; Level of difficulty: 1

Preheat the oven to 350°F/180°C/gas 4. • Butter a 13 x 9-inch (33 x 23-cm) baking pan. • Stir together the flour, sugar, baking powder, and salt in a large bowl. • Use a pastry blender to cut in the butter until the mixture resembles coarse crumbs. • Beat the eggs, milk, vanilla, and almond extract in a medium bowl. • Stir the egg mixture into the dry ingredients until just blended. • Spoon the batter into the prepared pan. Sprinkle with the raspberries and hazelnuts. • Bake for about 55 minutes, or until a toothpick inserted into the center comes out clean. Cool the cake in the pan on a rack. Serve warm.

INGREDIENTS

- 2 cups (300 g) all-purpose (plain) flour
- 1 cup (200 g) sugar
- 2 teaspoons baking powder
- ½ teaspoon salt
- ½ cup (125 g) butter
- 2 large eggs
- 1 cup (250 ml) milk
- 1 teaspoon vanilla extract
- 1 teaspoon almond extract
- 2 cups (200 g) raspberries
- ½ cup (50 g) chopped hazelnuts

Right: *Banana cinnamon breakfast cake*

Frosted citrus and coconut cake

Serves: 12-14; Preparation: 35 minutes + 30 minutes to chill; Cooking: 30 minutes; Level of difficulty: 2

Preheat the oven to 350°F/180°C/gas 4. • Butter three 9-inch (23-cm) round cake pans. Line with waxed paper. Butter the paper. • Sift the flour, baking powder, and salt into a large bowl. • Beat the butter, sugar, and orange zest in a large bowl with an electric mixer at medium speed until creamy. • Add the egg yolks, one at a time, beating until just blended after each addition. • With mixer at low speed, gradually beat in the dry ingredients and coconut, alternating with the orange juice and water. • With mixer at high speed, beat the egg whites in a large bowl until stiff peaks form. Use a large rubber spatula to fold them into the batter. • Spoon one-third of the batter into each of the prepared pans. • Bake for about 30 minutes, or until a toothpick inserted into the center comes out clean. • Cool the cakes in the pans for 10 minutes. Turn out onto racks. Carefully remove the paper and let cool completely. • Filling: Beat the egg yolks and sugar in a double boiler. Beat in the cornstarch, flour, and orange zest. Gradually add the orange juice, water, and butter. Place over barely simmering water and cook, stirring frequently, until the mixture lightly coats a metal spoon or registers 160°F (71°C) on an instant-read thermometer. Transfer to a clean bowl. Place a sheet of plastic wrap directly on the surface and refrigerate until cold. • Frosting: Beat the confectioners' sugar and butter in a medium bowl. Add enough of the lemon juice to make a thick, spreadable frosting. • Place one cake on a serving plate and spread with half the filling. Place another cake on top and spread with the remaining filling. Top with the remaining cake and spread with the frosting. Sprinkle with coconut. • Refrigerate for 30 minutes before serving.

INGREDIENTS

- 3 cups (450 g) all-purpose (plain) flour
- 4 teaspoons baking powder
- ½ teaspoon salt
- ¾ cup (200 g) butter
- 2 cups (400 g) sugar
- 2 tablespoons finely grated orange zest
- 3 large eggs, separated
- ½ cup (75 g) freshly grated coconut or shredded (desiccated) coconut
- ½ cup (125 ml) orange juice
- ½ cup (125 ml) water

FILLING

- 4 large egg yolks
- 1 cup (200 g) sugar
- ¼ cup (30 g) cornstarch (cornflour)
- 2 tablespoons all-purpose (plain) flour
- 1 tablespoon finely grated orange zest
- ½ cup (125 ml) lemon juice
- 4 tablespoons water
- 2 tablespoons butter

FROSTING

- 3 cups (450 g) confectioners' (icing) sugar
- 4 tablespoons butter
- 3–4 tablespoons lemon juice
- ½ cup (75 g) shredded (desiccated) coconut

Right: Frosted citrus and coconut cake

Pineapple and coconut cake

Serves: 8-10; Preparation: 25 minutes; Cooking: 1 hour; Level of difficulty: 1

Preheat the oven to 350°F/180°C/gas 4. • Butter and flour a 10-inch (25-cm) tube pan. • Sift the flour, baking powder, baking soda, and salt into a large bowl. Stir in the coconut. • Beat the butter, sugar, and coconut extract in a large bowl with an electric mixer at medium speed until creamy. • Add the eggs, one at a time, beating until just blended after each addition. • With mixer at low speed, gradually beat in the dry ingredients, alternating with the pineapple. Stir in the nuts. • Spoon the batter into the prepared pan. • Bake for about 1 hour, or until a toothpick inserted into the center comes out clean. • Cool the cake in the pan for 10 minutes. Turn out onto a rack to cool completely.

■ INGREDIENTS

- 2 cups (300 g) all-purpose (plain) flour
- 1 teaspoon baking powder
- 1 teaspoon baking soda
- ¼ teaspoon salt
- ¾ cup (120 g) shredded (desiccated) coconut
- ¾ cup (200 g) butter
- 1½ cups (300 g) sugar
- 1 teaspoon coconut extract
- 3 large eggs
- 1 can (20 oz/625 g) crushed pineapple, drained
- 1 cup (120 g) walnuts, coarsely chopped

Vegetable Cakes

ℭ

Pumpkin, carrots, zucchini, potatoes, and even beet root, can be combined with butter, sugar, eggs, flour, and spices to create some mouthwatering cakes. Vegetable cakes are often a more healthy choice than traditional recipes and are perfect for school lunches and snacks.

Pumpkin and walnut ring

Serve this luscious big cake at Thanksgiving, Christmas,
and other festive occasions throughout the fall and winter.

Serves: 12-14; Preparation: 30 minutes; Cooking: 1 hour 15 minutes; Level of difficulty: 1

Preheat the oven to 375°F/190°C/gas 5. • Butter and flour an 11-inch (28-cm) tube pan. • Sift the flour, baking powder, baking soda, cinnamon, ginger, nutmeg, and salt into a large bowl. • Beat the sugar and oil in a large bowl with an electric mixer at medium speed until well blended. • Add the eggs, one at a time, beating until just blended after each addition. • With mixer at low speed, gradually beat in the pumpkin and the dry ingredients. • By hand, stir in the walnuts. • Spoon the batter into the prepared pan. • Bake for about 1 hour and 15 minutes, or until a toothpick inserted into the center comes out clean. • Run a knife around the edges of the pan to loosen the cake. Cool the cake in the pan for 15 minutes. Turn out onto a rack to cool completely. • Dust with the confectioners' sugar.

> VARIATIONS
> – Spread with *Vanilla Frosting* (see page 30).
> – Replace the walnuts with the same quantity of hazelnuts or macadamias.

■ INGREDIENTS

- 2⅔ cups (400 g) all-purpose (plain) flour
- 2 teaspoons baking powder
- 1 teaspoon baking soda
- 1 teaspoon each ground cinnamon, ginger, and nutmeg
- ½ teaspoon salt
- 2 cups (400 g) sugar
- 1 cup (250 ml) vegetable oil
- 4 large eggs
- 2 cups (400 g) plain canned pumpkin purée
- ¾ cup (100 g) walnuts, finely chopped
- ⅓ cup (50 g) confectioners' (icing) sugar, to dust

Lemon pumpkin cake with wine syrup

Serves: 8-10; Preparation: 30 minutes; Cooking: 1 hour; Level of difficulty: 1

Preheat the oven to 350°F/180°C/gas 4. • Butter a 9-inch (23-cm) square baking pan. • Beat the butter, sugar, and lemon zest in a large bowl with an electric mixer at medium speed until creamy. • Add the egg yolks, one at a time, beating until just blended after each addition. • With mixer at low speed, gradually beat in the flour, baking powder, salt, and pumpkin. • With mixer at high speed, beat the egg whites in a medium bowl until stiff peaks form. Use a large rubber spatula to fold them into the batter. • Spoon the batter into the prepared pan. • Bake for about 1 hour, or until a toothpick inserted into the center comes out clean. • Cool the cake in the pan on a rack. • Wine Syrup: Stir together the sugar, wine, and lemon zest in a small saucepan over low heat until the sugar has dissolved. Bring to a boil and simmer for 2 minutes. • Poke holes in the cake with a skewer. Drizzle with the syrup.

■ INGREDIENTS

- 1 cup (250 g) butter
- 1 cup (200 g) sugar
- 4 tablespoons finely grated lemon zest
- 3 large eggs, separated
- 2 cups (300 g) all-purpose (plain) flour
- 1 teaspoon baking powder
- ¼ teaspoon salt
- 1 cup (200 g) plain canned pumpkin purée

WINE SYRUP

- ¾ cup (150 g) sugar
- ½ cup (125 ml) dry white wine
- 2 tablespoons finely grated lemon zest

Right: Pumpkin and walnut ring

Chocolate zucchini cake

Serves: 8-10; Preparation: 30 minutes; Cooking: 1 hour; Level of difficulty: 1

Preheat the oven to 350°F/180°C/gas 4. • Butter and flour a 10-inch (25-cm) tube pan. • Sift the flour, cocoa, baking powder, baking soda, cinnamon, and salt into a large bowl. • Beat the butter, sugar, and vanilla in a large bowl with an electric mixer at medium speed until creamy. • Add the eggs, one at a time, beating until just blended after each addition. • With mixer at low speed, gradually beat in the dry ingredients, orange zest, and zucchini, alternating with the milk. Stir in the pecans by hand. • Spoon the batter into the prepared pan. • Bake for about 1 hour, or a toothpick inserted into the center comes out clean. • Cool the cake in the pan for 10 minutes. Turn out onto a rack to cool completely. • Spread the frosting over the cake.

■ INGREDIENTS

- 1⅔ cups (250 g) all-purpose (plain) flour
- ⅔ cup (100 g) unsweetened cocoa powder
- 2 teaspoons baking powder
- 1 teaspoon baking soda
- 1 teaspoon ground cinnamon
- ½ teaspoon salt
- ¾ cup (200 g) butter
- 2 cups (400 g) sugar
- 2 teaspoons vanilla extract
- 3 large eggs
- 1 tablespoon finely grated orange zest
- 2 cups (300 g) grated zucchini
- ½ cup (125 ml) milk
- ¾ cup (100 g) pecans, chopped
- 1 quantity *Basic Chocolate Frosting* (see page 30)

Zucchini and walnut cake

Serves: 8-10; Preparation: 30 minutes; Cooking: 1 hour; Level of difficulty: 1

Preheat the oven to 350°F/180°C/gas 4. • Butter an 11 x 7-inch (28 x 18-cm) baking pan. • Sift the flour, cinnamon, baking powder, baking soda, and salt into a large bowl. • Beat the sugar, oil, and vanilla in a large bowl with an electric mixer at medium speed until well blended. • Add the eggs, one at a time, beating until just blended after each addition. • With mixer at low speed, gradually beat in the dry ingredients. • By hand, stir in the zucchini and walnuts. • Spoon the batter into the prepared pan. • Bake for about 1 hour, or until a toothpick inserted into the center comes out clean. • Cool the cake in the pan for 15 minutes. Turn out onto a rack to cool completely. • Spread the frosting over the cake.

■ INGREDIENTS

- 2 cups (300 g) all-purpose (plain) flour
- 2 teaspoons cinnamon
- 1 teaspoon baking powder
- ½ teaspoon baking soda
- ¼ teaspoon salt
- 2 cups (400 g) sugar
- 1 cup (250 ml) vegetable oil
- 1 teaspoon vanilla extract
- 3 large eggs
- 2 cups (300 g) grated zucchini
- 1 cup (150 g) coarsely chopped walnuts
- 1 quantity *Vanilla Frosting* (see page 30)

Right: Zucchini and walnut cake

Zucchini and apricot cake

Serves: 8-10; Preparation: 25 minutes; Cooking: 45 minutes; Level of difficulty: 1

Preheat the oven to 350°F/180°C/gas 4. • Butter a 9-inch (23-cm) square baking pan. Line with waxed paper. Butter the paper. • Sift both flours, baking powder, baking soda, and salt into a medium bowl. • Beat the butter, sugar, lemon zest, and lemon extract in a large bowl with an electric mixer at medium speed until creamy. • Add the eggs, one at a time, beating until just blended after each addition. • With mixer at low speed, beat in the zucchini, apricots, and dry ingredients, alternating with the milk. • Spoon the batter into the prepared pan. • Bake for about 45 minutes, or until a toothpick inserted into the center comes out clean. • Cool the cake in the pan for 10 minutes. Turn out onto a rack. Carefully remove the paper and let cool completely. • Frosting: Bring the apricots and water to a boil in a small saucepan over medium heat. Reduce the heat and simmer until the apricots are soft. Set aside to cool. • Beat the cream cheese, confectioners' sugar, and lemon juice in a large bowl. Stir in the apricot mixture. • Spread the cake with the frosting.

■ INGREDIENTS

- 1 cup (150 g) all-purpose (plain) flour
- ½ cup (75 g) whole-wheat (wholemeal) flour
- 1 teaspoon baking powder
- 1 teaspoon baking soda
- ¼ teaspoon salt
- ½ cup (125 g) butter
- ¾ cup (150 g) sugar
- 1 tablespoon finely grated lemon zest
- 1 teaspoon lemon extract
- 2 large eggs
- 1½ cups (225 g) grated zucchini
- ¼ cup (30 g) dried apricots, finely chopped
- 4 tablespoons milk

FROSTING

- ½ cup (60 g) chopped dried apricots
- ¾ cup (200 ml) water
- 1 cup (250 g) cream cheese
- 1 cup (150 g) confectioners' (icing) sugar
- 2 tablespoons lemon juice

Pumpkin spice ring

Serves: 12-14; Preparation: 25 minutes; Cooking: 1 hour 15 minutes; Level of difficulty: 1

Preheat the oven to 350°F/180°C/gas 4. • Butter and flour a 12-inch (30-cm) tube pan. • Sift the flour, baking powder, cinnamon, baking soda, cloves, and salt into a large bowl. • Beat the eggs, sugar, maple syrup, and butter in a medium bowl with an electric mixer at medium speed until well blended. • With mixer at low speed, gradually beat in the pumpkin, followed by the dry ingredients. • Spoon the batter into the prepared pan. • Bake for about 1 hour and 15 minutes, or until a toothpick inserted into the center comes out clean. • Cool the cake in the pan for 15 minutes. Turn out onto a rack to cool completely.

■ INGREDIENTS

- 3 cups (450 g) all-purpose (plain) flour
- 2 teaspoons baking powder
- 2 teaspoons cinnamon
- 1 teaspoon baking soda
- ½ teaspoon cloves
- ½ teaspoon salt
- 2 large eggs
- 1 cup (200 g) sugar
- ½ cup (125 ml) pure maple syrup
- 4 tablespoons butter
- 1 lb (500 g) canned pumpkin purée

Right: Zucchini and apricot cake

Carrot and apple loaf

Serves: 6-8; Preparation: 20 minutes; Cooking: 1 hour; Level of difficulty: 1

Preheat the oven to 350°F/180°C/gas 4. • Butter a 9 x 5-inch (23 x 13-cm) loaf pan. Line with aluminum foil, letting the edges overhang. Butter the foil. • Sift the flour, baking powder, baking soda, cinnamon, ginger, and salt into a large bowl. • Use a pastry blender to cut in the butter until the mixture resembles coarse crumbs. • Stir in the walnuts, apples, carrots, raisins, eggs, and orange zest and juice. • Spoon the batter into the prepared pan. • Bake for about 1 hour, or until a toothpick inserted into the center comes out clean. • Cool the loaf in the pan for 30 minutes. Using the foil as a lifter, remove from the pan. Carefully remove the foil and let cool completely.

■ INGREDIENTS

- 2 cups (300 g) whole-wheat (wholemeal) flour
- 1½ teaspoons baking powder
- 1 teaspoon baking soda
- 1 teaspoon ground cinnamon
- ½ teaspoon ground ginger
- ¼ teaspoon salt
- ½ cup (125 g) butter
- 1 cup (100 g) chopped walnuts
- 2 Granny Smith apples, peeled, cored, and grated
- 2 large carrots, grated
- ¾ cup (90 g) raisins
- 2 large eggs, lightly beaten
- 2 tablespoons finely grated orange zest
- 4 tablespoons orange juice

Mary's pumpkin loaves

Serves: 8-10; Preparation: 15 minutes; Cooking: 50 minutes; Level of difficulty: 1

Preheat the oven to 325°F/170°C/gas 3. • Butter two 8 x 4-inch (20 x 11-cm) loaf pans. Line with aluminum foil, letting the edges overhang. Butter the foil. • Beat the butter, sugar, and orange zest in a large bowl with an electric mixer at medium speed until creamy. • Add the eggs, one at a time, beating until just blended after each addition. • With mixer at low speed, gradually beat in the pumpkin, prunes, flour, baking powder, and salt, alternating with the milk. • Spoon the batter into the prepared pans. • Bake for about 50 minutes, or until a toothpick inserted into the centers comes out clean. • Cool the loaves in the pans for 15 minutes. Using the foil as a lifter, remove the loaves from the pans. Carefully remove the foil. Cool the loaves completely on racks. • Dust with the confectioners' sugar.

■ INGREDIENTS

- 1 cup (250 g) butter
- 1¼ cups (250 g) sugar
- 2 tablespoons finely grated orange zest
- 2 large eggs
- 1 cup (250 g) plain canned pumpkin purée
- 1⅓ cups (200 g) pitted prunes, chopped
- 2 cups (300 g) all-purpose (plain) flour
- 2 teaspoons baking powder
- ¼ teaspoon salt
- ½ cup (125 ml) milk
- confectioners' sugar, to dust

Left: *Carrot and apple loaf*

Beet and red currant cake

The beets combine beautifully with the other ingredients in this recipe to make a cake that will both please and surprise your friends and family when you make it. On special occasions, serve it frosted with Vanilla Frosting (see page 30) or Cream Cheese Frosting (see page 32).

Serves: 8-10; Preparation: 20 minutes; Cooking: 1 hour 15 minutes; Level of difficulty: 1

Preheat the oven to 350°F/180°C/gas 4. • Butter an 11 x 7-inch (28 x 18-cm) baking pan. • Beat the butter, sugar, and vanilla in a large bowl with an electric mixer at high speed until creamy. • With mixer at medium speed, add the eggs, one at a time, beating until just blended after each addition. • With mixer at low speed, beat in the beets, red currants, flour, baking powder, and salt. • Spoon the batter into the prepared pan. • Bake for about 1 hour and 15 minutes, or until a toothpick inserted into the center comes out clean. • Cool the cake completely in the pan on a rack.

■ INGREDIENTS

- 1 cup (250 g) butter
- 1 cup (200 g) sugar
- 1 teaspoon vanilla extract
- 4 large eggs
- 1 cup (225 g) cooked, peeled beets (beet root), coarsely grated
- 5 oz (150 g) fresh or frozen red or black currants
- 2 cups (300 g) all-purpose (plain) flour
- 2 teaspoons baking powder
- ¼ teaspoon salt

Frosted zucchini and ginger ring

Serves: 8-10; Preparation: 20 minutes; Cooking: 40 minutes; Level of difficulty: 1

Preheat the oven to 350°F/180°C/gas 4. • Butter and flour a 9-inch (23-cm) ring pan. • Sift the flour, baking powder, cinnamon, ginger, baking soda, and salt into a medium bowl. • Beat the butter, sugar, and vanilla in a large bowl with an electric mixer at medium speed until creamy. • Add the eggs, one at a time, beating until just blended after each addition. • With mixer at low speed, gradually beat in the dry ingredients. Stir in the zucchini and raisins. • Spoon the batter into the prepared pan. • Bake for about 40 minutes, or until a toothpick inserted into the center comes out clean. • Cool the cake in the pan for 15 minutes. Turn out onto a rack to cool completely. • Spread the cake with the frosting.

■ INGREDIENTS

- 1½ cups (225 g) all-purpose (plain) flour
- 1 teaspoon baking powder
- 1 teaspoon each ground cinnamon and ginger
- ½ teaspoon baking soda
- ¼ teaspoon salt
- ½ cup (125 g) butter
- ¾ cup (150 g) sugar
- 2 teaspoons vanilla extract
- 3 large eggs
- 1¼ cups (125 g) grated zucchini
- ½ cup (60 g) raisins
- 1 quantity *Vanilla Frosting* (see page 30)

Right: Beet and red currant cake

Frosted carrot and nut cake

Serves: 8-10; Preparation: 25 minutes; Cooking: 45 minutes; Level of difficulty: 1

Preheat the oven to 350°F/180°C/gas 4. • Butter and flour a 9-inch (23-cm) springform pan. • Sift the flour, baking powder, cinnamon, nutmeg, and salt into a large bowl. • Beat the sugar, eggs, and oil with an electric mixer at medium speed for 3 minutes. • With mixer at low speed, gradually beat in the dry ingredients. • Stir in the carrots, nuts, and currants. • Spoon the batter into the prepared pan. • Bake for about 45 minutes, or until a toothpick inserted into the center comes out clean. • Cool the cake in the pan for 15 minutes. Turn out onto a rack to cool completely. • Spread the frosting over the top and sides of the cake.

INGREDIENTS

- 1⅔ cups (250 g) all-purpose (plain) flour
- 2 teaspoons baking powder
- 1 teaspoon each ground cinnamon and nutmeg
- ½ teaspoon salt
- 1 cup (200 g) sugar
- 3 large eggs
- 1 cup (250 ml) vegetable oil
- 1½ cups (250 g) firmly packed grated carrots
- ½ cup (100 g) coarsely chopped walnuts
- ¾ cup (100 g) currants
- 1½ quantities *Cream Cheese Frosting* (see page 32)

Date and carrot ring

Serves: 10-12; Preparation: 25 minutes; Cooking: 55 minutes; Level of difficulty: 1

Preheat the oven to 350°F/180°C/gas 4. • Butter and flour a 10-inch (25-cm) tube pan. • Sift the flour, allspice, baking powder, baking soda, and salt into a medium bowl. • Beat the butter, sugar, corn syrup, and vanilla in a large bowl with an electric mixer at medium speed until creamy. • Add the eggs, one at a time, beating until just blended after each addition. • With mixer at low speed, gradually beat in the dry ingredients. Stir in the carrots, dates, and walnuts. • Spoon the batter into the prepared pan. • Bake for about 55 minutes, or until a toothpick inserted into the center comes out clean. • Cool the cake in the pan for 15 minutes. Turn out onto a rack to cool completely.

INGREDIENTS

- 1½ cups (225 g) all-purpose (plain) flour
- 1½ teaspoons allspice
- 1 teaspoon baking powder
- ½ teaspoon baking soda
- ¼ teaspoon salt
- ½ cup (125 g) butter
- 1 cup (200 g) sugar
- 2 tablespoons corn (golden) syrup
- 1 teaspoon vanilla extract
- 2 large eggs
- 2 cups (300 g) firmly packed grated carrots
- 1 cup (150 g) chopped dates
- 1 cup (150 g) walnuts, chopped

Right: *Frosted carrot and nut cake*

Perfect carrot and walnut cake

Serves: 12-14; Preparation: 20 minutes; Cooking: 50 minutes; Level of difficulty: 1

Preheat the oven to 350°F/180°C/gas 4. • Butter and flour a 12-inch (30-cm) springform pan. • Sift the flour, cinnamon, baking powder, baking soda, ginger, nutmeg, cloves, and salt into a large bowl. • Beat the butter, sugar, and vanilla in a large bowl with an electric mixer at medium speed until creamy. • Add the eggs, one at a time, beating until just blended after each addition. • With mixer at low speed, gradually beat in the dry ingredients. • Stir in the carrots, walnuts, and raisins. • Spoon the batter into the prepared pan. • Bake for about 50 minutes, or until a toothpick inserted into the center comes out clean. • Cool the cake in the pan for 10 minutes. Loosen and remove the pan sides. Invert the cake onto a rack. Loosen and remove the pan bottom and let cool completely. • Spread the top of the cake with the frosting. Decorate with walnut halves.

■ INGREDIENTS

- 2⅓ cups (350 g) all-purpose (plain) flour
- 2 teaspoons cinnamon
- 1 teaspoon baking powder
- 1 teaspoon baking soda
- 1 teaspoon ground ginger
- ½ teaspoon nutmeg
- ¼ teaspoon ground cloves
- ¼ teaspoon salt
- 1½ cups (375 g) butter
- 2 cups (400 g) sugar
- 2 teaspoons vanilla extract
- 4 large eggs
- 3 cups (425 g) firmly packed grated carrots
- 1 cup (100 g) walnuts
- ⅓ cup (30 g) raisins
- 1½ quantities *Cream Cheese Frosting* (see page 32)

Carrot cake with sunflower seeds

Serves: 12-14; Preparation: 30 minutes; Cooking: 1 hour 15 minutes; Level of difficulty: 1

Preheat the oven to 350°F/180°C/gas 4. • Butter and flour a 10-inch (25-cm) springform pan. • Sift the flour, baking powder, ginger, nutmeg, baking soda, and salt into a large bowl. • Beat the oil, brown sugar, and eggs in a large bowl with an electric mixer at high speed until creamy. • With mixer at low speed, gradually beat in the carrots, hazelnuts, sunflower seeds, and the dry ingredients. • Spoon the batter into the prepared pan. • Bake for about 1 hour and 15 minutes, or until a toothpick inserted into the center comes out clean. • Cool in the pan for 10 minutes. Loosen and remove the pan sides. Invert the cake onto a rack. Loosen and remove the pan bottom and let cool completely. • Spread the cake with the frosting.

■ INGREDIENTS

- 2½ cups (350 g) all-purpose (plain) flour
- 2 teaspoons baking powder
- 1 teaspoon ground ginger
- 1 teaspoon ground nutmeg
- ½ teaspoon baking soda
- ½ teaspoon salt
- 1 cup (250 ml) vegetable oil
- 1¼ cups (250 g) brown sugar
- 3 large eggs
- 3 cups (425 g) firmly packed grated carrots
- 1 cup (100 g) hazelnuts, coarsely chopped
- 2 tablespoons sunflower seeds
- 1 quantity *Orange Frosting* (see page 38)

Right: *Perfect carrot and walnut cake*

Easy zucchini, raisin, and nut cake

INGREDIENTS

- 1 package (18 oz/500 g) yellow cake mix
- 4 large eggs
- ½ cup (125 ml) vegetable oil
- 1 teaspoon ground cinnamon
- 1 teaspoon vanilla extract
- 2 cups (300 g) grated zucchini
- ½ cup (60 g) raisins
- ½ cup (75 g) coarsely chopped pecans
- confectioners' (icing) sugar, to dust (optional)

Serves: 12-14; Preparation: 15 minutes; Cooking: 45 minutes; Level of difficulty: 1

Preheat the oven to 350°F/180°C/gas 4. • Butter and flour a 10-inch (25-cm) tube pan. • With an electric mixer at medium speed, beat the cake mix, eggs, oil, cinnamon, and vanilla in a large bowl for 5 minutes. • Fold in the zucchini, raisins, and pecans. • Spoon the batter into the prepared pan. • Bake for about 45 minutes, or until golden brown and a toothpick inserted into the center comes out clean. • Cool the cake in the pan for 10 minutes. Turn out onto a rack to cool completely. • If liked, dust with the confectioners' sugar just before serving.

Dried Fruit and Nut Cakes

ℭℬ

Dried and candied fruit and nuts can be used to make hearty cakes that are most appreciated in fall and winter. Packed with goodness and energy, they are perfect to pack for lunch or snacks when skiing, hiking, cycling, or engaging in other active sports.

Broiled orange and lemon cake

Serves: 10-12; Preparation: 40 minutes; Cooking: 50 minutes; Level of difficulty: 1

Preheat the oven to 325°F/170°C/gas 3. • Butter and flour a 13 x 9-inch (33 x 23-cm) baking pan. • Sift the flour, baking powder, baking soda, and salt into a large bowl. • Beat the butter, brown sugar, and citrus zests in a large bowl with an electric mixer at medium speed until creamy. • Add the eggs, one at a time, beating until just blended after each addition. • With mixer at low speed, gradually beat in the dry ingredients, alternating with the buttermilk. Stir in the raisins and pecans. • Spoon the batter into the prepared pan. • Bake for about 45 minutes, or until a toothpick inserted into the center comes out clean. • Topping: Stir the sugar, orange juice, lemon juice, and butter in a medium bowl until well blended. Spoon the topping over the cake when it comes out of the oven. Turn on the broiler (grill). Broil 6 inches (15 cm) from the heat source for 3–5 minutes, or until golden brown and bubbly. Cool the cake completely in the pan on a rack. • Spread the cake with the whipped cream just before serving.

■ INGREDIENTS

- 2½ cups (375 g) all-purpose (plain) flour
- 2 teaspoons baking powder
- ½ teaspoon baking soda
- ¼ teaspoon salt
- ½ cup (125 g) butter
- 1 cup (200 g) brown sugar
- 2 tablespoons finely grated orange zest
- 1 tablespoon finely grated lemon or lime zest
- 2 large eggs
- 1 cup (250 ml) buttermilk
- 1 cup (125 g) raisins
- ¾ cup (100 g) pecans, chopped

TOPPING
- 1 cup (200 g) sugar
- 6 tablespoons orange juice
- 4 tablespoons lemon juice
- 1 tablespoon butter, melted
- 1 cup (250 ml) heavy (double) cream, beaten

Date and rum loaf

Serves: 6-8; Preparation: 15 minutes; Cooking: 40 minutes; Level of difficulty: 1

Preheat the oven to 350°F/180°C/gas 4. • Butter a 9 x 5-inch (23 x 13 cm) loaf pan. Line with aluminum foil, letting the edges overhang. Butter the foil. • Sift the flour, baking powder, and salt into a medium bowl. • Beat the egg yolks, butter, and sugar in a large bowl with an electric mixer at high speed until pale and thick. • With mixer at low speed, gradually beat in the dry ingredients, alternating with the milk and rum. Stir in the dates and walnuts. • With mixer at high speed, beat the egg whites until stiff peaks form. Use a large rubber spatula to fold them into the batter. • Spoon the batter into the prepared pan. • Bake for about 40 minutes, or until a toothpick inserted into the center comes out clean. • Cool the loaf in the pan for 5 minutes. • Using the foil as a lifter, remove the loaf from the pan. Carefully remove the foil. Cool the loaf completely on a rack.

■ INGREDIENTS

- 1 cup (150 g) all-purpose (plain) flour
- 2 teaspoons baking powder
- ¼ teaspoon salt
- 2 large eggs, separated
- ½ cup (125 g) butter
- ½ cup (100 g) sugar
- 6 tablespoons milk
- 3 tablespoons rum
- 1 cup (150 g) pitted dates, finely chopped
- ¾ cup (100 g) walnuts, finely chopped

Right: Broiled orange and lemon cake

Almond cake

This delicious big cake can be served any time of the day, from breakfast through to late afternoon. It freezes well and is an ideal cake to prepare in advance and keep in the freezer for unexpected visitors.

Serves: 10-12; Preparation: 20 minutes; Cooking: 50 minutes; Level of difficulty: 1

Preheat the oven to 350°F/180°C/gas 4. • Butter and flour a 13 x 9-inch (33 x 23-cm) baking pan. • Sift the flour, baking powder, cinnamon, and salt into a medium bowl. • Beat the butter, sugar, and almond and vanilla extracts in a large bowl with an electric mixer at medium speed until creamy. • Add the eggs, one at a time, beating until just blended after each addition. • With mixer at low speed, gradually beat in the dry ingredients, alternating with the sour cream. • Spoon the batter into the prepared pan and sprinkle with the almonds. • Bake for about 50 minutes, or until golden brown and a toothpick inserted into the center comes out clean. • Cool the cake completely in the pan on a rack.

■ INGREDIENTS

- 2 cups (300 g) all-purpose (plain) flour
- 2 teaspoons baking powder
- 1 teaspoon ground cinnamon
- ¼ teaspoon salt
- 1 cup (250 g) butter
- 2 cups (400 g) sugar
- 1 teaspoon almond extract
- ½ teaspoon vanilla extract
- 2 large eggs
- 1 cup (250 ml) sour cream
- ¾ cup (100 g) coarsely chopped almonds

Frosted pumpkin spice cake

Serves: 8-10; Preparation: 25 minutes; Cooking: 50 minutes; Level of difficulty: 1

Preheat the oven to 350°F/180°C/gas 4. • Butter and flour a 9-inch (23-cm) springform pan. • Sift the flour, baking powder, ginger, cinnamon, baking soda, nutmeg, and salt into a large bowl. Stir in the oats. • Beat the butter, honey, and lemon zest in a large bowl with an electric mixer at medium speed until creamy. • Add the egg, beating until just blended. • With mixer at low speed, gradually beat in the pumpkin, walnuts, and dry ingredients, alternating with the milk. • Spoon the batter into the prepared pan. • Bake for about 50 minutes, or until a toothpick inserted into the center comes out clean. • Cool the cake in the pan for 15 minutes. Loosen and remove the pan sides. Invert the cake onto a rack. Loosen and remove the pan bottom and let cool completely. • Spread the top and sides of the cake with the frosting.

■ INGREDIENTS

- 1⅔ cups (250 g) all-purpose (plain) flour
- 1 teaspoon each baking powder, ground ginger, and cinnamon
- ½ teaspoon baking soda
- ½ teaspoon nutmeg
- ¼ teaspoon salt
- 1 cup (150 g) rolled oats
- ½ cup (125 g) butter
- ⅔ cup (180 g) honey
- 1 tablespoon finely grated lemon zest
- 1 large egg
- 1 cup (250 g) plain canned pumpkin purée
- ½ cup (60 g) walnuts, coarsely chopped
- 4 tablespoons milk
- 1½ quantities *Cream Cheese Frosting* (see page 32)

VARIATION
– Substitute the honey with 1 cup (200 g) of firmly packed dark brown sugar.

Right: *Almond cake*

Candied ginger and walnut cake

INGREDIENTS

- ⅓ cup (75 g) walnuts, finely chopped
- 2¼ cups (330 g) all-purpose (plain) flour
- 2 teaspoons ground ginger
- 1½ teaspoons baking powder
- ¼ teaspoon salt
- 1 cup (250 g) butter
- 1½ cups (300 g) sugar
- 1 cup (250 g) cream cheese
- 2 teaspoons vanilla extract
- 4 large eggs
- ½ cup (50 g) coarsely chopped candied ginger

Serves: 10-12; Preparation: 30 minutes; Cooking: 1 hour 20 minutes; Level of difficulty: 1

Preheat the oven to 325°F/170°C/gas 3. • Butter and flour a 10-inch (25-cm) tube pan. Sprinkle the walnuts in the pan. • Sift the flour, ground ginger, baking powder, and salt into a large bowl. • Beat the butter, sugar, cream cheese, and vanilla in a large bowl with an electric mixer at medium speed until creamy. • Add the eggs, one at a time, beating until just blended after each addition. • With mixer at low speed, gradually beat in the dry ingredients and candied ginger. • Spoon the batter into the prepared pan. • Bake for about 1 hour and 20 minutes, or until a toothpick inserted into the center comes out clean. • Run a knife around the edges of the pan to loosen the cake. Cool the cake in the pan for 15 minutes. Turn out onto a rack to cool completely.

Pistachio and lemon torte

INGREDIENTS

- 1¾ cups (225 g) pistachios
- 1 cup (200 g) sugar
- 3 large eggs, separated
- 2 tablespoons finely grated lemon zest
- 1 teaspoon baking powder
- ½ teaspoon baking soda
- ¼ teaspoon salt

Serves: 6-8; Preparation: 30 minutes; Cooking: 30 minutes; Level of difficulty: 1

Preheat the oven to 350°F/180°C/gas 4. • Butter a 9-inch (23-cm) springform pan. • Plunge the pistachios into a pot of boiling water for 30 seconds. Drain. Rub dry with a clean kitchen towel, then carefully peel off the inner skins. • Chop the pistachios and sugar finely in a food processor. • Transfer to a large bowl and stir in the egg yolks, lemon zest, baking powder, baking soda, and salt. • Beat the egg whites in a medium bowl with an electric mixer at high speed until stiff peaks form. Use a large rubber spatula to fold them into the batter. • Spoon the batter into the prepared pan. • Bake for about 30 minutes, or until a toothpick inserted into the center comes out clean. • Cool the cake in the pan for 10 minutes. Loosen and remove the pan sides and let the cake cool completely on a rack.

Left: *Candied ginger and walnut cake*

Yogurt cake with pecan topping

Serves: 8-10; Preparation: 30 minutes; Cooking: 1 hour; Level of difficulty: 1

Preheat the oven to 350°F/180°C/gas 4. • Butter and flour a 9-inch (23-cm) square baking pan. • Topping: Stir together the pecans, sugar, flour, butter, cinnamon, and vanilla in a medium bowl. • Cake: Sift the flour, baking powder, and salt into a medium bowl. • Beat the butter, sugar, and vanilla in a large bowl with an electric mixer at medium speed until creamy. • Add the eggs, one at a time, beating until just blended after each addition. • With mixer at low speed, beat in the dry ingredients, alternating with the yogurt. • Spoon half the batter into the prepared pan. Sprinkle with half the topping. Spoon the remaining batter over the top and sprinkle with the remaining topping. • Bake for about 1 hour, or until a toothpick inserted into the center comes out clean. • Cool the cake completely in the pan on a rack. Serve warm or at room temperature.

■ INGREDIENTS

TOPPING

- 1 cup (100 g) pecans, coarsely chopped
- ½ cup (100 g) sugar
- ½ cup (75 g) all-purpose (plain) flour
- 4 tablespoons butter, melted
- 2 teaspoons cinnamon
- 1 teaspoon vanilla extract

CAKE

- 2 cups (300 g) all-purpose (plain) flour
- 2 teaspoons baking powder
- ¼ teaspoon salt
- ½ cup (125 g) butter
- 1 cup (200 g) sugar
- 2 teaspoons vanilla extract
- 2 large eggs
- 1 cup (250 ml) plain yogurt

Apricot and coconut sheet cake

Serves: 8-10; Preparation: 25 minutes + 1 hour to soak; Cooking: 45 minutes; Level of difficulty: 1

Mix the dried and canned apricots with their juice in a medium bowl. Set aside for 1 hour. • Preheat the oven to 350°F/180°C/gas 4. • Butter a 13 x 9-inch (33 x 23-cm) baking pan. • Beat the butter and brown sugar in a large bowl with an electric mixer at medium speed until creamy. • Add the egg yolks, one at a time, beating until just blended after each addition. Beat in the baking powder and salt. • With mixer at low speed, gradually beat in the coconut, flour, and apricot mixture. • With mixer at high speed, beat the egg whites in a medium bowl until stiff peaks form. Use a large rubber spatula to fold them into the batter. • Spoon the batter into the prepared pan. • Bake for about 45 minutes, or until a toothpick inserted into the center comes out clean. • Cool the cake completely in the pan on a rack. • Dust with the confectioners' sugar just before serving.

■ INGREDIENTS

- 1 cup (120 g) dried apricots, chopped
- 1 cup (200 g) canned apricots, chopped (reserve the juice)
- ½ cup (125 g) butter
- ¾ cup (150 g) firmly packed brown sugar
- 2 large eggs, separated
- 2 teaspoons baking powder
- ¼ teaspoon salt
- 1½ cups (225 g) shredded (desiccated) coconut
- 1½ cups (225 g) all-purpose (plain) flour
- confectioners' (icing) sugar, to dust

Right: Yogurt cake with pecan topping

Granny's potato cake

Serves: 6-8; Preparation: 20 minutes; Cooking: 50 minutes; Level of difficulty: 1

Preheat the oven to 325°F/170°C/gas 3. • Butter a 13 x 9-inch (33 x 23-cm) baking pan. Line with waxed paper. Butter the paper. • Sift the flour, ginger, baking powder, baking soda, and salt into a medium bowl. • Beat the butter, brown sugar, and corn syrup in a large bowl with an electric mixer at medium speed until creamy. • Add the eggs, one at a time, beating until just blended after each addition. • With mixer at low speed, gradually beat in the potato and dry ingredients, alternating with the milk. • Spoon the batter into the prepared pan. • Bake for about 50 minutes, or until a toothpick inserted into the center comes out clean. • Cool the cake in the pan for 10 minutes. Turn out onto a rack. Carefully remove the paper and let cool completely. • Frosting: Beat the confectioners' sugar, ginger, and butter in a medium bowl. Add enough lemon juice to make a spreadable frosting. • Spread the cake with the frosting and garnish with the candied ginger.

■ INGREDIENTS

- 1½ cups (225 g) all-purpose (plain) flour
- 2 teaspoons ground ginger
- 1 teaspoon baking powder
- ½ teaspoon baking soda
- ¼ teaspoon salt
- ¾ cup (200 g) butter
- ¾ cup (150 g) firmly packed brown sugar
- 6 tablespoons corn (golden) syrup
- 2 large eggs
- 1 cup (200 g) grated peeled raw potato
- 4 tablespoons milk

FROSTING
- 2 cups (300 g) confectioners' (icing) sugar
- 2 teaspoons ginger
- 2 tablespoons butter
- 2 tablespoons lemon juice
- candied ginger, to garnish

Macadamia nut cake

Serves: 6-8; Preparation: 15 minutes; Cooking: 35 minutes; Level of difficulty: 1

Preheat the oven to 350°F/180°C/gas 4. • Butter a 9-inch (23-cm) springform pan. • Sift the flour, baking powder, and salt into a medium bowl. • Beat the eggs, sugar, and vanilla in a large bowl with an electric mixer at high speed until pale and thick. • With mixer at low speed, gradually beat in the dry ingredients, alternating with the butter and brandy. Stir in the macadamias. Spoon the batter into the prepared pan. • Bake for about 35 minutes, or until a toothpick inserted into the center comes out clean. • Cool the cake in the pan for 10 minutes. Loosen and remove the pan sides and let cool completely.

■ INGREDIENTS

- 1⅓ cups (200 g) all-purpose (plain) flour
- 1½ teaspoons baking powder
- ¼ teaspoon salt
- 3 large eggs
- ¾ cup (150 g) sugar
- 1 teaspoon vanilla extract
- ¾ cup (180 g) butter, melted
- 2 tablespoons brandy
- 1½ cups (180 g) macadamia nuts, coarsely chopped

VARIATION
– Spread with *Vanilla Frosting* (see page 30) or *Lemon Frosting* (see page 30).

Right: *Granny's potato cake*

Cinnamon spice cake

This tasty—but not too sweet—cake is a perfect way to start the day.

Serves: 8-10; Preparation: 25 minutes; Cooking: 35 minutes; Level of difficulty: 1

Preheat the oven to 375°F/190°C/gas 5. • Butter and flour a 9-inch (23-cm) square baking pan. • Stir together the flour, brown sugar, baking powder, and salt in a large bowl. Use a pastry blender to cut in the butter until the mixture resembles fine crumbs. Stir in the milk and egg, then the raisins. The batter will be sticky and thick, like a cookie dough. • Spread the batter in the prepared pan. • Topping: Mix the sugar, cinnamon, allspice, and ginger in a small bowl. Sprinkle over the batter. Drizzle with the butter. • Bake for about 35 minutes, or until a toothpick inserted into the center comes out clean. • Cool the cake completely in the pan on a rack.

VARIATION
– Add ½ cup (60 g) of coarsely chopped toasted nuts (walnuts, pecans, hazelnuts, macadamias) to the batter along with the raisins.

■ INGREDIENTS

- 2 cups (300 g) all-purpose (plain) flour
- ⅓ cup (70 g) firmly packed brown sugar
- 2 teaspoons baking powder
- ½ teaspoon salt
- 4 tablespoons cold butter
- ½ cup (125 ml) milk
- 1 large egg, lightly beaten
- ½ cup (90 g) raisins

TOPPING
- 4 tablespoons sugar
- 1 teaspoon each ground cinnamon, allspice, and ginger
- 3 tablespoons butter, melted

Almond loaf

Serves: 6-8; Preparation: 20 minutes; Cooking: 45 minutes; Level of difficulty: 1

Preheat the oven to 350°F/180°C/gas 4. • Butter a 9 x 5-inch (23 x 13-cm) loaf pan. Line with aluminum foil, letting the edges overhang. Butter the foil. • Sift the flour, baking powder, and salt into a medium bowl. Stir in the almonds. • Beat the butter, sugar, and almond extract in a medium bowl with an electric mixer at medium speed until creamy. • Add the eggs, one at a time, beating until just blended after each addition. • Gradually beat in the dry ingredients. • Spoon the batter into the prepared pan. • Bake for about 45 minutes, or until a toothpick inserted into the center comes out clean. • Cool the loaf in the pan for 5 minutes. • Using the foil as a lifter, remove the loaf from the pan. Carefully remove the foil. Cool the loaf completely on a rack.

■ INGREDIENTS

- 1⅓ cups (200 g) all-purpose (plain) flour
- 2 teaspoons baking powder
- ¼ teaspoon salt
- ⅓ cup (70 g) almonds, finely chopped
- ½ cup (125 g) butter
- 1 cup (200 g) sugar
- ½ teaspoon almond extract
- 3 large eggs

Right: Cinnamon spice cake

Panforte

Panforte—literally, in Italian, "strong bread"—is a traditional, wonderfully chewy cake made every fall in the beautiful medieval town of Siena, in Tuscany. There are many variations but they are all based on a mixture of the new season's nuts, honey, and spices. This is our favorite recipe.

Serves: 10-12; Preparation: 25 minutes; Cooking: 35 minutes; Level of difficulty: 2

Preheat the oven to 350°F/180°C/gas 4. • Line a baking sheet with rice paper. • Mix the candied peels, nuts, flour, and spices in a large bowl. • Heat the brown sugar, honey, and water in a medium saucepan over medium heat, stirring constantly, until the sugar has dissolved. • Wash down the sides of the pan with a pastry brush dipped in cold water to prevent sugar crystals from forming. Cook, without stirring, until small bubbles form on the surface and the syrup registers 234°F (114°C) on a candy thermometer. • Remove from the heat and beat into the nut mixture. • Spoon onto the prepared sheet. Shape the dough into a round about ½-inch (1-cm) thick. • Bake for about 35 minutes, or until golden brown. • Cool the cake completely on the baking sheet. • Remove the excess rice paper from the edges before serving. If using, dust with the confectioners' sugar.

■ INGREDIENTS

- 1 cup (100 g) candied orange peel, coarsely chopped
- 2 tablespoons candied lemon peel, chopped
- 1⅔ cups (250 g) unblanched, toasted almonds, coarsely chopped
- ¾ cup (100 g) walnuts, coarsely chopped
- 1 cup (150 g) all-purpose (plain) flour
- 1 teaspoon each ground coriander, mace, cloves, and nutmeg
- 1 cup (200 g) firmly packed brown sugar
- ½ cup (125 ml) honey
- ½ cup (125 ml) water
- 4 tablespoons confectioners' (icing) sugar, to dust (optional)

Frosted hazelnut cake

Serves: 10-12; Preparation: 20 minutes; Cooking: 40 minutes; Level of difficulty: 2

Preheat the oven to 350°F/180°C/gas 4. • Butter and flour a 9-inch (23-cm) springform pan. • Sift the flour, cornstarch, baking powder, and salt into a medium bowl. Stir in the hazelnuts. • Beat the eggs and sugar in a large bowl with an electric mixer at high speed until pale and thick. • With mixer at medium speed, gradually beat in the butter. • With mixer at low speed, gradually add the dry ingredients and rum. • Spoon the batter into the prepared pan. • Bake for about 40 minutes, or until a toothpick inserted into the center comes out clean. • Cool the cake in the pan for 10 minutes. Loosen and remove the pan sides and let cool completely. • Spread the top of the cake with the frosting.

■ INGREDIENTS

- 1 cup (150 g) all-purpose (plain) flour
- 1 cup (150 g) cornstarch (cornflour)
- 2 teaspoons baking powder
- ¼ teaspoon salt
- 1¼ cups (175 g) hazelnuts, finely ground
- 3 large eggs
- 1 cup (200 g) sugar
- ½ cup (125 g) + 2 tablespoons butter
- 3 tablespoons rum
- ½ quantity *Lemon Frosting* or 1 quantity *Vanilla Frosting* (see page 30)

Right: *Panforte*

■ INGREDIENTS

TOPPING

- ⅓ cup (50 g) all-purpose (plain) flour
- ¼ cup (50 g) firmly packed brown sugar
- 1 teaspoon each ground cinnamon and nutmeg
- 4 tablespoons butter
- ½ cup (50 g) chopped nuts

CAKE

- 2 cups (300 g) all-purpose (plain) flour
- 1 teaspoon each baking powder and baking soda
- 1 teaspoon cinnamon
- ½ teaspoon salt
- 1 cup (250 g) butter
- 1 cup (200 g) firmly packed brown sugar
- 2 tablespoons dark molasses (treacle)
- 2 teaspoons vanilla extract
- 3 large eggs
- 1 cup (250 ml) sour cream

Sour cream cake with nut and spice topping

Serves: 8–10; Preparation: 25 minutes; Cooking: 55 minutes; Level of difficulty: 1

Preheat the oven to 325°F/170°C/gas 3. • Butter and flour a 13 x 9-inch (33 x 23-cm) baking pan. • Topping: Stir the flour, brown sugar, cinnamon, and nutmeg in a medium bowl. Use a pastry blender to cut in the butter until the mixture resembles fine crumbs. Stir in the nuts. • Cake: Sift the flour, baking powder, baking soda, cinnamon, and salt into a large bowl. • Beat the butter, brown sugar, molasses, and vanilla in a large bowl with an electric mixer at medium speed until creamy. • Add the eggs, one at a time, beating until just blended after each addition. • With mixer at low speed, gradually beat in the dry ingredients, alternating with the sour cream. • Spoon the batter into the prepared pan. Sprinkle with the topping. • Bake for about 55 minutes, or until a toothpick inserted into the center comes out clean. • Cool the cake completely in the pan on a rack.

■ INGREDIENTS

- 2 cups (300 g) all-purpose (plain) flour
- 1 teaspoon baking powder
- 1 teaspoon allspice
- ¼ teaspoon salt
- 1 lb (500 g) mixed dried fruit
- 1 cup (200 g) firmly packed brown sugar
- ½ cup (125 g) butter
- ½ cup (125 ml) water
- 3 large eggs, separated

Mixed fruitcake

Serves: 8–10; Preparation: 35 minutes; Cooking: 1 hour 30 minutes; Level of difficulty: 1

Preheat the oven to 300°F/150°C/gas 2. • Butter and flour a deep 8-inch (20-cm) square baking pan. • Sift the flour, baking powder, allspice, and salt into a large bowl. • Heat the mixed fruit, brown sugar, butter, and water in a large saucepan over medium heat. Bring to a boil and simmer gently for 15 minutes. Remove from the heat and set aside to cool. • Beat in the eggs, one at a time, followed by the dry ingredients. • Spoon the batter into the prepared pan. • Bake for about 1 hour and 30 minutes, or until the cake shrinks away from the pan sides and a toothpick inserted into the center comes out clean. • Cool the cake completely in the pan on a rack.

Left: Sour cream cake with nut and spice topping

Apricot brandy cake

Serves: 10-12; Preparation: 30 minutes; Cooking: 2 hours; Level of difficulty: 1

Drain the apricots, reserving ½ cup (125 ml) of the syrup. • Chop the apricots coarsely. Mix the apricots and the reserved apricot syrup in a large saucepan with the dried fruit, brown sugar, butter, preserves, and 4 tablespoons of brandy. Stir over low heat until the butter has melted and the sugar dissolved. Bring to a boil and simmer, covered, for 10 minutes. Set aside to cool. • Preheat the oven to 300°F/150°C/gas 2. • Butter a 9-inch (23-cm) square cake pan. Line with waxed paper. • Stir the eggs, flour, baking soda, and salt into the fruit mixture. • Spoon the batter into the prepared pan. • Bake for about 2 hours, or until a toothpick inserted into the center comes out clean. • Brush the cake with the remaining brandy. Cool the cake completely in the pan on a rack.

■ INGREDIENTS

- 1 can (15 oz/450 g) apricots in syrup
- 1 lb (500 g) mixed dried fruit
- 1¼ cups (250 g) firmly packed brown sugar
- 1 cup (250 g) butter
- 4 tablespoons apricot preserves (jam)
- 6 tablespoons brandy
- 3 large eggs, lightly beaten
- 2 cups (300 g) all-purpose (plain) flour
- 1 teaspoon baking soda
- ¼ teaspoon salt

Sunflower seed fruit cake

Serves: 10-12; Preparation: 20 minutes + 1 hour to cool; Cooking: 1 hour 45 minutes; Level of difficulty: 1

Stir the dried fruit, ½ cup (125 ml) of water, the raisins, brown sugar, butter, cinnamon, nutmeg, and cloves in a large saucepan over medium-low heat until the sugar has dissolved. Bring to a boil, reduce the heat to low, and simmer for 10 minutes, stirring constantly. • Set aside to cool for 1 hour. • Preheat the oven to 325°F/170°C/gas 3. • Butter a 9-inch (23-cm) square baking pan. Line with waxed paper. • Stir the eggs, walnuts, and sunflower seeds into the fruit mixture, followed by the flour, baking powder, baking soda, and salt. • Spoon the batter into the prepared pan. Sprinkle with the pumpkin and sunflower seeds. • Bake for about 1 hour and 45 minutes, or until a toothpick inserted into the center comes out clean. • Cool the cake completely in the pan. Turn out onto a rack. Carefully remove the paper before serving.

■ INGREDIENTS

- 1½ cups (150 g) dried fruit, chopped
- ½ cup (125 ml) water
- ¾ cup (125 g) raisins
- ¾ cup (150 g) brown sugar
- 2 tablespoons butter
- 1 teaspoon cinnamon
- 1 teaspoon nutmeg
- ½ teaspoon ground cloves
- 2 large eggs, lightly beaten
- 1 cup (125 g) walnuts
- ½ cup (75 g) sunflower seeds
- 2 cups (300 g) whole-wheat (wholemeal) flour
- 2 teaspoons baking powder
- ½ teaspoon baking soda
- ½ teaspoon salt
- 3 tablespoons pumpkin seeds
- 3 tablespoons raw sunflower seeds

Right: *Apricot brandy cake*

Dried apricot layer cake

Serves: 10-12; Preparation: 45 minutes; Cooking: 50 minutes; Level of difficulty: 2

Preheat the oven to 350°F/180°C/gas 4. • Butter a 9-inch (23-cm) springform pan. • Soak the apricots in the brandy for 15 minutes. • Sift the flour, baking powder, baking soda, and salt into a large bowl. • Beat the butter, 1 cup (200 g) sugar, and vanilla in a large bowl until creamy. • Add the egg yolks, beating until just blended after each addition. • Beat in the dry ingredients, alternating with the apricot mixture and sour cream. • Beat the egg whites and remaining sugar in a large bowl until stiff, glossy peaks form. Fold them into the batter. • Spoon the batter into the prepared pan. • Bake for about 50 minutes, or until a toothpick inserted into the center comes out clean. • Cool the cake in the pan for 10 minutes. Loosen and remove the pan sides. Turn out onto a rack. Let cool completely. • Frosting: Soak the apricots in the brandy for 15 minutes. • Beat the cream cheese, sour cream, and confectioners' sugar in a medium bowl until smooth. Stir in the apricot mixture. • Split the cake into thirds horizontally. Place one layer on a serving plate. Spread with a quarter of the frosting. Top with a second cake layer. Spread with a quarter of the frosting and top with the remaining cake layer. Spread the top and sides of the cake with the remaining frosting. • Press the almonds into the sides.

INGREDIENTS

- ½ cup (50 g) candied apricots, finely chopped
- 4 tablespoons apricot brandy
- 2½ cups (375 g) all-purpose (plain) flour
- 2 teaspoons baking powder
- ½ teaspoon baking soda
- ¼ teaspoon salt
- ½ cup (125 g) butter
- 1½ cups (300 g) sugar
- 2 teaspoons vanilla extract
- 3 large eggs, separated
- ⅔ cup (180 ml) sour cream

FROSTING

- ½ cup (50 g) candied apricots, finely chopped
- 6 tablespoons apricot brandy
- 1 cup (250 g) cream cheese
- 1 cup (250 ml) sour cream
- 2 cups (300 g) confectioners' (icing) sugar
- ½ cup (75 g) toasted slivered almonds

Prune and nut cake

Serves: 8-10; Preparation: 25 minutes; Cooking: 50 minutes; Level of difficulty: 1

Preheat the oven to 350°F/180°C/gas 4. • Butter a 9-inch (23-cm) springform pan. • Stir the brown sugar, prunes, milk, butter, and walnuts in a large saucepan over low heat. Bring to a boil and remove from the heat. • Stir in the baking soda and set aside for 10 minutes. • Beat in the eggs, flour, baking powder, and salt. • Spoon the batter into the prepared pan. • Bake for about 50 minutes, or until a toothpick inserted into the center comes out clean. • Cool the cake in the pan for 15 minutes. Loosen and remove the pan sides and let cool completely.

INGREDIENTS

- 1 cup (200 g) firmly packed brown sugar
- 1 cup (125 g) pitted prunes, coarsely chopped
- 1 cup (250 ml) milk
- ¾ cup (200 g) butter
- ½ cup (60 g) walnuts, coarsely chopped
- ½ teaspoon baking soda
- 2 large eggs, lightly beaten
- 2 cups (300 g) all-purpose (plain) flour
- 2 teaspoons baking powder
- ¼ teaspoon salt

Right: *Dried apricot layer cake*

Walnut torte

Serves: 10-12; Preparation: 35 minutes; Cooking: 55 minutes; Level of difficulty: 2

Preheat the oven to 350°F/180°C/gas 4. • Butter and flour a 9-inch (23-cm) springform pan. • Stir together the walnuts, flour, baking powder, and salt in a medium bowl. • Beat the butter, ¾ cup (150 g) of sugar, and vanilla in a large bowl with an electric mixer at medium speed until creamy. • Add the egg yolks, beating until just blended after each addition. • With mixer at high speed, beat the egg whites and remaining sugar in a large bowl until stiff, glossy peaks form. Fold them into the batter. • Fold in the dry ingredients. • Spoon the batter into the prepared pan. • Bake for about 55 minutes, or until a toothpick inserted into the center comes out clean. • Cool the cake in the pan for 10 minutes. Loosen and remove the pan sides. Invert onto a rack and let cool completely. • Frosting: Melt the chocolate in a double boiler over barely simmering water. Remove from the heat and gradually mix in the butter. • Split the cake horizontally. Place one layer on a serving plate. Spread with the marmalade. Top with the remaining layer. Spread with the frosting.

■ INGREDIENTS

- 2½ cups (330 g) walnuts, finely ground
- ⅓ cup (50 g) all-purpose (plain) flour
- ½ teaspoon baking powder
- ¼ teaspoon salt
- 1 cup (250 g) butter
- 1¼ cups (250 g) sugar
- 1 teaspoon vanilla extract
- 5 large eggs, separated

FROSTING
- 8 oz (250 g) semisweet chocolate, coarsely chopped
- ½ cup (125 g) butter
- ½ cup (160 g) orange marmalade

Rum and raisin loaf

Serves: 4-6; Preparation: 25 minutes; Cooking: 35 minutes; Level of difficulty: 1

Preheat the oven to 350°F/180°C/gas 4. • Butter a 9 x 5-inch (23 x 13-cm) loaf pan. Line with aluminum foil, letting the edges overhang. Butter the foil. • Sift the flour, baking powder, and salt into a large bowl. • Melt the butter and brown sugar in a medium saucepan over low heat until the sugar has dissolved. • Remove from the heat and stir in the raisins, rum, and vanilla. • Stir the raisin mixture, eggs, and milk into the dry ingredients. • Spoon the batter into the prepared pan. • Bake for about 35 minutes, or until a toothpick inserted into the center comes out clean. • Cool the loaf in the pan for 5 minutes. • Using the foil as a lifter, remove the loaf from the pan. Carefully remove the foil. Cool the loaf completely on a rack.

■ INGREDIENTS

- 1½ cups (225 g) all-purpose (plain) flour
- 2 teaspoons baking powder
- ¼ teaspoon salt
- ¾ cup (200 g) butter
- ½ cup (100 g) firmly packed brown sugar
- 1 cup (120 g) raisins
- 2 tablespoons dark rum
- ½ teaspoon vanilla extract
- 3 large eggs, lightly beaten
- 2 tablespoons milk

VARIATION
– For extra flavor, spread with *Vanilla Frosting* (see page 30) or *Lemon Frosting* (see page 30).

Right: *Walnut torte*

Nut bake

Serves: 10-12; Preparation: 30 minutes; Cooking: 55 minutes; Level of difficulty: 1

Preheat the oven to 350°F/180°C/gas 4. • Butter a 9-inch (23-cm) square baking pan. • Beat the butter, sugar, and lemon zest in a large bowl with an electric mixer at medium speed until creamy. • Add the eggs, one at a time, beating until just blended after each addition. • With mixer at low speed, gradually beat in the flour, baking powder, baking soda, and salt, alternating with the milk. Stir in the finely chopped nuts and lemon juice. • Spoon the batter into the prepared pan. • Sprinkle the coarsely chopped nuts and raw sugar over the batter. • Bake for about 55 minutes, or until a toothpick inserted into the center comes out clean. • Cool the cake completely in the pan on a rack.

■ INGREDIENTS

- ½ cup (125 g) butter
- 1¼ cups (250 g) sugar
- 2 tablespoons finely grated lemon zest
- 3 large eggs
- 1½ cups (225 g) all-purpose (plain) flour
- 1 teaspoon baking powder
- ½ teaspoon baking soda
- ¼ teaspoon salt
- ½ cup (125 ml) milk
- 2 tablespoons each walnuts, almonds, hazelnuts, pistachios, finely chopped
- 1 tablespoon lemon juice
- 2 tablespoons each walnuts, almonds, pistachios, hazelnuts, coarsely chopped
- 2 tablespoons raw sugar

Cherry vanilla loaves

Serves: 8-10; Preparation: 30 minutes; Cooking: 1 hour; Level of difficulty: 1

Preheat the oven to 350°F/180°C/gas 4. • Butter two 9 x 5-inch (23 x 13-cm) loaf pans. Line with aluminum foil, letting the edges overhang. Butter the foil. • Beat the butter, sugar, and vanilla in a large bowl with an electric mixer at medium speed until creamy. • Add the eggs, one at a time, beating until just blended after each addition. • With mixer at low speed, add the cherries and raisins. Gradually beat in the flour, baking powder, baking soda, and salt, alternating with the milk. • Spoon the batter into the prepared pan. • Bake for about 1 hour, or until a toothpick inserted into the center comes out clean. • Cool the loaves in the pans for 5 minutes. Using the foil as a lifter, remove the loaves from the pans. Carefully remove the foil. Cool the loaves completely on racks.

■ INGREDIENTS

- ¾ cup (200 g) butter
- 1¼ cups (250 g) sugar
- 1 teaspoon vanilla extract
- 4 large eggs
- ⅔ cup (80 g) sliced candied cherries
- ½ cup (60 g) raisins
- 3 cups (450 g) all-purpose (plain) flour
- 2 teaspoons baking powder
- ½ teaspoon baking soda
- ¼ teaspoon salt
- 1 cup (250 ml) milk

Right: *Nut bake*

Chocolate hazelnut torte

Serves: 10-12; Preparation: 25 minutes; Cooking: 50 minutes; Level of difficulty: 2

Preheat the oven to 325°F/170°C/gas 3. • Butter and flour a 13 x 9-inch (33 x 23-cm) baking pan. • Stir the chocolate, hazelnuts, sugar, wine, and bread crumbs in a large saucepan over medium-low heat until the chocolate is melted. Set aside to cool. • Beat the egg whites and salt in a large bowl with an electric mixer at high speed until stiff peaks form. • With mixer at medium speed, beat the egg yolks in a large bowl until pale. Fold the yolks into the chocolate mixture. Fold in the beaten whites. • Spoon the batter into the prepared pan. • Bake for about 50 minutes, or until a toothpick inserted into the center comes out clean. • Cool the cake completely in the pan on a rack. • Topping: With mixer at high speed, beat the cream, sugar, and vanilla in a medium bowl until stiff. Spread the cake with the cream and decorate with the hazelnuts.

■ INGREDIENTS

- 8 oz (250 g) semisweet chocolate, coarsely chopped
- 1¼ cups (275 g) hazelnuts, finely ground
- ¾ cup (150 g) sugar
- ¾ cup (200 ml) dry white wine
- 1 tablespoon fine dry bread crumbs
- 6 large eggs, separated
- ¼ teaspoon salt

TOPPING
- 1 cup (250 ml) heavy (double) cream
- 1 tablespoon sugar
- 1 teaspoon vanilla extract
- whole shelled hazelnuts, to decorate

Cornmeal fruit and nut cake

Serves: 8-10; Preparation: 1 hour; Cooking: 80 minutes; Level of difficulty: 1

Preheat the oven to 350°F/180°C/gas 4. • Butter and flour a 10-inch (25-cm) springform pan. • Stir together the almonds, candied peel and cherries, grappa, raisins, figs, and fennel seeds in a medium bowl. Stand for 15 minutes. • Bring the milk to a boil in a large saucepan over medium heat. Reduce the heat to low. Gradually beat in the cornmeal and flour, stirring constantly, for 15 minutes. Stir in the sugar, butter, oil, and salt and cook, stirring often, for 10 minutes more. • Remove from the heat. Stir in the fruit and grappa mixture. • Spoon the batter into the prepared pan. • Bake for about 55 minutes, or until lightly browned. After 30 minutes, cover the top of the cake loosely with a piece of foil to prevent it from drying out. • Cool the cake completely in the pan on a rack. Loosen and remove the pan sides to serve.

■ INGREDIENTS

- ⅓ cup (40 g) coarsely chopped almonds
- ⅓ cup (40 g) chopped candied peel and cherries
- 4 tablespoons grappa
- 3 tablespoons golden raisins (sultanas)
- 2 tablespoons chopped figs
- 1 teaspoon fennel seeds
- 1 quart (1 liter) milk
- 2½ cups (375 g) coarsely ground cornmeal
- ⅓ cup (50 g) all-purpose (plain) flour
- ½ cup (100 g) sugar
- 6 tablespoons cold butter
- 4 tablespoons vegetable oil
- ¼ teaspoon salt

Right: *Chocolate hazelnut torte*

Brazil nut and prune torte

■ INGREDIENTS

- 1 lb (500 g) Brazil nuts, coarsely chopped
- 1 lb (500 g) pitted prunes, coarsely chopped
- 1 cup (100 g) halved candied cherries
- ¾ cup (125 g) all-purpose (plain) flour
- ¾ cup (150 g) sugar
- ½ teaspoon baking powder
- ½ teaspoon salt
- 3 large eggs
- 1 tablespoon dry sherry
- ⅓ cup (50 g) confectioners' (icing) sugar, to dust

This cake is packed with energy. Pack in lunch boxes on sports days or prepare for hikers or skiers.

Serves: 10-12; Preparation: 20 minutes; Cooking: 1 hour 15 minutes; Level of difficulty: 2

Preheat the oven to 350°F/180°C/gas 4. • Butter a 9-inch (23-cm) springform pan. • Place the Brazil nuts, prunes, and cherries in a large bowl. • Stir in the flour, sugar, baking powder, and salt. • Beat the eggs and sherry in a medium bowl. Stir the egg mixture into the fruit mixture. • Spoon the batter into the prepared pan. • Bake for about 1 hour and 15 minutes, or until dark golden brown and a toothpick inserted into the center comes out clean. • Turn out onto a rack and let cool completely. • Dust with confectioners' sugar just before serving.

VARIATION
– For a different flavor, substitute the Brazil nuts with the same quantity of almonds, hazelnuts, or walnuts.

Emily's fruit and rice cake

■ INGREDIENTS

- 1 quart (1 liter) milk
- 1 teaspoon vanilla extract
- ¾ cup (150 g) sugar
- 1½ cups (300 g) short-grain rice
- ¼ teaspoon salt
- 2 large eggs + 2 egg yolks
- ⅓ cup (50 g) finely ground almonds
- ½ cup (90 g) golden raisins (sultanas)
- ⅓ cup (60 g) pine nuts
- 10 dates, preferably fresh, coarsely chopped

This is based on an old Italian recipe. In this case it has been revisited by my dear English friend, Emily, who has revamped it for modern palates. Serve it with cream as a family dessert.

Serves: 6-8; Preparation: 15 minutes; Cooking: 45 minutes; Level of difficulty: 1

Preheat the oven to 350°F/180°C/gas 4. • Butter and flour a 9-inch (23-cm) ring mold. • Bring the milk and vanilla to a boil in a large saucepan. • Stir in the sugar, rice, and salt. Cook, stirring constantly, for 15 minutes. Drain off any milk that has not been absorbed and transfer the rice to a large bowl. • Beat in the eggs, egg yolks, almonds, raisins, pine nuts, and dates with an electric mixer at low speed. • Spoon the batter into the prepared pan. • Bake for about 30 minutes, or until lightly browned. • Cool the cake in the pan for 15 minutes. • Invert onto a serving plate and serve warm.

Left: *Brazil nut and prune torte*

Pecan crunch cake

Serves: 10-12; Preparation: 25 minutes; Cooking: 1 hour; Level of difficulty: 1

Preheat the oven to 350°F/180°C/gas 4. • Butter and flour a 9-inch (23-cm) springform pan. • Pecan Crunch: Stir the brown sugar, flour, and cinnamon in a small bowl. Stir in the pecans and butter. • Cake: Sift the flour, baking powder, baking soda, and salt into a large bowl. • Beat the butter, brown sugar, and vanilla in a large bowl with an electric mixer at medium speed until creamy. • Add the eggs, one at a time, beating until just blended after each addition. • With mixer at low speed, gradually beat in the dry ingredients, alternating with the milk. • Spoon the batter into the prepared pan. Sprinkle with the pecan crunch. • Bake for about 1 hour, or until a toothpick inserted into the center comes out clean. • Cool the cake in the pan for 15 minutes. Loosen and remove the pan sides and let cool completely. Transfer the cake to the rack top-side up.

■ INGREDIENTS

PECAN CRUNCH
- ½ cup (100 g) brown sugar
- 2 tablespoons all-purpose (plain) flour
- 2 teaspoons cinnamon
- ¾ cup (100 g) chopped pecans
- 4 tablespoons butter, melted

CAKE
- 2 cups (300 g) all-purpose (plain) flour
- 1 teaspoon baking powder
- 1 teaspoon baking soda
- ¼ teaspoon salt
- ½ cup (125 g) butter
- 1 cup (200 g) brown sugar
- 1 teaspoon vanilla extract
- 3 large eggs
- 1 cup (250 ml) milk

Raisin cake with nut streusel

Serves: 4-6; Preparation: 30 minutes; Cooking: 45 minutes; Level of difficulty: 1

Nut Streusel: Stir the flour and brown sugar in a medium bowl. Use a pastry blender to cut in the butter until the mixture resembles coarse crumbs. Stir in the walnuts. • Raisin Cake: Preheat the oven to 350°F/180°C/gas 4. • Butter and flour an 8-inch (20-cm) springform pan. • Sift the flour, baking powder, baking soda, and salt into a medium bowl. • Beat the butter, brown sugar, honey, and vanilla in a large bowl with an electric mixer at medium speed until creamy. • Add the eggs, one at a time, beating until just blended after each addition. • With mixer at low speed, gradually beat in the raisins and dry ingredients, alternating with the milk. • Spoon the batter into the prepared pan. • Sprinkle with the nut streusel. • Bake for about 45 minutes, or until a toothpick inserted into the center comes out clean. • Cool the cake in the pan for 15 minutes. Loosen the sides and turn out onto a rack. Invert top-side up and let cool completely.

■ INGREDIENTS

NUT STREUSEL
- ⅔ cup (100 g) all-purpose (plain) flour
- 6 tablespoons brown sugar
- 6 tablespoons butter
- 1 cup (150 g) chopped walnuts

RAISIN CAKE
- 1⅓ cups (200 g) all-purpose (plain) flour
- 1 teaspoon baking powder
- ½ teaspoon baking soda
- ¼ teaspoon salt
- 6 tablespoons butter
- ¾ cup (150 g) brown sugar
- 2 tablespoons honey
- 1 teaspoon vanilla extract
- 2 large eggs
- 1 cup (120 g) raisins
- 4 tablespoons milk

Right: *Pecan crunch cake*

Hazelnut date ring

Serves: 12-14; Preparation: 30 minutes; Cooking: 1 hour 10 minutes; Level of difficulty: 1

Preheat the oven to 325°F/170°C/gas 3. • Butter and flour a 10-inch (25-cm) tube pan. • Sift the flour, baking powder, and salt into a large bowl. Stir in the coconut. • Beat the butter, sugar, and vanilla and lemon extracts in a large bowl with an electric mixer at medium speed until creamy. • Add the eggs, one at a time, beating until just blended after each addition. • With mixer at low speed, gradually beat in the dry ingredients, alternating with the milk. • Stir in the dates and hazelnuts. • Spoon the batter into the prepared pan. • Bake for about 1 hour, or until a toothpick inserted into the center comes out clean. • Run a knife around the edges of the pan to loosen the cake. Cool the cake in the pan for 15 minutes. Turn out onto a rack to cool completely. • Frosting: Beat the cream cheese, butter, and lemon extract in a medium bowl with mixer at high speed until creamy. With mixer at low speed, gradually beat in the confectioners' sugar. • Spread the cake with the frosting.

■ INGREDIENTS

- 3 cups (450 g) all-purpose (plain) flour
- 1 teaspoon baking powder
- ½ teaspoon salt
- 1 cup (125 g) shredded (desiccated) coconut
- 1 cup (250 g) butter
- 2 cups (400 g) sugar
- 1 teaspoon vanilla extract
- 1 teaspoon lemon extract
- 6 large eggs
- 1 cup (250 ml) milk
- 1½ cups (150 g) chopped pitted dates
- 1 cup (125 g) hazelnuts, coarsely chopped

FROSTING
- 3 oz (90 g) cream cheese
- 6 tablespoons butter
- 2 teaspoons lemon extract
- 3 cups (450 g) confectioners' (icing) sugar

Lemon and raisin cake

Serves: 8-10; Preparation: 15 minutes + 30 minutes to plump raisins; Cooking: 40 minutes; Level of difficulty: 1

Plump the raisins in the water in a small bowl for 30 minutes. • Drain well and dry with paper towels. • Preheat the oven to 350°F/180°C/gas 4. • Butter a 9-inch (23-cm) springform pan. • Sift the flour, baking powder, and salt into a large bowl. • Beat the eggs and sugar in a large bowl with an electric mixer at high speed until pale and thick. • With mixer at medium speed, beat in the oil and lemon zest. • With mixer at low speed, gradually beat in the dry ingredients, alternating with the milk. Stir in the raisins. • Spoon the batter into the prepared pan. • Bake for about 40 minutes, or until a toothpick inserted into the center comes out clean. • Cool in the pan for 10 minutes. Loosen and remove the pan sides and cool completely on a rack.

■ INGREDIENTS

- ½ cup (60 g) raisins
- 1 cup (250 ml) warm water
- 1⅔ cups (250 g) all-purpose (plain) flour
- 2 teaspoons baking powder
- ¼ teaspoon salt
- 2 large eggs
- ⅔ cup (170 g) sugar
- 2 tablespoons extra-virgin olive oil
- 2 tablespoons grated lemon zest
- 6 tablespoons milk

Right: *Hazelnut date ring*

Hazelnut cake with red wine zabaglione

Serves: 6-8; Preparation: 30 minutes; Cooking: 50 minutes; Level of difficulty: 1

Preheat the oven to 350°F/180°C/gas 4. • Butter a 9-inch (23-cm) springform pan. • Toast the hazelnuts for about 8 minutes, or until pale golden brown. Chop coarsely. • Sift the flour, baking powder, and salt into a large bowl. Stir in the hazelnuts. • Beat the butter and sugar in a large bowl with an electric mixer at high speed until pale and creamy. • With mixer at medium speed, add the eggs, one at a time, beating until just blended after each addition. • With mixer at low speed, gradually beat in the dry ingredients. • Spoon the batter into the prepared pan. • Bake for about 40 minutes, or until a toothpick inserted into the centers comes out clean. • Cool in the pan for 10 minutes. Loosen and remove the pan sides and cool completely on a rack. • Zabaglione: Beat the egg yolks and sugar in a heatproof bowl until pale and creamy. • Add the wine, then place in a double boiler over barely simmering water. Stir constantly for about 15 minutes, or until thick. • Serve wedges of cake with the zabaglione passed on the side.

■ INGREDIENTS

- ¾ cup (100 g) hazelnuts
- 1⅔ cups (250 g) all-purpose (plain) flour
- 2 teaspoons baking powder
- ¼ teaspoon salt
- ⅔ cup (180 g) butter
- 1 cup (200 g) sugar
- 3 large eggs

ZABAGLIONE
- 6 large egg yolks
- 6 tablespoons sugar
- ⅔ cup (180 ml) good quality, robust dry red wine

Whole-wheat fruit loaves

Serves: 10-12; Preparation: 20 minutes; Cooking: 45 minutes; Level of difficulty: 1

Preheat the oven to 350°F/180°C/gas 4. • Butter two 9 x 5-inch (23 x 13-cm) loaf pans. Line with aluminum foil, letting the edges overhang. Butter the foil. • Sift the flour, baking powder, baking soda, and salt into a large bowl. Stir in the wheat germ, brown sugar, and dates. • Beat in the milk, butter, eggs, banana, and carrot with an electric mixer at low speed. • Spoon half the batter into each of the prepared pans. Sprinkle with the peanuts. • Bake for about 45 minutes, or until a toothpick inserted into the centers comes out clean. • Cool the loaves in the pans for 5 minutes. Using the foil as a lifter, remove the loaves from the pans. Carefully remove the foil. Cool the loaves completely on racks.

■ INGREDIENTS

- 1½ cups (225 g) whole-wheat (wholemeal) flour
- 1½ teaspoons baking powder
- ½ teaspoon baking soda
- ¼ teaspoon salt
- 1 cup (150 g) wheat germ
- ¾ cup (150 g) brown sugar
- 1 cup (150 g) chopped dates
- 1¼ cups (310 ml) milk
- ½ cup (125 g) butter, melted
- 2 large eggs, lightly beaten
- 1 large ripe banana, mashed
- ½ cup (150 g) grated carrot
- ¾ cup (100 g) unsalted roasted peanuts, chopped

Right: *Hazelnut cake with red wine zabaglione*

Pine nut cake

Serves: 6-8; Preparation: 25 minutes; Cooking: 40 minutes; Level of difficulty: 1

Preheat the oven to 350°F/180°C/gas 4. • Butter a 9-inch (23-cm) springform pan. • Sift the flour, baking powder, and salt into a medium bowl. • Beat the egg yolks, whole egg, and sugar in a large bowl with an electric mixer at high speed until pale and thick. • Melt the butter and set aside to cool a little. • With mixer at low speed, gradually beat in the dry ingredients and half the pine nuts, followed by the butter. • Spoon the batter into the prepared pan. Sprinkle the remaining pine nuts over the top. • Bake for about 40 minutes, or until a toothpick inserted into the center comes out clean. • Cool in the pan for 10 minutes. Loosen and remove the pan sides and cool completely on a rack. • Dust with the confectioners' sugar just before serving.

■ INGREDIENTS

- 1⅓ cups (200 g) all-purpose (plain) flour
- ½ teaspoon baking powder
- ¼ teaspoon salt
- 2 large egg yolks + 1 large egg
- 1 cup (200 g) sugar
- ¾ cup (200 g) butter
- 1 cup (150 g) pine nuts
- ⅓ cup (50 g) confectioners' (icing) sugar, to dust

Mediterranean fig cake

Serves: 12-14; Preparation: 2 hours + 12 hours to soak; Cooking: 1 hour 30 minutes; Level of difficulty: 1

Trim the tough bits off the figs and place them in a bowl with just enough warm water to cover. Soak overnight. • Drain the figs, rinse well, and place in a saucepan with enough water to cover. Cook gently over medium heat until tender, about 30 minutes. • Preheat the oven to 350°F/180°C/gas 4. • Butter a 10-inch (25-cm) springform pan. • Drain the figs and pat dry with paper towels. Chop coarsely and place in a large bowl. • Stir in the oil, flour, chocolate, honey, walnuts, almonds, sugar, raisins, lemon peel, orange zest, port, nutmeg, and cinnamon until well blended. • Spoon the batter into the prepared pan. • Bake for about 1 hour, or until dark golden brown. • Cool the cake completely in the pan on a rack. Loosen and remove the pan sides to serve.

■ INGREDIENTS

- 1½ lb (750 g) dried figs
- ½ cup (125 ml) extra-virgin olive oil
- ⅔ cup (100 g) whole-wheat (wholemeal) flour
- 4 oz (125 g) bittersweet chocolate, coarsely chopped
- ½ cup (125 ml) honey
- ⅔ cup (100 g) toasted walnuts, coarsely chopped
- ½ cup (75 g) toasted almonds, coarsely chopped
- ⅓ cup (70 g) sugar
- ½ cup (90 g) golden or dark raisins
- ⅓ cup (40 g) candied lemon peel
- 3 tablespoons finely grated orange zest
- ½ cup (125 ml) port
- 1 teaspoon each ground nutmeg and cinnamon

Right: Pine nut cake

Pepper nut ring

Serves: 8-10; Preparation: 15 minutes; Cooking: 30 minutes; Level of difficulty: 1

Preheat the oven to 350°F/180°C/gas 4. • Grease a 10-inch (25-cm) ring mold with oil. • Mix the honey, sugar, and water in a large saucepan over medium heat. Stir until the sugar has dissolved. • Remove from the heat and stir in the flour, baking soda, pepper, and salt. • Add the almonds, pine nuts, candied peel, and chocolate and stir until well mixed. • Spoon the batter into the prepared pan. • Bake for about 30 minutes, or until a toothpick inserted into the center comes out clean. • Cool the cake in the pan for 15 minutes. • Invert onto a rack and let cool completely.

■ INGREDIENTS

- 6 tablespoons clear honey
- ½ cup (100 g) sugar
- ½ cup (125 ml) water
- 1⅓ cups (200 g) all-purpose (plain) flour
- 1 teaspoon baking soda
- 1 teaspoon freshly ground black pepper
- ¼ teaspoon salt
- ⅔ cup (100 g) chopped almonds
- generous ⅓ cup (75 g) pine nuts
- ⅔ cup (60 g) candied peel
- 2 oz (60 g) semisweet chocolate, finely grated

Chocolate fruit and nut cake

Serves: 4-6; Preparation: 35 minutes; Cooking: 55 minutes; Level of difficulty: 1

Preheat the oven to 350°F/180°C/gas 4. • Butter and flour a 10-inch (25-cm) springform pan. • Melt the chocolate in a double boiler over barely simmering water. Set aside to cool. • Sift the flour, cinnamon, baking powder, and salt into a large bowl. • Place the sugar, honey, and water in a large saucepan over medium-low heat, stirring until the sugar has dissolved. • Remove from the heat and gradually stir in the dry ingredients. • Stir in the chocolate, almonds, raisins, pine nuts, and orange peel. • Spoon the batter into the prepared pan. • Bake for about 55 minutes, or until a toothpick inserted into the center comes out clean. • Cool the cake in the pan for 15 minutes. Loosen and remove the pan sides. Invert the cake onto a rack. Loosen and remove the pan bottom and let cool completely.

■ INGREDIENTS

- 8 oz (250 g) bittersweet chocolate, coarsely chopped
- 2⅔ cups (400 g) all-purpose (plain) flour
- 1 tablespoon ground cinnamon
- 2 teaspoons baking powder
- ½ teaspoon salt
- 1 cup (200 g) sugar
- 1½ cups (375 ml) honey
- 1 cup (250 ml) cold water
- 1½ cups (150 g) almonds, coarsely chopped
- 1 cup (180 g) raisins
- ¾ cup (125 g) pine nuts
- ⅔ cup (70 g) candied orange peel, chopped

Right: *Pepper nut ring*

Poppy seed and apple cake

Serves: 8-10; Preparation: 30 minutes; Cooking: 40 minutes; Level of difficulty: 1

Preheat the oven to 325°F/170°C/gas 3. • Butter a 9-inch (23-cm) springform pan. • Beat the egg yolks, sugar, and vanilla in a large bowl with an electric mixer at high speed until pale and thick. • With mixer at low speed, gradually beat in the almonds, poppy seeds, baking powder, cinnamon, and salt, alternating with the lemon juice and rum. • Stir in the apples. • Spoon the batter into the prepared pan. • Bake for about 40 minutes, or until a toothpick inserted into the center comes out clean. • Cool in the pan for 10 minutes. Loosen and remove the pan sides and cool completely on a rack.

> VARIATION
> – This cake is equally good if made with finely ground hazelnuts instead of almonds.

■ INGREDIENTS

- 8 large egg yolks
- 1 cup (200 g) sugar
- 1 teaspoon vanilla extract
- 1⅓ cups (200 g) finely ground almonds
- 1½ cups (200 g) poppy seeds
- 2 teaspoons baking powder
- 1 teaspoon ground cinnamon
- ¼ teaspoon salt
- 6 tablespoons lemon juice
- 1 tablespoon rum
- 3 sweet apples, peeled, cored, and grated

Apricot and date crumble cake

Serves: 10-12; Preparation: 35 minutes; Cooking: 50 minutes; Level of difficulty: 1

Preheat the oven to 350°F/180°C/gas 4. • Butter and flour a 10-inch (25-cm) tube pan. • Beat the butter, sugar, and vanilla in a large bowl with an electric mixer at medium speed until creamy. • Add the eggs, one at a time, beating until just blended after each addition. • With mixer at low speed, gradually beat in the flour, baking powder, and baking soda, alternating with the sour cream. • Stir in the apricots and dates. • Spoon the batter into the prepared pan. • Crumble: Rub the brown sugar, butter, flour, cinnamon, and nutmeg in a small bowl until crumbly. Sprinkle over the batter. • Bake for about 50 minutes, or until a toothpick inserted into the center comes out clean. • Cool the cake in the pan for 10 minutes. Turn out onto a rack crumble-side up and let cool completely.

■ INGREDIENTS

- ½ cup (125 g) butter
- 1 cup (200 g) sugar
- 2 teaspoons vanilla extract
- 3 large eggs
- 2 cups (300 g) all-purpose (plain) flour
- 2 teaspoons baking powder
- ½ teaspoon baking soda
- ⅔ cup (180 ml) sour cream
- ½ cup (60 g) dried apricots, chopped
- ½ cup (60 g) pitted dates, coarsely chopped

CRUMBLE
- ½ cup (100 g) brown sugar
- 2 tablespoons butter
- 2 tablespoons all-purpose (plain) flour
- 1 teaspoon each ground cinnamon and nutmeg

Right: Poppy seed and apple cake

- 1 cup (250 ml) strong black tea
- ⅔ cup (100 g) raisins
- 4 oz (125 g) grapes
- ½ cup (100 g) candied peel
- 1 large egg, lightly beaten
- ¼ cup (50 g) raw sugar
- 1 cup (150 g) whole-wheat (wholemeal) flour
- 1 teaspoon baking powder
- ¼ teaspoon salt

Dried fruit and tea cake

Serves: 6-8; Preparation: 20 minutes + 12 hours to soak; Cooking: 50 minutes; Level of difficulty: 2

Place the tea in a medium bowl with the raisins, grapes, and candied peel. Let soak for 12 hours (or overnight). • Preheat the oven to 350°F/ 180°C/gas 4. • Butter a 9-inch (23-cm) springform pan. • Beat the egg and sugar in a large bowl with an electric mixer at medium speed until creamy. • With mixer at low speed, beat in the tea mixture, alternating with the flour, baking powder, and salt. • Spoon the batter into the prepared pan. • Bake for about 50 minutes, or until golden brown and a toothpick inserted into the center comes out clean. • Cool in the pan for 10 minutes. Loosen and remove the pan sides. Serve hot.

- 1½ cups (225 g) raisins
- 1½ cups (225 g) dates
- 1 cup (150 g) golden raisins
- ½ cup (75 g) candied fruit peel, chopped
- ½ cup (75 g) dried apricots, chopped
- ½ cup (75 g) candied cherries
- 1⅓ cups (330 ml) beer
- 4 tablespoons water
- 1½ cups (225 g) whole-wheat (wholemeal) flour
- 1½ cups (225 g) all-purpose (plain) flour
- 2 teaspoons baking powder
- 1 teaspoon each ground nutmeg, ginger, and cinnamon
- ½ teaspoon salt
- 1 cup (250 g) butter
- ¾ cup (200 g) honey
- ½ cup (125 g) corn syrup
- 3 large eggs
- ½ cup (60 g) almonds

Spicy beer fruit cake

Serves: 12-14; Preparation: 30 minutes + 12 hours to soak; Cooking: 2 hours 30 minutes; Level of difficulty: 2

Place the dried and candied fruits in a large bowl and pour in the beer. Cover and let stand for 12 hours. • Preheat the oven to 300°F/150°C/ gas 2. • Butter a deep 13 x 9-inch (33 x 23-cm) baking pan. Line with waxed paper. Butter the paper. • Sift the flours, baking powder, nutmeg, ginger, cinnamon, and salt into a large bowl. • Beat the butter, honey, and corn syrup in a large bowl with an electric mixer at medium speed until creamy. • Add the eggs, one at a time, beating until just blended after each addition. • With mixer at low speed, gradually beat in the dry ingredients and the fruit mixture. • Spoon the batter into the prepared pan. Sprinkle with the almonds. • Bake for about 2 hours and 30 minutes, or until dark brown at the edges and a toothpick inserted into the center comes out clean. • Cool the cake in the pan for 15 minutes. Turn out onto a rack. Carefully remove the paper and let cool completely.

Left: Dried fruit and tea cake

Frosted whisky fruitcake

Serves: 8-10; Preparation: 30 minutes; Cooking: 1 hour; Level of difficulty: 1

Place the raisins in a small saucepan with the water. Bring to a boil and simmer for 15 minutes. Drain well, reserving the liquid, and set aside to cool. • Preheat the oven to 350°F/180°C/gas 4. • Butter a 9 x 5-inch (23 x 13-cm) loaf pan. Line with aluminum foil, letting the edges overhang. Butter the foil. • Sift the flour, baking soda, nutmeg, and salt into a large bowl. • Beat the butter and sugar in a large bowl with an electric mixer at medium speed until creamy. • Add the egg, beating until just blended. • With mixer at low speed, gradually beat in the dry ingredients, alternating with 2 tablespoons of the reserved liquid. • Stir in the whisky, lemon juice, and walnuts. • Spoon the batter into the prepared pan. • Bake for about 45 minutes, or until dark brown at the edges and a toothpick inserted into the center comes out clean. • Cool the loaf in the pan for 5 minutes. Using the foil as a lifter, remove the loaf from the pan. Carefully remove the foil. Cool the loaf completely on a rack. • Slice in half horizontally and fill with half the frosting. Cover with the remaining cake layer and spread the top with frosting.

INGREDIENTS

- 1 cup (150 g) golden raisins (sultanas)
- 1 cup (250 ml) water
- 1⅓ cups (200 g) all-purpose (plain) flour
- 1 teaspoon baking soda
- ½ teaspoon ground nutmeg
- ¼ teaspoon salt
- ½ cup (125 g) butter
- ¾ cup (150 g) sugar
- 1 large egg
- 2 tablespoons whisky
- 1 tablespoon lemon juice
- ¾ cup (80 g) walnuts, coarsely chopped
- 1 quantity *Lemon Frosting* (see page 30) made with 1 teaspoon of whisky

Fruit cake with sherry

Serves: 10-12; Preparation: 25 minutes + 12 hours to stand; Cooking: 2 hours 30 minutes; Level of difficulty: 2

Mix the golden and dark raisins, prunes, currants, cherries, ½ cup (125 ml) sherry, and honey in a large bowl. Cover and let stand for 12 hours. • Preheat the oven to 300°F/150°C/gas 2. • Butter a deep 8-inch (20-cm) square cake pan. Line with aluminum foil, letting the edges overhang. Butter the foil. • Beat the butter and brown sugar in a large bowl with an electric mixer at medium speed until creamy. • Add the eggs, one at a time, beating until just blended after each addition. • With mixer at low speed, gradually beat in the flour, baking powder, and salt. Stir in the fruit mixture. • Spoon the batter into the prepared pan. • Bake for about 2 hours and 30 minutes, or until a toothpick inserted into the center comes out clean. • Remove from the oven and brush with the extra sherry. Cool the cake in the pan for 15 minutes. Using the foil as a lifter, remove the loaf from the pan. Carefully remove the foil and let cool completely on a rack.

INGREDIENTS

- 3 cups (350 g) golden raisins (sultanas)
- 2 cups (240 g) dark raisins
- 1½ cups (200 g) pitted prunes, coarsely chopped
- 1 cup (150 g) currants
- 1 cup (150 g) quartered candied red cherries
- ¾ cup (150 ml) dry sherry
- 6 tablespoons honey
- 1 cup (250 g) butter
- 1 cup (200 g) brown sugar
- 5 large eggs
- 1⅓ cups (200 g) all-purpose (plain) flour
- 1 teaspoon baking powder
- ¼ teaspoon salt

Left: Frosted whisky fruitcake

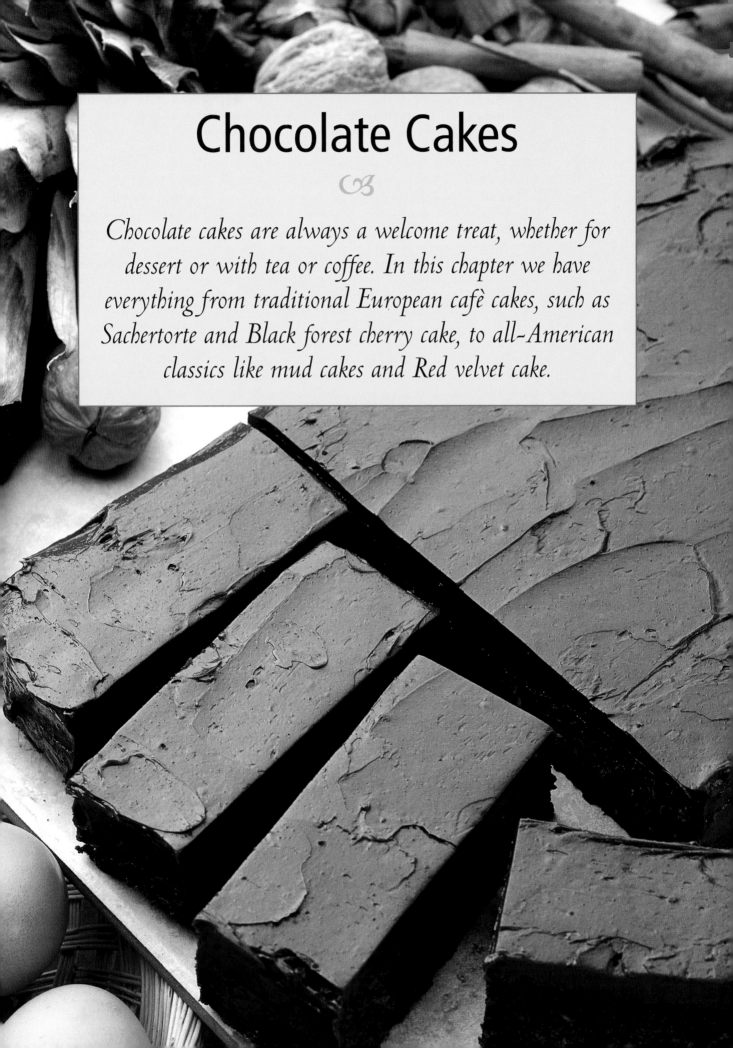

Chocolate Cakes

☙

Chocolate cakes are always a welcome treat, whether for dessert or with tea or coffee. In this chapter we have everything from traditional European cafè cakes, such as Sachertorte and Black forest cherry cake, to all-American classics like mud cakes and Red velvet cake.

Rich chocolate cake with marbled frosting

Serves: 10-12; Preparation: 45 minutes; Cooking: 55 minutes; Level of difficulty: 1

Preheat the oven to 350°F/180°C/gas 4. • Butter a 9-inch (23-cm) square baking pan. Line with waxed paper. Butter the paper. • Beat the flour, sugar, cocoa, baking powder, salt, butter, eggs, milk, water, vanilla, and vinegar in a large bowl with an electric mixer at medium speed until creamy. • Spoon the batter into the prepared pan. • Bake for about 55 minutes, or until a toothpick inserted into the center comes out clean. • Cool the cake in the pan for 5 minutes. Turn out onto a rack. Carefully remove the paper and let cool completely. • Frostings: Melt the chocolate and ½ cup (125 g) of butter in a double boiler over barely simmering water. Set aside to cool enough to spread (make sure it doesn't set). • With mixer at medium speed, beat the cream cheese and 6 tablespoons of butter in a small bowl until creamy. Add the honey and gradually beat in the confectioners' sugar. • Spoon alternate dollops of each of the frostings onto the top of the cake. Use a thin metal spatula to spread the frosting over. Use a fork to swirl the frostings together to create a marbled effect.

■ INGREDIENTS

- 2⅓ cups (350 g) all-purpose (plain) flour
- 1½ cups (300 g) sugar
- ⅔ cup (100 g) unsweetened cocoa powder
- 1 tablespoon baking powder
- ¼ teaspoon salt
- ¾ cup (200 g) butter
- 3 large eggs
- 1 cup (250 ml) milk
- ½ cup (125 ml) water
- 1 teaspoon vanilla extract
- 1 teaspoon white vinegar

FROSTINGS
- 4 oz (125 g) bittersweet chocolate, coarsely chopped
- ½ cup (125 g) butter
- 7 tablespoons cream cheese
- 6 tablespoons butter
- 1 tablespoon honey
- 1⅓ cups (200 g) confectioners' (icing) sugar

Chocolate potato ring

Serves: 8-10; Preparation: 20 minutes; Cooking: 35 minutes; Level of difficulty: 1

Preheat the oven to 350°F/180°C/gas 4. • Butter and flour a 10-inch (25-cm) tube pan. • Sift the flour, cocoa, baking powder, and salt into a medium bowl. • Beat the butter and sugar in a large bowl with an electric mixer at medium speed until creamy. • Add the eggs, one at a time, beating until just blended after each addition. • With mixer at low speed, gradually beat in the potato and dry ingredients, alternating with the milk. • Spoon the batter into the prepared pan. • Bake for about 35 minutes, or until a toothpick inserted into the center comes out clean. • Cool the cake in the pan for 30 minutes. Turn out onto a rack to cool completely. • Spread the top and sides of the cake with the frosting.

■ INGREDIENTS

- 2 cups (300 g) all-purpose (plain) flour
- ½ cup (75 g) cocoa powder
- 1½ teaspoons baking powder
- ¼ teaspoon salt
- ½ cup (125 g) butter
- ¾ cup (150 g) sugar
- 3 large eggs
- 1 cup (200 g) unseasoned mashed potato
- ½ cup (125 ml) milk
- 2 quantities *Basic Chocolate Frosting* (see page 30)

Right: *Rich chocolate cake with marbled frosting*

Hawaiian sheet cake

Serves: 8-10; Preparation: 30 minutes; Cooking: 40 minutes; Level of difficulty: 1

Preheat the oven to 350°F/180°C/gas 4. • Butter and flour a 13 x 9-inch (33 x 23-cm) baking pan. • Sift the flour, cocoa, baking powder, cinnamon, and salt into a medium bowl. • Beat the butter, sugar, and vanilla in a large bowl with an electric mixer at medium speed until creamy. • Add the eggs, one at a time, beating until just blended after each addition. • With mixer at low speed, gradually beat in the dry ingredients. • By hand, stir in the pineapple and walnuts. • Spoon the batter into the prepared pan. • Bake for about 40 minutes, or until a toothpick inserted into the center comes out clean. • Cool the cake completely in the pan on a rack. • Spread with the frosting.

■ INGREDIENTS

- 1 cup (150 g) all-purpose (plain) flour
- ½ cup (75 g) unsweetened cocoa powder
- 1 teaspoon baking powder
- 1 teaspoon cinnamon
- ¼ teaspoon salt
- ⅔ cup (180 g) butter
- 1½ cups (300 g) sugar
- 1 teaspoon vanilla extract
- 3 large eggs
- 1 cup (250 g) drained crushed pineapple
- 12 walnuts, chopped
- 2 quantities *Basic Chocolate Frosting* (see page 30)

Chocolate chip cake with amaretto frosting

Serves: 8-10; Preparation: 30 minutes; Cooking: 25 minutes; Level of difficulty: 1

Preheat the oven to 350°F/180°C/gas 4. • Butter and flour two 9-inch (23-cm) round cake pans. • Melt the chocolate and butter in a double boiler over barely simmering water. Set aside to cool. • Beat the eggs in a large bowl with an electric mixer at high speed until pale in color. Gradually beat in the sugar until pale and thick. • Use a large rubber spatula to fold in the cooled chocolate mixture. • Stir in 4 tablespoons of liqueur and the vanilla. • Sift the flour, baking powder, and salt into a large bowl. Gradually add the dry ingredients to the chocolate mixture. • Use a large rubber spatula to fold in the chocolate chips. • Spoon half the batter into each of the prepared pans. • Bake for about 25 minutes, or until a toothpick inserted into the center comes out clean. Cool the cakes in the pans for 10 minutes. Turn out onto racks to cool completely. • Frosting: Bring the cream to a boil in a medium saucepan. Remove from the heat. Stir in the chocolate chips. Cover and let stand for 10 minutes. • Stir in the amaretto until smooth. Place a cake on a serving plate. Drizzle with the remaining liqueur. • Spread with one-third of the frosting. Top with the remaining cake. Spread the remaining frosting over the cake.

■ INGREDIENTS

- 3 oz (90 g) bittersweet chocolate, chopped
- 6 tablespoons butter
- 2 large eggs
- 1⅓ cups (125 g) sugar
- ½ cup (125 ml) chocolate liqueur
- 1 teaspoon vanilla extract
- ⅔ cup (100 g) all-purpose (plain) flour
- ⅓ teaspoon baking powder
- ½ teaspoon salt
- 4 oz (125 g) bittersweet chocolate chips

FROSTING
- 1 cup (250 ml) heavy (double) cream
- 10 oz (350 g) bittersweet chocolate chips
- 2 tablespoons amaretto

Right: *Hawaiian sheet cake*

Chocolate banana cake

- 2 cups (300 g) all-purpose (plain) flour
- ½ cup (75 g) unsweetened cocoa powder
- 1½ teaspoons baking powder
- ½ teaspoon baking soda
- ¼ teaspoon salt
- ½ cup (100 g) sugar
- 2 large eggs
- ¾ cup (180 ml) hot water
- 2 bananas, mashed with a fork
- 2 teaspoons vanilla extract
- 1 quantity
  Rich Chocolate Frosting
  (see page 30)

Serves: 8-10; Preparation: 25 minutes; Cooking: 35 minutes; Level of difficulty: 1

Preheat the oven to 350°F/180°C/gas 4. • Butter a 9-inch (23-cm) square baking pan. Line with waxed paper. Butter the paper. • Sift the flour, cocoa, baking powder, baking soda, and salt into a large bowl. Stir in the sugar. • Beat in the eggs, water, bananas, and vanilla. • Spoon the batter into the prepared pan. • Bake for about 35 minutes, or until a toothpick inserted into the center comes out clean. • Cool the cake in the pan for 10 minutes. Turn out onto a rack. Carefully remove the paper and let cool completely. • Spread the cake with the frosting.

Chocolate orange cake with marbled frosting

- 2 cups (300 g) all-purpose (plain) flour
- 1½ cups (300 g) sugar
- ½ cup (75 g) unsweetened cocoa powder
- ½ cup (125 g) butter
- 2 tablespoons finely grated orange zest
- 7 tablespoons orange juice
- 3 large eggs
- 4 tablespoons water
- 2 teaspoons baking powder
- ½ teaspoon baking soda
- ¼ teaspoon salt

MARBLED FROSTING
- 4 tablespoons butter
- 1 tablespoon finely grated orange zest
- 2 cups (300 g) confectioners' (icing) sugar
- 2 tablespoons milk
- 2 tablespoons unsweetened cocoa powder

Left: *Chocolate banana cake*

Serves: 8-10; Preparation: 15 minutes; Cooking: 40 minutes; Level of difficulty: 1

Preheat the oven to 350°F/180°C/gas 4. • Butter an 11 x 7-inch (28 x 18-cm) baking pan. • Beat the flour, sugar, cocoa, butter, orange zest and juice, eggs, water, baking powder, baking soda, and salt in a large bowl with an electric mixer at low speed until just blended. Increase mixer speed to medium and beat for 5 minutes, or until the batter is smooth. • Spoon the batter into the prepared pan. • Bake for about 40 minutes, or until a toothpick inserted into the center comes out clean. • Cool the cake completely in the pan on a rack. • Marbled Frosting: With mixer at high speed, beat the butter and orange zest in a large bowl until creamy. Gradually beat in the confectioners' sugar and milk. • Place half the mixture in another bowl. Stir in the cocoa. • Place spoonfuls of orange and chocolate frosting next to each other on top of the cake. Swirl them together with a knife to create a marbled effect.

Chocolate cake with peanut butter frosting

Serves: 8-10; Preparation: 30 minutes; Cooking: 1 hour 20 minutes; Level of difficulty: 1

Preheat the oven to 325°F/170°C/gas 3. • Butter a 9-inch (23-cm) square baking pan. • Sift the flour, baking powder, and salt into a large bowl. • Melt the chocolate in a double boiler over barely simmering water. Set aside to cool. • Beat the butter, sugar, and vanilla in a large bowl with an electric mixer at medium speed until creamy. • Add the egg yolks, one at a time, beating until just blended after each addition. • With mixer at low speed, gradually beat in the chocolate and peanut butter, followed by the dry ingredients, alternating with the milk. • With mixer at high speed, beat the egg whites in a large bowl until stiff peaks form. Use a large rubber spatula to fold them into the chocolate mixture. • Spoon the batter into the prepared pan. • Bake for about 1 hour 20 minutes, or until a toothpick inserted into the center comes out clean. • Cool the cake in the pan for 10 minutes. Turn out onto a rack and let cool completely. • Peanut Butter Frosting: With mixer at high speed, beat the confectioners' sugar, butter, and peanut butter in a large bowl until smooth. • Spread the cake with the frosting.

■ INGREDIENTS

- 2 cups (300 g) all-purpose (plain) flour
- 2 teaspoons baking powder
- ¼ teaspoon salt
- 6 oz (180 g) semisweet chocolate, coarsely chopped
- ½ cup (125 g) butter
- 1¾ cups (350 g) sugar
- 1 teaspoon vanilla extract
- 4 large eggs, separated
- ½ cup (125 g) smooth peanut butter
- 1 cup (250 ml) milk

PEANUT BUTTER FROSTING
- 1½ cups (225 g) confectioners' (icing) sugar
- ½ cup (125 g) butter, melted
- ½ cup (125 g) smooth peanut butter

White chocolate and walnut mud cake

Serves: 8-10; Preparation: 30 minutes; Cooking: 1 hour; Level of difficulty: 2

Preheat the oven to 325°F/170°C/gas 3. • Butter a 9-inch (23-cm) round cake pan. Line with waxed paper. • Place the brown sugar, milk, butter, molasses, and chocolate in a saucepan and stir over low heat, without boiling, until smooth. Set aside to cool. • Sift the flour, baking powder, and salt into a medium bowl. Gradually stir the dry ingredients and eggs into the sugar mixture. • Spoon the batter into the prepared pan. • Bake for about 1 hour, or until a toothpick inserted into the center comes out clean. • Cool the cake completely in the pan. Turn out onto a rack. Carefully remove the paper and let cool completely. • Spread with the ganache.

■ INGREDIENTS

- 1 cup (200 g) firmly packed brown sugar
- 1 cup (250 ml) milk
- ¾ cup (200 g) butter
- 6 tablespoons molasses
- 6 oz (180 g) white chocolate, chopped
- 2 cups (300 g) all-purpose (plain) flour
- 2 teaspoons baking powder
- ¼ teaspoon salt
- 2 large eggs, lightly beaten
- 1 quantity *White Chocolate Ganache* (see page 32)

Right: *Chocolate cake with peanut butter frosting*

Black forest cherry cake

There are many versions of this striking chocolate layer cake. It is named after the Black Forest in southern Germany, although it was actually invented in Austria and has always been a classic in Viennese coffee houses. Despite its elaborate appearance, it is not an especially difficult cake to make. The chocolate cake can be prepared in advance. Always assemble the cake 3–4 hours in advance of serving and chill in the refrigerator.

Serves: 8-10; Preparation: 35 minutes; Cooking: 45 minutes; Level of difficulty: 2

Preheat the oven to 350°F/180°C/gas 4.• Butter two 9-inch (23-cm) round cake pans. Line with waxed paper. Butter the paper. • Sift the flour, baking powder, and salt into a large bowl. • Melt the chocolate and water in a double boiler over barely simmering water. Set aside to cool. • Beat the butter and brown sugar in a large bowl with an electric mixer at medium speed until creamy. • Add the eggs, one at a time, beating until just blended after each addition. • With mixer at low speed, gradually beat in the chocolate mixture, sour cream, and dry ingredients. • Spoon half the batter into each of the prepared pans. • Bake for about 45 minutes, or until a toothpick inserted into the centers comes out clean. • Cool the cakes in the pans for 10 minutes. Turn out onto racks. Carefully remove the waxed paper and let cool completely. • Split the cakes horizontally. • Filling: Mix the cherry jam and kirsch. • With mixer at high speed, beat the cream in a medium bowl until stiff. • Frosting: Melt the chocolate and butter in a double boiler over barely simmering water. • Place a layer of cake on a serving plate. Spread with one-third of the jam mixture and one-third of the whipped cream. Repeat with the remaining cake layers, finishing with a plain layer. Spread the frosting over the top and sides of the cake. Decorate with the candied cherries.

■ INGREDIENTS

- 1⅔ cups (250 g) all-purpose (plain) flour
- 1½ teaspoons baking powder
- ¼ teaspoon salt
- 5 oz (150 g) semisweet chocolate, coarsely chopped
- ½ cup (125 ml) water
- ½ cup (125 g) butter
- 1¼ cups (250 g) firmly packed brown sugar
- 2 large eggs
- ½ cup (125 ml) sour cream

FILLING
- 1½ cups (480 ml) cherry jam or preserves
- 3 tablespoons kirsch (cherry schnapps)
- 2 cups (500 ml) heavy (double) cream

FROSTING
- 8 oz (250 g) bittersweet chocolate, coarsely chopped
- 4 tablespoons butter
- candied cherries, to decorate

Right: *Black forest cherry cake*

Chocolate ladyfinger mousse

INGREDIENTS

- 1 lb (500 g) bittersweet chocolate
- 1¼ cups (250 g) sugar
- ¾ cup (200 ml) water
- 2 large eggs
- 8 large egg yolks
- 1 tablespoon unflavored gelatin
- 1½ cups (375 ml) heavy (double) cream
- 36 ladyfingers

Serves: 8-10; Preparation: 30 minutes + 6 hours to chill; Level of difficulty: 2

Set out the sides of a 10-inch (25-cm) springform pan. Place on a plate with a 10-inch (25-cm) disk of parchment paper. • Melt the chocolate in a double boiler over barely simmering water. Let cool. • Dissolve the sugar in ½ cup (125 ml) water in a saucepan over medium heat. Wash down the pan sides with a pastry brush dipped in cold water to prevent sugar crystals from forming. Cook, without stirring, until the mixture reaches 238°F (114°C), or the soft-ball stage. • Beat the eggs and egg yolks in a large bowl with an electric mixer at medium speed until frothy. With mixer at high speed, gradually beat in the sugar mixture, beating until thick. • Sprinkle the gelatin over the remaining water in a small saucepan. Let stand 1 minute. Cook over low heat until completely dissolved. • Add the gelatin mixture to the egg mixture. • With mixer at high speed, beat the cream in a large bowl until stiff. • Use a large rubber spatula to fold in the chocolate and then the cream. • Cover the parchment paper with a layer of ladyfingers. • Spoon the mousse into the mold and refrigerate for 6 hours, or until set. Carefully remove the pan sides before serving.

Chocolate mousse chantilly

INGREDIENTS

- 8 oz (250 g) bittersweet chocolate, coarsely chopped
- 4 tablespoons water
- 6 large eggs
- ¾ cup (200 g) butter
- ½ quantity *Chantilly Cream* (see page 26)
- fresh berries (raspberries, strawberries, etc), to decorate
- slivered almonds, to decorate

Serves: 6-8; Preparation: 30 minutes + 12 hours to chill; Cooking: 15 minutes; Level of difficulty: 2

Butter an 8-inch (20-cm) square baking pan. • Melt the chocolate and water in a double boiler over barely simmering water. Beat in the eggs, one at a time, until just blended. Cook until the mixture lightly coats a metal spoon or it registers 160°F (71°C) on an instant-read thermometer. Remove from the heat and stir in the butter. Immediately plunge the pan into a bowl of ice water and stir until the mixture has cooled. • Use a large rubber spatula to fold three-quarters of the Chantilly Cream into the chocolate mixture. • Spoon the mixture into the prepared pan and refrigerate for 12 hours, or until set. • Cover the pan with a serving plate and carefully turn upside down. • Spoon the remaining Chantilly Cream into a pastry bag and pipe the top of the mousse. Decorate with the berries and almonds.

Right: Chocolate ladyfinger mousse

Classic devil's food cake

Serves: 8-10; Preparation: 45 minutes; Cooking: 35 minutes; Level of difficulty: 2

Preheat the oven to 350°F/180°C/gas 4. • Butter two 9-inch (23-cm) round cake pans. Line with waxed paper. Butter the paper. • Melt the chocolate in a double boiler over barely simmering water. Set aside to cool. • Stir together the milk and lemon juice to make sour milk. Set aside. • Sift the flour, baking powder, baking soda, and salt into a large bowl. • Beat both sugars, butter, and vanilla in a large bowl with an electric mixer at medium speed until creamy. • Add the eggs, one at a time, beating until just blended after each addition. • With mixer at low speed, gradually beat in the dry ingredients, food coloring, and chocolate, alternating with the sour milk. • Spoon the batter into the prepared pans. • Bake for about 35 minutes, or until a toothpick inserted into the centers comes out clean. • Cool the cakes in the pans for 5 minutes. Turn out onto racks. Carefully remove the paper and let cool completely. • Place one cake on a serving plate. Spread with the raspberry preserves, followed by the Mock Cream. Top with the remaining cake. • Spread the top and sides with the frosting.

INGREDIENTS

- 5 oz (150 g) semisweet chocolate
- 1 cup (250 ml) milk
- 1 tablespoon lemon juice
- 2 cups (300 g) all-purpose (plain) flour
- 1 teaspoon baking powder
- ½ teaspoon baking soda
- ¼ teaspoon salt
- ¾ cup (150 g) sugar
- ¾ cup (150 g) firmly packed brown sugar
- ½ cup (125 g) butter
- 1 teaspoon vanilla extract
- 2 large eggs
- 1 teaspoon red food coloring
- ½ cup (160 ml) raspberry preserves (jam)
- 1 quantity *Mock Cream* (see page 40)
- 1 quantity *Rich Chocolate Frosting* (see page 30)

Rich chocolate sundae

Serves: 8-10; Preparation: 25 minutes; Cooking: 50 minutes; Level of difficulty: 2

Preheat the oven to 350°F/180°C/gas 4. • Butter a 13 x 9-inch (33 x 23-cm) baking pan. • Sift the flour, half the cocoa, baking powder, and salt into a large bowl. Stir in the sugar. • Mix the milk, butter, and vanilla in a medium bowl. Beat the milk mixture into the dry ingredients with an electric mixer at low speed. • By hand, stir in the nuts. • Spoon the batter into the prepared pan. Place the pan on a baking sheet. Mix the brown sugar and remaining cocoa in a medium bowl. Sprinkle over the batter and pour the water carefully over the cake. • Bake for about 50 minutes, or until a toothpick inserted into the center comes out clean. • Serve the cake from the pan while still warm, spooning a little of the sauce that forms in the bottom of the pan over each serving.

INGREDIENTS

- 1⅔ cups (250 g) all-purpose (plain) flour
- 1 cup (150 g) unsweetened cocoa powder
- 2 teaspoons baking powder
- ¼ teaspoon salt
- 1¼ cups (250 g) sugar
- 1 cup (250 ml) milk
- 6 tablespoons butter
- 2 teaspoons vanilla extract
- 1 cup (150 g) walnuts or pecans, chopped
- 1¾ cups (350 g) firmly packed brown sugar
- 1¼ cups (310 ml) boiling water

Right: *Classic devil's food cake*

Chocolate sour cream cake

Serves: 10-12; Preparation: 30 minutes; Cooking: 35 minutes; Level of difficulty: 2

Preheat the oven to 350°F/180°C/gas 4. • Butter two 9-inch (23-cm) round cake pans. Line with waxed paper. • Sift the flour, baking powder, and salt into a large bowl. • Melt the chocolate with the water in a double boiler over barely simmering water. Let cool. • Beat the butter, brown sugar, and vanilla in a large bowl with an electric mixer at medium speed until creamy. • Add the eggs, beating until just blended after each addition. • Gradually beat in the chocolate mixture, followed by the yogurt and dry ingredients. • Spoon half the batter into each of the prepared pans. • Bake for about 35 minutes, or until a toothpick inserted into the centers comes out clean. • Turn out onto racks and let cool completely. • Filling: With mixer at high speed, beat the cream, confectioners' sugar, and vanilla in a medium bowl until stiff. • Frosting: Melt the chocolate in a double boiler over barely simmering water. Remove from the heat. Stir in the sour cream and confectioners' sugar. Do not let the frosting cool completely or it will be too thick to spread. • Split each cake horizontally. Place one layer on a serving plate. Spread with one-third of the raspberry jam and top with a layer of frosting. Spread with one-third of the cream. Repeat with the remaining cake layers. • Spread the top and sides with the remaining frosting.

■ INGREDIENTS

- 2½ cups (375 g) all-purpose (plain) flour
- 2 teaspoons baking powder
- ¼ teaspoon salt
- 6 oz (180 g) semisweet chocolate, chopped
- ½ cup (125 ml) water
- ¾ cup (200 g) butter
- 1¾ cups (350 g) firmly packed brown sugar
- 1 teaspoon vanilla extract
- 3 large eggs
- ½ cup (125 ml) plain yogurt
- FILLING
- 1½ cups (375 ml) heavy (double) cream
- 3 tablespoons confectioners' (icing) sugar
- ½ teaspoon vanilla extract
- FROSTING
- 12 oz (350 g) semisweet chocolate, chopped
- ¾ cup (200 ml) sour cream
- 1½ cups (225 g) confectioners' (icing) sugar
- 1 cup (225 g) raspberry jelly

Viennese mud cake

Serves: 8-10; Preparation: 25 minutes; Cooking: 1 hour 10 minutes; Level of difficulty: 1

Preheat the oven to 325°F/170°C/gas 3. • Butter and flour a 9-inch (23-cm) springform pan. • Stir the butter, chocolate, brown sugar, milk, and corn syrup in a large saucepan over low heat until smooth. Do not boil. Set aside to cool. • Stir in the flour and baking powder. Add the eggs, one at a time, beating until just blended after each addition. • Spoon the batter into the prepared pan. • Bake for about 1 hour and 10 minutes, or until a toothpick inserted into the center comes out clean. • Cool the cake in the pan for 10 minutes. Loosen and remove the pan sides. Invert the cake onto a rack. Loosen and remove the pan bottom and let cool completely. • Spread the top and sides of the cake with the ganache.

■ INGREDIENTS

- ¾ cup (180 g) butter
- 5 oz (150 g) white chocolate, coarsely chopped
- 1 cup (200 g) firmly packed brown sugar
- 1 cup (250 ml) milk
- 6 tablespoons corn (golden) syrup
- 2 cups (300 g) all-purpose (plain) flour
- 2 teaspoons baking powder
- 2 large eggs, lightly beaten
- 1 quantity *White Chocolate Ganache* (see page 32)

Right: *Viennese mud cake*

Chocolate raisin cake

■ INGREDIENTS

- 1 cup (180 g) raisins
- 2 tablespoons dark rum
- 1 large egg
- ¾ cup (150 g) firmly packed dark brown sugar
- 7 oz (200 g) milk chocolate, coarsely chopped
- ½ cup (125 g) butter
- 1¼ cups (180 g) all-purpose (plain) flour
- 1 teaspoon baking powder
- ¼ teaspoon salt

RUM FROSTING

- 4 large egg yolks
- ⅓ cup (70 g) sugar
- 4 tablespoons light (single) cream
- 2 teaspoons dark rum
- 2 tablespoons butter
- 1 teaspoon unsweetened cocoa powder

Serves: 6-8; Preparation: 25 minutes + 1 hour to soak; Cooking: 30 minutes; Level of difficulty: 1
Preheat the oven to 350°F/180°C/gas 4. • Butter an 8-inch (20-cm) square baking pan. • Stir together the raisins and rum in a large bowl. Cover and soak for 1 hour. • Beat the egg and brown sugar in a large bowl with an electric mixer at medium speed until creamy. • Melt the chocolate and butter in a double boiler over barely simmering water. With mixer at medium speed, beat into the egg mixture. • Use a large rubber spatula to fold in the flour, baking powder, salt, and raisin mixture. • Spoon the batter into the prepared pan. • Bake for about 30 minutes, or until a toothpick inserted into the center comes out clean. Cool completely in the pan on a rack. • Rum Frosting: Beat the egg yolks, sugar, cream, and rum in a medium saucepan until well blended. Cook over low heat, stirring constantly with a wooden spoon, until the mixture lightly coats a metal spoon, or registers 160°F (71°C) on an instant-read thermometer. Immediately plunge the pan into a bowl of ice water and stir until cooled. • Beat the butter in a small bowl until creamy. Use a large rubber spatula to fold in the cocoa powder. Gradually fold the cocoa butter into the egg yolk mixture. • Cover and refrigerate for 10 minutes. • Spread the frosting over the cake.

Double chocolate tube cake

■ INGREDIENTS

- 2 cups (300 g) all-purpose (plain) flour
- ⅓ cup (50 g) unsweetened cocoa powder
- 2 teaspoons baking powder
- ¼ teaspoon salt
- ⅔ cup (180 g) butter
- 4 tablespoons vegetable shortening
- 2 cups (400 g) sugar
- 3 large eggs
- ⅔ cup (180 ml) milk
- 1 teaspoon vanilla extract
- ¾ cup (150 g) semisweet chocolate chips

Serves: 8-10; Preparation: 25 minutes; Cooking: 1 hour; Level of difficulty: 1
Preheat the oven to 325°F/170°C/gas 3. • Butter a 10-inch (25-cm) tube pan. Dust with cocoa. • Sift the flour, cocoa, baking powder, and salt into a medium bowl. • Beat the butter, shortening, and sugar in a large bowl with an electric mixer at medium speed until creamy. • Add the eggs, one at a time, beating until just blended after each addition. • With mixer at low speed, gradually beat in the dry ingredients, alternating with the milk and vanilla. • By hand, stir in the chocolate chips. • Spoon the batter into the prepared pan. • Bake for about 1 hour, or until a toothpick inserted into the center comes out clean. • Cool the cake in the pan for 10 minutes. Turn out onto a rack to cool completely.

Right: Chocolate raisin cake

Chocolate sour cream and rum cake

Serves: 8-10; Preparation: 25 minutes; Cooking: 50 minutes; Level of difficulty: 1

Preheat the oven to 350°F/180°C/gas 4. • Butter and flour two 9-inch (23-cm) cake pans. • Stir the water, cocoa, and baking soda in a saucepan over low heat until smooth. Set aside to cool. • Sift the flour, cornstarch, and salt into a medium bowl. • Beat the butter, sugar, and vanilla in a large bowl with an electric mixer at medium speed until creamy. • Add the eggs, one at a time, beating until just blended after each addition. • With mixer at low speed, gradually beat in the dry ingredients, alternating with the sour cream and cocoa mixture. • Spoon half the batter into each of the prepared pans. • Bake for about 50 minutes, or until a toothpick inserted into the center comes out clean. • Cool the cakes in the pans for 5 minutes. Turn out onto racks to cool completely. • Frosting: Mix the confectioners' sugar and cocoa in a large bowl. Add the butter, rum, and vanilla. Beat in enough of the milk to make a thick, spreadable frosting. • Place a cake on a serving plate. Spread with one-third of the frosting. Top with the remaining cake. Spread with the remaining frosting.

■ INGREDIENTS

- ½ cup (125 ml) water
- ½ cup (75 g) unsweetened cocoa powder
- 2 teaspoons baking soda
- 2 cups (300 g) all-purpose (plain) flour
- ½ cup (75 g) cornstarch (cornflour)
- ¼ teaspoon salt
- ⅔ cup (150 g) butter
- 1¾ cups (350 g) sugar
- 1½ teaspoons vanilla extract
- 2 large eggs
- 1 cup (250 ml) sour cream

FROSTING

- 2 cups (300 g) confectioners' (icing) sugar
- ⅓ cup (50 g) unsweetened cocoa powder
- ⅔ cup (150 g) butter, melted
- 1½ tablespoons rum
- 1 teaspoon vanilla extract
- 1–2 tablespoons milk

Dark chocolate Bundt cake

Serves: 8-10; Preparation: 15 minutes; Cooking: 55 minutes; Level of difficulty: 1

Preheat the oven to 350°F/180°C/gas 4. • Butter a 10-inch (25-cm) Bundt pan. Dust with cocoa. • Place all the ingredients except the chocolate chips in a large bowl and beat with an electric mixer at medium speed until well blended. • Fold in the chocolate chips. The batter will be thick. • Spoon the batter into the prepared pan. • Bake for about 55 minutes, or until a toothpick inserted into the center comes out clean. • Cool the cake in the pan for 10 minutes. Turn out onto a rack to cool completely.

■ INGREDIENTS

- 1 package (18 oz/500 g) dark chocolate cake mix
- 2 cups (500 ml) sour cream
- 3 large eggs
- ½ cup (125 ml) coffee liqueur
- 6 tablespoons vegetable oil
- 1 package (3.9 oz/120 g) instant chocolate pudding mix
- 1 package (12 oz/350 g) semisweet chocolate chips

Right: Chocolate sour cream and rum cake

Chocolate almond brittle cake

■ INGREDIENTS

ALMOND BRITTLE
- ½ cup (100 g) sugar
- ½ cup (75 g) almonds, finely ground

CAKE
- 8 oz (250 g) bittersweet chocolate, coarsely chopped
- 8 oz (250 g) milk chocolate, coarsely chopped
- 4 tablespoons butter
- ½ cup (90 g) raisins
- 2 tablespoons all-purpose (plain) flour
- 2 tablespoons sugar
- 2 large eggs, separated
- 2 tablespoons dark rum
- ¼ teaspoon salt

Serves: 6-8; Preparation: 25 minutes + 4 hours to chill; Cooking: 25 minutes; Level of difficulty: 1

Almond Brittle: Oil a cookie sheet. Place the sugar in a saucepan over medium heat and stir until dissolved. Bring to a boil and cook until a deep golden color. • Stir in the almonds, then pour onto the cookie sheet. Let cool. • Break into pieces. • Cake: Preheat the oven to 350°F/180°C/gas 4. • Butter a 9-inch (23-cm) round cake pan. Line with waxed paper. • Melt the two chocolates and butter in a double boiler over barely simmering water. Transfer to a large bowl and set aside until lukewarm. • Stir in the raisins, flour, sugar, egg yolks, and rum. • Beat the egg whites and salt in a small bowl with an electric mixer at high speed until stiff peaks form. Fold them into the batter. • Spoon the batter into the prepared pan. • Bake for 10 minutes. Sprinkle with the brittle and bake for 15 minutes. • Turn the oven off and leave the cake in the oven with the door ajar for 2 hours. • Turn out and wrap carefully in foil. • Refrigerate for at least 4 hours before serving.

Chocolate cream hazelnut torte

■ INGREDIENTS

CHOCOLATE CREAM
- 8 oz (250 g) bittersweet chocolate, chopped
- ¾ cup (200 ml) heavy (double) cream
- ⅓ cup (30 g) toasted hazelnuts, finely ground

HAZELNUT TORTE
- 6 large egg whites
- ¼ teaspoon salt
- 1 cup (200 g) sugar
- 1⅓ cups (150 g) toasted hazelnuts, finely ground
- ⅓ cup (50 g) confectioners' (icing) sugar
- hazelnuts, to decorate

Serves: 6-8; Preparation: 40 minutes; Cooking: 10 minutes; Level of difficulty: 2

Chocolate Cream: Melt the chocolate and cream in a double boiler over barely simmering water. Stir in the hazelnuts. Set aside to cool. • Hazelnut Torte: Preheat the oven to 400°F/200°C/gas 6. • Butter and flour a baking sheet. Cut two 8-inch (20-cm) squares of waxed paper and place on the baking sheet. • Beat the egg whites and salt in a large bowl with an electric mixer at medium speed until frothy. With mixer at high speed, gradually add the sugar, beating until stiff, glossy peaks form. • Use a rubber spatula to fold the hazelnuts into the beaten whites. • Spoon the batter onto the paper, spreading them with the back of the spoon. Leave a ½-inch (1-cm) border all around the edges of the paper. • Bake for about 10 minutes, or until a toothpick inserted into the centers comes out clean. Cool completely on a rack. • Trim the edges of the cakes so that they are straight. • Place one layer on a serving plate. Spread with the chocolate cream. Top with the remaining layer. • Dust with the confectioners' sugar. Decorate with the hazelnuts.

Right: *Chocolate almond brittle cake*

Peppy chocolate pound cake

Serves: 12–14; Preparation: 25 minutes; Cooking: 1 hour 30 minutes; Level of difficulty: 1

Preheat the oven to 350°F/180°C/gas 4. • Butter and flour a 12-inch (30-cm) tube pan. • Sift the flour, cocoa, baking powder, and salt into a large bowl. • Beat the butter, shortening, sugar, and vanilla in a large bowl with an electric mixer at medium speed until creamy. • Add the eggs, one at a time, beating until just blended after each addition. • With mixer at low speed, gradually beat in the dry ingredients, alternating with the milk. • Spoon the batter into the prepared pan. • Bake for 1 hour and 30 minutes, or until a toothpick inserted into the center comes out clean. • Run a knife around the edges of the pan to loosen the cake. Cool the cake in the pan for 15 minutes. Turn out onto a rack to cool completely. • Peppermint Frosting: With mixer at medium speed, beat the confectioners' sugar and butter in a large bowl until creamy. Add the cocoa, milk, and peppermint extract and beat until smooth. • Spread the top and sides of the cake with the frosting.

■ INGREDIENTS

- 3½ cups (500 g) all-purpose (plain) flour
- 1 cup (150 g) unsweetened cocoa powder
- 1 teaspoon baking powder
- ½ teaspoon salt
- 1 cup (250 g) butter
- ½ cup (125 g) vegetable shortening
- 3 cups (600 g) sugar
- 1 tablespoon vanilla extract
- 5 large eggs
- 1¼ cups (310 ml) milk

PEPPERMINT FROSTING

- 2 cups (300 g) confectioners' (icing) sugar
- 4 tablespoons butter
- ⅓ cup (50 g) unsweetened cocoa powder
- 1 tablespoon milk
- ½ teaspoon peppermint extract

Double chocolate cake with raspberry coulis

Serves: 6–8; Preparation: 35 minutes; Cooking: 35 minutes; Level of difficulty: 2

Cake: Preheat the oven to 325°F/170°C/gas 3. • Butter an 8-inch (20-cm) springform pan. • Melt the chocolate chips and butter in a double boiler over barely simmering water. • Let cool for 5 minutes. • Add the egg yolks, one at a time, beating until just blended after each addition. • With mixer at high speed, beat the egg whites and sugar in a large bowl until soft peaks form. Use a large rubber spatula to fold in the chocolate mixture and flour. • Pour the batter into the prepared pan. • Bake for about 35 minutes, or until a toothpick inserted into the center comes out clean. • Cool the cake in the pan on a rack for 10 minutes. • Loosen and remove the pan sides and let cool completely. • Frosting: Melt the chocolate chips with the butter and corn syrup in a small saucepan over medium heat. • Spread the frosting over the top of the cake. • Serve with the raspberry coulis passed on the side.

■ INGREDIENTS

CAKE

- 1 cup (180 g) semisweet chocolate chips
- ½ cup (125 g) butter
- 4 large eggs, separated
- ½ cup (100 g) sugar
- ½ cup (75 g) all-purpose (plain) flour

FROSTING

- ½ cup (90 g) semisweet chocolate chips
- 2 tablespoons butter
- 2 tablespoons corn (golden) syrup
- 1 quantity *Raspberry Coulis* (see page 34)

Right: Peppy chocolate pound cake

Exotic chocolate cake

■ INGREDIENTS

- 7 oz (200 g) bittersweet chocolate, chopped
- ½ cup (125 g) butter
- 1 cup (200 g) sugar
- 1 tablespoon finely grated orange zest
- 1 tablespoon orange juice
- 2 large eggs
- 1 cup (150 g) all-purpose (plain) flour
- 1 teaspoon baking powder
- ¼ teaspoon salt
- ½ cup (75 g) candied ginger, chopped
- confectioners' (icing) sugar, to dust

Serves: 6-8; Preparation: 25 minutes; Cooking: 45 minutes; Level of difficulty: 1

Preheat the oven to 350°F/180°C/gas 4. • Butter an 8-inch (20-cm) square baking pan. Line with waxed paper. Butter the paper. • Melt the chocolate and butter in a double boiler over barely simmering water. Transfer to a large bowl. • Beat in the sugar and orange zest and juice with an electric mixer at medium speed until creamy. • Add the eggs, one at a time, beating until just blended after each addition. • Use a large rubber spatula to fold in the flour, baking powder, salt, and ginger. • Spoon the batter into the prepared pan. • Bake for about 45 minutes, or until a toothpick inserted into the center comes out clean. Cool completely in the pan on a rack. • Dust with the confectioners' sugar.

Chocolate loaf with strawberries and cream

Serves: 6-8; Preparation: 30 minutes + 12 hours to chill; Cooking: 55 minutes; Level of difficulty: 1

Preheat the oven to 325°F/170°C/gas 3. • Butter a 9 x 5-inch (23 x 13-cm) loaf pan. Line with aluminum foil, letting the edges overhang. Butter the foil. • Melt the chocolate and butter in a double boiler over barely simmering water. Let cool. • Beat the eggs and egg yolk in a double boiler over barely simmering water with an electric mixer at medium speed until pale and thick. Fold into the chocolate mixture. • With mixer at high speed, beat the egg whites in a medium bowl until stiff peaks form. Fold into the chocolate mixture. • Spoon the batter into the prepared pan. • Place the pan in a larger pan and pour in hot water to measure 1 inch (2.5-cm) up the sides of the loaf pan. • Bake for about 55 minutes, or until a toothpick inserted into the center comes out clean. • Cool the loaf in the pan on a rack. Refrigerate for 12 hours. • Using the foil as a lifter, remove the loaf from the pan. Carefully remove the foil. • Beat the cream and confectioners' sugar until thick. • Serve with the cream and strawberries.

■ INGREDIENTS

- 8 oz (250 g) bittersweet chocolate, chopped
- ½ cup (125 g) butter
- 4 large eggs + 1 large egg yolk
- 2 large egg whites
- 1 cup (250 ml) heavy (double) cream
- 1 tablespoon confectioners' (icing) sugar
- 8 oz (250 g) fresh strawberries, hulled and sliced

Mocha mousse cake

Serves: 8-10; Preparation: 30 minutes + 1 hour to chill; Cooking: 35 minutes; Level of difficulty: 1

Preheat the oven to 300°F/150°C/gas 2. • Butter a 10-inch (25-cm) springform pan. Dust with cocoa. • Melt the chocolate, butter, and coffee in a double boiler over barely simmering water. Transfer to a large bowl. Cool to warm. • Beat the egg yolks and milk in a large bowl with an electric mixer at high speed until pale and thick. Fold them into the chocolate mixture. • With mixer at high speed, beat the egg whites and sugar in a large bowl until stiff peaks form. Fold them into the chocolate mixture. • Spoon the mixture into the prepared pan. • Bake for about 35 minutes, or until just firm in the center. • Cool completely in the pan on a rack. Loosen and remove the pan sides. Refrigerate for 1 hour before serving.

■ INGREDIENTS

- 12 oz (350 g) semisweet chocolate, coarsely chopped
- 1 cup (250 g) butter, cut up
- 1 teaspoon freeze-dried coffee granules
- 10 large eggs, separated
- 4 tablespoons milk
- 1½ cups (300 g) sugar

Right: *Chocolate loaf with strawberries and cream*

Chocolate peppermint cream cake

*This rich chocolate cake will be a hit with everyone
who enjoys the classic combination of chocolate and peppermint.*

Serves: 6-8; Preparation: 40 minutes; Cooking: 35 minutes; Level of difficulty: 2

Preheat the oven to 350°F/180°C/gas 4. • Butter a 9-inch (23-cm) round cake pan. Line with waxed paper. Butter the paper. • Melt the chocolate and water in a double boiler over barely simmering water. Set aside to cool. • Sift the flour, cocoa, baking powder, baking soda, and salt into a medium bowl. • Beat the butter and both sugars in a large bowl with an electric mixer at medium speed until creamy. • Add the eggs, one at a time, beating until just blended after each addition. • With mixer at low speed, gradually beat in the dry ingredients, alternating with the milk and chocolate. • Spoon the batter into the prepared pan. • Bake for about 35 minutes, or until a toothpick inserted into the center comes out clean. • Cool the cake in the pan for 10 minutes. Turn out onto a rack. Carefully remove the waxed paper and let cool completely. • Peppermint Filling: With mixer at high speed, beat the confectioners' sugar and butter in a medium bowl until creamy. Stir in the milk and peppermint extract. • Frosting: Stir together the confectioners' sugar and cocoa in a medium bowl. Beat in the butter and enough water to make a thick, spreadable frosting. • Split the cake horizontally. • Place one layer on a serving plate. Spread with the filling. Top with the remaining layer. Spread the top and sides with the frosting.

> VARIATIONS
> — For an over-the-top peppermint flavor, add ½ teaspoon of peppermint extract to the frosting.
> — For a different flavor, substitute the peppermint extract with almond or orange extract.

■ INGREDIENTS

- 4 oz (125 g) semisweet chocolate, coarsely chopped
- 4 tablespoons water
- 1¼ cups (180 g) all-purpose (plain) flour
- 2 tablespoons unsweetened cocoa powder
- 1 teaspoon baking powder
- 1 teaspoon baking soda
- ¼ teaspoon salt
- ½ cup (125 g) butter, melted
- 1 cup (200 g) sugar
- ⅓ cup (70 g) firmly packed brown sugar
- 2 large eggs
- 6 tablespoons milk

PEPPERMINT FILLING

- 3 cups (450 g) confectioners' (icing) sugar
- ½ cup (125 g) butter
- 1 tablespoon milk
- 1 teaspoon peppermint extract

FROSTING

- 2 cups (300 g) confectioners' (icing) sugar
- 2 tablespoons unsweetened cocoa powder
- 1 tablespoon butter
- 6 tablespoons hot water

Right: Chocolate peppermint cream cake

Mascarpone chocolate cake

Serves: 6-8; Preparation: 25 minutes; Cooking: 35 minutes; Level of difficulty: 2

Preheat the oven to 350°F/180°C/gas 4. • Butter a 9-inch (23-cm) round cake pan. Line with waxed paper. • Melt the chocolate and butter in a double boiler over barely simmering water. Let cool. • Beat the egg yolks and confectioners' sugar in a large bowl with an electric mixer at medium speed until pale and creamy. • With mixer at low speed, beat in the cornstarch and mascarpone, followed by the cooled chocolate mixture. • Beat the egg whites at high speed until stiff peaks form. Fold into the mixture. • Spoon the batter into the prepared pan. • Bake for about 35 minutes, or until a toothpick inserted into the center comes out clean. • Cool the cake in the pan for 10 minutes. Turn out onto a rack. Carefully remove the waxed paper and let cool completely. • Mascarpone Topping: With mixer at medium speed, beat the mascarpone and confectioners' sugar in a medium bowl until creamy. • Spread over the top of the cake. • Melt the chocolate in a double boiler over barely simmering water. Set aside to cool a little then drizzle over the cake.

■ INGREDIENTS

- 7 oz (200 g) bittersweet chocolate, coarsely chopped
- ⅔ cup (180 g) butter
- 4 large eggs, separated
- 1⅓ cups (200 g) confectioners' (icing) sugar
- 1 tablespoon cornstarch (cornflour)
- 1 tablespoon mascarpone cheese

MASCARPONE TOPPING
- 7 oz (200 g) mascarpone cheese
- 4 tablespoons confectioners' (icing) sugar
- 4 oz (125 g) bittersweet (dark) chocolate

Sachertorte

Serves: 6-8; Preparation: 25 minutes; Cooking: 55 minutes; Level of difficulty: 2

Preheat the oven to 325°F/170°C/gas 3. • Set out a 9-inch (23-cm) springform pan. • Melt the chocolate in a double boiler over barely simmering water. Set aside to cool. • Beat the butter and sugar in a large bowl with an electric mixer at medium speed until creamy. • Add the egg yolks, one at a time, beating until just blended after each addition. • Use a large rubber spatula to fold in the chocolate and flour. • With mixer at high speed, beat the egg whites until stiff peaks form. Fold them into the batter. • Spoon the batter into the prepared pan. • Bake for about 55 minutes, or until a toothpick inserted into the center comes out clean. • Cool the cake in the pan for 20 minutes. Loosen and remove the pan sides and let cool completely. • Split the cake horizontally. Place one layer on a serving plate. Spread with the preserves. Top with the remaining cake. • Frosting: Melt the butter and chocolate in a double boiler over barely simmering water. Add the coffee, confectioners' sugar, and vanilla. Beat well until smooth and creamy. • Spread the top and sides of the cake with the frosting.

■ INGREDIENTS

- 5 oz (150 g) semisweet chocolate, chopped
- 6 tablespoons butter
- ½ cup (100 g) sugar
- 5 large eggs, separated
- ⅔ cup (100 g) all-purpose (plain) flour
- 6 tablespoons apricot preserves (jam)

FROSTING
- 1 tablespoon butter
- 4 oz (125 g) semisweet chocolate, chopped
- 6 tablespoons strong cold coffee
- 2 cups (300 g) confectioners' (icing) sugar
- 1 teaspoon vanilla extract

Right: *Mascarpone chocolate cake*

Chocolate supreme truffle cake

This rich and delicious cake is for genuine chocolate lovers only!

Serves: 10-12; Preparation: 45 minutes; Cooking: 30 minutes; Level of difficulty: 3

Truffles: Melt the chocolate, cream, and butter in a double boiler over barely simmering water. Stir in the confectioners' sugar and orange liqueur until smooth. • Dust your hands with cocoa and roll spoonfuls of the mixture into marble-sized balls. Transfer to a plate and refrigerate for 30 minutes. • Cake: Preheat the oven to 350°F/180°C/gas 4. • Butter two 9-inch (23-cm) springform pans. • Sift the flour, cocoa, baking powder, baking soda, and salt into a large bowl. • Melt the chocolate in a double boiler over barely simmering water. Set aside to cool. • Beat the butter, sugar, and cream cheese in a large bowl with an electric mixer at medium speed until creamy. • Add the eggs, one at a time, beating until just blended after each addition. • With mixer at low speed, gradually beat in the chocolate, orange liqueur, and vanilla. • Beat in the dry ingredients, alternating with the water. • Spoon half the batter into each of the prepared pans. • Bake for about 30 minutes, or until a toothpick inserted into the centers comes out clean. • Cool the cakes in the pans for 10 minutes. Loosen and remove the pan sides. Invert the cakes onto racks. Loosen and remove the pan bottoms. • Filling: Melt the chocolate and cream in a double boiler over barely simmering water. Set aside to cool. • Frosting: Melt the chocolate in a double boiler over barely simmering water. Set aside to cool. • With mixer at medium speed, beat the butter in a medium bowl until creamy. Beat the butter into the chocolate until glossy and smooth. Cover and set aside. • Split each cake horizontally. Place a layer on a serving plate. Spread with one-third of the filling. Repeat with 2 more layers. Top with the remaining layer. • Spread the cake with the frosting. Decorate with the truffles.

■ INGREDIENTS

TRUFFLES
- 4 oz (125 g) bittersweet chocolate, chopped
- 3 tablespoons heavy (double) cream
- 1 tablespoon butter
- ⅓ cup (50 g) confectioners' (icing) sugar
- 2 tablespoons orange liqueur
- ⅓ cup (50 g) unsweetened cocoa powder

CAKE
- 2 cups (300 g) all-purpose (plain) flour
- ⅓ cup (50 g) unsweetened cocoa powder
- 1 teaspoon baking powder
- ½ teaspoon baking soda
- ¼ teaspoon salt
- 2 oz (60 g) bittersweet chocolate, chopped
- 6 tablespoons butter
- ¾ cup (150 g) sugar
- 7 tablespoons cream cheese
- 2 large eggs
- 1 tablespoon orange liqueur
- 1 teaspoon vanilla extract
- ¾ cup (200 ml) water

FILLING
- 8 oz (250 g) bittersweet chocolate, chopped
- 6 tablespoons heavy (double) cream

FROSTING
- 5 oz (150 g) bittersweet chocolate, chopped
- 10 tablespoons butter

Right: *Chocolate supreme truffle cake*

Frozen fudge pecan cake

Serves: 8-10; Preparation: 30 minutes + 12 hours to freeze; Cooking: 30 minutes; Level of difficulty: 2
Preheat the oven to 350°F/180°C/gas 4. • Butter a 9-inch (23-cm) springform pan. • Place the pecans and 1 tablespoon of flour in a food processor and chop finely. • Melt the chocolate, butter, liqueur, and vanilla in a double boiler over barely simmering water. Set aside to cool. • Beat the eggs, sugar, and salt in a large bowl with an electric mixer at medium speed until pale and thick. • Stir the remaining flour, chocolate mixture, and pecans into the egg mixture. • Spoon the batter into the prepared pan. • Bake for about 30 minutes, or until the top is set. • Cool the cake completely in the pan on a rack. • When cool, cover with foil and freeze for 12 hours. • Transfer to the refrigerator about 2 hours before serving. Loosen and remove the pan sides. • Topping: With mixer at high speed, beat the cream in a medium bowl until stiff. Spread over the cake and decorate with the extra pecans.

■ INGREDIENTS

- 1½ cups (200 g) pecans
- ⅓ cup (50 g) all-purpose (plain) flour
- 1 lb (500 g) semisweet chocolate, chopped
- ¾ cup (200 g) cold butter, cut up
- 1 tablespoon coffee liqueur
- 1 teaspoon vanilla extract
- 4 large eggs
- 2 tablespoons sugar
- ¼ teaspoon salt

TOPPING
- 1 cup (250 ml) heavy (double) cream
- extra pecans, to decorate

Bundt cake with chocolate sauce

Serves: 6-8; Preparation: 25 minutes; Cooking: 45 minutes; Level of difficulty: 1
Preheat the oven to 350°F/180°C/gas 4. • Butter a 9-inch (23-cm) Bundt pan. Dust with cocoa. • Sift the flour, cocoa, baking powder, baking soda, and salt into a large bowl. Stir in the sugars. • Beat the butter, buttermilk, milk, eggs, coffee mixture, and vanilla in a large bowl with an electric mixer at medium speed until well blended. • With mixer at low speed, beat the butter mixture into the dry ingredients. • Spoon the batter into the prepared pan. • Bake for about 45 minutes, or until a toothpick inserted into the center comes out clean. • Cool the cake in the pan for 15 minutes. Turn out onto a rack to cool completely. • Chocolate Sauce: Stir the chocolate and cream in a small saucepan over very low heat until the chocolate melts. Remove from the heat. Set aside to cool. • Spoon the sauce over the cake and serve.

■ INGREDIENTS

- 1⅓ cups (200 g) all-purpose (plain) flour
- ⅓ cup (50 g) unsweetened cocoa powder
- 1 teaspoon baking powder
- 1 teaspoon baking soda
- ¼ teaspoon salt
- ¾ cup (150 g) sugar
- ⅓ cup (70 g) firmly packed dark brown sugar
- 4 tablespoons butter, melted
- 1 cup (250 ml) buttermilk
- ½ cup (125 ml) milk
- 2 large eggs
- 1 tablespoon freeze-dried coffee granules, dissolved in 1 tablespoon milk
- 1 teaspoon vanilla extract

CHOCOLATE SAUCE
- ½ cup (100 g) bittersweet chocolate chips
- ½ cup (125 ml) heavy (double) cream

Right: *Frozen fudge pecan cake*

Chocolate orange cake

Serves: 8-10; Preparation: 25 minutes; Cooking: 40 minutes; Level of difficulty: 1

Preheat the oven to 350°F/180°C/gas 4. • Butter an 8-inch (20-cm) square baking pan. • Sift the flour, cocoa, and baking powder into a medium bowl. • Beat the butter and sugar in a large bowl with an electric mixer at medium speed until creamy. • Add the eggs, one at a time, beating until just blended after each addition. • Stir in the orange zest. • Mix the orange juice and brown sugar in a saucepan over low heat until the sugar has dissolved. Remove from the heat and set aside to cool. • With mixer at low speed, gradually beat the dry ingredients into the butter mixture, alternating with the orange mixture. • Spoon the batter into the prepared pan. • Bake for about 40 minutes, or until a toothpick inserted into the center comes out clean. • Cool the cake in the pan for 15 minutes. Turn out onto a rack to cool completely. • Spread the cake with the frosting.

Red velvet cake

Serves: 8-10; Preparation: 35 minutes; Cooking: 35 minutes; Level of difficulty: 1

Preheat the oven to 350°F/180°C/gas 4. • Butter two 9-inch (23-cm) round cake pans. Line with waxed paper. Butter the paper. • Sift the flour, cocoa, baking powder, baking soda, and salt into a large bowl. • Beat the butter, sugar, and vanilla in a large bowl with an electric mixer at medium speed until creamy. • Add the eggs, one at a time, beating until just blended after each addition. • With mixer at low speed, gradually beat in the dry ingredients, alternating with the buttermilk, food coloring, and vinegar. • Spoon half the batter into each of the prepared pans. • Bake for about 35 minutes, or until a toothpick inserted into the center comes out clean. • Cool the cakes in the pans for 10 minutes. Turn out onto racks. Carefully remove the paper and let cool completely. • Cream Cheese Frosting: With mixer at medium speed, beat the cream cheese, butter, and vanilla in a large bowl until creamy. Gradually beat in the confectioners' sugar until fluffy. • Place one cake on a serving plate. Spread with one-third of the frosting. Place the other cake on top. Spread with the remaining frosting.

■ INGREDIENTS

- 2 cups (300 g) all-purpose (plain) flour
- ½ cup (75 g) unsweetened cocoa powder
- 1 teaspoon baking powder
- ½ teaspoon baking soda
- ¼ teaspoon salt
- ½ cup (125 g) butter
- 1½ cups (300 g) sugar
- 1 teaspoon vanilla extract
- 3 large eggs
- 1 cup (250 ml) buttermilk
- 2 tablespoons red food coloring
- 1 tablespoon white vinegar

CREAM CHEESE FROSTING
- 1 cup (250 g) cream cheese
- ½ cup (125 g) butter
- 1 teaspoon vanilla extract
- 3 cups (450 g) confectioners' (icing) sugar

White chocolate mud cake

Serves: 8-10; Preparation: 35 minutes; Cooking: 55 minutes; Level of difficulty: 1

Preheat the oven to 325°F/170°C/gas 3. • Butter a 9-inch (23-cm) round baking pan. Line with waxed paper. Butter the paper. • Stir the butter, sugar, chocolate, and milk in a large saucepan over low heat until smooth. Do not boil. • Set aside to cool. • Sift the flour, baking powder, and salt into a medium bowl. Gradually stir the dry ingredients, eggs, and vanilla into the saucepan. • Spoon the batter into the prepared pan. • Bake for about 55 minutes, or until a toothpick inserted into the center comes out clean. • Cool the cake in the pan for 10 minutes. Turn out onto a rack. Carefully remove the paper and let cool completely. • Spread with the ganache.

■ INGREDIENTS

- 1 cup (250 g) butter
- 2 cups (400 g) sugar
- 6 oz (180 g) white chocolate, coarsely chopped
- 1 cup (250 ml) milk
- 2 cups (300 g) all-purpose (plain) flour
- 2 teaspoons baking powder
- ¼ teaspoon salt
- 2 large eggs, lightly beaten
- 1 teaspoon vanilla extract
- 1 quantity *White Chocolate Ganache* (see page 32)

Right: Red velvet cake

White chocolate cake

Serves: 10-12; Preparation: 30 minutes; Cooking: 1 hour 15 minutes; Level of difficulty: 1

Preheat the oven to 350°F/180°C/gas 4. • Butter and flour a 10-inch (25-cm) springform pan. Sprinkle the pan with 2 tablespoons of the sugar. • Sift the flour, baking powder, baking soda, and salt into a large bowl. • Beat the butter, remaining sugar, and vanilla and almond extracts in a large bowl with an electric mixer at medium speed until creamy. • Add the eggs, one at a time, beating until just blended after each addition. • With mixer at low speed, gradually beat in the dry ingredients, alternating with the yogurt and chocolate. • Spoon the batter into the prepared pan. • Bake for about 1 hour and 15 minutes, or until a toothpick inserted into the center comes out clean. • Cool the cake in the pan for 15 minutes. Turn out onto the rack to cool completely. • Spread the cake with the ganache.

VARIATION
– For a deeper, more traditional flavor, spread with dark Chocolate Ganache (see page 32).

■ INGREDIENTS

- 2 cups (400 g) sugar
- 3 cups (450 g) all-purpose (plain) flour
- 1 teaspoon baking powder
- ½ teaspoon baking soda
- ½ teaspoon salt
- 1 cup (250 g) butter
- 2 teaspoons vanilla extract
- 1 teaspoon almond extract
- 5 large eggs
- 1 cup (250 ml) plain yogurt
- 8 oz (250 g) semisweet chocolate, coarsely chopped

- 1 quantity
  White Chocolate Ganache
  (see page 32)

Almond fudge cake

Serves: 10-12; Preparation: 15 minutes; Cooking: 40 minutes; Level of difficulty: 1

Preheat the oven to 350°F/180°C/gas 4. • Butter and flour a 13 x 9-inch (33 x 23-cm) baking pan. • Sift the flour, cocoa, baking soda, and salt into a large bowl. Stir in the sugar. • Beat in the water, oil, and almond extract with an electric mixer at low speed until blended. • Spoon the batter into the prepared pan. • Bake for about 40 minutes, or until a toothpick inserted into the center comes out clean. • Cool the cake completely in the pan on a rack.

■ INGREDIENTS

- 3 cups (450 g) all-purpose (plain) flour
- ½ cup (75 g) unsweetened cocoa powder
- 2 teaspoons baking soda
- ½ teaspoon salt
- 2 cups (400 g) sugar
- 2 cups (500 ml) water
- ½ cup (125 ml) vegetable oil
- ½ teaspoon almond extract
- 1 quantity
  Rich Chocolate Frosting
  (see page 30)

Right: *White chocolate cake*

Chocolate cake with melon

Serves: 8-10; Preparation: 40 minutes + 4 hours to chill; Cooking: 40 minutes; Level of difficulty: 2

Preheat the oven to 350°F/180°C/gas 4. • Butter a 9-inch (23-cm) round cake pan. Dust with cocoa. • Melt the chocolate in a double boiler over barely simmering water. Set aside to cool. • Sift the flour, cocoa, baking powder, and salt into a medium bowl. • Beat the butter and sugar in a large bowl with an electric mixer at medium speed until creamy. • Add the egg yolks, one at a time, beating until just blended after each addition. • With mixer at low speed, gradually beat in the chocolate, followed by the dry ingredients. • With mixer at high speed, beat the egg whites in a medium bowl until stiff peaks form. Use a large rubber spatula to fold them into the batter. • Spoon the batter into the prepared pan. • Bake for about 40 minutes, or until a toothpick inserted into the center comes out clean. • Cool the cake in the pan for 10 minutes. Turn out onto a rack to cool completely. • Filling: Cut the cantaloupe into 2 pieces. Peel one piece with a knife and cut into chunks. Purée the melon chunks in a food processor until smooth. Use a melon baller to scoop the remaining melon into balls, reserving any juice. Refrigerate the purée, melon balls and juice. • Sprinkle the gelatin over the water in a saucepan. • Beat the egg yolks, milk, and sugar in a medium saucepan. Place over low heat and cook, stirring constantly with a wooden spoon, until the mixture lightly coats a metal spoon or registers 160°F (71°C) on an instant-read thermometer. Immediately plunge the pan into a bowl of ice water and stir until cooled. Beat the egg yolk mixture with a mixer at high speed until thick. Place the gelatin over low heat and stir until completely dissolved. • Stir the gelatin and puréed cantaloupe into the egg mixture. Use a large rubber spatula to fold in the whipped cream. • Split the cake horizontally. Place one layer in a 10-inch (25-cm) springform pan. • Drizzle with some reserved juice and spread with one-third of the cantaloupe filling. Place the remaining layer on top. Drizzle with the cantaloupe juice and spread the remaining filling over the top and sides. • Decorate with the cantaloupe balls and the grated chocolate. • Refrigerate for 4 hours. Loosen and remove the pan sides just before serving.

■ INGREDIENTS

- 4 oz (125 g) bittersweet chocolate, coarsely chopped
- 1⅓ cups (200 g) all-purpose (plain) flour
- ⅓ cup (50 g) unsweetened cocoa powder
- 1 teaspoon baking powder
- ¼ teaspoon salt
- ½ cup (125 g) butter
- ¾ cup (150 g) sugar
- 3 large eggs, separated

FILLING
- 1½ lb (750 g) cantaloupe (rock) melon
- 1 tablespoon unflavored gelatin
- 4 tablespoons water
- 3 large egg yolks
- 6 tablespoons milk
- ½ cup (100 g) sugar
- 2 cups (500 ml) heavy (double) cream, whipped
- 2 tablespoons coarsely grated bittersweet chocolate

Right: Chocolate cake with melon

Sponge Cakes

&

Sponge cakes generally contain little or no butter or fat of any kind and are leavened by well-beaten eggs rather than baking powder or other rising agents. Light and dry, they lend themselves beautifully to rich cream fillings and frostings.

Red currant and meringue sponge

INGREDIENTS

- ⅔ cup (100 g) all-purpose (plain) flour
- ½ teaspoon baking powder
- ¼ teaspoon salt
- 3 large eggs + 3 large egg yolks
- ½ cup (100 g) sugar
- 1 teaspoon vanilla extract

MERINGUE
- 8 large egg whites
- 1 cup (200 g) sugar

TOPPING
- 1½ cups (375 g) red currant jelly
- 1 tablespoon rum
- ½ cup (60 g) coarsely chopped almonds, to decorate

Serves: 6-8; Preparation: 45 minutes + 2 hours to chill; Cooking: 25 minutes; Level of difficulty: 2

Preheat the oven to 300°F/150°C/gas 2. • Butter and flour two 8-inch (20-cm) springform pans. • Sift the flour, baking powder, and salt into a medium bowl. • Beat the eggs, egg yolks, sugar, and vanilla in a large bowl with an electric mixer at high speed until pale and thick. • Use a large rubber spatula to fold in the dry ingredients. • Spoon the batter into the prepared pans. • Bake for about 25 minutes, or until springy to the touch. • Cool the cakes in the pans for 10 minutes. Loosen and remove the pan sides. • Transfer onto racks and let cool completely. • Meringue: With mixer at medium speed, beat the egg whites and sugar in a large bowl until stiff peaks form. • Heat gently to 160°F (71°C). Spread the meringue over the top of each cake and broil (grill) until the meringue is lightly golden. • Topping: Stir the jelly and rum in a bowl. • Place a cake layer on a serving plate and spread with half the topping. Cover with the remaining layer and spread with the remaining topping. Sprinkle with the almonds. • Refrigerate for 2 hours.

Rosita cake

INGREDIENTS

- 5 large oranges, very thinly sliced
- ½ cup (100 g) sugar
- 1½ quarts (1.5 liters) cold water

- 6 tablespoons orange liqueur
- 1 quantity *Pastry Cream* (see page 28)
- ¾ cup (200 ml) heavy (double) cream
- one 9-inch (23-cm) *Basic Sponge Cake* (see page 22)

Serves: 10-12; Preparation: 45 minutes + 24 hours to marinate + 6 hours to chill; Level of difficulty: 3

Simmer the oranges, sugar, and water in a large saucepan over medium-low heat for 2 hours. Let cool, cover, and set aside for 24 hours. • Line a 9-inch (23-cm) springform pan with aluminum foil. • Drain the oranges, reserving the syrup. • With the best-shaped orange slices, line the base and sides of the prepared pan. • Finely chop the remaining slices. • Stir the chopped oranges and liqueur into the pastry cream. • Beat the cream in a medium bowl with an electric mixer at high speed until stiff. Fold it into the pastry cream. • Spoon half the cream into the pan. • Split the cake horizontally. Place one layer on top of the cream and brush with some reserved syrup. Spread with the remaining pastry cream. Top with the remaining cake layer and brush with more syrup. Press down lightly on the cake with your fingertips. • Refrigerate for 6 hours. • Invert onto a serving plate. Loosen the sides and carefully remove the foil.

Left: *Red currant and meringue sponge*

Lemon frosted chiffon cake

Serves: 10-12; Preparation: 35 minutes; Cooking: 1 hour; Level of difficulty: 1

Preheat the oven to 325°F/170°C/gas 3. • Butter and flour a 10-inch (25-cm) tube pan. • Sift the flour, baking powder, and salt into a large bowl. Stir in the sugar. Add the oil, lemon zest and juice, and milk. • Beat the egg whites in a large bowl with an electric mixer at high speed until stiff peaks form. Fold them into the batter. • Spoon the batter into the prepared pan. • Bake for about 1 hour, or until a toothpick inserted into the center of the cake comes out clean. • Turn out onto a rack and let cool completely. • Turn top-side up and spread with the frosting.

■ INGREDIENTS

- 2 cups (300 g) cake flour
- 2 teaspoons baking powder
- ½ teaspoon salt
- 1½ cups (150 g) sugar
- ½ cup (125 ml) vegetable oil
- 1 tablespoon finely grated lemon zest
- 4 tablespoons lemon juice
- ½ cup (125 ml) milk
- 6 large egg whites
- 1 quantity *Lemon Frosting* (see page 30)

Cream sponge with passion fruit frosting

Serves: 10-12; Preparation: 30 minutes; Cooking: 20 minutes; Level of difficulty: 2

Preheat the oven to 375°F/190°C/gas 5. • Butter two 8-inch (20-cm) round cake pans. Line with parchment paper. • Sift the cornstarch, flour, baking powder, and salt into a small bowl. • Beat the egg yolks and sugar in a large bowl with an electric mixer at high speed until pale and thick. • Use a large rubber spatula to fold in the dry ingredients. • With mixer at high speed, beat the egg whites in a large bowl until stiff peaks form. Fold them into the batter. • Spoon half the batter into each of the prepared pans. • Bake for about 20 minutes, or until a toothpick inserted into the center comes out clean. • Cool the cakes in the pans for 5 minutes. Turn out onto racks. Carefully remove the paper and let cool completely. • Frosting: Beat the confectioners' sugar, passion fruit pulp, and butter in a medium bowl. • Place one cake on a serving plate. Spread with the Chantilly Cream. Top with the remaining cake. Spread with the frosting.

■ INGREDIENTS

- ¾ cup (125 g) cornstarch (cornflour)
- 3 tablespoons all-purpose (plain) flour
- ½ teaspoon baking powder
- ¼ teaspoon salt
- 4 large eggs, separated
- ¾ cup (150 g) sugar

FROSTING

- 1½ cups (225 g) confectioners' (icing) sugar
- 6 tablespoons passion fruit pulp
- 1 tablespoon butter, melted
- ½ quantity *Chantilly Cream* (see page 26)

Right: *Cream sponge with passion fruit frosting*

Chocolate angel cake with chocolate sauce

Serves: 8-10; Preparation: 25 minutes; Cooking: 45 minutes; Level of difficulty: 2

Preheat the oven to 350°F/180°C/gas 4. • Set out a 10-inch (25-cm) angel-food tube pan. • Sift the confectioners' sugar, flour, cocoa, and salt into a medium bowl. • Beat the egg whites and cream of tartar in a large bowl with an electric mixer at medium speed until frothy. • With mixer at high speed, gradually add the sugar, beating until stiff, glossy peaks form. Add the vanilla. • Use a large rubber spatula to fold in the dry ingredients. • Spoon the batter into the pan. • Bake for about 45 minutes, or until springy to the touch and the cake shrinks from the pan sides. • Cool the cake by inverting it onto the feet of its pan or hanging it on the neck of a heatproof bottle. • Remove from the pan and serve with the raspberries and chocolate sauce.

■ INGREDIENTS

- 1½ cups (225 g) confectioners' (icing) sugar
- 1 cup (150 g) cake flour
- 4 tablespoons unsweetened cocoa powder
- ¼ teaspoon salt
- 10 large egg whites
- 1½ teaspoons cream of tartar
- 1 cup (200 g) sugar
- 1 teaspoon vanilla extract
- 2 cups (400 g) raspberries, hulled
- 1 quantity *Chocolate Sauce* (see page 32)

Chocolate sponge with chantilly

Serves: 6-8; Preparation: 25 minutes; Cooking: 30 minutes; Level of difficulty: 2

Preheat the oven to 375°F/190°C/gas 5. • Butter two 8-inch (20-cm) round cake pans. Line with parchment paper. • Sift the flour, cocoa, baking powder, and salt into a medium bowl. • Beat the egg yolks and sugar in a large bowl with an electric mixer at high speed until pale and thick. • With mixer at low speed, gradually beat in the dry ingredients, alternating with the milk. • With mixer at high speed, beat the egg whites in a large bowl until stiff peaks form. Fold them into the batter. • Spoon half the batter into each of the prepared pans. • Bake for about 30 minutes, or until springy to the touch and the cake shrinks from the pan sides. • Cool the cakes in the pans for 5 minutes. Turn out onto racks. Carefully remove the paper and let cool completely. • Place one cake on a serving plate and spread with the Chantilly Cream. Top with the remaining cake. Spread the top with the frosting.

■ INGREDIENTS

- 1 cup (150 g) all-purpose (plain) flour
- 4 tablespoons unsweetened cocoa powder
- 1 teaspoon baking powder
- ¼ teaspoon salt
- 4 large eggs, separated
- ¾ cup (150 g) sugar
- 4 tablespoons milk
- ½ quantity *Chantilly Cream* (see page 26)
- 1 quantity *Rich Chocolate Frosting* (see page 30)

Right: *Chocolate sponge with chantilly*

Mandarin cream sponge

Serves: 8-10; Preparation: 25 minutes + 1 hour to chill; Level of difficulty: 2

Beat the cream, sugar, and vanilla in a medium bowl with an electric mixer at high speed until stiff. • Split the cake horizontally. Place one layer on a serving plate. Brush with half the orange juice. Spread with the cream. Top with the remaining layer and brush with the remaining orange juice. • Warm ½ cup (125 ml) marmalade in a small saucepan over low heat. Brush the cake with the marmalade. Cover with plastic wrap and refrigerate for 1 hour. • Decorate with the mandarin segments. Warm the remaining marmalade and brush over the fruit just before serving.

■ INGREDIENTS

- 1 cup (250 ml) heavy (double) cream
- 2 tablespoons sugar
- 1 teaspoon vanilla extract
- one *Basic Sponge Cake* (see page 22), baked in a 9-inch (23-cm) square pan
- 1 cup (250 ml) orange juice
- ½ cup (125 g) + 2 tablespoons orange marmalade
- mandarin orange segments, to decorate

Orange ladyfinger delight

Serves: 8-10; Preparation: 45 minutes + 3 hours to chill; Level of difficulty: 2

Filling: Beat the egg yolks and confectioners' sugar in a large bowl with an electric mixer at medium speed until pale and thick. • Add the cream cheese and orange juice and zest. • Heat gently to 160°F (71°C). • Sprinkle the gelatin over the liqueur in a saucepan. Let stand 1 minute. Stir over low heat until the gelatin has completely dissolved. Stir the gelatin mixture into the cream cheese mixture. • With mixer at high speed, beat the cream in a medium bowl until stiff. • Fold the cream into the cream cheese mixture. • Place the cake in a 9-inch (23-cm) springform pan. • Spread with one-third of the filling. Top with a layer of ladyfingers and spread with one-third of the remaining filling. Lightly press down and top with another layer of ladyfingers. Spread with the remaining filling. • Refrigerate for 3 hours. • Loosen and remove the pan sides and place on a serving plate. • Spread the top and sides with the Chantilly Cream. If liked, decorate with the fresh fruit.

VARIATION
– Change the flavor to lemon by replacing the orange juice and zest with the same quantities of lemon juice and zest. Replace the orange liqueur with Limoncello or another sweet lemon liqueur.

■ INGREDIENTS

FILLING
- 5 large egg yolks
- ⅔ cup (100 g) confectioners' (icing) sugar
- 1 cup (250 g) cream cheese
- 4 tablespoons orange juice
- 2 tablespoons finely grated orange zest
- 2 tablespoons unflavored gelatin
- 3 tablespoons orange liqueur
- 1 cup (250 ml) heavy (double) cream

- one 9-inch (23-cm) *Basic Sponge Cake* (see page 22)
- 25 ladyfingers
- ½ quantity *Chantilly Cream* (see page 26)
- sliced fresh fruit, to decorate (optional)

Right: *Mandarin cream sponge*

Lemon cloud cake

Serves: 8-10; Preparation: 25 minutes; Cooking: 45 minutes; Level of difficulty: 2

Preheat the oven to 350°F/180°C/gas 4. • Set out a 10-inch (25-cm) angel-food tube pan. • Sift the confectioners' sugar, flour, and salt into a medium bowl. • Beat the egg whites, vanilla, and cream of tartar in a large bowl with an electric mixer at medium speed until frothy. • With mixer at high speed, gradually add the sugar, beating until stiff, glossy peaks form. • Gently fold in the dry ingredients. • Place half the batter in another bowl. • Beat the egg yolks in a large bowl until pale and thick. Add the lemon zest. • Fold the beaten egg yolks into one bowl of beaten whites. • Place alternate spoonfuls of the batter into the pan. • Bake for about 45 minutes, or until springy to the touch. • Cool the cake by inverting it onto the feet of its pan or hanging it on the neck of a heatproof bottle. • Remove from the pan and spread with the frosting.

Apricot layered sponge

Serves: 8-10; Preparation: 45 minutes + 1 hour to chill; Level of difficulty: 2

Dissolve the sugar in a small bowl with the water and 3 tablespoons of rum. • Stir the remaining rum into the apricot preserves. • Cut each sponge in half horizontally. • Brush each layer of sponge with the rum and sugar mixture. • Place one layer on a serving plate and spread with half the apricot mixture. Cover with another layer and spread with half the custard. Cover with a third layer and spread with the remaining apricot mixture. Cover with the remaining cake layer and spread with the remaining custard. • Top with the apricot halves and decorate the sides of the cake with slices of banana. • Spoon the Chantilly Cream into a piping bag and decorate the top of the cake. • Refrigerate for 1 hour before serving.

■ INGREDIENTS

- ¼ cup (50 g) sugar
- 3 tablespoons water
- 4 tablespoons rum
- ½ cup (125 g) apricot preserves (jam)
- two 9-inch (23-cm) *Basic Sponge Cakes* (see page 22)
- 1 quantity *Vanilla Custard* (see page 28)
- 8 oz (250 g) canned apricot halves, well drained
- 1 banana, peeled, sliced, and drizzled with lemon juice
- ½ quantity *Chantilly Cream* (see page 26)

Carrot and almond torte

Make sure the carrots are very finely grated in this delicately flavored cake. They will help the cake to rise and give it texture as well as taste.

Serves: 8-10; Preparation: 25 minutes; Cooking: 1 hour; Level of difficulty: 2

Preheat the oven to 350°F/180°C/gas 4. • Butter and flour a 10-inch (25-cm) springform pan. • Sift the flour, baking powder, and salt into a large bowl. Stir in the almonds. • Beat the egg yolks, sugar, and lemon zest in a large bowl with an electric mixer at high speed until pale and thick. • With mixer at low speed, gradually beat in the carrots and dry ingredients. • With mixer at high speed, beat the egg whites in a large bowl until stiff peaks form. Use a large rubber spatula to fold them into the batter. • Spoon the batter into the prepared pan. • Bake for about 1 hour, or until a toothpick inserted into the center comes out clean. • Cool the cake in the pan for 10 minutes. Loosen and remove the pan sides and let cool completely. • Dust with the confectioners' sugar.

■ INGREDIENTS

- ½ cup (75 g) all-purpose (plain) flour
- ¾ teaspoon baking powder
- ¼ teaspoon salt
- 2 cups (300 g) almonds, finely ground
- 5 large eggs, separated
- 1½ cups (300 g) sugar
- 1 tablespoon finely grated lemon zest
- 2 cups (250 g) firmly packed finely grated carrots
- 4–6 tablespoons confectioners' (icing) sugar, to dust

Right: *Apricot layered sponge*

INGREDIENTS

- 5 large eggs
- ¾ cup (150 g) sugar
- ¼ teaspoon salt
- 1⅓ cups (200 g) all-purpose (plain) flour
- 1 teaspoon vanilla extract
- finely grated zest of 1 orange
- 2 teaspoons orange liqueur
- 1¼ cups (310 ml) heavy (double) cream
- 1 tablespoon confectioners' (icing) sugar
- 1½ cups (180 g) candied orange peel, finely chopped
- ½ cup (125 ml) heavy (double) cream, beaten until stiff
- 1 orange, in segments

INGREDIENTS

- 4 large eggs, separated
- ½ cup (100 g) sugar
- ¼ teaspoon salt
- ¾ cup (125 g) all-purpose (plain) flour

FILLING
- 2 cups (400 g) strawberries, hulled
- ⅓ cup (50 g) confectioners' (icing) sugar
- ¾ cup (200 ml) heavy (double) cream

Orange delight

Serves: 10-12; Preparation: 45 minutes + 2 hours to chill; Cooking: 40 minutes; Level of difficulty: 2

Preheat the oven to 325°F/170°C/gas 3. • Butter and flour a 10-inch (25-cm) round cake pan. • Beat the eggs, sugar, and salt in a large bowl with an electric mixer at high speed until pale and thick. Use a large rubber spatula to fold in the flour, vanilla, and orange zest. • Spoon the batter into the prepared pan. • Bake for about 30 minutes, or until a toothpick inserted into the center comes out clean. • Cool the cake in the pan for 5 minutes. Turn out onto a rack and let cool completely. • Use a sharp knife to hollow out the cake leaving a ¾-inch (3-cm) border. Cut the removed cake into cubes. • Place the hollowed out cake onto a baking sheet. Drizzle with liqueur. Return to the oven until crisp, about 8 minutes. • With mixer at high speed, beat the cream in a large bowl until stiff. Fold in the confectioners' sugar, cake cubes, and orange peel. • Spoon the cream mixture into the cake. • Refrigerate for 2 hours. • Carefully transfer to a serving plate. Spoon the beaten cream into a pastry bag and pipe on top. Decorate with the orange.

Summertime picnic cake

Serves: 6-8; Preparation: 30 minutes; Cooking: 10 minutes; Level of difficulty: 2

Preheat the oven to 400°F/200°C/gas 6. • Butter and flour a 13 x 9-inch (33 x 23-cm) baking pan. Line with parchment paper. • Beat the egg yolks and half the sugar in a large bowl with an electric mixer at medium speed until pale and thick. • With mixer at medium speed, beat the egg whites and salt in a large bowl until frothy. With mixer at high speed, gradually add the remaining sugar, beating until stiff, glossy peaks form. Fold into the beaten yolks. • Fold in the flour. • Spoon the batter into the prepared pan. • Bake for about 10 minutes, or until lightly browned. • Turn out onto a rack. Carefully remove the paper and let cool completely. • Filling: Cut most of the strawberries in small pieces and dust with confectioners' sugar. • With mixer at high speed, beat the cream in a medium bowl until stiff. Stir in the chopped strawberries. • Split the cake vertically. • Place one layer on a serving plate. Spread with half the cream filling. Top with the remaining layer of cake. • Spread with the remaining cream and decorate with the remaining strawberries.

Left: Orange delight

Chocolate-filled roulade

Serves: 6-8; Preparation: 30 minutes + 2 hours to chill; Cooking: 15 minutes; Level of difficulty: 3

Preheat the oven to 350°F/180°C/gas 4. • Line a 10 x 15-inch (25 x 35-cm) jelly-roll pan with parchment paper. • Beat the egg yolks, confectioners' sugar, and vanilla in a large bowl until pale and creamy. • Fold in the flour and cornstarch. • Beat the egg whites and salt with an electric mixer at high speed until stiff. Gently fold them into the batter. • Spoon the batter into the prepared pan. • Bake for about 15 minutes, or until risen and golden. • Dust a clean kitchen towel with confectioners' sugar. Turn the cake out onto the towel. Roll up the cake, using the towel as a guide. Leave, seam side down, until cool. • Unroll the sponge. Drizzle with the rum and cover with the chocolate spread. Roll up using the towel as a guide. Wrap the roulade in foil. Chill for 2 hours. • Unwrap and transfer to a serving dish. • Dust with the confectioners' sugar and sprinkle with flakes of chocolate.

■ INGREDIENTS

- 1 cup (150 g) confectioners' (icing) sugar + extra, to dust
- 4 large eggs, separated
- ⅓ cup (50 g) all-purpose (plain) flour
- 1 teaspoon vanilla extract
- 2 tablespoons cornstarch (cornflour)
- ¼ teaspoon salt
- 3 tablespoons rum
- ½ cup (125 g) chocolate hazelnut spread (Nutella)
- 4 tablespoons dark chocolate flakes

Chocolate cream roll

Serves: 6-8; Preparation: 25 minutes; Cooking: 15 minutes; Level of difficulty: 2

Preheat the oven to 400°F/200°C/gas 6. • Line a 10 x 15-inch (25 x 35-cm) jelly-roll pan with parchment paper. • Beat the egg whites in a large bowl with an electric mixer at medium speed until frothy. • Add the sugar, beating until stiff, glossy peaks form. Fold in the egg yolks, followed by the cocoa and flour. • Spoon the batter into the prepared pan. • Bake for about 15 minutes, or until a toothpick inserted into the center comes out clean. • Dust a clean kitchen towel with confectioners' sugar. Turn the cake out onto the towel. Roll up the cake, using the towel as a guide. Leave, seam side down, until cool. • With mixer at high speed, beat the cream in a medium bowl until stiff. • Unroll the cake and spread evenly with the cream, leaving a 1-inch (2.5-cm) border. Reroll the cake and place on a serving plate. • Frosting: With mixer at high speed, beat the butter and sugar in a medium bowl until creamy. Stir in the cocoa. • Spread the roll with the frosting. Decorate with the walnuts.

■ INGREDIENTS

- 6 large egg whites
- ¼ cup (50 g) sugar
- 2 large egg yolks, beaten
- ½ cup (75 g) unsweetened cocoa powder
- 1 tablespoon all-purpose (plain) flour
- 2 tablespoons confectioners' (icing) sugar
- 1 cup (250 ml) heavy (double) cream

FROSTING
- ⅔ cup (180 g) butter
- ½ cup (100 g) sugar
- ½ cup (75 g) cocoa powder
- ¾ cup (90 g) walnuts, coarsely chopped

Right: *Chocolate-filled roulade*

Raspberry jelly roll

- 1 cup (150 g) all-purpose (plain) flour
- 1½ teaspoons baking powder
- ¼ teaspoon salt
- 3 large eggs, separated
- ¾ cup (150 g) sugar
- 1 teaspoon vanilla extract
- 4 tablespoons milk
- ¼ teaspoon cream of tartar

FILLING
- 1 cup (125 g) fresh raspberries
- 1½ cups (375 ml) heavy (double) cream
- ¼ cup (50 g) sugar
- ¼ cup (25 g) pistachios, coarsely chopped
- 4 tablespoons confectioners' (icing) sugar, to dust

Serves: 6-8; Preparation: 25 minutes; Cooking: 15 minutes; Level of difficulty: 2

Preheat the oven to 400°F/200°C/gas 6. • Butter and flour a 10 x 15-inch (25 x 35-cm) jelly-roll pan. Line with parchment paper. • Sift the flour, baking powder, and salt into a medium bowl. • Beat the egg yolks, sugar, and vanilla in a large bowl with an electric mixer at high speed until pale and thick. • With mixer at low speed, gradually beat in the dry ingredients, alternating with the milk. • With mixer at high speed, beat the egg whites and cream of tartar in a large bowl until stiff peaks form. • Gently fold them into the batter. • Spoon the batter into the prepared pan. • Bake for about 15 minutes, or until lightly browned. • Dust a clean kitchen towel with confectioners' sugar. Turn the cake out onto the towel. Roll up the cake, using the towel as a guide. Leave, seam side down, until cool. • Filling: Process the raspberries until smooth. Strain out the seeds. • Beat the cream and sugar in a large bowl until stiff. Fold in the raspberries and pistachios. • Unroll the cake and spread with the filling. Reroll the cake. Place on a serving dish and dust with the confectioners' sugar.

Fruit-filled jelly roll

- 1 jelly roll (see recipe above), before filling

FILLING
- 1 tablespoon gelatin
- 3¼ cups (800 ml) cold water
- 2 cups (400 g) strawberries, hulled
- 1½ cups (300 g) sugar
- 4 tablespoons orange liqueur
- ¾ cup (200 ml) orange juice
- 2 bananas, peeled and thinly sliced

Serves: 8-10; Preparation: 30 minutes + 6 hours to chill; Cooking: 15 minutes; Level of difficulty: 3

Prepare the jelly roll to the stage where it is cooled completely. • Filling: Sprinkle the gelatin over 4 tablespoons of water in a saucepan. Let stand 1 minute. Stir over low heat until the gelatin has completely dissolved. • Purée ½ cup (100 g) strawberries, ¼ cup (50 g) sugar, and the liqueur in a food processor. • Unroll the cake and spread with the strawberry mixture, leaving a border. Reroll the cake. • Stir the remaining water and sugar in a medium saucepan over medium heat until the sugar has dissolved. Stir in the gelatin mixture and orange juice. Set aside to cool. • Slice the remaining strawberries (reserving a few to decorate). • Cut the cake into 10 slices and place in a 9-inch (23-cm) springform pan, cutting to fit. • Slice the bananas and drizzle with the lemon juice. Arrange around the pan sides. Fill with the fruit jelly mixture. • Refrigerate for 6 hours. • Decorate with the strawberries.

Left: *Raspberry jelly roll*

Spiced jelly roll with apple filling

Serves: 8-10; Preparation: 25 minutes; Cooking: 15 minutes; Level of difficulty: 2

Preheat the oven to 375°F/190°C/gas 5. • Butter a 10 x 15-inch (25 x 35-cm) jelly-roll pan. Line with parchment paper. • Sift the flour, baking powder, cinnamon, and ginger into a medium bowl. • Beat the egg yolks and sugar in a large bowl with an electric mixer at high speed until pale and thick. • With mixer at high speed, beat the egg whites and salt in a large bowl until stiff peaks form. Fold them into the egg yolk mixture. • Gradually fold the dry ingredients into the batter. • Spoon the batter into the prepared pan. • Bake for about 15 minutes, or until springy to the touch. • Dust a clean kitchen towel with confectioners' sugar. Turn the cake out onto the towel. Roll up the cake, using the towel as a guide. Leave, seam side down, until cool. • Filling: Bring the apples and water to a boil in a saucepan. Cover and simmer until tender. Stir in the sugar and lemon juice. Drain off some of the juice and set aside to cool. • Beat the cream in a large bowl until stiff. • Unroll the cake and spread with the cream. Spoon the apples over the cream. Reroll the cake. Dust with the confectioners' sugar.

■ INGREDIENTS

- 1 cup (150 g) cake flour
- 1 teaspoon baking powder
- 1 teaspoon each ground cinnamon and ginger
- 3 large eggs, separated
- ½ cup (100 g) sugar
- ¼ teaspoon salt

FILLING

- 2 large tart green apples, peeled, cored, and chopped
- 4 tablespoons water
- 2 tablespoons sugar
- 1 tablespoon lemon juice
- 1 cup (250 ml) heavy (double) cream
- 6 tablespoons confectioners' (icing) sugar

Jelly roll with peach filling

Serves: 8-10; Preparation: 35 minutes; Cooking: 35 minutes; Level of difficulty: 2

Filling: Cook the peaches, sugar, and lemon zest in a large saucepan over medium heat, stirring often, for about 20 minutes, or until the peaches are tender. Set aside to cool. • Jelly Roll: Preheat the oven to 350°F/180°C/gas 4. • Butter a 10 x 15-inch (25 x 35-cm) jelly-roll pan. Line with parchment paper. • Beat the eggs, sugar, and salt in a large bowl with an electric mixer at high speed until pale and thick, about 20 minutes. • Use a large rubber spatula to fold the flour and vanilla into the beaten eggs. • Spoon the batter into the prepared pan. • Bake for about 15 minutes, or until golden brown. • Dust a clean kitchen towel with confectioners' sugar. Turn the cake out onto the towel. Roll up the cake, using the towel as a guide. Leave, seam side down, until cool. • Unroll the cake and brush with the rum. Spread evenly with the peach filling. • Reroll the cake, wrap in plastic wrap (cling film), and refrigerate for 1 hour. • Decorate with the chopped peach and dust with the confectioners' sugar.

■ INGREDIENTS

FILLING

- 1 lb (500 g) peaches, peeled, pitted, and chopped
- 1 cup (200 g) sugar
- 2 teaspoons finely grated lemon zest

JELLY ROLL

- 2 large eggs
- ⅓ cup (70 g) sugar
- ¼ teaspoon salt
- ½ cup (75 g) cake flour
- ½ teaspoon vanilla extract
- 3 tablespoons dark rum
- 1 large fresh peach, peeled and finely chopped
- confectioners' (icing) sugar, to dust

Right: *Spiced jelly roll with apple filling*

Chocolate jelly roll

Serves: 6-8; Preparation: 30 minutes; Cooking: 20 minutes; Level of difficulty: 2

Preheat the oven to 350°F/180°C/gas 4. • Butter a 10 x 15-inch (25 x 35-cm) jelly-roll pan. Line with parchment paper. • Melt the chocolate in a double boiler over barely simmering water. Let cool. • Beat the egg yolks and sugar in a large bowl until pale and thick. • Gradually beat in the chocolate. • Beat the egg whites and salt in a large bowl until stiff peaks form. Fold them into the chocolate mixture. • Spoon the batter into the prepared pan. • Bake for about 20 minutes, or until springy to the touch. • Cool the cake in the pan for 5 minutes. • Dust a clean kitchen towel with confectioners' sugar. Turn the cake out onto the towel. Roll up the cake, using the towel as a guide. Leave, seam side down, until cool. • Unroll the cake and spread with half the frosting. • Reroll the cake and spread with the remaining frosting.

■ INGREDIENTS

- 8 oz (250 g) bittersweet chocolate, coarsely chopped
- 8 large eggs, separated
- 1¼ cups (250 g) sugar
- ¼ teaspoon salt
- 1 quantity *Rich Chocolate Frosting* (see page 30)

Almond jelly roll with crunchy topping

Serves: 6-8; Preparation: 30 minutes; Cooking: 40 minutes; Level of difficulty: 3

Preheat the oven to 350°F/180°C/gas 4. • Butter a 10 x 15-inch (25 x 35-cm) jelly-roll pan. Line with parchment paper. • Crunchy Topping: Oil a baking sheet. Cook the sugar and almonds in a saucepan over low heat, stirring constantly, until the sugar melts. Continue cooking, stirring frequently, until deep golden brown. • Pour onto the prepared sheet and set aside to cool. • When cool, crush into small pieces. • Almond Jelly Roll: Beat the egg yolks and sugar in a large bowl with an electric mixer at high speed until pale and thick. • Add the finely ground almonds and almond extract. • With mixer at high speed, beat the egg whites and salt in a large bowl until stiff peaks form. Fold them into the almond mixture. • Spoon the batter into the prepared pan. • Bake for about 20 minutes, or until a toothpick inserted into the center comes out clean. • Dust a clean kitchen towel with confectioners' sugar. Turn the cake out onto the towel. Roll up the cake, using the towel as a guide. Leave, seam side down, until cool. • With mixer at high speed, beat the cream in a large bowl until stiff. • Unroll the cake and spread evenly with the cream, leaving a 1-inch (2.5-cm) border. Reroll the cake. • Press the pieces of crunchy topping into the outside of the roll.

■ INGREDIENTS

CRUNCHY TOPPING
- 1½ cups (300 g) sugar
- ¾ cup (100 g) blanched whole almonds

ALMOND JELLY ROLL
- 5 large eggs, separated
- ¾ cup (150 g) sugar
- ⅓ cup (50 g) almonds, finely ground
- 1 teaspoon almond extract
- ¼ teaspoon salt
- 3 tablespoons sugar, to dust
- 1½ cups (375 ml) heavy (double) cream

Right: *Chocolate jelly roll*

Chocolate jelly roll with raspberry filling

Serves: 6-8; Preparation: 25 minutes; Cooking: 20 minutes; Level of difficulty: 2

■ INGREDIENTS

- 3 oz (90 g) bittersweet chocolate, chopped
- ½ cup (75 g) all-purpose (plain) flour
- ½ teaspoon each baking powder and baking soda
- ¼ teaspoon salt
- 4 large eggs
- ¾ cup (150 g) sugar
- 1 teaspoon vanilla extract
- 2 tablespoons cold water
- 2 tablespoons confectioners' (icing) sugar
- ½ quantity Chantilly Cream (see page 26)
- 2 cups (400 g) raspberries

Preheat the oven to 375°F/190°C/gas 5. • Butter a 10 x 15-inch (25 x 35-cm) jelly-roll pan. Line with parchment paper. • Melt the chocolate in a double boiler over barely simmering water. Let cool. • Sift the flour, baking powder, baking soda, and salt into a medium bowl. • Beat the eggs, sugar, and vanilla in a large bowl with an electric mixer at high speed until pale and thick. • Fold the dry ingredients into the egg mixture, alternating with the water and chocolate. • Spoon the batter into the prepared pan. • Bake for about 20 minutes, or until springy to the touch. • Dust a clean kitchen towel with confectioners' sugar. Turn the cake out onto the towel. Roll up the cake, using the towel as a guide. Leave, seam side down, until cool. • Unroll the cake and spread the Chantilly Cream. Sprinkle with the raspberries. • Reroll the cake.

Coffee jelly roll

Serves: 6-8; Preparation: 30 minutes; Cooking: 20 minutes; Level of difficulty: 2

Preheat the oven to 400°F/200°C/gas 6. • Butter a 10 x 15-inch (25 x 35-cm) jelly-roll pan. Line with parchment paper. • Sift the flour, baking powder, and salt into a large bowl. • Beat the eggs and 1 cup (200 g) sugar in a large bowl with an electric mixer at high speed until pale and thick. • With mixer at low speed, gradually beat in the dry ingredients, alternating with the butter and coffee mixture. • Spoon the batter into the prepared pan. • Bake for about 20 minutes, or until springy to the touch. • Dust a clean kitchen towel with confectioners' sugar. Turn the cake out onto the towel. Roll up the cake, using the towel as a guide. Leave, seam side down, until cool. • Unroll the cake and spread evenly with the coffee-flavored Chantilly Cream. Reroll the cake.

INGREDIENTS

- 1 cup (150 g) all-purpose (plain) flour
- 1 teaspoon baking powder
- ¼ teaspoon salt
- 5 large eggs
- 1 cup (200 g) + 2 tablespoons sugar
- 6 tablespoons butter, melted
- 2 tablespoons freeze-dried coffee granules dissolved in 1 tablespoon boiling water
- ½ quantity *Chantilly Cream* (see page 26), flavored with 2 tablespoons freeze-dried coffee granules

Pistachio jelly roll with lemon filling

Serves: 6-8; Preparation: 30 minutes + 1 hour to chill; Cooking: 15 minutes; Level of difficulty: 2

Preheat the oven to 350°F/180°C/gas 4. • Butter a 10 x 15-inch (25 x 35-cm) jelly-roll pan. Line with parchment paper. • Process the pistachios and 2 tablespoons of sugar in a food processor until finely chopped. • Beat the egg yolks, remaining sugar, and vanilla in a medium bowl with an electric mixer at high speed until pale and thick. • With mixer at low speed, gradually beat in the flour and pistachio mixture. • With mixer at high speed, beat the egg whites and salt in a medium bowl until stiff peaks form. Fold them into the batter. • Spoon the batter into the prepared pan. • Bake for about 15 minutes, or until springy to the touch. • Dust a clean kitchen towel with confectioners' sugar. Turn the cake out onto the towel. Roll up the cake, using the towel as a guide. Leave, seam side down, until cool. • Unroll the cake and drizzle with the rum. Spread with the preserves. • Reroll the cake and refrigerate for 1 hour. • Remove the towel and cut into slices. • Spread the pastry cream on a serving plate and arrange the slices on top. Sprinkle with the almonds.

INGREDIENTS

- ½ cup (60 g) shelled and peeled pistachios
- ½ cup (100 g) sugar
- 2 large eggs, separated
- ½ teaspoon vanilla extract
- ½ cup (75 g) all-purpose (plain) flour
- ¼ teaspoon salt
- ¾ cup (125 g) confectioners' (icing) sugar
- 2 tablespoons rum
- ¾ cup (200 g) lemon preserves (jam)
- 1 quantity *Pastry Cream* (see page 28)
- 4 tablespoons slivered almonds

Right: *Coffee jelly roll*

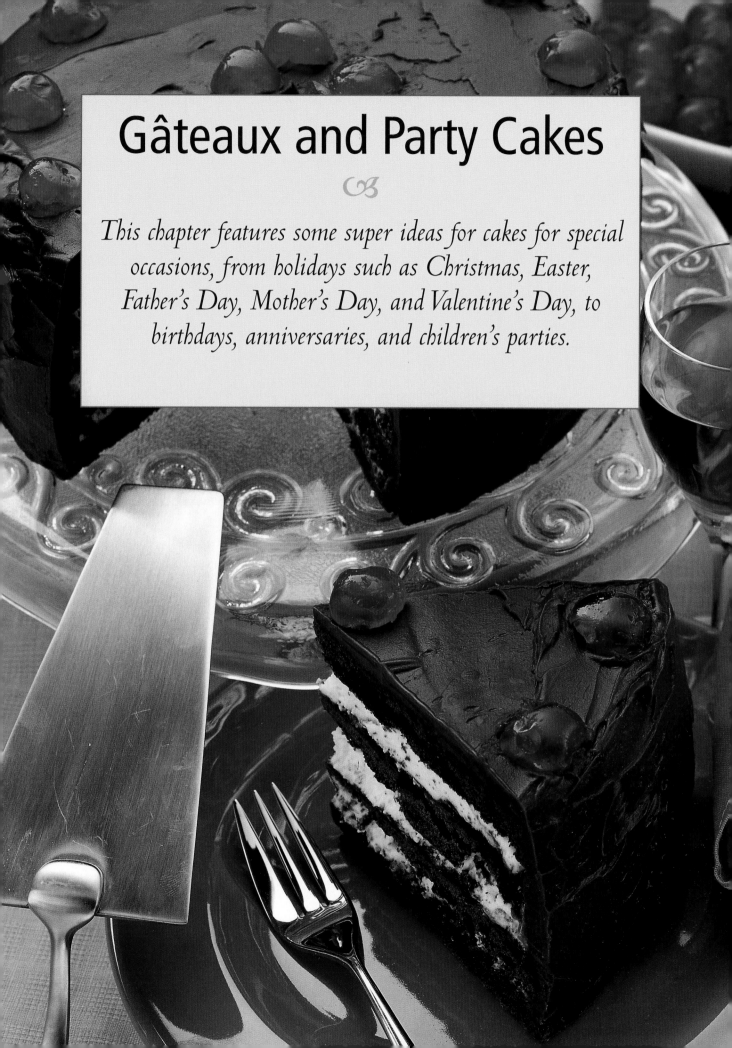

Gâteaux and Party Cakes

This chapter features some super ideas for cakes for special occasions, from holidays such as Christmas, Easter, Father's Day, Mother's Day, and Valentine's Day, to birthdays, anniversaries, and children's parties.

St. Valentine's heart tart

Serves: 6-8; Preparation: 20 minutes; Cooking: 20 minutes; Level of difficulty: 1

Preheat the oven to 400°F/200°C/gas 6. • Butter and flour a 9-inch (23-cm) heart-shaped pan. • Unfold or unroll the pastry on a lightly floured surface into a 13-inch (33-cm) round. Fit the pastry into the prepared pan. Fold over and crimp the edges. Prick all over with a fork. • Line the pastry shell with foil and fill with dried beans or pie weights. Bake for 10 minutes, then remove the foil with the beans. Bake until crisp and golden brown. • Cool on a rack for 10 minutes. Carefully remove from the pan and let cool completely. • Arrange the strawberries on the cooled pastry, rounded side up. • Warm the red currant jelly and kirsch in a small saucepan. Brush over the strawberries. • Beat the cream and sugar in a medium bowl until stiff. Pipe rosettes over the cake.

■ INGREDIENTS

- 8 oz (250 g) frozen puff pastry, thawed
- 1½ lb (750 g) fresh strawberries (preferably all about the same size), hulled and cut in half
- ¾ cup (240 ml) red currant jelly
- 2 tablespoons kirsch or other fruit liqueur
- ½ cup (125 ml) heavy (double) cream
- 1 tablespoon sugar

Valentine's coffee cake with truffles

Serves: 6-8; Preparation: 45 minutes + 1 hour to chill; Level of difficulty: 3

Prepare the cake. • Truffles: Melt the chocolate with the cream in a double boiler over barely simmering water. Set aside to cool. • Dissolve the coffee in the liqueur and stir into the chocolate mixture. Refrigerate for 1 hour, or until thick and malleable. • Roll teaspoonfuls of the chocolate mixture into round truffles and place on a dish lined with waxed paper. This should yield about 12 truffles. Cover and refrigerate until firm. • Coffee Buttercream: Melt the white chocolate with the cream in a double boiler over barely simmering water. Set aside to cool. • Beat the butter in a large bowl with an electric mixer at high speed until creamy. Gradually beat in the confectioners' sugar. • Beat in the chocolate mixture and dissolved coffee. • Split the cake horizontally. Place one layer on a serving plate and spread with a quarter of the buttercream. Place the remaining layer on top. Spread the top and sides with the remaining buttercream. • Press the hazelnuts into the sides of the cake and arrange the truffles on top. Dust with the cocoa.

■ INGREDIENTS

- one *Basic Yellow Cake* (see page 44), baked in a 9-inch (23-cm) heart-shaped pan

TRUFFLES
- 4 oz (125 g) bittersweet chocolate, chopped
- 3 tablespoons heavy (double) cream
- 2 teaspoons coffee granules
- 2 teaspoons coffee liqueur

COFFEE BUTTERCREAM
- 10 oz (300 g) white chocolate, chopped
- ⅔ cup (180 ml) heavy (double) cream
- 1¾ cups (450 g) butter
- 1 cup (150 g) confectioners' (icing) sugar
- 1 tablespoon coffee granules dissolved in 1 tablespoon warm water
- 1 cup (100 g) hazelnuts, toasted and chopped
- 2 tablespoons cocoa

Right: *St. Valentine's heart tart*

Children's party hedgehog cake

Serves: 8-10; Preparation: 35 minutes; Level of difficulty: 2

Cut the sponge cake into ½-inch (1-cm) thick slices. • Dip the slices of cake briefly in the marsala. • Beat the butter, confectioners' sugar, and brandy in a large bowl until creamy. • Spread the cake slices with a layer of the buttercream. Dip in the coffee and spread with another layer of buttercream. • Layer the cake slices in a ring shape with a pointed edge to resemble the hedgehog in the photo. • Cover the cake with buttercream and decorate with the almonds to resemble the spikes. • Decorate with the coffee beans to resemble eyes and the sugared almonds to resemble the ears.

■ INGREDIENTS

• 1 *Basic Sponge Cake* (see page 22)
• ½ cup (125 ml) marsala
• 1 cup (250 g) butter
• 1⅔ cups (250 g) confectioners' (icing) sugar
• 4 tablespoons brandy
• 1 cup (250 ml) strong hot coffee
• 1 cup (100 g) flaked almonds, toasted
• 2 coffee beans
• 2 sugared almonds

Birthday berry gâteau

Serves: 8-10; Preparation: 1 hour; Cooking: 1 hour 30 minutes; Level of difficulty: 3

Preheat the oven to 350°F/180°C/gas 4. • Butter one deep 10-inch (25-cm) round pan and one deep 7-inch (18-cm) round pan. • Sift the flour, baking powder, baking soda, and salt into a large bowl. Add the almonds. • Beat the butter and sugar in a large bowl until creamy. • Add the eggs, beating until just blended. • Gradually beat in the dry ingredients, sour cream, raspberries, and blackberries. • Spoon three-quarters of the batter into the prepared 10-inch (25-cm) pan. Spoon the remaining batter into the 7-inch (18-cm) pan. • Bake the 10-inch (25-cm) cake for about 1 hour and 30 minutes, or until a toothpick inserted into the center comes out clean. Bake the remaining cake for about 1 hour, or until a toothpick inserted into the center comes out clean. • Turn out onto racks. Let cool completely. • Place the large cake on a plate. Spread with two-thirds of the ganache. Center the smaller cake on top. Spread with the remaining ganache. • Melt the white chocolate in a double boiler over barely simmering water. • Melt the semisweet chocolate in a double boiler over barely simmering water. • Cut 1 strip of parchment paper to measure 2 x 27½ inches (5 x 70 cm). Cut another strip to measure 3 x 40 inches (8 x 100 cm). Cut a wave pattern ½-inch (1-cm) from the top. Spread the short strip with the white chocolate. Spread the long strip with the dark chocolate. Wrap the smaller strip around the top layer of cake. Wrap the larger strip around the bottom layer. Carefully remove the paper. • Decorate with the fruit.

■ INGREDIENTS

• 3 cups (450 g) all-purpose (plain) flour
• 2 teaspoons baking powder
• ½ teaspoon baking soda
• ½ teaspoon salt
• 2 cups (300 g) finely ground almonds
• 2 cups (500 g) butter
• 4 cups (800 g) sugar
• 12 large eggs
• 1¼ cups (310 ml) sour cream
• 1¼ cups (310 g) fresh or frozen and thawed raspberries
• 1¼ cups (310 g) fresh or frozen and thawed blackberries
• 2 recipes *White Chocolate Ganache* (see page 32)
• 5 oz (150 g) white chocolate, chopped
• 10 oz (300 g) semisweet chocolate, chopped
• 2⅔ cups (680 g) mixed fresh berries

Right: *Children's party hedgehog cake*

Lisa's ladybug cake

INGREDIENTS

- two 10-inch (25-cm) store-bought round sponge cakes
- 1 quantity *Rich Chocolate Frosting* (see page 30)
- 1½ quantities *Vanilla Frosting* (see page 30)
- 1 teaspoon red food coloring
- M&M's, to decorate

Serves: 10-12; Preparation: 15 minutes; Level of difficulty: 1

Place one cake on a serving plate. Spread the top and sides of the cake with the chocolate frosting. • Slice the remaining cake in half vertically. • Mix the vanilla frosting and the red food coloring in a medium bowl until well blended. Spread the top and sides of the cake with the red frosting. Place the two halves of cake on top of the chocolate-frosted cake to resemble wings. • Decorate with the M&M's.

Ice cream clown cake

INGREDIENTS

- 3 large eggs, separated
- ½ cup (100 g) sugar
- 1 cup (150 g) finely ground almonds
- ⅔ cup (100 g) all-purpose (plain) flour
- ¼ teaspoon salt

ALMOND ICE CREAM
- 3 large eggs, separated
- ½ cup (100 g) sugar
- 1 teaspoon vanilla extract
- ½ teaspoon almond extract
- 2 cups (500 ml) heavy (double) cream

TOPPING
- 4 ice cream sugar cones
- brightly colored candy to make eyes, noses, and mouths on the clowns

Serves: 8-10; Preparation: 45 minutes + 3 hours to freeze; Cooking: 30 minutes; Level of difficulty: 2

Preheat the oven to 350°F/180°C/gas 4. • Butter and flour a 9-inch (23-cm) springform pan. • Beat the egg yolks and sugar in a large bowl with an electric mixer at high speed until pale and thick. • Gradually beat in the almonds and flour. • Beat the egg whites and salt with an electric mixer at high speed until stiff peaks form. Fold them into the batter. • Spoon the batter into the prepared pan. • Bake for about 30 minutes, or until a toothpick inserted into the center comes out clean. • Cool in the pan on a rack. • Almond Ice Cream: Beat the egg yolks, sugar, vanilla, and almond extract in a large bowl with an electric mixer at high speed until pale and thick. • Transfer to a double boiler. Cook over low heat until the mixture lightly coats a metal spoon or registers 160°F (71°C) on an instant-read thermometer. Plunge the pan into a bowl of ice water and stir until the egg mixture has cooled. • Beat the cream in a medium bowl until stiff. • Fold the cream into the cooled egg mixture. • Place in a freezer-proof bowl and freeze for 2 hours, stirring at frequent intervals to prevent ice crystals forming. • Use a small ice cream scoop to make four 1½-inch (4-cm) balls. Set aside on a plate in the freezer. • Spread the remaining ice cream on the cake and return to the freezer for 1 hour. • Loosen and remove the pan sides and place the cake on a serving plate. • Place the balls of ice cream on top and top each one with an upside-down ice cream cone to make a clown hat. • Use the candy to give each clown eyes, a nose, and a mouth.

Left: Lisa's ladybug cake

Easy cat cake

Serves: 6-8; Preparation: 45 minutes; Cooking: 50 minutes; Level of difficulty: 2

Preheat the oven to 350°F/180°C/gas 4. • Butter a 9 x 3-inch (23 x 8-cm) round cake pan. Line with waxed paper. Butter the paper. • Melt the chocolate in a double boiler over barely simmering water. Set aside to cool. • Sift the flour, baking powder, and salt into a large bowl. • Beat the butter and sugar in a large bowl with an electric mixer at medium speed until creamy. • Add the egg yolks, beating until just blended. • With mixer at low speed, gradually beat in the dry ingredients, alternating with the chocolate. • With mixer at high speed, beat the egg whites in a large bowl until stiff peaks form. Use a large rubber spatula to fold them into the batter. • Spoon the batter into the prepared pan. • Bake for about 50 minutes, or until a toothpick inserted into the center comes out clean. • Cool the cake in the pan for 10 minutes. Turn out onto a rack. Carefully remove the paper and let cool completely. • Split the cake horizontally. Place one layer on a serving plate. Spread with half the preserves. Top with the remaining layer. Spread with the remaining preserves. • Spread with the frosting. • Form the eyes and mouth with the cherries.

■ INGREDIENTS

- 8 oz (250 g) bittersweet chocolate, coarsely chopped
- 1⅓ cups (200 g) all-purpose (plain) flour
- 1 teaspoon baking powder
- ¼ teaspoon salt
- ¾ cup (200 g) butter
- 1 cup (200 g) sugar
- 8 large eggs, separated
- ½ cup (160 ml) apricot preserves (jam)
- 1 quantity *Rich Chocolate Frosting* (see page 30)
- candied cherries, for the eyes and mouth

Children's birthday cake

Serves: 6-8; Preparation: 20 minutes; Cooking: 30 minutes; Level of difficulty: 1

Preheat the oven to 325°F/170°C/gas 3. • Butter and flour a 9-inch (23-cm) square pan. • Sift the flour, baking powder, and salt into a medium bowl. Stir in the coconut. • Beat the butter, sugar, and vanilla in a large bowl with an electric mixer at medium speed until creamy. • Add the eggs, beating until just blended after each addition. • With mixer at low speed, gradually beat in the dry ingredients, alternating with the milk. • Stir in three-quarters of the M&M's. • Spoon the batter into the prepared pan. Sprinkle with the remaining M&M's. • Bake for about 30 minutes, or until a toothpick inserted into the center comes out clean. • Cool the cake completely in the pan.

■ INGREDIENTS

- 1⅓ cups (200 g) all-purpose (plain) flour
- 1½ teaspoons baking powder
- ¼ teaspoon salt
- ⅔ cup (90 g) shredded (desiccated) coconut
- ½ cup (125 g) butter
- ½ cup (100 g) sugar
- 2 teaspoons vanilla extract
- 3 large eggs
- 3 tablespoons milk
- scant 1 cup (90 g) plain M & M's

Right: *Easy cat cake*

Parisian raspberry gâteau

Serves: 8-10; Preparation: 45 minutes + 2 hours to soak and chill; Level of difficulty: 2

Place the raspberries, 1 cup (150 g) of confectioners' sugar, and kirsch in a large bowl. Soak for 1 hour. • Drain the raspberries, reserving the syrup. • Beat the cream cheese, remaining confectioners' sugar, and lemon zest in a large bowl until creamy. Mix in the raspberries. • Sprinkle the gelatin over the water in a saucepan. Let stand 1 minute. Stir over low heat until the gelatin has dissolved. • Beat the cream in a medium bowl until stiff. Fold the cream and the gelatin mixture into the raspberry mixture. • Split the cake in three horizontally. Place one layer on a serving plate. Brush with the syrup. Spread with half the raspberry mixture. Top with a second layer and spread with the remaining raspberry mixture. Top with the remaining layer. • Brush with the remaining syrup. • Heat the raspberry jelly in a saucepan until liquid. Spread over the cake. • Decorate with the raspberries. • Refrigerate for 1 hour.

INGREDIENTS

- 1 lb (500 g) raspberries (reserve 12 to decorate)
- 1⅔ cups (250 g) confectioners' (icing) sugar
- 1 cup (250 ml) kirsch
- 1 cup (250 g) cream cheese
- 1 tablespoon finely grated lemon zest
- 1¼ cups (310 ml) heavy (double) cream
- 2 tablespoons gelatin
- 4 tablespoons cold water
- one 9-inch (23-cm) *Basic Sponge Cake* (see page 22)
- 1 cup (325 ml) raspberry jelly

Divine strawberry cream cake

Serves: 6-8; Preparation: 45 minutes + 4 hours to chill; Cooking: 10 minutes; Level of difficulty: 3

Butter a 9-inch (23-cm) springform pan. • Cherry Syrup: Boil the water and sugar in a small saucepan until the sugar dissolves, stirring constantly. Remove from the heat and stir in the kirsch. Let cool. • Strawberry Filling: Sprinkle the gelatin over the water in a medium saucepan. Let stand 5 minutes. • Purée half the strawberries in a food processor. Stir the puréed strawberries, sugar, and lemon juice into the gelatin. Stir over low heat until the gelatin has dissolved. • Set aside, stirring often, until cool and thick. • Beat the cream in a large bowl until stiff. Fold into the cooled strawberry mixture. • Split the cake horizontally. Trim the cake to 8 inches (20 cm). Crumble the excess cake and set aside. • Place one layer in the prepared pan and brush with half the syrup. Spread half the filling over the cake. Arrange the remaining strawberries on the cake. Top with the remaining layer and drizzle with the remaining syrup. Spread with the remaining filling. Cover with plastic wrap (cling film) and refrigerate for 4 hours. • Press the cake crumbs onto the sides of the cake. • Decorate with the chantilly cream and strawberries.

INGREDIENTS

CHERRY SYRUP
- 6 tablespoons water
- 3 tablespoons sugar
- 6 tablespoons kirsch

STRAWBERRY FILLING
- 1 tablespoon gelatin
- 6 tablespoons cold water
- 1 lb (500 g) strawberries, hulled and sliced
- ¾ cup (150 g) sugar
- 1 tablespoon lemon juice
- 2 cups (500 ml) heavy (double) cream, chilled
- one 9-inch (23-cm) *Basic Sponge Cake* (see page 22)
- ¼ quantity *Chantilly Cream* (see page 26)
- 8–10 perfect strawberries, to decorate

Right: *Parisian raspberry gâteau*

Gluten-free lemon cake

■ INGREDIENTS

- 9 large eggs, separated
- 1⅓ cups (200 g) confectioners' (icing) sugar
- juice of 1½ lemons
- ½ cup (75 g) potato starch (potato flour)
- ½ cup (75 g) matzo meal

Serves: 6-8; Preparation: 30 minutes; Cooking: 50 minutes; Level of difficulty: 1

Preheat the oven to 375°F/190°C/gas 5. • Set out a 9-inch (23-cm) tube pan with a removable bottom. • Beat the egg whites in a large bowl with an electric mixer at medium speed until frothy. With mixer at high speed, add the confectioners' sugar, beating until stiff, glossy peaks form. • With mixer at high speed, beat the egg yolks and lemon juice in a large bowl until pale and thick. • Use a large rubber spatula to fold the yolk mixture into the beaten whites, followed by the potato starch and matzo meal. • Pour into the pan. • Bake for about 50 minutes, or until a toothpick inserted into the pan comes out clean. • Let cool completely.

Caramel layer cake

Serves: 10-12; Preparation: 35 minutes; Cooking: 45 minutes; Level of difficulty: 2

Preheat the oven to 350°F/180°C/gas 4. • Butter a deep 10-inch (25-cm) springform pan. • Sift the flour, baking powder, baking soda, and salt into a large bowl. • Beat the butter, brown sugar, and caramel flavoring in a large bowl until creamy. • Add the egg yolks, beating until just blended. • Gradually beat in the dry ingredients and milk. • Beat the egg whites in a large bowl until stiff peaks form. Fold them into the batter. • Spoon the batter into the prepared pan. • Bake for about 45 minutes, or until golden brown. • Cool in the pan for 15 minutes. Turn out onto a rack and let cool completely. • Caramel Frosting: Bring the brown sugar and milk to a boil in a medium saucepan over medium heat, stirring constantly until the sugar has dissolved. Cook until the mixture is thick and it registers 234°–240°F (112°–115°C) on a candy thermometer. Remove from the heat. Stir in the butter and let cool to warm. • Filling: Beat the cream, sugar, and vanilla in a medium bowl until stiff. • Split the cake in three horizontally. Place one layer on a plate and spread with half the filling. Top with a second layer and spread with the remaining filling. Place the remaining layer on top. Spread the top and sides with the frosting.

INGREDIENTS

- 3 cups (450 g) all-purpose (plain) flour
- 2 teaspoons baking powder
- 1 teaspoon baking soda
- ¼ teaspoon salt
- 1 cup (250 g) butter
- 1½ cups (300 g) firmly packed brown sugar
- 2 teaspoons caramel or butterscotch flavoring
- 5 large eggs, separated
- 1 cup (250 ml) milk

CARAMEL FROSTING
- 2 cups (400 g) firmly packed brown sugar
- 1¼ cups (310 ml) milk
- 5 tablespoons butter

FILLING
- 1 cup (250 ml) heavy (double) cream
- 2 tablespoons sugar
- 1 teaspoon vanilla extract

Walnut and brandy New Year's cake

Serves: 12-14; Preparation: 15 minutes; Cooking: 50 minutes; Level of difficulty: 1

Preheat the oven to 350°F/180°C/gas 4. • Butter and flour a 12-inch (30-cm) springform pan. • Beat the egg whites in a large bowl with an electric mixer at high speed until stiff peaks form. • Beat the butter and sugar in a large bowl until creamy. Add the egg yolks. Add the brandy and orange juice and zest. • With mixer at low speed, gradually beat in the flour and baking powder. • Fold in the egg whites. • Spoon the batter into the prepared pan. Sprinkle with the walnuts. • Bake for about 50 minutes, or until a toothpick inserted into the center comes out clean. • Cool the cake completely in the pan on a rack. Loosen and remove the pan sides.

INGREDIENTS

- 8 large eggs, separated
- 1 cup (250 g) butter
- 3 cups (600 g) sugar
- 4 tablespoons brandy
- finely grated zest and juice of 4 oranges
- 4 cups (600 g) all-purpose (plain) flour
- 2 teaspoons baking powder
- ½ cup (50 g) walnuts

Right: Caramel layer cake

Shooting star cake

Serves: 6-8; Preparation: 1 hour + 3 hours to freeze; Level of difficulty: 3

Line a 1½-quart (1.5-liter) star-shaped baking pan with waxed paper. • Warm the milk and coffee beans in a small saucepan over low heat. • Beat the egg yolks, ½ cup (100 g) sugar, and salt in a large bowl with an electric mixer at medium speed until frothy. Mix in the coffee granules and flour. • Strain the milk, discarding the coffee beans. Add the milk to the egg yolk mixture. • Transfer the mixture to a large saucepan and bring to a boil over low heat. Cook and stir until thick. Let cool. • Briefly dip the ladyfingers in the coffee. Arrange half the ladyfingers in the prepared pan. • Stir the egg whites, ¼ cup (50 g) sugar, water, and cream of tartar in a saucepan until blended. Cook over low heat, beating constantly until the whites register 160°F (71°C) on an instant-read thermometer. Transfer to a bowl and beat at high speed until soft peaks form. Beat in the remaining sugar until stiff peaks form. Fold them into the batter. • Pour the batter into the prepared pan. Cover with the remaining ladyfingers. Freeze for 3 hours, or until set. • Turn out onto a serving plate. Carefully remove the paper.

■ INGREDIENTS

- 2⅔ cups (680 ml) milk
- 10 coffee beans
- 5 large eggs
- 1 cup (200 g) sugar
- ¼ teaspoon salt
- 2 tablespoons freeze-dried coffee granules
- ⅓ cup (50 g) all-purpose (plain) flour
- 35 ladyfingers
- ½ cup (125 ml) strong cold coffee
- 1⅔ cups (430 g) egg whites
- 5 teaspoons water
- ¼ teaspoon cream of tartar

French epiphany cake

Serves: 8-10; Preparation: 20 minutes; Cooking: 25 minutes; Level of difficulty: 1

Preheat the oven to 400°F/200°C/gas 6. • Butter and flour a 10-inch (25-cm) springform pan. • Beat the butter and sugar in a large bowl with an electric mixer at medium speed until creamy. • Add 2 eggs, beating until just blended. Gradually beat in the ground almonds. • Unfold or unroll the pastry on a lightly floured work surface. Cut out two 10-inch (25-cm) rounds. Fit one pastry round into the prepared pan. Spoon the almond mixture over the top. • Beat the remaining egg in a small bowl. • Brush the pastry with some of the beaten egg. Place the remaining pastry round on top. Use a knife to score patterns in the pastry and brush with the remaining beaten egg. • Bake for about 25 minutes, or until golden brown. • Cool the cake in the pan on a rack for 15 minutes. Loosen and remove the pan sides and serve warm.

■ INGREDIENTS

- ½ cup (125 g) butter
- ¾ cup (150 g) sugar
- 3 large eggs
- 1⅓ cups (200 g) finely ground almonds
- 1 lb (500 g) frozen puff pastry, thawed

Right: Shooting star cake

Christmas tree cake

Serves: 8-10; Preparation: 40 minutes; Cooking: 30 minutes; Level of difficulty: 2

Preheat the oven to 375°F/190°C/gas 5. • Butter and flour a 1½-quart (1.5-liter) Christmas tree pan. • Bring the butter, salt, and water to a boil in a saucepan over a medium heat. Beat in the flour until the mixture leaves the pan sides. Remove from the heat and add the eggs, one at a time, beating until just blended after each addition. • Stir in the cherries, lemon peel, and almonds. • Spoon the batter into the prepared pan. • Bake for about 30 minutes, or until golden brown. • Cool in the pan for 5 minutes. Turn out onto a serving plate. Dust with the confectioners' sugar.

■ INGREDIENTS

- 6 tablespoons butter
- ⅛ teaspoon salt
- 1 cup (250 ml) water
- 1 cup (150 g) all-purpose (plain) flour
- 4 large eggs
- 4 oz (125 g) candied cherries, coarsely chopped
- ⅔ cup (70 g) candied lemon peel, chopped
- ⅔ cup (70 g) almonds, finely chopped
- confectioners' (icing) sugar, to dust

Dorothy's christmas fruitcakes

Serves: 12-14; Preparation: 45 minutes + 1 week to soak; Cooking: 2 hours; Level of difficulty: 2

Mix the raisins, prunes, currants, candied cherries, candied peel, sherry, and rum in a large bowl. Soak for 1 week. • Stir 1¾ cups (350 g) brown sugar and water in a saucepan over medium heat until the sugar has dissolved and the syrup boils. Reduce the heat and gently boil the syrup until reduced to about 1 cup (250 ml). Set aside to cool. • Preheat the oven to 350°F/180°C/gas 4. • Butter two 8-inch (20-cm) springform pans. • Sift the flour, baking powder, baking soda, nutmeg, cinnamon, cloves, and salt into a large bowl. • Beat the butter, remaining brown sugar, and vanilla in a large bowl with an electric mixer at medium speed until creamy. • Add the eggs, beating until just blended. • Gradually beat in the dry ingredients, alternating with the syrup. Stir in the fruit mixture. • Spoon half the batter into each of the prepared pans. • Bake for about 2 hours, or until dark brown and the cakes shrink from the pan sides. • Cool the cakes completely in the pans on racks. Loosen and remove the pan sides. Invert onto the racks. Loosen and remove the pan bottoms. Carefully remove the paper. Wrap in foil and store until ready to serve, up to 4 months. • Form the almond paste into 2 equal balls. Dust a surface lightly with confectioners' sugar. Roll out one ball of almond paste to an 8-inch (20-cm) round. Fit the almond paste over one of the cakes, trimming the edges if needed. Repeat with the remaining paste. • Spread with the frosting.

■ INGREDIENTS

- 15 oz (450 g) raisins
- 2 cups (360 g) pitted prunes, chopped
- 1½ cups (360 g) currants
- 8 oz (250 g) candied cherries, chopped
- 8 oz (250 g) mixed candied peel, chopped
- 2 cups (500 ml) sherry
- 2 cups (500 ml) dark rum
- 3¾ cups (750 g) firmly packed dark brown sugar
- ¾ cup (200 ml) water
- 3¼ cups (480 g) all-purpose (plain) flour
- 1 tablespoon baking powder
- 1 teaspoon each baking soda, ground nutmeg, and cinnamon
- ½ teaspoon each ground cloves and salt
- 1½ cups (375 g) butter
- 2 teaspoons vanilla extract
- 7 large eggs
- 8 oz (250 g) almond paste
- 1 quantity *Sherry Frosting* (see page 28)

Right: *Christmas tree cake*

INGREDIENTS

- 1⅔ cups (250 g) all-purpose (plain) flour
- 1½ teaspoons baking powder
- 5 oz (150 g) semisweet chocolate, chopped
- ½ cup (125 ml) water
- ½ cup (125 g) butter
- 1¼ cups (250 g) firmly packed brown sugar
- 2 large eggs
- ½ cup (125 ml) sour cream

CHERRY CREAM FILLING
- 1 cup (320 ml) cherry preserves (jam)
- 3 tablespoons kirsch
- 2 cups (500 ml) heavy (double) cream
- 1 quantity *Basic Chocolate Frosting* (see page 30)
- candied cherries

Chocolate cherry cream gâteau

Serves: 6-8; Preparation: 30 minutes; Cooking: 45 minutes; Level of difficulty: 2

Preheat the oven to 350°F/180°C/gas 4. • Butter two 9-inch (23-cm) round pans. • Sift the flour and baking powder into a large bowl. • Melt the chocolate and water in a double boiler over barely simmering water. • Beat the butter and brown sugar in a large bowl until creamy. • Add the eggs, one at a time, beating until just blended. • Gradually beat in the chocolate mixture, sour cream, and dry ingredients. • Spoon half the batter into each of the prepared pans. • Bake for about 45 minutes, or until golden. • Let cool completely. • Split the cakes horizontally. • Cherry Cream Filling: Mix the preserves and kirsch. • Beat the cream in a medium bowl until stiff. • Place one layer on a serving plate. Spread with one-third of the preserves mixture and one-third of the whipped cream. Repeat with the remaining cake layers, finishing with a plain layer. Spread the frosting over the top and sides of the cake. Decorate with the cherries.

INGREDIENTS

- 1⅔ cups (250 g) all-purpose (plain) flour
- 2 teaspoons baking powder
- ¼ teaspoon salt
- 1 cup (250 g) butter
- 1¼ cups (250 g) sugar
- 1 teaspoon vanilla extract
- 4 large eggs

FILLING AND TOPPING
- 1 lb (500 g) canned peaches, drained
- 2 tablespoons sugar
- ¼ teaspoon almond extract
- 1½ tablespoons gelatin
- 5 tablespoons kirsch
- ¼ cup (80 ml) apricot preserves (jam)
- ½ cup (50 g) flaked almonds, toasted

Viennese almond and peach gâteau

Serves: 8-10; Preparation: 30 minutes + 4 hours to chill; Cooking: 35 minutes; Level of difficulty: 2

Preheat the oven to 400°F/200°C/gas 6. • Butter and flour a 10-inch (25-cm) springform pan. • Sift the flour, baking powder, and salt into a large bowl. • Beat the butter, sugar, and vanilla in a large bowl until creamy. • Add the eggs, beating until just blended. • Beat in the dry ingredients. • Spoon the batter into the prepared pan. • Bake for about 35 minutes, or until golden. • Cool in the pan for 10 minutes. Invert onto a rack and let cool completely. • Filling and Topping: Mash the peaches, sugar, and almond extract in a medium bowl until smooth. • Place ¼ of the peach syrup in a saucepan. Sprinkle with the gelatin. Let stand for 1 minute. Stir over low heat until dissolved. • Stir into the peach mixture. Refrigerate until set. • Split the cake horizontally. Place one layer in the cleaned springform pan. • Add 4 tablespoons kirsch to the remaining syrup and drizzle over the cake. Spread with the apricot mixture and top with the remaining cake. Refrigerate for 4 hours • Heat the preserves and remaining kirsch in a saucepan over low heat. • Remove the pan sides. • Brush with the preserves. Sprinkle with the almonds.

Left: Chocolate cherry cream gâteau

Coconut and walnut celebration cake

Serves: 8-10; Preparation: 30 minutes; Cooking: 25 minutes; Level of difficulty: 1

Preheat the oven to 350°F/180°C/gas 4. • Butter two 10-inch (25-cm) round cake pans. • Mix the buttermilk, baking soda, and salt in a bowl and set aside. • Beat the shortening, butter, sugar, vanilla, and almond extract in a large bowl until creamy. • Add the egg yolks, one at a time, beating until just blended. • Gradually beat in the flour, alternating with the buttermilk mixture. • Stir in the coconut and walnuts. • Beat the egg whites in a large bowl until stiff peaks form. Fold them into the batter. • Spoon the batter into the prepared pans. • Bake for about 25 minutes, or until a toothpick inserted into the center comes out clean. • Cool the cakes in the pans for 5 minutes. Turn out onto racks. Carefully remove the paper and let cool completely. • Place one cake on a serving dish and spread with one-third of the frosting. Top with the remaining cake. Spread with the remaining frosting. Decorate with the walnuts and bananas.

■ INGREDIENTS

- ½ cup (125 ml) buttermilk
- 1 teaspoon baking soda
- 1 teaspoon salt
- ½ cup (125 g) shortening
- ½ cup (125 g) butter
- 2 cups (400 g) sugar
- 1 teaspoon vanilla extract
- ½ teaspoon almond extract
- 5 large eggs, separated
- 2 cups (300 g) all-purpose (plain) flour
- ½ cup (60 g) shredded (desiccated) coconut
- 1 cup (100 g) chopped walnuts
- 2 quantities *Cream Cheese Frosting* (see page 32)
- ½ cup (50 g) walnuts, to decorate
- ½ cup (50 g) banana slices, to decorate

Exotic pineapple and coconut layer cake

Serves: 10-12; Preparation: 15 minutes; Cooking: 35 minutes; Level of difficulty: 1

Preheat the oven to 350°F/180°C/gas 4. • Butter and flour a 13 x 9-inch (33 x 23-cm) baking pan. • Stir together the flour, sugar, and baking powder in a large bowl. Use a large rubber spatula to fold in the eggs, nuts, coconut, and pineapple. • Spoon the batter into the prepared pan. • Bake for about 35 minutes, or until a toothpick inserted into the center comes out clean. • Cool the cake completely in the pan on a rack. • Beat the cream cheese, butter, vanilla, and confectioners' sugar in a large bowl with an electric mixer at high speed until creamy. Spread the frosting over the cake.

■ INGREDIENTS

- 2 cups (300 g) all-purpose (plain) flour
- 2 cups (400 g) sugar
- 2 teaspoons baking powder
- 2 large eggs, lightly beaten
- 1 cup (100 g) mixed nuts, finely chopped
- 1 cup (120 g) shredded (desiccated) coconut
- 2 cups (500 g) crushed canned pineapple
- 1 cup (250 g) cream cheese
- 4 tablespoons butter
- 1 teaspoon vanilla extract
- 1½ cups (225 g) confectioners' (icing) sugar

Right: *Coconut and walnut celebration cake*

Viennese kaffeehaus gâteau

Serves: 4-6; Preparation: 30 minutes; Cooking: 35 minutes; Level of difficulty: 2

Preheat the oven to 400°F/200°C/gas 6. • Butter a 9-inch (23-cm) springform pan. Line with parchment paper. • Beat the eggs and confectioners' sugar in a large heatproof bowl. Fit the bowl into a large saucepan of barely simmering water over low heat. Beat the eggs with an electric mixer at high speed until tripled in volume and thick. • Gradually fold the hazelnuts and flour into the batter. • Spoon the batter into the prepared pan. • Bake for about 35 minutes, or until a toothpick inserted into the center comes out clean. • Cool in the pan for 5 minutes. Loosen and remove the pan sides. Invert onto a rack. Loosen and remove the pan bottom. Carefully remove the paper. Turn top-side up and let cool completely. • Almond Butter Filling: Beat the egg yolks and sugar in a double boiler until well blended. • Mix the cornstarch and milk in a small bowl. Stir in the yolk mixture. Place over barely simmering water and cook, stirring constantly with a wooden spoon, until the mixture lightly coats a metal spoon or registers 160°F (71°C) on an instant-read thermometer. • Beat until the mixture thickens. Remove from the heat. • Gradually beat in the butter. Add the almonds and coffee. • Split the cake horizontally. Place one layer on a serving plate. Spread with two-thirds of the filling. Top with the remaining layer. • Frosting: Heat the coffee, kirsch, and confectioners' sugar in a saucepan over low heat. • Spread the cake with the frosting. Set aside. • Spoon the remaining filling into a pastry bag. Pipe on top in a decorative manner.

INGREDIENTS

CAKE
- 8 large eggs
- 1 cup (150 g) + 1 tablespoon confectioners' (icing) sugar
- 1⅓ cups (200 g) toasted hazelnuts, finely ground
- 1 cup (150 g) cake flour

ALMOND BUTTER FILLING
- 5 large egg yolks
- ½ cup (100 g) sugar
- 1 tablespoon cornstarch (cornflour)
- 1 cup (250 ml) milk
- ¾ cup (200 g) butter
- 1 cup (150 g) almonds, finely ground
- 1–2 tablespoons cold strong coffee

FROSTING
- 3–4 tablespoons cold strong coffee
- 1 tablespoon kirsch
- 1⅔ cups (250 g) confectioners' (icing) sugar

Yule chocolate log

Serves: 6-8; Preparation: 40 minutes + 4 hours to chill; Cooking: 1 hour 20 minutes; Level of difficulty: 3

Preheat the oven to 250°F/130°C/gas ½. • Meringue: Line a baking sheet with parchment paper. • Beat the egg whites and sugar in a large bowl until stiff, glossy peaks form. • Fold in the confectioners' sugar and hazelnuts. • Spoon the meringue into a pastry bag fitted with a plain nozzle and pipe two long bands of meringue onto the prepared sheet. • Bake for about 1 hour and 20 minutes, or until crisp. • Vanilla Filling: Sprinkle the gelatin over the cold water in a saucepan. Let stand 1 minute. Cook until dissolved. • Beat the cream in a large bowl until stiff.

INGREDIENTS

MERINGUE
- 5 large egg whites
- ¾ cup (150 g) sugar
- ½ cup (75 g) confectioners' (icing) sugar
- ¾ cup (125 g) finely ground hazelnuts

VANILLA FILLING
- 1 tablespoon gelatin
- 4 tablespoons cold water

Right: Viennese kaffeehaus gâteau

- 1 cup (250 ml) cream
- ½ teaspoon vanilla extract
- ¼ quantity
  Pastry Cream
  (see page 28)

HAZELNUT FILLING
- 3 oz (90 g) bittersweet
  chocolate
- ½ cup (125 g) butter
- 3 large eggs, separated
- ¾ cup (200 ml) chocolate
  hazelnut cream
- ¼ cup (50 g) sugar
- ½ teaspoon cream of
  tartar
- 1 quantity
  Chocolate Ganache
  (see page 32)

Mix the cream, gelatin mixture, and vanilla into the pastry cream. •
Hazelnut Filling: Melt the chocolate in a double boiler over barely
simmering water. • Beat the butter, egg yolks, chocolate hazelnut cream,
and chocolate in a saucepan. Cook over low heat, stirring constantly
with a wooden spoon until it registers 160°F (71°C) on an instant-read
thermometer. Plunge the pan into a bowl of ice water and stir until
cooled. • Stir the whites, sugar, and cream of tartar in a heavy saucepan
until blended. Cook over low heat until the whites register 160°F (71°C)
on an instant-read thermometer. Transfer to a bowl and beat until stiff
peaks form. Fold in the chocolate mixture. • Line a 14-inch (35-cm)
Bûche de Nöel mold with plastic wrap (cling film). Spoon in the vanilla
filling until half full. Top with a band of meringue. Spoon the hazelnut
filling over and top with the remaining meringue band. • Refrigerate for
4 hours, or until firmly set. • Spread the cake with the ganache.

Caramel and cream layered gâteau

Serves: 6-8; Preparation: 15 minutes; Cooking: 3 minutes; Level of difficulty: 1

Cut the sponge cakes in half horizontally. • Caramel Frosting: Melt the butter with the brown sugar in a medium saucepan over medium heat. Bring to a boil and stir for 1 minute, or until slightly thickened. • Cool slightly. • Beat in the coffee-flavored milk and confectioners' sugar until smooth. • Beat the cream in a large bowl until stiff. • Place one layer of cake on a serving plate. Spread with one-third of the cream. Top with a layer of cake. Spread the cake with one-third of the frosting. Cover with another layer of cake and spread with half the remaining cream. Finish with the remaining cake layer. • Spread the top and sides of the cake with the remaining frosting. Pipe the remaining cream in rosettes over the cake.

■ INGREDIENTS

- 2 *Basic Sponge Cakes* (see page 22)

CARAMEL FROSTING
- ½ cup (125 g) butter, melted
- ¾ cup (150 g) brown sugar
- 1 teaspoon instant coffee granules dissolved in 2 tablespoons warm milk
- 2 cups (300 g) confectioners' (icing) sugar
- 1 cup (250 ml) heavy (double) cream

Golden layer cake

Serves: 6-8; Preparation: 30 minutes; Cooking: 25 minutes; Level of difficulty: 1

Preheat the oven to 350°F/180°C/gas 4. • Butter and flour three 9-inch (23-cm) round cake pans. • Sift the flour, baking soda, and salt into a large bowl. • Beat the butter, sugar, and vanilla in a large bowl until creamy. • Add the eggs, one at a time, beating until just blended after each addition. • Gradually beat in the dry ingredients, alternating with the sour cream. • Spoon one-third of the batter into each of the prepared pans. • Bake for about 25 minutes, or until a toothpick inserted into the center comes out clean. • Cool the cakes in the pans for 15 minutes. Turn out onto racks to cool completely. • Golden Frosting: Melt the butter in a large saucepan over low heat. Stir in the brown sugar and milk and simmer for 5 minutes, stirring constantly. Remove from the heat and stir in the vanilla. • Beat in the confectioners' sugar until smooth. Set aside to cool. • Place one cake on a serving plate and spread with some frosting. Top with another cake and spread with frosting. Top with the remaining cake. Spread the top and sides of the cake with the remaining frosting.

■ INGREDIENTS

- 2⅔ cups (400 g) all-purpose (plain) flour
- 1 teaspoon baking soda
- ¼ teaspoon salt
- 1 cup (250 g) butter
- 2 cups (400 g) sugar
- 2 teaspoons vanilla extract
- 6 large eggs
- 1 cup (250 ml) sour cream

GOLDEN FROSTING
- 6 tablespoons butter
- 1 cup (200 g) firmly packed brown sugar
- ¾ cup (200 ml) milk
- 2 teaspoons vanilla extract
- 2 cups (300 g) confectioners' (icing) sugar

Right: *Caramel and cream layered gâteau*

Filled Italian Christmas cake

An Italian Christmas cake, called a panettone, *is light and bread-like in texture. They are not easy to make and even in Italy people buy one from their favorite bakery or local supermarket. Like many Italian foods, panettone are now easy to find in specialist bakeries or Italian delicatessens.*

Serves: 10-12; Preparation: 25 minutes + 12 hours to rest; Cooking: 5 minutes; Level of difficulty: 1

Preheat the oven to 400°F/200°C/gas 6. • Butter a baking sheet. • Use a knife to slice off the top third of the panettone horizontally. Use the knife to hollow out the base of the panettone, leaving a shell about ½-inch (1-cm) thick. • Brush the top third of the panettone with the butter and place on the baking sheet. Sprinkle with the almonds and dust with 2 tablespoons of confectioners' sugar. • Bake for about 5 minutes, or until crisp and golden brown. • Beat the cream and remaining confectioners' sugar in a medium bowl with an electric mixer at high speed until stiff. • Brush the bottom and sides of the hollowed-out panettone with the rum. • Spread one-third of the cream inside the panettone. Cover with half the strawberries and pineapple. Repeat, then finish with cream. • Refrigerate for 12 hours. • Place the toasted lid on top just before serving.

■ INGREDIENTS

- 1 panettone, weighing about 2 lb (1 kg)
- 2 tablespoons butter, melted
- 2 tablespoons slivered almonds
- 2 tablespoons confectioners' (icing) sugar
- 1 cup (250 ml) heavy (double) cream
- 4 tablespoons rum
- 1 cup (250 g) sliced strawberries
- 6 slices pineapple, chopped

Celebration panettone

Serves: 10-12; Preparation: 40 minutes + 6 hours to chill; Level of difficulty: 2

Sprinkle the gelatin over the water in a small saucepan. Let stand 1 minute. Cook over low heat until completely dissolved. • Beat the egg yolks and sugar in a saucepan until well blended. Cook over low heat, stirring constantly with a wooden spoon, until the mixture lightly coats a metal spoon or registers 160°F (71°C) on an instant-read thermometer. • Add the vanilla and Champagne and continue cooking, beating constantly until thick. • Stir in the gelatin mixture until completely dissolved. Set aside to cool. Make sure it does not set. • Invert the panettone. Cut a round into the bottom 1 inch (2.5 cm) from the edge. Remove the cake round and set aside. Remove the interior of the panettone, leaving the sides intact. • Spoon the egg mixture into the panettone. • Replace the cake round. • Transfer to a large bowl, bottom-side up, wrap with plastic wrap (cling film), and refrigerate for 6 hours, or until set. • Turn out onto a serving plate.

■ INGREDIENTS

- 1 tablespoon unflavored gelatin
- 4 tablespoons water
- 6 large eggs
- 1 cup (200 g) superfine (caster) sugar
- 1 teaspoon vanilla extract
- 1⅔ cups (430 ml) Champagne
- 1 panettone, weighing about 2 lb (1 kg)

Left: *Filled Italian Christmas cake*

Italian chocolate gâteau

Serves: 8-10; Preparation: 50 minutes; Cooking: 20 minutes; Level of difficulty: 2

Preheat the oven to 375°F/190°C/gas 5. • Butter two 9-inch (23-cm) round cake pans. • Stir the almonds, flour, cocoa, baking powder, and salt in a large bowl. • Beat the egg yolks, 1 cup (200 g) sugar, vanilla, and almond extract in a large bowl until pale and thick. • Gradually beat in the dry ingredients, alternating with the milk. • Beat the egg whites and remaining sugar in a large bowl until stiff, glossy peaks form. • Fold them into the batter. • Spoon half the batter into each of the prepared pans. • Bake for about 20 minutes, or until a toothpick inserted into the center comes out clean. • Cool in the pans for 10 minutes. Turn out onto racks and let cool completely. • Ricotta Filling: Beat the cream in a medium bowl until stiff. • Process the ricotta, confectioners' sugar, and candied peel in a food processor until smooth. Transfer to a large bowl. • Fold the cream into the ricotta mixture. • Split the cakes horizontally. Place one layer on a serving plate. Spread with one-third of the filling. Repeat with two more layers. Place the remaining layer on top. • Spread with the frosting. Decorate with the chocolate shavings.

■ INGREDIENTS

- 1½ cups (225 g) almonds, finely ground
- ⅔ cup (100 g) cake flour
- ⅔ cup (100 g) cocoa powder
- 1½ teaspoons baking powder
- ¼ teaspoon salt
- 8 large eggs, separated
- 1½ cups (300 g) sugar
- 2 teaspoons vanilla extract
- ½ teaspoon almond extract
- ½ cup (125 ml) milk

RICOTTA FILLING
- 1 cup (250 ml) cream
- 2 cups (500 g) ricotta
- ½ cup (75 g) confectioners' (icing) sugar
- ½ cup (50 g) chopped peel
- ½ quantity *Basic Chocolate Frosting* (see page 30)
- shavings of bittersweet chocolate, to decorate

Frosted red buttermilk cake

Serves: 6-8; Preparation: 35 minutes; Cooking: 25 minutes; Level of difficulty: 1

Preheat the oven to 350°F/180°C/gas 4. • Butter two 9-inch (23-cm) round cake pans. • Sift the flour, cocoa, baking powder, baking soda, and salt into a large bowl. • Beat the butter, sugar, and vanilla in a large bowl until creamy. • Add the eggs, one at a time, beating until just blended. • Gradually beat in the dry ingredients, alternating with the buttermilk, food coloring, and vinegar. • Spoon half the batter into each of the prepared pans. • Bake for about 25 minutes, or until a toothpick inserted into the center comes out clean. • Cool the cakes in the pans for 10 minutes. Turn out onto racks and let cool completely. • Place one cake on a serving plate. Spread with one-third of the frosting. Place the other cake on top. Spread with the remaining frosting.

■ INGREDIENTS

- 2 cups (300 g) all-purpose (plain) flour
- ½ cup (75 g) cocoa powder
- 1 teaspoon baking powder
- ½ teaspoon baking soda
- ¼ teaspoon salt
- ½ cup (125 g) butter
- 1½ cups (300 g) sugar
- 1 teaspoon vanilla extract
- 3 large eggs
- 1 cup (250 ml) buttermilk
- 2 tablespoons red coloring
- 1 tablespoon white vinegar
- 2 quantities *Cream Cheese Frosting* (see page 32)

Right: *Italian chocolate gâteau*

Basic savarin

A savarin is a French cake made with sugar, yeast, flour, and eggs which is bathed in liqueur or another sweet syrup. It was invented by two French cooks, the Julien brothers, and named for the famed French gastronomist Jean Anthelme Brillat-Savarin.

Serves: 8-10; Preparation: 30 minutes + 1 hour 40 minutes to rise; Cooking: 35 minutes; Level of difficulty: 2

Butter a 10-inch (25-cm) savarin mold. • Mix the yeast, sugar, and water. Set aside for 10 minutes. • Sift the flour and salt into a large bowl. • Beat the eggs, butter, and rum in a large bowl until creamy. • Stir in the yeast mixture. Gradually fold in the dry ingredients. • Knead on a lightly floured work surface until a smooth dough is formed, about 5–10 minutes. • Place in an oiled bowl and let rise in a warm place for 1 hour, or until doubled in bulk. • Punch down the dough, transfer to the prepared pan, and let rise for 40 minutes, or until doubled in bulk. • Preheat the oven to 375°F/190°C/gas 5. • Bake for about 35 minutes, or until golden. • Cool in the pan for 15 minutes. Turn out onto a rack to cool completely.

■ INGREDIENTS

- ½ oz (15 g) fresh yeast or 1 package (¼ oz/7 g) active dry yeast
- ¼ cup (50 g) sugar
- 4 tablespoons warm water
- 1⅔ cups (250 g) all-purpose (plain) flour
- 1 teaspoon salt
- 3 large eggs
- ½ cup (125 g) butter
- 4 tablespoons dark rum

Cream-filled lemon savarin

Serves: 8-10; Preparation: 45 minutes + 1 hour to rise; Cooking: 20 minutes; Level of difficulty: 2

Prepare the dough according to the recipe directions through punching down the dough after the first rise. • Butter a 10-inch (25-cm) tube pan. • Place the savarin dough in the pan. Let rise in a warm place for 1 hour. • Preheat the oven to 400°F/200°C/gas 6. • Bake for about 20 minutes, or until golden brown. • Turn out onto a rack to cool. • Bring the sugar, water, lemon zest, and cinnamon stick to a boil in a saucepan. • Place the cake (still on the rack) on a large plate. • Remove the cinnamon stick from the syrup. Drizzle the hot syrup over the cake. Scoop up any excess syrup with a spoon and drizzle over the cake. • Drizzle with the rum. • Heat the apricot preserves in a saucepan until liquid. Pour over the cake and set aside to cool. • Beat the cream and confectioners' sugar in a medium bowl with an electric mixer at high speed until stiff. • Spoon the cream into the center. • Decorate with the cherries and almonds.

■ INGREDIENTS

- 1 *Basic Savarin* (see above)
- 1½ cups (300 g) sugar
- 2 cups (500 ml) cold water
- 2 tablespoons finely grated lemon zest
- 1 cinnamon stick
- 2 cups (500 ml) rum
- ½ cup (160 ml) apricot preserves
- 1½ cups (375 ml) heavy (double) cream
- ⅓ cup (50 g) confectioners' (icing) sugar
- candied cherries and almonds, to decorate

Right: *Cream-filled lemon savarin*

Boozy raspberry savarin

Serves: 6-8; Preparation: 25 minutes + 1 hour to rise; Cooking: 25 minutes; Level of difficulty: 2

Prepare the dough according to the recipe directions through punching down the dough after the first rise. • Butter a 9-inch (23-cm) savarin pan. • Place the dough in the pan. Set aside in a warm place to rise for 1 hour. • Preheat the oven to 400°F/200°C/gas 6. • Bake for about 25 minutes, or until golden. • Cool in the pan for 15 minutes. • Place the cake on a large plate and poke holes all over with a fork. • Mix the orange juice and rum in a small bowl. Drizzle over the cake. • Fill the center of the savarin with the raspberries. • Beat the cream in a large bowl until stiff. • Spoon the cream into a pastry bag and pipe over the savarin in a decorative manner. • Decorate with the raspberries.

■ INGREDIENTS

- 1 *Basic Savarin* (see page 304)
- 2 tablespoons orange juice
- ½ cup (125 ml) dark rum
- 2 cups (500 g) raspberries
- ⅔ cup (180 ml) heavy (double) cream

English Easter fruitcake

Serves: 8-10; Preparation: 40 minutes; Cooking: 2 hours; Level of difficulty: 2

Preheat the oven to 325°F/170°C/gas 3. • Butter a 9-inch (23-cm) springform pan. • Sift the flour, nutmeg, allspice, baking powder, baking soda, and salt into a large bowl. • Beat the butter and sugar in a large bowl until creamy. • Add the eggs, one at a time, beating until just blended after each addition. • Gradually beat in the dried fruit, 3 tablespoons sherry, and the orange and lemon zests. Gradually beat in the dry ingredients. • Roll out half the marzipan on a board dusted with confectioners' sugar to a 9-inch (23-cm) round. Spoon half the batter into the prepared pan. Place the marzipan on top. Spoon the remaining batter over the top. • Bake for about 2 hours, or until golden brown and a toothpick inserted into the center comes out clean. • Cool the cake in the pan for 1 hour. Loosen and remove the pan sides. Invert onto a rack. Loosen and remove the pan bottom. • Turn top-side up and let cool completely. • Roll out the remaining marzipan to a 9-inch (23-cm) round. Trim around the marzipan with a fluted pastry cutter to make a decorative edge. • Brush the cake with the remaining sherry and cover with the marzipan. Use a fork to make patterns on the top.

■ INGREDIENTS

- 2 cups (300 g) all-purpose (plain) flour
- 1 teaspoon each ground nutmeg, allspice, and baking powder
- ½ teaspoon baking soda
- ¼ teaspoon salt
- ¾ cup (200 g) butter
- 1 cup (200 g) sugar
- 4 large eggs
- 3 cups (300 g) chopped mixed dried fruit
- 4 tablespoons dry sherry
- 2 tablespoons finely grated orange zest
- 2 tablespoons finely grated lemon zest
- 1 lb (500 g) marzipan
- ribbons, sugar eggs, and marzipan animals, to decorate

Right: Boozy raspberry savarin

Basic crêpes

Makes: 12 crêpes; Preparation: 20 minutes + 30 minutes to chill; Cooking: 30 minutes; Level of difficulty: 1

Beat the eggs in a large bowl until pale and thick. • Stir together the flour, sugar, and salt in a large bowl. Beat in the milk. Beat the batter into the eggs until smooth. • Refrigerate for 30 minutes. • Melt 1 tablespoon of the butter in an 8-inch (20-cm) crêpe pan. Pour a ladleful of batter into the pan. Rotate the pan so that the batter covers the bottom in an even layer. • Place over medium heat and cook until golden brown. Flip the crêpe. Brown on the other side, then transfer to a serving plate. • Add more butter and continue cooking.

Orange and pineapple crêpe cake

Serves: 4-6; Preparation: 20 minutes; Cooking: 3 minutes; Level of difficulty: 2

Beat the first measure of cream in a large bowl until stiff. • Place a crêpe on a serving dish and spread with a layer of cream. Drizzle with 1 teaspoon of liqueur and top with some pineapple. Place another crêpe on top and repeat until all have been stacked and layered. • Cook the sugar in a saucepan, stirring until the sugar has dissolved. Continue cooking, without stirring, over low heat until deep gold. Stir in the orange juice and cook until reduced. • Add the second measure of cream and bring to a boil. Boil for 2–3 minutes. Set aside to cool. • Stir in the remaining liqueur. Pour over the crêpes and serve.

Ice cream-filled pancakes

Serves: 4-6; Preparation: 20 minutes; Level of difficulty: 1

Prepare the crêpe batter and use it to make 7 thick pancakes. • Leave the ice cream at room temperature to soften for 10 minutes. • Beat the cream in a medium bowl until stiff. • Place one pancake on a serving dish. Spread with half the cherry ice cream. Place another pancake on top and spread with half the whipped cream. Place another pancake on top and spread with half the strawberry ice cream. • Repeat so that all the pancakes and ice cream are stacked, finishing with a pancake. • Decorate with the strawberries.

Left: Orange and pineapple crêpe cake

Coconut gâteau

Serves: 10-12; Preparation: 30 minutes + 30 minutes to chill; Cooking: 25 minutes; Level of difficulty: 2

Preheat the oven to 350°F/180°C/gas 4. • Butter two 9-inch (23-cm) round cake pans. • Sift the flour, baking powder, and salt into a large bowl. • Beat the butter, sugar, and vanilla and coconut extracts in a large bowl with an electric mixer at medium speed until creamy. • Add the eggs, one at a time, beating until just blended after each addition. • Gradually beat in the dry ingredients, alternating with the milk. Stir in the nuts. • Spoon half the batter into each of the prepared pans. • Bake for about 25 minutes, or until a toothpick inserted into the center comes out clean. • Cool the cakes in the pans for 10 minutes. Turn out onto racks and let cool completely. • Filling: With mixer at medium speed, beat the cream cheese, butter, and vanilla in a large bowl until smooth. Add the confectioners' sugar and coconut. • Topping: Beat the cream, confectioners' sugar, and vanilla in a medium bowl until stiff. • Split each cake horizontally. Place one layer on a serving plate. Spread with one-third of the filling. Repeat with two more layers. Place the remaining cake layer on top. Spread with the topping and sprinkle with the coconut. • Refrigerate for 30 minutes before serving.

INGREDIENTS

- 2½ cups (375 g) all-purpose (plain) flour
- 2½ teaspoons baking powder
- ½ teaspoon salt
- 1 cup (250 g) butter
- 2 cups (400 g) sugar
- 1 teaspoon each vanilla and coconut extracts
- 4 large eggs
- 1 cup (250 ml) milk
- ½ cup (50 g) macadamia nuts, chopped

FILLING
- 1 cup (250 ml) cream cheese
- 2 tablespoons butter
- 2 teaspoons vanilla extract
- 2 cups (300 g) confectioners' (icing) sugar
- 1 cup (120 g) shredded fresh coconut

TOPPING
- 1 cup (250 ml) cream
- 2 tablespoons confectioners' (icing) sugar
- 1 teaspoon vanilla extract
- ½ cup (60 g) shredded fresh coconut

Simple berry and hazelnut cake

Serves: 6-8; Preparation: 20 minutes; Level of difficulty: 1

Mix the berries and 3 tablespoons rum in a small bowl. Soak for 10 minutes. • Split the cake horizontally. Place one layer on a serving plate. Drizzle with the remaining rum. Spread with half the pastry cream and cover with the fruit mixture. Top with the remaining cake layer. • Spread with the remaining pastry cream. Sprinkle with the hazelnuts. • Dust with the confectioners' sugar.

INGREDIENTS

- 1 cup (250 g) mixed berries
- 4 tablespoons rum
- one 9-inch (23-cm) *Basic Sponge Cake* (see page 22)
- 1 quantity *Pastry Cream* (see page 28)
- 2 cups (200 g) chopped hazelnuts
- 4 tablespoons confectioners' (icing) sugar

Right: Coconut gâteau

Anniversary cake

Serves: 6-8; Preparation: 30 minutes; Cooking: 25 minutes; Level of difficulty: 2

Preheat the oven to 325°F/170°C/gas 3. • Set out a baking sheet. • Bring the milk, coffee beans, and lemon zest to a boil in a saucepan over medium heat. • Remove from the heat and add the vanilla. • Beat the egg yolks and sugar in a large bowl with an electric mixer at high speed until pale and thick. • Use a large rubber spatula to fold in the flour. • Gradually add the milk mixture. Return the mixture to the saucepan and cook over low heat, stirring constantly with a wooden spoon, until the mixture lightly coats a metal spoon or registers 160°F (71°C) on an instant-read thermometer. Discard the coffee beans and lemon zest. • Split the cake horizontally. Drizzle with the amaretto. • Place one layer on the baking sheet. Spread with the filling. Top with the remaining layer. • Topping: With mixer at high speed, beat the egg whites in a large bowl until stiff peaks form. Add the liqueur. • Spread the top of the cake with the frosting. Bake for about 25 minutes, or until lightly browned. • Decorate with the marzipan flowers.

■ INGREDIENTS

- 2 cups (500 ml) milk
- 3 coffee beans
- zest of 1 lemon, in one piece
- 1 teaspoon vanilla extract
- 4 large egg yolks
- ¾ cup (150 g) sugar
- ⅓ cup (50 g) all-purpose (plain) flour
- 1 *Basic Sponge Cake* (see page 22)
- 2 tablespoons amaretto (almond liqueur)

TOPPING
- 2 large egg whites
- 2 tablespoons confectioners' (icing) sugar
- 1 teaspoon Alchermes liqueur or marsala wine
- marzipan flowers, to decorate

Banana passover cake

Serves: 6-8; Preparation: 20 minutes; Cooking: 25 minutes; Level of difficulty: 1

Preheat the oven to 350°F/180°C/gas 4. • Butter two 9-inch (23-cm) round cake pans. Dust with matzo meal. • Beat the egg yolks, sugar, and salt in a large bowl with an electric mixer at high speed until pale and thick. • Use a large rubber spatula to fold in the bananas, potato starch, and walnuts. • With mixer at high speed, beat the egg whites in a large bowl until stiff peaks form. Fold them into the batter. • Spoon half the batter into each of the prepared pans. • Bake for about 25 minutes, or until a toothpick inserted into the center comes out clean. • Cool the cakes completely in the pans on racks. Turn out onto racks. • With mixer at high speed, beat the cream in a large bowl until stiff. • Place one cake on a serving plate. Spread with the cream and the banana slices. Top with the remaining layer.

■ INGREDIENTS

- 7 large eggs, separated
- 1 cup (200 g) sugar
- ¼ teaspoon salt
- 1 cup (250 g) very ripe mashed bananas
- ¾ cup (125 g) potato starch (potato flour)
- 1 cup (100 g) walnuts, coarsely chopped
- 1 cup (250 ml) heavy (double) cream
- 1 banana, peeled and thinly sliced

Right: Anniversary cake

Grape harvest cake

Serves: 6-8; Preparation: 45 minutes; Cooking: 35 minutes; Level of difficulty: 1

Preheat the oven to 375°F/190°C/gas 5. • Butter and flour a 9-inch (23-cm) springform pan. • Rinse the grapes under cold running water and dry each one carefully. Cut each grape in half. • Sift the flour, baking powder, and salt into a medium bowl. • Beat the butter, sugar, and vanilla in a large bowl with an electric mixer at medium speed until creamy. • Add the eggs, one at a time, beating until just blended. • Gradually beat in the dry ingredients and the lemon juice. • Stir in the grape halves. • Spoon the batter into the prepared pan. • Bake for about 35 minutes, or until a toothpick inserted into the center comes out clean. • Cool the cake in the pan for 10 minutes. Loosen and remove the pan sides and let cool completely. • Heat the apricot preserves and brandy in a small saucepan over low heat. Set aside to cool for 10 minutes. • Brush the cake with some preserves and decorate with the grape halves. Brush with the remaining preserves.

■ INGREDIENTS

- 2 cups (200 g) white seedless grapes + extra, halved, for decoration
- 2 cups (200 g) black seedless grapes + extra, halved, for decoration
- 1½ cups (225 g) all-purpose (plain) flour
- 1½ teaspoons baking powder
- ¼ teaspoon salt
- ½ cup (125 g) butter
- ¾ cup (150 g) sugar
- 1 teaspoon vanilla extract
- 3 large eggs
- 1 tablespoon lemon juice
- ½ cup (160 ml) apricot preserves (jam)
- 1 tablespoon apricot brandy (or other fruit liqueur)

Nutty Easter cake

Serves: 6-8; Preparation: 20 minutes + 12 hours to chill; Level of difficulty: 1

Set out a deep pudding mold and line with moist muslin. • Beat the butter and ¾ cup (150 g) sugar in a large bowl with an electric mixer at medium speed until creamy. Beat in the cream cheese. • Beat the egg yolks, the remaining sugar, and 4 tablespoons of cream in a double boiler until well blended. Cook over low heat, stirring constantly with a wooden spoon, until the mixture lightly coats a metal spoon or registers 160°F (71°C) on an instant-read thermometer. Immediately plunge the pan into a bowl of ice water and stir until the egg mixture has cooled. • With mixer at low speed, beat the egg yolk mixture into the cream cheese mixture, followed by the remaining cream, vanilla, ⅔ cup (70 g) candied peel, pistachios, and almonds. • Spoon the mixture into the prepared mold. • Refrigerate for at least 12 hours, or until firmly set. • Invert onto a serving plate, removing the muslin. • Decorate with the remaining candied peel in the form of a cross.

■ INGREDIENTS

- 1 cup (250 g) butter
- 1 cup (200 g) sugar
- 2 cups (500 g) cream cheese
- 2 large egg yolks
- ½ cup (125 ml) heavy (double) cream
- ½ teaspoon vanilla extract
- ⅔ cup (120 g) raisins
- ⅔ cup (70 g) mixed candied peel, finely chopped + 1 cup (100 g) to decorate
- 1 tablespoon pistachios, finely chopped
- 1 cup (100 g) almonds, finely chopped

Right: *Grape harvest cake*

Meringue Cakes

℅

Light as air, melt-in-your mouth meringue is always a winner. Use it to finish cakes or bake it in crisp layers and sandwich them together with fruit and whipped cream. Add finely chopped nuts to the basic meringue mixture to make classic dacquoise.

Banana vacherin with chantilly

■ INGREDIENTS

- 5 large egg whites
- 1½ cups (300 g) firmly packed light brown sugar
- 1 teaspoon vanilla extract
- 1½ cups (375 ml) heavy (double) cream
- 2 tablespoons confectioners' (icing) sugar
- 2 medium very ripe (but not brown) bananas, peeled and very thinly sliced
- ½ quantity *Chantilly Cream* (see page 26)

Serves: 6-8; Preparation: 30 minutes; Cooking: 1 hour; Level of difficulty: 2

Preheat the oven to 250°F/130°C/gas ½. • Line a baking sheet with parchment paper and mark two 9-inch (23-cm) circles on the paper. • Beat the egg whites and brown sugar in a large bowl with an electric mixer at high speed until stiff, glossy peaks form. • Add the vanilla. • Spoon the mixture into a pastry bag fitted with a ½-inch (1-cm) tip and pipe the mixture into two spiral disks, starting at the center of the circles and filling each one. • Bake for about 1 hour, or until crisp. Turn off the oven and let cool. Carefully remove the paper. • Beat the cream and confectioners' sugar in a large bowl until stiff. • Place two-thirds of the cream in a bowl and fold in the bananas (reserve a few slices to decorate). • Place a meringue layer on a serving plate. Spread with the cream. Top with the remaining layer and spread with the remaining cream. • Top with the Chantilly Cream and decorate with the remaining slices of banana.

Apricot almond dacquoise

■ INGREDIENTS

- 5 large egg yolks
- ½ cup (100 g) sugar
- ½ cup (125 ml) milk
- 1¼ cups (310 g) butter
- 2 tablespoons coffee extract
- 2 cans (15-oz/450-g) apricot halves, drained
- 3 *Basic Dacquoise* rounds (see page 26)
- ¾ cup (120 g) flaked almonds
- 2 tablespoons confectioners' (icing) sugar

Serves: 8-10; Preparation: 30 minutes; Cooking: 20 minutes; Level of difficulty: 2

Beat the egg yolks and sugar in a large bowl with an electric mixer at high speed until pale and thick. • Bring the milk to a boil in a large saucepan over medium heat. Remove from the heat. Slowly beat the hot milk into the egg mixture. • Transfer the mixture to the saucepan. Cook over low heat, stirring constantly with a wooden spoon, until the mixture lightly coats a metal spoon or registers 160°F (71°C) on an instant-read thermometer. Immediately plunge the pan into a bowl of ice water and stir until the egg mixture has cooled. • Add the butter and the coffee extract. Transfer to a bowl. Press plastic wrap (cling film) directly on the surface and refrigerate. • Reserve 3–4 apricot halves and chop the rest coarsely. • Spoon half the filling into another bowl and fold in the apricots. • Place one dacquoise round on a serving plate and spread with half the apricot filling. Top with another dacquoise round and spread with the remaining apricot filling. Place the remaining dacquoise on top. Spread with the plain filling. • Sprinkle with the almonds and decorate with the reserved apricots. Dust with the confectioners' sugar.

Right: *Banana vacherin with chantilly*

Coffee liqueur vacherin

Serves: 6-8; Preparation: 30 minutes; Cooking: 1 hour; Level of difficulty: 2

Preheat the oven to 250°F/130°C/gas ½. • Line a baking sheet with parchment paper and mark two 9-inch (23-cm) circles on the paper. • Beat the egg whites in a large bowl with an electric mixer at medium speed until frothy. • With mixer at high speed, gradually beat in the sugar until stiff, glossy peaks form. Add 1 tablespoon coffee liqueur. • Spoon the mixture into a pastry bag fitted with a ½-inch (1-cm) tip and pipe into two spiral disks, starting at the center of the circles and filling each one. • Bake for about 1 hour, or until crisp. Turn off the oven and leave the door ajar until the meringues are completely cool. • Carefully remove the paper. • Beat the cream, confectioners' sugar, and remaining coffee liqueur in a large bowl with mixer at high speed until stiff. • Place a meringue layer on a serving plate. Spread with three-quarters of the cream. Top with the remaining meringue layer. Spoon the remaining cream into a pastry bag and decorate the top of the vacherin with 8–10 rosettes. Top each one with a coffee bean.

■ INGREDIENTS

- 5 large egg whites
- 1½ cups (300 g) sugar
- 3 tablespoons coffee liqueur
- 1½ cups (375 ml) heavy (double) cream
- 2 tablespoons confectioners' (icing) sugar
- whole coffee beans, to decorate

Caramel vacherin

Serves: 6-8; Preparation: 30 minutes; Cooking: 1 hour; Level of difficulty: 2

Preheat the oven to 250°F/130°C/gas ½. • Line a baking sheet with parchment paper and mark two 9-inch (23-cm) circles on the paper. • Beat the egg whites in a large bowl with an electric mixer at medium speed until frothy. • With mixer at high speed, gradually add both sugars, beating until stiff, glossy peaks form. • Add the vanilla. • Spoon the mixture into a pastry bag fitted with a ½-inch (1-cm) tip and pipe the mixture into two spiral disks, starting at the center of the circles and filling each one. • Bake for about 1 hour, or until crisp. Turn off the oven and leave the door ajar until the meringues are completely cool. • Carefully remove the paper. • Beat the cream and confectioners' sugar in a large bowl with mixer at high speed until stiff. • Place a meringue layer on a serving plate. Spread with three-quarters of the cream. Top with the remaining meringue layer and spread with the remaining cream. • Decorate with the caramel sauce.

■ INGREDIENTS

- 5 large egg whites
- ¾ cup (150 g) sugar
- ¾ cup (150 g) firmly packed light brown sugar
- 1 teaspoon vanilla extract
- 1½ cups (375 ml) heavy (double) cream
- 2 tablespoons confectioners' (icing) sugar
- caramel ice cream topping (plastic squeeze bottle)

Right: Chocolate vacherin

Chocolate vacherin

INGREDIENTS

- 5 large egg whites
- 1½ cups (300 g) sugar
- ⅓ cup (50 g) unsweetened cocoa powder
- 1 teaspoon vanilla extract
- 1 quantity Chocolate Ganache (see page 32)
- 1 cup (250 ml) heavy (double) cream
- 2 oz (60 g) bittersweet chocolate, finely grated

Serves: 6-8; Preparation: 30 minutes; Cooking: 1 hour; Level of difficulty: 2

Preheat the oven to 250°F/130°C/gas ½. • Line a baking sheet with parchment paper and mark two 9-inch (23-cm) circles on the paper. • Beat the egg whites in a large bowl with an electric mixer at medium speed until frothy. • With mixer at high speed, gradually add the sugar, beating until stiff, glossy peaks form. • Fold in the cocoa and vanilla. • Spoon the mixture into a pastry bag fitted with a ½-inch (1-cm) tip and pipe the mixture into two spiral disks. • Bake for about 1 hour, or until crisp. • Turn off the oven and let cool. • Carefully remove the paper. • Place a meringue layer on a serving plate. Spread with the ganache. Top with the remaining meringue layer. • Beat the cream in a large bowl until stiff. Spread over the cake. Sprinkle with the chocolate.

Chocolate hazelnut supreme

Serves: 6-8; Preparation: 1 hour; Cooking: 2 hours; Level of difficulty: 2

Preheat the oven to 250°F/130°C/gas ½. • Line two baking sheets with parchment paper and mark four 9-inch (23-cm) circles on the paper. • Meringue: Cook the sugar and water in a saucepan over medium heat until the sugar has dissolved. • Beat the egg whites and salt in a large bowl with an electric mixer at high speed until frothy. With mixer at high speed, beat in the hot sugar mixture and confectioners' sugar, beating until stiff, glossy peaks form. • Spoon the mixture into a pastry bag with a ½-inch (1-cm) tip and pipe the mixture into four spiral disks, starting at the center and filling the circles. • Bake for about 2 hours, or until crisp. • Turn off the oven and leave the meringues in the oven with the door slightly ajar until completely cool. • Remove from the oven and carefully remove the paper. • Filling: Beat the cream in a large bowl with an electric mixer at high speed until stiff. • Fold the chocolate cream into the beaten cream. • Place a meringue round on a serving plate and spread with one-third of the filling. Top with the another round of meringue and cover with one-third of the filling. Top with another round of meringue and spread with the remaining filling. Crumble the fourth meringue over the cake. • Serve immediately.

■ INGREDIENTS

MERINGUE
• 1 cup (200 g) sugar
• ½ cup (125 ml) water
• 4 large egg whites
• ⅛ teaspoon salt
• 1⅓ cups (200 g) confectioners' (icing) sugar

FILLING
• 2 cups (500 ml) heavy (double) cream
• ½ cup (125 g) chocolate hazelnut cream (Nutella), melted

Dacquoise with chocolate buttercream

Serves: 6-8; Preparation: 15 minutes + 30 minutes to chill; Level of difficulty: 1

Place one dacquoise round on a serving plate. Spread with half of the chocolate buttercream. Cover with a second round and spread with the remaining buttercream. • Dust with the confectioners' sugar and stick the almonds all around the sides. • Refrigerate for 30 minutes before serving.

■ INGREDIENTS

• 3 *Basic Dacquoise* rounds (see page 26)
• 1 quantity *Chocolate Buttercream* (see page 36)
• ⅓ cup (50 g) confectioners' (icing) sugar
• ¾ cup (120 g) flaked toasted almonds

Right: Chocolate hazelnut supreme

Strawberry meringue cake

■ INGREDIENTS

- 9 large egg whites
- 3 cups (600 g) sugar
- ⅛ teaspoon salt
- 3 cups (750 ml) heavy (double) cream
- ⅓ cup (50 g) confectioners' (icing) sugar
- 1 teaspoon vanilla extract
- 3 cups (500 g) coarsely chopped strawberries, hulled

Serves: 10-12; Preparation: 45 minutes; Cooking: 1 hour 10 minutes; Level of difficulty: 2

Preheat the oven to 250°F/130°C/gas ½. • Cut three 9-inch (23-cm) rounds of parchment paper and place on two baking sheets. Cut one 8 x 12-inch (20 x 30-cm) rectangle of parchment paper and place on one of the baking sheets. • Beat the egg whites, sugar, and salt in a large bowl with an electric mixer at high speed until stiff, glossy peaks form. • Spread a quarter of the meringue onto each parchment round. • Use the remaining meringue to make 6–8 small meringues. Place them on the paper rectangle. • Bake for about 1 hour. Remove the small meringues and bake the rounds for about 10 minutes more, or until crisp. Turn the oven off and let cool. Carefully remove the paper. • Beat the cream, confectioners' sugar, and vanilla in a large bowl until stiff. • Place one meringue round on a serving plate. Spread with one-third of the cream and top with one-third of the strawberries. Top with another meringue round. Spread with one-third of the cream and sprinkle with one-third of the strawberries. Top with another round and spread with the cream. Top with the remaining strawberries and the small meringues.

Pavlova with fresh fruit

■ INGREDIENTS

- 4 large egg whites
- ⅛ teaspoon salt
- 1¼ cups (250 g) sugar
- 2 tablespoons water
- 1 tablespoon cornstarch (cornflour)
- 2 teaspoons vanilla extract
- 1 teaspoon white vinegar
- 1 cup (250 ml) heavy (double) cream
- 2 tablespoons confectioners' (icing) sugar
- fresh fruit, to decorate

This is a classic dessert cake in Australia and New Zealand. It was created in the early 1930s in honor of the brilliant Russian ballet dancer Anna Pavlova, who toured the region at that time.

Serves: 6-8; Preparation: 20 minutes; Cooking: 50 minutes; Level of difficulty: 1

Preheat the oven to 250°F/130°C/gas ½. • Butter a baking sheet. Line with waxed paper. Drizzle a little water over the paper. • Beat the egg whites and salt in a large bowl with an electric mixer at medium speed until frothy. • Gradually beat in the sugar until stiff, glossy peaks form. • Beat in the water, cornstarch, 1 teaspoon vanilla, and vinegar. • Spoon the meringue mixture onto the prepared sheet. Do not spread much; the meringue will spread as it bakes. • Bake for about 50 minutes, or until crisp and pale gold. Turn the oven off and leave in the oven until cold. Invert onto a rack and carefully remove the paper. Transfer to a serving plate. • Beat the cream, confectioners' sugar, and remaining vanilla in a medium bowl until stiff. • Spread the cream over the meringue and decorate with the fruit.

Left: Pavlova with fresh fruit

Meringue cakes with chocolate mint sauce

Serves: 4; Preparation: 1 hour; Cooking: 2 hours; Level of difficulty: 2

Preheat the oven to 250°F/130°C/gas ½. • Line a baking sheet with parchment paper and mark eight 5-inch (13-cm) circles on the paper. • Meringue: Cook 1 cup (200 g) sugar and water in a saucepan over medium heat until the sugar has dissolved. • Beat the egg whites and salt in a large bowl with an electric mixer at medium speed until frothy. • With mixer at high speed, beat in the remaining sugar and sugar syrup until stiff, glossy peaks form. • Spoon the mixture into a pastry bag with a ½-inch (1-cm) tip and pipe the mixture into 8 spiral disks on the paper. • Bake for about 2 hours, or until crisp. • Turn off the oven and let cool. • Carefully remove the paper. • Chocolate Mint Sauce: Mix the egg yolks, sugar, vanilla, cornstarch, and milk in a saucepan. • Cook over low heat, stirring constantly, until the mixture thickens. Set aside to cool. • Stir the peppermint extract and food coloring into the sauce and spoon onto 4 dessert plates. • Place a meringue on each plate. Spread with chocolate ice cream. Top with a second meringue. • Dust with the cocoa.

■ INGREDIENTS

MERINGUE
- 1¼ cups (250 g) sugar
- 5 tablespoons water
- 6 large egg whites
- ⅛ teaspoon salt

CHOCOLATE MINT SAUCE
- 4 large egg yolks
- ⅓ cup (70 g) sugar
- 1 teaspoon vanilla extract
- 1 teaspoon cornstarch (cornflour)
- 1 cup (250 ml) milk
- 2 teaspoons peppermint extract
- 1 teaspoon green food coloring
- 1 cup (250 ml) chocolate ice cream, softened
- unsweetened cocoa powder, to dust

Chocolate dacquoise with almonds

Serves: 6-8; Preparation: 45 minutes; Cooking: 1 hour; Level of difficulty: 2

Preheat the oven to 300°F/150°C/gas 3. • Butter three 8-inch (20-cm) round cake pans. Line with parchment paper. • Beat the egg whites in a large bowl with an electric mixer at medium speed until frothy. • With mixer at high speed, gradually add the sugar, beating until stiff, glossy peaks form. • Fold the almonds and almond extract into the batter. • Spoon the batter evenly into the prepared pans. • Bake for about 1 hour, or until pale gold and crisp. • Cool the meringues in the pans for 10 minutes. Turn out onto racks. Carefully remove the paper and let cool completely. • Split the cake into three horizontally. Place a layer on a serving plate. Spread with one-third of the buttercream. Top with a meringue layer, followed by a cake layer. Spread with half the remaining buttercream. Top with another meringue layer and the remaining cake layer, finishing with a layer of buttercream.

■ INGREDIENTS

- 3 large egg whites
- ½ cup (100 g) sugar
- ⅔ cup (100 g) almonds, finely ground
- 1 teaspoon almond extract
- 1 *Basic Chocolate Sponge Cake* (see page 22)
- 1 quantity *Chocolate Buttercream* (see page 36)

Right: Meringue cakes with chocolate mint sauce

Dacquoise with coffee buttercream

Vary this dessert by changing the flavor of the buttercream.
See the various possibilities for different buttercreams on page 36.

Serves: 6-8; Preparation: 15 minutes + 30 minutes to chill; Level of difficulty: 1

INGREDIENTS

- 3 *Basic Dacquoise* rounds (see page 26)
- 1 quantity *Coffee Buttercream* (see page 36)
- ⅓ cup (50 g) confectioners' (icing) sugar
- 1 cup (125 g) flaked toasted almonds

Place one dacquoise round on a serving plate. Spread with half of the coffee buttercream. Cover with a second round and spread with the remaining buttercream. • Dust with the confectioners' sugar and stick the almonds all around the sides. • Refrigerate for 30 minutes before serving.

Meringue with chocolate and candied chestnuts

The meringue for this cake can be cooked a day or two in advance. Store in an airtight container until ready to use. Assemble the cake just before serving so that the meringue is fresh and crisp.

Serves: 6-8; Preparation: 30 minutes; Cooking: 1 hour 30 minutes; Level of difficulty: 2

Preheat the oven to 250°F/130°C/gas ½. • Cut four 8-inch (20-cm) rounds of parchment paper and place on two baking sheets. • Mix the sugar and confectioners' sugar in a medium bowl. • Beat the egg whites with half the sugar mixture and the salt in a large bowl with an electric mixer at medium speed until stiff, glossy peaks form. Gradually beat in the remaining sugar mixture. • Spread a third of the meringue onto each parchment round. • Bake for about 1 hour 30 minutes, or until crisp and pale gold. • Turn the oven off and let cool. Carefully remove the paper. • Beat the cream and vanilla in a large bowl until stiff. • Fold in the chocolate chips and candied chestnuts. • Place one meringue round on a serving plate. Spread with one-third of the cream. Top with another meringue round and spread with one-third of the cream. Top with the last round and spread with the remaining cream. • Crumble the remaining meringue round over the cake.

■ INGREDIENTS
- 1 cup (200 g) sugar
- ⅔ cup (100 g) confectioners' (icing) sugar
- 6 large egg whites
- ¼ teaspoon salt
- 2 cups (500 ml) heavy (double) cream
- ½ teaspoon vanilla extract
- 6 tablespoons chocolate chips
- 4 candied chestnuts, crumbled or coarsely chopped

Strawberry dacquoise

Serves: 6-8; Preparation: 15 minutes + 30 minutes to chill; Level of difficulty: 1

Place one dacquoise round on a serving plate. • Stir the strawberries into the buttercream. Spread the dacquoise with one-third of the buttercream. Cover with a second round and spread with one-third of the buttercream. Cover with the final round and spread with the remaining buttercream • Dust with the confectioners' sugar and press the almonds into the buttercream all around the sides. Decorate with the whole strawberries. • Refrigerate for 30 minutes before serving.

■ INGREDIENTS
- 3 *Basic Dacquoise* rounds (see page 26)
- 1 cup (200 g) strawberries, hulled and finely chopped + 6 whole, to decorate
- 1 quantity *Vanilla Buttercream* (see page 36)
- ⅓ cup (50 g) confectioners' (icing) sugar
- ¾ cup (75 g) slivered toasted almonds

Right: *Meringue with chocolate and candied chestnuts*

Meringues with raspberries and cream cheese

INGREDIENTS
- ½ cup (100 g) sugar
- ⅔ cup (100 g) confectioners' (icing) sugar
- 3 large egg whites
- ¼ teaspoon salt

FILLING
- 1 cup (250 ml) cream cheese
- ¼ cup (50 g) sugar
- 2 tablespoons kirsch
- 1 tablespoon finely grated lemon zest
- 8 oz (250 g) raspberries + 20 raspberries, to decorate
- ½ cup (125 ml) heavy (double) cream, whipped

Serves: 4; Preparation: 30 minutes; Cooking: 1 hour 30 minutes; Level of difficulty: 2

Preheat the oven to 250°F/130°C/gas ½. • Line a baking sheet with parchment paper. Butter and flour the paper. • Mix the sugar and confectioners' sugar together in a medium bowl. • Beat the egg whites with half the sugar mixture and the salt in a large bowl with an electric mixer at medium speed until stiff, glossy peaks form. Gradually beat in the remaining sugar mixture, 1 tablespoon at a time. • Spoon the mixture into a pastry bag with a ½-inch (1-cm) tip and pipe four 3-inch (8-cm) spiral disks on the baking sheet. Finish each circle with 3 rounds of meringue to form little baskets. • Bake for about 1 hour and 30 minutes, or until crisp. • Turn the oven off and let the meringues cool in the oven with the door ajar. Carefully remove the paper. • Filling: Place the cream cheese and sugar in a small bowl and beat until smooth. Stir in the kirsch and lemon zest. • Divide the raspberries among the four meringue "baskets." • Fold the cream into the cream cheese and spoon the mixture over the raspberries. • Top with the remaining raspberries and serve.

Meringues with chocolate and raspberries

INGREDIENTS
MERINGUE
- 1¼ cups (250 g) sugar
- 1⅓ cups (300 g) confectioners' (icing) sugar
- 2 tablespoons cornstarch (cornflour)
- 8 large egg whites
- ⅛ teaspoon salt

FILLING
- ½ cup (125 ml) red wine
- ¾ cup (150 g) sugar

Serves: 8-10; Preparation: 45 minutes; Cooking: 1 hour and 30 minutes; Level of difficulty: 3

Meringue: Preheat the oven to 250°F/130°C/gas ½. • Line a baking sheet with parchment paper. Butter and flour the paper. • Mix the sugar, confectioners' sugar, and cornstarch in a medium bowl. • Beat the egg whites with half the sugar mixture and the salt in a large bowl with an electric mixer at medium speed until stiff, glossy peaks form. Gradually beat in the remaining sugar mixture. • Spoon the mixture into a pastry bag with a ½-inch (1-cm) tip and pipe 3-inch (8-cm) spiral disks on the baking sheet. • Bake for about 1 hour and 30 minutes, or until the meringue is crisp. • Turn the oven off and let the meringues cool in the oven with the door ajar. Carefully remove the paper. • Filling: Bring the wine, half the sugar, and the cornstarch to a boil in a small saucepan

Right: Meringues with raspberries and cream cheese

- 4 tablespoons cornstarch (cornflour)
- 14 oz (400 g) raspberries
- 3 tablespoons raspberry liqueur
- 1½ cups (375 ml) heavy (double) cream
- 4 oz (125 g) bittersweet chocolate, melted

- fresh raspberries, to decorate

over medium heat, stirring constantly. • Add two-thirds of the raspberries and bring back to a boil. Add the raspberry liqueur and let reduce to about half the original volume, 8-10 minutes. • Remove from the heat and let cool. • Purée the remaining raspberries in a blender and strain them through a fine mesh strainer to remove the seeds. • Whip the cream with the remaining sugar in a large bowl. Add the raspberry purée and mix well. • Drizzle each of the meringues with a little of the melted chocolate. • Pipe a border of raspberry cream onto half of the meringues. Spoon the raspberry sauce into the center of each one and then cover them with the remaining meringues. • Arrange on a serving dish and garnish with raspberries.

Spicy chocolate meringue slice

Serves: 6-8; Preparation: 30 minutes; Cooking: 1 hour; Level of difficulty: 2

Preheat the oven to 325°F/170°C/gas 3. • Butter and flour a 9-inch (23-cm) square baking pan. • Sift the flour, baking powder, allspice, and salt into a medium bowl. • Beat the butter and sugar in a large bowl with an electric mixer at medium speed until creamy. • Add the eggs, one at a time, beating until just blended after each addition. • Beat in the chocolate. • With mixer at low speed, gradually beat in the dry ingredients, alternating with the milk. • Spoon the batter into the prepared pan. • Meringue: With mixer at high speed, beat the egg whites and sugar in a medium bowl until stiff peaks form. Gently spread the meringue over the batter. • Spice Topping: Chop the almonds coarsely. • Mix all the ingredients in a small bowl. Sprinkle over the meringue. • Bake for about 1 hour, or until golden and a toothpick inserted into the center comes out clean. • Cool the cake completely in the pan on a rack.

■ INGREDIENTS

- 1½ cups (225 g) all-purpose (plain) flour
- 1½ teaspoons baking powder
- 1 teaspoon allspice
- ¼ teaspoon salt
- ½ cup (125 g) butter
- ⅔ cup (140 g) sugar
- 3 large eggs
- 4 oz (125 g) bittersweet chocolate, coarsely grated
- ⅔ cup (180 ml) milk

MERINGUE
- 2 large egg whites
- ½ cup (100 g) sugar

SPICE TOPPING
- ½ cup (60 g) almonds
- 2 tablespoons shredded (desiccated) coconut
- 1 tablespoon sugar
- 1 teaspoon ground cinnamon

Walnut meringue torte

Serves: 6-8; Preparation: 30 minutes + 30 minutes to chill; Cooking: 25 minutes; Level of difficulty: 1

Preheat the oven to 350°F/180°C/gas 4. • Butter two 9-inch (23-cm) cake pans. Line with waxed paper. Butter the paper. • Beat the egg whites and sugar in a large bowl with an electric mixer at high speed until stiff, glossy peaks form. • Fold in the walnuts, vinegar, and vanilla. • Spoon the mixture evenly into the prepared pans and smooth the tops with a thin metal spatula. • Bake for about 25 minutes, or until crisp. • Cool the cakes in the pans for 20 minutes. Turn out onto racks. Carefully remove the paper and let cool. • Beat the cream in a large bowl until stiff. • Place a meringue layer on a serving plate. Spread with two-thirds of the cream. Cover with sliced strawberries. Top with the remaining meringue and spread with the remaining cream. Decorate with the strawberries and dust with the confectioners' sugar. • Refrigerate for 30 minutes before serving.

■ INGREDIENTS

- 5 large egg whites
- 1½ cups (300 g) sugar
- 1 cup (125 g) walnuts, finely ground
- 1 teaspoon white wine vinegar
- 1 teaspoon vanilla extract
- 1½ cups (375 ml) heavy (double) cream
- 14 oz (400 g) strawberries, sliced + a few whole, to decorate
- 2 tablespoons confectioners' (icing) sugar

Right: Spicy chocolate meringue slice

Almond meringue cake

Serves: 6-8; Preparation: 25 minutes; Cooking: 35 minutes; Level of difficulty: 2

Preheat the oven to 350°F/180°C/gas 4. • Butter two 9-inch (23-cm) cake pans. Line with waxed paper. Butter the paper. • Sift the flour, cocoa, baking powder, and salt into a medium bowl. • Beat the butter and ½ cup (100 g) sugar in a large bowl with an electric mixer at medium speed until creamy. • Add the egg yolks, one at a time, beating until just blended after each addition. • Fold in the dry ingredients, followed by the buttermilk and sour cream. • Spoon half the batter into each of the prepared pans. • With mixer at high speed, beat the egg whites and remaining sugar in a large bowl until stiff, glossy peaks form. • Spoon the meringue over the batter. Sprinkle the almonds over one of the cakes. • Bake for 10 minutes. Cover loosely with foil and bake for 25 minutes more. • Remove the foil and cool the cakes in the pans for 5 minutes. Turn out onto racks and carefully remove the paper. Turn meringue-side up and let cool completely. • Filling: With mixer at high speed, beat the cream and sugar until stiff. • Place the cake without almonds on a serving plate. Spread with the cream and arrange the strawberries on the cream. Top with the remaining almond cake.

■ INGREDIENTS

- 1 cup (150 g) all-purpose (plain) flour
- ½ cup (75 g) unsweetened cocoa powder
- 1 teaspoon baking powder
- ¼ teaspoon salt
- ½ cup (125 g) butter
- 1¼ cups (250 g) sugar
- 4 large eggs, separated
- ½ cup (125 ml) buttermilk
- ½ cup (125 ml) sour cream
- 4 tablespoons chopped almonds

FILLING
- 1 cup (250 ml) heavy (double) cream
- 2 tablespoons sugar
- 10 oz (300 g) strawberries, hulled and thickly sliced

Meringue with chocolate filling

Serves: 6-8; Preparation: 30 minutes; Cooking: 1 hour; Level of difficulty: 1

Preheat the oven to 250°F/130°C/gas ½. • Line a baking sheet with parchment paper and mark two 9-inch (23-cm) circles on the paper. • Beat the egg whites and confectioners' sugar in a large bowl with an electric mixer at high speed until stiff, glossy peaks form. • Spoon the mixture into a pastry bag with a plain ½-inch (1-cm) tip and pipe into two spiral disks. • Bake for about 1 hour, or until crisp and dry. Turn off the oven and leave the door ajar until completely cool. • With mixer at high speed, beat the cream, sugar, and vanilla in a small bowl until stiff. • Carefully remove one meringue layer from the paper and place on a serving plate. Spread with the pastry cream. Top with the remaining meringue layer. • Spread with the cream and decorate with the strawberries.

■ INGREDIENTS

- 5 large egg whites
- 1½ cups (225 g) confectioners' (icing) sugar
- ⅔ cup (180 ml) heavy (double) cream
- 1 tablespoon sugar
- ½ teaspoon vanilla extract
- 1 quantity Chocolate Pastry Cream (see page 28), chilled
- strawberries, to decorate

Right: *Almond meringue cake*

Sugar plum dessert

Serves: 8-10; Preparation: 50 minutes; Cooking: 1 hour 30 minutes; Level of difficulty: 3

Preheat the oven to 250°F/130°C/gas ½. • Line a large baking sheet with parchment paper. • Meringue: Beat the egg whites and lemon juice in a large bowl with an electric mixer at medium speed until soft peaks form. Gradually add the sugar, beating until stiff, glossy peaks form. • Place the meringue in a piping bag and pipe into fingers on the prepared baking sheet. • Bake for 1 hour, or until dry. • Remove from the oven and let cool. • Poach the plums in the wine in a large saucepan over medium heat for 20 minutes. • Remove from the heat and let cool. • Filling: Bring the milk to a boil in a large saucepan. • Beat the egg yolks and sugar until pale and creamy. Add the milk and mix well. Return to the saucepan and cook over low heat until thick. Remove from heat and let cool slightly. • Add the butter and mix well. • Drain the plums, reserving the juice. Chop the plums and add to the custard. • Place a layer of cake on a serving dish and drizzle with the plum juice. Spread with half the custard and cover with half the meringue fingers. Top with the remaining custard. Crumble the remaining meringues over the top.

■ INGREDIENTS

MERINGUE
- 6 large egg whites
- juice of ½ lemon
- 2½ cups (500 g) sugar

- 10 oz (300 g) plums, pitted
- ½ cup (125 ml) red wine

FILLING
- 1 cup (250 ml) milk
- 3 large egg yolks
- ⅓ cup (70 g) sugar
- ⅔ cup (180 g) butter

- one 9-inch (23-cm) *Basic Sponge Cake* (see page 22), cut in half horizontally

Cherry chocolate meringue cake

Serves: 8-10; Preparation: 30 minutes; Cooking: 35 minutes; Level of difficulty: 2

Preheat the oven to 325°F/170°C/gas 3. • Butter and flour an 8-inch (20-cm) round cake pan. Line with waxed paper. Butter the paper. • Sift the flour and baking powder into a large bowl. • Beat the butter, sugar, and eggs in a large bowl with an electric mixer at high speed until creamy. Add the cocoa mixture. • With mixer at low speed, gradually beat in the dry ingredients. Stir in the walnuts and cherries. • Spoon the batter into the prepared pan. • Bake for about 25 minutes, or until a toothpick inserted into the center comes out clean. • Cool the cake in the pan for 15 minutes. Invert onto a rack and carefully remove the paper. • Topping: Beat the egg whites, sugar, water, cream of tartar, and salt with mixer at high speed until stiff, glossy peaks form. • Spread the meringue over the cake. • Bake for about 10 minutes, or until golden.

■ INGREDIENTS

- ⅔ cup (100 g) all-purpose (plain) flour
- 1 teaspoon baking powder
- 6 tablespoons butter
- ½ cup (100 g) sugar
- 2 large eggs
- 3 tablespoons cocoa powder dissolved in 3 tablespoons hot water
- ½ cup (60 g) walnuts, coarsely chopped
- 12 sour cherries, chopped

TOPPING
- 2 large egg whites
- 6 tablespoons sugar
- 2 teaspoons water
- ⅛ teaspoon cream of tartar
- ⅛ teaspoon salt

Right: Sugar plum dessert

Florentine baked alaska

Serves: 8-10; Preparation: 1 hour + 12 hours to chill; Cooking: 5 minutes; Level of difficulty: 3

Filling: Crumble the almond paste in a medium saucepan and add the water and milk. Cook over low heat until dissolved. • Add the almond extract and gelatin and stir until dissolved. • Remove from heat and set aside to cool and set. • Beat the cream in a large bowl until stiff. • Fold the almond mixture into the cream. • Line a 2-quart (2-liter) dome-shaped pudding mold with plastic wrap (cling film) and line with slices of cake. Brush with the rum mixture and fill with half the almond filling. Cover with a layer of cake and brush with rum mixture. Fill with the remaining almond filling and remaining cake. • Refrigerate for 12 hours. • Preheat the oven to 350°F/180°C/gas 4. • Meringue: Beat the egg whites, sugar, and salt in a large bowl with an electric mixer at high speed until stiff peaks form. • Unmold the cake carefully. Place on an ovenproof plate, dome-side up. • Spread the meringue over the cake and sprinkle with the almonds. • Bake for 5 minutes, or until golden brown.

■ INGREDIENTS

FILLING
- 7 oz (200 g) almond paste (marzipan)
- ⅔ cup (180 ml) water
- 4 tablespoons milk
- ½ teaspoon almond extract
- 2 tablespoons gelatin
- 1½ cups (375 ml) heavy (double) cream
- 1 *Basic Sponge Cake* (see page 22), sliced
- 3 tablespoons rum mixed with 3 tablespoons water

MERINGUE
- 4 large egg whites
- ½ cup (100 g) sugar
- ⅛ teaspoon salt
- 2 tablespoons slivered almonds

Caramel layer cake with meringue

Serves: 10-12; Preparation: 50 minutes; Cooking: 55 minutes; Level of difficulty: 3

Preheat the oven to 325°F/170°C/gas 3. • Butter a 9-inch (23-cm) springform pan. • Sift the flour and salt into a medium bowl. • Beat the eggs, egg yolks, and sugar in a large bowl with an electric mixer at high speed until pale and thick. • Fold the dry ingredients into the batter. • Spoon the batter into the prepared pan. • Bake for about 45 minutes, or until a toothpick inserted into the center comes out clean. • Invert onto a rack. Let cool completely. • Syrup: Bring the sugar and water to a boil in a saucepan. Boil for 5 minutes, stirring constantly. Remove from heat and stir in the walnuts and caramel. • Preheat the oven to 350°F/180°C/gas 4. • Slice the cake in three horizontally. Place one layer in the bottom of a dish with tall sides and only slightly larger than the cake itself. • Spoon one-third of the syrup over the cake. Repeat with the remaining two layers and the syrup. • Meringue: Beat the egg whites, sugar, water, and cream of tartar with an electric mixer at high speed until stiff, glossy peaks form. • Spread the meringue over the cake. • Bake for 8–10 minutes, or until lightly browned.

■ INGREDIENTS

- 1⅓ cups (200 g) all-purpose (plain) flour
- ¼ teaspoon salt
- 3 large eggs + 5 large egg yolks
- ¾ cup (150 g) sugar

SYRUP
- 1½ cups (300 g) sugar
- 1 cup (250 ml) water
- 1 cup (120 g) walnuts, coarsely chopped
- 3 tablespoons caramel flavoring

MERINGUE
- 5 large egg whites
- ¼ cup (50 g) sugar
- 5 teaspoons water
- ¼ teaspoon cream of tartar

Right: *Florentine baked alaska*

Cheesecakes

Classic cheesecakes have a crumbled cookie base with a smooth, slightly tangy, cream cheese filling. These can be either covered with fresh fruit or smothered in chocolate or caramel toppings. We have included the classics, plus some unusual recipes with sponge cake bases or mascarpone filling. Enjoy!

Cheesecake with sour cream

Serves: 8-10; Preparation: 30 minutes + 7 hours to chill; Cooking: 65 minutes; Level of difficulty: 2

Butter a 10-inch (25-cm) springform pan. • Crust: Melt the butter and mix with the crumbs, sugar, cinnamon, and ginger in a medium bowl. • Press into the bottom and partway up the sides of the prepared pan. Refrigerate for 1 hour. • Filling: Preheat the oven to 375°F/190°C/gas 5. • Beat the cream cheese, sugar, vanilla, and almond extract in a large bowl with an electric mixer at medium speed until smooth. • Add the eggs, one at a time, beating until just blended after each addition. • With mixer at low speed, add the cinnamon, ginger, and nutmeg. • Spoon the filling into the crust. • Bake for about 50 minutes, or until set. • Cool the cake in the pan for 10 minutes. • Topping: Beat together the sour cream, sugar, and vanilla in a medium bowl. Spread over the cheesecake. • Bake for about 15 more minutes, or until set. • Cool in the pan on a rack. • Refrigerate for 6 hours. Loosen and remove the pan sides to serve.

■ INGREDIENTS

CRUST
- 4 tablespoons butter
- 2 cups (300 g) graham cracker (digestive biscuit) crumbs
- 6 tablespoons raw sugar
- 1 teaspoon each ground cinnamon and ginger

FILLING
- 1½ lb (750 g) cream cheese
- 1 cup (200 g) sugar
- 2 teaspoons vanilla extract
- 1 teaspoon almond extract
- 3 large eggs
- 1 teaspoon each ground cinnamon, ginger, nutmeg

TOPPING
- 2 cups (500 ml) sour cream
- 1 tablespoon sugar
- 1 teaspoon vanilla extract

Vanilla cheesecake with fruit and chantilly

Serve this cheesecake with raspberries, chopped strawberries, or peeled and chopped fresh peaches, nectarines, or apricots.

Serves: 8-10; Preparation: 30 minutes + 6 hours to chill; Cooking: 70 minutes; Level of difficulty: 1

Preheat the oven to 400°F/200°C/gas 6. • Butter a 10-inch (25-cm) springform pan. • Crust: Melt the butter and mix with the crumbs, sugar, and cinnamon in a medium bowl. • Press into the bottom and partway up the sides of the prepared pan. • Bake for about 10 minutes, or until lightly browned. • Cool the crust completely in the pan on a rack. • Filling: Beat the cream cheese, sugar, and vanilla in a large bowl with an electric mixer at medium speed until smooth. • Add the eggs, one at a time, beating until just blended after each addition. • With mixer at low speed, beat in the cream and flour. • Spoon the filling into the crust. • Bake for 10 minutes, then lower the oven to 250°F/130°C/gas ½ and bake for about 50 minutes more, or until set. • Cool the cake in the pan on a rack. • Refrigerate for 6 hours. • Loosen and remove the pan sides. Spread the top with the Chantilly Cream and cover with the fresh fruit.

■ INGREDIENTS

CRUST
- 4 tablespoons butter
- 2 cups (300 g) graham cracker (digestive biscuit) crumbs
- ½ cup (100 g) raw sugar
- 1 teaspoon cinnamon

FILLING
- 1½ lb (750 g) cream cheese
- 1¾ cups (350 g) sugar
- 2 teaspoons vanilla extract
- 4 large eggs
- 4 tablespoons heavy (double) cream
- 2 tablespoons all-purpose (plain) flour
- ½ quantity *Chantilly Cream* (see page 26)
- 2 cups (400 g) chopped fresh fruit

Right: Cheesecake with sour cream

Basic vanilla cheesecake

■ INGREDIENTS

- 1 *Basic Cheesecake Crust* (see page 22)

- 1 lb (500 g) cream cheese
- ¾ cup (150 g) sugar
- 2 teaspoons vanilla extract
- 1 teaspoon lemon extract
- 1 cup (250 ml) heavy (double) cream

Serves: 6-8; Preparation: 15 minutes + 6 hours to chill; Level of difficulty: 1

Preheat the oven to 350°F/180°C/gas 4. • Butter a 9-inch (23-cm) springform pan. • Beat the cream cheese, sugar, vanilla, and lemon extract in a large bowl with an electric mixer at medium speed until smooth. • With mixer at high speed, beat the cream in a large bowl until stiff. Fold the cream into the cheese mixture. • Spoon the filling into the crust. Refrigerate for 6 hours. Loosen and remove the pan sides.

Cheesecake with carrot and raisin filling

Serves: 8-10; Preparation: 30 minutes + 6 hours to chill; Cooking: 1 hour; Level of difficulty: 2

Preheat the oven to 350°F/180°C/gas 4. • Butter a 10-inch (25-cm) springform pan. • Coarsely chop the nuts. Melt the butter and mix with the crumbs, nuts, sugar, and cinnamon in a large bowl. • Press into the bottom and partway up the sides of the prepared pan. • Bake for about 10 minutes, or until lightly browned. • Cool completely in the pan on a rack. • Filling: Finely grate the carrots. • Beat the cream cheese, sugar, cornstarch, and vanilla in a large bowl with an electric mixer at medium speed until creamy. • Add the eggs, one at a time, beating until just blended after each addition. • With mixer at low speed, beat in the carrots, raisins, half the orange zest and all the juice, nutmeg, ginger, and cinnamon. • Spoon the filling into the crust. • Bake for about 50 minutes, or until set. • Cool the cake in the pan on a rack. • Refrigerate for 6 hours. • Topping: With mixer at medium speed, beat the cream cheese, confectioners' sugar, sour cream, and orange juice in a medium bowl until smooth. Loosen and remove the pan sides. Spread with the topping. Decorate with the remaining orange zest.

Almond cheesecake with candied ginger

Serves: 8-10; Preparation: 30 minutes + 7 hours to chill; Cooking: 50 minutes; Level of difficulty: 2

Butter a 9-inch (23-cm) springform pan. • Prepare the crust. • Press into the bottom and partway up the sides of the prepared pan. • Refrigerate for 1 hour. • Preheat the oven to 350°F/180°C/gas 4. • Filling: Beat the cream cheese, sugar, honey, and vanilla in a large bowl with an electric mixer at medium speed until creamy. • Add the eggs, one at a time, beating until just blended after each addition. • With mixer at low speed, beat in the sour cream and ginger. • Spoon the filling into the crust. Sprinkle with the almonds. • Bake for about 50 minutes, or until set. • Cool the cake in the pan on a rack. Refrigerate for 6 hours. Loosen and remove the pan sides to serve.

■ INGREDIENTS

CRUST
- ½ cup (60 g) nuts
- 4 tablespoons butter
- 1½ cups (225 g) graham cracker (digestive biscuit) crumbs
- ½ cup (100 g) raw sugar
- 1 teaspoon cinnamon

FILLING
- 2 medium carrots
- 1 lb (500 g) cream cheese
- ½ cup (100 g) sugar
- ½ cup (75 g) cornstarch
- 1 teaspoon vanilla extract
- 4 large eggs
- ½ cup (75 g) raisins
- 2 teaspoons finely grated orange zest
- 4 tablespoons orange juice
- 1 teaspoon each nutmeg, ginger, and cinnamon

TOPPING
- 4 oz (125 g) cream cheese
- 1 cup (150 g) confectioners' (icing) sugar
- 4 tablespoons sour cream
- 1 tablespoon orange juice

■ INGREDIENTS

- 1 *Basic Cheesecake Crust* (see page 22)

FILLING
- 1 lb (500 g) cream cheese
- ½ cup (100 g) sugar
- ½ cup (125 g) honey
- 1 teaspoon vanilla extract
- 3 large eggs
- 1 cup (250 ml) sour cream
- 3 tablespoons candied ginger, finely chopped
- ⅔ cup (80 g) flaked almonds

Right: Cheesecake with carrot and raisin filling

Brownie cheesecake

Serves: 8-10; Preparation: 1 hour + 6 hours to chill; Cooking: 1 hour 30 minutes; Level of difficulty: 2

Preheat the oven to 350°F/180°C/gas 4. • Butter and flour a 10-inch (25-cm) springform pan. • Melt the chocolate and butter in a double boiler over barely simmering water. Set aside to cool for 15 minutes. • Transfer to a bowl. Beat in the sugar with an electric mixer at medium speed. • Add the eggs, one at a time, beating until just blended after each addition. • With mixer at low speed, gradually beat in the flour and salt, alternating with the milk and vanilla extract. Stir in the walnuts. • Spoon the batter into the prepared pan. • Bake for about 30 minutes, or until set. • Cool completely in the pan on a rack. • Filling: With mixer at medium speed, beat the cream cheese, sugar, and vanilla in a large bowl until smooth. Add the sour cream and the eggs, one at a time, until just blended after each addition. • Spoon the filling over the brownie. • Bake for about 1 hour, or until set. • Cool the cake in the pan on a rack. • Refrigerate for 6 hours.

■ INGREDIENTS

- 4 oz (125 g) bittersweet chocolate, chopped
- ½ cup (125 g) butter
- 1½ cups (300 g) sugar
- 2 large eggs
- 1 cup (150 g) all-purpose (plain) flour
- ¼ teaspoon salt
- 4 tablespoons milk
- 1 teaspoon vanilla extract
- ½ cup (60 g) walnuts, coarsely chopped

FILLING
- 1½ lb (750 g) cream cheese
- ½ cup (100 g) sugar
- 2 teaspoons vanilla extract
- ½ cup (125 ml) sour cream
- 4 large eggs

Chocolate cheesecake with mandarins

Serves: 8-10; Preparation: 25 minutes + 6 hours to chill; Cooking: 1 hour; Level of difficulty: 2

Preheat the oven to 375°F/190°F/gas 5. • Butter a 9-inch (23-cm) springform pan. • Prepare the crust. • Press into the bottom and partway up the sides of the prepared pan. • Bake for 10 minutes, or until lightly browned. • Cool completely in the pan on a rack. • Filling: Beat the cream cheese, sugar, and orange extract in a large bowl with electric mixer at medium speed. • Add the eggs, one at a time, beating until just blended after each addition. • With mixer at low speed, gradually beat in the flour. Stir in the chocolate chips. • Spoon the filling into the crust. • Bake for about 40 minutes, or until set. Cool the cake in the pan for 15 minutes. • Topping: With mixer at medium speed, beat the sour cream, sugar, and vanilla. Spread the topping over the cheesecake. • Bake for 10 minutes more, or until set. • Cool the cake in the pan on a rack. • Refrigerate for 6 hours. • Loosen and remove the pan sides. Decorate with the mandarins and chocolate chips.

■ INGREDIENTS

- 1 Basic Cheesecake Crust (see page 22)

FILLING
- 1 lb (500 g) cream cheese
- ¾ cup (150 g) sugar
- 1 teaspoon orange extract
- 3 large eggs
- 2 tablespoons all-purpose (plain) flour
- ½ cup (75 g) semisweet chocolate chips

TOPPING
- 1 cup (250 ml) sour cream
- 2 tablespoons sugar
- 1 teaspoon vanilla extract
- 1 can (11 oz/300 g) mandarin oranges, drained
- ½ cup (75 g) semisweet chocolate chips

Right: Brownie cheesecake

Chocolate and orange cheesecake

INGREDIENTS

- 1 *Basic Cheesecake Crust* (see page 22), made with 3 tablespoons unsweetened cocoa powder

FILLING
- 8 oz (250 g) bittersweet chocolate, chopped
- 1 lb (500 g) cream cheese
- ½ cup (125 ml) sour cream
- 1 tablespoon finely grated orange zest
- 5 large eggs
- 1 cup (250 ml) heavy (double) cream

Serves: 8-10; Preparation: 30 minutes + 7 hours to chill; Cooking: 1 hour; Level of difficulty: 2

Preheat the oven to 350°F/180°C/gas 4. • Butter a 9-inch (23-cm) springform pan. • Prepare the crust. • Press into the bottom and halfway up the pan sides. • Refrigerate for 1 hour. • Melt the chocolate in a double boiler over barely simmering water. • Beat the cream cheese in a large bowl with an electric mixer at high speed until creamy. • Beat in the sour cream, orange zest, remaining sugar, and the melted chocolate. • With mixer at medium speed, add the eggs, one at a time, beating until just blended after each addition. • Spoon the filling into the crust. • Bake for 1 hour, or until set. • Cool the cake in the pan on a rack. • Refrigerate for 6 hours. • Loosen and remove the pan sides. Transfer to a serving plate. • With mixer at high speed, beat the cream in a medium bowl until stiff. Spread over the cheesecake.

Chocolate cheesecake with candied cherries

- 1 *Basic Cheesecake Crust* (see page 22)

FILLING
- 6 oz (180 g) semisweet chocolate, chopped
- 1 lb (500 g) cream cheese
- ¾ cup (150 g) sugar
- 1 teaspoon vanilla extract
- 2 large eggs

TOPPING
- 1 cup (250 ml) heavy (double) cream
- 2 tablespoons confectioners' (icing) sugar
- ½ teaspoon vanilla extract
- candied cherries, to decorate

Serves: 6-8; Preparation: 30 minutes + 6 hours to chill; Cooking: 55 minutes; Level of difficulty: 1

Preheat the oven to 350°F/180°C/gas 4. • Butter a 9-inch (23-cm) springform pan. • Prepare the crust. • Press into the bottom and partway up the sides of the prepared pan. • Bake for about 10 minutes, or until lightly browned. • Cool completely in the pan on a rack. • Filling: Melt the chocolate in a double boiler over barely simmering water. Set aside to cool. • Beat the cream cheese, sugar, and vanilla in a large bowl with an electric mixer at medium speed until creamy. • Add the eggs, one at a time, beating until just blended after each addition. • With mixer at low speed, beat in the chocolate. • Spoon the filling into the crust. • Bake for about 45 minutes, or until set. • Cool the cake in the pan on a rack. • Refrigerate for 6 hours. • Topping: With mixer at high speed, beat the cream, confectioners' sugar, and vanilla in a medium bowl until stiff. • Loosen and remove the pan sides. • Pipe the top of the cheesecake with rosettes of cream and decorate with the candied cherries.

Nutty brown sugar cheesecake

- 1 *Basic Cheesecake Crust* (see page 22)

FILLING
- 1½ lb (750 g) cream cheese
- 1 cup (200 g) firmly packed brown sugar
- 1 teaspoon vanilla extract
- 3 large eggs
- ½ cup (125 ml) sour cream
- ½ cup (60 g) nuts

TOPPING
- 1½ cups (375 ml) sour cream
- 4 tablespoons raw sugar
- 1 teaspoon vanilla extract

Serves: 8-10; Preparation: 30 minutes + 6 hours to chill; Cooking: 1 hour; Level of difficulty: 1

Preheat the oven to 350°F/180°C/gas 4. • Butter a 9-inch (23-cm) springform pan. • Prepare the crust. • Press into the bottom and partway up the sides of the prepared pan. • Bake for 10 minutes, or until lightly browned. • Cool completely in the pan on a rack. • Filling: Beat the cream cheese, brown sugar, and vanilla in a large bowl with an electric mixer at medium speed until creamy. • Add the eggs, one at a time, beating until just blended after each addition. • With mixer at low speed, add the sour cream, followed by the nuts. • Spoon the filling into the crust. • Bake for about 40 minutes, or until set. • Topping: With mixer at medium speed, beat the sour cream, sugar, and vanilla in a medium bowl. Spread over the cheesecake. • Bake for about 10 minutes, or until set. • Cool the cake in the pan on a rack. • Refrigerate for 6 hours. • Loosen and remove the pan sides just before serving.

Left: *Chocolate cheesecake with candied cherries*

Chocolate almond cheesecake

Serves: 8-10; Preparation: 30 minutes + 7 hours to chill; Cooking: 1 hour; Level of difficulty: 1

Butter a 9-inch (23-cm) springform pan. • Prepare the crust. • Press into the bottom and partway up the sides of the prepared pan. Refrigerate for 1 hour. • Filling: Melt the chocolate in a double boiler over barely simmering water. Set aside to cool. • Preheat the oven to 350°F/ 180°C/gas 4. • Beat the cream cheese, sugar, almond extract, and vanilla in a large bowl with an electric mixer at medium speed until smooth. • Add the eggs, one at a time, beating until just blended after each addition. • With mixer at low speed, beat in the chocolate. • Spoon the filling into the crust. • Bake for about 1 hour, or until set. • Cool the cake in the pan on a rack. • Refrigerate for 6 hours. • Topping: With mixer at high speed, beat the cream and confectioners' sugar in a small bowl until stiff. Pipe the cream over the cheesecake. • Loosen and remove the pan sides just before serving.

■ INGREDIENTS

- 1 *Basic Cheesecake Crust* (see page 22), made with amaretti cookie crumbs

FILLING
- 6 oz (180 g) bittersweet chocolate, chopped
- 1½ lb (750 g) cream cheese
- 1 cup (200 g) sugar
- 1 teaspoon almond extract
- ½ teaspoon vanilla extract
- 4 large eggs

TOPPING
- 1 cup (250 ml) heavy (double) cream
- 2 tablespoons confectioners' (icing) sugar

White chocolate and orange cheesecake

Serves: 10-12; Preparation: 30 minutes + 6 hours to chill; Cooking: 1 hour; Level of difficulty: 2

Preheat the oven to 350°F/180°C/gas 4. • Butter a 10-inch (25-cm) springform pan. • Prepare the crust. • Press into the bottom and partway up the sides of the prepared pan. • Bake for about 10 minutes, or until lightly browned. • Cool in the pan on a rack. • Filling: Melt the white chocolate in a double boiler over barely simmering water. Set aside to cool. • Boil the strip of orange zest and orange juice in a saucepan until reduced to about 4 tablespoons. Discard the orange zest and set aside to cool. • Beat the cream cheese, sugar, liqueur, grated orange zest, and reduced juice in a large bowl with an electric mixer at medium speed until smooth. • Add the eggs, one at a time, beating until just blended after each addition. • With mixer at low speed, beat in the white chocolate. • Spoon the filling into the crust. • Bake for about 50 minutes, or until set. • Cool the cake in the pan on a rack. • Refrigerate for 6 hours before serving.

■ INGREDIENTS

- 1 *Basic Cheesecake Crust* (see page 22)

FILLING
- 6 oz (180 g) white chocolate, chopped
- 2-inch (5-cm) long piece orange zest
- 1½ cups (375 ml) orange juice
- 2 lb (1 kg) cream cheese
- ¾ cup (150 g) sugar
- 2 tablespoons orange liqueur
- 1 tablespoon finely grated orange zest
- 4 large eggs

Right: Chocolate almond cheesecake

Tangy vanilla and orange cheesecake

Serves: 8-10; Preparation: 30 minutes + 7 hours to chill; Cooking: 50 minutes; Level of difficulty: 1

Butter a 9-inch (23-cm) springform pan. • Prepare the crust. • Press into the bottom and partway up the sides of the prepared pan. Refrigerate for 1 hour. • Filling: Preheat the oven to 350°F/180°C/gas 4. • Beat the cream cheese, sugar, orange zest, and vanilla in a large bowl with an electric mixer at medium speed until smooth. • Add the eggs, one at a time, beating until just blended after each addition. • With mixer at low speed, add the sour cream. • Spoon the filling into the crust. • Bake for about 50 minutes, or until set. • Cool the cake in the pan on a rack. • Refrigerate for 6 hours. Loosen and remove the pan sides to serve.

■ INGREDIENTS

• 1 *Basic Cheesecake Crust* (see page 22)

FILLING

• 1½ lb (750 g) cream cheese
• 1½ cups (300 g) sugar
• 2 tablespoons finely grated orange zest
• 2 teaspoons vanilla extract
• 4 large eggs
• 2 cups (500 ml) sour cream

Orange marmalade cheesecake

Serves: 8-10; Preparation: 30 minutes + 8 hours to chill; Cooking: 50 minutes; Level of difficulty: 1

Preheat the oven to 325°F/170°C/gas 3. • Butter and flour a 9-inch (23-cm) springform pan. • Prepare the crust. • Press into the bottom and partway up the sides of the prepared pan. • Bake for about 10 minutes, or until lightly browned. • Cool in the pan on a rack. • Filling: Beat the cream cheese, sugar, and vanilla in a large bowl with an electric mixer at medium speed until creamy. • Add the eggs, one at a time, beating until just blended after each addition. • Spoon the filling into the crust. • Bake for about 40 minutes, or until set. • Cool the cake completely in the pan on a rack. • Refrigerate for 6 hours. • Topping: With mixer at high speed, beat the cream and sugar in a medium bowl until stiff. Fold the marmalade into the cream and spread over the cake. Refrigerate for 2 hours. Loosen and remove the pan sides to serve.

■ INGREDIENTS

• 1 *Basic Cheesecake Crust* (see page 22)

FILLING

• 1½ lb (750 g) cream cheese
• ½ cup (100 g) sugar
• 2 teaspoons vanilla extract
• 2 large eggs

TOPPING

• 1 cup (250 ml) heavy (double) cream
• 1 tablespoon sugar
• 4 tablespoons orange marmalade

VARIATION
– For a different flavor, substitute the orange marmalade with raspberry or cherry preserves (jam.)

Right: Tangy vanilla and orange cheesecake

Caramel cheesecake with nuts

Serves: 8-10; Preparation: 30 minutes + 6 hours to chill; Cooking: 1 hour; Level of difficulty: 1

Preheat the oven to 350°F/180°C/gas 4. • Butter a 9-inch (23-cm) springform pan. • Prepare the crust. • Press into the bottom and partway up the sides of the prepared pan. • Bake for about 10 minutes, or until lightly browned. • Cool completely in the pan on a rack. • Filling: Beat the cream cheese, sugar, and vanilla in a large bowl with an electric mixer at medium speed until creamy. • Add the eggs, one at a time, beating until just blended after each addition. • Spoon the filling into the crust. • Bake for about 50 minutes, or until set. • Cool the cake in the pan on a rack. • Topping: Mix the caramel topping and nuts in a small bowl. Spread over the cheesecake. Refrigerate for 6 hours. • Loosen and remove the pan sides to serve.

■ INGREDIENTS

- 1 *Basic Cheesecake Crust* (see page 22)

FILLING
- 1 lb (500 g) cream cheese
- ½ cup (100 g) sugar
- 1 teaspoon vanilla extract
- 2 large eggs

TOPPING
- 6 tablespoons caramel ice cream topping
- 1 cup (125 g) mixed toasted nuts, coarsely chopped

Pumpkin cheesecake

This cheesecake will be popular at Halloween, or at any time throughout the fall and winter time.

Serves: 8-10; Preparation: 30 minutes + 7 hours to chill; Cooking: 1 hour 15 minutes; Level of difficulty: 1

Preheat the oven to 325°F/170°C/gas 3. • Butter a 9-inch (23-cm) springform pan. • Prepare the crust. • Press into the bottom and partway up the sides of the prepared pan. • Refrigerate for 1 hour. • Filling: Beat the cream cheese, brown sugar, and vanilla in a large bowl with an electric mixer at medium speed until creamy. • Add the eggs, one at a time, beating until just blended after each addition. • With mixer at low speed, beat in the pumpkin, cream, maple syrup, cinnamon, and allspice. • Spoon the filling into the crust. • Bake for about 1 hour and 15 minutes, or until set. • Cool the cake completely in the pan on a rack. • Refrigerate for 6 hours. • Loosen and remove the pan sides to serve.

■ INGREDIENTS

- 1 *Basic Cheesecake Crust* (see page 22), made with gingersnap cookie crumbs

FILLING
- 1½ lb (750 g) cream cheese
- 1 cup (200 g) firmly packed brown sugar
- 2 teaspoons vanilla extract
- 4 large eggs
- 1½ cups (375 g) canned pumpkin purée
- ½ cup (125 ml) heavy (double) cream
- 4 tablespoons maple syrup
- 1 teaspoon each ground cinnamon and allspice

Right: Caramel cheesecake with nuts

■ INGREDIENTS

- 1 *Basic Cheesecake Crust* (see page 22)

FILLING

- 1½ tablespoons unflavored gelatin
- ⅔ cup (180 ml) dry white wine
- 1 cup (250 g) cream cheese
- ¾ cup (150 g) sugar
- 4 tablespoons lemon juice
- 1½ cups (375 ml) heavy (double) cream
- ⅔ cup (150 g) drained, sliced canned apricots
- 1 cup (200 g) mixed fresh berries

Berryfruit cheesecake

Serves: 6-8; Preparation: 30 minutes + 5 hours to chill; Cooking: 5 minutes; Level of difficulty: 2

Butter a 9-inch (23-cm) springform pan. • Prepare the crust. • Press into the bottom and partway up the sides of the prepared pan. • Refrigerate for 1 hour. • Sprinkle the gelatin over 4 tablespoons of wine in a saucepan. Let stand 1 minute. Stir over low heat until the gelatin has completely dissolved. • Beat the cream cheese, sugar, lemon juice, and remaining wine in a large bowl with an electric mixer at medium speed until creamy. Stir in the gelatin mixture. • With mixer at high speed, beat the cream in a medium bowl until stiff. • Use a large rubber spatula to fold the cream into the cheese mixture. • Spoon one-third of the filling into the crust. Top with the apricots and two-thirds of the berries. Spread with the remaining filling. Refrigerate for 4 hours, or until set. • Loosen and remove the pan sides. Decorate with the remaining berries.

■ INGREDIENTS

- one 10-inch (25-cm) *Italian Sponge Cake* (see page 24)

FILLING

- 2 cups (500 ml) milk
- 2 tablespoons finely grated lemon zest
- ¼ teaspoon salt
- 1 cup (200 g) short-grain rice
- ¼ cup (50 g) sugar
- 1 tablespoon gelatin
- ¼ cup cold water
- 1 cup (250 ml) heavy (double) cream
- 1 cup (250 g) mascarpone cheese
- 1 teaspoon vanilla extract

TOPPING

- 2 cups (400 g) mixed red berries
- ½ cup (125 ml) apricot preserves (jam)

Italian cheesecake

This cheesecake calls for a disk of fat-free sponge cake. Either make an Italian sponge cake (see page 24) or buy a 10-inch (25-cm) disk ready made. If making the Italian sponge cake at home, you will only need half of it for this recipe. These rest can be frozen for later use.

Serves: 6-8; Preparation: 1 hour + 3 hours 30 minutes to chill; Cooking: 30 minutes; Level of difficulty: 3

Prepare the cake and let cool. • Filling: Bring the milk, lemon zest, and salt to a boil in a saucepan over medium heat. Stir in the rice and sugar and simmer for about 25 minutes, or until the rice is very tender, stirring occasionally. Remove from the heat and let cool. • Sprinkle the gelatin over the water in a saucepan. Let stand 1 minute. Stir over low heat until completely dissolved. Stir the gelatin into the rice mixture and refrigerate for 15 minutes. • Beat the cream in a large bowl with an electric mixer at high speed until stiff. • Stir the mascarpone, vanilla, and cream into the rice mixture. • Cut the cake in half horizontally. Place a layer on the bottom of a buttered 10-inch (25-cm) springform pan. Place the sides of the springform pan around the cake and tighten. Spoon the filling over the cake. Refrigerate for 3 hours, or until set. • Decorate with the berries. • Warm the preserves in a saucepan over low heat. Brush over the fruit. Refrigerate for 15 minutes. • Loosen and remove the pan sides.

Left: *Berryfruit cheesecake*

Mini amaretti cheesecakes

Serves: 12; Preparation: 30 minutes + 3 hours to chill; Cooking: 25 minutes; Level of difficulty: 1

Preheat the oven to 325°F/170°C/gas 3. • Prepare the crust. • Butter 12 medium muffin cups and press the crust mixture into the bottoms and partway up the sides. • Filling: Beat the cream cheese, sugar, vanilla, and almond extract in a large bowl with an electric mixer at medium speed until smooth. • Add the eggs, one at a time, beating until just blended after each addition. • Spoon the filling into the prepared cups, filling each three-quarters full. • Bake for about 25 minutes, or until set. • Cool the cakes in the pans on racks. Refrigerate for 2 hours. • Topping: Stir the marmalade and rum in a small saucepan until liquid. Remove from the heat and let cool slightly. Drizzle some jelly over each cheesecake. • Refrigerate for 1 hour more. Carefully remove from the muffin cups just before serving.

■ INGREDIENTS

- 1 *Basic Cheesecake Crust* (see page 22), made with amaretti cookie crumbs

FILLING
- 2 cups (500 g) cream cheese
- ½ cup (100 g) sugar
- 1 teaspoon vanilla extract
- ½ teaspoon almond extract
- 2 large eggs

TOPPING
- ½ cup (125 ml) orange marmalade
- 1 tablespoon rum

Easy no-bake cheesecake

In this recipe we have made a classic lemon-flavored filling. You can vary this by substituting the lemon zest and juice with lime or orange. You may also eliminate the citrus flavor altogether, replacing it with 2 teaspoons of vanilla, rum, or butterscotch extracts or 1 teaspoon of almond extract.

Serves: 6-8; Preparation: 30 minutes + 5 hours to chill; Level of difficulty: 1

Butter a 9-inch (23-cm) springform pan. • Prepare the crust. • Press into the bottom and partway up the sides of the prepared pan. • Refrigerate for 1 hour. • Filling: Beat the condensed milk, cream cheese, cream, and lemon zest in a large bowl with an electric mixer at low speed until creamy. Beat in the lemon juice. • Spoon the filling into the crust. • Refrigerate for 4 hours. Loosen and remove the pan sides. • Topping: With mixer at high speed, beat the cream in a medium bowl until stiff. Spread the cream over the cheesecake. Decorate with the fruit.

■ INGREDIENTS

- 1 *Basic Cheesecake Crust* (see page 22)

FILLING
- 1 can (14 oz/400 g) sweetened condensed milk
- 1 cup (250 ml) reduced-fat cream cheese, softened
- ½ cup (125 ml) heavy (double) cream
- 2 tablespoons finely grated lemon zest
- 4 tablespoons lemon juice

TOPPING
- 1 cup (250 ml) heavy (double) cream
- sliced ripe fresh fruit, to decorate

Right: Mini amaretti cheesecakes

Apple and ginger cheesecake

Serves: 8-10; Preparation: 30 minutes + 7 hours to chill; Cooking: 55 minutes; Level of difficulty: 1

Preheat the oven to 350°F/180°C/gas 4. • Butter a 9-inch (23-cm) springform pan. • Mix the flour, sugar, and ginger in a medium bowl. Use a pastry blender to cut in the butter until the mixture resembles coarse crumbs. • Press into the bottom and partway up the sides of the prepared pan. Prick all over with a fork. • Bake for 10 minutes, or until lightly browned. • Cool completely in the pan on a rack. • Filling: Beat the cream cheese, half the sugar, and the vanilla and lemon extracts in a large bowl with an electric mixer at medium speed until creamy. • Add the eggs, one at a time, beating until just blended after each addition. • Spoon the filling into the crust. • Arrange the apple slices on top. • Mix the remaining sugar with the ginger and lemon zest in a small bowl. Sprinkle over the apples. • Bake for about 45 minutes, or until set. • Cool the cake completely in the pan on a rack. • Refrigerate for 6 hours. • Brush the preserves over the apples. • Refrigerate for 1 more hour. • Loosen and remove the pan sides to serve.

■ INGREDIENTS

- 1 cup (150 g) all-purpose (plain) flour
- ½ cup (100 g) sugar
- 1 teaspoon ground ginger
- ½ cup (125 g) butter

FILLING

- 2 cups (500 ml) cream cheese
- 1 cup (200 g) sugar
- 1 teaspoon vanilla extract
- 1 teaspoon lemon extract
- 2 large eggs
- 3 medium Golden Delicious apples, peeled, cored, and thinly sliced
- 4 tablespoons candied ginger, finely chopped
- 1 tablespoon lemon zest
- ½ cup (125 ml) apricot preserves (jam), warmed

Sour cream and sweet potato cheesecake

Serves: 10-12; Preparation: 30 minutes + 6 hours to chill; Cooking: 1 hour; Level of difficulty: 2

Preheat the oven to 350°F/180°C/gas 4. • Butter and flour a 10-inch (25-cm) springform pan. • Prepare the crust. • Press into the bottom and partway up the sides of the prepared pan. • Bake for 10 minutes, or until lightly browned. Cool completely in the pan on a rack. • Filling: Halve the sweet potatoes and spoon the insides into a medium bowl. Mash until smooth. • Beat the cream cheese, sugar, and vanilla in a large bowl with an electric mixer at medium speed until creamy. • Beat in the sweet potatoes. Add the eggs, one at a time, beating until just blended after each addition. • With mixer at low speed, beat in the sour cream and cream. • Spoon the filling into the crust. • Bake for about 1 hour, or until set. • Cool the cake in the pan on a rack. • Topping: Stir the brown sugar and butter in a saucepan over low heat until the sugar has dissolved. • Increase the heat and bring to a boil. Remove from the heat and stir in the nuts and cream. Spread over the cheesecake. • Refrigerate for 6 hours. Loosen and remove the pan sides.

■ INGREDIENTS

- 1 *Basic Cheesecake Crust* (see page 22)

FILLING

- 1½ lb (750 g) sweet potatoes, baked
- 1½ lb (750 g) cream cheese
- ¾ cup (150 g) sugar
- 1 teaspoon vanilla extract
- 3 large eggs
- 6 tablespoons sour cream
- 4 tablespoons cream

TOPPING

- ¾ cup (150 g) firmly packed brown sugar
- 4 tablespoons butter
- 1 cup (125 g) walnuts, coarsely chopped
- 4 tablespoons cream

Right: *Apple and ginger cheesecake*

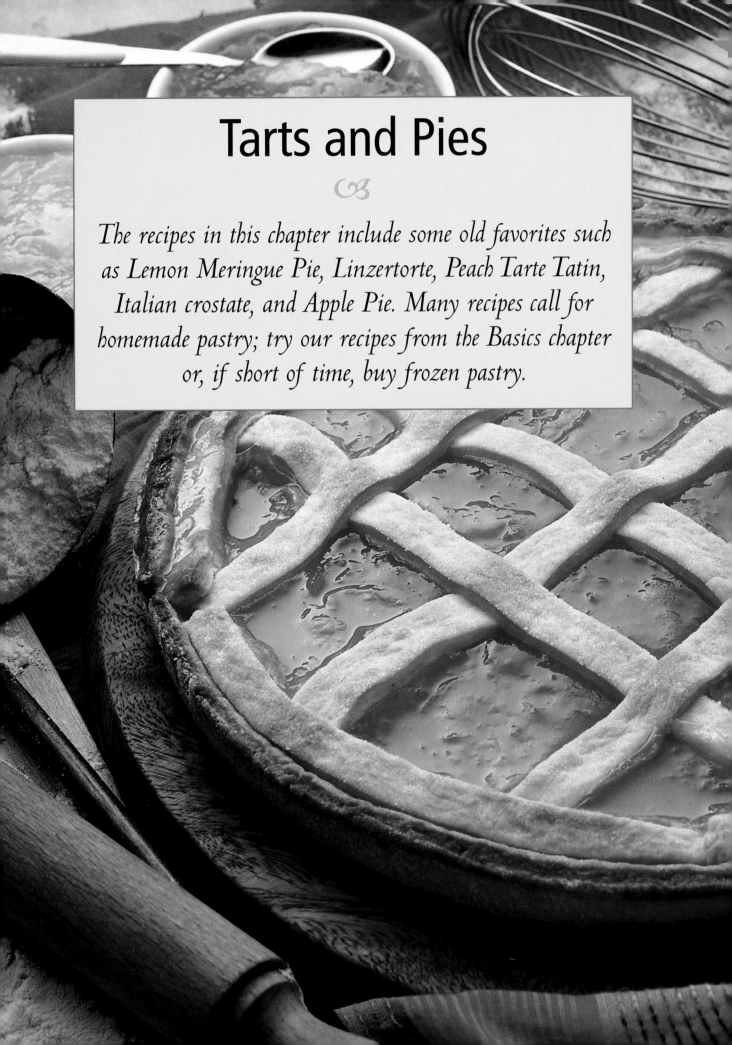

Tarts and Pies

☙

The recipes in this chapter include some old favorites such as Lemon Meringue Pie, Linzertorte, Peach Tarte Tatin, Italian crostate, and Apple Pie. Many recipes call for homemade pastry; try our recipes from the Basics chapter or, if short of time, buy frozen pastry.

Summer tart

Serves: 10-12; Preparation: 30 minutes + 1 hour 30 minutes to chill; Cooking: 40 minutes; Level of difficulty: 2

Pastry: Sift the flour and salt into a large bowl. Add the sugar and lemon zest. • Rub in the butter using your fingertips until the mixture resembles bread crumbs. • Add the egg and port and mix to make a smooth dough. • Wrap in plastic wrap (cling film) and refrigerate for 30 minutes. • Preheat the oven to 400°F/200°C/gas 6. • Butter a 10-inch (25-cm) pie plate. • Roll out the pastry on a floured work surface and use it to line the prepared pan. Cover with waxed paper and fill with dried beans. • Bake blind for 30 minutes. • Let cool. Discard the beans and waxed paper. Transfer to a serving dish. • Filling: Bring the milk to a boil in a large saucepan. • Beat the egg yolks, flour, and sugar in a large bowl until pale and creamy. • Add the hot milk and beat well. Return the mixture to the saucepan and cook over low heat for 5–8 minutes, stirring constantly, until thickened. • Add the vanilla. • Remove from the heat and let cool slightly. • Pour into the pastry case and refrigerate for 1 hour. • Arrange the strawberries on the top of the tart and brush with the apricot preserves.

INGREDIENTS

PASTRY
- 1⅓ cups (200 g) all-purpose (plain) flour
- ⅛ teaspoon salt
- ½ cup (100 g) sugar
- finely grated zest of 1 lemon
- 6 tablespoons cold butter, cut into pieces
- 1 large egg, lightly beaten
- 2 tablespoons port

FILLING
- 1¼ cups (310 ml) milk
- 2 large egg yolks
- 1 tablespoon all-purpose (plain) flour
- ½ cup (100 g) sugar
- 1 teaspoon vanilla extract
- 10 oz (300 g) strawberries, hulled and sliced
- ½ cup (125 g) apricot preserves (jam), melted

Dreamy chocolate tart

Serves: 6-8; Preparation: 30 minutes + 4 hours to chill; Level of difficulty: 1

Mix the wafers, almonds, and butter in a large bowl. • Press into the bottom and partway up the sides of a 9-inch (23-cm) pie plate. • Refrigerate for 2 hours, or until set. • Spoon the pastry cream into the pastry and refrigerate for 2 hours. • Decorate with the berries and brush with the preserves.

INGREDIENTS

PASTRY
- 1½ cups (180 g) finely crushed vanilla wafers
- ⅔ cup (100 g) almonds, finely ground
- ¾ cup (200 g) butter, melted

FILLING
- 1 quantity *Chocolate Pastry Cream* (see page 28)
- 1¼ cups (310 g) mixed berries
- ½ cup (125 g) apricot preserves (jam), melted

Right: *Summer tart*

Banana meringue tart

Serves: 6-8; Preparation: 40 minutes + time to prepare pastry; Cooking: 50 minutes; Level of difficulty: 2

If using homemade pastry, prepare the dough and set aside to rest. • Preheat the oven to 425°F/220°C/gas 7. • Butter a 10-inch (25-cm) pie plate. • Roll out the pastry on a lightly floured work surface and use it to line the prepared pan. Prick the base with a fork. Cover with waxed paper and fill with dried beans. • Bake blind for 15 minutes. • Let cool. Discard the beans and waxed paper. • Filling: Bring the milk and vanilla pod to a boil in a small saucepan over low heat. Remove from the heat and discard the vanilla. • Beat the egg yolks and sugar in a large bowl with an electric mixer at high speed until pale and creamy. • Mix the banana, dates, nuts, and cinnamon in a large bowl. • Pour in the egg mixture and gradually stir in the milk. • Spoon the filling into the pastry case. • Bake for 25 minutes. • With mixer at high speed, beat the egg whites and confectioners' sugar in a large bowl until stiff, glossy peaks form. • Remove the tart from the oven and spread with the meringue. • Return to the oven and bake for 10 minutes more, or until the meringue is lightly browned.

INGREDIENTS

- 1 quantity *Shortcrust Pastry* (see page 16)

FILLING
- ¾ cup (200 ml) milk
- 1 vanilla pod
- 3 large eggs, separated
- ¼ cup (50 g) sugar
- 1 large banana, sliced
- ⅓ cup (60 g) dates, chopped
- ¾ cup (75 g) chopped walnuts
- ½ teaspoon ground cinnamon
- ⅓ cup (50 g) confectioners' (icing) sugar

Linzertorte

Serves: 6-8; Preparation: 20 minutes; Cooking: 35 minutes; Level of difficulty: 1

Mix the flour, sugar, almonds, cinnamon, nutmeg, and salt in a large bowl. Stir in the egg yolks, rum, and lemon zest. • Use a pastry blender to cut in the butter until the mixture resembles coarse crumbs. • Divide the dough into ¾ and ¼ portions and shape each into a disk. Roll the larger disk of dough out on a lightly floured work surface to a 10-inch (25-cm) round. Fit into a 9-inch (23-cm) springform pan, forming a ½ inch (1-cm) rim around the edge. • Spread the preserves over the pastry. • Use your hands to roll the remaining dough into long, thin sausage shapes. Arrange in a lattice pattern over the top, sealing well. • Preheat the oven to 375°F/190°C/gas 5. • Bake for about 35 minutes, or until lightly browned. • Cool the tart completely in the pan on a rack. Loosen and remove the pan sides. Dust with the confectioners' sugar.

INGREDIENTS

- 1½ cups (225 g) all-purpose (plain) flour
- ¾ cup (150 g) sugar
- ½ cup (75 g) finely ground almonds
- ½ teaspoon each ground cinnamon and nutmeg
- ¼ teaspoon salt
- yolks of 3 hard-boiled eggs
- 3 tablespoons rum
- 1 tablespoon finely grated lemon zest
- ½ cup (125 g) cold butter
- ⅔ cup (140 g) raspberry preserves (jam)
- 2 tablespoons confectioners' (icing) sugar

Right: Banana meringue tart

Zesty citrus crostata

Serves: 8-10; Preparation: 30 minutes + 1 hour to chill; Cooking: 35 minutes; Level of difficulty: 2

INGREDIENTS

- 1⅓ cups (200 g) all-purpose (plain) flour
- scant ⅔ cup (140 g) butter
- generous ⅓ cup (80 g) sugar
- ⅛ teaspoon salt
- generous ⅓ cup (130 g) orange marmalade
- generous ⅓ cup (130 g) lemon marmalade

Preheat the oven to 350°F/180°C/gas 4. • Use your hands to mix the flour, butter, sugar, and salt in a large bowl until a smooth dough has formed. • Cover and refrigerate for 1 hour. • Butter an 11-inch (28-cm) pie plate. • Roll out three-quarters of the pastry on a lightly floured surface and use it to line the prepared pan. • Spread the orange marmalade in the base of the pastry case. Top with the lemon marmalade. • Roll out the remaining dough and cut into thin strips. • Lay over the crostata in a lattice pattern. • Bake for about 35 minutes, or until golden brown. • Serve warm or at room temperature.

Lemon meringue pie

Serves: 6-8; Preparation: 30 minutes; Cooking: 1 hour 10 minutes; Level of difficulty: 2

Preheat the oven to 400°F/200°C/gas 6. • Pastry: Sift the flour and salt into a large bowl. Stir in the sugar and almonds. • Rub in the butter using your fingertips until the mixture resembles bread crumbs. • Press the mixture into a 9-inch (23-cm) springform pan. Cover with waxed paper and dried beans or pie weights. • Bake blind for 15 minutes. Discard the paper and beans or pie weights. • Filling: Beat the eggs and sugar in a large bowl with an electric mixer at high speed until frothy. Add the lemon zest and juice. • Beat in the melted butter until well blended. • Pour the filling into the pastry case and bake for 30 minutes. • Lower the oven temperature to 300°F/150°C/gas 2. • Meringue: With mixer at high speed, beat the egg whites and sugar in a large bowl until stiff, glossy peaks form. • Spread the meringue over the filling. • Bake for about 25 minutes, or until the meringue is lightly browned. • Serve warm or at room temperature.

■ INGREDIENTS

PASTRY
- 1 cup (150 g) all-purpose (plain) flour
- ¼ teaspoon salt
- ¼ cup (50 g) sugar
- ⅓ cup (50 g) finely ground almonds
- ½ cup (125 g) butter

FILLING
- 3 large eggs
- ¾ cup (150 g) sugar
- finely grated zest of 2 lemons
- juice of 1 lemon
- ⅔ cup (150 g) butter, melted

MERINGUE
- 2 large egg whites
- ½ cup (100 g) sugar

Sour cherry tart

Serves: 6-8; Preparation: 30 minutes + time to prepare pastry; Cooking: 1 hour; Level of difficulty: 2

Preheat the oven to 400°F/200°C/gas 6. • Roll the dough out on a lightly floured work surface to a 12-inch (30-inch) round. • Fit into a 9-inch (23-cm) pie plate, trimming the edges if needed. Line with a sheet of waxed paper and fill with dried beans or pie weights. • Bake blind for 15 minutes. • Discard the paper with the beans. • Bake for 5 minutes more, or until crisp. • Let cool completely. • Lower the oven temperature to 350°F/180°C/gas 4. • Beat the eggs, egg yolks, milk, cream, sugar, and flour in a large bowl. Add the cherries. • Spoon the filling into the pastry shell. • Bake for about 40 minutes, or until set. • Cool the tart in the pan on a rack. • Dust with the confectioners' sugar. • Serve warm.

■ INGREDIENTS

- 1 quantity *Sweet Shortcrust Pastry* (see page 16)
- 2 large eggs + 2 large egg yolks, lightly beaten
- ⅔ cup (180 ml) milk
- ⅔ cup (180 ml) light (single) cream
- ½ cup (100 g) sugar
- 1 tablespoon all-purpose (plain) flour
- 1½ cups (375 g) wild black or sour cherries, pitted
- ⅓ cup (50 g) confectioners' (icing) sugar, to dust

Right: *Lemon meringue pie*

Orange marmalade pie

■ INGREDIENTS

- 1½ cups (225 g) all-purpose (plain) flour
- 1 teaspoon baking powder
- ¼ teaspoon salt
- 6 tablespoons butter
- ½ cup (100 g) sugar
- 1 tablespoon grated lime zest
- 2 large eggs
- 1 cup (360 g) chunky orange marmalade
- 1 tablespoon lime juice

Serves: 8-10; Preparation: 25 minutes; Cooking: 35 minutes; Level of difficulty: 1

Preheat the oven to 350°F/180°C/gas 4. • Sift the flour, baking powder, and salt into a large bowl. • Beat the butter, sugar, and lime zest in a medium bowl with an electric mixer at medium speed until creamy. • Add the eggs, one at a time, beating until just blended after each addition. • With mixer at low speed, gradually beat in the dry ingredients. • Press the mixture into a 10-inch (25-cm) pie plate with a removable bottom. • Mix the marmalade and lime juice. Spread over the dough, leaving a ½-inch (1-cm) border. • Bake for about 35 minutes, or until golden brown and the marmalade is bubbly. • Cool completely in the pan on a rack.

Fresh raspberry tart

■ INGREDIENTS

PASTRY

- 1⅔ cups (250 g) all-purpose (plain) flour
- ⅓ cup (70 g) sugar
- ¼ teaspoon salt
- ½ cup (125 g) butter
- 1 large egg
- 3–4 tablespoons water

TOPPING

- 1 lb (500 g) fresh raspberries, hulled
- ¾ cup (250 g) raspberry jelly, warmed
- 2 tablespoons confectioners' (icing) sugar (optional)

This tart is equally good when made with small or sliced strawberries.
Use the same weight of fruit and replace the raspberry jelly with strawberry jelly.

Serves: 6-8; Preparation: 30 minutes + 30 minutes to chill; Cooking: 30 minutes; Level of difficulty: 1

Pastry: Sift the flour, sugar, and salt into a large bowl. • Rub in the butter using your fingertips until the mixture resembles bread crumbs. • Add the egg and enough water to make a smooth dough. • Press into a 9-inch (23-cm) springform pan, forming a ½-inch (1-cm) thick rim around the edge. Prick all over with a fork. • Refrigerate for 30 minutes. • Preheat the oven to 375°F/190°C/gas 5. • Line with waxed paper and fill with dried beans or pie weights. Bake blind for 20 minutes. • Discard the paper and beans or pie weights. • Bake for 8 minutes more, or until lightly browned. • Let cool completely. • Arrange the raspberries over the top and drizzle with the warm jelly. • Dust with the confectioners' sugar, if liked.

Left: Orange marmalade pie

Caramelized grape tart

Serves: 6-8; Preparation: 20 minutes + time to prepare pastry; Cooking: 30 minutes; Level of difficulty: 2

If using homemade pastry, prepare the dough, adding ½ cup (75 g) ground almonds. Set aside to rest for 30 minutes. • Roll the dough out on a lightly floured work surface to a 12-inch (30-cm) round. • Fit the dough into a 9-inch (23-cm) pie plate, trimming the edges if needed. • Preheat the oven to 350°F/180°C/gas 4. • Sauté the grapes in the butter in a saucepan over medium heat for 5 minutes. • Increase the heat to high and add the brown sugar and rum. Stir well and remove from the heat. • Sprinkle the amaretti over the pastry. Add the grapes and their juices. Sprinkle with the remaining almonds. • Bake for about 25 minutes, or until lightly browned. • Cool completely in the pan on a rack.

■ INGREDIENTS

- 1 quantity *Shortcrust Pastry* (see page 16)
- 1 cup (150 g) almonds, finely ground
- 1½ lb (750 g) seedless white grapes, halved
- 1 tablespoon butter
- 1 tablespoon firmly packed brown sugar
- 1 tablespoon dark rum
- 5 amaretti cookies, crushed

Frosted caramel and walnut pie

Serves: 8-10; Preparation: 45 minutes + overnight to chill; Cooking: 20 minutes; Level of difficulty: 2

Chop the walnuts with the sugar in a food processor. • Beat the butter, confectioners' sugar, and walnut mixture in a large bowl until creamy. • Add the eggs, beating until just blended after each addition. • With mixer at low speed, gradually beat in the flour and salt. • Shape into a disk, wrap in plastic wrap (cling film), and refrigerate overnight. • Roll out the dough on a lightly floured work surface to a 12-inch (30-cm) round. Fit into a 10-inch (25-cm) pie plate, trimming the edges if needed. Refrigerate for 1 hour. • Preheat the oven to 350°F/180°C/gas 4. • Line with a sheet of waxed paper and fill with dried beans or pie weights. • Bake for 15 minutes. Discard the paper and beans or pie weights and let cool. • Caramel Filling: Stir the water, sugar, and corn syrup in a saucepan over medium heat until the sugar has dissolved. Wash down the pan sides with a pastry brush dipped in cold water to prevent sugar crystals from forming. Cook, without stirring, until the mixture reaches 238°F (114°C), or the soft-ball stage. • Remove from the heat and beat in the butter and cream. Fold in the walnuts and vanilla. Pour into the pastry shell. Cool to room temperature. • Refrigerate for 2 hours. • Spread with the chocolate ganache.

■ INGREDIENTS

PASTRY

- ½ cup (75 g) toasted walnuts
- ½ cup (100 g) sugar
- ⅔ cup (180 g) butter
- ⅔ cup (100 g) confectioners' (icing) sugar
- 2 large eggs
- 2⅔ cups (400 g) all-purpose (plain) flour
- ¼ teaspoon salt

CARAMEL FILLING

- 4 tablespoons cold water
- 1 cup (200 g) sugar
- 2 tablespoons corn (golden) syrup
- 4 tablespoons butter
- 6 tablespoons heavy (double) cream
- ¾ cup (100 g) toasted walnuts, finely chopped
- ½ teaspoon vanilla extract
- 1 quantity *Chocolate Ganache* (see page 32)

Right: Caramelized grape tart

Easy apricot tart

INGREDIENTS

- 1 quantity
Sweet Shortcrust Pastry
(see page 16)
- 1 *Italian Sponge Cake*
(see page 24),
thinly sliced
- 2 tablespoons raisin wine
or sweet dessert wine
- 1¼ lb (575 g) apricots,
peeled, pitted, and
thinly sliced
- 4 large egg yolks
- ¼ cup (50 g) sugar
- 2 tablespoons
confectioners' (icing)
sugar, to dust

Serves: 8-10; Preparation: 45 minutes + 1 hour to chill + time to prepare pastry; Cooking: 35 minutes; Level of difficulty: 2

Preheat the oven to 375°F/190°C/gas 5. • Roll the pastry out on a lightly floured work surface to a 12-inch (30-cm) round. • Fit into a 10-inch (25-cm) round cake pan, trimming the edges if needed. • Line with a sheet of waxed paper and fill with dried beans or pie weights. • Bake blind for 20 minutes. Discard the paper and beans or pie weights. Let cool completely. • Refrigerate for 1 hour. • Arrange the cake slices in the pastry shell. Drizzle with 1 tablespoon of wine. Arrange the apricot slices on top. • Beat the egg yolks, sugar, and remaining wine with an electric mixer at medium speed until pale and thick. • Spoon the egg mixture over the apricots. • Dust with the confectioners' sugar. • Bake for about 15 minutes more, or until lightly browned. • Cool the tart in the pan for 15 minutes. • Transfer to a serving plate and serve warm.

Berryfruit clafoutis

INGREDIENTS

- 3 large eggs
- ⅓ cup (70 g) firmly
packed brown sugar
- finely grated zest
of 1 lemon
- 1½ cups (375 ml) milk
- ½ cup (125 ml) lowfat
yogurt
- ½ cup (75 g) all-purpose
(plain) flour
- 8 oz (250 g) bilberries
- 8 oz (250 g) blackberries

Serves: 4-6; Preparation: 25 minutes; Cooking: 45 minutes; Level of difficulty: 1

Preheat the oven to 400°F/200°C/gas 6. • Line an 8-inch (20-cm) flan dish with waxed paper. • Beat the eggs, sugar, and lemon zest in a large bowl with an electric mixer at medium speed until pale and thick. • With mixer at low speed, mix in the milk, yogurt, and flour. • Arrange the bilberries and blackberries in the prepared dish. • Pour the egg mixture over the berry fruit. • Bake for about 45 minutes, or until browned and set. • Serve warm.

Left: Easy apricot tart

Special occasion crostata

This eyecatching crostata must be made with the best-quality fruit.
If you are using bananas, brush with lemon juice to prevent discoloring.

Serves: 6-8; Preparation: 40 minutes + 30 minutes to chill; Cooking: 30 minutes; Level of difficulty: 2

Sift the flour, sugar, and salt into a large bowl. Cut in the butter with your fingertips until the mixture resembles coarse crumbs. • Add the egg yolk and water and mix to form a smooth pastry. Shape into a ball, wrap in plastic wrap (cling film), and refrigerate for 30 minutes. • Roll the dough out on a lightly floured surface to a 12-inch (30-cm) round. Fit into a 9-inch (23-cm) tart pan, trimming the edges if needed. • Preheat the oven to 375°F/190°C/gas 5. • Line the pastry shell with a sheet of waxed paper and fill with dried beans or pie weights. • Bake for 15 minutes. Discard the paper and beans or pie weights. • Bake for about 15 minutes more, or until crisp. • Let cool completely. • Topping: Spoon the custard into the pastry case. Arrange the fruit on top and brush with the preserves.

■ INGREDIENTS

PASTRY
- 1 cup (150 g) all-purpose (plain) flour
- 2 tablespoons sugar
- ⅛ teaspoon salt
- 6 tablespoons cold butter, cut up
- 1 large egg yolk
- 1 tablespoon ice water

TOPPING
- 1 quantity *Vanilla Custard* (see page 28)
- 2 cups (500 g) sliced fresh fruit or whole berries
- ¼ cup (80 g) apricot preserves (jam), warmed

Upside-down peach crostata

Serves: 6-8; Preparation: 30 minutes; Cooking: 35 minutes; Level of difficulty: 1

Preheat the oven to 400°F/200°C/gas 6. • Sift the flour and salt into a large bowl and make a well in the center. • Beat in the butter, egg, milk, and sugar with an electric mixer at medium speed. Shape into a ball and set aside. • Arrange the peaches in a 9-inch (23-cm) pie plate and sprinkle with the remaining sugar. • Roll the dough out on a lightly floured surface into a 9-inch (23-cm) round. • Place over the peaches, pressing down gently with your fingertips. Prick all over with a fork. • Bake for about 35 minutes, or until lightly browned. • Cool the tart in the pan for 10 minutes. • Invert onto a serving plate, peach-side up. • With mixer at high speed, beat the cream, confectioners' sugar, and vanilla in a medium bowl until stiff. • Spoon the cream into a pastry bag and decorate the top. • Serve warm or at room temperature.

■ INGREDIENTS

PASTRY
- 2 cups (300 g) all-purpose (plain) flour
- ¼ teaspoon salt
- ½ cup (125 g) butter, melted
- 1 large egg
- 4 tablespoons milk
- 6 tablespoons sugar

FILLING
- 4 large yellow peaches, peeled and thinly sliced
- 4 tablespoons sugar
- ¾ cup (200 g) heavy (double) cream
- 1 tablespoon confectioners' (icing) sugar
- ½ teaspoon vanilla extract

Right: *Special occasion crostata*

Creamy fig tart

Serves: 10-12; Preparation: 30 minutes + 30 minutes to chill; Cooking: 30 minutes; Level of difficulty: 2

Pastry: Sift the flour and salt into a large bowl. • Rub in the butter with your fingertips until the mixture resembles bread crumbs. • Mix in the egg yolks, sugar, and vanilla to make a smooth dough. • Shape into a ball, wrap in plastic wrap (cling film), and refrigerate for 30 minutes. • Preheat the oven to 400°F/200°C/gas 6. • Custard: Bring the milk to a boil in a large saucepan over low heat. • Beat the egg yolks, 1 cup (150 g) of confectioners' sugar, and flour in a large bowl. Pour in the milk, beating well. • Return this mixture to the saucepan and cook over low heat, stirring constantly for 5 minutes, or until thickened. • Add the vanilla, remove from the heat, and let cool. • Butter an 11-inch (28-cm) pie plate. • Roll out the pastry on a floured surface to ¼ inch (5 mm) thick and use it to line the prepared pan. Prick with a fork. • Bake blind for 20 minutes. • Turn out onto a rack. Fill with the cooled custard and top with the figs. • Dust with the remaining confectioners' sugar. Brush the figs with the preserves.

INGREDIENTS

PASTRY
- 1⅔ cups (250 g) all-purpose (plain) flour
- ⅛ teaspoon salt
- ¾ cup (200 g) butter, cut into pieces
- 2 large egg yolks
- ½ cup (100 g) sugar
- 1 teaspoon vanilla extract

CUSTARD
- 2 cups (500 ml) milk
- 4 large egg yolks
- 1¼ cups (180 g) confectioners' (icing) sugar
- 2 tablespoons all-purpose (plain) flour
- 1 teaspoon vanilla extract
- 8 ripe figs, segmented
- 3 tablespoons apricot preserves (jam), melted

Pineapple and plum pie

Serves: 6-8; Preparation: 25 minutes + 1 hour 30 minutes to chill and macerate; Cooking: 35 minutes; Level of difficulty: 1

Topping: Place the pineapple and plums in a bowl with the brandy. Soak for 1 hour. • Butter and flour a 9-inch (23-cm) springform pan. • Pastry: Sift the flour and salt into a large bowl. • Rub in the butter with your fingertips until the mixture resembles bread crumbs. • Mix in the egg, sugar, and brandy to make a smooth dough. • Set a quarter of the dough aside and press the rest into the bottom and halfway up the sides of the prepared pan. Refrigerate for 30 minutes. • Preheat the oven to 375°F/190°C/gas 5. • Spread the jelly over the pastry and top with the pineapple and plum mixture. Drizzle any remaining liquid in the bowl over the fruit. • Use your hands to roll the remaining dough into long, thin sausage shapes. Place in a lattice pattern over the fruit. • Bake for about 35 minutes, or until lightly browned. • Cool the tart in the pan on a rack. Loosen and remove the pan sides. • Serve warm or at room temperature.

INGREDIENTS

TOPPING
- 4 rings pineapple, chopped
- 6 oz (180 g) dark red Italian-style plums, pitted and coarsely chopped
- 4 tablespoons brandy
- ¼ cup (80 g) pineapple jelly, warmed

PASTRY
- 1⅔ cups (400 g) all-purpose (plain) flour
- ¼ teaspoon salt
- ½ cup (125 g) butter
- 1 large egg
- ⅓ cup (70 g) sugar
- 1 tablespoon brandy

Right: Creamy fig tart

Autumnal pear tart

Serves: 8-10; Preparation: 25 minutes + time to prepare the pastry + 30 minutes to chill; Cooking: 25 minutes; Level of difficulty: 1

Prepare the pastry and set aside to chill. • Preheat the oven to 350°F/ 180°C/gas 4. • Butter a 10-inch (25-cm) springform pan. • Roll three-quarters of the dough out on a lightly floured work surface to ½-inch (1-cm) thick and use it to line the prepared pan. • Cut the pears into small cubes and sprinkle with the sugar and cinnamon. • Spread the pear mixture over the pastry. • Roll out the remaining pastry and cut into thin strips. Arrange the strips in a lattice pattern on top of the filling. • Bake for about 25 minutes, or until the pastry is golden brown. • Serve warm.

- 1 quantity
  Sweet Shortcrust Pastry
  (see page 16)
- 2 large firm-ripe pears
- ½ cup (100 g) sugar
- ⅛ teaspoon ground
  cinnamon

Crunchy honey crostata

■ INGREDIENTS

Serves: 4-6; Preparation: 25 minutes + 30 minutes to chill; Cooking: 25 minutes; Level of difficulty: 2

Sift the flour and salt into a large bowl. • Stir in the sugar, egg, and oil to make a soft dough. Shape into a ball, wrap in plastic wrap (cling film), and refrigerate for 30 minutes. • Filling: Stir the honey, amaretti crumbs, almonds, pine nuts, lemon zest, and butter in a saucepan over low heat. • Roll the dough out on a lightly floured work surface to a 10-inch (25-cm) round. • Preheat the oven to 400°F/200°C/gas 6. • Fit the dough into an 8-inch (20-cm) springform pan, leaving the long edges draped over the sides. • Spoon the filling into the pastry and fold the edges over onto the pie. • Bake for about 25 minutes, or until golden brown. • Loosen and remove the pan sides. • Serve warm.

- 1⅓ cups (200 g) all-purpose (plain) flour
- ¼ teaspoon salt
- ¼ cup (50 g) sugar
- 1 large egg
- 2 tablespoons extra-virgin olive oil

FILLING
- ¼ cup (60 g) honey
- ½ cup (60 g) crushed amaretti cookies
- ⅓ cup (40 g) almonds, coarsely chopped
- 2 tablespoons pine nuts
- 1 tablespoon finely grated lemon zest
- 4 tablespoons butter

Right: *Autumnal pear tart*

Creamy lemon tart

PASTRY

- 2⅓ cups (350 g) all-purpose (plain) flour
- ¼ teaspoon salt
- ½ cup (100 g) sugar
- ½ cup (125 g) butter
- 3 large eggs
- ½ teaspoon vanilla extract

LEMON FILLING

- 4 tablespoons butter
- 2 tablespoons all-purpose (plain) flour
- juice of 3 lemons
- 2 cups (500 ml) milk
- ½ cup (100 g) sugar

Serves: 6-8; Preparation: 45 minutes + 1 hour to chill; Cooking: 45 minutes; Level of difficulty: 2

Sift the flour and salt into a large bowl. Stir in the sugar. • Rub in the butter with your fingertips until the mixture resembles coarse crumbs. • Mix in the eggs and vanilla to form a stiff dough. • Shape into a ball, wrap in plastic wrap (cling film), and refrigerate for 1 hour. • Preheat the oven to 350°F/180°C/gas 4. • Butter a 9-inch (23-cm) springform pan. • Lemon Filling: Melt the butter in a medium saucepan and mix in the flour. • Remove from heat and gradually mix in the lemon juice, milk, and sugar. Return to the heat and bring to a boil. Boil for 1-2 minutes, stirring constantly. • Roll out three-quarters of the dough on a lightly floured work surface to ½-inch (1-cm) thick and use it to line the prepared pan. • Pour the filling into the pastry case. • Roll out the remaining dough and cut into thin strips. Arrange the strips in a lattice pattern on top of the filling. • Bake for about 45 minutes, or until the filling has set and the pastry is lightly browned. • Serve at room temperature.

Peach and banana crostata

- 1½ cups (225 g) all-purpose (plain) flour
- ¼ teaspoon salt
- ⅓ cup (70 g) sugar
- 6 tablespoons butter
- 1 large egg yolk

- 1 quantity *Vanilla Custard* (see page 28)
- 1 large banana, peeled and sliced
- 2 medium peaches, peeled and sliced
- 2 tablespoons all-purpose (plain) flour
- 1 tablespoon butter
- 2 tablespoons sugar
- ½ teaspoon ground cinnamon

Serves: 4-6; Preparation: 25 minutes + 30 minutes to chill; Cooking: 35 minutes; Level of difficulty: 1

Sift the flour and salt into a large bowl. Stir in the sugar. • Rub in the butter with your fingertips until the mixture resembles coarse crumbs. • Mix in the egg yolk to form a stiff dough. • Press into the bottom and sides of a 9-inch (23-cm) springform pan. Refrigerate for 30 minutes. • Preheat the oven to 400°F/200°C/gas 6. • Spoon the custard into the pastry. Top with the banana and peaches. • Mix the flour, butter, sugar, and cinnamon in a small bowl. Sprinkle over the fruit. • Bake for about 35 minutes, or until set. • Loosen and remove the pan sides. Serve warm.

Left: *Creamy lemon tart*

Peach pie

Serves: 8-10; Preparation: 45 minutes + time to prepare pastry; Cooking: 35 minutes; Level of difficulty: 1

Preheat the oven to 375°F/190°C/gas 5. • Roll the pastry out on a lightly floured work surface to a 12-inch (30-cm) round. • Fit into a 10-inch (25-cm) round cake pan, trimming the edges if needed. • Line the pastry shell with a sheet of waxed paper and fill with dried beans or pie weights. • Bake blind for 20 minutes. Discard the paper and beans or pie weights. • Cool completely in the pan. • Refrigerate until chilled. • Arrange the cake slices in the pastry shell. Drizzle with 1 tablespoon of wine. Arrange the peach slices on top. • Beat the egg yolks, sugar, and remaining wine with an electric mixer at medium speed until pale and thick. Spoon over the peaches. • Dust with the confectioners' sugar. • Bake for about 15 minutes, or until lightly browned. • Cool the tart in the pan for 15 minutes. • Transfer onto a serving plate. Serve warm.

■ INGREDIENTS

- 1 quantity *Sweet Shortcrust Pastry* (see page 16)
- 1 *Italian Sponge Cake* (see page 24), thinly sliced
- 2 tablespoons raisin wine or sweet dessert wine
- 1¼ lb (575 g) peaches, peeled, pitted, and thinly sliced
- 4 large egg yolks
- ¼ cup (50 g) sugar
- 2 tablespoons confectioners' (icing) sugar, to dust

Apple custard pie

Serves: 6-8; Preparation: 25 minutes + 30 minutes to chill; Cooking: 35 minutes; Level of difficulty: 1

Sift the flour and salt into a large bowl. Stir in the sugar. • Rub in the butter with your fingertips until the mixture resembles coarse crumbs. • Mix in the egg and brandy to form a stiff dough. • Press into the bottom and halfway up the sides of a 9-inch (23-cm) springform pan. Refrigerate for 30 minutes. • Preheat the oven to 400°F/200°C/gas 6. • Topping: Arrange the apple slices in circles on the pastry. • Bake for about 25 minutes, or until lightly browned. • Beat the egg, egg yolk, sugar, cornstarch, vanilla, and salt in a medium saucepan. Gradually pour in the milk. Place over medium heat and stir until the mixture thickens. • Spoon the cream over the apples in the pastry. • Bake for about 10 minutes more, or until golden brown. • Loosen and remove the pan sides. Serve warm or at room temperature.

■ INGREDIENTS

PASTRY
- 1⅔ cups (400 g) all-purpose (plain) flour
- ¼ teaspoon salt
- ⅓ cup (70 g) sugar
- ½ cup (125 g) butter
- 1 large egg
- 1 tablespoon brandy

TOPPING
- 2 medium apples, peeled, cored, and cut into wedges
- 1 large egg + 1 large egg yolk
- ⅓ cup (70 g) sugar
- 2 teaspoons cornstarch (cornflour)
- 1 teaspoon vanilla extract
- ¼ teaspoon salt
- ⅔ cup (180 ml) milk

Right: Peach pie

Blackberry crostata

Serves: 6-8: Preparation: 40 minutes; Cooking: 40 minutes; Level of difficulty: 2

Preheat the oven to 350°F/180°C/gas 4. • Butter a 10-inch (25-cm) springform pan. • Wash and dry the blackberries. Mix the berries, 4 tablespoons of sugar, and half the mint leaves in a large saucepan. Cook over medium heat for 15 minutes, or until the blackberries have softened slightly. • Roll the pastry out on a lightly floured work surface and use it to line the prepared pan. • Sprinkle with the hazelnuts and top with the blackberries. • Beat the egg, remaining sugar, and cream in a large bowl with an electric mixer at high speed until pale and thick. Pour the mixture over the blackberries. • Bake for about 40 minutes, or until set. • Garnish with the remaining mint leaves.

INGREDIENTS

- 1 lb (500 g) blackberries
- ½ cup (100 g) sugar
- 1 sprig fresh mint
- 1 quantity *Sweet Shortcrust Pastry* (see page 16)
- 1 cup (100 g) chopped hazelnuts
- 1 large egg
- 3 tablespoons heavy (double) cream

Summer berry pie

Serves: 6-8: Preparation: 30 minutes + 30 minutes to chill; Cooking: 50 minutes; Level of difficulty: 2

Sift the flour and salt into a large bowl. • Rub in the butter and lard with your fingertips until the mixture resembles coarse crumbs. Mix in the water to form a stiff dough. • Set one-third of the dough aside and roll the rest into a disk large enough to line an 8-inch (20-cm) springform pan. Place in the pan, trimming the edges if needed. Refrigerate for 30 minutes. • Preheat the oven to 375°F/190°C/gas 5. • Filling: Mix the crumbs, sugar, raisins, almonds, candied peel, cinnamon, nutmeg, cloves, and liqueur in a large bowl. • Spread two-thirds of the crumb mixture over the pastry shell. Top with the apple and pear. Sprinkle with the remaining crumb mixture. • Roll the remaining dough out into a disk large enough to cover the top of the pie. Fit into the pan and seal the edges. Use a sharp knife to make five long openings in a star shape in the top. • Bake for about 50 minutes, or until lightly browned. • Loosen and remove the pan sides. Serve warm.

INGREDIENTS

PASTRY
- 1½ cups (225 g) all-purpose (plain) flour
- ½ teaspoon salt
- 4 tablespoons butter
- 4 tablespoons lard or vegetable shortening
- 2 tablespoons water

FILLING
- ½ cup (60 g) graham cracker (digestive biscuit) crumbs
- ⅓ cup (70 g) sugar
- ⅓ cup (90 g) raisins
- ⅔ cup (70 g) almonds, chopped
- ⅓ cup (60 g) chopped candied peel
- 1 teaspoon cinnamon
- ½ teaspoon nutmeg
- ¼ teaspoon cloves
- 3 tablespoons orange liqueur or brandy
- 1 small apple, peeled, cored, and thinly sliced
- 1 small pear, peeled, cored, and thinly sliced

Right: *Blackberry crostata*

Banana coconut tart

Serves: 4-6: Preparation: 40 minutes + time to prepare pastry; Cooking: 25 minutes; Level of difficulty: 2

Preheat the oven to 350°F/180°C/gas 4. • Roll the pastry out on a lightly floured work surface to ½-inch (1-cm) thick and use it to line a 10-inch (25-cm) springform pan. Prick all over with a fork. • Bake blind for 15 minutes. • Filling: Beat the eggs in a large bowl until frothy. Mix in the coconut and ½ cup (100 g) of sugar. • Bring the milk to a boil and gradually add the coconut mixture. • Boil for 2 minutes, until the mixture begins to thicken. • Remove from the heat and mix in the rum. • Pour the filling into the pastry case and top with the bananas. • Bake for about 10 minutes, or until golden brown. • Serve warm.

■ INGREDIENTS

- 1 quantity
Sweet Shortcrust Pastry
(see page 16)

FILLING

- 2 large eggs
- ½ cup (60 g) shredded (desiccated) coconut
- ¾ cup (150 g) sugar
- ½ cup (125 ml) milk
- 4 tablespoons rum
- 5 bananas, sliced

Coconut pie

Orange-flower water can be found in gourmet food stores.

Serves: 4-6; Preparation: 30 minutes + 12 hours to soak; Cooking: 30 minutes; Level of difficulty: 2

Topping: Place the coconut and 4 tablespoons of water in a medium bowl. Set aside for 12 hours. • Pastry: Sift the flour and salt into a large bowl. • Stir in the sugar. • Rub in the butter with your fingertips until the mixture resembles coarse crumbs. Mix in the egg yolks to form a stiff dough. • Press into a 9-inch (23-cm) springform pan. Refrigerate for 30 minutes. • Preheat the oven to 375°F/190°C/gas 5. • Line the pastry with a sheet of waxed paper and fill with dried beans or pie weights. Bake blind for 20 minutes. • Discard the paper and beans or pie weights. • Filling: Beat the egg yolks, flour, sugar, and salt in a saucepan. • Bring the milk to a boil in a pan over medium heat. Gradually pour it into the egg mixture. Place the saucepan over low heat and stir until thick. Add the orange-flower water. • Pour the filling into the pastry shell. • Topping: Boil the remaining water and sugar in a saucepan for 2 minutes. Add the coconut and lemon juice and cook for 2 minutes, stirring often. • Spread over the filling. • Bake for about 10 minutes, or until browned. • Cool the tart completely in the pan. Loosen and remove the pan sides to serve.

■ INGREDIENTS

TOPPING

- 1 cup (125 g) shredded (desiccated) coconut
- 1⅔ cups (430 ml) water
- ¼ cup (50 g) sugar
- 1 tablespoon lemon juice

PASTRY

- 1½ cups (225 g) all-purpose (plain) flour
- ¼ teaspoon salt
- ⅓ cup (70 g) sugar
- ½ cup (125 g) cold butter
- 2 large egg yolks

FILLING

- 3 large egg yolks
- 2 tablespoons all-purpose (plain) flour
- ⅓ cup (70 g) sugar
- ¼ teaspoon salt
- 1¼ cups (310 ml) milk
- 2 tablespoons orange-flower water

Right: Banana coconut tart

Caramel apple pie

- 2½ lb (1.25 kg) Golden Delicious apples
- juice of ½ lemon
- 1¼ cups (250 g) brown sugar
- ½ cup (125 g) butter
- 1 quantity *Sweet Shortcrust Pastry* (see page 16)
- 1 quantity *Pastry Cream* (see page 28)

Serves: 6-8; Preparation: 45 minutes + time to make pastry and pastry cream; Cooking: 40 minutes; Level of difficulty: 2

Preheat the oven to 350°F/180°C/gas 4. • Peel, core, and dice the apples. • Cook the apples with the lemon juice and half the sugar in the butter in a saucepan over medium heat until softened. • Roll out the dough and use it to line a 10-inch (25-cm) springform pan. Prick the base with a fork. • Bake blind for 30 minutes. • Spoon the pastry cream into the pastry case and top with the cooked apples. • Sprinkle with the remaining sugar and broil until the sugar caramelizes. • Serve hot.

Light almond tart

Serves: 6-8; Preparation: 30 minutes; Cooking: 45 minutes; Level of difficulty: 1

Preheat the oven to 350°F/180°C/gas 4. • Butter a 12-inch (30-cm) flan pan and sprinkle with the slivered almonds. • Chop the almonds with 1 tablespoon of sugar in a food processor until finely ground. • Sift the flour and cornstarch into a large bowl. • Stir in the ground almonds. • Beat the egg whites and remaining sugar in a large bowl with an electric mixer at high speed until stiff, glossy peaks form. Gently fold in dry ingredients and melted butter. • Pour the mixture into the prepared pan. • Bake for about 45 minutes, or until the filling is set. • Let cool completely.

■ INGREDIENTS

• 1 cup (120 g) slivered almonds
• ½ cup (60 g) almonds
• 1 cup (200 g) sugar
• ⅓ cup (50 g) all-purpose (plain) flour
• ⅓ cup (50 g) cornstarch (cornflour)
• 6 large egg whites
• ½ cup (125 g) butter, melted

Plum and yogurt tart

Serves: 6-8; Preparation: 45 minutes + time to make pastry + 1 hour to chill; Cooking: 35 minutes; Level of difficulty: 2

Preheat the oven to 400°F/200°C/gas 6. • Butter a 10-inch (25-cm) pie plate. • Roll the dough out on a lightly floured work surface to a 12-inch (30-cm) round. Fit into the prepared pan. • Line with waxed paper and fill with dried beans or pie weights. • Bake blind for 15 minutes. • Discard the paper and beans or pie weights. Bake for about 5 minutes more, or until crisp. • Let cool completely. • Yogurt Cream: Sprinkle the gelatin over the water in a saucepan. Let stand 1 minute. Stir over low heat until the gelatin has completely dissolved. • Mix the yogurt and gelatin in a large bowl until thickened. • Filling: Bring the sugar, water, and lemon juice to a boil over medium heat in a large saucepan. Add the plums and cook over low heat for 10 minutes. • Drain the plums. • Brush the jelly over the pastry. • Spoon the yogurt cream over the top. Spoon the plums over. • Warm the apricot preserves and liqueur in a saucepan over low heat until liquid. Brush over the plums. • Beat the cream with an electric mixer at high speed until stiff. Spoon into a pastry bag and decorate the top.

■ INGREDIENTS

• 1 quantity *Sweet Shortcrust Pastry* (see page 16)

YOGURT CREAM
• 1½ teaspoons gelatin
• 2 tablespoons cold water
• ½ cup (125 ml) plain yogurt

FILLING
• ¾ cup (150 g) sugar
• 2 cups (500 ml) water
• juice of 1 lemon
• 1¾ lb (850 g) plums, pitted
• 2 tablespoons raspberry jelly
• ¼ cup (80 g) apricot preserves (jam)
• 1 tablespoon fruit liqueur
• ⅔ cup (180 ml) heavy (double) cream

Right: Light almond tart

Peach tarte tatin

In the late 19th century, French hotel cook Stéphanie Tatin was so busy that she baked her delicious apple pie upside down. She served it anyway, straight from the oven, and it was immensely popular. This equally luscious version should always be served warm.

Serves: 6-8; Preparation: 30 minutes + 30 minutes to chill; Cooking: 30 minutes; Level of difficulty: 1

Sift the flour and salt into a large bowl. • Rub in the butter with your fingertips until the mixture resembles coarse crumbs. • Mix in the egg to form a stiff dough. • Shape the dough into a ball, wrap in plastic wrap (cling film), and refrigerate for 30 minutes. • Preheat the oven to 350°F/180°C/gas 4. • Butter an 10-inch (25-cm) baking pan. Sprinkle with sugar. • Cut the peaches in half and remove the pits. Peel and cut into slices. Arrange the peaches in the pan. Sprinkle with the sugar. • Roll the pastry out on a lightly floured work surface to a 12-inch (30-cm) round and use it to cover the fruit in the prepared pan. • Bake for 30 minutes, or until the pastry is golden brown. • Invert, peach-side up, on a serving dish. Serve immediately.

■ INGREDIENTS

PASTRY
• 1⅓ cups (200 g) all-purpose (plain) flour
• ⅛ teaspoon salt
• ½ cup (125 g) butter
• 1 large egg

TOPPING
• ½ cup (100 g) sugar
• 2 lb (1 kg) peaches

Upside-down cherry pie

Serves: 6-8; Preparation: 30 minutes + 30 minutes to chill; Cooking: 25 minutes; Level of difficulty: 2

Stir together the flour, sugar, lemon zest, and salt in a large bowl. • Use a pastry blender to cut in the butter until the mixture resembles coarse crumbs. • Shape into a ball, wrap in plastic wrap (cling film), and refrigerate for 30 minutes. • Dust a 9-inch (23-cm) pie plate with the confectioners' sugar. • Preheat the oven to 400°F/200°C/gas 6. • Place the cherries in the plate with their rounded, stalkless sides upward. • Roll the dough out on a lightly floured surface into a 9-inch (23-cm) round. Place over the cherries, pressing down gently with your fingertips. • Bake for about 25 minutes, or until the pastry is golden brown. • Invert, cherry-side up, on a serving dish. Let cool completely.

■ INGREDIENTS

• 1 cup (150 g) all-purpose (plain) flour
• ¼ cup (50 g) sugar
• 1 tablespoon finely grated lemon zest
• ¼ teaspoon salt
• ½ cup (125 g) cold butter, cut up
• ⅓ cup (50 g) confectioners' (icing) sugar
• 2 cups (500 g) ripe fresh sweet cherries, pitted

Right: *Peach tarte tatin*

Red currant crostata

INGREDIENTS

PASTRY
- 1⅓ cups (200 g) all-purpose (plain) flour
- ⅓ cup (50 g) cornstarch (cornflour)
- ⅛ teaspoon salt
- finely grated zest of ½ lemon
- ½ cup (125 g) butter
- 1 large egg
- 1 teaspoon vanilla extract

- 1 quantity *Vanilla Custard* (see page 26)
- 10 oz (300 g) red currants, cleaned

Serves: 6-8; Preparation: 30 minutes + 30 minutes to chill; Cooking: 35 minutes; Level of difficulty: 2

Pastry: Sift the flour, cornstarch, and salt into a large bowl. Stir in the lemon zest. • Rub in the butter with your fingertips until the mixture resembles coarse crumbs. • Mix in the egg and vanilla to form a smooth dough. • Shape the dough into a ball, wrap in plastic wrap (cling film), and refrigerate for 30 minutes. • Preheat the oven to 400°F/200°C/gas 6. • Butter and flour an 8-inch (20-cm) pie plate. • Roll the pastry out on a lightly floured surface to ½ inch (1 cm) thick and use it to line the prepared pan. Fill with dried beans or pie weights. • Bake blind for 15 minutes. • Discard the paper and beans or pie weights. Bake for 5 minutes more. • Prepare the custard and let cool completely. • Pour the custard into the pastry case. Cover with the red currants. • Bake for 10 minutes. • Serve warm or at room temperature.

Blackberry pie

INGREDIENTS

- 1 quantity *Sweet Shortcrust Pastry* (see page 16)
- 1½ cups (360 g) blackberry preserves (jam)
- 1 large egg yolk

We have suggested blackberry preserves as a topping, but other flavored preserves can be used with equal success.

Serves: 6-8; Preparation: 20 minutes + time to make the pastry; Cooking: 30 minutes; Level of difficulty: 1

Preheat the oven to 375°F/190°C/gas 5. • Prepare the pastry. • Butter and flour a 10-inch (25-cm) pie plate. • Break off two-thirds of the dough and roll it out so that it is just large enough to line the prepared pan. Leave a narrow border of the pastry hanging over the sides. • Spread the blackberry preserves evenly over the pastry. • Roll out the remaining pastry into a square sheet. Use a fluted pastry wheel to cut it into ½-inch (1-cm) wide strips. Place over the preserves in a lattice pattern. Fold the overhanging pastry border over the ends of the lattice to form a rolled edging. • Beat the egg yolk and brush over the top of the pie. • Bake for 30 minutes. • Serve warm.

Left: *Red currant crostata*

Strawberries and cream pie

Serves: 6-8; Preparation: 30 minutes + time to make pastry; Cooking: 1 hour 10 minutes; Level of difficulty: 2

Preheat the oven to 375°F/190°C/gas 5. • Butter a 10-inch (25-cm) pie pan. • Roll the pastry out on a lightly floured work surface into a 12-inch (30-cm) round. • Fit into the prepared pan, trimming the edges if needed. Prick all over with a fork. • Line with waxed paper and fill with dried beans or pie weights. • Bake blind for 25 minutes. • Discard the paper and beans or pie weights. • Lower the oven temperature to 300°F/150°C/gas 3. • Bake for 10 minutes more, or until crisp. • Arrange the strawberries in the pastry shell. • Beat the milk, cream, eggs and egg yolk, and sugar in a large bowl. • Spoon the egg mixture over the strawberries. • Bake for about 35 minutes, or until set. • Transfer to a serving plate. • Serve warm.

■ INGREDIENTS

- 1 quantity *Sweet Shortcrust Pastry* (see page 16)
- 1 lb (500 g) strawberries, hulled and sliced
- 2 cups (500 ml) milk
- ½ cup (125 ml) light (single) cream
- 2 large eggs + 1 large egg yolk, lightly beaten
- ¼ cup (50 g) sugar

Pear, almond, and cornmeal pie

Serves: 6-8; Preparation: 30 minutes + 1 hour to chill; Cooking: 50 minutes; Level of difficulty: 2

Stir together the flour, cornmeal, and salt in a large bowl. Stir in ½ cup (100 g) of sugar. • Rub in the butter with your fingertips until the mixture resembles coarse crumbs. • Mix in the egg yolks to form a dough. • Roll out two-thirds of the pastry to line the bottom and sides of a buttered 9-inch (23-cm) pie plate. • Refrigerate for 1 hour. • Rinse the pears and dry well. Peel and core them. Cut lengthwise into quarters. Cut each quarter lengthwise into 3 slices. • Place the pears in a saucepan. Add ¼ cup (50 g) of sugar, the wine, and cinnamon and cook gently over medium heat for 10 minutes. • Pour off the cooking liquid and sprinkle with the cocoa. Let cool. • Preheat the oven to 400°F/200°C/gas 6. • Sprinkle the pastry shell with the crumbled amaretti cookies and arrange the pears on top. • Roll out the remaining dough into a round slightly larger than the diameter of the pie pan. Place this on top of the pears, pinching the pastry edges together to seal. Pierce a few little holes in the pie lid with a fine skewer. • Bake for about 40 minutes, or until golden brown. • Let cool completely. Serve at room temperature.

■ INGREDIENTS

PASTRY

- 2 cups (300 g) all-purpose (plain) flour
- 1 cup (150 g) fine yellow cornmeal
- ⅛ teaspoon salt
- ⅔ cup (180 g) butter
- 3 large egg yolks

FILLING

- 2 lb (1 kg) firm cooking pears
- ¾ cup (150 g) sugar
- 1¼ cups (310 ml) full-bodied dry red wine
- ⅛ teaspoon ground cinnamon
- 2 tablespoons unsweetened cocoa powder
- 12 amaretti cookies, coarsely crushed

Right: Strawberries and cream pie

Apple pie

Serves: 6-8; Preparation: 40 minutes + 30 minutes to chill; Cooking: 45 minutes; Level of difficulty: 1

Pastry: Sift the flour and salt into a large bowl. Rub in the butter and lard with your fingertips until the mixture resembles coarse crumbs. Mix in the lemon juice and enough water to form a stiff dough. Shape the dough into a ball, wrap in plastic wrap (cling film), and refrigerate for 30 minutes. • Preheat the oven to 350°F/180°C/gas 4. • Butter a 10-inch (25-cm) pie plate. • Set aside one-quarter of the dough. Roll out the remaining dough on a lightly floured work surface to ½-inch (1-cm) thick and use it to line the prepared pan. • Peel and core the apples. Cut into thin slices and arrange in the pastry case. Sprinkle with the brown sugar, nutmeg, and orange and lemon zests. Drizzle with the melted butter. • Roll out the remaining pastry to a 10-inch (25-cm) round and place on top of the filling. • Sprinkle with the sugar. • Bake for about 45 minutes, or until lightly browned. • Serve warm.

■ INGREDIENTS

PASTRY
- 2 cups (300 g) all-purpose (plain) flour
- ¼ teaspoon salt
- 6 tablespoons butter
- 3 tablespoons lard
- juice of ½ lemon
- 4 tablespoons cold water

FILLING
- 4 medium apples
- ⅓ cup (70 g) brown sugar
- ⅛ teaspoon freshly grated nutmeg
- 1 tablespoon finely grated orange zest
- 1 tablespoon finely grated lemon zest
- 3 tablespoons butter, melted
- ⅓ cup (70 g) sugar

Almond and grape crostata

Serves: 6-8; Preparation: 10 minutes + time to make the pastry; Cooking: 35 minutes; Level of difficulty: 1

Preheat the oven to 350°F/180°C/gas 4. • Prepare the pastry, working 2 tablespoons of sugar and half the ground almonds into the dough. Add extra water if the dough is too stiff. • Rinse the grapes and cut them in half. Sauté the grapes in the butter in a large saucepan over medium heat for 4-5 minutes. • Turn the heat up to high and add the sugar and rum. Stir quickly and remove from heat. • Sprinkle the pastry with the amaretti cookies. Spoon the grapes and their juice over the top. Sprinkle with the remaining almonds. • Bake for 30 minutes. • Serve warm.

■ INGREDIENTS

- 1 quantity *Sweet Shortcrust Pastry* (see page 16)
- 2 tablespoons sugar
- ½ cup (75 g) finely ground almonds
- 1¾ lb (850 g) white grapes
- 2 tablespoons butter
- 2 tablespoons brown sugar
- 2 tablespoons dark rum
- 6 amaretti cookies, crumbled
- 1 tablespoon butter

Right: *Apple pie*

Lemon almond pie

- 1 quantity *Sweet Shortcrust Pastry* (see page 16)
- 2 large eggs + 2 large egg whites
- ⅛ teaspoon salt
- 1 cup (200 g) sugar
- 1½ cups (225 g) ground almonds
- 6 tablespoons butter, melted
- finely ground zest and juice of 2 lemons
- 10 pieces candied peel
- 2 tablespoons confectioners' (icing) sugar

Serves: 6-8; Preparation: 15 minutes + time to make the pastry; Cooking: 40 minutes; Level of difficulty: 1

Preheat the oven to 350°F/180°C/gas 4. • Prepare the pastry. • Roll the pastry out so that it is large enough to line a fairly shallow 10-inch (25-cm) pie pan. Butter and flour the pan and line it with the pastry. Prick well with a fork. • Beat the egg whites and salt in a large bowl with an electric mixer at high speed until stiff. • Beat the eggs and sugar in a large bowl until frothy. Gently fold in the almonds, egg whites, butter, and lemon zest and juice. • Spread this mixture evenly over the dough. • Bake for 40 minutes. • Decorate with the candied peel and sprinkle with the confectioners' sugar. • Serve chilled.

Strawberry almond crostata

Serves: 6-8; Preparation: 30 minutes + 30 minutes to chill; Cooking: 35 minutes; Level of difficulty: 2

Sift 1 cup (150 g) flour, ¼ cup (30 g) confectioners' sugar, baking powder, and salt into a large bowl. Add the butter, wine, egg yolk, and lemon zest. Shape into a ball, wrap in plastic wrap (cling film), and refrigerate for 30 minutes. • Preheat the oven to 400°F/200°C/gas 6. • Butter a 9-inch (23-cm) pie pan. • Beat the egg, remaining confectioners' sugar, remaining flour, and vanilla in a saucepan. Gradually add the milk, whisking constantly. Bring to a boil over medium heat and cook, stirring constantly, until thickened. • Remove from the heat and add the liqueur. • Roll out the dough on a lightly floured work surface to an 11-inch (28-cm) round. Fit into the prepared pan, trimming the edges to fit. Prick all over with a fork. • Sprinkle with the amaretti crumbs, drizzle with the amaretto, and spread with the cream. • Arrange the strawberries in the cream. • Bake for about 35 minutes, or until lightly browned. • Cool in the pan on a rack. • Brush the preserves over the strawberries. • Serve warm or at room temperature.

■ INGREDIENTS

- 1⅓ cups (200 g) all-purpose (plain) flour
- ⅔ cup (100 g) confectioners' (icing) sugar
- ½ teaspoon baking powder
- ¼ teaspoon salt
- ½ cup (125 g) butter, melted
- 2 tablespoons white wine
- 1 large egg yolk + 1 large egg
- 1 tablespoon finely grated lemon zest
- ½ teaspoon vanilla extract
- ⅔ cup (180 ml) milk
- 1 tablespoon orange liqueur
- ½ cup (60 g) amaretti cookies, crushed
- 6 tablespoons amaretto
- 20 medium strawberries, hulled and sliced
- ½ cup (130 ml) strawberry preserves (jam), warmed

Strawberry and lemon tart

Serves: 6-8; Preparation: 30 minutes; Cooking: 35 minutes; Level of difficulty: 2

Preheat the oven to 375°F/190°C/gas 5. • Butter a 10-inch (25-cm) round cake pan. • Beat the eggs and sugar in a large bowl with an electric mixer at high speed until pale and thick. • Fold the flour and baking powder into the batter. • Mix the oil and milk in a small bowl. Add the lemon zest. Mix the oil mixture into the batter. • Spoon half the batter into the prepared pan. Arrange half the strawberries on top. • Spoon in the remaining batter. Arrange the remaining strawberries on top. • Bake for about 35 minutes, or until a toothpick inserted into the center comes out clean. • Transfer to a serving plate and let cool completely. • Dust with the confectioners' sugar. Serve with whipped cream.

■ INGREDIENTS

- 3 large eggs
- ¾ cup (150 g) sugar
- 1⅓ cups (200 g) all-purpose (plain) flour
- 2 teaspoons baking powder
- 2 tablespoons oil
- 4 tablespoons milk
- finely grated zest of 1 lemon
- 1½ cups (375 g) strawberries, hulled
- confectioners' (icing) sugar, to dust
- whipped cream, to serve

Right: *Strawberry almond crostata*

Apple and raisin pie

■ INGREDIENTS

- 1 lb (500 g) apples
- grated zest and juice of 1 lemon
- 1 cup (150 g) all-purpose (plain) flour
- ¼ cup (50 g) sugar
- 3 large eggs
- 7 tablespoons milk
- 1 tablespoon rum
- 2 tablespoons butter, melted
- ½ cup (60 g) golden raisins (sultanas)
- 2 tablespoons confectioners' (icing) sugar, to dust

Serves: 4-6; Preparation: 30 minutes; Cooking: 45 minutes; Level of difficulty: 1

Preheat the oven to 325°F/170°C/gas 3. • Butter and flour a 9-inch (23-cm) springform pan. • Peel and core the apples. Slice them thinly and drizzle with the lemon juice. • Sift the flour into a large bowl. • Stir in the sugar, lemon zest, and eggs. • Gradually mix in the milk and rum. Add the butter, apples, and raisins until well blended. • Spoon the batter into the prepared pan. • Bake for about 45 minutes, or until a toothpick inserted into the center comes out clean. • Loosen the pan sides and place on a serving dish. Dust half the pie with the confectioners' sugar.

Cornmeal apple pie

■ INGREDIENTS

- 2 cups (300 g) all-purpose (plain) flour
- 1 cup (150 g) finely ground cornmeal
- 1 teaspoon baking powder
- 2 large eggs
- 1 cup (200 g) sugar
- ¾ cup (200 g) extra-virgin olive oil
- 4 tablespoons dry white wine
- 1 apple
- juice of ½ lemon
- 2 tablespoons brown sugar

Serves: 6-8; Preparation: 20 minutes; Cooking: 50 minutes; Level of difficulty: 1

Preheat the oven to 350°F/180°C/gas 4. • Butter and flour a 9-inch (23-cm) cake pan. • Stir together the flour, cornmeal, and baking powder in a large bowl. • Beat the eggs and sugar in a large bowl with an electric mixer until creamy. • Mix in the dry ingredients. • Gradually mix in the oil and wine and continue beating until the mixture is smooth and creamy. • Spoon the batter into the prepared pan. • Peel and core the apple and slice it thinly. Drizzle with the lemon juice. Arrange the apple slices on top of the tart and sprinkle with the brown sugar. • Bake for about 50 minutes, or until a toothpick inserted into the center comes out clean. • Serve at room temperature.

Left: *Apple and raisin pie*

Dark chocolate pie

Serves: 6-8; Preparation: 35 minutes + 1 hour to chill; Cooking: 15 minutes; Level of difficulty: 1

Pastry: Mix the egg yolks with the vanilla in a small bowl. • Process the almonds and confectioners' sugar in a food processor. • Add the flour and pulse until well blended. • Add the butter and process for 10 seconds. • Add the egg yolks and process until a stiff dough starts to form. • Shape the dough into a ball, wrap in plastic wrap (cling film), and refrigerate for 1 hour. • Preheat the oven to 375°F/190°C/gas 5. • Butter a 10-inch (25-cm) springform pan. • Roll the pastry out on a lightly floured work surface and use it to line the prepared pan. • Filling: Bring the milk and cream to a boil in a large saucepan. • Remove from the heat and add the chocolate, stirring constantly, until it melts completely. • Pour the filling into the pastry case. • Bake for about 15 minutes, or until the filling has set and the pastry is golden brown. • Serve at room temperature.

■ INGREDIENTS

PASTRY
- 2 large egg yolks
- 1 teaspoon vanilla extract
- ⅓ cup (50 g) finely ground almonds
- ¾ cup (125 g) confectioners' (icing) sugar
- 1⅓ cups (200 g) all-purpose (plain) flour
- ½ cup (125 g) butter

FILLING
- 3 cups (750 ml) milk
- 1 tablespoon heavy (double) cream
- 7 oz (200 g) semisweet chocolate (70% cocoa solids), coarsely chopped

Rum and mocha pie

Serves: 6-8; Preparation: 45 minutes; Cooking: 35 minutes; Level of difficulty: 1

Preheat the oven to 350°F/180°C/gas 4. • Butter and flour a 10-inch (25-cm) springform pan. • Sift the flour, baking powder, and salt into a large bowl. Stir in the sugar. • Rub in the butter with your fingertips until the mixture resembles fine bread crumbs. • Mix in the egg yolks and rum to form a smooth dough. • Filling: Mix the almonds, sugar, and cocoa in a large bowl. • Stir in the egg yolks and coffee. • Roll out the pastry on a lightly floured work surface and use it to line the prepared pan. • Pinch the edge of the pastry to obtain a fluted effect. • Fill the pie shell with the filling. • Bake for about 35 minutes, or until the filling has set and the pastry is golden brown. • Serve warm.

■ INGREDIENTS

PASTRY
- 2 cups (300 g) all-purpose (plain) flour
- 2 teaspoons baking powder
- ⅛ teaspoon salt
- ¼ cup (50 g) sugar
- ½ cup (125 g) butter, cut in small pieces
- 2 large egg yolks
- 2 tablespoons rum

FILLING
- 1 cup (100 g) toasted almonds, finely chopped
- ⅔ cup (140 g) sugar
- ⅓ cup (50 g) unsweetened cocoa powder
- 2 large egg yolks
- 5 tablespoons strong coffee, cooled

Right: *Dark chocolate pie*

Creamy chocolate crostata

Serves: 6-8; Preparation: 30 minutes + 30 minutes to chill; Cooking: 50 minutes; Level of difficulty: 2

Preheat the oven to 375°F/190°C/gas 5. • Butter a 9-inch (23-cm) springform pan. Sprinkle with the crumbs. • Roll the dough out on a lightly floured work surface into a 9-inch (23-cm) round. Fit into the prepared pan. Refrigerate for 30 minutes. • Chocolate Filling: Melt the butter in a saucepan over low heat. Stir in the sugar, chocolate, cornstarch, and vanilla. Add the milk and egg yolks and continue cooking, stirring constantly, for about 10 minutes, or until the filling thickens. Remove from the heat and set aside to cool. • Beat the egg whites in a large bowl with an electric mixer at medium speed until stiff peaks form. • Use a large rubber spatula to fold the beaten whites and cream into the chocolate filling. • Spoon into the pastry shell. • Bake for about 50 minutes, or until set. • Cool completely in the pan on a rack. • Loosen and remove the pan sides. Transfer to a serving plate. Dust with the cocoa.

INGREDIENTS

- 1 quantity *Sweet Shortcrust Pastry* (see page 16)
- 2–3 tablespoons vanilla wafer crumbs

CHOCOLATE FILLING
- ½ cup (125 g) butter
- 1 cup (200 g) sugar
- 6 oz (180 g) bittersweet chocolate, coarsely chopped
- 2 tablespoons cornstarch (cornflour)
- 1 teaspoon vanilla extract
- 4 tablespoons milk
- 4 large eggs, separated
- 1 cup (250 ml) heavy (double) cream
- 2 tablespoons cocoa powder, to dust

Almond and chocolate pie

Serves: 6-8; Preparation: 30 minutes + 1 hour to chill; Cooking: 1 hour; Level of difficulty: 2

Pastry: Mix the flour, sugar, butter, whole egg and yolk, baking powder, amaretti cookies, and rum in a large bowl to form a firm dough. • Shape into a ball, wrap in plastic wrap (cling film), and refrigerate for 1 hour. • Preheat the oven to 350°F/180°C/gas 4. • Roll out the pastry and use half of it to line an 8-inch (20-cm) springform pan. • Cover with a layer of pastry cream followed by a layer of amaretti cookies and ladyfingers briefly dipped in the liqueur, and a layer of chocolate. Repeat until all the ingredients are in the pan. • Cover with the other half of the pastry dough. • Prick all over with a fork. • Bake for 1 hour. • Serve at room temperature.

INGREDIENTS

PASTRY
- 2¼ cups (330 g) all-purpose (plain) flour
- ½ cup (100 g) sugar
- ½ cup (125 g) butter
- 1 large egg and 1 egg yolk
- 1 teaspoon baking powder
- 4 amaretti cookies, crushed
- 1 tablespoon dark rum

FILLING
- 1 quantity *Pastry Cream* (see page 28)
- 15 amaretti cookies, crushed
- 10 ladyfingers
- 1¾ cups (400 ml) Alchermes liqueur or rum
- 10 oz (300 g) semisweet chocolate, coarsely grated

Right: Creamy chocolate crostata

Coconut and chocolate pie

■ INGREDIENTS

- ⅔ cup (180 g) butter, melted
- 1⅓ cups (200 g) confectioners' (icing) sugar
- 1 teaspoon vanilla extract
- ⅛ teaspoon salt
- 2 large eggs
- ⅓ cup (50 g) all-purpose (plain) flour
- 1 cups (120 g) shredded (desiccated) coconut + extra to dust
- 7 oz (200 g) semisweet chocolate, coarsely chopped
- 4 tablespoons coconut milk

Serves: 6-8; Preparation: 30 minutes + 3 hours to stand; Cooking: 35 minutes; Level of difficulty: 2

Preheat the oven to 350°F/180°C/gas 4. • Butter and flour a 10-inch (25-cm) springform pan. • Mix the melted butter, confectioners' sugar, vanilla, and salt in a large bowl until creamy. • Add the eggs, one at a time, beating until just blended. Mix in the flour and coconut. • Spoon the batter into the prepared pan. • Bake for 35 minutes, or until a toothpick inserted into the center comes out clean. • Let cool completely in the pan. • Melt the chocolate with the coconut milk in a double boiler over barely simmering water. • Set aside to cool. • Spread the chocolate over the top of the cake and sprinkle with the extra coconut. • Serve chilled or at room temperature.

Chocolate and almond crostata

■ INGREDIENTS

- 4 oz (125 g) bittersweet chocolate, coarsely chopped
- 1⅓ cups (200 g) all-purpose (plain) flour
- 1⅓ cups (200 g) finely ground almonds
- ½ cup (100 g) sugar
- ½ teaspoon salt
- ¾ cup (200 g) butter
- 3 large egg yolks
- 1 quantity *Chocolate Pastry Cream*, chilled (see page 28)
- 1 cup (250 ml) heavy (double) cream

Serves: 6-8; Preparation: 30 minutes + 1 hour to chill; Cooking: 25 minutes; Level of difficulty: 2

Melt the chocolate in a double boiler over barely simmering water. Set aside to cool. • Stir together the flour, almonds, sugar, and salt in a large bowl. • Beat in the butter and egg yolks with an electric mixer at medium speed. • With mixer at low speed, beat in the chocolate. • Shape into a smooth ball. Wrap in plastic wrap (cling film) and refrigerate for 1 hour. • Preheat the oven to 350°F/180°C/gas 4. • Butter a 9-inch (23-cm) pie plate. • Roll the dough out on a lightly floured work surface and fit into the prepared pan. Prick all over with a fork. • Bake for about 25 minutes, or until firm. • Cool the crust completely in the pan on a rack. • Fill with the pastry cream. • With mixer at high speed, beat the cream in a medium bowl until stiff. • Spread with the cream.

Left: *Coconut and chocolate pie*

Apple and golden raisin pie

INGREDIENTS

FILLING

- 1½ lb (750 g) apples
- ¼ cup (50 g) sugar
- 3 tablespoons lemon juice
- ⅓ cup (60 g) golden raisins (sultanas)

PASTRY

- 2 cups (300 g) all-purpose (plain) flour
- 2 teaspoons baking powder
- ¼ teaspoon salt
- ½ cup (100 g) sugar
- 7 tablespoons butter
- 1 large egg, lightly beaten
- 2 ladyfingers
- 4 tablespoons confectioners' (icing) sugar

Serves: 6-8; Preparation: 30 minutes; Cooking: 40 minutes; Level of difficulty: 2

Preheat the oven to 400°F/200°C/gas 6. • Butter and flour a 9-inch (23-cm) springform pan. • Filling: Wash and dry the apples. Peel and core them and cut into small cubes. • Cook the apples with the sugar, lemon juice, and raisins in a medium saucepan very low heat for 10 minutes, until softened but not broken down. • Remove from heat and let cool. • Pastry: Sift the flour, baking powder, and salt into a large bowl. Stir in the sugar. • Rub in the butter until the mixture resembles coarse crumbs. • Mix in the egg to form a smooth dough. • Roll out two-thirds of the dough and fit into the prepared pan. Prick all over with a fork. • Crumble the ladyfingers over the dough. • Top with the apple mixture. • Roll out the remaining dough and cut into thin strips. Arrange the strips in a rectangle on top of the filling. • Bake for about 40 minutes, or until the pastry is golden brown. • Loosen the pan sides and transfer to a serving plate. Let cool completely. • Dust with the confectioners' sugar.

Apple crostata

INGREDIENTS

PASTRY

- 1½ cups (225 g) all-purpose (plain) flour
- ¼ teaspoon salt
- ⅓ cup (70 g) sugar
- 4 tablespoons cold butter, cut up
- 3 large egg yolks

TOPPING

- 4 medium apples, peeled, cored, and grated
- 4 tablespoons lemon juice
- ⅓ cup (70 g) sugar
- 2–3 tablespoons brandy (optional)

Serves: 6-8; Preparation: 20 minutes + 30 minutes to chill; Cooking: 50 minutes; Level of difficulty: 2

Butter a 9-inch (23-cm) springform pan. • Pastry: Sift the flour and salt into a large bowl. Stir in the sugar. • Rub in the butter with your fingertips until the mixture resembles fine bread crumbs. • Mix in the egg yolks to form a smooth dough. • Set one-quarter of the dough aside and press the rest into the bottom and sides of the pan. Refrigerate for 30 minutes. • Preheat the oven to 375°F/190°C/gas 5. • Topping: Drizzle the apples with the lemon juice. Soak for 3 minutes. • Squeeze out most of the lemon juice. Spread a layer of apple over the pastry. Sprinkle with sugar. Cover with more apple. Repeat until all of the apple is in the pan, reserving 1 tablespoon of sugar. Drizzle with the brandy, if desired. • Use your hands to roll the remaining dough into long, thin sausage shapes. Place in a lattice pattern over the top. • Bake for about 50 minutes, or until lightly browned. After 40 minutes, sprinkle the apple (not the pastry sides) with the reserved sugar. • Loosen and remove the pan sides. Serve warm.

Left: *Spiced apple pie*

Apple and rosemary syrup tart

Serves: 6-8; Preparation: 15 minutes; Cooking: 35 minutes; Level of difficulty: 2

Line an 9-inch (23-cm) baking pan with waxed paper. • Roll the pastry out on a lightly floured surface to a 10-inch (25-cm) round. Refrigerate until ready to use. • Melt the butter with the sugar and honey in a medium saucepan over medium heat, stirring occasionally until golden brown. • Cut the apples into quarters and add to the pan. Add the lemon zest and rosemary. Cook over medium heat until the apples have softened, but not broken down. Use a slotted spoon to remove the apples and place in the prepared pan. • Boil the syrup for 1-2 minutes, or until it thickens slightly. Pour the syrup over the apples and let cool completely. • Preheat the oven to 400°F/200°C/gas 6. • Cover the apples with the chilled pastry and prick all over with a fork. • Bake for 20 minutes. • Invert, apple-side up, onto a serving plate. • Serve warm.

INGREDIENTS

- 10 oz (300 g) frozen puff pastry, thawed
- ⅔ cup (180 g) butter
- 1 cup (200 g) sugar
- 2 tablespoons honey
- 4 apples, peeled and cored
- finely grated zest of 1 lemon
- 1 tablespoon rosemary leaves

Boozy apricot and cherry pie

Serves: 6-8; Preparation: 10 minutes + time to make the pastry and sponge cake; Cooking: 35 minutes; Level of difficulty: 2

Prepare the pastry. • Prepare the sponge cake. • Preheat the oven to 375°F/190°C/gas 5. • Butter and flour a 10-inch (25-cm) pie pan. • Rinse the apricots and dry well. Pit them and cut in half. • Break off a piece of pastry about the size of a tennis ball and reserve. • Roll the rest out so that it is large enough to line the prepared pan. Leave a narrow border of the pastry hanging over the sides. Prick well with a fork. • Slice the sponge cake and arrange in the pastry case. Drizzle with the liqueur and sprinkle with the almonds. • Arrange the apricot halves, cut side down on top. Sprinkle with the sugar. • Roll out the remaining pastry into a square sheet. Use a fluted pastry wheel to cut it into ¼-inch (5-mm) wide strips. Place over the apricots in a lattice pattern. Fold the overhanging pastry border over the ends of the lattice to form a rolled edging. • Brush the top of the pie with the egg yolk. • Bake for about 35 minutes, or until golden brown. • Serve warm.

INGREDIENTS

- 1 lb (500 g) small apricots
- 1 quantity *Sweet Shortcrust Pastry* (see page 16)
- ½ quantity *Basic Sponge Cake* (see page 22)
- 4 tablespoons Maraschino or Kirsch (cherry liqueur)
- ¼ cup (50 g) finely chopped almonds
- ⅓ cup (70 g) sugar
- 1 large egg yolk

Right: Apple and rosemary syrup tart

Strludels

Austria is renowned today for its apple strudel made with light flaky pastry and scrumptious apple and spice filling, but food historians think that strudel recipes probably date back to ancient Greece. They are thought to be related to the modern-day Greek specialty, baklava.

Tropical strudel

Serves: 10-12; Preparation: 45 minutes; Cooking: 25 minutes; Level of difficulty: 1

Prepare the pastry for the strudel. Set aside to rest. • Preheat the oven to 400°F/200°C/gas 6. • Butter a baking sheet. • Cover a work surface with a large clean cloth. • Roll the strudel pastry out very thinly on a floured surface. It should be almost transparent. • Transfer to the cloth and brush with melted butter. • Mix the mangoes, sugar, lemon zest, cashew nuts, and bread crumbs in a large bowl. • Spoon the filling onto half of the pastry, leaving a wide border around the edges. Fold the end of the pastry over the filling and, using the cloth as a guide, roll the strudel up until all the filling is contained. Tuck in the ends and seal. Brush with butter and slide onto the baking sheet. • Bake for about 25 minutes, or until golden brown. • Serve the strudel hot or warm with the sauce passed separately.

INGREDIENTS

- 1 quantity *Strudel Pastry* (see page 20)
- ½ cup (125 g) butter, melted
- 3 lb (1.5 kg) mangoes, peeled and diced
- 4 tablespoons sugar
- 2 tablespoons finely grated lemon zest
- ½ cup (90 g) unsalted cashew nuts
- 6 tablespoons fine dry bread crumbs
- 1 quantity *Citrus Sauce* (see page 34)

Bavarian strudel

Serves: 10-12; Preparation: 45 minutes; Cooking: 25 minutes; Level of difficulty: 2

Butter a large baking sheet. • Place the water, sugar, and ginger in a pan large enough to hold all the pears. Stir over low heat until the sugar has dissolved. Increase the heat so that the liquid simmers. • Add the pears and poach for 15–20 minutes, or until the pears can be easily pierced with a toothpick. Cool and refrigerate. • Preheat the oven to 400°F/200°C/gas 6. • Almond Cream: Process the almonds and confectioners' sugar until smooth. • Beat the butter in a large bowl with an electric mixer at medium speed until creamy. • With mixer at low speed, gradually beat in the almond mixture and flour. • Add the eggs, beating until just blended. Add the rum. • Halve the poached pears and cut out the cores. Slice each half pear thinly lengthwise and set aside. • Lay the sheets of dough out flat and cover with waxed paper and a damp kitchen towel. (This will stop them from drying out.) Brush the first sheet with melted butter. Top with another sheet and brush with butter. Repeat with 4 more sheets. • Spoon half the almond cream on the top layer, leaving a border. Fan out a pear half on one end of the dough. Roll up the strudel. • Transfer to the baking sheet. Brush with butter. Repeat with the remaining dough, almond cream, and pear halves. • Bake for about 10 minutes, or until lightly browned. • Serve warm.

INGREDIENTS

- 1 quart (1 liter) water
- 1 cup (200 g) sugar
- 1½ inches (4 cm) fresh ginger, peeled and sliced ½-inch (1-cm) thick
- 2 firm-ripe pears, peeled

ALMOND CREAM
- ¾ cup (90 g) flaked almonds
- 1 cup (150 g) confectioners' (icing) sugar
- ½ cup (125 g) butter
- ⅓ cup (50 g) all-purpose (plain) flour
- 2 large eggs
- 1 tablespoon dark rum
- 12 sheets phyllo dough, thawed if frozen
- ½ cup (125 g) butter, melted

Right: Tropical strudel

Apple and pineapple strudel

Serves: 8-10; Preparation: 45 minutes; Cooking: 15 minutes; Level of difficulty: 1

Preheat the oven to 400°F/200°C/gas 6. • Butter a large baking sheet. • Lay the sheets of dough out flat and cover with waxed paper and a damp kitchen towel. (This will stop them from drying out.) • Brush the first sheet with butter. Top with a second sheet and brush with butter. Repeat with three more sheets. • Mix the apples, pineapple, cornstarch, allspice, vanilla, and honey in a large bowl. • Spread the dough with the pineapple mixture. • Cover with the remaining sheet of dough. Brush with butter. Roll up the strudel. Transfer to the baking sheet. • Bake for 10–15 minutes, or until lightly browned. • Serve warm.

■ INGREDIENTS

- 6 sheets phyllo dough, thawed if frozen
- 6 tablespoons butter, melted
- 3 apples, peeled, cored, and thinly sliced
- 8 oz (250 g) crushed pineapple, drained
- 1 tablespoon cornstarch (cornflour)
- 2 teaspoons allspice
- 1 teaspoon vanilla extract
- 3 tablespoons honey

Viennese horseshoe

Serves: 10-12; Preparation: 1 hour; Cooking: 50 minutes; Level of difficulty: 2

Pastry: Stir together the flour, sugar, and salt in a large bowl. Stir in the butter, eggs, and milk until well blended. • Knead the dough on a lightly floured surface until smooth and elastic, about 10 minutes. Set aside to rest for 15 minutes. • Filling: Mix the walnuts, raisins, almonds, figs, pineapple, chocolate, and cocoa in a large bowl. • Beat the sugar, egg, and butter in a medium bowl with an electric mixer at medium speed until creamy. • Preheat the oven to 375°F/190°C/gas 5. • Line a large baking sheet with waxed paper. • Roll the dough out very thinly on a lightly floured work surface into an oval shape. • Brush the sugar mixture over the pastry, leaving a ½-inch (1-cm) border on all sides. Gently spread with the fruit mixture, leaving a ½-inch (1-cm) border. Roll the strudel up, pinching the ends together. • Carefully transfer the strudel to the prepared sheet. Gently pull it into a horseshoe shape. If the dough breaks while you are moving it, take a little dough from the end to make a patch. • Mix the egg yolk, sugar, and milk in a small bowl and brush over the strudel. • Bake for about 50 minutes, or until golden brown. • Slide onto a rack to cool. • Serve warm or at room temperature.

■ INGREDIENTS

PASTRY
- 2 cups (300 g) all-purpose (plain) flour
- ¼ cup (50 g) sugar
- ¼ teaspoon salt
- 4 tablespoons butter, melted
- 2 large eggs, lightly beaten
- 2 tablespoons milk

FILLING
- 1 cup (100 g) walnuts, coarsely chopped
- ⅔ cup (100 g) raisins
- ⅓ cup (40 g) flaked almonds
- 6 dried figs, chopped
- 5 canned pineapple rings, well drained and chopped
- 3 oz (90 g) semisweet chocolate, coarsely chopped
- ⅓ cup (50 g) unsweetened cocoa powder
- ¾ cup (150 g) sugar
- 1 large egg
- 4 tablespoons butter
- 1 large egg yolk
- 2 tablespoons sugar
- 1 tablespoon milk

Right: *Apple and pineapple strudel*

Maria's peach and berry strudel

■ INGREDIENTS

- ½ cup (60 g) whole almonds, toasted
- 1¼ cups (120 g) old-fashioned rolled oats
- ½ cup (100 g) firmly packed brown sugar
- ¼ cup (50 g) sugar
- 2 teaspoons ground cinnamon
- 3 medium peaches, peeled, pitted, and diced
- 1 cup (200 g) raspberries
- ½ teaspoon vanilla extract
- 6 sheets phyllo dough
- 6 tablespoons butter, melted

Serves: 8-10; Preparation: 45 minutes; Cooking: 20 minutes; Level of difficulty: 1

Preheat the oven to 375°F/190°C/gas 5. • Butter a large baking sheet. • Chop the almonds and oats finely in a food processor. Add the sugars and 1 teaspoon of cinnamon. • Mix the peaches, raspberries, remaining cinnamon, and vanilla in a large bowl. • Lay the sheets of dough out flat and cover with waxed paper and a damp kitchen towel. • Brush one sheet with melted butter. Top with another sheet and brush with butter. • Spoon a quarter of the almond mixture over half the pastry. Top with a sheet of dough and brush with butter. Repeat until the almond mixture and phyllo are used up. Gently spread with the peach mixture, leaving a ½-inch (1-cm) border. Roll the strudel up, pinching the ends together. • Transfer to the baking sheet. • Bake for about 20 minutes, or until crisp. • Serve warm.

Blackberry custard strudel

Serves: 8-10; Preparation: 45 minutes; Cooking: 35 minutes; Level of difficulty: 1

Custard: Bring the cream to a boil in a small saucepan over low heat. • Beat the egg yolks and sugar in a large bowl until pale and creamy. • Add the cream and mix well. Return the mixture to the saucepan over low heat. Stir constantly for 5–10 minutes, until thickened. Remove from the heat and let cool. • Preheat the oven to 425°F/220°C/gas 7. • Roll the pastry out on a lightly floured work surface to ¼ inch (5 mm) thick. Transfer to a sheet of waxed paper. • Mix the blueberries, banana, and sugar in a large bowl. • Spread the pastry with the custard, leaving a ½-inch (1-cm) border. Spoon the fruit in an even layer on top of the custard. • Roll the strudel up, pinching the ends together. Transfer to the baking sheet. • Bake for 20 minutes. • Dust with the confectioners' sugar. • Bake for about 5 minutes more, or until golden brown. • Serve warm.

■ INGREDIENTS

CUSTARD
- ½ cup (125 ml) cream
- 2 large egg yolks
- ¼ cup (50 g) sugar

- 15 oz (450 g) puff pastry
- 10 oz (300 g) blueberries
- 1 large banana, peeled and sliced
- 2 tablespoons sugar
- 2 tablespoons confectioners' (icing) sugar, to dust

Thanksgiving strudel

Serves: 6-8; Preparation: 45 minutes; Cooking: 30 minutes; Level of difficulty: 1

Preheat the oven to 425°F/220°C/gas 7. • Butter a large baking sheet. • Lay the sheets of dough out flat and cover with waxed paper and a damp kitchen towel. (This will stop them from drying out.) • Brush the first sheet with melted butter. Sprinkle with some bread crumbs. Top with another sheet and brush with butter. Repeat with 4 more sheets, finishing with a phyllo layer. • Sauté the apples in 2 tablespoons of butter in a large saucepan over medium heat for 5 minutes. Stir in the blackberries and sugar and cook, stirring, for 8–10 minutes. • Stir in the apricots, pecans, and cinnamon. Drain any juice and set aside to cool. • Gently spread the pastry with the blackberry mixture, leaving a ½-inch (1-cm) border. • Roll the strudel up, pinching the ends together. Transfer to the baking sheet. • Brush with the remaining butter. • Bake for about 20 minutes, or until lightly browned. • Serve warm.

■ INGREDIENTS

- 6 sheets phyllo dough, thawed if frozen
- ½ cup (125 g) + 2 tablespoons butter, melted
- 4 tablespoons fine dry bread crumbs
- 2 tart cooking apples, peeled, cored, and thinly sliced
- 1½ cups (300 g) blackberries
- ¾ cup (150 g) sugar
- ½ cup (75 g) dried apricots, finely chopped
- 1 cup (120 g) pecans, toasted and coarsely chopped
- 1 teaspoon ground cinnamon

Right: *Blackberry custard strudel*

Best nut strudel

Serves: 14-16; Preparation: 2 hours; Cooking: 30 minutes; Level of difficulty: 2

Preheat the oven to 375°F/190°C/gas 5. • Line 2 baking sheets with waxed paper. • Mix the mixed nuts, almonds, pine nuts, raisins, chocolate, sugar, candied peel, orange juice, rum, vanilla, and salt in a large bowl. • Roll out half the pastry on a lightly floured surface into a rectangle. Use your hands to stretch it out on a clean kitchen towel until paper-thin. • Brush with 1 tablespoon of butter. Spoon half the mixture evenly onto the rectangle, leaving a ½-inch (1-cm) border. • Gently spread with the nut mixture, leaving a border. • Roll the strudel up, pinching the ends together. Transfer to the baking sheet. • Repeat with remaining pastry and filling. • Mix the egg, sugar, and milk in a small bowl. • Brush the strudels with the milk mixture. • Bake for about 30 minutes, or until browned. • Serve warm.

INGREDIENTS

- 4 cups (500 g) mixed nuts, finely chopped
- 1½ cups (150 g) almonds, chopped
- 1 cup (180 g) pine nuts
- 2¼ cups (375 g) golden raisins (sultanas)
- 3 oz (90 g) semisweet chocolate, grated
- 1 cup (200 g) sugar
- ½ cup (75 g) candied lemon peel
- juice of 2 oranges
- 4 tablespoons rum
- 1 teaspoon vanilla extract
- ¼ teaspoon salt
- 2 recipes *Strudel Pastry* (see page 20)
- 2 tablespoons butter, melted
- 1 large egg, lightly beaten
- 2 tablespoons sugar
- 1 teaspoon milk

Zesty apple and apricot strudel

Serves: 8-10; Preparation: 30 minutes; Cooking: 30 minutes; Level of difficulty: 2

Preheat the oven to 375°F/190°C/gas 5. • Butter a large baking sheet. • Lay the 2 sheets of dough out flat and cover with waxed paper and a damp kitchen towel. (This will stop them from drying out.) • Brush the first sheet with melted butter. Top with another sheet and brush with butter. Sprinkle with bread crumbs. • Mix the apples, sugar, raisins, apricots, almonds, and lemon zest and juice in a large bowl. • Gently spread with the nut mixture, leaving a ½-inch (1-cm) border. • Roll the strudel up, pinching the ends together. Transfer to the baking sheet. • Brush with the remaining melted butter. Sprinkle with the sugar and cinnamon. • Repeat with the remaining two sheets of dough and the remaining apple mixture. • Bake for about 30 minutes, or until lightly browned. • Serve warm.

INGREDIENTS

- 4 sheets phyllo dough
- 4 tablespoons butter, melted
- ⅓ cup (50 g) fine dry bread crumbs
- 3 cups (300 g) apple chunks
- ½ cup (100 g) sugar
- ¼ cup (40 g) raisins
- ½ cup (75 g) dried apricots, chopped
- ¼ cup (30 g) almonds, coarsely chopped
- ¼ teaspoon lemon zest
- ½ teaspoon lemon juice
- 1 tablespoon sugar
- ½ teaspoon cinnamon

Right: *Best nut strudel*

Savory apple, stilton, and thyme strudel

- 1 lb (500 g) apples, peeled, cored, and coarsely chopped
- finely grated zest and juice of 1 lemon
- 8 oz (250 g) stilton cheese, crumbled
- 2 tablespoons walnuts, coarsely chopped
- 1 tablespoon finely chopped fresh thyme
- ⅛ teaspoon freshly grated nutmeg
- ⅛ teaspoon freshly ground black pepper
- 10 sheets phyllo dough, thawed if frozen
- ½ cup (125 g) butter, melted
- ½ cup (75 g) dry bread crumbs

■ INGREDIENTS

- 1⅔ cups (250 g) all-purpose (plain) flour
- ¼ teaspoon salt
- 4 tablespoons butter, melted
- 4 tablespoons milk

FILLING
- 1½ cups (375 g) ricotta cheese
- ⅓ cup (70 g) sugar
- 4 tablespoons butter, melted
- 2 tablespoons brandy
- 1 tablespoon lemon zest
- 1 cup (150 g) raisins
- ⅓ cup (40 g) walnuts, coarsely chopped
- ½ cup (60 g) graham cracker (digestive biscuit) crumbs
- 1 large egg
- 2 tablespoons sugar

Left: *Savory apple, stilton, and thyme strudel*

Serves: 10-12; Preparation: 45 minutes; Cooking: 30 minutes; Level of difficulty: 1

Preheat the oven to 350°F/180°C/gas 4. • Butter a large baking sheet. • Sprinkle the apples with the lemon juice in a large bowl. Add the lemon zest, stilton, walnuts, thyme, nutmeg, and black pepper. • Lay the sheets of dough out flat and cover with waxed paper and a damp kitchen towel. (This will stop them from drying out.) • Place two sheets of dough on the baking sheet. Brush with some melted butter and sprinkle with bread crumbs. • Top with another two sheets and repeat until all the phyllo is used up, finishing with a little butter and some bread crumbs. • Gently spread with the apple mixture, leaving a ½-inch (1-cm) border. • Roll the strudel up, pinching the ends together. Transfer to the baking sheet. • Brush with the remaining butter and sprinkle with the remaining bread crumbs. • Bake for about 30 minutes, or until lightly browned. • Serve warm.

Raisin and ricotta strudel

Serves: 8-10; Preparation: 45 minutes; Cooking: 50 minutes; Level of difficulty: 1

Sift the flour and salt into a medium bowl. Stir in the butter and milk until well blended. • Knead the dough on a lightly floured work surface until smooth and elastic, about 10 minutes. • Shape into a ball, place in a clean bowl, and cover with a tea towel. Set aside to rest for 30 minutes. • Filling: Beat the ricotta, sugar, butter, brandy, and lemon zest in a large bowl with an electric mixer at low speed until well blended. Beat in the raisins and nuts. • Preheat the oven to 375°F/190°C/gas 5. • Line a large baking sheet with waxed paper. • Roll the pastry out very thinly on a lightly floured work surface into an oval shape. • Sprinkle with the graham cracker crumbs. Gently spread with the ricotta mixture, leaving a ½-inch (1-cm) border. • Roll the strudel up, pinching the ends together. Transfer to the baking sheet. Gently pull into a horseshoe shape. • Mix the egg and sugar in a small bowl. Brush over the strudel. • Bake for about 50 minutes, or until golden brown. • Slide onto a rack to cool. • Serve warm or at room temperature.

Cheese and pear strudel

For a quick version of this strudel and the other strudel recipes on these pages,
replace the homemade dough with 1 lb (500 g) of store-bought puff pastry.

Serves: 8-10; Preparation: 45 minutes; Cooking: 35 minutes; Level of difficulty: 2

Prepare the strudel pastry. • Preheat the oven to 350°F/180°C/gas 4. •
Roll the pastry out on a lightly floured work surface to very thin. It
should be almost transparent. • Brush all over with the half the melted
butter. • Filling: Pulse the goat's cheese, gorgonzola, and cream in a food
processor or blender until smooth. • Peel and core the pears. Cut into
very thin slices. • Spread the cheese mixture over the pastry. • Arrange
the pears in a single layer over the top. Sprinkle with the emmental.
Season with a little salt and a generous grinding of pepper. • Carefully
roll the strudel up. Fold in the ends and press to seal. Brush the top with
the remaining butter. • Carefully transfer to a large baking sheet. • Bake
for about 35 minutes, or until golden brown. • Serve warm.

■ INGREDIENTS

- 1 quantity *Strudel Pastry* (see page 20)
- 4 tablespoons butter, melted

FILLING
- ⅔ cup (180 g) fresh creamy goat's cheese
- ⅔ cup (180 g) gorgonzola cheese
- 2 tablespoons heavy (double) cream
- 2 large sweet pears
- 1¼ cups (150 g) freshly grated emmental cheese
- salt and freshly ground black pepper to taste

Potato and onion strudel

Serves: 6-8; Preparation: 45 minutes; Cooking: 55 minutes; Level of difficulty: 2

Prepare the strudel pastry. • Filling: Boil the potatoes in lightly salted
water for 10–15 minutes, or until tender. • Mash the potatoes with the
cream in a large bowl until puréed. Season with salt and pepper. • Sauté
the onions in the oil in a large frying pan for 10 minutes, or until golden
brown. • Preheat the oven to 350°F/180°C/gas 4. • Roll the pastry out
on a lightly floured work surface to very thin. It should be almost
transparent. • Brush all over with the half the melted butter. • Spread
the potato purée evenly over the pastry. • Spread the onions over the top
and sprinkle with the cilantro. • Carefully roll the strudel up. Fold in the
ends and press to seal. Brush the top with the remaining butter. •
Carefully transfer to a large baking sheet. • Bake for about 35 minutes, or
until golden brown. • Serve warm.

■ INGREDIENTS

- 1 quantity *Strudel Pastry* (see page 20)

FILLING
- 4 large potatoes, peeled and cut into pieces
- 2 tablespoons heavy (double) cream
- salt and freshly ground black pepper to taste
- 2 large onions, thinly sliced
- 2 tablespoons extra-virgin olive oil
- 2 tablespoons finely chopped cilantro (coriander)
- 4 tablespoons butter, melted

Right: *Cheese and pear strudel*

Mushroom strudel

Serves: 6-8; Preparation: 45 minutes; Cooking: 45 minutes; Level of difficulty: 2

Prepare the strudel pastry. • Clean the mushrooms and slice thinly. • Sauté the mushrooms and garlic in the oil in a large frying pan for 10 minutes, or until tender and all the water they produce has evaporated. Season with salt and pepper. • Preheat the oven to 350°F/180°C/gas 4. • Roll the pastry out on a lightly floured surface to very thin. It should be almost transparent. • Brush all over with the half the melted butter. • Spread the mushroom mixture evenly over the pastry. • Sprinkle with the marjoram. • Carefully roll the strudel up. Fold in the ends and press to seal. Brush the top with the remaining butter. • Carefully transfer to a large baking sheet. • Bake for about 35 minutes, or until golden brown. • Serve warm.

■ INGREDIENTS

- 1 quantity *Strudel Pastry* (see page 20)

FILLING
- 1½ lb (750 g) white mushrooms
- 2 cloves garlic, finely chopped
- 4 tablespoons extra-virgin olive oil
- salt and freshly ground black pepper to taste
- 1 tablespoon finely chopped marjoram
- 4 tablespoons butter, melted

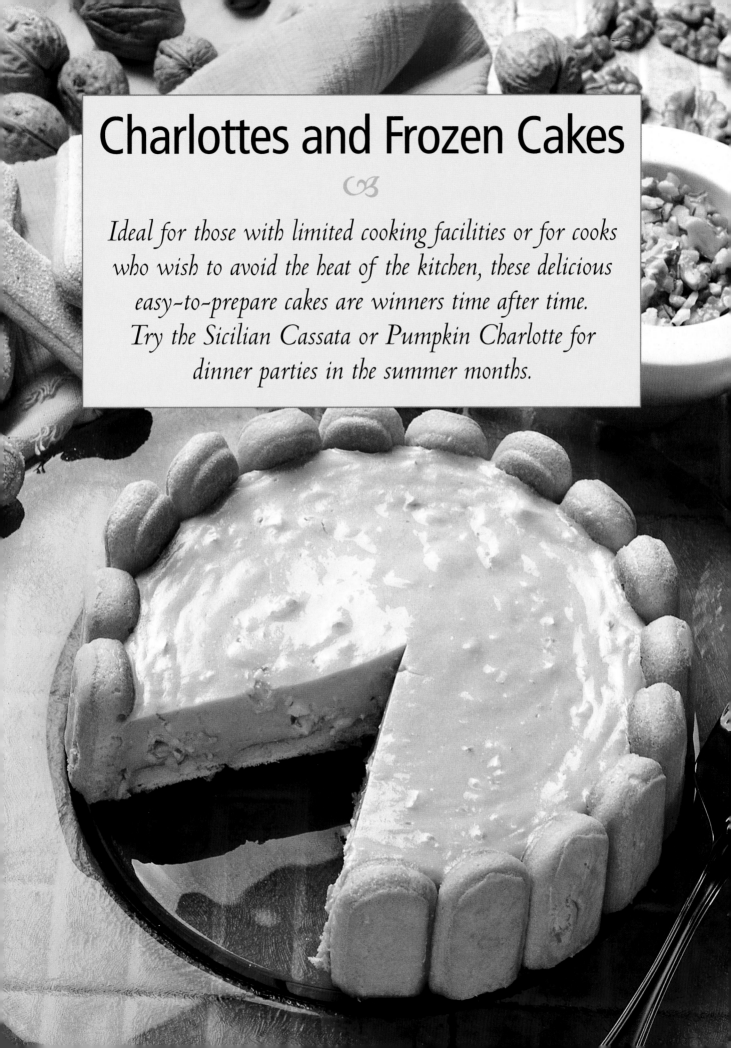

Charlottes and Frozen Cakes

⁂

Ideal for those with limited cooking facilities or for cooks who wish to avoid the heat of the kitchen, these delicious easy-to-prepare cakes are winners time after time. Try the Sicilian Cassata or Pumpkin Charlotte for dinner parties in the summer months.

Chocolate supreme charlotte

Serves: 8-10; Preparation: 30 minutes + 6 hours to chill; Level of difficulty: 2

Set out a 10-inch (25-cm) springform pan. Line with waxed paper. • Dissolve the 1 cup (200 g) of sugar in ½ cup (125 ml) of water in a saucepan over medium heat. Wash down the pan sides with a pastry brush dipped in cold water to prevent sugar crystals from forming. Cook until the mixture reaches 238°F (115°C), or the soft-ball stage. • Beat the eggs and egg yolks and remaining sugar in a double boiler over barely simmering water until blended. Cook, stirring constantly with a wooden spoon, until the mixture lightly coats a metal spoon or registers 160°F (71°C) on an instant-read thermometer. Immediately plunge the pan into a bowl of cold water and beat until cooled. • With mixer at high speed, gradually add the sugar mixture, beating until thick. • Sprinkle the gelatin over the remaining water in a small saucepan. Let stand 1 minute. Cook over low heat until completely dissolved. • Add the gelatin mixture to the egg mixture. • With mixer at high speed, beat the cream in a large bowl until stiff. • Fold the chocolate and cream into the mixture. • Line the pan bottom and sides with ladyfingers. Trim the ladyfingers for the pan sides to fit. • Spoon the mousse into the mold and refrigerate for 6 hours, or until set.

■ INGREDIENTS

- 1¼ cups (250 g) sugar
- ¾ cup (200 ml) water
- 2 large eggs
- 8 large egg yolks
- 1 tablespoon unflavored gelatin
- 1½ cups (375 ml) heavy (double) cream
- 1 lb (500 g) bittersweet chocolate, melted
- 36 ladyfingers

No-bake chocolate mascarpone cake

Serves: 6-8; Preparation: 40 minutes + 6 hours to chill; Level of difficulty: 2

Butter a 9-inch (23-cm) springform pan. • Melt the white chocolate in a double boiler over barely simmering water. Set aside to cool. Repeat with the semisweet chocolate and set aside to cool. • Beat the egg yolks, sugar, brandy, and white wine in a double boiler with an electric mixer at medium speed over barely simmering water until the mixture falls in ribbons, about 20 minutes. • Fold half the egg mixture into each of the cooled chocolate mixtures. • Stir half the mascarpone into each mixture until well blended. • Cut the cake horizontally and place one layer in the prepared pan. (Freeze the remaining half for later use.) • Spoon in the white and dark mixtures alternately and swirl with a knife to create a marbled pattern. Refrigerate for 6 hours. Loosen and remove the pan sides. Remove the paper.

■ INGREDIENTS

- 4 oz (125 g) white chocolate, chopped
- 4 oz (125 g) semisweet chocolate, chopped
- 3 large egg yolks
- ⅔ cup (140 g) sugar
- 4 tablespoons brandy
- 3 tablespoons white wine
- 1½ cups (375 g) mascarpone cheese
- one 9-inch (23-cm) *Basic Sponge Cake* (see page 22)

Right: *No-bake chocolate mascarpone cake*

Candied chestnut charlotte

■ INGREDIENTS

- 4 tablespoons dark rum
- ½ cup (125 ml) water
- about 30 ladyfingers
- 2 cups (500 ml) heavy (double) cream
- ½ cup (100 g) sugar
- 14 oz (400 g) candied chestnuts, crumbled

Serves: 4-6; Preparation: 20 minutes + 12 hours to chill; Level of difficulty: 2

Mix the rum and water in a large bowl. Dip the ladyfingers in the rum mixture. • Line a 1-quart (1-liter) charlotte mold with the ladyfingers, pressing them against the sides so that they stay in place. • Beat the cream and sugar in a large bowl with an electric mixer at high speed until stiff. • Use a large rubber spatula to fold the chestnuts into the cream. Repeat layers of chestnut cream and ladyfingers in the mold until all the ingredients have been used up, finishing with ladyfingers. • Refrigerate for 12 hours, or overnight. • Invert onto a serving plate just before serving.

Ladyfinger cake with maple syrup

Serves: 6-8; Preparation: 40 minutes + 6 hours to chill; Level of difficulty: 2

Lightly oil a 10-inch (25-cm) springform pan. • Sprinkle the gelatin over the water in a small saucepan. Let stand 1 minute. • Warm the maple syrup and stir into the gelatin mixture. Refrigerate until thickened, about 20 minutes. • Beat the cream in a large bowl with an electric mixer at high speed until stiff. • Use a large rubber spatula to fold the cream into the maple syrup mixture. Stir in the walnuts. • Trim the bottoms of the ladyfingers so that they will stand straight and use them to line the sides of the pan. Line the bottom of the pan with the remaining ladyfingers. • Spoon the filling into the pan. • Refrigerate for 6 hours, or until set. • Loosen the sides of the springform pan and carefully remove them. • If liked, warm the extra maple syrup and drizzle it over the cake.

■ INGREDIENTS

- 1 tablespoon unflavored gelatin
- 4 tablespoons water
- 1 cup (250 ml) maple syrup + extra to drizzle (optional)
- 2 cups (500 ml) heavy (double) cream
- ¾ cup (100 g) walnuts, coarsely chopped
- about 30 ladyfingers

Dried apricot charlotte

Serves: 6-8; Preparation: 30 minutes + 4 hours to chill; Cooking: 25 minutes; Level of difficulty: 2

Line a 9-inch (23-cm) springform pan with ladyfingers. • Place the apricots in a bowl with hot water to cover. Microwave at medium heat for 8 minutes. Drain. • Mix in the sugar and 1 cup (250 ml) of water. Microwave for 15 minutes. • Sprinkle the gelatin over 4 tablespoons of water in a small saucepan. Let stand 1 minute. Stir over low heat until completely dissolved. • Process the apricot mixture until puréed. Add the gelatin mixture. Refrigerate until thickened. • Beat the cream and confectioners' sugar in a large bowl with an electric mixer at high speed until stiff. • Use a large rubber spatula to fold it into the apricot mixture. • Pour half the mixture into the pan and top with ladyfingers. Pour in the remaining mixture. • Refrigerate for 4 hours. Loosen the pan sides and carefully remove them.

■ INGREDIENTS

- about 30 ladyfingers
- 2 cups (300 g) dried apricots
- ⅓ cup (70 g) sugar
- 1¼ cups (310 ml) water
- 2 tablespoons unflavored gelatin
- 2 cups (500 ml) heavy (double) cream
- ½ cup (75 g) confectioners' (icing) sugar

Right: Ladyfinger cake with maple syrup

Ladyfinger cake with bananas and cream

Serves: 6-8; Preparation: 30 minutes + 4 hours to chill; Level of difficulty: 1

Lightly oil a 10-inch (25-cm) springform pan. • Sprinkle 1 tablespoon of gelatin over 4 tablespoons of the cold water. Add the hot water and stir until completely dissolved. • Pour a thin layer of gelatin into the pan. When set, cut several slices of banana and arrange on top of the gelatin. Pour over enough of the gelatin mixture to cover the bananas and let set. • Trim the bottoms of the ladyfingers so that they will stand straight and use them to line the sides of the pan. • Process the remaining bananas until puréed. Add the lemon juice, sugar, and nuts. • Beat 1½ cups (375 ml) of the cream in a large bowl with an electric mixer at high speed until stiff. • Sprinkle the remaining gelatin over the remaining cold water in a small saucepan. Let stand 1 minute. Stir over low heat until completely dissolved. • Fold the whipped cream and the gelatin mixture into the banana mixture. Pour the mixture into the mold. Refrigerate for 4 hours, or until set. • Loosen and remove the sides of the pan and place on a serving plate. • Beat the remaining cream until stiff and use it to decorate the top of the cake.

■ INGREDIENTS

- 2 tablespoons unflavored gelatin
- ½ cup (125 ml) cold + ½ cup (125 ml) hot water
- 7 ripe bananas, peeled
- about 24 ladyfingers
- 2 tablespoons lemon juice
- 4 tablespoons sugar
- ½ cup (60 g) walnuts, coarsely chopped
- 2 cups (500 ml) heavy (double) cream

Frozen raspberry charlotte

Serves: 8-10; Preparation: 30 minutes + 1 hour to freeze; Level of difficulty: 1

Mix the wine and kirsch and drizzle over the cake slices. • Use the slices to line a 2-quart (2-liter) straight-sided mold or soufflé dish. • Spoon one-third of the ice cream over the cake, smoothing the top. Top with one-third of the raspberries. Cover with cake slices. Repeat with the ice cream, raspberries, and cake slices until they have all been used, finishing with a layer of ice cream. • Freeze for 1 hour. • Soak the mold in hot water for 10 seconds. Turn out onto a serving dish, then turn again, so that the ice cream-side is facing up. • Beat the cream with an electric mixer at high speed until stiff. Decorate with the cream and raspberries.

■ INGREDIENTS

- ½ cup (125 ml) dry white wine
- 4 tablespoons kirsch
- 1 *Classic Pound Cake* (see page 55), cut into ½-inch (1-cm) thick slices
- 3 cups (750 g) vanilla ice cream, softened
- 1 lb (500 g) raspberries, cleaned (reserve 12 to decorate)
- 1 cup (250 ml) heavy (double) cream

VARIATION
— Substitute the raspberries with the same quantity of strawberries.

Right: Ladyfinger cake with bananas and cream

Pumpkin charlotte

■ INGREDIENTS

- about 30 ladyfingers
- 2 tablespoons unflavored gelatin
- 4 tablespoons cold water
- ⅔ cup (180 ml) milk
- 6 tablespoons dark rum
- 4 large eggs, separated
- ⅔ cup (140 g) firmly packed brown sugar
- 2 cups (200 g) mashed pumpkin
- 2 teaspoons finely grated orange zest
- 1 teaspoon each ground cinnamon, nutmeg, and ginger
- 1½ cups (375 ml) heavy (double) cream
- 4 teaspoons water
- ¼ teaspoon cream of tartar
- ½ cup (60 g) toasted hazelnuts, coarsely chopped

Serves: 6-8; Preparation: 20 minutes + 6 hours to chill; Level of difficulty: 2

Butter a 9-inch (23-cm) springform pan. • Trim the ends off the ladyfingers. Arrange the ladyfingers around the edges of the pan. • Sprinkle the gelatin over the cold water and let soften for 5 minutes. • Stir the gelatin, milk, rum, egg yolks, and ⅓ cup (70 g) brown sugar in a large saucepan over low heat until the mixture coats a metal spoon or reaches 160°F (71°C) on an instant-read thermometer. Remove from the heat and stir in the pumpkin, orange zest, and spices. • Beat the cream in a large bowl with an electric mixer at high speed until stiff. • Stir the egg whites, remaining brown sugar, water, and cream of tartar in a saucepan until blended. Cook over low heat, beating constantly, until the whites register 160°F (71°C) on an instant-read thermometer. Transfer to a large bowl. • With an electric mixer at high speed, beat until stiff, glossy peaks form. • Use a large rubber spatula to fold the beaten whites and cream into the pumpkin mixture. Add the hazelnuts. • Spoon the mixture into the prepared pan. • Refrigerate for 6 hours, or until set. • Loosen and remove the pan sides.

Chestnut charlotte

■ INGREDIENTS

- 4 tablespoons dark rum
- ½ cup (125 ml) water
- about 30 ladyfingers
- 2 cups (500 ml) heavy (double) cream
- ½ cup (100 g) sugar
- 14 oz (450 g) candied chestnuts, crumbled

Serves: 8-10; Preparation: 20 minutes + 12 hours to chill; Level of difficulty: 2

Mix the rum and water in a large bowl. Dip the ladyfingers in the rum mixture. • Line a 1-quart (1-liter) charlotte mold with ladyfingers. • Beat the cream and sugar in a large bowl with an electric mixer at high speed until stiff. • Use a large rubber spatula to fold the chestnuts into the cream. • Repeat layers of the chestnut cream and ladyfingers in the mold until all the ingredients are used up, finishing with ladyfingers. • Refrigerate for 12 hours, or overnight. • Invert onto a serving plate.

Caramel apple ladyfinger cake

Serves: 6-8; Preparation: 20 minutes + 1 hour 30 minutes to soak and stand; Level of difficulty: 2

Butter a 9-inch (23-cm) springform pan. • Sprinkle the apples with lemon zest and juice in a large bowl. Soak for 1 hour. • Heat the apple juice and water in a saucepan. Add the brown sugar, cinnamon, and nutmeg and cook over medium heat until the sugar has dissolved. Simmer for 5 minutes. • Add the apples and soaking juices, stirring often, and cook until tender. Transfer the apples to a plate. • Dip the ladyfingers briefly in the apple syrup. • Line the bottom and sides of mold with ladyfingers, trimming to fit. Spoon in the apples and top with ladyfingers. Drizzle with the syrup. Place a plate on top and let stand 30 minutes. • Loosen the pan sides and place on a serving plate. • Caramel Sauce: Cook the sugar and water in a saucepan, stirring over low heat until the sugar has dissolved. Continue cooking, without stirring, until deep golden brown. • Bring the cream to a boil in a separate saucepan. • Remove the sugar from the heat and stir in the cream. • Return to medium heat for 3 minutes, beating constantly. • Remove from the heat and add the butter. • Serve the charlotte with the sauce, still warm, passed on the side.

INGREDIENTS

- 2 lb (1 kg) Granny Smith apples, peeled, cored, and thinly sliced
- finely grated zest and juice of 1 lemon
- ¾ cup (200 ml) apple juice
- ½ cup (125 ml) water
- ¾ cup (150 g) firmly packed brown sugar
- 1 teaspoon each ground cinnamon and nutmeg
- about 30 ladyfingers

CARAMEL SAUCE
- 1 cup (200 g) sugar
- 6 tablespoons cold water
- 1 cup (250 ml) heavy (double) cream
- 2 tablespoons butter

Lime ladyfinger cake

Serves: 8-10; Preparation: 30 minutes + 4 hours to chill; Level of difficulty: 2

Line a 1½-quart (1.5-liter) charlotte mold with waxed paper. Butter the paper. • Line with one-third of the ladyfingers. • Beat the sugar, cornstarch, lime zest and juice, water, eggs, and salt in a saucepan until blended. Cook over low heat, beating constantly with a wooden spoon, until the mixture lightly coats a metal spoon or registers 160°F (71°C) on an instant-read thermometer. Immediately plunge the pan into a bowl of ice water and stir until the egg mixture has cooled. • With mixer at medium speed, beat the butter in a medium bowl until creamy. Gradually add the egg mixture and almonds. • Spoon half the mixture into the prepared pan. Top with one-third of the ladyfingers. Spoon in the remaining mixture and top with ladyfingers. • Refrigerate for 4 hours. • Invert onto a serving plate.

INGREDIENTS

- about 30 ladyfingers
- 1 cup (200 g) sugar
- 3 tablespoons cornstarch (cornflour)
- 1 tablespoon finely grated lime zest
- ½ cup (125 ml) lime juice
- ½ cup (125 ml) cold water
- 4 large eggs, lightly beaten
- ¼ teaspoon salt
- ½ cup (125 g) butter
- 1½ cups (150 g) flaked almonds

Right: Caramel apple ladyfinger cake

Strawberry amaretto ladyfinger cake

Serves: 6-8; Preparation: 30 minutes; Cooking: 50 minutes; Level of difficulty: 2

Preheat the oven to 350°F/180°C/gas 4. • Butter and flour an 11 x 7-inch (28 x 18-cm) baking pan. • Arrange half the ladyfingers in the pan. Drizzle with 2 tablespoons of amaretto and top with the strawberries. Cover with the remaining ladyfingers and drizzle with the remaining amaretto. • Beat the eggs and egg yolk, sugar, vanilla, and salt in a large bowl with an electric mixer at medium speed until pale and thick. Add the milk. • Pour over the ladyfingers. Set aside for 5 minutes. • Dot with the butter. • Bake for 35 minutes. • Remove from the oven and cover with aluminum foil. Return to the oven and bake for 15 minutes more, or until lightly browned. • Cool completely in the pan. • Spread with the whipped cream and arrange the strawberries on top.

■ INGREDIENTS

• 7 oz (200 g) ladyfingers
• 4 tablespoons amaretto (almond liqueur)
• 1 cup (250 g) strawberries, hulled
• 2 large eggs + 1 large egg yolk
• ½ cup (100 g) sugar
• 1 teaspoon vanilla extract
• ⅛ teaspoon salt
• ½ cup (125 ml) milk
• 4 tablespoons cold butter, cut up
• 1 cup (250 ml) whipped cream, to serve
• halved strawberries, to decorate

Boozy orange charlotte

Serves: 4-6; Preparation: 35 minutes + 2 hours to freeze; Level of difficulty: 2

Butter a 7-inch (18-cm) charlotte mold. Line the sides of the mold with the pirouette cookies. Freeze for 1 hour. • Spoon 2 cups (500 g) of the sorbet into the mold and top with a layer of ladyfingers. • Spoon in the remaining sorbet and top with the remaining ladyfingers. Freeze for 1 hour. • Beat the egg yolks and sugar in a double boiler over barely simmering water until well blended. Cook, stirring constantly with a wooden spoon, until the mixture lightly coats a metal spoon or registers 160°F (71°C) on an instant-read thermometer. Beat with an electric mixer until pale and creamy. Stir in the liqueur. • Invert the mold onto a serving plate and drizzle with the caramel topping and orange sauce.

■ INGREDIENTS

• 30 pirouette cookies
• 3 cups (750 g) orange sorbet
• about 14 ladyfingers
• 4 large egg yolks
• ½ cup (100 g) sugar
• 4 tablespoons orange liqueur
• 4 tablespoons caramel ice-cream topping

Right: Strawberry amaretto ladyfinger cake

Coffee and cream ladyfinger cake

■ INGREDIENTS

- 4 tablespoons apricot preserves (jam), melted
- about 24 ladyfingers
- 4 large egg yolks
- 1 cup (150 g) confectioners' (icing) sugar
- 4 teaspoons coffee extract
- 3 tablespoons dark rum
- 3 cups (750 ml) heavy (double) cream
- 4 oz (125 g) semisweet chocolate, coarsely grated

Serves: 6-8; Preparation: 20 minutes + 8 hours to freeze; Level of difficulty: 2

Brush the sides of a 9-inch (23-cm) springform pan with the apricot preserves. • Trim the ladyfingers and stand them around the sides of the pan. • Beat the egg yolks, confectioners' sugar, coffee extract, and rum in a saucepan until blended. Cook over low heat, beating constantly with a wooden spoon, until the mixture lightly coats a metal spoon or registers 160°F (71°C) on an instant-read thermometer. Immediately plunge the pan into a bowl of ice water and stir until the egg mixture has cooled. • Beat the cream in a large bowl with an electric mixer at high speed until stiff. • Use a large rubber spatula to fold the cream into the egg yolk mixture. • Spoon the mixture into the prepared pan. • Freeze for 8 hours, or until set. • Loosen and remove the pan sides and turn out onto a serving plate. Decorate with the grated chocolate.

Almond lemon charlotte

■ INGREDIENTS

- about 30 ladyfingers
- 1 cup (200 g) sugar
- 3 tablespoons cornstarch (cornflour)
- 1 tablespoon finely grated lemon zest
- ½ cup (125 ml) lemon juice
- ½ cup (125 ml) cold water
- 4 large eggs, lightly beaten
- ¼ teaspoon salt
- ½ cup (125 g) butter
- 1½ cups (150 g) flaked almonds

Serves: 8-10; Preparation: 30 minutes + 4 hours to chill; Level of difficulty: 2

Line a 1½-quart (1.5-liter) charlotte mold with waxed paper. Butter the paper. • Line with one-third of the ladyfingers. • Beat the sugar, cornstarch, lemon zest and juice, water, eggs, and salt in a saucepan until blended. Cook over low heat, beating constantly with a wooden spoon, until the mixture lightly coats a metal spoon or registers 160°F (71°C) on an instant-read thermometer. Immediately plunge the pan into a bowl of ice water and stir until cooled. • With mixer at medium speed, beat the butter in a medium bowl until creamy. Gradually add the lemon mixture and almonds. • Spoon half the mixture into the prepared pan. Top with a layer of ladyfingers. Spoon in the remaining mixture and top with ladyfingers. • Refrigerate for 4 hours. • Invert onto a serving plate.

Left: *Coffee and cream ladyfinger cake*

Chocolate hazelnut cream cake

Serves: 6-8; Preparation: 30 minutes + 8 hours to chill; Level of difficulty: 1

Set out a 9-inch (23-cm) springform pan. • Bring the milk to a boil in a saucepan over low heat. Remove from the heat. • Beat the egg yolks, sugar, and vanilla in a large bowl with an electric mixer at high speed until pale and thick. • With mixer at low speed, gradually add the cornstarch. • Pour the hot milk into the egg mixture. Return the mixture to the saucepan over low heat and cook, stirring constantly with a wooden spoon, until the mixture lightly coats a metal spoon or registers 160°F (71°C) on an instant-read thermometer. Immediately plunge the pan in a bowl of ice water and stir until cooled. • Stir the hazelnut cream into the custard. Line the pan with half the ladyfingers and cover with custard. Repeat. • Refrigerate for 8 hours. • Loosen and remove the pan sides. Transfer to a serving plate. • Decorate the top of the cake with the fruit.

■ INGREDIENTS

- 1 quart (1 liter) milk
- 6 large egg yolks
- 1 cup (200 g) sugar
- 1 teaspoon vanilla extract
- ⅓ cup (50 g) + 2 tablespoons cornstarch (cornflour)
- 28 ladyfingers
- 6 tablespoons chocolate hazelnut cream (Nutella)
- ½ cup (125 g) sliced fresh fruit (such as strawberries, kiwifruit, bananas, or pineapple), to decorate

No-bake pineapple and banana delight

Serves: 8-10; Preparation: 30 minutes + 1 hour to chill; Level of difficulty: 1

Butter a 13 x 9-inch (33 x 23-cm) baking pan. • Mix the crumbs and butter in a large bowl. • Press into the prepared pan. • Beat the cream cheese and 1⅔ cups (250 g) confectioners' sugar with an electric mixer at high speed until creamy. • Spread the cheese mixture over the crust. • Spoon the pineapple over the cream cheese and top with bananas. • With mixer at high speed, beat the cream, the remaining confectioners' sugar, and vanilla in a large bowl until stiff. • Spread the cream over and sprinkle with the nuts. • Refrigerate for 1 hour.

■ INGREDIENTS

- 4 cups (500 g) vanilla wafer crumbs
- 1 cup (250 g) butter, melted
- 1 cup (250 g) cream cheese
- 1⅔ cups (250 g) + 2 tablespoons confectioners' (icing) sugar
- 1 can (1 lb/500 g) crushed pineapple, drained
- 6 bananas, peeled and sliced
- 1½ cups (375 ml) heavy (double) cream
- 1 teaspoon vanilla extract
- ¼ cup (60 g) nuts, coarsely chopped

Right: *Chocolate hazelnut cream cake*

Tropical charlotte

Serves: 8-10; Preparation: 50 minutes + 4 hours to chill; Level of difficulty: 2

Sprinkle the gelatin over the water in a saucepan. Let stand 1 minute. Stir over low heat until the gelatin has completely dissolved. • Beat the egg yolks, sugar, and orange juice in a medium saucepan. Cook over low heat, stirring constantly with a wooden spoon, until the mixture lightly coats a metal spoon or registers 160°F (71°C) on an instant-read thermometer. Immediately plunge the pan into a bowl of ice water and stir until cooled. • Add the gelatin mixture, 2 tablespoons of liqueur, and the lemon juice. Transfer to a large bowl. Cover and refrigerate until thick. • Beat the cream in a large bowl until stiff. • Fold the cream into the orange mixture. • Butter a 9-inch (23-cm) springform pan. Line with some of the ladyfingers. Fill any gaps with ladyfinger pieces. Drizzle with 2 tablespoons of liqueur. • Spoon in the orange cream. Cover and refrigerate for 3 hours. • Transfer to a serving dish. • Stir the preserves and the remaining liqueur in a saucepan over low heat. Trim the ladyfingers to just taller than the filling. Brush each ladyfinger with a little preserves and press against the filling, making a border. • Decorate with the fruit and brush the remaining preserves over the top.

■ INGREDIENTS

- 1½ tablespoons unflavored gelatin
- 4 tablespoons cold water
- 2 large egg yolks
- ¾ cup (150 g) sugar
- 1 cup (250 ml) orange juice
- 5 tablespoons orange liqueur
- 2 tablespoons lemon juice
- 1¼ cups (310 ml) heavy (double) cream
- 7 oz (200 g) ladyfingers
- ½ cup (160 g) apricot preserves (jam)
- 1½ cups (375 g) mixed sliced fresh fruit (such as strawberries, kiwifruit, peaches, and raspberries)

Peach and strawberry ladyfinger cake

Serves: 4-6; Preparation: 30 minutes + 4 hours to chill; Level of difficulty: 1

Butter an 8-inch (20-cm) springform pan. • Beat the cream and 1 tablespoon of kirsch in a large bowl with an electric mixer at medium speed until stiff. • Mix the remaining liqueur and water. • Trim the ladyfingers so that 15 can be placed in a spokelike pattern to cover the pan bottom. Arrange strawberry slices around the pan sides. • Reserve a few slices to decorate. • Dip the ladyfinger trimmings in the liqueur mixture. Mix three-quarters of the cream, remaining fruit, and ladyfinger trimmings. • Spoon the mixture over the ladyfingers. Arrange the remaining ladyfingers in a spokelike pattern to cover the top. • Refrigerate for 4 hours, or until set. • Loosen and remove the pan sides. Transfer onto a serving dish. Decorate with the remaining cream and fruit.

■ INGREDIENTS

- 1⅔ cups (400 ml) heavy (double) cream
- ⅔ cup (180 ml) kirsch
- ⅔ cup (180 ml) water
- about 30 ladyfingers
- 10 oz (300 g) thinly sliced strawberries
- 10 oz (300 g) peeled and thinly sliced peaches

Right: *Tropical charlotte*

Chocolate and coffee ice cream cake

Serves: 6-8; Preparation: 30 minutes + 2 hours to freeze; Level of difficulty: 1

Ice Cream: Bring the milk and cream to a boil in a saucepan over medium heat. Remove from the heat. • Beat the egg yolks, sugar, and hot milk mixture in a double boiler until well blended. Cook over low heat, stirring constantly with a wooden spoon, until the mixture lightly coats a metal spoon or registers 160°F (71°C) on an instant-read thermometer. Add the vanilla. Immediately plunge the pan into a bowl of ice water and stir until the egg mixture has cooled. • Press plastic wrap (cling film) directly onto the surface and refrigerate until chilled. • Freeze in an ice cream machine according to manufacturer's directions. • Pack into a freezer-proof container dusted with confectioners' sugar. Freeze the ice cream for 1 hour. • Divide the ice cream into two equal portions. Stir the chocolate into one portion and the coffee into the other. • Spoon the mixture into a 9-inch (23-cm) ring mold in layers. Freeze for 1 hour. • Topping: Beat the cream, brandy, and confectioners' sugar in a medium bowl with an electric mixer at high speed until stiff. • Unmold onto a serving plate. Pipe the cream over the cake in a decorative manner. Decorate with the coffee beans.

■ INGREDIENTS

ICE CREAM
- 1¼ cups (310 ml) milk
- 1 cup (250 ml) heavy (double) cream
- 4 large egg yolks
- ½ cup (100 ml) sugar
- 1 tablespoon vanilla extract
- 7 oz (200 g) semisweet chocolate, finely grated
- 2 teaspoons freeze-dried coffee granules dissolved in 2 tablespoons hot water

TOPPING
- 1 cup (250 ml) heavy (double) cream
- 1 tablespoon brandy
- 4 tablespoons confectioners' (icing) sugar
- coffee beans, to decorate

Mocha ice cream cake

Serves: 6-8; Preparation: 20 minutes + 2 hours 30 minutes to chill; Level of difficulty: 1

Mix the crumbs, butter, and liqueur in a medium bowl until well blended. Press into the bottom of a 9-inch (23-cm) springform pan. Refrigerate for 30 minutes. • Filling: Beat the ice cream in a large bowl with an electric mixer at low speed until fluffy. • Spread the ice cream evenly into the crust. Freeze for 2 hours. • Loosen and remove the pan sides. Place the cake on a serving plate and sprinkle with the chocolate. Let stand at room temperature for 10 minutes.

■ INGREDIENTS

- 1½ cups (180 g) vanilla wafer crumbs
- 6 tablespoons butter, melted
- 1 tablespoon coffee liqueur

FILLING
- 1 quart (1 liter) packed chocolate ice cream, softened
- 7 oz (200 g) bittersweet chocolate, coarsely grated

Right: Three-flavor ice cream cake

Three-flavor ice cream cake

■ INGREDIENTS

- 3 pints (750 g) pistachio ice cream, softened
- 2 pints (750 g) strawberry ice cream, softened
- 1 cup (250 ml) heavy (double) cream
- ½ cup (60 g) candied cherries, coarsely chopped

Serves: 10-12; Preparation: 15 minutes + 2 hours 30 minutes to freeze; Level of difficulty: 1

Line a 2½-quart (2.5-liter) loaf pan with plastic wrap (cling film). • Beat the pistachio ice cream in a large bowl with an electric mixer at low speed until smooth. Spread pistachio ice cream in the prepared pan. Freeze for 1 hour. • With mixer at low speed, beat the strawberry ice cream in a large bowl until smooth. Spread strawberry ice cream over the pistachio layer. Freeze for 1 hour. • With mixer at high speed, beat the cream in a large bowl until stiff. Use a large rubber spatula to fold in the cherries. Spread the cream over the strawberry ice cream. Freeze for 30 minutes. • Dip the mold in warm water and invert onto a serving plate.

Italian trifle mold

Serves: 10-12; Preparation: 1 hour + 3 hours to chill; Level of difficulty: 2

Set out a domed 2-quart (2-liter) mold or a stainless steel bowl. • Warm the milk and lemon zest in a saucepan over medium heat. • Beat the egg yolks and ¾ cup (150 g) sugar in a large bowl with an electric mixer at high speed until pale and thick. Stir in the flour and warm milk. • Discard the lemon zest. • Return the mixture to the saucepan and bring to a boil, stirring constantly, over medium heat. Simmer for 5 minutes until thick and creamy. • Add the vanilla. • Transfer half of the mixture to a medium bowl. • Melt the chocolate in a double boiler over barely simmering water. • Stir the chocolate into one of the bowls. • Cook the remaining sugar and water in a saucepan over medium heat until the sugar has dissolved. • Remove from the heat and add the liqueur. • Line the mold with half the cake slices. Drizzle with the liqueur mixture. Spoon the vanilla filling into the mold. Top with half the remaining cake slices. Spoon the chocolate mixture over the top. Cover with the remaining cake slices. • Refrigerate for 3 hours. • Dip the mold briefly into cold water. Invert onto a serving plate.

■ INGREDIENTS

- 2 cups (500 ml) milk
- zest of ½ lemon, in one long piece
- 4 large egg yolks
- 1 cup (200 g) sugar
- 1 tablespoon all-purpose (plain) flour
- 1 teaspoon vanilla extract
- 5 oz (150 g) semisweet chocolate, coarsely chopped
- 4 tablespoons water
- ⅔ cup (180 ml) Alchermes liqueur or Marsala wine
- 1 *Basic Sponge Cake* (see page 22), cut into ¼-inch (5-mm) thick slices

Italian mocha cake

Serves: 6-8; Preparation: 1 hour + 12 hours to chill; Level of difficulty: 2

Line a 1-quart (1-liter) mold or a stainless steel bowl with plastic wrap (cling film). • Cut the cake into small pieces and dip in the rum until moist. Line the prepared mold with the cake slices. • Melt the chocolate with 2 tablespoons of rum and the coffee in a double boiler over barely simmering water. • Set aside to cool. • Beat the 1½ cups (375 ml) of cream, confectioners' sugar, and vanilla in a large bowl until stiff. • Gently fold half the cream into the melted chocolate. • Fold the candied fruit and almonds into the remaining cream. • Spoon the chocolate mixture into the mold. Spoon the candied fruit cream over the top, smoothing the top. • Cover with a sheet of waxed paper and refrigerate for 12 hours, or overnight. • Invert and turn out the mold onto a serving plate. • Beat the remaining cream in a medium bowl until stiff. Spread the cream over the top and dust with the cocoa.

■ INGREDIENTS

- ¼ *Basic Sponge Cake* (see page 22)
- 4 tablespoons rum
- 3 oz (90 g) semisweet chocolate, chopped
- 2 tablespoons instant coffee granules
- 2 cups (500 ml) heavy (double) cream
- 2 tablespoons confectioners' (icing) sugar
- 1 teaspoon vanilla extract
- ⅔ cup (60 g) chopped mixed candied fruit
- ½ cup (50 g) chopped almonds
- ⅓ cup (50 g) unsweetened cocoa powder

Right: Italian mocha cake

Frozen Florentine trifle

Serves: 10-12; Preparation: 45 minutes + 5 hours to chill; Level of difficulty: 2

Mix the sugar and water in a saucepan over medium heat until the sugar has dissolved and it comes to a boil. Boil for 5 minutes. Remove from the heat. Add the brandy and rum and let cool. • Moisten the edges of a domed 2-quart (2-liter) mold with a little syrup and line with half the cake slices. Brush with the syrup. • Gently fold the confectioners' sugar, nuts, candied fruit, and grated chocolate into the cream. Spoon the cream into the mold and top with the cake slices. • Refrigerate for 5 hours. • Dip the mold into cold water. Invert onto a serving plate.

■ INGREDIENTS

- 1 cup (200 g) sugar
- 1 cup (250 ml) water
- 3 tablespoons brandy
- 3 tablespoons rum
- 1 *Basic Sponge Cake* (see page 22), cut into ¼-inch (5-mm) thick slices
- ⅓ cup (50 g) confectioners' (icing) sugar
- ⅓ cup (50 g) almonds, finely ground
- ⅓ cup (50 g) hazelnuts, finely ground
- ¼ cup (50 g) mixed candied fruit, chopped
- 6 oz (180 g) semisweet chocolate, grated
- 1 quart (1 liter) whipped cream

Chilled chocolate rum trifle

Serves: 6-8; Preparation: 30 minutes + 3-4 hours to chill; Cooking: 20 minutes; Level of difficulty: 1

Beat the sugar, egg yolks, and 2 tablespoons of milk in a double boiler until blended. Cook over low heat, stirring constantly with a wooden spoon, until the mixture lightly coats a metal spoon or registers 160°F (71°C) on an instant-read thermometer. Immediately plunge the pan into a bowl of ice water and stir until the egg mixture has cooled. • Gradually beat in the flour and the remaining milk. • Fit the bowl into a saucepan of gently simmering water, without letting the bowl touch the water. Cook, stirring, until the mixture thickens. • Remove from the heat and pour half the mixture into another bowl. • Stir the chocolate into the mixture remaining in the first bowl over barely simmering water until the chocolate is melted. Remove from the heat. Press plastic wrap (cling film) directly on the surface of each bowl. Refrigerate until cooled. • Butter a 9-inch (23-cm) springform pan. Line with cake slices. Brush with half the rum to moisten. Brush with the preserves. • Spread with the plain custard. Top with the chocolate custard. Top with the remaining cake slices and brush with the remaining rum. • Refrigerate for 3–4 hours.

■ INGREDIENTS

- ½ cup (100 g) sugar
- 3 large egg yolks
- 3 cups (750 ml) warm milk
- ½ cup (75 g) all-purpose (plain) flour
- 5 oz (150 ml) bittersweet chocolate, coarsely grated
- 1 *Basic Sponge Cake* (see page 22), thinly sliced
- ½ cup (125 ml) rum
- ¾ cup (200 ml) cherry or plum preserves, warmed

Right: *Frozen Florentine trifle*

Ricotta and candied fruit cakes with raspberry sauce

Serves: 6-8; Preparation: 30 minutes + 2 hours to chill; Level of difficulty: 2

Preheat the oven to 375°F/190°C/gas 5. • Set out six individual terrine dishes or ramekins. • Dissolve half the sugar in the water in a small saucepan over medium heat. • Sprinkle the gelatin over the sugar mixture. Let stand 1 minute. Place over low heat and stir until the gelatin has completely dissolved. • Place the ricotta in a large bowl. Stir in the sugar mixture. Mix in the candied fruit, chocolate, and kirsch. • Spoon into the dishes. • Refrigerate for 2 hours. • Process the raspberries and the remaining sugar in a food processor until puréed. • Turn out onto individual plates. • Serve with the raspberry sauce passed on the side.

■ INGREDIENTS

- ½ cup (100 g) sugar
- 4 tablespoons water
- 1 tablespoon unflavored gelatin
- 2 cups (500 g) ricotta cheese
- ½ cup (75 g) chopped mixed candied fruit
- 3 oz (90 g) semisweet chocolate, grated
- 1 tablespoon kirsch
- 1 cup (150 g) raspberries

Sicilian cassata

Cassata is a traditional dessert from Sicily. There are many variations on the basic theme of sponge cake lined with apricot preserves and filled with ricotta cheese, candied fruit, and chocolate. This is one of our favorites.

Serves: 6-8; Preparation: 1 hour + 2 hours to chill; Level of difficulty: 2

Cut the sponge cake into ½-inch (1-cm) thick slices. • Line a 9-inch (23-cm) cake pan with waxed paper. Line with the cake slices. • Warm the apricot preserves and water in a small saucepan over low heat until liquid. Fill the spaces between the slices of cake in the pan with the preserves mixture. • Filling: Heat the sugar, water, and vanilla in a saucepan over medium heat, stirring constantly, until the sugar has dissolved. • Place the ricotta in a large bowl and gradually beat in the sugar mixture with an electric mixer at high speed until stiff. • Use a wooden spoon to stir in the candied peel, pistachios, and kirsch. • Spoon the mixture into the pan over the cake slices. • Top with the remaining slices of cake. • Refrigerate for 2 hours. • Dip the pan briefly into cold water. Invert onto a serving plate. • Glaze: Stir the confectioners' sugar, preserves, and orange-flower water in a saucepan over medium heat until liquid. Drizzle over the cake. • Arrange the candied peel on top in a decorative manner.

■ INGREDIENTS

- 1 *Basic Sponge Cake* (see page 22)
- 4 tablespoons apricot preserves
- 2 teaspoons water

FILLING
- 1¼ cups (250 g) sugar
- 1 tablespoon water
- ½ teaspoon vanilla extract
- 2 cups (500 g) ricotta cheese
- 2 cups (300 g) mixed candied peel, chopped
- 2 tablespoons pistachios
- 1 tablespoon kirsch

GLAZE
- 1⅓ cups (200 g) confectioners' (icing) sugar
- ½ cup (125 g) apricot preserves
- 1 tablespoon orange-flower water
- ½ cup (75 g) mixed candied peel, to decorate

Right: *Ricotta and candied fruit cakes with raspberry sauce*

Marbled ice cream cake with fresh fruit

Serves: 6-8; Preparation: 25 minutes + 2 hours to freeze; Level of difficulty: 1

Line a 9-inch (23-cm) round cake pan with muslin. • Spoon the vanilla ice cream into the prepared pan, followed by the chocolate ice cream. Swirl the two flavors with a fork to create a marbled effect. • Cover with plastic wrap (cling film) and freeze for 2 hours. • Beat the cream, confectioners' sugar, and vanilla in a large bowl with an electric mixer at high speed until stiff. • Turn the ice cream cake out onto a serving plate. • Spread with cream and decorate with the fruit.

■ INGREDIENTS

- 2 cups (500 g) vanilla ice cream, softened
- 2 cups (500 g) chocolate ice cream, softened
- 2 cups (500 ml) heavy (double) cream
- 4 tablespoons confectioners' (icing) sugar
- 1 teaspoon vanilla extract
- about 24 raspberries, cleaned
- 3 kiwifruit, peeled and thickly sliced

Mint ice-cream layer cake

Serves: 6-8; Preparation: 35 minutes + 2 hours to freeze; Level of difficulty: 1

Coarsely chop half the peppermint candies in a food processor. Set aside. • Repeat with the remaining candies, but leave in the food processor. Add the water and process until syrupy. • Beat the cream, confectioners' sugar, and vanilla in a medium bowl with an electric mixer at high speed until stiff. • Split the cake into three horizontally. • Place one layer on a serving plate. Drizzle with 2 tablespoons of syrup. Spread with ½ cup (125 ml) of cream and sprinkle with the chopped candy. Top with the second layer, drizzle with syrup, and spread with ½ cup (125 ml) cream. Sprinkle with the candy. Invert the remaining layer and drizzle the cut side with the remaining syrup. Place top-side up on the cake. • Spread the remaining cream over the cake. Sprinkle with the chopped candies. • Scoop up about 10 small ice cream balls and arrange on top. • Freeze for 2 hours before serving.

■ INGREDIENTS

- 1 cup (150 g) hard peppermint-flavored candies
- 4 tablespoons water
- 1½ cups (375 ml) heavy (double) cream
- ⅓ cup (50 g) confectioners' (icing) sugar
- 1 teaspoon vanilla extract
- 1 *Basic Sponge Cake* (see page 22)
- 2 cups (500 g) vanilla ice cream

Ice cream cakes with berry sauce

Serves: 6-8; Preparation: 30 minutes + 3 hours to freeze; Cooking: 5 minutes; Level of difficulty: 1

Set out six 2-inch (5-cm) individual domed molds. • Berry Sauce: Sprinkle the gelatin over the orange juice in a saucepan. Let stand 1 minute. Stir in the sugar. Warm over low heat until the gelatin has completely dissolved. Bring to a boil, stirring constantly. Add the berries and stir until completely covered. • Remove from the heat. Pour into a medium bowl and set aside to cool. • Freeze for 1 hour, then refrigerate for 30 minutes. • Filling: Drizzle 4 tablespoons of orange juice over the peaches in a large bowl. Let soak 15 minutes. • Mix the remaining orange juice, orange liqueur, and sugar in a large bowl. • Soak the bread in the orange mixture. • Mix the ice cream, cream, and fruit and juices in a large bowl. • Line the prepared molds with the bread slices. Spoon in the ice cream mixture. • Cover with aluminum foil and freeze for 2 hours. • Dip the molds briefly into cold water. Invert each onto individual dessert plates. • Spoon the berry sauce over the tops.

■ INGREDIENTS

BERRY SAUCE
- 1½ teaspoons unflavored gelatin
- juice of 1 orange
- 3 tablespoons sugar
- 1¼ cups (310 g) mixed berries

FILLING
- juice of 2 oranges
- 1½ cups (325 g) chopped canned peaches, drained
- 4 tablespoons orange liqueur
- 2 tablespoons sugar
- 8 slices white sandwich bread
- 1⅔ cups (580 g) vanilla ice cream, softened
- 1¼ cups (310 ml) whipped cream

Right: Mint ice-cream layer cake

Raisin and cookie ice cream cake

Serves: 8-10; Preparation: 20 minutes + 3 hours to freeze; Level of difficulty: 1

Line a 2-quart (2-liter) loaf pan with plastic wrap (cling film). • Beat the cream, sugar, and orange liqueur in a large bowl with an electric mixer at high speed until stiff. Use a large rubber spatula to fold in the ice cream, cookie crumbs, two-thirds of the chocolate chips, and raisins. Spoon the mixture into the prepared pan, pressing down firmly. Freeze for 3 hours. • With mixer at high speed, beat the cream, confectioners' sugar, and vanilla in a medium bowl until stiff. • Turn out onto a serving plate. Remove the plastic wrap (cling film). Sprinkle with the remaining chocolate chips and serve with the cream passed separately.

■ INGREDIENTS

- 1 cup (250 ml) heavy (double) cream
- ⅓ cup (70 g) sugar
- 2 tablespoons orange liqueur
- 2 cups (500 g) vanilla ice cream, softened
- 1 cup (150 g) graham cracker (digestive biscuit) crumbs
- ¾ cup (100 g) semisweet chocolate chips
- ½ cup (60 g) raisins
- 1 cup (250 ml) heavy (double) cream
- 2 tablespoons confectioners' (icing) sugar
- 1 teaspoon vanilla extract

Strawberry ricotta cake

Serves: 10-12; Preparation: 30 minutes + 6 hours to soak and chill; Level of difficulty: 1

Sprinkle the lemons with ¼ cup (50 ml) sugar and the lemon liqueur in a large bowl. Soak for 2 hours. • Beat the egg yolks, remaining sugar, and vanilla in a large bowl with an electric mixer at high speed until pale and thick. • Transfer to a double boiler over barely simmering water. Cook over low heat, stirring constantly with a wooden spoon, until the mixture lightly coats a metal spoon or registers 160°F (71°C) on an instant-read thermometer. Immediately plunge the pan in a bowl of ice water and stir until the egg mixture has cooled. • Mix the ricotta, orange zest, and strawberries in a large bowl. • Sprinkle the gelatin over 4 tablespoons of cream in a saucepan. Let soften for 1 minute. Stir over low heat until the gelatin has completely dissolved. • With mixer at high speed, beat the remaining cream in a medium bowl until stiff. • Stir the gelatin mixture into the ricotta mixture. • Use a large rubber spatula to fold in the whipped cream. • Rinse a 2-quart (2-liter) bowl with cold water. Line with the sliced lemons, overlapping them slightly. • Carefully spoon in the ricotta mixture, taking care not to disturb the lemons. • Refrigerate for 4 hours. • Top with a serving plate and invert the mold.

■ INGREDIENTS

- 2 large lemons, peeled and very thinly sliced
- ¾ cup (150 g) sugar
- ½ cup (125 ml) lemon liqueur
- 4 large egg yolks
- 1 teaspoon vanilla extract
- 2 cups (500 g) ricotta cheese
- 2 tablespoons finely grated orange zest
- 1½ cups (375 ml) finely chopped fresh strawberries
- 1 tablespoon unflavored gelatin
- 1 cup (250 ml) heavy (double) cream

Right: Raisin and cookie ice cream cake

Nut, dried fruit, and cookie cake

Serves: 6-8; Preparation: 15 minutes + 5 hours to chill; Level of difficulty: 1

Butter a 9-inch (23-cm) springform pan. Line with aluminum foil. Butter the foil. • Melt the chocolate and butter in a double boiler over barely simmering water. • Remove from the heat and add the eggnog. • Stir in the fruit, walnuts (reserving some to decorate), and cookie pieces until well blended. • Spoon into the prepared pan, pressing it down with the back of the spoon. Refrigerate for 5 hours. • Loosen and remove the pan sides. Turn out onto a serving plate. Remove the foil and turn top-side up. • Spread the frosting over the cake. Decorate with the walnut pieces.

Fig and chocolate ice cream cake

■ INGREDIENTS

Serves: 4-6; Preparation: 25 minutes + 3 hours to freeze; Level of difficulty: 1

Beat the cocoa and ¾ cup (200 ml) milk in a large saucepan until smooth. Beat in the remaining milk and cream. Bring to a boil over medium heat, stirring constantly. Remove from the heat. • Beat the egg yolks, sugar, and 2 tablespoons of the milk mixture in a saucepan until well blended. Cook over low heat, stirring constantly with a wooden spoon, until the mixture lightly coats a metal spoon or registers 160°F (71°C) on an instant-read thermometer. Add the remaining milk mixture. Immediately plunge the pan into a bowl of ice water and stir until the egg mixture has cooled. Transfer to a large bowl. Press plastic wrap (cling wrap) directly onto the surface. Refrigerate until chilled. • Freeze in an ice cream machine according to manufacturer's directions. • Butter an 8-inch (20-cm) round cake pan. Spoon the ice cream into the prepared pan. Freeze for 3 hours. • Turn out onto a serving dish. Decorate with the figs and raspberries.

- 1 cup (150 g) unsweetened cocoa powder
- 1¼ cups (310 ml) milk
- 1 cup (250 ml) heavy (double) cream
- 4 large egg yolks
- ½ cup (100 g) sugar
- 4 fresh figs, peeled and sliced
- 1 cup (250 g) fresh raspberries, hulled

Marsala and pear mold

■ INGREDIENTS

Serves: 4-6; Preparation: 1 hour + 2 hours to freeze; Level of difficulty: 2

Mix the egg yolks, sugar, and Marsala in a saucepan until well blended. Cook over low heat, stirring constantly with a wooden spoon, until the mixture lightly coats a metal spoon or registers 160°F (71°C) on an instant-read thermometer. Immediately plunge the pan into a bowl of ice water and stir until the egg mixture has cooled. • Gradually stir in the milk and cream. • Freeze in an ice cream machine, according to manufacturer's directions. • Sauté the pears in the butter in a large saucepan over medium heat until softened. Sprinkle with the brown sugar. Drizzle with the rum. • Line a domed 2-quart (2-liter) mold or a stainless steel bowl with half the cake slices. Arrange the pears over the cake slices and up the sides of the mold. Spoon in the ice cream to fill the mold. Top with the remaining cake slices. Place a serving plate on top. • Freeze for 2 hours, or until firmly set. • Refrigerate for 15 minutes before serving. • Dip the mold briefly into cold water, then invert onto a serving plate. • Dust with the cocoa.

- 6 large egg yolks
- ¾ cup (150 g) sugar
- ½ cup (125 ml) dry Marsala wine
- ¾ cup (200 ml) milk
- ¾ cup (200 ml) light (single) cream
- 4 large pears, peeled, thinly sliced, and drained
- 1 teaspoon butter
- 2 teaspoons firmly packed brown sugar
- 1 teaspoon light rum
- 1 *Basic Sponge Cake* (see page 22), thinly sliced
- unsweetened cocoa powder, to dust

Right: Fig and chocolate ice cream cake

Pastries

℘

Baklava, millefeuille, éclairs—all of these classic desserts are made from a delicate pastry base. Some of the recipes in this chapter are time-consuming, but rewarding in the eating and presentation. If you are short of time, use frozen and thawed pastry.

Almond and walnut baklava

Serves: 10-12; Preparation: 40 minutes; Cooking: 40 minutes; Level of difficulty: 2

Preheat the oven to 400°F/200°C/gas 6. • Butter a large jelly-roll pan. • Lay the sheets of dough out flat and cover with waxed paper and a damp kitchen towel. (This will stop them from drying out.) • Mix the almonds, walnuts, cinnamon, and cloves in a large bowl. • Fit one phyllo sheet in the pan and brush with butter. Fit another sheet on top and brush with butter. Place another 3 sheets on top and sprinkle with the nut mixture. Brush each sheet with more butter. Repeat until all the almond mixture is used up, finishing with a layer of pastry. • Cut the baklava into squares and drizzle with the remaining butter. • Bake for about 30 minutes, or until golden brown. • Syrup: Place all the ingredients in a medium saucepan and bring to a boil. Boil over low heat for 10–15 minutes, or until deep golden brown and syrupy. • Drizzle the syrup over the baklava after removing it from the oven.

■ INGREDIENTS

- 10 sheets phyllo pastry, thawed if frozen
- 3 cups (300 g) chopped almonds
- 3 cups (300 g) chopped walnuts
- 1 tablespoon ground cinnamon
- 1 teaspoon ground cloves
- ⅔ cup (180 g) butter, melted

SYRUP
- 2¼ cups (450 g) sugar
- 1¼ cups (310 ml) water
- 6 tablespoons honey
- 2 teaspoons lemon juice
- ½ teaspoon vanilla extract

Almond and cinnamon baklava

Serves: 10-12; Preparation: 45 minutes; Cooking: 40 minutes; Level of difficulty: 2

Preheat the oven to 325°F/170°C/gas 3. • Butter a 9-inch (23-cm) square baking pan. • Lay the sheets of dough out flat and cover with waxed paper and a damp kitchen towel. (This will stop them from drying out.) • Mix the almonds, sugar, and cinnamon in a large bowl. • Fit one pastry sheet in the pan and brush with butter. Fit another sheet on top and brush with butter. Sprinkle with a little almond filling. Place another sheet on top, brush with butter, and sprinkle with filling. Repeat until all the almond mixture is used up. You should have about 12 layers of filled dough. • Fold the remaining sheets and place on top. Brush with butter. • Cut the pastry into diamond shapes about 2 inches (5-cm) in length. Be sure to cut through all the layers to the bottom of the pan. • Bake for about 40 minutes, or until golden brown. • Honey Syrup: Bring the honey, water, and sugar to a boil in a saucepan over low heat until the sugar has dissolved. Add the rose water. • Drizzle the syrup over the baklava after removing it from the oven. Sprinkle with the almonds. • Cool the cake completely in the pan on a rack.

■ INGREDIENTS

- 14 sheets phyllo dough, thawed if frozen
- 2½ cups (375 g) almonds, finely ground
- ⅔ cup (140 g) sugar
- 2 teaspoons ground cinnamon
- 1 cup (250 g) butter, melted

HONEY SYRUP
- 1 cup (250 ml) honey
- 4 tablespoons water
- ¼ cup (50 g) sugar
- 1½ tablespoons rose water
- 2 tablespoons almonds, chopped, to decorate

Right: Almond and walnut baklava

Turkish pistachio baklava

■ INGREDIENTS

- 12 sheets phyllo dough, thawed if frozen
- 5 cups (750 g) almonds
- 2 cups (300 g) pistachios
- 1 cup (150 g) confectioners' (icing) sugar
- 3 tablespoons orange-flower water or rose water
- 1 teaspoon ground cardamom
- 1 cup (250 g) butter, melted
- 1 cup (150 g) whole almonds
- 1¼ cups (310 ml) honey
- ½ cup (50 g) candied cherries, to decorate

Serves: 10-12; Preparation: 2 hours + 24 hours to rest; Cooking: 50 minutes; Level of difficulty: 2

Preheat the oven to 350°F/180°C/gas 4. • Butter a large jelly-roll pan. • Lay the sheets of phyllo out flat and cover with waxed paper and a damp kitchen towel. (This will stop them from drying out.) • Butter a baking sheet. • Process 4 cups (600 g) of almonds with the pistachios, confectioners' sugar, orange-flower water, and cardamom in a food processor until very finely chopped. • Place a phyllo sheet in the prepared pan and brush with butter. Cover with 6 more sheets, brushing each one with butter. • Spread with the almond mixture and top with the remaining 5 sheets, brushing each with butter. • Use a knife to cut into diamond shapes. Sprinkle with the remaining almonds and brush with butter. • Bake for about 50 minutes, or until browned. • Heat the honey in a saucepan until liquid. Drizzle the honey over the baklava. • Split into diamonds and rest overnight. Decorate with the cherries.

American-style baklava

■ INGREDIENTS

- 12 sheets phyllo dough, thawed if frozen
- 1 cup (250 g) butter, melted
- 1 lb (500 g) pecans, coarsely chopped
- ½ cup (100 g) sugar
- 2 teaspoons ground cinnamon

SYRUP
- 2 cups (400 g) sugar
- 2 cups (500 ml) water
- juice of ½ lemon

Serves: 10-12; Preparation: 50 minutes + 30 minutes to chill; Cooking: 65 minutes; Level of difficulty: 2

Preheat the oven to 350°F/180°C/gas 4. • Butter a large jelly-roll pan. • Lay the sheets of phyllo out flat and cover with waxed paper and a damp kitchen towel. (This will stop them from drying out.) • Mix the pecans, sugar, and cinnamon in a large bowl. • Place the first sheet on the prepared pan and brush with butter. Sprinkle with a little pecan mixture. Top with another sheet and brush with butter. Repeat with 10 more sheets. • Refrigerate for 30 minutes. Cut into diamond shapes. • Drizzle with the remaining butter. • Bake for about 45 minutes, or until golden. • Syrup: Bring the sugar, water, and lemon juice to a boil in a saucepan over medium heat. Boil for 20 minutes. Set aside to cool. • Pour the syrup over the cake.

Left: *American-style baklava*

Easy peach puff

INGREDIENTS

- 1¼ lb (575 g) peaches, peeled, pitted, and cut into cubes
- 1 cup (100 g) slivered almonds
- ½ cup (50 g) pistachios, chopped
- 3 amaretti cookies, lightly crushed
- 1 teaspoon sugar
- 4 tablespoons vanilla extract
- 1 lb (500 g) fresh or frozen puff pastry, thawed if frozen
- 1 large egg, lightly beaten
- confectioners' (icing) sugar, to dust

Serves: 6-8; Preparation: 30 minutes; Cooking: 40 minutes; Level of difficulty: 1

Preheat the oven to 400°F/200°C/gas 6. • Set out a baking sheet. • Mix the peaches, almonds, pistachios, amaretti crumbs, sugar, and vanilla in a large bowl. • Roll the pastry out on a lightly floured work surface to a ⅛-inch (3-mm) thick rectangle or square. Prick all over with a fork. Place the pastry on the prepared sheet. • Spoon the peach mixture into the center. Fold the pastry over. • Cut slashes into the top of the pastry and seal the ends with a fork. • Brush with the beaten egg and dust with the confectioners' sugar. • Bake for about 40 minutes, or until golden. • Serve warm.

Cream-filled chocolate éclairs

INGREDIENTS

- 1 quantity *Choux Pastry* (see page 18)
- 1 large egg
- 1 teaspoon water
- ½ cup (125 ml) heavy (double) cream
- 1 quantity *Pastry Cream* (see page 28), cooled
- 1 quantity *Rich Chocolate Frosting* (see page 30)

Serves: 4-6; Preparation: 45 minutes + time to make the pastry + 15 minutes to chill; Cooking: 30 minutes; Level of difficulty: 3

Preheat the oven to 425°F/220°C/gas 7. • Line a baking sheet with parchment paper. • Place the choux pastry in a pastry bag fitted with a ¾-inch (2-cm) tip and pipe ten 4-inch (10-cm) strips of pastry onto the baking sheet. • Lightly beat the egg with the water and brush over the pastry. Score the top of the pastry with a fork to keep the pastry flat during baking. • Bake for 15 minutes. Reduce the oven temperature to 400°F/200°C/gas 6 and bake for 15 minutes more. Remove from the oven and turn off the heat. Use the point of a sharp knife to make a few small cuts along the sides of the éclairs to release steam. Return the éclairs to the oven and leave the door slightly ajar for 10 minutes. • Transfer to racks to cool. • Beat the cream with an electric mixer at high speed until stiff. Fold it into the pastry cream. • Just before serving, place the cream filling in a pastry bag fitted with a ¼-inch (5-mm) tip. Make a hole in one end of each éclair and fill with 3 tablespoons of the filling. • Spread the top of each éclair with frosting. Refrigerate for 15 minutes before serving.

Right: *Easy peach puff*

Apple turnovers

Serves: 4; Preparation: 45 minutes; Cooking: 30 minutes; Level of difficulty: 2

Preheat the oven to 450°F/230°C/gas 8. • Butter a baking sheet. • Cook half the apples with the pear liqueur and half the sugar in a medium saucepan over low heat for 15 minutes. • Cook the remaining apples with the cider, cinnamon, and remaining sugar in a medium saucepan over low heat for 15 minutes. • Strain both apple mixtures and mash until smooth. • Roll the pastry out on a lightly floured surface to ⅛ inch (3 mm) thick. Cut out four 5-inch (13-cm) rounds. Transfer the pastry to the prepared baking sheet. Prick all over with a fork and dampen the edges with water. • Spoon the apple purée into the centers of the rounds. Fold in half and seal well. Brush the pastries with the beaten egg. • Bake for 15 minutes, or until golden brown and puffed. • Beat the cream in a large bowl until stiff. Spoon the cream into a pastry bag and pipe in a decorative manner over the turnovers. Serve warm with any remaining apple purée passed on the side.

INGREDIENTS

- 6 apples, peeled and cut into cubes
- 1 cup (250 ml) pear liqueur
- ¾ cup (150 g) sugar
- 1 cup (250 ml) apple cider
- ⅛ teaspoon ground cinnamon
- 8 oz (250 g) frozen puff pastry, thawed
- 1 large egg, lightly beaten
- ½ cup (125 ml) heavy (double) cream

Ice cream profiteroles

Serves: 6-8; Preparation: 45 minutes + time to prepare the pastry; Cooking: 20 minutes; Level of difficulty: 3

Preheat the oven to 400°F/200°C/gas 6. • Butter a baking sheet. • Fit a pastry bag with a ¾-inch (2-cm) tip and fill the bag half-full with batter. Pipe the batter out onto the baking sheet in 24 small mounds. • Bake for about 20 minutes, or until lightly browned. • Transfer to a rack to cool. • Cream Topping: Beat the cream and sugar in a medium bowl with an electric mixer at high speed until stiff. • Leave the ice cream at room temperature to soften, 10 minutes. Cut a "lid" off each cream puff. Use a teaspoon to hollow out the larger piece, if necessary. Fill with ice cream. Cover each puff with its lid and place on a large serving plate with 1-inch (2.5-cm) sides. Spoon a little cream onto the top of each. Sprinkle with the chocolate. • Pour three-quarters of the chocolate sauce into the base of a serving plate. Place the cream puffs in a pyramid shape on the sauce. Drizzle the remaining sauce over the top.

INGREDIENTS

- 1 quantity *Choux Pastry* (see page 18)

CREAM TOPPING
- 1 cup (250 ml) heavy (double) cream
- 1 tablespoon sugar

- 2 cups (500 ml) firmly packed vanilla ice cream
- ¼ cup (30 g) milk chocolate, grated
- 1 quantity *Chocolate Sauce* (see page 32)

Right: *Apple turnovers*

Turin puff

INGREDIENTS

- 4 firm-ripe pears, peeled, cored, and halved
- 2 tablespoons lemon juice
- 1½ cups (300 g) sugar
- 4 tablespoons white wine
- 8 oz (250 g) fresh or frozen puff pastry, thawed if frozen
- 1 large egg, lightly beaten
- 40 hazelnuts, lightly toasted

Serves: 4-6; Preparation: 35 minutes; Cooking: 45 minutes; Level of difficulty: 1

Preheat the oven to 350°F/180°C/gas 4. • Butter a large baking pan. • Drizzle the pears with the lemon juice. Use a sharp knife to make deep cuts in the pears lengthwise. Place in the baking pan, curved-side up and sprinkle with ¾ cup (150 g) sugar. • Bake for 10 minutes. Drizzle with the wine. Bake for 12 minutes more. • Roll out the pastry to fit a 10-inch (25-cm) pie plate. • Brush the pastry with the egg and sprinkle with the remaining sugar and the nuts. • Bake for about 20 minutes, or until golden brown. • Scoop a few of the nuts off the pastry with a spoon and arrange the pears on the pastry, curved-sides up. Sprinkle with the nuts. • Serve warm or at room temperature.

Simple lemon puff

INGREDIENTS

- 4 tablespoons butter
- ½ cup (100 g) firmly packed brown sugar
- 2 large lemons, very thinly sliced
- 1 lb (500 g) frozen puff pastry, thawed

Serves: 8-10; Preparation: 15 minutes + 30 minutes to chill; Cooking: 20 minutes; Level of difficulty: 1

Line a 10-inch (25-cm) pie plate with parchment paper. Dampen the paper. • Beat the butter and brown sugar in a small bowl with an electric mixer at high speed until creamy. Spread in the prepared pie plate. Refrigerate for 30 minutes. • Arrange the slices of lemon on the prepared base, overlapping them slightly. • Preheat the oven to 350°F/ 180°C/gas 4. • Roll the pastry out on a lightly floured surface to a 10-inch (25-cm) round. Place the pastry over the lemons. Prick all over with a fork. • Bake for about 20 minutes, or until crisp and golden brown. • Invert onto a serving plate. Carefully remove the paper and serve. • If the surface is not caramelized, place under the broiler for a few minutes.

Left: *Turin puff*

Banana millefeuille

Serves: 6-8; Preparation: 20 minutes; Cooking: 20 minutes; Level of difficulty: 2

Preheat the oven to 375°F/190°C/gas 5. • Butter two or three baking sheets. • Roll the pastry out on a lightly floured surface to ¼ inch (5 mm) thick. Cut out three 10-inch (25-cm) disks. • Bake for about 10 minutes, or until golden brown. • Let cool completely on racks. • Bring the milk to a boil in a large saucepan. • Beat the egg yolks and sugar in a large bowl until pale and creamy. • Stir in the vanilla and flour. • Gradually beat in the milk. • Return the mixture to the saucepan and place over low heat. Bring to a boil and cook, stirring constantly, for 5 minutes, or until the custard thickens. • Remove from heat, stir in the butter, and let cool. • Peel and slice the bananas. Drizzle with the lemon juice. • Place a pastry round on a serving dish and spread with slightly less than half the custard. Cover with slightly less than half the bananas and oranges. • Cover with the second disk of pastry and repeat. • Top with the remaining pastry and decorate with the remaining fruit and custard.

■ INGREDIENTS

- 14 oz (400 g) frozen puff pastry, thawed
- 2 cups (500 ml) milk
- 4 large egg yolks
- ½ cup (100 g) sugar
- 1 teaspoon vanilla extract
- ⅓ cup (50 g) all-purpose (plain) flour
- 2 tablespoons butter
- 3 large bananas
- juice of 1 lemon
- 2 oranges, peeled and cut into segments

Creamy thousand-layer puff

Serves: 6-8; Preparation: 40 minutes; Cooking: 30 minutes; Level of difficulty: 2

Preheat the oven to 350°F/180°C/gas 4. • Roll the pastry out into 4 very thin rectangles of equal size. Place on baking sheets and prick all over with a fork. • Bake for about 10 minutes, or until golden brown. • Beat the egg yolks and sugar in a saucepan until pale and creamy. • Stir in the Marsala and place the saucepan in a larger pan of simmering water over low heat. Cook, stirring constantly, until the cream is smooth and thick. • Remove from heat and pour into a bowl to cool. • Beat the cream and fold it carefully into the cooled egg mixture. • Place one sheet of cooled pastry on a large plate and cover with one-third of the cream. Cover with another sheet of pastry and layer of cream. Repeat and cover with the fourth sheet of pastry. • Place the confectioners' sugar in a small bowl with the butter and vanilla extract. Stir in enough boiling water to make a thick glaze. Spread over the top sheet of pastry. Sprinkle with the almonds. • Serve as soon as possible so that the pastry doesn't have time to become soggy.

■ INGREDIENTS

- 14 oz (400 g) frozen puff pastry, thawed
- 3 large egg yolks
- ¾ cup (150 g) sugar
- 4 tablespoons Marsala wine
- ⅔ cup (180 ml) heavy (double) cream
- ½ cup (75 g) confectioners' (icing) sugar
- 2 tablespoons butter
- ½ teaspoon vanilla extract
- 2 tablespoons boiling water
- 1 cup (100 g) almond shavings

Right: *Banana millefeuille*

Saint-Honoré

This is a classic French dessert. It is time-consuming to make but well worth the effort.

Serves: 10-12; Preparation: 1 hour 45 minutes; Cooking: 35 minutes; Level of difficulty: 3

Preheat the oven to 400°F/200°C/gas 6. • Stir together the flour and sugar in a medium bowl. Use a pastry blender to cut in the butter until the mixture resembles coarse crumbs. Stir in the egg yolk until a smooth dough is formed. • Roll the dough out on a lightly floured surface to form a 10-inch (25-cm) round. Prick all over with a fork and place on a baking sheet. Brush a little beaten egg around the edge. • Prepare the Choux Pastry. Fit a pastry bag with a plain ¾-inch (2-cm) tip and fill half-full with pastry. • Pipe the pastry around the edge of the pastry round. • Set aside the remaining pastry. • Brush some beaten egg over the top. • Bake for about 20 minutes, or until golden. • Cool the pastry completely on a rack. • Line a baking sheet with waxed paper. • Fill a pastry bag with the remaining choux pastry. Pipe heaps the size of small nuts on the prepared sheet. Brush with the remaining beaten egg. • Bake for about 15 minutes, or until golden. Cool the pastry puffs completely on racks. • Filling: Warm the milk in a saucepan over low heat. • Beat the egg yolks and sugar in a large bowl with an electric mixer at high speed until pale and thick. Use a large rubber spatula to fold in the flour. Gradually stir in the hot milk. • Transfer the mixture to a medium saucepan. Bring to a boil, stirring constantly, and cook until thickened. Remove from the heat and stir in the rum and vanilla. Set aside to cool completely. • Caramel Glaze: Heat the sugar and water in a saucepan over medium heat until the sugar has dissolved. Continue cooking, without stirring, until pale gold in color. Remove from the heat. • Spoon the cooled filling into the pastry base. • Dip the tops of the choux puffs in the caramel to glaze. Dip the bases of the puffs in the caramel and stick around the edges of the cake at regular intervals, pressing down lightly. • Frosting: Mix the confectioners' sugar and enough water to make a smooth frosting. Spoon half the frosting over the filling. • Trace crossing diagonal lines on the frosting with a small knife. Stir the cocoa into the remaining frosting. Spoon the frosting into a pastry bag. Use the lines as a guide to pipe thin chocolate lines over the filling.

INGREDIENTS

- 1⅓ cups (200 g) all-purpose (plain) flour
- 1 tablespoon sugar
- 7 tablespoons cold butter
- 1 large egg yolk + 1 large egg, lightly beaten
- ½ quantity *Choux Pastry* (see page 18)
- 1 large egg, lightly beaten

FILLING
- 2 cups (500 ml) milk
- 4 large egg yolks
- ¾ cup (150 g) sugar
- ½ cup (75 g) all-purpose (plain) flour
- 1 tablespoon dark rum
- 1 teaspoon vanilla extract

CARAMEL GLAZE
- 1 cup (200 g) sugar
- 2 tablespoons water

FROSTING
- ⅔ cup (100 g) confectioners' (icing) sugar
- 2 tablespoons boiling water
- 1 tablespoon unsweetened cocoa powder

Right: Saint-Honoré

Almond and chocolate millefeuille

INGREDIENTS

- 1½ lb (650 g) fresh or frozen puff pastry, thawed if frozen
- 3 tablespoons confectioners' (icing) sugar
- 3 cups (450 ml) *Pastry Cream* (see page 28)
- 8 oz (250 g) white chocolate, coarsely chopped
- 1 oz (30 g) bittersweet chocolate, chopped
- 1 cup (100 g) flaked almonds

Serves: 10-12; Preparation: 45 minutes; Cooking: 20 minutes; Level of difficulty: 3

Preheat the oven to 400°F/200°C/gas 6. • Line 2 baking sheets with waxed paper. • Roll the pastry into three equal squares. Place on the prepared sheets and prick with a fork. • Bake for about 15 minutes, or until golden brown. Sprinkle with 1 tablespoon confectioners' sugar and broil (grill) for 5 minutes to caramelize. • Cool on racks. • Place one pastry layer on a plate and spread with half the pastry cream. Cover with another pastry layer and repeat with the remaining cream and pastry. • Melt the white chocolate in a double boiler over barely simmering water. Spread over the cake. • Melt the bittersweet chocolate in a double boiler over barely simmering water. Spoon into a pastry bag. • Pipe over the top of the cake in a decorative manner. Press the almonds onto the sides of the cake.

Millefeuille with zabaglione

Be sure to assemble this cake just before serving so that the pastry does not become soggy.

Serves: 6-8; Preparation: 30 minutes; Cooking: 25 minutes; Level of difficulty: 2

Preheat the oven to 350°F/180°C/gas 4. • Butter a large baking sheet. • Roll the pastry out on a floured surface to ¼ inch (5 mm) thick. Cut out three 10-inch (25-cm) rounds. Brush with beaten egg and sprinkle with sugar. • Transfer to the prepared baking sheet. • Bake for 15 minutes, or until golden brown. • Cool completely on racks. • Zabaglione: Beat the egg yolks and sugar in a large bowl until pale and creamy. Add the marsala. Transfer to a double boiler over low heat and cook, stirring constantly, for about 15 minutes, or until the mixture thickens. Do not allow it to boil. • Remove from the heat and divide between two bowls. Add the melted chocolate to one of the bowls and mix well. Let cool. • Place one of the pastry rounds on a serving dish and spread with the plain zabaglione. Cover with a pastry round and spread with the chocolate zabaglione. Cover with the remaining pastry round and dust with the confectioners' sugar.

■ INGREDIENTS

PASTRY
- 14 oz (400 g) fresh or frozen puff pastry, thawed if frozen (see page 18)
- 1 small egg, lightly beaten
- 1 tablespoon sugar

ZABAGLIONE
- 4 large egg yolks
- ⅓ cup (70 g) sugar
- 6 tablespoons Marsala wine
- 4 oz (125 g) semisweet chocolate
- 2 tablespoons confectioners' (icing) sugar, to dust

Chestnut cream millefeuille

Serves: 6-8; Preparation: 30 minutes; Cooking: 15 minutes; Level of difficulty: 1

Preheat the oven to 400°F/200°C/gas 6. • Line a baking sheet with waxed paper. • Unfold or unroll the pastry on a lightly floured work surface. Place on the prepared sheet and prick all over with a fork. • Bake for about 15 minutes, or until golden brown. • Cool the pastry on a rack. • Use a sharp knife to cut into 4 rectangles, measuring about 4 x 9 inches (10 x 23-cm). • Chestnut Cream Filling: Purée the candied chestnuts, rum, and milk in a food processor until smooth. • Place one pastry layer on a serving plate. Spread with a thin layer of chestnut cream. Cover with another pastry layer and repeat until all the pastry and cream has been used up. • Finish with a pastry layer. Dust with the confectioners' sugar. Decorate with the candied chestnuts and chocolate leaves.

■ INGREDIENTS

- 1 lb (500 g) fresh or frozen puff pastry, thawed if frozen

CHESTNUT CREAM FILLING
- 12 oz (300 g) candied chestnuts, coarsely chopped
- 2 tablespoons rum
- 6 tablespoons milk
- 1¼ cups (310 ml) heavy (double) cream
- 2–3 tablespoons confectioners' (icing) sugar, to dust
- candied chestnuts, to decorate
- chocolate leaves, to decorate

Right: *Millefeuille with zabaglione*

Apple cinnamon puff

- 1 lb (500 g) fresh or frozen puff pastry, thawed if frozen
- 2 cups (500 ml) unsweetened applesauce
- ⅓ cup (70 g) sugar
- 1 tablespoon finely grated lemon zest
- 1 teaspoon ground cinnamon
- 1 large egg yolk, lightly beaten

Serves: 8-10; Preparation: 30 minutes; Cooking: 30 minutes; Level of difficulty: 1

Preheat the oven to 400°F/200°C/gas 6. • Set aside one-quarter of the pastry and roll the remainder out on a lightly floured surface to form a 13-inch (33-cm) square. Fit into a 12-inch (30-cm) square tart pan, pressing up the sides. Prick all over with a fork. • Stir the applesauce, sugar, lemon zest, and cinnamon in a large bowl. Spread evenly over the pastry. • Roll out the remaining dough and cut into long strips. Arrange the strips over the apple filling in a lattice pattern, sealing them to the pastry sides. Brush the egg yolk over the pastry. • Bake for about 30 minutes, or until golden brown. • Serve warm.

Pineapple and pistachio puff

- 1 tablespoon butter
- ⅓ cup (70 g) sugar
- 2 tablespoons lemon juice
- 1 fresh pineapple, weighing about 2 lb (1 kg), peeled and finely chopped
- 1 lb (500 g) fresh or frozen puff pastry, thawed if frozen
- ¾ cup (120 g) pistachios
- 3 ladyfingers
- 1 large egg, lightly beaten
- 2 tablespoons confectioners' (icing) sugar, to dust

Serves: 8-10; Preparation: 40 minutes; Cooking: 30 minutes; Level of difficulty: 2

Preheat the oven to 400°F/200°C/gas 6. • Set out a 12-inch round pie plate. • Cook the butter, ¼ cup (50 g) sugar, and lemon juice in a saucepan over medium heat until golden brown. • Add the pineapple and cook until the mixture is dry, about 10 minutes. Set aside to cool. • Unroll or unfold the pastry on a lightly floured surface and roll out to form two 13-inch (33-cm) rounds. Use one round to line the pan, folding the edges over to form a raised rim. Prick all over with a fork. • Finely chop the pistachios, ladyfingers, and remaining sugar in a food processor. • Sprinkle the pistachio mixture over the pastry. Spread with the pineapple mixture. • Run a pastry cutting wheel over the remaining round of pastry to create an open spider's web pattern and drape the pastry over the pineapple. • Brush the pastry with the egg. • Dust with the confectioners' sugar. • Bake for about 20 minutes, or until golden brown. • Serve warm or at room temperature.

Left: *Apple cinnamon puff*

Small Cakes

These bite-sized treats are ideal finger or party food for adults and children alike. Create the delectable Cannoli or Custard-filled Carnival Fritters for a taste of the Mediterranean. Or try one of the many tartlet recipes for outdoor summer dining.

Custard-filled carnival fritters

Makes: about 12 fritters; Preparation: 30 minutes; Cooking: 30 minutes; Level of difficulty: 3

Custard: Beat the egg yolks, sugar, and flour in a large bowl until pale and creamy. • Bring the milk to a boil with the lemon zest in a large saucepan. • Gradually pour the milk over the egg mixture and beat well. Return the mixture to the saucepan and place over low heat. Cook for 7–8 minutes, stirring constantly, until the custard thickens. • Remove from the heat and let cool. • Fritters: Bring the butter and water to a boil in a large saucepan. • Sift in the flour and salt and stir until the mixture comes away from the sides of the pan and forms a ball. Remove from the heat and beat in the sugar. • Let cool slightly. Add the lemon zest and eggs, beating until just blended. • Cut twelve 3-inch (8-cm) squares of waxed paper. • Heat the oil in a large, deep frying pan until very hot. • Use a pastry bag to pipe 2 inch (5-cm) rounds of the batter onto each piece of paper. Pipe a border around the edge of each round. • Fry in small batches with their paper still attached for 3–4 minutes, or until golden. The paper will fall off during frying. • Remove with a slotted spoon and drain well on paper towels. • Arrange on a serving dish and fill each one with the custard. Decorate with the cherries and dust with the confectioners' sugar.

■ INGREDIENTS

CUSTARD
- 3 large egg yolks
- ¼ cup (50 g) sugar
- 2 tablespoons all-purpose (plain) flour
- 1 cup (250 ml) milk
- finely grated zest of ½ lemon

FRITTERS
- 6 tablespoons butter
- 1 cup (250 ml) water
- 1 cup (150 g) all-purpose (plain) flour
- ⅛ teaspoon salt
- 2 tablespoons sugar
- finely grated zest of 1 lemon
- 3 large eggs
- 1 quart (1 liter) olive oil, for frying
- fresh or candied cherries, to decorate
- 4 tablespoons confectioners' (icing) sugar, to dust

Carol's pistachio moments

Makes: 10-12 small cakes; Preparation: 45 minutes; Cooking: 20 minutes; Level of difficulty: 1

Preheat the oven to 325°F/170°C/gas 3. • Butter and flour 10–12 little cake molds (or a muffin tray). • Mix the pistachios and sugar in a large bowl. • Beat the egg whites in a large bowl with an electric mixer at high speed until stiff peaks form. • Stir the egg yolks and orange zest into the pistachio mixture. • Use a large rubber spatula to gradually fold the pistachio mixture into the beaten whites, alternating with the cornstarch. • Spoon the batter into the prepared molds, filling each about three-quarters full. • Bake for about 20 minutes, or until a toothpick inserted into the center comes out clean. • Cool the cakes on racks.

■ INGREDIENTS

- 1¼ cups (200 g) pistachios, blanched and finely ground
- 1 cup (200 g) sugar
- 4 large eggs, separated
- 2 tablespoons finely grated orange zest
- ½ cup (75 g) cornstarch (cornflour)

Right: Citrus bites

Citrus bites

■ INGREDIENTS

- 1½ cups (225 g) all-purpose (plain) flour
- 6 tablespoons butter, melted
- 1 tablespoon finely grated lemon zest
- 2 teaspoons baking powder
- 1 large egg, lightly beaten
- ⅓ cup (70 g) sugar
- 2 tablespoons lemon juice
- ⅔ cup (120 g) raisins
- 4 tablespoons raw sugar

Makes: about 12-15 small cakes; Preparation: 10 minutes; Cooking: 15 minutes; Level of difficulty: 1

Preheat the oven to 375°F/190°C/gas 5. • Butter a baking sheet. • Beat the flour, butter, lemon zest, and baking powder in a large bowl with an electric mixer at medium speed until well blended. • Add the egg, sugar, lemon juice, and raisins. • Drop heaping tablespoons of the batter onto the prepared sheet, spacing them about 2 inches (5 cm) apart. Sprinkle with the raw sugar. • Bake for about 15 minutes, or until golden brown. • Cool the cakes on racks.

Spiced nutty chocolate cakes

Makes: 12-15 small cakes; Preparation: 10 minutes; Cooking: 30 minutes; Level of difficulty: 1

Preheat the oven to 350°F/180°C/gas 4. • Butter a large baking sheet. • Mix the honey, sugar, baking soda, and pepper in a large bowl. • Add the water and flour and mix well. • Add the almonds, pine nuts, candied peel, and chocolate and beat until well blended. • Drop tablespoons of the batter well spaced onto the prepared sheet. • Bake for about 30 minutes, or until firm to the touch. • Cool on the sheet until firm. Transfer to a rack to cool completely.

■ INGREDIENTS

- 6 tablespoons clear honey
- ½ cup (100 g) sugar
- 1 teaspoon baking soda
- 1 teaspoon freshly ground black pepper
- ½ cup (125 ml) boiling water
- 1⅓ cups (200 g) all-purpose (plain) flour
- ¾ cup (75 g) chopped almonds
- generous ⅓ cup (75 g) pine nuts
- ⅔ cup (60 g) diced candied peel
- 2 oz (60 g) semisweet chocolate, finely grated

Proust's madeleines

These delicious little cakes are associated with the town of Commercy in France. The French writer, Marcel Proust made madeleines famous when he wrote about them in his novel, "Remembrance of Things Past."

Makes: about 12 small cakes; Preparation: 15 minutes; Cooking: 10 minutes; Level of difficulty: 1

Preheat the oven to 400°F/200°C/gas 6. • Butter and flour a 12-cup madeleine tray. • Spoon the batter into the prepared tray, filling each half full. • Bake for about 10 minutes, or until a toothpick inserted into the center comes out clean. • Cool the cakes in the tray for 15 minutes. Turn out onto racks and let cool completely. • Brush each cake with a thin layer of lemon curd. Place the coconut on a plate and roll each cake until well coated. • Decorate with the candied cherries.

■ INGREDIENTS

- 1 quantity *Basic Sponge Cake* batter (see page 22)
- 1 cup (250 ml) lemon curd
- 1 cup (125 g) shredded (desiccated) coconut
- 12 candied cherries, to decorate

Right: *Spiced nutty chocolate cakes*

Fisherman's cakes

Makes: about 15 small cakes; Preparation: 10 minutes; Cooking: 25 minutes; Level of difficulty: 1

Preheat the oven to 375°F/190°C/gas 5. • Line a cookie sheet with waxed paper. • Process all the ingredients in a food processor until smooth. • Alternatively, place all the ingredients in a large bowl and beat with an electric mixer at low speed until blended. • Use your hands to spread the dough out to about ½-inch (1-cm) thick on a lightly floured work surface. • Use a plain cookie cutter or glass to cut out rounds. • Transfer the rounds to the prepared sheet. Reroll the remaining dough and cut into disks. • Bake for about 25 minutes, or until golden brown and firm to the touch. • Cool the cakes on racks.

■ INGREDIENTS

- 1⅓ cups (200 g) all-purpose (plain) flour
- ¾ cup (135 g) raisins
- ¾ cup (150 g) sugar
- ¾ cup (200 ml) milk
- 6 tablespoons smooth peanut butter
- 1 large egg
- 2 tablespoons oil
- 2 teaspoons baking powder
- 1 teaspoon vanilla extract

Queen of hearts tarts

Makes: 12 tarts; Preparation: 15 minutes + time to prepare pastry; Cooking: 20 minutes; Level of difficulty: 2

Preheat the oven to 400°F/200°C/gas 6. • Set out twelve 2½-inch (5-cm) tartlet molds. • Roll the pastry out on a lightly floured work surface to 3-inch (7-cm) disks and use them to line the tartlet molds. Prick all over with a fork. Line the pastry shells with foil and fill the foil with dried beans or pie weights. • Bake for 5 minutes, then remove the foil and beans or pie weights and bake for about 10 minutes, or until they are just beginning to become crisp. • Use a teaspoon to spoon the preserves into the tarts. • Bake for about 10 minutes more, or until the pastry is golden brown and the preserves begin to bubble. • Cool the tarts completely in the molds on racks.

■ INGREDIENTS

- ½ quantity *Sweet Shortcrust Pastry* (see page 16)
- 1 cup (300 g) raspberry preserves (jam)

Right: *Fisherman's cakes*

Cupid cupcakes

■ INGREDIENTS

- 1¾ cups (275 g) all-purpose (plain) flour
- 2 teaspoons baking powder
- ½ teaspoon baking soda
- ¼ teaspoon salt
- ½ cup (125 g) butter
- ½ cup (100 g) sugar
- 1 teaspoon vanilla extract
- 2 large eggs
- 1 cup (250 ml) heavy (double) cream
- 4 oz (125 g) milk chocolate, finely chopped
- 12 small heart-shaped milk chocolates

Makes: about 12 cupcakes; Preparation: 20 minutes; Cooking: 20 minutes; Level of difficulty: 1

Preheat the oven to 350°F/180°C/gas 4. • Butter and flour a 12-cup muffin pan, or line with foil or paper baking cups. • Sift the flour, baking powder, baking soda, and salt into a medium bowl. • Beat the butter, sugar, and vanilla in a large bowl with an electric mixer at medium speed until creamy. • Add the eggs one at a time, beating until just blended. • Gradually beat in the dry ingredients, alternating with the cream. Stir in the chopped chocolate. • Spoon the batter into the prepared cups, filling each one about three-quarters full. • Bake for about 20 minutes, or until a toothpick inserted into the center comes out clean. • Cool the cakes on racks. • When the cupcakes are still warm, press a chocolate into the top of each. • Let cool completely.

Classic butterflies

These dainty little cakes are perfect to serve at afternoon tea.

Makes: about 18 cakes; Preparation: 25 minutes; Cooking: 15 minutes; Level of difficulty: 1

Preheat the oven to 350°F/180°C/gas 4. • Set out about 18 foil or paper baking cups. • Sift the flour, baking powder, and salt into a medium bowl. • Beat the butter and sugar in a medium bowl with an electric mixer at high speed until pale and creamy. • With mixer at medium speed, beat in the egg. • Gradually beat in the dry ingredients, alternating with the milk. • Spoon the batter into the baking cups, filling each one about two-thirds full. • Bake for about 15 minutes, or until risen and golden brown. • Cool the cakes on racks. • Use a sharp knife to cut a circle about ½-inch (1-cm) deep from the top of each cake. • Beat the cream with the confectioners' sugar and vanilla in a medium bowl until thick. • Spoon a little cream into each cake. • Cut the tops in half and arrange on the cakes like butterfly wings.

INGREDIENTS

- 1 cup (150 g) all-purpose (plain) flour
- 1 teaspoon baking powder
- ¼ teaspoon salt
- ½ cup (125 g) butter
- ½ cup (100 g) sugar
- 1 large egg
- 2 tablespoons milk
- 1 cup (250 ml) heavy (double) cream
- 2 tablespoons confectioners' (icing) sugar
- ¼ teaspoon vanilla extract

Lemon and strawberry butterflies

Makes: about 20-24 cakes; Preparation: 15 minutes; Cooking: 15 minutes; Level of difficulty: 1

Preheat the oven to 350°F/180°C/gas 4. • Arrange 20–24 foil or paper baking cups on baking sheets. • Sift the flour, baking powder, and salt into a medium bowl. • Beat the butter, sugar, and vanilla in a large bowl with an electric mixer at medium speed until creamy. • Add the eggs one at a time, beating until just blended after each addition. • Gradually beat in the dry ingredients, alternating with the milk and lemon juice. • Spoon the batter into the baking cups, filling each one about two-thirds full. • Bake for about 15 minutes, or until golden brown. • Cool the cakes on racks. • With mixer at high speed, beat the cream in a medium bowl until stiff. • Cut a small circle about ½-inch (1-cm) deep from the top of each cake. Fill with ½ teaspoon of jam and 2–3 teaspoons of whipped cream. Cut the tops in half and arrange on the cakes like butterfly wings.

INGREDIENTS

- 2 cups (300 g) all-purpose (plain) flour
- 2 teaspoons baking powder
- ¼ teaspoon salt
- ⅔ cup (180 g) butter
- ¾ cup (150 g) sugar
- 1 teaspoon vanilla extract
- 2 large eggs
- ½ cup (125 ml) milk
- 1 tablespoon lemon juice
- ½ cup (160 g) strawberry preserves (jam)
- 1 cup (250 ml) heavy (double) cream

Right: *Classic butterflies*

Easy fruit rounds

Makes: 6 small cakes; Preparation: 10 minutes + time to prepare the sponge; Level of difficulty: 1

Place the fruit in a medium bowl and drizzle with the lemon juice. • Cut the sponge cake in half horizontally and use a sharp-edged cookie cutter or glass to cut out six rounds of cake. Arrange on serving dishes and spread with half of the preserves. • Melt the remaining preserves in a small saucepan over low heat. • Arrange the fruit on top of the cake and brush with the melted preserves. • Pipe rosettes of the cream on top of the cakes just before serving.

■ INGREDIENTS

- 12 raspberries, hulled
- 2 kiwifruit, peeled and cut into segments
- 2 large bananas, peeled and sliced
- juice of 1 lemon
- 1 *Basic Sponge Cake* (see page 22)
- ⅓ cup (100 g) apricot preserves (jam)
- whipped cream, to decorate

Mini almond cakes with coffee mousse

Makes: 8 cakes; Preparation: 1 hour + 12 hours to chill; Cooking: 15 minutes; Level of difficulty: 2

Preheat the oven to 375°F/190°C/gas 5. • Butter a baking sheet. Line with waxed paper. • Cake: Mix the almonds and ½ cup (100 g) of sugar in a large bowl. Stir in the egg yolks, flour, and salt. • Beat the egg whites and remaining sugar in a large bowl until stiff, glossy peaks form. Fold them into the almond mixture. • Spread the batter onto the prepared sheet to about ¼-inch (5-mm) thick. • Bake for about 15 minutes, or until lightly browned. Cool for 10 minutes. Cut out eight 3-inch (8-cm) disks. Carefully remove the paper and let cool. • Coffee Mousse: Beat the egg yolks, sugar, and 1 tablespoon of coffee in a double boiler. Cook over barely simmering water until the mixture lightly coats a metal spoon or registers 160°F (71°C) on an instant-read thermometer. Immediately plunge the pan into a bowl of ice water and stir until the egg mixture has cooled. Transfer to a large bowl and let cool. • Sprinkle the gelatin over 2 tablespoons of coffee in a saucepan. Let stand 1 minute. Stir over low heat until the gelatin has completely dissolved. Stir into the egg and sugar mixture. • Beat the cream in a large bowl until stiff. Fold the cream into the cooled egg mixture. Refrigerate until it begins to set. • Dip the bases into the remaining coffee. • Set out on serving plates and place a metal ring around each one. Spoon the mousse over each of the bases. Refrigerate for 12 hours. • Remove the metal rings and dust with the cocoa. • Topping: Beat the cream in a large bowl until stiff. • Spoon into a pastry bag and pipe onto each mousse. Decorate with the raspberries.

■ INGREDIENTS

CAKE
- 1 cup (150 g) finely ground almonds
- ¾ cup (150 g) sugar
- 3 large eggs, separated + 3 large egg whites
- ⅓ cup (50 g) all-purpose (plain) flour
- ¼ teaspoon salt

COFFEE MOUSSE
- 3 large egg yolks
- ¼ cup (50 g) sugar
- ½ cup (125 ml) cold strong coffee
- 1½ teaspoons unflavored gelatin
- 1 cup (250 ml) heavy (double) cream
- 2 tablespoons unsweetened cocoa powder

TOPPING
- ½ cup (125 ml) heavy (double) cream
- raspberries, to decorate

Right: *Easy fruit rounds*

Tuscan fall tarts

■ INGREDIENTS

PASTRY
- 1⅓ cups (200 g) all-purpose (plain) flour
- ¼ teaspoon salt
- ⅓ cup (70 g) sugar
- generous ⅓ cup (100 g) butter
- 2 large egg yolks

FILLING
- 1¼ cups (400 g) fig preserves
- fresh figs, cut into segments, to decorate

Makes: 12 tartlets; Preparation: 30 minutes + 1 hour to chill the pastry; Cooking: 20 minutes; Level of difficulty: 2

Pastry: Sift the flour and salt into a large bowl and make a well in the center. Stir in the sugar. • Rub in the butter with your fingertips • Add the egg yolks and mix to make a smooth dough. • Wrap in plastic wrap (cling film) and chill for 1 hour. • Preheat the oven to 375°F/190°C/gas 5. • Grease 12 tartlet pans. • Roll out the dough on a lightly floured work surface. Cut out rounds and use them to line the pans. • Fill each one with 2–3 tablespoons of preserves. • Bake for 20 minutes. • Remove from the oven and let cool. Transfer to serving dishes and decorate with the fresh figs.

Ricotta and strawberry summer tarts

■ INGREDIENTS

- 12 store-bought tartlet shells or homemade (see recipe *Tuscan Fall Tarts,* above)
- 1 cup (250 g) strawberries + about 12 extra, to decorate
- ⅔ cup (100 g) confectioners' (icing) sugar
- ½ cup (125 ml) raspberry liqueur
- finely grated zest and juice of 1 lemon
- ⅔ cup (180 ml) fresh ricotta cheese
- 1 cup (250 ml) plain yogurt
- 1½ tablespoons unflavored gelatin
- 4 tablespoons cold water
- 1½ cups (375 ml) heavy (double) cream

Makes: 12 tartlets; Preparation: 50 minutes + 1 hour to chill; Level of difficulty: 1

If using homemade tartlet shells, follow the recipe above, then bake the shells at 375°F/190°C/gas 5 for about 12 minutes, or until crisp and golden brown. Let cool completely. • Process 1 cup (250 g) of strawberries in a food processor until puréed. • Transfer the strawberries to a large bowl and mix in the confectioners' sugar, liqueur, lemon zest and juice, ricotta, and yogurt. • Sprinkle the gelatin over the water in a saucepan. Let stand 1 minute. Stir over low heat until the gelatin has completely dissolved. • Stir the gelatin into the strawberry mixture and refrigerate until thickened. • Beat the cream in a medium bowl with an electric mixer at medium speed until stiff. Fold the cream into the strawberry mixture. • Spoon the raspberry mixture into a pastry bag with a ¼-inch (5-mm) plain tip. Pipe into the tartlets. Decorate with the extra strawberries. Refrigerate for 1 hour.

Left: *Tuscan fall tarts*

Swiss boats with white chocolate mousse

You will need about 16 plain or fluted barquette ("sailing boat") molds to make these delicious little tartlets. These are readily available in specialty baking stores. .

Makes: about 16 boats; Preparation: 30 minutes + 30 minutes to chill; Cooking: 10 minutes; Level of difficulty: 2

Boats: Melt the bittersweet chocolate in a double boiler over barely simmering water. • Pour about 1 tablespoon of chocolate into a mold and swirl it around so that it covers the bottom and sides in an even layer. Set aside to cool and set. Repeat with the remaining molds. • Melt the white chocolate in a double boiler over barely simmering water. Remove from the heat and let cool a little. • Beat the cream and kirsch in a medium bowl until very thick. • Fold the cream into the white chocolate to make a thick cream. • Remove the chocolate "boats" from the molds. • Spoon a little of the cream into each one and decorate with the fruit. • Let cool completely, then refrigerate for 30 minutes before serving.

VARIATIONS
— Invert the types of chocolate to make white boats with chocolate filling.
— Decorate with coarsely chopped walnuts or almonds in place of the fruit.

■ INGREDIENTS

BOATS
- 8 oz (250 g) bittersweet chocolate, coarsely chopped

MOUSSE
- 2 oz (60 g) white chocolate, coarsely chopped
- ½ cup (125 ml) heavy (double) cream
- 2 teaspoons kirsch (or other colorless liqueur)
- 4–6 tablespoons fresh small berryfruit (red, white, or black currants or blueberries), to decorate

Raisin cupcakes

Makes: 18-20 small cakes; Preparation: 10 minutes; Cooking: 20 minutes; Level of difficulty: 1

Preheat the oven to 350°F/180°C/gas 4. • Arrange 18–20 foil baking cups on a baking sheet. • Sift the flour, baking powder, and salt into a large bowl. Stir in the sugar and raisins. • Stir in the egg, cream, butter, and vanilla. • Spoon a generous tablespoon of batter into each cup. • Bake for about 20 minutes, or until golden. • Cool the cakes on racks. • Dust with the confectioners' sugar.

■ INGREDIENTS

- 1½ cups (225 g) all-purpose (plain) flour
- 2 teaspoons baking powder
- ⅛ teaspoon salt
- ½ cup (100 g) sugar
- ¾ cup (135 g) raisins
- 1 large egg, lightly beaten
- 4 tablespoons heavy (double) cream
- 4 tablespoons butter, melted
- 1 teaspoon vanilla extract
- 2 tablespoons confectioners' (icing) sugar, to dust

Right: *Swiss boats with white chocolate mousse*

Springtime boats

These tartlets can be made in oval barquette ("sailing boat") molds or in round tartlet molds. The tartlet shells can be baked in advance and stored in an airtight container. Be sure to fill the tartlets just before serving so that the pastry will still be buttery and crisp.

Makes: about 12 tartlets; Preparation: 45 minutes + 30 minutes to rest; Cooking: 10 minutes; Level of difficulty: 2

Pastry: Mix the butter, sugar, flour, egg yolk, lemon zest, and salt in a food processor until just mixed. Do not overbeat. • Shape the pastry into a ball and wrap in plastic wrap (cling film). Refrigerate for 30 minutes. • Preheat the oven to 400°F/200°C/gas 6. • Butter 12 oval or round tartlet molds. • Roll the pastry out on a lightly floured work surface to ⅛ inch (3 mm) thick. Cut out pieces large enough to line the tartlet molds. • Line the molds with the pastry and prick all over with a fork. • Bake blind for about 10 minutes, or until golden brown. • Let cool for 15 minutes, then carefully remove the tartlet shells from the molds. Let cool completely. • Filling: Fill each tartlet with preserves. • Beat the cream in a small bowl with an electric mixer at high speed until thick. • Pipe rosettes of the cream on top of the tartlets. Decorate the each tartlet with a raspberry and a fresh mint leaf.

> VARIATION
> – Replace the raspberry jam with apricot jam laced with 1 tablespoon of rum and decorate with whipped cream and coarsely chopped walnuts.

■ INGREDIENTS

PASTRY
- ½ cup (125 g) butter
- ½ cup (100 g) sugar
- 1⅓ cups (200 g) all-purpose (plain) flour
- 1 large egg yolk
- grated zest of ½ lemon
- ¼ teaspoon salt

FILLING
- 1 cup (200 g) raspberry preserves (jam)
- ½ cup (125 ml) heavy (double) cream
- 12 fresh raspberries
- 12 fresh mint leaves

Pineapple tarts

Makes: 12 tartlets; Preparation: 30 minutes + time to make tartlet shells and pastry cream; Level of difficulty: 1

If using homemade tartlet shells, follow the recipe on page 495, then bake the shells at 375°F/190°C/gas 5 for about 12 minutes, or until crisp and golden brown. Let cool completely. • Spread each tartlet with ½ tablespoon apricot preserves. Cover with 2–3 tablespoons of pastry cream. Top each tartlet with pineapple chunks and pieces of strawberry. • Dust with the confectioners' sugar.

■ INGREDIENTS

- 12 store-bought tartlet shells, or homemade (see recipe *Tuscan Fall Tarts*, page 495)
- ½ cup (160 g) apricot preserves (jam)
- 1 quantity *Pastry Cream* (see page 28)
- 24 pieces canned pineapple chunks
- 12 large strawberries, halved
- 2 tablespoons confectioners' (icing) sugar, to dust

Right: *Springtime boats*

Chocolate raspberry tarts

Makes: 12 tartlets; Preparation: 30 minutes + time to make tartlet shells and pastry cream; Level of difficulty: 1

- 12 store-bought tartlet shells, or homemade (see recipe *Tuscan Fall Tarts*, page 495)
- ½ cup (160 ml) raspberry preserves (jam)
- 1 quantity *Chocolate Pastry Cream* (see page 28)
- 24 large raspberries,
- 2 tablespoons confectioners' (icing) sugar

If using homemade tartlet shells, follow the recipe on page 495, then bake the shells at 375°F/190°C/gas 5 for about 12 minutes, or until crisp and golden brown. Let cool completely. • Spread each tartlet with ½ tablespoon raspberry preserves. • Fill each with 2–3 tablespoons of the chocolate pastry cream. Place two raspberries on each tartlet. • Dust with the confectioners' sugar.

Filled orange tartlets

Makes: about 24 tartlets; Preparation: 45 minutes + 30 minutes to rest; Cooking: 25 minutes; Level of difficulty: 2

Pastry: Finely chop the almonds in a food processor. • Sift the flour and salt into a large bowl and cut in the butter. Mix in enough water to make a firm dough. • Wrap in plastic wrap (cling film) and refrigerate for 30 minutes. • Preheat the oven to 350°F/180°C/gas 4. • Butter 12 oval or round tartlet molds. • Orange Custard: Mix the egg yolks, sugar, flour, and orange zest in a medium bowl. • Heat the milk in a medium saucepan until almost boiling. • Remove from the heat and gradually pour into the egg mixture. Return the mixture to the saucepan over medium heat. Bring to a boil and cook, stirring constantly, for 5 minutes. • Remove from the heat and stir in the liqueur. Set aside to cool. • Beat the cream in a medium bowl with an electric mixer at high speed until thick. • Fold the cream into the custard. • Roll the pastry out on a lightly floured work surface to ⅛ inch (3 mm) thick. Cut out 12 disks large enough to line the base and sides of the pans. Fill with the custard. Roll out 12 smaller disks and use them to cover each tartlet. • Bake for about 15 minutes, or until golden brown. • Cool on racks for 5 minutes, then carefully remove from the molds.

■ INGREDIENTS

PASTRY
- ½ cup (80 g) shelled almonds
- 2 cups (300 g) all-purpose (plain) flour
- ¼ teaspoon salt
- ½ cup (125 g) butter
- ½ cup (125 ml) water

ORANGE CUSTARD
- 2 large egg yolks
- ⅓ cup (70 g) sugar
- 2 tablespoons all-purpose (plain) flour
- finely grated zest of 1 orange
- 1 cup (250 ml) milk
- 3 tablespoons orange liqueur
- ¾ cup (200 ml) heavy (double) cream

Catherine's classic tartlets

Makes: 24 tartlets; Preparation: 30 minutes; Cooking: 15 minutes; Level of difficulty: 1

Preheat the oven to 350°F/180°C/gas 4. • Butter two 12-cup mini muffin pans. • Beat the butter and sugar in a large bowl until creamy. • Add the almond extract and the egg, beating until just blended. Mix in the flour to form a smooth dough. • Divide the dough into 24 equal pieces. Press each into the bottom and up the sides of the prepared cups. • Bake for 15 minutes, or until lightly browned. • Filling: Mix the confectioners' sugar, corn syrup, and butter in a medium saucepan. Bring to a boil and boil for 1 minute. Fill the shells with the filling. Top each one with pecans. • Bake for 5 more minutes. • Let cool completely.

■ INGREDIENTS

PASTRY
- ½ cup (125 g) butter
- ½ cup (100 g) sugar
- ½ teaspoon almond extract
- 1 large egg
- 1⅓ cups (200 g) all-purpose (plain) flour

FILLING
- 1 cup (150 g) confectioners' (icing) sugar
- 4 tablespoons corn (golden) syrup
- ½ cup (125 g) butter
- 1 cup (100 g) chopped pecans

Right: Filled orange tartlets

Grandmother's tartlets

Serve these sweet tartlets with fresh fruit, such as raspberries, strawberries, black currants, red currants, or sliced fresh peaches or apricots.

Makes: 6 tartlets; Preparation: 30 minutes + 30 minutes to chill; Cooking: 20 minutes; Level of difficulty: 2

Pastry: Mix the flour, butter, water, sugar, and salt in a large bowl to make a smooth dough. • Wrap in plastic wrap (cling film) and refrigerate for 30 minutes. • Preheat the oven to 400°F/200°C/gas 6. • Butter 6 tartlet pans. • Filling: Process the almonds with 2 tablespoons of sugar in a food processor until very finely chopped. • Beat the egg yolks, remaining sugar, and vanilla and almond extracts in a large bowl until pale and creamy. • Add the chopped almonds and ricotta. • Roll out the pastry on a lightly floured surface to ¼ inch (5 mm) thick. Line the prepared tartlet pans with the pastry. Spoon the filling evenly into the tartlets. • Sprinkle with the flaked almonds. • Bake for about 20 minutes, or until golden brown. • Let cool slightly.

Peach upside-down cakes

Makes: 16 cakes; Preparation: 30 minutes; Cooking: 25 minutes; Level of difficulty: 1

Preheat the oven to 325°F/170°C/gas 5. • Butter and flour 16 individual 4-inch (10-cm) tartlet pans. • Beat the butter, confectioners' sugar, and salt in a large bowl with an electric mixer at medium speed until creamy. • Add the eggs one at a time, beating until just blended after each addition. • Use a large rubber spatula to fold in the flour and baking powder. Stir in the vanilla and lemon zest. • Arrange the fruit in the prepared pans. Spoon the batter over the fruit. • Bake for about 25 minutes, or until golden brown. • Cool the cakes in the pans for 15 minutes. • Invert onto individual serving plates to cool completely. Dust with the extra confectioners' sugar.

Left: Grandmother's tartlets

Elegant dinner tartlets

Makes: 12 tartlets; Preparation: 30 minutes + 4 hours 15 minutes to chill and rest; Cooking: 20 minutes; Level of difficulty: 2

Pastry: Mix the flour, sugar, egg yolks, and butter to make a smooth dough. • Wrap in plastic wrap (cling film) and refrigerate for 15 minutes. • Preheat the oven to 350°F/180°C/gas 4. • Butter twelve 2-inch (5-cm) barquette molds (or other small tartlet pans). • Roll the pastry out on a floured surface to ⅛ inch (3 mm) thick. Cut out 3-inch (8-cm) discs and line the tartlet pans. • Filling: Beat the eggs and egg yolk, sugar, milk, and brandy in a large bowl. Spoon the mixture into the tartlet cases and sprinkle with the almonds. • Bake for 20 minutes. • Let cool completely. • Rest for 4 hours before serving.

■ INGREDIENTS

PASTRY
- 1⅓ cups (200 g) all-purpose (plain) flour
- ½ cup (100 g) sugar
- 2 egg yolks, lightly beaten
- generous ⅓ cup (100 g) butter

FILLING
- 3 large eggs
- 1 large egg yolk
- ½ cup (100 g) sugar
- 6 tablespoons milk
- 1 tablespoon brandy
- ⅓ cup (50 g) blanched almonds, chopped and toasted

Miniature soufflés

Makes: 8 mini soufflés; Preparation: 30 minutes; Cooking: 20 minutes; Level of difficulty: 2

Preheat the oven to 400°F/200°C/gas 6. • Butter eight individual ramekins. • Bring the milk, ½ cup (100 g) sugar, and mandarin zest to a boil in a saucepan. • Remove from the heat. • Melt the 4 tablespoons of butter and stir in the flour until smooth. Add the egg yolks, beating until just blended. Pour the hot milk mixture over the top and return to the heat. Bring to a boil, stirring constantly. • Remove from heat and let cool completely. • Beat the egg whites and salt in a large bowl with an electric mixer at high speed until frothy. With mixer at high speed, beat in the remaining sugar, beating until stiff, glossy peaks form. • Use a large rubber spatula to fold them into the cooled egg yolk mixture. • Heat the remaining butter and brown sugar in a saucepan. Sauté the mandarin segments until softened, 5 minutes. Drizzle with the liqueur. • Place 2 segments in each prepared ramekin. Spoon the batter evenly into the ramekins. • Bake for about 15 minutes, or until risen and lightly browned. • Dust with the confectioners' sugar. • Serve warm.

■ INGREDIENTS

- 2 cups (500 ml) milk
- ¾ cup (150 g) sugar
- finely grated zest of 1 mandarin orange + 16 mandarin segments
- ½ cup (75 g) all-purpose (plain) flour
- 4 tablespoons + 1 tablespoon cold butter
- 5 large eggs, separated
- ⅛ teaspoon salt
- 2 tablespoons firmly packed dark brown sugar
- 1 teaspoon orange liqueur
- confectioners' (icing) sugar, to dust

Right: *Elegant dinner tartlets*

Peach and pistachio tarts

Makes: 6 tartlets; Preparation: 30 minutes; Cooking: 20 minutes; Level of difficulty: 1

Preheat the oven to 350°F/180°C/gas 4. • Butter six 4-inch (10-cm) tartlet pans. • Roll the pastry out on a floured surface to ¼ inch (5 mm) thick. Cut out 6 discs and use them to line the tartlet pans. • Press the pastry into the pans and prick all over with a fork. • Line with waxed paper and fill with dried beans or pie weights. • Bake blind for 20 minutes. • Discard the paper and beans or pie weights and let cool completely. Turn the tartlets out onto serving dishes. • Melt the preserves with the liqueur in a small saucepan over low heat. Spoon the mixture into the tartlet cases. • Arrange the peaches over the layer of preserves. Sprinkle with the pistachios and serve.

■ INGREDIENTS

- 1 quantity *Sweet Shortcrust Pastry* (see page 16)
- ¼ cup (80 g) peach preserves (jam)
- 4 tablespoons peach liqueur
- 8 oz (250 g) canned peaches, sliced
- 2 tablespoons chopped pistachios

Lemon and pistachio tarts

Makes: 8 tartlets; Preparation: 30 minutes + 3 hours to chill; Cooking: 20 minutes; Level of difficulty: 1

Pastry: Preheat the oven to 350°F/180°C/gas 4. • Butter eight 4-inch (10-cm) tartlet pans. • Process the macadamia nuts, coconut, pistachios, and brown sugar in a food processor or blender until finely chopped. • Transfer the mixture to a large bowl. • Beat the egg whites in a large bowl with an electric mixer at high speed until soft peaks form. Fold them into the processed mixture. • Press the mixture into the bottoms and sides of the tartlet pans. • Bake for about 20 minutes, or until golden brown. • Cool in the pans for 5 minutes. • Turn out onto racks and let cool completely. • Filling: Beat the sugar, lemon juice, and egg yolks in a double boiler over barely simmering water. Beat until the mixture thickens and registers 160°F (71°C) on an instant-read thermometer. • Remove from the heat. • Gradually add the butter, beating until melted and well blended. Press plastic wrap (cling film) directly onto the surface of the filling. • Refrigerate for 3 hours. • Fill each pastry case with 4 tablespoons of filling. • Sprinkle with the chopped nuts.

■ INGREDIENTS

PASTRY
- 2 cups (300 g) roasted macadamia nuts
- 1½ cups (180 g) sweetened shredded (desiccated) coconut
- 1¼ cups (180 g) shelled pistachios
- ½ cup (100 g) firmly packed light brown sugar
- 3 large egg whites

FILLING
- 1 cup (200 g) sugar
- ¾ cup (200 ml) lemon juice
- 8 large egg yolks
- ½ cup (125 g) cold butter
- ½ cup (50 g) coarsely chopped macadamia or pistachio nuts, to decorate

Right: *Peach and pistachio tarts*

Siennese kisses

■ INGREDIENTS

- 2 large eggs + 2 large egg yolks
- 1⅓ cups (200 g) confectioners' (icing) sugar
- ½ teaspoon vanilla extract
- ⅔ cup (100 g) all-purpose (plain) flour
- 4 tablespoons butter, melted
- 1 tablespoon clear honey
- ⅔ cup (180 ml) ricotta cheese
- ½ cup (50 g) diced candied peel
- 2 oz (60 g) semisweet chocolate, coarsely chopped

Makes: 6 small cakes; Preparation: 35 minutes; Cooking: 30 minutes; Level of difficulty: 1

Preheat the oven to 350°F/180°C/gas 4. • Butter 12 tartlet pans. • Beat the eggs, ⅔ cup (100 g) of confectioners' sugar, and vanilla in a large bowl until pale and thick. • Add the egg yolks and continue beating until thick. • Beat in the flour, melted butter, and honey. • Pour the batter into the prepared pans, filling them half-full. • Bake for 30 minutes. • Turn out onto racks and let cool completely. • Mix the ricotta, ⅓ cup (50 g) of confectioners' sugar, candied peel, and chocolate in a large bowl. Stick the rounds together in pairs with the ricotta mixture. Dust with the remaining confectioners' sugar.

Tangy citrus cupcakes

■ INGREDIENTS

- ⅔ cup (100 g) all-purpose (plain) flour
- 3 tablespoons cornstarch (cornflour)
- 1½ teaspoons baking powder
- ¼ teaspoon salt
- 6 tablespoons butter
- ¾ cup (150 g) sugar
- 2 tablespoons finely grated orange zest
- 2 large eggs
- 1 tablespoon orange juice
- ½ quantity *Vanilla Buttercream* mixed with 1 tablespoon orange liqueur (see page 36) (optional)
- 1–2 clementines, peeled and divided into sections

Makes: 12 small cakes; Preparation: 20 minutes; Cooking: 20 minutes; Level of difficulty: 1

Preheat the oven to 375°F/190°C/gas 5. • Butter and flour a 12-cup muffin pan or line with foil or paper baking cups. • Sift the flour, cornstarch, baking powder, and salt into a medium bowl. • Beat the butter, sugar, and orange zest in a large bowl with an electric mixer at medium speed until creamy. • Add the eggs one at a time, beating until just blended after each addition. • Beat in the dry ingredients, alternating with the orange juice. • Spoon the batter into the prepared cups, filling each one half-full. • Bake for about 20 minutes, or until a toothpick inserted into the center comes out clean. • Cool the cakes on racks. If desired, spread with the buttercream. Top each cupcake with a piece of clementine.

Right: *Siennese cookies*

Dublin apple cakes

Makes: about 12 small cakes; Preparation: 40 minutes + 1 hour to chill; Cooking: 30 minutes; Level of difficulty: 1

Sift the flour and baking powder into a large bowl. Stir in the sugar. • Use your fingertips to rub in the butter until the mixture resembles coarse crumbs. • Mix in the egg to form a smooth dough. Wrap in plastic wrap (cling film) and refrigerate for 1 hour. • Preheat the oven to 350°F/180°C/gas 4. • Bake the apples in a roasting pan for 15 minutes, or until softened. • Peel the apples and mash the flesh in a large bowl until puréed. • Roll the dough out on a lightly floured surface to ½ inch (1 cm) thick. Cut out 2-inch (5-cm) rounds. • Spoon the apple purée onto the center of each round. Fold in half and pinch the edges together to seal them. Arrange on a large baking sheet. • Bake for about 15 minutes, or until golden brown. • Serve warm or cold.

■ INGREDIENTS

- 1⅔ cups (250 g) all-purpose (plain) flour
- 1½ teaspoons baking powder
- ¾ cup (150 g) sugar
- ⅔ cup (180 g) butter
- 1 large egg, lightly beaten
- 3 apples, cored

Devilish chocolate cakes

Makes: 6 cakes; Preparation: 15 minutes; Cooking: 10 minutes; Level of difficulty: 2

Preheat the oven to 400°F/200°C/gas 6. • Butter 6 custard cups. • Melt the chocolate in a double boiler over barely simmering water. Set aside to cool. • Sift the flour, baking soda, and salt into a small bowl. Beat the butter and ½ cup (100 g) of sugar in a large bowl with an electric mixer at medium speed until creamy. • Add the eggs one at a time, beating until just blended after each addition. • With mixer at low speed, gradually beat in the dry ingredients, chocolate, and vanilla. • Spoon the batter into the prepared dishes and place them on a baking sheet. • Bake for about 10 minutes, or until springy to the touch at the edges and the center is molten but "set." • While the cakes are baking, beat the cream and the remaining sugar with a mixer at high speed until stiff. • Invert onto dessert plates and serve with the cream on the side.

■ INGREDIENTS

- 14 oz (400 g) bittersweet chocolate, coarsely chopped
- ½ cup (75 g) all-purpose (plain) flour
- ½ teaspoon baking soda
- ¼ teaspoon salt
- 4 tablespoons butter
- ½ cup (100 g) + 2 tablespoons sugar
- 4 large eggs
- 1 teaspoon vanilla extract
- 1 cup (250 ml) heavy (double) cream

Right: Dublin apple cakes

Creamy apricot cakes

■ INGREDIENTS

- 18 canned apricot halves
- 6 tablespoons firmly packed brown sugar
- 1 cup (150 g) all-purpose (plain) flour
- 1½ teaspoons baking powder
- ¼ teaspoon salt
- 4 tablespoons butter
- ½ cup (100 g) sugar
- 1 teaspoon vanilla extract
- 1 large egg
- 4 tablespoons milk
- ¾ cup (200 ml) heavy (double) cream

Makes: 6 small cakes; Preparation: 20 minutes; Cooking: 25 minutes; Level of difficulty: 1

Preheat the oven to 375°F/190°C/gas 5. • Butter 6 custard cups. • Slice the apricot halves and arrange them in the cups. Sprinkle with 1 tablespoon of sugar. Place the custard cups on a jelly-roll pan for easier handling. • Sift the flour, baking powder, and salt into a large bowl. • Beat the butter, sugar, and vanilla in a medium bowl until creamy. • Add the egg, beating until just blended. • Gradually beat in the dry ingredients, alternating with the milk. • Spoon the batter into the cups. • Bake for about 25 minutes, or until a toothpick inserted into the center comes out clean. • Cool the cakes in the cups for 10 minutes. Invert the cakes onto dessert plates. • With mixer at high speed, beat the cream in a small bowl until stiff. Spoon the cream over the cakes.

Cannoli

Cannoli are a traditional Sicilian sweet, best eaten freshly made. For this recipe you will need Cannoli molds, which are a kind of pipe which you wrap the pastry around before frying it. You can get these from a good kitchen equipment store or catalog.

Makes: 12 cannoli; Preparation: 30 minutes; Cooking: 5 minutes; Level of difficulty: 3

Cannoli: Sift the flour and cocoa into a medium bowl. • Stir in the sugar, lard, eggs, and marsala to make a smooth dough. • Roll the dough out on a lightly floured surface to ⅛ inch (3 mm) thick and cut into twelve 4-inch (10-cm) disks. • Heat the oil in a deep-fryer over medium heat. • Wrap a pastry disk around each cannoli molds, pressing the overlapping edges together to seal. • Fry the cannoli, still on the mold, in small batches, for about 5 minutes, or until bubbly and golden brown. • Remove with a slotted spoon and drain on paper towels. Let cool slightly before carefully removing the mold. • Filling: Beat the ricotta with the sugar and vanilla with a wooden spoon in a large bowl. Add the chocolate and candied fruit. • Just before serving, fill the pastry tubes with the filling and arrange on a serving dish. • Dust with the confectioners' sugar and serve.

■ INGREDIENTS

CANNOLI
- 1⅓ cups (200 g) all-purpose (plain) flour
- 1 tablespoon unsweetened cocoa powder
- 2 tablespoons sugar
- generous 1 tablespoon (20 g) lard, softened
- 2 large eggs, lightly beaten
- 2 tablespoons marsala
- 1 quart (1 liter) oil, for frying

FILLING
- 2 cups (500 g) ricotta cheese
- 1½ cups (300 g) sugar
- 1 teaspoon vanilla extract
- 4 oz (125 g) semisweet chocolate, chopped
- 1 cup (200 g) chopped candied pumpkin, or other chopped candied fruit or peel

Fried cinnamon spirals

Makes: 4 cakes; Preparation: 20 minutes; Cooking: 20 minutes; Level of difficulty: 1

Sift the flour, baking soda, cream of tartar, cinnamon, and salt into a large bowl. Stir in the sugar. • Beat the egg and milk in a large bowl with an electric mixer at high speed until well blended. • With mixer at low speed, gradually beat in the dry ingredients. • Heat the oil in a large, deep frying pan until very hot. • Pour ½ cup (125 ml) of batter through a funnel into the oil with a circular motion to form a spiral. Fry until golden brown, turning over once. Remove from the pan and drain on paper towels. • Dust with the confectioners' sugar.

■ INGREDIENTS

- 1⅔ cups (250 g) all-purpose (plain) flour
- ¾ teaspoon baking soda
- ½ teaspoon cream of tartar
- ½ teaspoon ground cinnamon
- ¼ teaspoon salt
- 2 tablespoons sugar
- 1 large egg
- 1 cup (250 ml) milk
- 2 cups (500 ml) vegetable oil, for frying
- 4 tablespoons confectioners' (icing) sugar, to dust

Right: Cannoli

Rum baba cakes

Makes: about 12 cakes; Preparation: 25 minutes + 30 minutes to rise; Cooking: 25 minutes; Level of difficulty: 2

Butter twelve 2 x 3-inch (4 x 8-cm) baba molds. • Stir together the yeast, water, and 1 teaspoon sugar. Set aside for 10 minutes. • Beat the eggs and remaining sugar in a large bowl with an electric mixer at high speed until pale and thick. • Stir in the oil, butter, and the yeast mixture. • Stir in the flour and salt. • Transfer to a lightly floured surface and knead until smooth. • Roll the dough into a fat sausage and cut into twelve equal pieces. Place in the prepared molds. Cover with plastic wrap and let rise in a warm place until the dough has risen to just below the top of each mold, about 30 minutes. • Preheat the oven to 350°F/180°C/gas 4. • Bake for about 15 minutes, or until lightly browned. • Rum Syrup: Stir the water and sugar in a saucepan over medium heat until the mixture comes to a boil. Boil for about 10 minutes, or until syrupy and thick. • Stir in the rum and lemon. Let cool. • Cool the babas in the molds for 15 minutes. Soak in the rum syrup.

■ INGREDIENTS

- 1 oz (30 g) fresh yeast or 2 packages (¼-oz/7-g each) active dry yeast
- 4 tablespoons warm water
- 2 tablespoons sugar
- 5 large eggs
- ½ cup (125 ml) extra-virgin olive oil
- 4 tablespoons butter, melted and cooled
- 2⅓ cups (350 g) all-purpose (plain) flour
- ¼ teaspoon salt

RUM SYRUP
- 2 cups (500 ml) water
- 1½ cups (300 g) sugar
- ½ cup (125 ml) rum
- 1 lemon, sliced

Cherry doughnuts

Makes: 20 doughnuts; Preparation: 40 minutes + 30 minutes to rest; Cooking: 10 minutes; Level of difficulty: 2

Stir together the yeast and milk. Set aside for 10 minutes. • Stir together the flour, yeast mixture, sugar, salt, and eggs in a large bowl. Transfer to a lightly floured surface and knead until smooth. • Beat the butter in a medium bowl with an electric mixer at medium speed until creamy. Work the butter into the dough and continue kneading until well mixed. Set aside to rest in a large bowl for about 30 minutes, or until doubled in bulk. • Roll the dough out on a lightly floured surface to about ½ inch (1 cm) thick. Use 3-inch (8-cm) pastry cutters to cut out rounds. • Brush half the disks with the jelly. Place the remaining halves on top and seal the edges well. • Heat the oil in a large, deep frying pan until very hot. • Fry the doughnuts in small batches until golden brown all over. • Drain well on paper towels. • Dust with the confectioners' sugar.

■ INGREDIENTS

- ½ oz (15 g) fresh yeast or 1 package (¼-oz/7-g) active dry yeast
- 1 cup (250 ml) warm milk
- 4⅓ cups (650 g) all-purpose (plain) flour
- ¾ cup (150 g) sugar
- ½ teaspoon salt
- 2 large eggs
- ½ cup (125 g) butter
- 4 tablespoons cherry jelly
- 2 cups (500 ml) vegetable oil, for frying
- confectioners' sugar, to dust

Right: Rum baba cakes

Muffins

Ideal for breakfast or mid-morning snacks,
muffins are simple to make and always well-received.
Try our classic Chocolate Orange Muffins for
picnics or the elegant Ginger Muffins with
Two Sauces to finish a dinner party.

Chocolate hazelnut cream muffins

Makes: about 12 muffins; Preparation: 15 minutes; Cooking: 20 minutes; Level of difficulty: 1

Preheat the oven to 350°F/180°C/gas 4. • Butter a 12-cup muffin pan. • Sift the flour, cocoa, baking powder, and salt into a large bowl. • Beat the butter, honey, and sugar in a large bowl with an electric mixer at high speed until pale and creamy. • Add the eggs, one at a time, beating until just blended after each addition. • With mixer at low speed, gradually add the ground almonds and dry ingredients. • Spoon the batter evenly into the prepared muffin pan, filling each about three-quarters full. • Bake for about 20 minutes, or until a toothpick inserted into the center comes out clean. • Cool the muffins on racks. • Spread the hazelnut cream over the muffins and sprinkle with the slivered almonds.

> VARIATION
> – Replace the almonds with the same quantity of coarsely chopped walnuts.

■ INGREDIENTS

- 2 cups (300 g) all-purpose (plain) flour
- 4 tablespoons unsweetened cocoa powder
- 1½ teaspoons baking powder
- ¼ teaspoon salt
- ½ cup (125 g) butter
- 4 tablespoons clear honey
- ¾ cup (150 g) sugar
- 3 large eggs
- ½ cup (50 g) ground almonds
- ½ cup (125 g) chocolate hazelnut spread (Nutella)
- 2 tablespoons slivered almonds

Frosted apple and walnut muffins

Makes: about 18 muffins; Preparation: 20 minutes; Cooking: 25 minutes; Level of difficulty: 1

Preheat the oven to 400°F/200°C/gas 6. • Butter about 18 muffin pan cups, or set out about 18 foil or paper baking cups. • Sift the flour, baking powder, nutmeg, salt, and cloves into a large bowl. • Stir in the apple and walnuts. • Beat the eggs, brown sugar, apple juice, and butter in a large bowl. Stir the egg mixture into the dry ingredients. Stir in the bran. • Spoon the batter evenly into the prepared cups, filling each about three-quarters full. • Bake for about 25 minutes, or until a toothpick inserted into the center comes out clean. • Cool the muffins completely on racks.

■ INGREDIENTS

- 2 cups (300 g) all-purpose (plain) flour
- 2 teaspoons baking powder
- ½ teaspoon nutmeg
- ½ teaspoon salt
- ⅛ teaspoon cloves
- 1 cup (100 g) peeled, cored, and shredded apple
- ½ cup (60 g) walnuts, chopped
- 2 large eggs
- ½ cup (100 g) firmly packed brown sugar
- ⅔ cup (180 ml) apple juice
- 4 tablespoons butter, melted
- 1 cup (150 g) wheat bran

Right: *Chocolate hazelnut cream muffins*

Ginger muffins with two sauces

Makes: about 12 muffins; Preparation: 15 minutes; Cooking: 25 minutes; Level of difficulty: 1
Preheat the oven to 325°F/170°C/gas 3. • Butter a 12-cup muffin pan. •
Sift the flour, potato starch, and baking powder into a large bowl. • Beat
the butter and ⅔ cup (100 g) of confectioners' sugar in a large bowl until
creamy. • Add the ginger and the egg and egg yolks, beating until just
blended after each addition. • Add the chocolate and dry ingredients to
make a smooth batter. • Spoon the batter evenly into the prepared cups,
filling each about three-quarters full. • Bake for about 25 minutes, or
until well risen and springy to the touch. • Let cool slightly and turn
out onto serving dishes. • Dust with the remaining confectioners' sugar
and spoon a little of each sauce onto the dishes around the base of the
muffins. • Decorate the muffins with the almonds. Garnish with the
whipped cream. • Serve warm.

- ⅓ cup (50 g) all-purpose (plain) flour
- 2 tablespoons potato starch
- 1 teaspoon baking powder
- 6 tablespoons butter
- 1 cup (150 g) confectioners' (icing) sugar
- 1 tablespoon freshly grated gingerroot
- 1 large egg + 3 large egg yolks
- 2 oz (60 g) semisweet chocolate, melted
- ½ quantity *Chocolate Sauce* (see page 32)
- ½ quantity *Tropical morning coulis* (see page 34)
- flaked almonds, to decorate
- whipped cream, to serve

Basic muffins

For vanilla muffins, add 1 teaspoon vanilla extract.

Makes: about 12 muffins; Preparation: 10 minutes; Cooking: 25 minutes; Level of difficulty: 1
Preheat the oven to 375°F/190°C/gas 5. • Butter a 12-cup muffin pan, or
line with foil or paper baking cups. • Sift the flour, baking powder, and
salt into a large bowl. Stir in the sugar. • Make a well in the center and
mix in the eggs, milk, and butter. • Spoon the batter evenly into the
prepared cups. • Bake for about 25 minutes, or until a toothpick inserted
into the center comes out clean. • Cool the muffins on racks.

- 2 cups (300 g) all-purpose (plain) flour
- 2 teaspoons baking powder
- ¼ teaspoon salt
- ½ cup (100 g) sugar
- 2 large eggs, lightly beaten
- ½ cup (125 ml) milk
- ½ cup (125 g) butter, melted

Right: *Ginger muffins with two sauces*

Chocolate orange muffins

Makes: abut 12 muffins; Preparation: 20 minutes; Cooking: 20 minutes; Level of difficulty: 1

Preheat the oven to 400°F/200°C/gas 6. • Butter and flour a 12-cup muffin pan, or line with foil or paper baking cups. • Melt the chocolate and butter in a double boiler over barely simmering water. Set aside. • Sift the flour, cocoa, and baking powder into a large bowl. • Stir in the sugar. • Add the eggs, milk, and orange zest until well blended. • Beat in the melted chocolate mixture. • Spoon the batter evenly into the muffin cups to fill them three-quarters full. • Bake for about 20 minutes, or until a toothpick inserted comes out clean. • Cool the muffins in the pan for 5 minutes. Turn out onto a rack and let cool completely. • Frosting: Melt the chocolate and butter in a double boiler over barely simmering water. • Remove from the heat and mix in the Cointreau. • Spread the frosting over the tops of the muffins. Decorate with the shredded orange zest and let stand until the frosting has set.

Chocolate cherry-topped muffins

Makes: about 12 muffins; Preparation: 15 minutes; Cooking: 20 minutes; Level of difficulty: 1

Preheat the oven to 375°F/190°C/gas 5. • Butter and flour a 12-cup muffin pan, or line with foil or paper baking cups. • Sift the flour, cocoa, baking powder, and salt into a large bowl. • Beat the eggs, brown sugar, and butter in a medium bowl until creamy. • Add the dry ingredients, alternating with the milk. • Spoon the batter evenly into the prepared cups, filling each one about three-quarters full. • Press four pieces of candied cherry into each muffin, leaving 1 or 2 pieces visible on top. • Bake for about 20 minutes, or until a toothpick inserted comes out clean. • Cool the muffins on racks.

■ INGREDIENTS

- 5 oz (150 g) semisweet chocolate, coarsely chopped
- 6 tablespoons butter
- 2½ cups (375 g) all-purpose (plain) flour
- 3 tablespoons unsweetened cocoa powder
- 2 teaspoons baking powder
- 3 tablespoons sugar
- 2 large eggs
- 1 cup (250 ml) milk
- 1 tablespoon finely grated orange zest

FROSTING

- 7 oz (200 g) semisweet chocolate, chopped
- 4 tablespoons butter
- 1 tablespoon Cointreau
- finely grated orange zest

■ INGREDIENTS

- 1½ cups (225 g) all-purpose (plain) flour
- ⅓ cup (50 g) unsweetened cocoa powder
- 2 teaspoons baking powder
- ¼ teaspoon salt
- 2 large eggs
- ½ cup (100 g) firmly packed brown sugar
- ½ cup (125 g) butter, melted
- ¾ cup (200 ml) milk
- 24 red candied cherries, halved

Left: *Chocolate orange muffins*

Pear and pecan muffins

Makes: about 20 muffins; Preparation: 15 minutes; Cooking: 25 minutes; Level of difficulty: 1

Preheat the oven to 400°F/200°C/gas 6. • Butter and flour two 12-cup muffin pans, or line with foil or paper baking cups. • Sift the flour, baking powder, cinnamon, and nutmeg into a large bowl. • Stir in the brown sugar, chopped pecans, and pears. • Add the eggs, milk, and vanilla until well blended. • Stir in the butter. • Spoon the batter evenly into the prepared cups, filling them three-quarters full. • Top each cup with half a pecan. • Bake for about 25 minutes, or until a toothpick inserted into the center comes out clean. • Cool the muffins in the pan for 5 minutes. Turn out onto a rack and let cool completely. • Dust with the confectioners' sugar.

■ INGREDIENTS

- 3 cups (450 g) all-purpose (plain) flour
- 2 teaspoons baking powder
- 1 teaspoon ground cinnamon
- ½ teaspoon grated nutmeg
- ½ cup (100 g) firmly packed brown sugar
- 1 cup (100 g) chopped pecan nuts, toasted
- 14 oz (400 g) firm-ripe pears, peeled, cored, and thinly sliced
- 2 large eggs
- 1½ cups (375 ml) milk
- 1 teaspoon vanilla extract
- ½ cup (125 g) butter
- 10 pecan nuts, halved to decorate
- confectioners' (icing) sugar, to dust

Gluten-free muffins

Your friends who have gluten allergies will appreciate these muffins. Most of the ingredients can be found in the natural-foods section of a good supermarket.

Makes: 14 muffins; Preparation: 15 minutes; Cooking: 25 minutes; Level of difficulty: 1

Preheat the oven to 375°F/190°C/gas 5. • Arrange about 14 foil baking cups on a baking sheet. • Stir together the flour, bran, baking powder, ginger, nutmeg, and salt in a large bowl. • Beat the egg, brown sugar, and oil in a medium bowl. • Beat in the bananas, milk, apricots, and raisins. Stir the banana mixture into the dry ingredients. • Spoon the batter evenly into the cups, filling each three-quarters full. • Bake for about 25 minutes, or until a toothpick inserted into the center comes out clean. • Cool the muffins on racks.

■ INGREDIENTS

- 1⅓ cups (200 g) brown rice flour
- 1 cup (150 g) rice bran
- 2 teaspoons gluten-free baking powder
- 1 teaspoon ground ginger
- 1 teaspoon ground nutmeg
- ¼ teaspoon salt
- 1 large egg
- ½ cup (100 g) brown sugar
- 4 tablespoons vegetable oil
- 1 cup (250 g) ripe bananas
- ¾ cup (200 ml) milk
- ½ cup (50 g) finely chopped dried apricots
- ½ cup (90 g) raisins

Right: Pear and pecan muffins

Banana and chocolate chip muffins

Makes: about 20 muffins; Preparation: 20 minutes; Cooking: 20 minutes; Level of difficulty: 1

Preheat the oven to 375°F/190°C/gas 5. • Arrange about 20 foil baking cups on baking sheets. • Sift both flours, baking powder, baking soda, and salt into a large bowl. • Beat the butter and sugar in a large bowl with an electric mixer at medium speed until creamy. • Add the eggs one at a time, beating until just blended after each addition. • Beat in the bananas, followed by the dry ingredients, alternating with the milk. • Stir in the chocolate chips and walnuts by hand. • Spoon the batter evenly into the cups, filling each about three-quarters full. • Bake for about 20 minutes, or until a toothpick inserted into the center comes out clean. • Cool the muffins on racks.

■ INGREDIENTS

- 1 cup (150 g) whole-wheat (wholemeal) flour
- 1 cup (150 g) all-purpose (plain) flour
- 2 teaspoons baking powder
- ½ teaspoon baking soda
- ¼ teaspoon salt
- ½ cup (125 g) butter
- 1 cup (200 g) sugar
- 3 large eggs
- 2 large very ripe bananas, mashed with a fork
- 4 tablespoons milk
- 1 cup (180 g) semisweet chocolate chips
- 1 cup (100 g) walnuts, chopped

Apple muffins

Makes: about 18 muffins; Preparation: 20 minutes; Cooking: 20 minutes; Level of difficulty: 1

Preheat the oven to 400°F/200°C/gas 6. • Arrange about 18 foil baking cups on baking sheets. • Sift the flour, baking powder, 2 teaspoons of cinnamon, and nutmeg into a large bowl. Stir in the sugar. • Melt the butter and honey in a small saucepan over low heat. • Beat the eggs and milk into the dry ingredients. • Mix in the butter mixture and apples until well blended. • Pour the batter evenly into the prepared cups, filling them three-quarters full. • Dust with the remaining cinnamon. • Bake for about 20 minutes, or until a toothpick inserted into the center comes out clean. • Cool the muffins in the pan for 5 minutes. Turn out onto a rack and let cool completely.

■ INGREDIENTS

- 2½ cups (375 g) all-purpose (plain) flour
- 2 teaspoons baking powder
- 1 tablespoon ground cinnamon
- 1 teaspoon grated nutmeg
- ⅓ cup (70 g) sugar
- ⅔ cup (180 g) butter
- 2 tablespoons honey
- 2 large eggs
- ⅔ cup (180 ml) milk
- 3 green apples, peeled, cored, and cut into cubes

Right: *Banana and chocolate chip muffins*

Strawberry and white chocolate muffins

Makes: about 16 muffins; Preparation: 15 minutes; Cooking: 25 minutes; Level of difficulty: 1

Preheat the oven to 350°F/180°C/gas 4. • Arrange about 16 foil baking cups on baking sheets. • Sift the flour, baking powder, and salt into a large bowl. Stir in the sugar. • Beat the butter, milk, egg, and vanilla in a medium bowl. • Gradually add the dry ingredients, followed by the chocolate chips. • Spoon three-quarters of the batter into the prepared cups. Spoon a heaping 1 teaspoon strawberry preserves into each muffin, making a hole in the batter. Top with the remaining batter. • Bake for about 25 minutes, or until a toothpick inserted into the center comes out clean. • Cool the muffins on racks.

■ INGREDIENTS

- 1½ cups (225 g) all-purpose (plain) flour
- 2 teaspoons baking powder
- ¼ teaspoon salt
- ½ cup (100 g) sugar
- ½ cup (125 g) butter, melted
- ½ cup (125 ml) milk
- 1 large egg
- ½ teaspoon vanilla extract
- 1½ cups (270 g) white chocolate chips
- ½ cup (160 g) strawberry preserves (jam)

Cinnamon and apple muffins

Makes: about 20 muffins; Preparation: 25 minutes; Cooking: 20 minutes; Level of difficulty: 1

Cinnamon Crumble: Stir together the flour, brown sugar, and cinnamon in a medium bowl. Use a pastry blender to cut in the butter until the mixture resembles coarse crumbs. • Muffins: Place the apples and water in a saucepan over medium heat. Cover and cook until tender, about 10 minutes. Mash until smooth and set aside to cool. • Preheat the oven to 400°F/200°C/gas 6. • Arrange 20 foil baking cups on baking sheets. • Sift the flour, baking powder, cinnamon, and salt into a large bowl. Stir in the brown sugar. • Beat in the milk, oil, and egg, followed by the applesauce and walnuts. • Spoon the batter evenly into the cups. • Sprinkle the crumble over the muffins. • Bake for about 20 minutes, or until a toothpick inserted into the center comes out clean. • Cool the muffins on racks.

■ INGREDIENTS

CINNAMON CRUMBLE

- ½ cup (75 g) all-purpose (plain) flour
- ¼ cup (50 g) firmly packed brown sugar
- 1½ teaspoons ground cinnamon
- 6 tablespoons butter

MUFFINS

- 2 large apples, peeled, cored, and chopped
- 2 tablespoons water
- 2¼ cups (330 g) all-purpose (plain) flour
- 1 tablespoon baking powder
- 2 teaspoons ground cinnamon
- ¼ teaspoon salt
- ¾ cup (150 g) firmly packed brown sugar
- ⅔ cup (180 ml) milk
- 6 tablespoons vegetable oil
- 1 large egg, lightly beaten
- ½ cup (50 g) chopped walnuts

Right: *White chocolate muffins*

White chocolate muffins

Makes: about 20 muffins; Preparation: 10 minutes; Cooking: 15 minutes; Level of difficulty: 1

Preheat the oven to 400°F/200°C/gas 6. • Arrange about 20 foil baking cups on baking sheets. • Sift the flour, baking powder, and salt into a large bowl. Stir in the sugar and chocolate chips. Make a well in the center. • Stir in the milk, butter, egg, honey, and vanilla. • Spoon the batter evenly into the cups, filling each three-quarters full. • Bake for about 15 minutes, or until a toothpick inserted into the center comes out clean. Cool the muffins on racks.

■ INGREDIENTS

- 2 cups (300 g) all-purpose (plain) flour
- 2½ teaspoons baking powder
- ¼ teaspoon salt
- ¼ cup (50 g) sugar
- 1½ cups (270 g) white chocolate chips
- 1 cup (250 ml) milk
- 4 tablespoons butter, melted
- 1 large egg, lightly beaten
- 2 tablespoons honey
- 2 teaspoons vanilla extract

Rice muffins

Makes: about 12 muffins; Preparation: 20 minutes; Cooking: 20 minutes; Level of difficulty: 1

Preheat the oven to 400°F/200°C/gas 6. • Butter and flour a 12-cup muffin pan, or line with foil or paper baking cups. • Mix the flour, baking powder, and milk in a large bowl. • Add the eggs one at a time, beating until just blended after each addition. • Beat in the butter, sugar, rum, and salt. • Stir in the rice. • Spoon the batter evenly into the prepared cups, filling them two-thirds full. • Bake for about 20 minutes, or until a toothpick inserted into the center comes out clean. • Cool the muffins in the pan for 5 minutes. Turn out onto a rack and let cool completely. • Dust with the confectioners' sugar.

INGREDIENTS

- 1 cup (150 g) all-purpose (plain) flour
- 1 teaspoon baking powder
- 1 cup (250 ml) milk
- 3 large eggs
- 4 tablespoons butter, melted
- 2 tablespoons sugar
- 1 teaspoon dark rum
- ½ teaspoon salt
- ¾ cup (75 g) boiled rice
- ⅓ cup (50 g) confectioners' (icing) sugar, to dust

Rhubarb and raspberry muffins

Makes: about 18 muffins; Preparation: 20 minutes; Cooking: 20 minutes; Level of difficulty: 1

Preheat the oven to 375°F/190°C/gas 5. • Arrange about 18 foil baking cups on baking sheets. • Sift both flours, baking powder, cinnamon, nutmeg, and salt into a large bowl. • Beat the brown sugar, egg yolks, milk, preserves, butter, and vanilla in a large bowl with an electric mixer at medium speed until smooth. • Stir in the rhubarb and raspberries, followed by the dry ingredients. • Beat the egg whites in a medium bowl until stiff peaks form. Use a large rubber spatula to fold them into the batter. • Spoon the batter evenly into the cups, filling each about two-thirds full. • Streusel: Mix the flour, sugar, oats, and cinnamon in a medium bowl. Use a pastry blender to cut in the butter until the mixture resembles coarse crumbs. Sprinkle over the muffins. • Bake for about 20 minutes, or until a toothpick inserted into the center comes out clean. • Cool the muffins on racks.

INGREDIENTS

- 1 cup (150 g) all-purpose (plain) flour
- 1 cup (150 g) whole-wheat (wholemeal) flour
- 2 teaspoons baking powder
- 1 teaspoon cinnamon
- ¼ teaspoon nutmeg
- ¼ teaspoon salt
- ½ cup (100 g) brown sugar
- 2 large eggs, separated
- ¾ cup (200 ml) milk
- 3 tablespoons raspberry preserves (jam)
- 2 tablespoons butter, melted
- 1 teaspoon vanilla extract
- 1½ cups (375 g) chopped rhubarb
- 1 cup (250 g) raspberries

STREUSEL
- ½ cup (75 g) all-purpose (plain) flour
- ½ cup (100 g) brown sugar
- ½ cup (50 g) rolled oats
- 1 teaspoon cinnamon
- 4 tablespoons cold butter

Right: Rice muffins

Spiced raisin muffins

Makes: about 12 muffins; Preparation: 15 minutes; Cooking: 20 minutes; Level of difficulty: 1

Preheat the oven to 400°F/200°C/gas 6. • Butter and flour a 12-cup muffin pan, or line with foil or paper baking cups. • Sift both flours, baking powder, ginger, and allspice into a large bowl. • Mix in the raisins and brown sugar. • Beat in the milk and eggs. • Mix in the butter until well blended. • Spoon the batter evenly into the prepared cups, filling them three-quarters full. • Bake for about 20 minutes, or until a toothpick inserted into the center comes out clean. • Cool the muffins in the pan for 5 minutes. Turn out onto a rack and let cool completely. • Spread the buttercream over the tops of the muffins.

INGREDIENTS

- 1 cup (150 g) all-purpose (plain) flour
- ⅔ cup (100 g) whole-wheat (wholemeal) flour
- 2 teaspoons baking powder
- ½ teaspoon ground ginger
- ½ teaspoon ground allspice
- 1⅔ cups (300 g) golden raisins (sultanas)
- ½ cup (100 g) brown sugar
- ¾ cup (200 ml) milk
- 2 large eggs
- ½ cup (125 g) butter, melted
- 1 quantity *Vanilla Buttercream* (see page 36)

Strawberry muffins

Serve these muffins still warm and fresh from the oven accompanied by a bowl of sweet strawberries or some homemade strawberry preserves.

Makes: about 12 muffins; Preparation: 10 minutes; Cooking: 20 minutes; Level of difficulty: 1

Preheat the oven to 400°F/200°C/gas 6. • Butter and flour a 12-cup muffin pan, or line with foil or paper baking cups. • Sift both flours, baking powder, baking soda, and salt into a large bowl. Stir in the brown sugar and make a well in the center. • Beat in the milk, eggs, and butter with an electric mixer at low speed. • Stir in the strawberries. • Spoon the batter evenly into the prepared cups, filling each about three-quarters full. • Bake for about 20 minutes, or until a toothpick inserted into the center comes out clean. • Cool the muffins on racks.

INGREDIENTS

- 1½ cups (225 g) all-purpose (plain) flour
- ⅔ cup (100 g) whole-wheat (wholemeal) flour
- 2 teaspoons baking powder
- ½ teaspoon baking soda
- ¼ teaspoon salt
- ½ cup (100 g) brown sugar
- 1 cup (250 ml) milk
- 2 large eggs, lightly beaten
- 4 tablespoons butter, melted
- 1 cup (250 g) strawberries, hulled and chopped

Right: Spiced raisin muffins

■ INGREDIENTS

- 1½ cups (225 g) whole-wheat (wholemeal) flour
- 1 teaspoon baking powder
- ½ teaspoon baking soda
- ½ teaspoon pumpkin pie spice
- ¼ teaspoon salt
- 2 large eggs
- ½ cup (100 g) brown sugar
- ½ cup (125 ml) vegetable oil
- 1½ cups (375 g) mashed ripe banana
- ¾ cup (200 ml) milk

Banana muffins

Makes: about 12 muffins; Preparation: 10 minutes; Cooking: 20 minutes; Level of difficulty: 1

Preheat the oven to 375°F/190°C/gas 5. • Butter and flour a 12-cup muffin pan, or line with foil or paper baking cups. • Sift the flour, baking powder, baking soda, pumpkin pie spice, and salt into a large bowl. • Beat the eggs, brown sugar, and oil in a medium bowl. Beat in the mashed banana and milk. Stir the banana mixture into the dry ingredients. • Spoon the batter evenly into the prepared cups, filling each three-quarters full. • Bake for about 20 minutes, or until springy to the touch. • Cool the muffins on racks.

Chocolate and mint muffins

INGREDIENTS

- 2 cups (300 g) all-purpose (plain) flour
- ½ cup (75 g) unsweetened cocoa powder
- 1 teaspoon baking powder
- ½ teaspoon baking soda
- ¼ teaspoon salt
- ⅔ cup (180 g) butter
- 1½ cups (300 g) sugar
- 3 large eggs
- ¾ cup (200 ml) milk
- 1 teaspoon peppermint extract
- 12 chocolate cream after-dinner mints, chopped

CHOCOLATE GLAZE
- 6 oz (180 g) semisweet chocolate, coarsely chopped
- ½ cup (125 g) butter
- 1 teaspoon peppermint extract

Makes: about 20 muffins; Preparation: 20 minutes; Cooking: 20 minutes; Level of difficulty: 1

Preheat the oven to 350°F/180°C/gas 6. • Arrange about 20 foil baking cups on baking sheets. • Sift the flour, cocoa, baking powder, baking soda, and salt into a large bowl. • Beat the butter and sugar in a large bowl with an electric mixer at medium speed until creamy. • Add the eggs one at a time, beating until just blended after each addition. • With mixer at low speed, beat in the dry ingredients, alternating with the milk and peppermint extract. Stir in the chopped chocolate mints. • Spoon the batter evenly into the prepared cups, filling each about three-quarters full. • Bake for about 20 minutes, or until a toothpick inserted into the center comes out clean. • Cool the cakes on racks. • Chocolate Glaze: Melt the chocolate and butter in a double boiler over barely simmering water. Add the mint extract. Let cool to warm. • Drizzle the glaze over the muffins.

Nutty chocolate muffins

INGREDIENTS

- 1¾ cups (275 g) all-purpose (plain) flour
- 2 teaspoons baking powder
- ½ teaspoon baking soda
- ¼ teaspoon salt
- ½ cup (125 g) butter
- ½ cup (100 g) sugar
- 1 teaspoon rum extract
- 2 large eggs
- 1 cup (250 ml) heavy (double) cream
- 4 oz (125 g) nut chocolate, chopped
- 6 oz (180 g) milk chocolate, chopped

Makes: about 12 muffins; Preparation: 20 minutes; Cooking: 20 minutes; Level of difficulty: 1

Preheat the oven to 350°F/180°C/gas 6. • Butter and flour a 12-cup muffin pan, or line with foil or paper baking cups. • Sift the flour, baking powder, baking soda, and salt into a medium bowl. • Beat the butter, sugar, and rum extract in a large bowl with an electric mixer at medium speed until creamy. • Add the eggs one at a time, beating until just blended after each addition. • Gradually beat in the dry ingredients, alternating with the cream. Stir in the nut chocolate. • Spoon the batter evenly into the prepared cups, filling each about three-quarters. • Bake for about 20 minutes, or until a toothpick inserted into the center comes out clean. • Cool the muffins on racks. • Melt the milk chocolate in a double boiler over barely simmering water. Let cool a little, then drizzle over the muffins.

Left: *Chocolate and mint muffins*

Zucchini and citrus muffins

Makes: about 18 muffins; Preparation: 20 minutes; Cooking: 20 minutes; Level of difficulty: 1

Preheat the oven to 400°F/200°C/gas 6. • Arrange about 18 foil baking cups on baking sheets. • Sift the flour, baking powder, baking soda, and salt into a large bowl. Stir in the brown sugar, lemon zest, walnuts, and raisins. • Beat the eggs, oil, lime juice, and milk in a large bowl. Stir the egg mixture into the dry ingredients. Fold in the zucchini. • Spoon the batter evenly into the prepared cups, filling each about two-thirds full. • Bake for about 20 minutes, or until a toothpick inserted into the center comes out clean. • Cool the muffins on racks. • Citrus Frosting: Beat the cream cheese and confectioners' sugar in a medium bowl with an electric mixer at medium speed until creamy. Beat in the lime zest and enough juice to make a thick, spreadable frosting. • Spread the frosting over the cooled muffins.

■ INGREDIENTS

- 2 cups (300 g) all-purpose (plain) flour
- 2 teaspoons baking powder
- 1 teaspoon baking soda
- ½ teaspoon salt
- ½ cup (100 g) firmly packed brown sugar
- 1 tablespoon lemon zest
- ¾ cup (75 g) chopped walnuts
- ½ cup (180 g) raisins
- 2 large eggs
- 6 tablespoons vegetable oil
- 4 tablespoons lime juice
- 4 tablespoons milk
- 1 cup (250 g) shredded zucchini

CITRUS FROSTING

- 3 oz (90 g) cream cheese
- 1 cup (150 g) confectioners' (icing) sugar
- 1 tablespoon lime zest
- 1 tablespoon lime juice

Cream-topped ginger muffins

Makes: about 12 muffins; Preparation: 20 minutes; Cooking: 15 minutes; Level of difficulty: 1

Preheat the oven to 375°F/190°C/gas 5. • Butter and flour a 12-cup muffin pan, or line with foil or paper baking cups. • Sift the flour, ground ginger, baking powder, and salt into a medium bowl. • Beat the butter, sugar, honey, and vanilla in a large bowl with an electric mixer at medium speed until creamy. • Add the egg, beating until just blended. • With mixer at low speed, gradually beat in the dry ingredients, alternating with the milk. Stir in 2 tablespoons of the crystallized ginger. • Spoon the batter evenly into the prepared cups, filling each three-quarters full. • Bake for about 15 minutes, or until a toothpick inserted into the center comes out clean. • Cool the muffins on racks. • Spread with the Mock Cream and sprinkle with the remaining ginger.

■ INGREDIENTS

- 1½ cups (225 g) all-purpose (plain) flour
- 1½ teaspoons ground ginger
- 1 teaspoon baking powder
- ¼ teaspoon salt
- ½ cup (125 g) butter
- ¾ cup (150 g) sugar
- 1 tablespoon honey
- 1 teaspoon vanilla extract
- 1 large egg
- 6 tablespoons milk
- 3 tablespoons finely chopped crystallized ginger
- 1 quantity *Mock Cream* (see page 40)

Right: *Zucchini and citrus muffins*

Zesty lemon muffins

■ INGREDIENTS

- 2 cups (300 g) all-purpose (plain) flour
- 2½ teaspoons baking powder
- ¼ teaspoon salt
- ¾ cup (150 g) sugar
- 2 large eggs
- 1 cup (250 ml) plain yogurt
- 6 tablespoons butter, melted
- 2 tablespoons finely grated lemon zest
- ½ cup (125 ml) lemon juice

Makes: 12 muffins; Preparation: 15 minutes; Cooking: 15 minutes; Level of difficulty: 1

Preheat the oven to 400°F/200°C/gas 6. • Butter a 12-cup muffin pan, or line with foil or paper baking cups. • Sift the flour, baking powder, and salt into a large bowl. Stir in the sugar and make a well in the center. • Beat the eggs, yogurt, butter, and lemon zest and juice in a medium bowl. Stir the yogurt mixture into the dry ingredients. • Spoon the batter evenly into the prepared cups, filling each about three-quarters full. • Bake for about 15 minutes or until a toothpick inserted into the center comes out clean. • Cool the muffins on racks.

Sherry fruit muffins

Makes: about 20 muffins; Preparation: 15 minutes + 12 hours to soak; Cooking: 20 minutes; Level of difficulty: 1

Mix the dried fruit, sherry, and water in a small bowl. Cover and let soak overnight. • Preheat the oven to 375°F/190°C/gas 5. • Arrange about 20 foil baking cups on baking sheets. • Sift the flour, baking powder, baking soda, and salt into a large bowl. • Beat the butter, sugar, and vanilla in a large bowl with an electric mixer at medium speed until creamy. • Add the eggs, beating until just blended. • With mixer at low speed, gradually beat in the dry ingredients, alternating with the milk. • Drain the dried fruit, if needed. • Stir the fruit into the batter. • Spoon the batter evenly into the prepared cups, filling each about three-quarters full. • Bake for about 20 minutes, or until a toothpick inserted into the center comes out clean. • Cool the muffins on racks.

■ INGREDIENTS

- 1 cup (250 g) mixed dried fruit, chopped
- ½ cup (125 ml) dry sherry
- ½ cup (125 ml) water
- 3 cups (450 g) all-purpose (plain) flour
- 2 teaspoons baking powder
- 1 teaspoon baking soda
- ¼ teaspoon salt
- ½ cup (125 g) butter
- 1 cup (200 g) sugar
- 2 teaspoons vanilla extract
- 2 large eggs
- ½ cup (125 ml) milk

Lemon-frosted carrot muffins

Makes: about 12 muffins; Preparation: 15 minutes; Cooking: 20 minutes; Level of difficulty: 1

Preheat the oven to 350°F/180°C/gas 6. • Butter and flour a 12-cup muffin pan, or line with foil or paper baking cups. • Sift both flours, baking powder, and salt into a large bowl. Stir in the brown sugar. • Add the butter, eggs, carrots, milk, and lemon juice. • Spoon the batter evenly into the prepared cups, filling each about two-thirds full. • Bake for about 20 minutes, or until a toothpick inserted into the center comes out clean. • Cool the muffins on racks. • Lemon Frosting: Beat the cream cheese, confectioners' sugar, and lemon zest in a medium bowl with an electric mixer at high speed until creamy. • Spread the frosting over the tops of the muffins.

■ INGREDIENTS

- 2 cups (300 g) all-purpose (plain) flour
- ½ cup (75 g) whole-wheat (wholemeal) flour
- 1 tablespoon baking powder
- ¼ teaspoon salt
- ⅔ cup (140 g) firmly packed brown sugar
- ½ cup (125 g) butter, melted
- 2 large eggs, lightly beaten
- 1½ cups (375 g) finely grated carrots
- ½ cup (125 ml) milk
- 4 tablespoons lemon juice

LEMON FROSTING

- 1 cup (250 g) cream cheese
- ½ cup (75 g) confectioners' (icing) sugar
- 1 tablespoon finely grated lemon zest

Right: *Sherry fruit muffins*

Pumpkin and raisin muffins

- 1⅓ cups (200 g) all-purpose (plain) flour
- 1 teaspoon each baking powder and baking soda
- 1 teaspoon each ground ginger, nutmeg, and cinnamon
- ¼ teaspoon salt
- ⅔ cup (180 g) butter
- ¾ cup (150 g) brown sugar
- ½ teaspoon vanilla extract
- 2 large eggs
- 1 cup (250 g) pumpkin purée
- 6 tablespoons corn (golden) syrup
- ½ cup (90 g) raisins

Makes: about 12 muffins; Preparation: 15 minutes; Cooking: 20 minutes; Level of difficulty: 1

Preheat the oven to 400°F/200°C/gas 6. • Butter and flour a 12-cup muffin pan, or line with foil or paper baking cups. • Sift the flour, baking powder, baking soda, ginger, nutmeg, cinnamon, and salt into a medium bowl. • Beat the butter, brown sugar, and vanilla with an electric mixer at medium speed until creamy. • Add the eggs one at a time, beating until just blended after each addition. Beat in the pumpkin and corn syrup. • With mixer at low speed, gradually beat in dry ingredients. • Stir in the raisins. • Spoon the batter evenly into the prepared cups, filling each about two-thirds full. • Bake for about 20 minutes, or until a toothpick inserted into the center comes out clean. • Cool the muffins on racks.

Berry muffins

Makes: about 12 muffins; Preparation: 10 minutes; Cooking: 20 minutes; Level of difficulty: 1

Preheat the oven to 400°F/200°C/gas 6. • Butter and flour a 12-cup muffin pan, or line with foil or paper baking cups. • Sift the flour, baking powder, salt, and nutmeg into a large bowl. Stir in the sugar. • Mix in the raspberries, blueberries, eggs, and butter to make a smooth batter. • Spoon the batter evenly into the prepared cups, filling each about three-quarters full. • Bake for about 20 minutes, or until well risen and browned. • Turn out onto serving dishes. • Serve hot or cold.

■ INGREDIENTS

- 2 cups (300 g) all-purpose (plain) flour
- 2 teaspoons baking powder
- ⅛ teaspoon salt
- ⅛ teaspoon ground nutmeg
- ½ cup (100 g) sugar
- 4 oz (125 g) raspberries, hulled
- 2 oz (60 g) blueberries
- 2 large eggs, lightly beaten
- generous ⅓ cup (100 g) melted butter

Raspberry jam muffins

Makes: about 15 muffins; Preparation: 15 minutes; Cooking: 25 minutes; Level of difficulty: 1

Preheat the oven to 375°F/190°C/gas 5. • Arrange about 15 foil baking cups on a baking sheet. • Sift the flour, baking powder, and salt into a large bowl. • Beat the butter, sugar, and almond extract in a large bowl with an electric mixer at medium speed until creamy. • Add the eggs one at a time, beating until just blended after each addition. • With mixer at low speed, gradually beat in the dry ingredients, alternating with the milk. • Stir in the almonds. • Spoon the batter evenly into the cups, filling each about three-quarters full. Top each muffin with a heaping teaspoon of raspberry jam. • Bake for about 25 minutes, or until a toothpick inserted into the center comes out clean. • Cool the muffins on racks.

■ INGREDIENTS

- 2½ cups (375 g) all-purpose (plain) flour
- 1 tablespoon baking powder
- ¼ teaspoon salt
- ½ cup (125 g) butter
- 1 cup (200 g) sugar
- 1 teaspoon almond extract
- 2 large eggs
- 1 cup (250 ml) milk
- 1 cup (100 g) sliced unblanched almonds
- about ½ cup (160 ml) raspberry jam

Right: *Berry muffins*

Cranberry and walnut muffins

Makes: about 12 muffins; Preparation: 15 minutes; Cooking: 20 minutes; Level of difficulty: 1

Preheat the oven to 400°F/200°C/gas 6. • Butter and flour a 12-cup muffin pan, or line with foil or paper baking cups. • Sift the flour, baking powder, cinnamon, nutmeg, and salt into a large bowl. • Stir in the cranberries and walnuts. • Beat the buttermilk, brown sugar, eggs, and butter in a medium bowl with an electric mixer at medium speed. • Stir the egg mixture into the dry ingredients. • Spoon the batter evenly into the prepared cups, filling each about two-thirds full. • Bake for about 20 minutes, or until a toothpick inserted into the center comes out clean. • Cool the muffins on racks.

■ INGREDIENTS

- 2 cups (300 g) all-purpose (plain) flour
- 2 teaspoons baking powder
- 1 teaspoon ground cinnamon
- ½ teaspoon nutmeg
- ¼ teaspoon salt
- 1 cup (250 g) cranberries
- ½ cup (50 g) toasted walnuts, chopped
- 1 cup (250 ml) buttermilk
- ½ cup (100 g) firmly packed brown sugar
- 2 large eggs
- 4 tablespoons butter, melted

Tropical muffins

Makes: about 12 muffins; Preparation: 15 minutes; Cooking: 20 minutes; Level of difficulty: 1

Preheat the oven to 350°F/180°C/gas 4. • Butter and flour a 12-cup muffin-pan, or line with foil or paper baking cups. • Sift the flour, baking powder, baking soda, and salt into a large bowl. • Beat the butter and sugar in a large bowl with an electric mixer at medium speed until creamy. • Add the eggs one at a time, beating until just blended after each addition. • With mixer at low speed, gradually beat in the dry ingredients, alternating with the cream. • Stir in the mango and passion fruit pulp. • Spoon the batter evenly into the prepared cups, filling each about two-thirds full. • Bake for about 15 minutes, or until a toothpick inserted into the center comes out clean. • Cool the muffins on racks. • Yogurt Cream Filling: With mixer at high speed, beat the cream and yogurt in a medium bowl until stiff. Fold in the lemon zest and passion fruit pulp. • Cut a small ½-inch (1-cm) deep hole in the top of each cooled muffin. Fill with the cream and cover with the removed piece from each muffin.

■ INGREDIENTS

- 2 cups (300 g) all-purpose (plain) flour
- 2 teaspoons baking powder
- ½ teaspoon baking soda
- ¼ teaspoon salt
- ½ cup (125 g) butter
- ⅔ cup (140 g) sugar
- 2 large eggs
- ½ cup (125 ml) heavy (double) cream
- ½ cup (50 g) chopped candied mango
- 4 tablespoons passion fruit pulp

YOGURT CREAM FILLING
- ½ cup (125 ml) heavy (double) cream
- ½ cup (125 ml) plain yogurt
- 2 teaspoons finely grated lemon zest
- 1 tablespoon fresh passion fruit pulp

Right: *Chocolate chip and orange muffins*

Chocolate chip and orange muffins

- 2 cups (300 g) all-purpose (plain) flour
- 2 teaspoons baking powder
- ½ teaspoon baking soda
- ¼ teaspoon salt
- 1 cup (200 g) sugar
- 1 large egg
- ¾ cup (200 ml) milk
- ½ cup (125 ml) vegetable oil
- 2 tablespoons finely grated orange zest
- 2 teaspoons vanilla extract
- 1 cup (180 g) semisweet chocolate chips

Makes: about 12 muffins; Preparation: 15 minutes; Cooking: 20 minutes; Level of difficulty: 1

Preheat the oven to 375°F/190°C/gas 5. • Butter and flour a 12-cup muffin pan, or line with foil or paper baking cups. • Sift the flour, baking powder, baking soda, and salt into a large bowl. • Beat the sugar, egg, milk, oil, orange zest, and vanilla in a medium bowl. Stir the orange mixture into the dry ingredients. • Fold in the chocolate chips. • Spoon the batter evenly into the prepared cups, filling each three-quarters full. • Bake for about 20 minutes, or until a toothpick inserted into the center comes out clean. • Cool the muffins on racks.

Coconut and yogurt muffins

Makes: about 12 muffins; Preparation: 20 minutes; Cooking: 20 minutes; Level of difficulty: 1

Preheat the oven to 350°F/180°C/gas 4. • Butter and flour a 12-cup muffin pan. • Sift the flour, baking powder, baking soda, and salt into a large bowl. Stir in the coconut. • Beat the butter, sugar, and vanilla in a large bowl with an electric mixer at medium speed until creamy. • Add the egg, beating until just blended. • With mixer at low speed, gradually beat in the dry ingredients, alternating with the yogurt. • Spoon the batter evenly into the prepared cups, filling each about three-quarters full. • Bake for about 20 minutes, or until a toothpick inserted into a center comes out clean. • Cool the muffins on racks. • Coconut Frosting: Beat the mascarpone, confectioners' sugar, and coconut in a medium bowl until creamy. • Spread the muffins with the frosting and decorate with the kiwifruit.

INGREDIENTS

- 2 cups (300 g) all-purpose (plain) flour
- 2½ teaspoons baking powder
- ½ teaspoon baking soda
- ¼ teaspoon salt
- ½ cup (60 g) shredded (desiccated) coconut
- 6 tablespoons butter
- ¾ cup (150 g) sugar
- ½ teaspoon vanilla extract
- 1 large egg
- 1 cup (250 ml) plain yogurt

COCONUT FROSTING

- 1 cup (250 ml) mascarpone cheese
- ⅓ cup (50 g) confectioners' (icing) sugar
- ¾ cup (90 g) shredded (desiccated) coconut
- 2–3 fresh kiwifruit, peeled and sliced, to decorate

Soft pineapple muffins

Makes: about 12 muffins; Preparation: 15 minutes; Cooking: 20 minutes; Level of difficulty: 1

Preheat the oven to 350°F/180°C/gas 4. • Butter and flour a 12-cup muffin pan. • Sift the flour, baking powder, baking soda, and salt in a large bowl. Stir in the oats. • Beat the butter, sugar, and vanilla in a large bowl with an electric mixer at medium speed until creamy. • Add the egg, beating until just blended. • Gradually beat in the dry ingredients, alternating with the pineapple and milk. • Spoon the batter evenly into the prepared cups, filling each about two-thirds full. • Bake for about 20 minutes, or until a toothpick inserted into a center comes out clean. • Cool the muffins on racks.

INGREDIENTS

- 1 cup (150 g) all-purpose (plain) flour
- 2½ teaspoons baking powder
- ½ teaspoon baking soda
- ¼ teaspoon salt
- 1 cup (150 g) rolled oats
- 6 tablespoons butter
- ½ cup (100 g) sugar
- ½ teaspoon vanilla extract
- 1 large egg
- ½ cup (125 g) canned crushed pineapple
- ¾ cup (200 ml) milk

Right: *Coconut and yogurt muffins*

Wake-up muffins

Makes: about 12 muffins; Preparation: 15 minutes; Cooking: 15 minutes; Level of difficulty: 1

Preheat the oven to 375°F/190°C/gas 5. • Butter and flour a 12-cup muffin pan or line with foil or paper baking cups. • Sift the flour, baking powder, and salt into a large bowl. Stir in the brown sugar. • Beat the egg and cream in a small bowl. • Beat the cream mixture and coffee into the dry ingredients with an electric mixer at low speed. • Spoon the batter evenly into the prepared cups, filling each about two-thirds full. • Bake for about 15 minutes, or until a toothpick inserted into the center comes out clean. • Cool the muffins on racks. • Dust with the confectioners' sugar.

■ INGREDIENTS

- 2 cups (300 g) all-purpose (plain) flour
- 1 tablespoon baking powder
- ¼ teaspoon salt
- ½ cup (100 g) firmly packed brown sugar
- 1 large egg
- 4 tablespoons heavy (double) cream
- 1 cup (250 ml) very strong cold black coffee
- 4 tablespoons confectioners' (icing) sugar, to dust

Easter Sunday muffins

Makes: about 12 muffins; Preparation: 10 minutes; Cooking: 15 minutes; Level of difficulty: 1

Preheat the oven to 350°F/180°C/gas 4. • Butter and flour a 12-cup muffin pan or line with foil or paper baking cups. • Beat the flour, sugar, cocoa, eggs, butter, milk, vanilla, and baking powder in a large bowl with an electric mixer at medium speed until well blended. • Spoon half the batter evenly into the cups. Place a chocolate egg in each. Top each with some of the remaining batter. • Sprinkle each with a few chocolate chips, if using. • Bake for about 15 minutes, or until springy to the touch. • Cool the muffins on racks.

■ INGREDIENTS

- 1½ cups (225 g) all-purpose (plain) flour
- ½ cup (100 g) sugar
- ½ cup (75 g) unsweetened cocoa powder
- 2 large eggs, lightly beaten
- 6 tablespoons butter, melted
- 6 tablespoons milk
- 2 teaspoons vanilla extract
- 1 tablespoon baking powder
- 20 small solid chocolate Easter eggs
- 2 tablespoons miniature chocolate chips (optional)

Right: *Chocolate, rum, and raisin muffins*

Chocolate, rum, and raisin muffins

■ INGREDIENTS

- 1¼ cups (225 g) raisins
- 6 tablespoons rum
- 2½ cups (375 g) all-purpose (plain) flour
- ½ cup (75 g) unsweetened cocoa powder
- 1 tablespoon baking powder
- ¼ teaspoon salt
- 1 cup (200 g) sugar
- 1 cup (250 ml) light (single) cream
- 2 eggs, lightly beaten
- 6 tablespoons butter
- 1 cup (180 g) semisweet chocolate chips

Makes: about 20 muffins; Preparation: 10 minutes + 30 minutes to soak; Cooking: 20 minutes; Level of difficulty: 1

Plump the raisins in the rum in a small bowl for 30 minutes. • Preheat the oven to 400°F/200°C/gas 6. • Butter and flour two 12-cup muffin pans or line with foil or paper baking cups. • Sift the flour, cocoa, baking powder, and salt into a large bowl. Stir in the sugar and make a well in the center. • Beat in the raisin mixture, cream, eggs, and butter until smooth. Stir in the chocolate chips. • Spoon the batter evenly into the prepared cups. • Bake for about 20 minutes, or until a toothpick inserted into the center comes out clean. • Cool the muffins on racks.

Easy chocolate muffins

Makes: about 18 muffins; Preparation: 20 minutes; Cooking: 20 minutes; Level of difficulty: 1

Preheat the oven to 350°F/180°C/gas 4. • Arrange about 18 foil baking cups on baking sheets. • Melt the chocolate with the cream in a double boiler over barely simmering water. Set aside to cool. • Sift the flour, baking powder, and salt into a large bowl. • Beat the butter and sugar in a large bowl with an electric mixer at medium speed until creamy. • Add the eggs, beating until just blended. • With mixer at low speed, gradually beat in the chocolate, followed by the dry ingredients, alternating with the milk and vanilla. • Spoon the batter evenly into the prepared pans, filling each about two-thirds full. • Bake for about 20 minutes, or until a toothpick inserted into the center comes out clean. • Cool the muffins on racks. • Spread the frosting over the tops.

■ INGREDIENTS

- 4 oz (125 g) semisweet chocolate, coarsely chopped
- 1 tablespoon heavy (double) cream
- 2 cups (300 g) all-purpose (plain) flour
- 2 teaspoons baking powder
- ¼ teaspoon salt
- ¾ cup (200 g) butter
- 1½ cups (300 g) sugar
- 3 large eggs
- ⅔ cup (180 ml) milk
- 2 teaspoons vanilla extract
- 1 quantity *Rich Chocolate Frosting* (see page 30)

Apricot and coconut muffins

Makes: about 15 muffins; Preparation: 20 minutes; Cooking: 15 minutes; Level of difficulty: 1

Preheat the oven to 350°F/180°C/gas 4. • Arrange about 15 foil baking cups on baking sheets. • Sift the flour and baking powder into a large bowl. Use your fingertips to rub in the butter. • Stir in the sugar, apricots, coconut, milk, and eggs until well blended. • Spoon the batter into the prepared cups, filling each about half full. • Bake for about 15 minutes, or until a toothpick inserted into the center comes out clean. • Cool the muffins in the pan for 10 minutes. • Turn out onto racks and let cool completely.

■ INGREDIENTS

- 2 cups (300 g) all-purpose (plain) flour
- 1 tablespoon baking powder
- ½ cup (125 g) butter
- ¾ cup (150 g) sugar
- 1 cup (250 g) chopped dried apricots
- ¾ cup (90 g) shredded (desiccated) coconut
- ¾ cup (200 ml) milk
- 2 large eggs, lightly beaten

Right: *Easy chocolate muffins*

Cherry and almond muffins

Makes: about 18 muffins; Preparation: 20 minutes; Cooking: 25 minutes; Level of difficulty: 1

Preheat the oven to 375°F/190°C/gas 5. • Arrange about 18 foil baking cups on baking sheets. • Sift the flour, baking powder, and salt into a large bowl. • Beat the butter, 1 cup (200 g) sugar, and almond extract in a large bowl with an electric mixer at medium speed until creamy. • Add the eggs one at a time, beating until just blended after each addition. • With mixer at low speed, gradually beat in the dry ingredients, alternating with the milk. • Stir in the cherries and almonds. • Spoon the batter evenly into the cups, filling each about two-thirds full. Dust with the remaining sugar. • Bake for about 25 minutes, or until a toothpick inserted into the center comes out clean. • Cool the muffins on racks.

■ INGREDIENTS

- 2 cups (300 g) all-purpose (plain) flour
- 2 teaspoons baking powder
- ¼ teaspoon salt
- ½ cup (125 g) butter
- 1¼ cups (250 g) sugar
- 1 teaspoon almond extract
- 2 large eggs
- ½ cup (125 ml) milk
- 2 cups (200 g) dark sweet cherries, pitted, coarsely chopped, and drained
- ¾ cup (75 g) sliced almonds, lightly toasted

Raspberry muffins

Makes: about 18 muffins; Preparation: 20 minutes; Cooking: 25 minutes; Level of difficulty: 1

Preheat the oven to 375°F/190°C/gas 5. • Arrange about 18 foil baking cups on baking sheets. • Beat the eggs, sugar, oil, yogurt, and 3 tablespoons of jelly in a large bowl with an electric mixer at high speed. • With mixer at low speed, gradually beat in the flour and baking powder. • Spoon the batter into the prepared cups, filling each one about half full. • Place a piece of cream cheese in the center and top each with 2 teaspoons of jelly. • Spoon the remaining batter on top. • Bake for about 25 minutes, or until a toothpick inserted into the center comes out clean. • Cool in the pans for 10 minutes. • Turn out onto racks and let cool completely. • Dust with the confectioners' sugar.

■ INGREDIENTS

- 3 large eggs
- ¾ cup (150 g) sugar
- 6 tablespoons vegetable oil
- 6 tablespoons raspberry yogurt
- 3 tablespoons raspberry jelly + ½ cup (160 ml)
- 2½ cups (375 g) all-purpose (plain) flour
- 2 teaspoons baking powder
- 6 tablespoons cream cheese
- 4 tablespoons confectioners' (icing) sugar

Right: *Cherry and almond muffins*

Lemon curd muffins

INGREDIENTS

- 2 cups (300 g) all-purpose (plain) flour
- 1 tablespoon baking powder
- ¼ teaspoon salt
- ⅓ cup (70 g) sugar
- 1 cup (250 ml) milk
- ½ cup (160 ml) lemon curd
- 2 large eggs
- 4 tablespoons butter

Makes: about 18 muffins; Preparation: 15 minutes; Cooking: 12 minutes; Level of difficulty: 1

Preheat the oven to 375°F/190°C/gas 5. • Arrange about 18 foil baking cups on a baking sheet. • Sift the flour, baking powder, and salt into a large bowl. Stir in the sugar. • Mix in the milk, lemon curd, eggs, and butter. • Spoon the batter evenly into the cups, filling each about two-thirds full. • Bake for about 15 minutes, or until a toothpick inserted into the center comes out clean. • Let cool completely.

Apricot muffins

Makes: about 12 muffins; Preparation: 15 minutes; Cooking: 15 minutes; Level of difficulty: 1

Preheat the oven to 350°F/180°C/gas 4. • Butter and flour a 12-cup muffin pan, or line with foil or paper baking cups. • Sift the flour, baking powder, and salt into a large bowl. • Bring the apricots and water in a saucepan over medium heat to a boil. Reduce the heat and simmer for 5 minutes. Remove from the heat and beat in the butter and brown sugar until the sugar has dissolved. • Stir in the milk, eggs, and vanilla. Stir the apricot mixture into the dry ingredients. • Spoon the batter evenly into the prepared cups, filling each about two-thirds full. • Bake for about 15 minutes, or until a toothpick inserted into the center comes out clean. • Cool the muffins on racks.

■ INGREDIENTS

- 2 cups (300 g) all-purpose (plain) flour
- 2 teaspoons baking powder
- ¼ teaspoon salt
- ⅔ cup (150 g) chopped dried apricots
- ¾ cup (200 ml) cold water
- ½ cup (125 g) butter
- ¾ cup (150 g) firmly packed brown sugar
- ½ cup (125 ml) milk
- 1 large egg, lightly beaten
- 2 teaspoons vanilla extract

Peach muffins

Makes: about 18 muffins; Preparation: 20 minutes; Cooking: 30 minutes; Level of difficulty: 1

Preheat the oven to 400°F/200°C/gas 6. • Arrange about 18 foil baking cups on baking sheets. • Sift the flour, baking powder, allspice, nutmeg, cinnamon, and salt into a large bowl. Stir in the brown sugar. • Stir in the milk, eggs, oil, and peaches. • Spoon the batter evenly into the cups, filling each about three-quarters full. Sprinkle with sugar. • Bake for about 30 minutes, or until a toothpick inserted into the center comes out clean. • Cool the muffins on racks.

■ INGREDIENTS

- 3 cups (450 g) all-purpose (plain) flour
- 1 tablespoon baking powder
- 1 teaspoon ground allspice
- 1 teaspoon each ground nutmeg and cinnamon
- ½ teaspoon salt
- 1½ cups (300 g) firmly packed dark brown sugar
- ⅔ cup (180 ml) milk
- 2 large eggs, lightly beaten
- ½ cup (125 ml) vegetable oil
- 3 large peaches, diced
- ¼ cup (50 g) sugar

Right: *Apricot muffins*

Bars and Brownies

☙

*All-American classic brownies are universally loved.
In this chapter, we have included our favorite variations
on the basic brownie recipe, as well as a host
of nutty, caramel, and seed-based bar cookies.
Just add cream to create a filling dessert.*

Amazing nutty brownies

Delicious brownies are always greeted with enthusiasm.
The hazelnut chocolate cream in this recipes adds some extra flavor.
Try serving them hot as a dessert to finish a family meal.
In that case, whip up a cup (250 ml) of cream and pipe it over the top.

Serves: 6-8; Preparation: 15 minutes; Cooking: 35 minutes; Level of difficulty: 1

Preheat the oven to 325°F/170°C/gas 3. • Butter a 9-inch (23-cm) square baking pan. • Melt the chocolate hazelnut spread and butter in a small saucepan over low heat. • Beat the eggs and sugar in a large bowl with an electric mixer at high speed until pale and creamy. • With mixer at medium speed, beat in the chocolate mixture and vanilla. • Fold in the flour, baking powder, and hazelnuts. • Spoon the batter into the prepared pan. • Bake for about 35 minutes, or until a toothpick inserted in the center comes out clean. • Let cool in the pan. • Cut into squares and transfer to a serving dish. • Serve with the whipped cream, if liked.

■ INGREDIENTS

- ½ cup (125 g) chocolate hazelnut spread (Nutella)
- 3 tablespoons butter
- 4 large eggs
- 1 cup (200 g) sugar
- ½ teaspoon vanilla extract
- 1⅓ cups (200 g) all-purpose (plain) flour
- 1 teaspoon baking powder
- 2 cups (200 g) coarsely chopped hazelnuts
- 1 cup (250 ml) heavy (double) cream, whipped (optional)

Mississippi brownies

Serves: 6-8; Preparation: 15 minutes; Cooking: 35 minutes; Level of difficulty: 1

Preheat the oven to 325°F/170°C/gas 3. • Butter a 9-inch (23-cm) square baking pan. • Melt the butter and chocolate in a double boiler over barely simmering water, mixing until glossy and smooth. • Remove from the heat and beat in the eggs. • Add the sugar, flour, baking powder, salt, and nuts and beat until well mixed. • Spoon the batter into the prepared pan. • Bake for about 35 minutes, or until a toothpick inserted in the center comes out clean. • Remove from the oven and let cool. • Let cool before cutting into squares.

■ INGREDIENTS

- ½ cup (125 g) butter
- 3 oz (90 g) semisweet chocolate
- 2 large eggs, lightly beaten
- 1¼ cups (250 g) sugar
- 1 cup (150 g) all-purpose (plain) flour
- 1 teaspoon baking powder
- ¼ teaspoon salt
- 1¼ cups (125 g) coarsely chopped walnuts

Right: *Mississippi brownies*

Frozen chocolate pecan cake

Serves: 6-8; Preparation: 25 minutes + 12 hours to freeze; Cooking: 25 minutes; Level of difficulty: 2

Preheat the oven to 350°F/180°C/gas 4. • Butter a 9-inch (23-cm) springform pan. • Place the pecans and 1 tablespoon of flour in a food processor and process until finely ground. • Melt the chocolate, butter, liqueur, and vanilla in a double boiler over barely simmering water. Set aside to cool. • Beat the eggs, sugar, and salt in a large bowl with an electric mixer at medium speed until pale and thick. • Stir the remaining flour, chocolate mixture, and pecans into the egg mixture. • Spoon the batter into the prepared pan. • Bake for about 25 minutes, or until the top is set. • Cool the cake completely in the pan on a rack. • When cool, cover with foil and freeze for 12 hours. • Transfer to the refrigerator about 2 hours before serving. Loosen and remove the pan sides. Topping: With mixer at high speed, beat the cream in a small bowl until stiff. Spread over the cake. Sprinkle with the chocolate. Cut into wedges and serve.

■ INGREDIENTS

- 1½ cups (200 g) pecans
- ⅓ cup (50 g) all-purpose (plain) flour
- 1 lb (500 g) semisweet chocolate, coarsely chopped
- ¾ cup (200 g) cold butter
- 1 tablespoon coffee liqueur
- 1 teaspoon vanilla extract
- 4 large eggs
- 2 tablespoons sugar
- ¼ teaspoon salt

TOPPING
- ¾ cup (200 ml) heavy (double) cream
- 3 oz (90 g) bittersweet chocolate, grated

Double chocolate macadamia bars

Serves: 6-8; Preparation: 20 minutes; Cooking: 30 minutes; Level of difficulty: 1

Preheat the oven to 350°F/180°C/gas 4. • Butter an 8-inch (20-cm) square baking pan. Line with waxed paper. Butter the paper. • Melt both types of chocolate with the butter in a double boiler over barely simmering water. Remove from the heat. • Stir in the brown sugar and honey. • Add the eggs one at a time, beating until just blended after each addition. • Use a large rubber spatula to fold in the flour, baking powder, salt, and nuts. • Spoon the batter into the prepared pan. • Bake for about 30 minutes, or until a toothpick inserted into the center comes out clean. • Cool in the pan for 15 minutes. Cut into bars to serve.

■ INGREDIENTS

- 3 oz (90 g) semisweet chocolate, coarsely chopped
- 3 oz (90 g) milk chocolate, coarsely chopped
- ½ cup (125 g) butter
- ½ cup (100 g) firmly packed dark brown sugar
- 2 tablespoons honey
- 2 large eggs, lightly beaten
- 1 cup (150 g) all-purpose (plain) flour
- 1 teaspoon baking powder
- ¼ teaspoon salt
- ⅔ cup (100 g) macadamia nuts, finely chopped

Right: *Frozen chocolate pecan cake*

Southern slices

Serves: 6-8; Preparation: 30 minutes + 6 hours to chill; Cooking: 15 minutes; Level of difficulty: 2

Line a 9-inch (23-cm) square baking pan with plastic wrap (cling film). • Melt the chocolate and butter in a double boiler over barely simmering water. Pour into the prepared pan. • Sprinkle the crumbs on top and press down lightly. Set aside at room temperature. • Topping: Mix the cream, honey, brown sugar, butter, and vanilla in a saucepan over low heat until the sugar has dissolved. Boil for about 15 minutes, without stirring, until caramel in color. Stir in the nuts. • Use a thin metal spatula to spread the topping over the chocolate base. • Refrigerate for 6 hours, or until set. • Cut into bars.

■ INGREDIENTS

- 8 oz (250 g) semisweet chocolate, coarsely chopped
- 1 tablespoon butter
- 2 cups (250 g) graham cracker (digestive biscuit) crumbs

TOPPING
- 1¼ cups (310 ml) heavy (double) cream
- ½ cup (125 ml) honey
- 1 cup (200 g) firmly packed brown sugar
- 1 tablespoon butter
- 1 teaspoon vanilla extract
- ½ cup (50 g) macadamia nuts, coarsely chopped
- ½ cup (90 g) pine nuts
- ½ cup (50 g) pecans, coarsely chopped
- ½ cup (50 g) pistachios, coarsely chopped

Piedmontese squares

Serves: 8-10; Preparation: 30 minutes; Cooking: 40 minutes; Level of difficulty: 1

Preheat the oven to 350°F/180°C/gas 4. • Butter an 11 x 7-inch (28 x 18-cm) baking pan. • Sift the flour, cocoa, baking powder, cinnamon, and salt into a medium bowl. • Beat the butter, brown sugar, and vanilla in a large bowl with an electric mixer at high speed until creamy. • Add the eggs one at a time, beating until just blended after each addition. • Mix in the dry ingredients, followed by the milk and cornmeal. • Stir in the chocolate chips, pecans, and coarsely chopped Brazil nuts by hand until well blended. • Spoon the mixture into the prepared pan. • Sprinkle with the finely chopped Brazil nuts. • Bake for 30 minutes. If the topping is fairly brown, cover with aluminum foil. Bake for 10 minutes more, or until a toothpick inserted into the center comes out clean. • Cool completely in the pan before cutting into squares.

■ INGREDIENTS

- ½ cup (75 g) all-purpose (plain) flour
- 1½ tablespoons cocoa
- 1 teaspoon baking powder
- ¼ teaspoon cinnamon
- ⅛ teaspoon salt
- ⅔ cup (180 g) butter
- ¾ cup (150 g) firmly packed brown sugar
- 1 teaspoon vanilla extract
- 2 large eggs
- 4 tablespoons milk
- ⅓ cup (50 g) cornmeal
- ¼ cup (45 g) milk chocolate chips
- ½ cup (50 g) chopped pecans
- ½ cup (50 g) coarsely chopped Brazil nuts
- ⅔ cup (70 g) finely chopped Brazil nuts

Right: Southern slices

Martha's date squares

Serves: 8-10; Preparation: 20 minutes; Cooking: 20 minutes; Level of difficulty: 1

Preheat the oven to 375°F/190°C/gas 5. • Line a 13 x 9-inch (33 x 23-cm) baking pan with aluminum foil, letting the edges overhang. Butter the foil. • Sift the flour, cornstarch, and salt into a large bowl. • Beat the butter, brown sugar, and egg in a large bowl with an electric mixer at high speed until well blended. • Mix in the dry ingredients, dates, and pecans to form a stiff dough. • Firmly press the mixture into the prepared pan to form a smooth, even layer. • Brush with the milk and sprinkle with the sugar. • Bake for about 20 minutes, or until just golden. • Cool completely in the pan on a rack. • Using the foil as handles, lift onto a cutting board. Peel off the foil. Cut into squares.

■ INGREDIENTS

- ⅔ cup (100 g) all-purpose (plain) flour
- ⅔ cup (100 g) cornstarch (cornflour)
- ⅛ teaspoon salt
- ½ cup (125 g) butter
- ½ cup (100 g) firmly packed light brown sugar
- 1 large egg
- ⅔ cup (120 g) finely chopped pitted dates
- 1 cup (100 g) coarsely chopped pecans
- 2 tablespoons milk
- 2 tablespoons sugar

Citrus and date bars

Serves: 8-10; Preparation: 20 minutes + 15 minutes to soak the dates; Cooking: 30 minutes; Level of difficulty: 1

Preheat the oven to 350°F/180°C/gas 4. • Butter an 8-inch (20-cm) square baking pan. • Heat the milk in a small saucepan over low heat. • Pour the milk into a large bowl, add the dates, and let soak for 15 minutes. • Sift the flour, baking powder, cinnamon, and salt into a medium bowl. • Beat the egg, butter, and orange zest into the date mixture. • Add the dry ingredients, followed by the orange flesh, beating until well blended. • Spoon the batter into the prepared pan. • Bake for about 30 minutes, or until a toothpick inserted into the center comes out clean. • Cool completely before cutting into bars.

■ INGREDIENTS

- ⅔ cup (180 ml) milk
- ½ cup (90 g) finely chopped dates
- ¾ cup (125 g) whole-wheat (wholemeal) flour
- ½ teaspoon baking powder
- ½ teaspoon ground cinnamon
- ⅛ teaspoon salt
- 1 large egg, lightly beaten
- 4 tablespoons butter, melted
- finely grated zest and chopped flesh of 1 orange

Right: Energy squares

Energy squares

■ INGREDIENTS

- 1⅔ cups (250 g) old-fashioned rolled oats
- 1½ cups (225 g) corn flakes
- 1 cup (120 g) shredded (desiccated) coconut
- 1 cup (200 g) firmly packed brown sugar
- 1 cup (180 g) pitted dates, coarsely chopped
- ¼ teaspoon salt
- ½ cup (125 g) butter, melted
- 2 tablespoons honey, warmed

Serves: 8-10; Preparation: 10 minutes; Cooking: 25 minutes; Level of difficulty: 1

Preheat the oven to 350°F/180°C/gas 4. • Butter an 11 x 7-inch (28 x 18-cm) baking pan. • Stir together the oats, corn flakes, coconut, brown sugar, dates, and salt in a large bowl. • Stir in the butter and honey. • Spoon the batter into the prepared pan and press down gently, using the back of the spoon. • Bake for about 25 minutes, or until lightly browned. • Cool completely before cutting into squares.

Louisiana mud bars

- 8 large egg whites
- 1 cup (200 g) firmly packed brown sugar
- 1 cup (250 g) butter
- 8 oz (250 g) bittersweet chocolate, coarsely chopped
- 3 tablespoons coffee liqueur
- 1 tablespoon vanilla extract
- 1 tablespoon strong, cold black coffee

Serves: 8-10; Preparation: 20 minutes + 3 hours to chill; Cooking: 35 minutes; Level of difficulty: 1

Preheat the oven to 300°F/150°C/gas 2. • Butter and flour a 10-inch (25-cm) springform pan. • Beat the egg whites with an electric mixer at medium speed until frothy. • With mixer at high speed, gradually add the brown sugar, beating until stiff peaks form. • Melt the butter in a medium saucepan over low heat. Remove from the heat and stir in the chocolate until melted. • Use a large rubber spatula to gradually fold the liqueur, vanilla, coffee, and chocolate mixture into the beaten whites. • Spoon the batter into the prepared pan. • Bake for about 35 minutes, or until a toothpick inserted into the center comes out clean. • Cool the cake completely in the pan on a rack. • Refrigerate for at least 3 hours, or until set before serving. Cut into bars.

Chocolate dominoes

- 1 cup (150 g) all-purpose (plain) flour
- 1 tablespoon unsweetened cocoa powder
- 2 teaspoons baking powder
- ½ cup (125 g) butter
- ½ cup (100 g) sugar
- 2 large eggs
- 2 tablespoons milk

VANILLA FROSTING
- 6 tablespoons butter, melted
- 1 cup (150 g) confectioners' (icing) sugar
- 1 teaspoon vanilla extract
- 7 oz (200 g) candy-covered chocolates

Serves: 8-10; Preparation: 25 minutes; Cooking: 40 minutes; Level of difficulty: 1

Preheat the oven to 350°F/180°C/gas 4. • Butter an 11 x 7-inch (28 x 18-cm) baking pan. Line with waxed paper. • Sift the flour, cocoa, and baking powder into a large bowl. • Beat the butter and sugar in a large bowl until creamy. • Add the eggs one at a time, beating until just blended after each addition. • Mix in the dry ingredients, alternating with the milk. • Spoon the batter into the prepared pan. • Bake for about 40 minutes, or until a toothpick inserted into the center comes out clean. • Cool completely in the pan. • Vanilla Frosting: Beat the butter, confectioners' sugar, and vanilla in a large bowl until creamy. • Spread the frosting over the top of the cake. Cut into bars and decorate with the candy-coated chocolates.

Left: *Chocolate dominoes*

Classic almond brittle

Serves: 10-12; Preparation: 10 minutes; Cooking: 20 minutes; Level of difficulty: 2

Cook the sugar with the water in a large saucepan over low heat, stirring constantly with a wooden spoon, for about 10 minutes, or until golden brown. • Add the almonds and orange zest. Mix well and continue to cooking for about 10 minutes, or until dark golden brown. Remove from the heat. • Oil a sheet of waxed paper with the sweet almond oil. • Pour the mixture out onto the prepared paper. Spread the brittle out on the paper; it should be about ½ inch (1 cm) thick. Let cool slightly. • While the mixture is still pliable, cut into squares with a sharp knife. Let cool completely.

■ INGREDIENTS

- 2½ cups (500 g) sugar
- 4 tablespoons water
- generous 3¼ cups (500 g) blanched almonds
- finely grated zest of 1 orange
- 1 tablespoon sweet almond oil

Crispy three-seed wedges

Serves: 10-12; Preparation: 20 minutes + 24 hours to rest; Cooking: 1 hour; Level of difficulty: 1

Preheat the oven to 350°F/180°C/gas 4. • Butter a 10-inch (25-cm) springform pan. • Beat the egg whites in a large bowl with an electric mixer at medium speed until frothy. With mixer at high speed, gradually add the sugar, beating until stiff, glossy peaks form. • Use a large rubber spatula to fold in the flour, pine nuts, pumpkin seeds, sunflower seeds, and sesame seeds. • Spoon the batter into the prepared pan. • Bake for about 45 minutes, or until lightly browned. Cool the cake completely in the pan on a rack. • Loosen and remove the pan sides. Wrap the cake tightly in aluminum foil. • Set aside to rest for 24 hours. • Preheat the oven to 350°F/180°C/gas 4. • Cut the cake into wedges and arrange on baking sheets. • Bake for about 15 minutes, or until crisp. • Let cool completely before serving.

■ INGREDIENTS

- 3 large egg whites
- ½ cup (100 g) sugar
- 1 cup (150 g) all-purpose (plain) flour
- ⅓ cup (60 g) pine nuts
- ⅓ cup (50 g) pumpkin seeds
- ⅓ cup (50 g) sunflower seeds
- 2 tablespoons sesame seeds

Right: *Classic almond brittle*

Caribbean coconut bars

Serves: 10-12; Preparation: 20 minutes; Cooking: 35 minutes; Level of difficulty: 1

Preheat the oven to 350°F/180°C/gas 4. • Butter a 10½ x 15½-inch (27 x 37-cm) jelly-roll pan. • Cake: Sift the flour, coconut, sugar, baking powder, and salt into a large bowl. Add the butter and beat until well mixed. • Spoon the batter into the prepared pan. • Bake for about 10 minutes, or until light golden brown. • Cool in the pan for 15 minutes. • Filling: Mix the condensed milk, corn syrup, brown sugar, and butter in a large bowl. • Topping: Beat the eggs and sugar with an electric mixer at high speed until pale and thick. Fold in the coconut. • Use a thin metal spatula to spread the filling over the cake. Sprinkle with the topping. • Bake for 25 minutes more, or until the topping has browned. • Let cool completely in the pan on a rack. Cut into bars.

■ INGREDIENTS

CAKE
- 1 cup (150 g) all-purpose (plain) flour
- ½ cup (60 g) shredded (desiccated) coconut
- ½ cup (100 g) sugar
- 2 teaspoons baking powder
- ¼ teaspoon salt
- ½ cup (125 g) butter, melted

FILLING
- 1 can (14 oz/400 g) sweetened condensed milk
- 2 tablespoons light corn (golden) syrup
- ¼ cup (50 g) firmly packed dark brown sugar
- 4 tablespoons butter, melted

TOPPING
- 4 large eggs
- ⅔ cup (140 g) sugar
- 2¾ cups (300 g) shredded coconut flesh

Buttery coconut bars

Serves: 10-12; Preparation: 15 minutes; Cooking: 40 minutes; Level of difficulty: 1

Preheat the oven to 350°F/180°C/gas 4. • Butter an 11 x 7-inch (28 x 18-cm) baking pan. • Sift the flour, baking powder, and salt into a large bowl. • Stir in the coconut, walnuts, almonds, oats, and sugar. • Use a pastry blender to cut in the butter until the mixture resembles coarse crumbs. • Dissolve the corn syrup in the milk in a small saucepan over low heat. Add the egg, beating until just blended. • Pour the egg mixture into the dry ingredients and mix well. • Spread the mixture evenly in the baking pan. • Bake for about 40 minutes, or until golden brown. • Cool completely before cutting into bars.

■ INGREDIENTS

- ¾ cup (125 g) all-purpose (plain) flour
- ½ teaspoon baking powder
- ¼ teaspoon salt
- ½ cup (60 g) shredded (desiccated) coconut
- ½ cup (50 g) finely chopped walnuts
- 2 tablespoons finely ground almonds
- ⅓ cup (50 g) rolled oats
- ¾ cup (150 g) sugar
- ½ cup (125 g) butter
- 1 tablespoon corn (golden) syrup
- 1 tablespoon milk
- 1 large egg

Right: *Caribbean coconut bars*

Emily's best coconut squares

Serves: 6-8; Preparation: 15 minutes; Cooking: 15 minutes; Level of difficulty: 1

■ INGREDIENTS

- 10 oz (300 g) semisweet chocolate, coarsely chopped
- ½ cup (125 g) butter
- 1½ cups (300 g) sugar
- 2 large eggs
- ⅔ cup (70 g) candied cherries, coarsely chopped
- 2 cups (240 g) shredded coconut

Preheat the oven to 325°F/170°C/gas 3. • Line a 10½ x 15½-inch (26 x 36-cm) jelly-roll pan with aluminum foil. • Melt the chocolate in a double boiler over barely simmering water. Spread the chocolate over the foil and set aside to cool. • Beat the butter and sugar in a large bowl with an electric mixer at high speed until creamy. • Add the eggs, beating until just blended after each addition. • Use a large rubber spatula to fold in the cherries and coconut. • Spread over the cooled chocolate. • Bake for about 15 minutes, or until a toothpick inserted into the center comes out clean. • Cool completely before cutting into squares.

Almond and orange bars

This recipe comes from Sicily where fresh oranges and almonds abound.

Serves: 15-20; Preparation: 15 minutes + 2 days to soak the orange zest; Cooking: 30 minutes; Level of difficulty: 3

Soak the orange zest in a bowl of water for 2 days, changing the water twice a day. • Drain the orange and cut into small thin strips with a sharp knife. • Transfer to a large saucepan. • Add the sugar and almonds. Cook over medium heat for about 30 minutes, stirring constantly, until the mixture is a dark golden brown color. • Turn the mixture out onto a marble cutting board and let cool. • Cut into bars.

■ INGREDIENTS

- 1 lb (500 g) orange zest, removed in long strips with a very sharp knife
- 2½ cups (500 g) sugar
- ⅔ cup (100 g) blanched almonds, toasted and coarsely chopped

Apricot and banana crisp

Serves: 10-12; Preparation: 55 minutes; Cooking: 30 minutes; Level of difficulty: 1

Bring the lemon juice, honey, and water to a boil with the apricots and bananas in a medium saucepan over medium heat. • Reduce the heat and simmer over low heat for 30 minutes, or until the fruit has softened. • Remove from the heat and let cool for 15 minutes. • Butter an 8-inch (20-cm) baking pan. • Melt the butter with the brown sugar in a medium saucepan over low heat until the sugar has dissolved completely. • Mix in the corn flakes until well coated. • Firmly press half the corn flake mixture into the prepared pan to form a smooth, even layer. Spoon the apricot and banana mixture evenly over the base and cover with the remaining corn flake mixture. • Cool completely before cutting into squares or bars.

■ INGREDIENTS

- 2 tablespoons lemon juice
- 2 tablespoons honey
- ⅔ cup (180 ml) water
- 2¼ cups (300 g) coarsely chopped dried apricots
- 2¼ cups (300 g) coarsely chopped dried bananas
- ½ cup (125 g) butter
- 1 cup (200 g) firmly packed light brown sugar
- 1¼ cups (180 g) corn flakes

Right: *Almond and orange bars*

Chocolate raisin crunch

Serves: 14-16; Preparation: 35 minutes; Cooking: 30 minutes; Level of difficulty: 3

Preheat the oven to 350°F/180°C/gas 4. • Butter a 10 x 7-inch (25 x 18-cm) baking pan. • Sift the flour, cornstarch, confectioners' sugar, baking powder, and salt into a large bowl. • Use your fingertips to rub in the butter until the mixture resembles coarse crumbs. • Add the raisins, milk, and vanilla and mix to form a firm dough. • Roll the dough out on a lightly floured work surface. • Transfer to the prepared pan, pressing it into the pan with your hands. Smooth the surface with the back of a spoon and prick all over with a fork. • Bake for about 30 minutes, or until lightly browned. • Remove from the oven and let cool slightly. • Melt the chocolate in a double boiler and pour over the raisin crunch in the pan. Before the chocolate has begun to set, make a zigzag pattern on each square with a fork. • Cut into squares.

■ INGREDIENTS

- 1⅔ cups (250 g) all-purpose (plain) flour
- 2 tablespoons cornstarch (cornflour)
- ½ cup (75 g) confectioners' (icing) sugar
- 1 teaspoon baking powder
- ⅛ teaspoon salt
- ¾ cup (200 g) butter, cut into pieces
- scant ½ cup (75 g) raisins
- 2 tablespoons milk
- ½ teaspoon vanilla extract
- 8 oz (250 g) semisweet chocolate, cut into pieces

Andrea's marble squares

Serves: 12-14; Preparation: 30 minutes; Cooking: 50 minutes; Level of difficulty: 1

Preheat the oven to 350°F/180°C/gas 4. • Butter and flour a 9-inch (23-cm) square baking pan. • Melt the chocolate and 3 tablespoons of butter in a double boiler over barely simmering water. Set aside to cool. • Beat the remaining butter, confectioners' sugar, and vanilla and coconut extracts in a large bowl with an electric mixer at medium speed until creamy. Add one egg and beat until just blended. • With mixer at low speed, beat in the chocolate mixture, followed by the flour and baking powder. • Spoon the batter into the prepared pan. • With mixer at medium speed, beat the cream cheese and sugar in a medium bowl until smooth. • Beat in the remaining egg. • Spread the cream cheese mixture over the chocolate layer. Use a sharp knife to swirl the batters together in a marble pattern. • Bake for about 50 minutes, or until a toothpick inserted into the center comes out clean. • Cool in the pan for 15 minutes. Cut into squares.

■ INGREDIENTS

- 3 oz (90 g) semisweet chocolate, coarsely chopped
- 6 tablespoons butter
- ½ cup (75 g) confectioners' (icing) sugar
- 1 teaspoon vanilla extract
- ½ teaspoon coconut extract
- 2 large eggs
- ½ cup (75 g) all-purpose (plain) flour
- ½ teaspoon baking powder
- 1 cup (250 g) cream cheese
- ¼ cup (50 g) sugar

Right: *Chocolate raisin crunch*

Crumb-topped toffee squares

Serves: 10-12; Preparation: 30 minutes; Cooking: 1 hour; Level of difficulty: 1

Preheat the oven to 350°F/180°C/gas 4. • Butter and flour a 9-inch (23-cm) square baking pan. • Sift the flour and salt into a large bowl. Stir in both sugars. • Use a pastry blender to cut in the butter until the mixture resembles fine crumbs. • Place ¾ cup (100 g) of the crumb mixture into a medium bowl and set aside. • Beat the buttermilk, egg, vanilla, and baking soda into the large bowl of crumb mixture until well blended. Spoon the batter into the prepared pan. • Mix the reserved crumb mixture with the toffee and walnuts. • Sprinkle the batter with the crumb mixture. • Bake for 1 hour, or until golden brown and the cake shrinks from the pan sides. • Cool in the pan for 15 minutes. Cut into squares.

■ INGREDIENTS

- 2 cups (300 g) all-purpose (plain) flour
- ¼ teaspoon salt
- 1 cup (200 g) firmly packed brown sugar
- ½ cup (100 g) sugar
- ½ cup (125 g) cold butter
- 1 cup (250 ml) buttermilk
- 1 large egg
- 1½ teaspoons vanilla extract
- 1 teaspoon baking soda
- 4 oz (125 g) toffee candies (Werther's Original Toffees are a good choice), crushed in a food processor to make ½ cup (50 g)
- ½ cup (50 g) walnuts, coarsely chopped

Classic mid-morning bars

Serves: 6-8; Preparation: 30 minutes; Cooking: 30 minutes; Level of difficulty: 1

Preheat the oven to 350°F/180°C/gas 4. • Butter a 9-inch (23-cm) baking pan. • Almond Toffee Topping: Melt the butter with both sugars in a small saucepan over low heat. • Add the milk and bring to a boil, stirring constantly. • Remove from the heat and stir in the almonds. • Cookie Base: Sift the flour, baking powder, and salt into a medium bowl. • Beat the butter and sugar in a large bowl with an electric mixer at high speed until creamy. • Add the egg, beating until just blended. • Mix in the dry ingredients and lemon zest. • Firmly press the mixture into the prepared pan to form a smooth, even layer. • Spread the almond toffee topping evenly over the cookie base. • Bake for about 30 minutes, or until just golden. • Cut into bars while the topping is still warm.

■ INGREDIENTS

ALMOND TOFFEE TOPPING
- 6 tablespoons butter
- ½ cup (100 g) sugar
- 2 tablespoons brown sugar
- 2 tablespoons milk
- 2½ cups (375 g) flaked almonds

COOKIE BASE
- 1⅓ cups (200 g) all-purpose (plain) flour
- 1 teaspoon baking powder
- ¼ teaspoon salt
- ½ cup (125 g) butter
- ⅔ cup (140 g) sugar
- 1 large egg
- 1 teaspoon finely grated lemon zest

Right: *Crumb-topped toffee squares*

Almond meringue squares

Serves: 10-12; Preparation: 15 minutes; Cooking: 40 minutes; Level of difficulty: 1

Preheat the oven to 275°F/140°C/gas 1. • Line a baking sheet with waxed paper. • Beat the egg whites with the salt in a large bowl until stiff. • Fold in the sugar, almonds, and confectioners' sugar. • Spoon the mixture onto the prepared baking sheet. • Bake for about 40 minutes, or until golden brown all over. • Cool in the pan for 15 minutes. Cut into squares.

■ INGREDIENTS

- 2 large egg whites
- ⅛ teaspoon salt
- 1 tablespoon sugar
- 1⅓ cups (200 g) blanched almonds, toasted and finely chopped
- 1 cup (150 g) confectioners' (icing) sugar

Christmas cherry bars

Serves: 10-12; Preparation: 30 minutes; Cooking: 30 minutes; Level of difficulty: 1

Preheat the oven to 350°F/180°C/gas 4. • Butter a 10-inch (25-cm) square baking pan. • Sift the flour and confectioners' sugar into a large bowl. • With an electric mixer at medium speed, beat in the butter and whole egg until well blended. • Firmly press the mixture into the prepared pan to form a smooth, even layer. • Bake for 10 minutes. • Reduce the oven temperature to 300°F/150°C/gas 2. • Warm the preserves in a small saucepan over low heat until liquid. • Spread the preserves over the base. • With mixer at medium speed, beat the egg whites in a large bowl until soft peaks form. • With mixer at high speed, gradually add the sugar and nutmeg, beating until stiff, glossy peaks form. • Gently fold in the cherries. • Spread the meringue on top of preserves. • Bake for about 20 minutes, or until the meringue is lightly browned. • Cool in the pan for 15 minutes. • Cut into bars.

■ INGREDIENTS

- ⅔ cup (100 g) all-purpose (plain) flour
- ½ cup (75 g) confectioners' (icing) sugar
- 6 tablespoons butter, melted
- 1 large egg + 2 large egg whites
- ⅔ cup (300 g) cherry preserves (jam)
- ½ cup (100 g) sugar
- 1 teaspoon freshly grated nutmeg
- ½ cup (50 g) finely chopped candied cherries

Right: Almond meringue squares

Spiced meringue bars

Serves: 12-14; Preparation: 30 minutes; Cooking: 30 minutes; Level of difficulty: 1

INGREDIENTS

- ⅔ cup (100 g) all-purpose (plain) flour
- ½ cup (75 g) confectioners' (icing) sugar
- ⅛ teaspoon salt
- 6 tablespoons butter, melted
- 1 large egg + 2 large egg whites
- ⅔ cup (210 g) raspberry preserves (jam)
- ½ cup (100 g) sugar
- 1 teaspoon ground cinnamon

Preheat the oven to 350°F/180°C/gas 4. • Butter a 10-inch (25-cm) square baking pan. • Sift the flour, confectioners' sugar, and salt into a large bowl. • Beat in the butter and whole egg. • Firmly press the mixture into the prepared pan to form a smooth, even layer. • Bake for 10 minutes. • Reduce the oven temperature to 300°F/150°C/gas 2. • Warm the preserves in a small saucepan over low heat. • Spread the preserves over the base. • Beat the egg whites in a large bowl until soft peaks form. • With mixer at high speed, gradually add the sugar and cinnamon, beating until stiff, glossy peaks form. • Spread the meringue on top of the preserves. • Bake for about 20 minutes, or until lightly browned. • Cut into bars and let cool completely.

Broiled chocolate oat bars

■ INGREDIENTS

- 4 oz (125 g) bittersweet chocolate, chopped
- ½ cup (125 g) butter
- 1 cup (250 ml) water
- 1 cup (150 g) rolled oats
- 1 cup (200 g) sugar
- 1 cup (200 g) firmly packed brown sugar
- 3 large eggs
- ½ cup (125 ml) coffee liqueur
- ½ cup (50 g) walnuts, coarsely chopped
- 1 teaspoon vanilla extract
- 2 cups (300 g) all-purpose (plain) flour
- 2 teaspoons baking powder
- ½ teaspoon salt

TOPPING

- ½ cup (125 g) butter, cut up
- 1 cup (200 g) firmly packed brown sugar
- 1 cup (100 g) walnuts, coarsely chopped
- 6 tablespoons heavy (double) cream

Serves: 10-12; Preparation: 30 minutes; Cooking: 55 minutes; Level of difficulty: 1

Preheat the oven to 350°F/180°C/gas 4. • Butter and flour a 13 x 9-inch (33 x 23-cm) baking pan. • Melt the chocolate and butter in a double boiler over barely simmering water. • Stir in the water and bring to a boil. • Remove from the heat. Beat in the oats, both sugars, eggs, liqueur, walnuts, and vanilla. • Stir in the flour, baking powder, and salt. • Spoon the batter into the prepared pan. • Bake for about 45 minutes, or until a toothpick inserted into the center comes out clean. Cool the cake completely in the pan on a rack. • Topping: Turn on the broiler (grill). • Bring the butter, brown sugar, nuts, and cream to a boil in a saucepan over low heat. Cook, stirring constantly, for 2–3 minutes, or until the mixture thickens. Pour over the hot cake. • Broil (grill) 4–6 inches (10–15 cm) from the heat source for about 5 minutes, or until the topping is lightly browned. • Cool completely in the pan on a rack. Cut into bars.

Jamaican bars

■ INGREDIENTS

- 1½ cups (225 g) all-purpose (plain) flour
- 1½ teaspoons baking powder
- ⅛ teaspoon salt
- ½ cup (125 g) butter
- 1 cup (200 g) firmly packed light brown sugar
- 2 large bananas, peeled and mashed with a fork
- ½ teaspoon vanilla extract
- ½ cup (50 g) finely chopped pecans

Serves: 8-10; Preparation: 20 minutes; Cooking: 35 minutes; Level of difficulty: 1

Preheat the oven to 350°F/180°C/gas 4. • Butter an 11 x 7-inch (28 x 18-cm) baking pan. • Sift the flour, baking powder, and salt into a medium bowl. • Beat the butter, brown sugar, bananas, and vanilla in a large bowl with an electric mixer at high speed until well blended. • Mix in the dry ingredients, followed by the pecans. • Pour the mixture into the prepared pan. • Bake for about 35 minutes, or until a toothpick inserted into the center comes out clean. • Cool completely before cutting into bars.

Left: *Broiled chocolate oat bars*

Nutty chocolate squares

Serves: 8-10; Preparation: 35 minutes; Cooking: 20 minutes; Level of difficulty: 1

Preheat the oven to 350°F/180°C/gas 4. • Butter an 8-inch (20-cm) square baking pan. • Sift the flour, baking powder, and salt into a large bowl. • Melt the chocolate in a double boiler over barely simmering water. • Beat the butter and sugar in a large bowl with an electric mixer at high speed until pale and creamy. • Add the egg, beating just until blended. • Mix in the dry ingredients, followed by the walnuts, melted chocolate, and vanilla. • If the batter is very stiff, add a little milk. • Spoon the batter into the prepared pan. • Bake for about 20 minutes, or until the top is lightly browned and springy to the touch. • Cool completely before cutting into squares.

■ INGREDIENTS

- ⅔ cup (100 g) all-purpose (plain) flour
- ¼ teaspoon baking powder
- ¼ teaspoon salt
- 2½ oz (75 g) semisweet chocolate, coarsely chopped
- 6 tablespoons butter
- ⅓ cup (70 g) sugar
- 1 large egg, lightly beaten
- ¾ cup (90 g) walnuts, coarsely chopped
- 1 teaspoon vanilla extract
- 1 tablespoon milk (optional)

Maya squares

Serves: 8-10; Preparation: 20 minutes; Cooking: 25 minutes; Level of difficulty: 1

Preheat the oven to 350°F/180°C/gas 4. • Butter an 8-inch (20-cm) baking pan. • Melt the butter and maple syrup in a double boiler over barely simmering water. • Stir in the oats, dates, carob, coconut, and salt until well mixed. Beat in the egg. • Spoon the mixture into the prepared pan, smoothing the top. • Bake for about 25 minutes, or until firm to the touch. • Cool completely in the pan. • Cut into squares.

■ INGREDIENTS

- ½ cup (125 g) butter
- 1 tablespoon maple syrup
- 1 cup (150 g) old-fashioned rolled oats
- 1 cup (180 g) finely chopped dates
- ⅔ cup (100 g) carob powder
- ½ cup (120 g) shredded (desiccated) coconut
- ⅛ teaspoon salt
- 1 large egg

Right: *Nutty chocolate squares*

Fall bars

Serves: 8–10; Preparation: 20 minutes; Cooking: 25 minutes; Level of difficulty: 1

Preheat the oven to 350°F/180°C/gas 4. • Butter an 8-inch (20-cm) square baking pan. • Sift the flour, cocoa, cinnamon, baking soda, and salt into a large bowl. • Use a pastry blender to cut in the butter until the mixture resembles coarse crumbs. • Stir together the pears, lemon juice, egg, and sugar in a large bowl until well blended. • Mix in the dry ingredients, cherries, and pear juice. • Spoon the mixture evenly into the prepared pan. • Bake for about 25 minutes, or until firm to the touch. • Cool completely in the pan. • Cut into bars.

■ INGREDIENTS

- 1 cup (150 g) all-purpose (plain) flour
- 2 tablespoons unsweetened cocoa powder
- ½ teaspoon ground cinnamon
- ½ teaspoon baking soda
- ¼ teaspoon salt
- 2 tablespoons butter
- 2 large firm-ripe pears, peeled, cored, and chopped
- 2 tablespoons lemon juice
- 1 large egg, lightly beaten
- 4 tablespoons sugar
- ½ cup (50 g) dried sour cherries
- 1 tablespoon pear juice

Children's party bars

Serves: 12–15; Preparation: 30 minutes; Cooking: 20 minutes; Level of difficulty: 1

Preheat the oven to 350°F/180°C/gas 4. • Line a 13 x 9-inch (33 x 23-cm) baking pan with aluminum foil, letting the edges overhang. • Sift the flour, cocoa, baking powder, and salt into a medium bowl. • Beat the butter and brown sugar in a large bowl with an electric mixer at high speed until creamy. • Add the eggs and vanilla, beating until just blended. • Mix in the dry ingredients, cherries, 2 cups (270 g) of chocolate chips, and ¾ cup (120 g) of hazelnuts. • Spoon the mixture into the prepared pan. • Bake for about 15 minutes, or until set but slightly moist in the center. • Sprinkle with the remaining chocolate chips, ¼ cup (30 g) hazelnuts, and marshmallows. • Return to the oven and bake for 5 minutes more, or until the chocolate and marshmallows have melted. • Using the foil as handles, lift onto a rack and let cool completely. • Remove the foil and cut into bars.

■ INGREDIENTS

- 1¾ cups (275 g) all-purpose (plain) flour
- 2 tablespoons cocoa powder
- 1 teaspoon baking powder
- ¼ teaspoon salt
- ½ cup (125 g) butter
- 1 cup (200 g) brown sugar
- 2 large eggs
- ½ teaspoon vanilla extract
- ¾ cup (90 g) finely chopped candied cherries
- 3 cups (540 g) semisweet chocolate chips
- 1 cup (120 g) finely chopped hazelnuts
- 1 cup (50 g) mini marshmallows

Right: *Fall bars*

Buttery apple bars

Serves: 8-10; Preparation: 25 minutes; Cooking: 20 minutes; Level of difficulty: 1

Preheat the oven to 400°F/200°C/gas 6. • Butter a 13 x 9-inch (33 x 23-cm) baking pan. • Sift the flour, baking powder, and salt into a medium bowl. • Beat the eggs and 1¼ cups (250 g) sugar in a large bowl with an electric mixer at high speed until pale and thick. • Bring the cream and butter to a boil in a small saucepan over medium heat. • Stir into the beaten egg mixture until well blended. • Mix in the dry ingredients. • Spoon the mixture into the prepared pan. • Arrange the apple slices on top of the batter and sprinkle with the remaining sugar. • Bake for about 20 minutes, or until golden brown and a toothpick inserted into the center comes out clean. • Cool completely before cutting into squares.

■ INGREDIENTS

- 1⅓ cups (200 g) all-purpose (plain) flour
- 2 teaspoons baking powder
- ⅛ teaspoon salt
- 2 large eggs
- 1¼ cups (250 g) + 2 tablespoons sugar
- ⅔ cup (180 ml) light (single) cream
- ½ cup (125 g) butter
- 4 tart apples, peeled, cored, and thinly sliced

Fresh mint bars

Serves: 10-12; Preparation: 30 minutes; Cooking: 30 minutes; Level of difficulty: 1

Preheat the oven to 400°F/200°C/gas 6. • Butter a 13 x 9-inch (33 x 23-cm) baking pan. • Base: Sift the flour and salt into a medium bowl. • Stir in the sugar. • Use a pastry blender to cut in the butter until the mixture resembles fine crumbs. • Add enough water to form a stiff dough. • Divide the dough in half. • Roll out half on a lightly floured surface to a thickness of ⅛ inch (3 mm) and to the size of the cookie sheet. • Trim the edges and transfer to the prepared pan. • Mint Currant Filling: Sprinkle the currants over the base, leaving a border of ½ inch (5 mm). • Dot with the butter. • Mix the brown sugar and mint in a small bowl and sprinkle over the currants. • Roll out the remaining dough to the same size. • Place the dough on top of the currant filling. • Brush with the beaten egg. • Bake for about 30 minutes, or until just golden. • Cool completely before cutting into bars.

■ INGREDIENTS

BASE
- 2 cups (300 g) all-purpose (plain) flour
- ⅛ teaspoon salt
- ¼ cup (50 g) sugar
- ¾ cup (180 g) butter
- 6 tablespoons ice water

MINT CURRANT FILLING
- 1¼ cups (215 g) dried currants
- 4 tablespoons butter, cut up
- ¼ cup (50 g) firmly packed light brown sugar
- 3 tablespoons finely chopped fresh mint
- 1 large egg, lightly beaten

Right: Buttery apple bars

Farmland bars

Serves: 10-12; Preparation: 40 minutes; Cooking: 1 hour; Level of difficulty: 1

Preheat the oven to 350°F/180°C/gas 4. • Butter an 11 x 7-inch (28 x 18-cm) baking pan. • Cookie Base: Sift the flour, baking powder, and salt into a large bowl. Stir in the coconut. • Melt the butter with the brown sugar in a small saucepan over low heat until the sugar has dissolved completely. • Stir the butter mixture into the dry ingredients until well blended. • Reserve 1 cup (150 g) of the cookie mixture. Firmly press the remaining mixture into the prepared pan to form a smooth, even layer. • Bake for 8–10 minutes, or until lightly browned. • Apple Oat Topping: Cook the apples with the butter and water in a saucepan over medium heat for 15–20 minutes, stirring frequently, until the apples have softened. • Plump the raisins in hot water to cover in a small bowl for 10 minutes. • Drain well and pat dry with paper towels. • Spread the apple mixture over the cookie base. • Mix together the reserved cookie mixture, raisins, oats, cinnamon, and nutmeg. Sprinkle the mixture over the apples. • Bake for about 30 minutes, or until golden brown. • Cool completely before cutting into bars.

INGREDIENTS

COOKIE BASE
- 1⅓ cups (200 g) all-purpose (plain) flour
- 2 teaspoons baking powder
- ¼ teaspoon salt
- 1 cup (120 g) shredded (desiccated) coconut
- ⅔ cup (180 g) butter
- ¾ cup (150 g) firmly packed light brown sugar

APPLE OAT TOPPING
- 4 large tart apples, peeled, cored, and chopped
- 2 tablespoons butter
- 2 tablespoons water
- ¼ cup (45 g) golden raisins (sultanas)
- ⅓ cup (50 g) old-fashioned rolled oats
- ¼ teaspoon ground cinnamon
- ¼ teaspoon freshly grated nutmeg

Apple and sunflower seed bars

Serves: 10-12; Preparation: 15 minutes; Cooking: 30 minutes; Level of difficulty: 1

Preheat the oven to 350°F/180°C/gas 4. • Oil an 11 x 7-inch (28 x 18-cm) baking pan. • Process the cashew nuts, sunflower seeds, and oil in a food processor or blender until smooth. (If you don't have a food processor or blender, grind with a pestle and mortar.) • Stir together the cashew and sunflower seed mixture, apple juice, coconut, vanilla, and salt in a large bowl until well blended. • Press the mixture into the prepared pan, smoothing the top. • Bake for about 30 minutes, or until golden brown. • Cool completely before cutting into bars.

INGREDIENTS

- ¾ cup (120 g) cashew nuts, shelled
- 4 cups (400 g) sunflower seeds
- 1 teaspoon vegetable or sesame oil
- 6 tablespoons apple juice concentrate or maple syrup
- 1 cup (120 g) shredded (desiccated) coconut
- ½ teaspoon vanilla extract
- ¼ teaspoon salt

Right: Farmland bars

■ INGREDIENTS

- 1¼ cups (180 g) all-purpose (plain) flour
- ½ teaspoon baking powder
- ⅛ teaspoon salt
- ½ cup (125 g) butter
- ½ cup (100 g) sugar
- 3 large eggs
- 1 cup (150 g) finely ground almonds
- ¼ cup (90 g) raspberry preserves (jam)
- 1¼ cups (180 g) confectioners' (icing) sugar
- 2 tablespoons boiling water + more as needed

Cocktail fingers

Serves: 8-10; Preparation: 20 minutes; Cooking: 25 minutes; Level of difficulty: 1

Preheat the oven to 350°F/180°C/gas 4. • Butter an 11 x 7-inch (28 x 18-cm) baking pan. • Sift the flour, baking powder, and salt into a medium bowl. • Beat the butter and sugar in a large bowl with an electric mixer at high speed until creamy. • Add the eggs one at a time, beating until just blended after each addition. • Mix in the dry ingredients and almonds. • Firmly press the dough into the prepared pan to form a smooth, even layer. Prick all over with a fork. • Bake for about 25 minutes, or until golden. • Cool completely before cutting into bars. • Stick the bars together in pairs with the preserves. • Beat the confectioners' sugar with enough water in a small bowl to make a spreadable frosting. • Spread the tops of the bars with the frosting.

■ INGREDIENTS

BASE
- ½ cup (125 g) butter
- ⅔ cup (180 g) firmly packed light brown sugar
- ⅔ cup (100 g) all-purpose (plain) flour
- ¼ cup (30 g) rolled oats
- ¼ cup (30 g) wheat germ
- 1 tablespoon finely grated orange zest
- ⅛ teaspoon salt

TOPPING
- 2 large eggs, lightly beaten
- ¼ cup (50 g) firmly packed brown sugar
- ¾ cup (90 g) blanched almonds, halved
- ½ cup (60 g) shredded (desiccated) coconut

Welsh bars

Serves: 10-12; Preparation: 30 minutes; Cooking: 35 minutes; Level of difficulty: 1

Preheat the oven to 350°F/180°C/gas 4. • Butter an 8-inch (20-cm) square baking pan. • Base: Beat the butter and brown sugar in a large bowl with an electric mixer at high speed until creamy. • Mix in the flour, oats, wheat germ, orange juice, and salt until well blended. • Firmly press the mixture into the prepared pan to form a smooth, even layer. • Topping: With mixer at high speed, beat the eggs and brown sugar in a large bowl until pale and thick. • Stir in the almonds and coconut. • Spread the topping evenly over the base. • Bake for about 30 minutes, or until just golden. • Cool completely before cutting into bars.

Left: *Cocktail fingers*

Red apple bars

Serves: 10-12; Preparation: 20 minutes; Cooking: 20 minutes; Level of difficulty: 2

Preheat the oven to 350°F/180°C/gas 4. • Butter an 11 x 7-inch (28 x 18-cm) baking pan. • Sift the flour, baking powder, and salt into a medium bowl. • Process the apples, butter, sugar, corn syrup, and orange-flower water in a food processor until puréed. • Add the egg, processing until just blended. • Mix in the dry ingredients. • Firmly press the mixture into the baking pan to form a smooth, even layer. • Bake for about 20 minutes, or until firm to the touch. • Cool completely in the pan. • Cut into bars.

INGREDIENTS

- 2⅔ cups (400 g) all-purpose (plain) flour
- 1 teaspoon baking powder
- ½ teaspoon salt
- 2 red apples, peeled, cored, and finely chopped
- ¾ cup (200 g) butter
- ⅓ cup (70 g) sugar
- 6 tablespoons corn (golden) syrup
- 1 tablespoon orange-flower water or orange juice
- 1 large egg

Latticed bars

Serves: 10-12; Preparation: 50 minutes + 30 minutes to chill; Cooking: 30 minutes; Level of difficulty: 1

Butter an 11 x 7-inch (28 x 18-cm) baking pan. • Sift the flour and salt into a medium bowl. • Rub in ½ cup (125 g) butter until the mixture resembles fine crumbs. • Add 1 egg yolk and enough water to form a soft dough. • Press the dough into a disk, wrap in plastic wrap, and refrigerate for 30 minutes. • Preheat the oven to 425°F/220°C/gas 7. • Roll out the dough on a lightly floured surface to a 11 x 7-inch (28 x 18-cm) rectangle. • Gather the dough scraps and set aside. • Fit the dough rectangle into the prepared pan. Prick all over with a fork. Finely grate the apples. Place in a fine-mesh sieve and press with the back of a wooden spoon to remove as much juice as possible. • Coarsely grate the marzipan. Sprinkle the grated marzipan over the base. • Use a wooden spoon to beat the remaining butter and sugar in a medium bowl until creamy. Mix in the grated apple. • Beat the 2 egg whites in a medium bowl with an electric mixer at high speed until stiff peaks form. Use a large rubber spatula to fold them into the apple mixture. • Spread the mixture evenly over the base. • Gather the dough scraps and re-roll into ¼-inch (5-mm) wide strips and arrange over the apple mixture. Brush the remaining egg yolk over the strips. • Bake for about 30 minutes, or until lightly browned. • Cool completely before cutting into bars.

INGREDIENTS

- 1½ cups (225 g) all-purpose (plain) flour
- ⅛ teaspoon salt
- ¾ cup (200 g) butter
- 2 large eggs, separated
- 1-2 tablespoons ice water
- 1½ lb (750 g) tart apples, such as Granny Smiths, peeled and cored
- 4 oz (125 g) ready-made marzipan
- 2 tablespoons sugar

Right: Red apple bars

Delicious walnut bars

Serves: 10-12; Preparation: 30 minutes + 30 minutes to chill; Cooking: 40 minutes; Level of difficulty: 1

Base: Sift the flour and salt into a medium bowl. • Use a pastry blender to cut in the butter until the mixture resembles fine crumbs. • Mix in the lemon juice and enough water to form a soft dough. • Shape the dough into a ball, wrap in plastic wrap (cling film), and refrigerate for 30 minutes. • Preheat the oven to 375°F/190°C/gas 5. • Butter an 8-inch baking pan. • Roll out the dough on a lightly floured surface to an 8-inch (20-cm) square. • Fit the dough into the prepared pan. • Topping: Melt the butter in a small saucepan over low heat. • Mix in the honey, brown sugar, and vanilla until well blended. • Add the eggs one at a time, beating until just blended after each addition. • Stir in the walnuts. • Spread the mixture evenly over the base. • Bake for about 40 minutes, or until lightly browned and firm to the touch. • Cool completely before cutting into bars.

■ INGREDIENTS

BASE
- ¾ cup (125 g) all-purpose (plain) flour
- ⅛ teaspoon salt
- 4 tablespoons butter
- 2 teaspoons lemon juice
- 1–2 tablespoons ice water

TOPPING
- 4 tablespoons butter
- 5 tablespoons honey
- ½ cup (100 g) firmly packed light brown sugar
- ½ teaspoon vanilla extract
- 2 large eggs
- 1 cup (100 g) finely chopped walnuts

Maple syrup bars

Serves: 8-10; Preparation: 25 minutes; Cooking: 30 minutes; Level of difficulty: 1

Preheat the oven to 325°F/170°C/gas 3. • Butter an 8-inch (20-cm) baking pan. • Spread the nuts out on a large baking sheet. Toast for 7 minutes, or until lightly golden. • Increase the oven temperature to 375°F/190°C/gas 5. • Let the nuts cool completely, then chop them coarsely. • Sift the flour and salt into a large bowl. • Melt the butter in a large saucepan over low heat. • Remove from the heat and stir in the sugar, maple syrup, and vanilla. • Add the eggs, beating until just blended. • Mix in the dry ingredients and nuts until well blended. • Pour the mixture into the prepared pan. • Bake for about 30 minutes, or until dry on the top and barely firm to the touch. Do not overbake. • Cool completely before cutting into squares.

■ INGREDIENTS

- ⅔ cup (100 g) almonds or macadamia nuts
- 1¼ cups (180 g) all-purpose (plain) flour
- ¼ teaspoon salt
- ¾ cup (200 g) butter
- ¾ cup (150 g) sugar
- ¾ cup (200 g) pure maple syrup
- 1 teaspoon vanilla extract
- 2 large eggs, lightly beaten

Right: Delicious walnut bars

Spiced fruitcake bars

Serves: 12-14; Preparation: 1 hour; Cooking: 30 minutes; Level of difficulty: 1

Cake: Preheat the oven to 350°F/180°C/gas 4. • Butter a 13 x 9-inch (33 x 23-cm) baking pan. Line with waxed paper. Butter the paper. • Beat the eggs, sugar, and vanilla in a large bowl with an electric mixer at high speed until pale and thick. Beat in the oil and milk. • Use a large rubber spatula to fold in the flour, hazelnuts, cocoa, allspice, cinnamon, and baking powder. • Spoon the batter into the prepared pan. • Bake for about 30 minutes, or until a toothpick inserted into the center comes out clean. • Cool the cake in the pan for 10 minutes. Turn out onto a rack. Carefully remove the paper and let cool completely. • Filling: Flavor the vanilla pastry cream with the rum. • Split the cake horizontally. Place a cake on a serving plate. Warm the jelly in a small saucepan. Brush over the cake. • Spread the filling over the jelly. Top with the remaining cake. • Frosting: Warm the preserves in a saucepan until liquid. • Use your hands to knead the confectioners' sugar into the almond paste on a surface dusted with confectioners' sugar. Roll out a rectangle to the size of the cake. • Brush the cake with the warmed preserves. • Cover with the rectangle of almond paste. • Slice the cake in half lengthways and cut into 1½-inch (4-cm) slices. • Mix the confectioners' sugar, water, and red food coloring. Spoon into a pastry bag and pipe over the slices in a decorative manner.

■ INGREDIENTS

CAKE
- 5 large eggs
- 1 cup (200 g) sugar
- 1 teaspoon vanilla extract
- 1 cup (250 ml) vegetable oil
- 4 tablespoons milk
- 2 cups (300 g) all-purpose (plain) flour
- ½ cup (75 g) hazelnuts, finely ground
- 1 tablespoon unsweetened cocoa powder
- 1 teaspoon each ground allspice and cinnamon
- ½ teaspoon baking powder

FILLING
- 1 cup (250 ml) *Pastry Cream* (see page 28)
- 1 tablespoon dark rum
- 3 tablespoons red currant jelly

FROSTING
- 2 tablespoons apricot preserves
- ½ cup (75 g) + 2 tablespoons confectioners' (icing) sugar
- 4 oz (125 g) almond paste
- 2 teaspoons water
- ½ teaspoon red food coloring, to decorate

Left: *Spiced fruitcake bars*

Cookies

⁓

In this chapter, we have included many of our favorite classic recipes, as well as some more complicated cookies, such as Italian-style (twice-baked) biscotti. Here you will find a trove of cookie recipes to bake on rainy afternoons and winter evenings.

Chocolate almond cookies

Makes: about 80 cookies; Preparation: 45 minutes + 1 hour to chill; Cooking: 15 minutes; Level of difficulty: 2

Sift the flour, baking powder, and salt into a large bowl. • Beat the eggs and sugar in a large bowl with an electric mixer at high speed until pale and thick. • Add the cinnamon and cloves. • Fold in the nuts, butter, and grated chocolate, followed by the dry ingredients. • Shape into a ball, wrap in plastic wrap (cling film), and refrigerate for 1 hour. • Preheat the oven to 350°F/180°C/gas 4. • Butter and flour a large baking sheet. • Turn the dough out onto a lightly floured surface. Roll out the dough to a rectangle about 4 inches (10 cm) thick. Transfer to the prepared baking sheet. • Bake for about 15 minutes, or until golden brown. • Use a sharp knife to cut into 2 x ¾-inch (5 x 2-cm) fingers. Transfer to racks to cool. • Glaze: Mix 1 tablespoon of lemon juice, kirsch, if using, and water in a small bowl. Stir in the confectioners' sugar to make a thick paste, adding more lemon juice or water if needed. • Drizzle the glaze over the tops of the cookies.

■ INGREDIENTS

- 3 cups (450 g) all-purpose (plain) flour
- 1 teaspoon baking powder
- ⅛ teaspoon salt
- 5 large eggs
- 2½ cups (500 g) sugar
- 1 tablespoon ground cinnamon
- 1 teaspoon ground cloves
- 5 cups (500 g) blanched almonds or hazelnuts, coarsely chopped
- 2 tablespoons butter, melted
- 8 oz (250 g) semisweet chocolate, grated

GLAZE
- 1–2 tablespoons lemon juice
- 1 tablespoon kirsch or rum (optional)
- 1 tablespoon cold water or more as needed
- 1½ cups (225 g) confectioners' (icing) sugar

Sorrento munchies

Makes: about 30 cookies; Preparation: 20 minutes; Cooking: 35 minutes; Level of difficulty: 2

Preheat the oven to 350°F/180°C/gas 4. • Butter a cookie sheet. • Sift the flour, baking powder, and salt into a medium bowl. • Beat the butter and sugar in a large bowl with an electric mixer at high speed until creamy. • Mix in the egg, dry ingredients, cornmeal, and pecans. • Form the dough into two logs 1 inch (2.5 cm) in diameter and place 3 inches (8 cm) apart on the prepared cookie sheet. • Bake for about 25 minutes, or until firm to the touch. • Transfer to a cutting board to cool for 15 minutes. • Cut on the diagonal into ½-inch (1-cm) slices. • Arrange the slices cut-side up on two cookie sheets and bake, one sheet at a time, for about 10 minutes, or until golden and toasted. • Transfer to racks to cool.

■ INGREDIENTS

- 1¼ cups (180 g) all-purpose (plain) flour
- 1 teaspoon baking powder
- ⅛ teaspoon salt
- 4 tablespoons butter
- ½ cup (100 g) sugar
- 1 large egg
- 2 tablespoons finely ground yellow cornmeal
- ¾ cup (75 g) finely chopped pecans

Right: *Chocolate almond cookies*

Easy honey hearts

Makes: about 36 cookies; Preparation: 40 minutes + 30 minutes to chill; Cooking: 20 minutes; Level of difficulty: 2

Sift the flour, cornstarch, powdered milk, baking soda, cream of tartar, and salt into a medium bowl. • Beat the butter and sugar in a large bowl with an electric mixer at high speed until creamy. • Add the egg, honey, and vanilla, beating until just blended. • Mix in the dry ingredients to form a smooth dough. Shape the dough into a ball, wrap in plastic wrap (cling film), and refrigerate for 30 minutes. • Preheat the oven to 300°F/150°C/gas 2. • Line three cookie sheets with parchment paper. • Roll out the dough on a lightly floured surface to a thickness of ¼ inch (5 mm). • Use a 2-inch (5-cm) heart-shaped cookie cutter to stamp out the cookies. Transfer to the prepared cookie sheets, placing them 2 inches (5 cm) apart. • Bake, one sheet at a time, for about 20 minutes, or until lightly browned. • Transfer to racks to cool.

■ INGREDIENTS

- 1¾ cups (275 g) all-purpose (plain) flour
- 2 tablespoons cornstarch (cornflour)
- 1 teaspoon powdered milk
- ½ teaspoon baking soda
- ½ teaspoon cream of tartar
- ⅛ teaspoon salt
- ½ cup (125 g) butter
- ½ cup (100 g) sugar
- 1 large egg
- 1 tablespoon honey
- ¼ teaspoon vanilla extract

Fresh ginger cookies

Makes: 64 cookies; Preparation: 40 minutes + 30 minutes to chill; Cooking: 15 minutes; Level of difficulty: 2

Melt the butter with the corn syrup, molasses, and brown sugar in a small saucepan over low heat. • Mix in the ginger, remove from the heat, and let cool. • Sift the flour, baking powder, allspice, and salt into a large bowl. Stir in the sugar. • Add the eggs, beating until just blended. • Mix in the corn syrup mixture to form a smooth dough. • Form the dough into four logs, each 8 inches (20 cm) long and 2 inches (5 cm) in diameter. Wrap in plastic wrap (cling film) and refrigerate for 30 minutes. • Preheat the oven to 325°F/170°C/gas 3. • Line two cookie sheets with parchment paper. • Slice the dough ½ inch (1 cm) thick and place each cookie 1 inch (2.5 cm) apart on the prepared cookie sheets. • Bake for about 15 minutes, or until the edges are firm but the center still gives a little to the touch. • Cool on the sheets until the cookies firm slightly. • Transfer to racks to cool completely.

■ INGREDIENTS

- ⅔ cup (180 g) butter
- 6 tablespoons light corn (golden) syrup
- 6 tablespoons dark molasses (treacle)
- ¾ cup (150 g) brown sugar
- 2 teaspoons finely grated fresh ginger root
- 2⅔ cups (400 g) all-purpose (plain) flour
- 1½ teaspoons baking powder
- 1 teaspoon ground allspice
- ⅛ teaspoon salt
- 2 tablespoons sugar
- 2 large eggs, lightly beaten

Right: Easy honey hearts

Bob's bran cookies

Makes: 64 cookies; Preparation: 40 minutes + 30 minutes to chill; Cooking: 10 minutes; Level of difficulty: 1

Sift the flour, baking powder, and salt into a medium bowl. • Beat the butter and sugar in a large bowl with an electric mixer at high speed until creamy. • Add the egg, beating until just blended. • Mix in the dry ingredients and bran to form a stiff dough. • Form the dough into two 8-inch (20-cm) logs, wrap in plastic wrap (cling film), and refrigerate for 30 minutes. • Preheat the oven to 400°F/200°C/gas 6. • Set out four cookie sheets. • Slice the dough ¼ inch (5 mm) thick and place 1 inch (2.5 cm) apart on the cookie sheets. • Bake, one sheet at a time, for about 10 minutes, or until pale gold. • Transfer to racks to cool.

■ INGREDIENTS

- 1½ cups (225 g) all-purpose (plain) flour
- 1 teaspoon baking powder
- ⅛ teaspoon salt
- ¾ cup (200 g) butter
- 1 cup (200 g) demerara sugar
- 1 large egg
- ⅓ cup (50 g) bran

INGREDIENTS

- ¾ cup (135 g) golden raisins (sultanas)
- 1 cup (150 g) all-purpose (plain) flour
- ½ teaspoon baking powder
- ½ teaspoon salt
- ½ teaspoon ground cinnamon
- ¼ teaspoon freshly grated nutmeg
- 4 tablespoons butter
- ½ cup (100 g) dark brown sugar
- 1 large egg
- ¼ cup (25 g) finely chopped walnuts

Afternoon tea bites

Makes: about 20 cookies; Preparation: 25 minutes; Cooking: 20 minutes; Level of difficulty: 1

Preheat the oven to 350°F/180°C/gas 4. • Butter two cookie sheets. • Plump the raisins in hot water to cover in a small bowl for 10 minutes. • Drain well and pat dry with paper towels. • Sift the flour, baking powder, salt, cinnamon, and nutmeg into a medium bowl. • Beat the butter and brown sugar in a large bowl with an electric mixer at high speed until creamy. • Add the egg, beating until just blended. • Stir in the dry ingredients, walnuts, and raisins. • Drop heaping teaspoons of the dough 1½ inches (4 cm) apart onto the prepared cookie sheets. • Bake for about 20 minutes, or until lightly browned and firm to the touch, rotating the sheets halfway through for even baking. • Transfer to racks to cool.

INGREDIENTS

COOKIES
- 2¼ cups (330 g) all-purpose (plain) flour
- 2 tablespoons rice flour
- ⅛ teaspoon salt
- 1 cup (250 g) butter
- ⅓ cup (70 g) sugar

PASSIONFRUIT DRIZZLE
- 1 cup (150 g) confectioners' (icing) sugar
- 2 tablespoons passionfruit pulp
- 1 tablespoon butter
- 1 tablespoon cold water
- 2 oz (60 g) white chocolate, coarsely chopped

Susan's summertime cookies

Makes: about 35 cookies; Preparation: 40 minutes + 1 hour 30 minutes to chill and set; Cooking: 15 minutes; Level of difficulty: 2

Cookies: Sift both flours and salt into a medium bowl. • Beat the butter and sugar in a large bowl with an electric mixer at high speed until creamy. • Mix in the dry ingredients to form a soft dough. • Turn the dough out onto a lightly floured surface and knead until smooth. • Shape the dough into a ball, wrap in plastic wrap (cling film), and refrigerate for 30 minutes. • Preheat the oven to 300°F/150°C/gas 2. • Line four cookie sheets with parchment paper. • Roll out the dough on a lightly floured surface to a thickness of ¼ inch (5 mm). • Cut into 1½-inch (4-cm) diamonds. • Transfer the cookies to the prepared cookie sheets, placing them 1 inch (2.5 cm) apart. • Bake for about 15 minutes, or until just golden at the edges. • Transfer to racks to cool. • Passionfruit Drizzle: Mix the confectioners' sugar, passionfruit pulp, butter, and water in a double boiler over barely simmering water until smooth. • Drizzle the tops of the cookies with the icing. • Let stand for 30 minutes until set. • Melt the white chocolate in a double boiler over barely simmering water and drizzle over the cookies. Let stand for 30 minutes before serving.

Left: *Afternoon tea bites*

Jamaican coconut crisps

Makes: about 15 cookies; Preparation: 15 minutes + 30 minutes to stand; Cooking: 15 minutes; Level of difficulty: 1

Preheat the oven to 350°F/180°C/gas 4. • Set out a cookie sheet. • Sift the flour, baking powder, and salt into a large bowl. Stir in the oats and coconut. • Melt the butter with the sugar and molasses in a medium saucepan over medium heat. Bring to a boil, stirring constantly. • Remove from the heat and add the baking soda mixture. • Pour the butter mixture into the dry ingredients and mix until well blended. • Let stand for 30 minutes, or until firm. • Form the dough into balls the size of walnuts and place 1½ inches (4 cm) apart on the cookie sheet. • Bake for about 15 minutes, or until firm to the touch. • Cool the cookies on the cookie sheet for 15 minutes. • Transfer to racks to cool.

■ INGREDIENTS

- ¾ cup (125 g) all-purpose (plain) flour
- 1 teaspoon baking powder
- ½ teaspoon salt
- ¾ cup (125 g) rolled oats
- ¼ cup (30 g) shredded (desiccated) coconut
- ½ cup (125 g) butter
- ¾ cup (150 g) sugar
- 2 tablespoons light molasses (treacle)
- 1 teaspoon baking soda dissolved in 1 tablespoon milk

Coconut cut-outs

Makes: about 25 cookies; Preparation: 40 minutes + 30 minutes to chill; Cooking: 25 minutes; Level of difficulty: 1

Preheat the oven to 300°F/150°C/gas 2. • Butter two cookie sheets. • Sift the flour and salt into a large bowl. • Use a pastry blender to cut in the shortening until the mixture resembles fine crumbs. • Stir in the coconut, oats, and sugar. • Mix the water, molasses, and baking soda in a small bowl. • Stir the baking soda liquid into the oat mixture to form a stiff dough. • Shape the dough into a ball, wrap in plastic wrap (cling film), and refrigerate for 30 minutes. • Roll out the dough on a lightly floured surface to a thickness of ¼ inch (5 mm). • Use a 3-inch (8-cm) cookie cutter to cut out the cookies. Gather the dough scraps, re-roll, and continue cutting out cookies until all the dough is used. • Transfer the cookies to the prepared cookie sheet, placing them 1 inch (2.5 cm) apart. • Bake for about 25 minutes, or until just golden at the edges. • Transfer to racks and let cool completely.

■ INGREDIENTS

- ¾ cup (125 g) all-purpose (plain) flour
- ⅛ teaspoon salt
- ½ cup (125 g) vegetable shortening
- 1 cup (120 g) shredded coconut
- 1 cup (150 g) rolled oats
- ½ cup (100 g) sugar
- 2 tablespoons cold water
- 1 tablespoon light molasses
- 1 teaspoon baking soda

Right: Jamaican coconut crisps

Mardi Gras cookies

Makes: about 16 cookies; Preparation: 40 minutes + 30 minutes to chill; Cooking: 12 minutes; Level of difficulty: 1

Preheat the oven to 350°F/180°C/gas 4. • Set out a cookie sheet. • Sift the flour, baking soda, cinnamon, and aniseeds into a medium bowl. • Beat the butter and ¼ cup (50 g) sugar in a large bowl with an electric mixer at high speed until creamy. • Add the egg yolk, beating until just blended. • Beat in the lemon and orange zests, cream, and coconut. • Mix in the dry ingredients to form a smooth dough. • Shape the dough into a ball, wrap in plastic wrap (cling film), and refrigerate for 30 minutes. • Roll out the dough on a lightly floured work surface to a thickness of ¼ inch (5 mm). • Use a 2½-inch (6-cm) cookie cutter to cut out the cookies. • Gather the dough scraps, re-roll, and continue cutting out cookies until all the dough is used. • Use a spatula to transfer the cookies to the cookie sheet, placing them 1 inch (2.5 cm) apart. • Brush the cookies with the beaten egg and sprinkle with the remaining sugar. • Bake for about 12 minutes, or until just golden at the edges. • Transfer to racks to cool.

■ INGREDIENTS

- 1 cup (150 g) all-purpose (plain) flour
- ¼ teaspoon baking soda
- ¼ teaspoon ground cinnamon
- ⅛ teaspoon ground aniseeds
- 6 tablespoons butter
- ¼ cup (50 g) + 2 tablespoons sugar
- 1 large egg + 1 large egg yolk, lightly beaten
- 1 teaspoon finely grated lemon zest
- 1 teaspoon finely grated orange zest
- 2 tablespoons heavy (double) cream
- 1 tablespoon shredded (desiccated) coconut

Licorice cookies

Makes: about 25 cookies; Preparation: 40 minutes + 30 minutes to chill; Cooking: 15 minutes; Level of difficulty: 1

Stir together the flour, sugar, and salt in a large bowl. • Gradually mix in the oil and wine until well blended. • Add the anisette and aniseeds and knead until a smooth dough has formed. • Shape the dough into a ball, wrap in plastic wrap (cling film), and refrigerate for 30 minutes. • Preheat the oven to 350°F/180°C/gas 4. • Butter and flour two cookie sheets. • Roll out the dough on a lightly floured surface to a thickness of ¼ inch (3 mm). • Use a 2-inch (5-cm) cookie cutter to cut out the cookies. • Gather the dough scraps, re-roll, and continue cutting out cookies until all the dough is used. • Transfer the cookies to the prepared cookie sheets. Prick all over with a fork. • Brush the cookies with the beaten egg and sprinkle with the brown sugar. • Bake for about 15 minutes, or until just golden. • Transfer to racks and let cool completely.

■ INGREDIENTS

- 2 cups (300 g) all-purpose (plain) flour
- 1 cup (200 g) sugar
- ⅛ teaspoon salt
- 4 tablespoons extra-virgin olive oil
- 4 tablespoons Muscatel wine
- 2 tablespoons anisette
- 1 tablespoon aniseeds
- 1 large egg, lightly beaten
- 1 tablespoon brown sugar

Right: *Mardi Gras cookies*

Blarney moments

Makes: about 25 cookies; Preparation: 40 minutes + 30 minutes to chill; Cooking: 15 minutes; Level of difficulty: 1

Plump the raisins in hot water to cover in a small bowl for 10 minutes. • Drain well and pat dry with paper towels. • Sift the flour, baking powder, and salt into a large bowl. • Stir in the raisins, oats, walnuts, and sugar. • Mix in the butter, milk, and egg. • Shape the dough into a ball, wrap in plastic wrap (cling film), and refrigerate for 30 minutes. • Preheat the oven to 425°F/220°C/gas 7. • Line two cookie sheets with parchment paper. • Roll out the dough on a lightly floured work surface to a thickness of ½ inch (1 cm). • Use a sharp knife to cut the dough into 2-inch (5-cm) diamonds. • Transfer the cookies to the prepared cookie sheets, placing them 1 inch (2.5 cm) apart. • Bake for about 15 minutes, or until just golden at the edges, rotating the sheets halfway through for even baking. • Transfer to racks to cool.

■ INGREDIENTS

- ⅓ cup (60 g) golden raisins (sultanas)
- 1¼ cups (180 g) all-purpose (plain) flour
- ½ teaspoon baking powder
- ⅛ teaspoon salt
- ½ cup (75 g) rolled oats
- ½ cup (50 g) coarsely chopped walnuts
- 2 tablespoons sugar
- 6 tablespoons butter, melted
- 4 tablespoons milk
- 1 large egg, lightly beaten

Peanut wonders

Makes: about 45 cookies; Preparation: 20 minutes; Cooking: 15 minutes; Level of difficulty: 1

Preheat the oven to 350°F/180°C/gas 4. • Butter three cookie sheets. • Sift the flour, baking soda, and salt into a large bowl. • Beat the butter and both sugars in a large bowl with an electric mixer at high speed until creamy. • Add the vanilla and egg, beating until just blended. • Mix in the dry ingredients, oats, raisins, and peanuts. • Drop heaping teaspoons of the dough 2 inches (5 cm) apart onto the prepared cookie sheets. • Bake, one sheet at a time, for about 15 minutes, or until lightly browned. • Transfer to racks and let cool completely.

■ INGREDIENTS

- 1¼ cups (180 g) all-purpose (plain) flour
- ½ teaspoon baking soda
- ½ teaspoon salt
- ½ cup (125 g) butter
- ½ cup (100 g) sugar
- ½ cup (100 g) firmly packed brown sugar
- ½ teaspoon vanilla extract
- 1 large egg, lightly beaten
- ⅓ cup (50 g) rolled oats
- ½ cup (90 g) raisins
- ⅔ cup (70 g) coarsely chopped peanuts

Right: Blarney moments

Sophie's favorites

Makes: about 28 cookies; Preparation: 40 minutes + 30 minutes to chill; Cooking: 15 minutes; Level of difficulty: 1

Sift the flour, semolina, cocoa, and salt into a medium bowl. • Beat the butter and sugar in a large bowl until creamy. • Add the egg, beating until just blended. • Mix in the dry ingredients. • Shape the dough into a ball, wrap in plastic wrap (cling film), and refrigerate for 30 minutes. • Preheat the oven to 375°F/190°C/gas 5. • Set out two cookie sheets. • Roll out the dough on a lightly floured surface to a thickness of ¼ inch (5 mm). • Use a 2-inch (5-cm) cookie cutter to cut out the cookies. Gather the dough scraps, re-roll, and continue cutting out cookies until all the dough is used. Transfer the cookies to the cookie sheets. • Bake for about 15 minutes, or until lightly browned. • Transfer to racks to cool completely.

■ INGREDIENTS

- ⅔ cup (100 g) all-purpose (plain) flour
- ½ cup (75 g) semolina flour
- 2 tablespoons unsweetened cocoa powder
- ⅛ teaspoon salt
- 6 tablespoons butter
- ½ cup (100 g) sugar
- 1 large egg, lightly beaten

Chilean cookies

Makes: about 25 cookies; Preparation: 20 minutes; Cooking: 15 minutes; Level of difficulty: 1

Preheat the oven to 350°F/180°C/gas 4. • Butter two cookie sheets. • Sift the flour, red pepper, baking powder, and salt into a medium bowl. • Beat the butter and both sugars in a large bowl with an electric mixer at high speed until creamy. • Add the egg and vanilla, beating until just blended. • Mix in the dry ingredients and chopped chocolate. • Drop teaspoons of the dough 1 inch (2.5 cm) apart onto the prepared cookie sheets. • Bake for about 15 minutes, or until firm to the touch, rotating the sheets halfway through for even baking. • Transfer to racks to cool.

■ INGREDIENTS

- ¾ cup (125 g) all-purpose (plain) flour
- 1 teaspoon ground red pepper
- ½ teaspoon baking powder
- ⅛ teaspoon salt
- ½ cup (125 g) butter
- 2 tablespoons sugar
- ¼ cup (50 g) brown sugar
- 1 large egg
- ½ teaspoon vanilla extract
- 3 oz (90 g) semisweet chocolate, finely chopped

Right: *Sophie's favorites*

Cocoa and cereal treats

INGREDIENTS

- 2 cups (300 g) all-purpose (plain) flour
- 1 tablespoon cocoa powder
- 1 teaspoon baking powder
- ⅛ teaspoon salt
- ½ cup (75 g) corn flakes
- 2 tablespoons rolled oats
- 2 tablespoons shredded (desiccated) coconut
- ½ cup (125 g) butter
- ⅔ cup (140 g) sugar
- 1 tablespoon corn (golden) syrup
- 1 teaspoon baking soda dissolved in 1 tablespoon milk

Makes: about 35 cookies; Preparation: 15 minutes; Cooking: 15 minutes; Level of difficulty: 1

Preheat the oven to 350°F/180°C/gas 4. • Butter two cookie sheets. • Sift the flour, cocoa, baking powder, and salt into a large bowl. • Stir in the corn flakes, oats, and coconut. • Melt the butter, sugar, and corn syrup in a small saucepan over low heat. • Add the baking soda mixture. • Stir the butter mixture into the dry ingredients. • Drop teaspoons of the dough 1½ inches (4 cm) apart onto the prepared cookie sheets, pressing down firmly with a fork. • Bake for about 15 minutes, or until crisp. • Transfer to racks to cool.

Matterhorn cookies

Makes: about 30 cookies; Preparation: 40 minutes + 30 minutes to chill; Cooking: 10 minutes; Level of difficulty: 1

Sift the flour, cinnamon, and salt into a medium bowl. • Beat the lard and butter in a large bowl with an electric mixer at high speed until well blended. • Add the sugar, egg yolk, and orange zest. • Mix in the dry ingredients to form a smooth dough. • Shape the dough into a ball, wrap in plastic wrap (cling film), and refrigerate for 30 minutes. • Preheat the oven to 350°F/180°C/gas 4. • Butter two cookie sheets. • Roll out the dough on a lightly floured work surface to a thickness of ¼ inch (5 mm). • Use a 3-inch (8-cm) fluted cookie cutter to cut out the cookies. Gather the dough scraps, re-roll, and continue cutting out cookies until all the dough is used. • Transfer the cookies to the prepared cookie sheets, placing them 1 inch (2.5 cm) apart. • Bake for about 10 minutes, or until just golden. • Transfer to racks to cool.

INGREDIENTS

- 2 cups (300 g) all-purpose (plain) flour
- ½ teaspoon ground cinnamon
- ⅛ teaspoon salt
- ⅔ cup (180 g) lard or vegetable shortening
- 6 tablespoons butter
- ½ cup (100 g) sugar
- 1 large egg yolk
- 1 teaspoon finely grated orange zest

Children's party cookies

Makes: 24 cookies; Preparation: 40 minutes + 30 minutes to chill; Cooking: 8 minutes; Level of difficulty: 2

Sift the flour, baking powder, and salt into a medium bowl. • Beat the butter, shortening, and sugar in a large bowl with an electric mixer at high speed until creamy. • Add the egg, milk, and vanilla. • Mix in the dry ingredients to form a smooth dough. • Divide the dough in half. Shape into two balls, wrap in plastic wrap (cling film), and refrigerate for 30 minutes. • Preheat the oven to 350°F/180°C/gas 4. • Set out four cookie sheets. • Roll out the dough on a lightly floured surface into a 12 x 9-inch (30 x 23-cm) rectangle. • Cut into twelve 3-inch (8-cm) squares. • Repeat with the remaining dough. • Transfer the cookies to the sheets. Do not place more than six cookies on each sheet as there must be space for the craft sticks. • Sprinkle with the crushed candies, pressing them lightly into the dough. • Cut 1-inch (2.5-cm) slits in each corner toward the center of the square. Fold every other corner into the center to make a windmill shape. • Press craft sticks into the base of the squares, pressing the dough around them so that they are firmly held. • Bake for about 8 minutes, or until just golden at the edges. • Transfer to racks to cool completely.

INGREDIENTS

- 2 cups (300 g) all-purpose (plain) flour
- 1½ teaspoons baking powder
- ¼ teaspoon salt
- 6 tablespoons butter
- 6 tablespoons vegetable shortening
- ¾ cup (150 g) sugar
- 1 large egg, lightly beaten
- 1 tablespoon milk
- ½ teaspoon vanilla extract
- ½ cup (50 g) crushed peppermint candies

Left: Matterhorn cookies

Orange-glazed valentines

Makes: about 35 cookies; Preparation: 45 minutes + 1 hour to chill and set; Cooking: 12 minutes; Level of difficulty: 2

Sift the flour, cinnamon, cloves, and salt into a medium bowl. • Beat the eggs and sugar in a large bowl with an electric mixer at high speed until very pale and thick. • Mix in the dry ingredients, nuts, lemon zest, and orange flower water to form a smooth dough. • Shape the dough into a ball, wrap in plastic wrap (cling film), and refrigerate for 30 minutes. • Preheat the oven to 325°F/170°C/gas 3. • Line two cookie sheets with parchment paper. • Roll out the dough to a thickness of ¼ inch (5 mm). • Use 1½-inch (4-cm) star- and crescent-shaped cookie cutters to cut out the cookies. Continue until all the dough is used. • Transfer the cookies to the prepared cookie sheets, placing them 1 inch (2.5 cm) apart. • Bake for about 12 minutes, or until just golden at the edges. • Transfer to racks to cool. • Orange Glaze: Mix the confectioners' sugar, orange juice, and water in a small bowl until smooth. • Drizzle the glaze over the cookies and let stand for 30 minutes until set.

■ INGREDIENTS

- 1⅔ cups (250 g) all-purpose (plain) flour
- 1 teaspoon ground cinnamon
- ½ teaspoon ground cloves
- ⅛ teaspoon salt
- 2 large eggs
- 1¼ cups (250 g) sugar
- 2½ cups (250 g) finely ground almonds or hazelnuts
- grated zest of 1 lemon
- 1 tablespoon orange flower water

ORANGE GLAZE
- 1⅓ cups (200 g) confectioners' (icing) sugar
- 2 tablespoons orange juice
- 1 tablespoon warm water

Hannukah holiday cookies

Makes: 32 cookies; Preparation: 30 minutes + 30 minutes to chill; Cooking: 15 minutes; Level of difficulty: 2

Beat the butter and cream cheese in a large bowl with an electric mixer at high speed until creamy. • Mix in the flour to form a smooth dough. Divide the dough in half and shape each half into a ball. Wrap in plastic wrap (cling film) and refrigerate for 30 minutes. • Preheat the oven to 375°F/190°C/gas 5. • Set out two cookie sheets. • Mix the raisins, sugar, and cinnamon in a small bowl. • Roll out one piece of the dough on a lightly floured work surface to a circle with a thickness of ¼ inch (5 mm). • Cut the circle into sixteen wedges. • Sprinkle half the raisin mixture over the entire surface, leaving a ¼-inch (5-mm) border. • Roll up each wedge from the wide end to the point, tucking the point under. • Transfer the cookies to the cookie sheets. • Bake for about 15 minutes, or until the bottoms are lightly browned. • Transfer to racks and let cool completely. • Dust with the confectioners' sugar.

■ INGREDIENTS

- 2 cups (500 g) butter
- 1 lb (500 g) cream cheese
- 2 cups (300 g) all-purpose (plain) flour
- ½ cup (90 g) golden raisins (sultanas)
- 2 tablespoons sugar
- 1 tablespoon ground cinnamon
- 4 tablespoons confectioners' (icing) sugar, to dust

Right: Orange-glazed valentines

Winter warming cookies

Makes: about 60 cookies; Preparation: 20 minutes; Cooking: 10 minutes; Level of difficulty: 1

Preheat the oven to 350°F/180°C/gas 4. • Butter four cookie sheets. • Sift the flour, baking soda, and salt into a medium bowl. • Beat the butter and brown sugar in a large bowl with an electric mixer at high speed until creamy. • Add the maple syrup and egg, beating until just blended. • Mix in the dry ingredients. • Shape the dough into balls the size of walnuts and place 2 inches (5 cm) apart on the prepared cookie sheets, flattening them slightly. • Bake, one sheet at a time, for about 10 minutes, or until lightly browned. • Transfer to racks and let cool completely. • Dust with the confectioners' sugar.

■ INGREDIENTS

- 4 cups (600 g) all-purpose (plain) flour
- 2 teaspoons baking soda
- ½ teaspoon salt
- 1 cup (250 g) butter
- 1 cup (200 g) light brown sugar
- 1 cup (250 ml) maple syrup
- 1 large egg, lightly beaten
- ⅓ cup (50 g) confectioners' (icing) sugar, to dust

Piped ginger cookies

Makes: about 60 cookies; Preparation: 30 minutes; Cooking: 10 minutes; Level of difficulty: 2

Preheat the oven to 375°F/190°C/gas 5. • Butter four cookie sheets. • Sift the flour, ginger, cloves, and salt into a medium bowl. • Beat the butter and sugar in a large bowl with an electric mixer at high speed until creamy. • Add the egg and lemon zest and juice, beating until just blended. • Mix in the dry ingredients to form a stiff dough. • Insert the chosen design plate into a cookie press by sliding it into the head and locking in place. Press out the cookies, spacing about 1 inch (2.5 cm) apart on the prepared cookie sheets. • Decorate each cookie with crystallized ginger and sprinkle with sugar crystals. • Bake, one sheet at a time, for about 10 minutes, or until firm to the touch and golden at the edges. • Transfer to racks to cool.

■ INGREDIENTS

- 3⅓ cups (500 g) all-purpose (plain) flour
- 1 teaspoon ground ginger
- ¼ teaspoon ground cloves
- ⅛ teaspoon salt
- 1½ cups (375 g) butter
- 1¼ cups (250 g) sugar
- 1 large egg
- 1 teaspoon finely grated lemon zest
- 1 tablespoon lemon juice
- 1 tablespoon chopped crystallized ginger
- 1 tablespoon colored sugar crystals

Right: *Winter warming cookies*

Spiced walnut cookies

INGREDIENTS

- 2 cups (300 g) all-purpose (plain) flour
- 1 teaspoon ground cinnamon
- 1 teaspoon ground ginger
- ⅛ teaspoon salt
- 1 cup (250 g) butter
- 1 cup (200 g) sugar
- 1 teaspoon almond extract
- 1 large egg, separated
- 1 tablespoon cold water
- 1 cup (100 g) finely chopped walnuts

Makes: about 18 cookies; Preparation: 20 minutes; Cooking: 15 minutes; Level of difficulty: 1

Preheat the oven to 350°F/180°C/gas 4. • Butter a 10½ x 15½-inch (26 x 36-cm) jelly-roll pan. • Sift the flour, cinnamon, ginger, and salt into a medium bowl. • Beat the butter and sugar in a large bowl with an electric mixer at high speed until creamy. • Add the almond extract and egg yolk, beating until just blended. • Mix in the dry ingredients to form a smooth dough. • Firmly press the dough into the prepared pan to form a smooth, even layer. • Beat the egg white and water in a small bowl and brush it over the dough. Sprinkle with walnuts. • Score the dough into 1-inch (2.5-cm) diamonds. • Bake for about 15 minutes, or until lightly browned. • Cool completely in the pan. • Cut along the lines and divide into diamonds.

Jenny's zesty cookies

Makes: about 12 cookies; Preparation: 20 minutes; Cooking: 15 minutes; Level of difficulty: 1

Preheat the oven to 350°F/180°C/gas 4. • Butter a cookie sheet. • Sift the flour and salt into a medium bowl. • Beat the butter and sugar in a large bowl with an electric mixer at high speed until creamy. • Add the vanilla and egg and egg yolks, beating until just blended. • Mix in the lemon zest and dry ingredients. • Drop teaspoons of the dough about 2 inches (5 cm) apart onto the prepared cookie sheet. • Bake for about 15 minutes, or until just golden. • Transfer to racks to cool. • In a small saucepan or in a microwave, heat the marmalade until liquid. Brush the marmalade over the cookies and dust with the confectioners' sugar.

■ INGREDIENTS

- 1 cup (150 g) all-purpose (plain) flour
- ⅛ teaspoon salt
- ½ cup (125 g) butter
- ½ cup (100 g) sugar
- ½ teaspoon vanilla extract
- 1 large egg + 2 large egg yolks
- 1 teaspoon finely grated lemon zest
- 2 tablespoons orange marmalade
- ⅓ cup (50 g) confectioners' (icing) sugar, to dust

Parisian cookies

Makes: about 12 cookies; Preparation: 20 minutes; Cooking: 6 minutes; Level of difficulty: 3

Preheat the oven to 425°F/220°C/gas 7. • Line two cookie sheets with parchment paper. Set out two rolling pins. • Sift the flour and cocoa into a small bowl. • Beat the egg whites and salt in a large bowl with an electric mixer at medium speed until frothy. With mixer at high speed, gradually add the sugar, beating until stiff, glossy peaks form. • Use a large rubber spatula to fold in the dry ingredients. • Fold in the cream and butter until well blended. • Drop tablespoons of the dough onto the cookie sheet, placing them 3 inches (8 cm) apart. Do not drop more than six cookies onto each sheet. Sprinkle with the almonds. • Bake, one sheet at a time, for about 6 minutes, or until the cookies are faintly tinged with gold and slightly darker at the edges. • Working quickly, use a spatula to lift each cookie from the sheet and drape it over a rolling pin. Slide each cookie off the pin and onto racks to finish cooling.

■ INGREDIENTS

- 1 tablespoon all-purpose (plain) flour
- 1 tablespoon unsweetened cocoa powder
- 2 large egg whites
- ⅛ teaspoon salt
- ¼ cup (50 g) sugar
- 1 tablespoon heavy (double) cream
- 1 tablespoon butter, melted
- 2 tablespoons flaked almonds

Right: Jenny's zesty cookies

Sarah's honey sandwiches

Makes: about 12 cookies; Preparation: 45 minutes + 30 minutes to chill; Cooking: 10 minutes; Level of difficulty: 1

Preheat the oven to 325°F/170°C/gas 3. • Spread the hazelnuts on a large baking sheet. Toast for 7 minutes, or until lightly golden. • Transfer to a large cotton kitchen towel. Fold the towel over the nuts and rub them through the towel to remove the thin inner skins. Pick out the nuts and transfer to a food processor with 1 tablespoon sugar. Process until very finely ground. • Increase the oven temperature to 375°F/190°C/gas 5. • Line two cookie sheets with parchment paper. • Sift the flour and salt into a medium bowl. • Use a wooden spoon to beat the ½ cup (125 g) butter and 3 tablespoons sugar in a large bowl until creamy. • Mix in the dry ingredients and hazelnut mixture to form a smooth dough. • Shape the dough into a ball, wrap in plastic wrap (cling film), and refrigerate for 30 minutes. • Roll out the dough on a lightly floured work surface to a thickness of ¼ inch (5 mm). • Use a 2-inch (5-cm) cookie cutter to cut out the cookies. Gather the dough scraps, re-roll, and continue cutting out cookies until all the dough is used. • Use a spatula to transfer the cookies to the prepared cookie sheets, placing them 1 inch (2.5 cm) apart. • Bake for about 10 minutes, or until golden brown. • Transfer to racks to cool. • Melt the remaining butter with the honey and remaining 2 tablespoons sugar in a small saucepan. Bring to a boil, stirring constantly. • Stick the cookies together in pairs with the honey mixture.

INGREDIENTS

- ½ cup (75 g) hazelnuts
- 6 tablespoons sugar
- 1 cup (150 g) all-purpose (plain) flour
- ⅛ teaspoon salt
- ½ cup (125 g) + 1 tablespoon butter
- 4 tablespoons honey

Simple peanut butter cookies

Makes: about 12 cookies; Preparation: 20 minutes; Cooking: 10 minutes; Level of difficulty: 1

Preheat the oven to 350°F/180°C/gas 4. • Butter a cookie sheet. • Mix the egg, peanut butter, and sugar in a large bowl until well blended. • Form the dough into balls the size of walnuts and place 2 inches (5 cm) apart on the prepared cookie sheet, flattening them slightly. • Bake for about 10 minutes, or until just golden. • Transfer to racks to cool.

INGREDIENTS

- 1 large egg, lightly beaten
- 1 cup (250 ml) smooth peanut butter
- 1 cup (200 g) sugar

Right: *Sarah's honey sandwiches*

■ INGREDIENTS

- 1⅔ cups (250 g) all-purpose (plain) flour
- ¼ teaspoon salt
- ⅓ cup (60 g) pine nuts
- ¼ cup (50 g) sugar
- ¾ cup (200 g) butter
- ⅔ cup (100 g) confectioners' (icing) sugar
- 3 large egg yolks
- ½ teaspoon vanilla extract
- 12 candied cherries, cut in half

Delicate cherry-topped cookies

Makes: about 24 cookies; Preparation: 40 minutes + 30 minutes to chill; Cooking: 15 minutes; Level of difficulty: 1

Sift the flour and salt into a large bowl. • Process the pine nuts and sugar until very finely ground. • Beat the butter and confectioners' sugar in a large bowl until creamy. • Add the egg yolks and vanilla. • Mix in the pine nut mixture and dry ingredients to form a stiff dough. • Shape the dough into a ball, wrap in plastic wrap (cling film), and refrigerate for 30 minutes. • Preheat the oven to 350°F/180°C/gas 4. • Butter two cookie sheets. • Roll out the dough to a thickness of ¼ inch (5 mm). • Cut into 1-inch (2.5-cm) squares. • Transfer the cookies to the prepared cookie sheets, placing them 1 inch apart. Press a half cherry into each cookie top. • Bake for about 15 minutes, or until just golden. • Transfer to racks to cool.

INGREDIENTS

- 5 cups (500 g) finely chopped toasted hazelnuts
- ½ cup (100 g) sugar
- 3 large eggs
- ½ teaspoon ground cinnamon
- ½ teaspoon ground cloves
- Grated zest of ½ lemon
- ⅛ teaspoon salt

Hazelnut crunchies

Makes: about 40 cookies; Preparation: 15 minutes; Cooking: 20 minutes; Level of difficulty: 1

Preheat the oven to 350°F/180°C/gas 4. • Line three cookie sheets with parchment paper. • Use a wooden spoon to mix the hazelnuts, sugar, eggs, cinnamon, cloves, lemon zest, and salt until a stiff dough has formed. • Form the dough into balls the size of walnuts and place 1 inch (2.5 cm) apart on the prepared cookie sheets, flattening them slightly. • Bake, one sheet at a time, for about 20 minutes, or until just golden at the edges. • Cool the cookies completely on the cookie sheets.

INGREDIENTS

- 1⅔ cups (250 g) all-purpose (plain) flour
- ¼ teaspoon salt
- ¾ cup (200 g) butter
- ¾ cup (150 g) sugar
- ⅓ cup (50 g) semolina flour
- 2 tablespoons currants
- ½ teaspoon almond extract
- 1 teaspoon cinnamon
- finely grated zest of ½ lemon
- 1 large egg yolk mixed with 2–3 tablespoons water
- ⅓ cup (50 g) confectioners' (icing) sugar
- 1 tablespoon water
- ¼ teaspoon green food coloring
- candied cherries, halved
- ½ quantity *Chocolate Buttercream* (see page 36)
- silver balls, to decorate
- ½ cup (160 g) raspberry preserves (jam)

Christmas cookies

Makes: about 40 cookies; Preparation: 1 hour; Cooking: 15 minutes; Level of difficulty: 2

Preheat the oven to 425°F/220°C/gas 7. • Butter four cookie sheets. • Sift the flour and salt into a large bowl. • Rub in the butter until the mixture resembles fine crumbs. • Stir in the sugar and semolina flour. • Divide the mixture into four bowls. • Mix the currants into one bowl of the mixture, the almond extract into the second bowl, the cinnamon into the third, and the lemon zest into the remaining bowl. • Add enough of the egg yolk mixture to the bowls to form each into a stiff dough. • Christmas Wreaths: Roll out the currant mixture on a lightly floured surface to a thickness of ¼ inch (5 mm). • Cut out ring-shaped cookies. • Star Cookies: Roll out the almond extract mixture to the same thickness. • Use a star-shaped cookie cutter to cut out the cookies. • Bell Cookies: Roll out the cinnamon mixture to the same thickness. • Use a bell-shaped cookie cutter to cut out cookies. • Christmas Tree Cookies: Roll out the lemon zest mixture to the same thickness. • Use a tree cookie cutter to cut out the cookies. • Transfer the cookies to the prepared sheets. • Bake for about 15 minutes, or until lightly browned. • Transfer to racks to cool. • Mix the confectioners' sugar with the water. Stir in the green food coloring. Spread the tops of the star cookies with the frosting and decorate with a half-cherry. • Stick the bell cookies together in pairs with the chocolate frosting and decorate with silver balls. • Warm the preserves in a small saucepan over low heat. • Stick the tree cookies together in pairs with the preserves.

Left: *Hazelnut crunchies*

Sicilian pine nut chewies

Makes: about 30 cookies; Preparation: 40 minutes + 30 minutes to chill; Cooking: 20 minutes; Level of difficulty: 1

Plump the raisins in hot water to cover in a small bowl for 10 minutes. • Drain well and pat dry with paper towels. • Sift the flour, baking powder, and salt into a large bowl and make a well in the center. • Mix in the sugar, olive oil, and water to form a smooth dough. • Knead in the raisins and pine nuts. • Shape the dough into a ball, wrap in plastic wrap (cling film), and refrigerate for 30 minutes. • Preheat the oven to 350°F/ 180°C/gas 4. • Butter two cookie sheets. • Roll out the dough on a lightly floured work surface to a thickness of ¼ inch (5 mm). • Use a 2-inch (5-cm) cookie cutter to cut out the cookies. Gather the dough scraps, re-roll, and continue cutting out cookies until all the dough is used. • Transfer the cookies to the prepared cookie sheets, placing them 1 inch (2.5 cm) apart. • Bake for about 20 minutes, or until just golden. • Transfer to racks to cool completely.

■ INGREDIENTS

- ⅓ cup (60 g) golden raisins (sultanas)
- 2⅔ cups (400 g) all-purpose (plain) flour
- 2 teaspoons baking powder
- ⅛ teaspoon salt
- ½ cup (100 g) sugar
- 6 tablespoons extra-virgin olive oil
- 6 tablespoons water
- ⅓ cup (60 g) pine nuts

Currant cookie strips

Makes: about 56 cookies; Preparation: 40 minutes + 30 minutes to chill; Cooking: 12 minutes; Level of difficulty: 1

Sift the flour, confectioners' sugar, and salt into a large bowl. • Use a pastry blender to cut in the butter until the mixture resembles fine crumbs. • Add the whole egg to form a stiff dough. • Divide the dough in half. Shape each half into a ball, wrap in plastic wrap (cling film), and refrigerate for 30 minutes. • Preheat the oven to 400°F/200°C/gas 6. • Butter four cookie sheets. • Roll out one disk on a lightly floured work surface to a thickness of ⅛ inch (3 mm) and to a 14 x 12-inch (35 x 30-cm) rectangle. Sprinkle with the currants. • Roll out the remaining dough to the same dimensions and place on top of the currants, pressing down lightly. • Cut into 2 x 1½-inch (5 x 4-cm) strips. • Transfer the cookies to the prepared cookie sheets, placing them 1 inch (2.5 cm) apart. Brush with the remaining beaten egg yolk. • Bake, one sheet at a time, for about 12 minutes, or until golden brown. • Transfer to racks to cool.

■ INGREDIENTS

- 2⅓ cups (350 g) all-purpose (plain) flour
- ⅔ cup (100 g) confectioners' (icing) sugar
- ⅛ teaspoon salt
- ¾ cup (200 g) butter
- 1 large egg + 1 large egg yolk, lightly beaten
- ⅓ cup (60 g) dried currants

Right: Sicilian pine nut chewies

Remembrance cookies

Makes: about 30 cookies; Preparation: 40 minutes + 30 minutes to chill; Cooking: 15 minutes;
Level of difficulty: 1

Sift the flour and salt into a medium bowl. • Beat the butter and brown sugar in a large bowl with an electric mixer at high speed until creamy. • Add the egg yolk and lemon zest and juice, beating until just blended. • Mix in the dry ingredients and rosemary to form a stiff dough. • Shape the dough into a ball, wrap in plastic wrap (cling film), and refrigerate for 30 minutes. • Preheat the oven to 350°F/180°C/gas 4. • Butter two cookie sheets. • Roll out the dough on a lightly floured work surface to a thickness of ¼ inch (5 mm). • Use a 3-inch (8-cm) heart-shaped cookie cutter to cut out the cookies. Gather the dough scraps, re-roll, and continue cutting out cookies until all the dough is used. • Transfer the cookies to the prepared cookie sheets, placing them 1 inch (2.5 cm) apart. • Bake for about 15 minutes, or until pale gold. • Transfer to racks to cool.

INGREDIENTS

- 1⅓ cups (200 g) all-purpose (plain) flour
- ⅛ teaspoon salt
- 4 tablespoons butter
- ⅔ cup (140 g) firmly packed light brown sugar
- 1 large egg yolk
- finely grated zest and juice of 1 lemon
- 1 tablespoon finely chopped rosemary

Scented cookies

Makes: about 20 cookies; Preparation: 20 minutes; Cooking: 12 minutes; Level of difficulty: 1

Preheat the oven to 450°F/230°C/gas 8. • Line two cookie sheets with parchment paper. • Sift the flour, baking powder, and salt into a large bowl. • Beat the butter and sugar in a large bowl with an electric mixer at high speed until creamy. • Add the egg yolk, beating until just blended. • Mix in the dry ingredients and lavender leaves. • Turn the dough out onto a lightly floured surface and knead to form a soft dough. • Roll out the dough to a thickness of ¼ inch (5 mm). • Sprinkle the dough with the lavender flowers, pressing in the heads with a rolling pin. • Use 2-inch (5-cm) cookie cutters to cut out the cookies. Gather the dough scraps, re-roll, and continue cutting out cookies until all the dough is used. • Transfer the cookies to the prepared cookie sheets. • Bake for about 12 minutes, or until firm to the touch and lightly browned. • Transfer to racks to cool.

INGREDIENTS

- 1¼ cups (180 g) all-purpose (plain) flour
- 1 teaspoon baking powder
- ⅛ teaspoon salt
- 6 tablespoons butter
- ¼ cup (50 g) sugar
- 1 large egg yolk
- 2 tablespoons fresh lavender leaves, rinsed, dried, and chopped
- 1 teaspoon lavender flowers (heads only), rinsed and dried

Right: *Remembrance cookies*

Filled cookies, Mantua-style

Makes: about 15 cookies; Preparation: 30 minutes + 30 minutes to chill the pastry; Cooking: 35 minutes; Level of difficulty: 2

Pastry: Sift the flour and confectioners' sugar into a large bowl. Make a well in the center and add the egg yolks and butter. Mix to make a smooth dough. Wrap in plastic wrap (cling film) and refrigerate for 30 minutes. • Preheat the oven to 350°F/180°C/gas 4. • Butter a large baking sheet. • Filling: Sift the flour and cornstarch into a medium bowl. Stir in the confectioners' sugar. • Add the butter and egg yolks. • Beat 2 egg whites in a large bowl with an electric mixer at high speed until stiff peaks form. Fold them into the mixture. • Roll the dough out on a lightly floured work surface to ⅛ inch (3 mm) thick. Cut into 3-inch (8-cm) rounds. • Brush each one with the remaining egg white. Spoon the filling into the center of each round. Fold in half and seal well. • Transfer to the prepared baking sheet. • Bake for 35 minutes. • Let cool completely. Dust with the confectioners' sugar just before serving.

■ INGREDIENTS

PASTRY
- 1⅔ cups (250 g) all-purpose (plain) flour
- ⅓ cup (50 g) confectioners' (icing) sugar
- 2 large egg yolks
- 6 tablespoons butter

FILLING
- ½ cup (75 g) all-purpose (plain) flour
- 2 tablespoons cornstarch (cornflour)
- ⅔ cup (100 g) confectioners' (icing) sugar
- 1 tablespoon butter, melted and cooled slightly
- 2 large eggs, separated
- 1 egg white, lightly beaten

Chocolate cream cookies

Makes: about 15 cookies; Preparation: 40 minutes + 1 hour to chill and set; Cooking: 10 minutes; Level of difficulty: 2

Sift the flour and salt into a large bowl. • Use a pastry blender to cut in the butter until the mixture resembles coarse crumbs. • Mix in the cream. • Shape the dough into a ball, wrap in plastic wrap (cling film), and refrigerate for 30 minutes. • Preheat the oven to 375°F/190°C/gas 5. • Line two cookie sheets with parchment paper. • Roll out the dough on a lightly floured work surface to a thickness of ⅛ inch (3-mm). • Use a 1½-inch (4-cm) cookie cutter to cut out the cookies. Gather the dough scraps, reroll, and continue cutting out cookies until all the dough is used. • Use a spatula to transfer the cookies to the cookie sheet, spacing them 1½ inches (4-cm) apart. • Sprinkle with the sugar. • Bake for about 10 minutes, or until just golden at the edges. • Transfer to racks to cool. • Chocolate Filling: Melt the chocolate in a double boiler over barely simmering water. Remove from the heat and mix in the confectioners' sugar and cream. • Stick the cookies together in pairs with the filling. • Let the cookies stand for 30 minutes to set.

■ INGREDIENTS

- 1 cup (150 g) all-purpose (plain) flour
- ⅛ teaspoon salt
- 6 tablespoons butter
- 4 tablespoons light (single) cream
- ⅓ cup (70 g) sugar

CHOCOLATE FILLING
- 2 oz (60 g) semisweet chocolate, coarsely chopped
- 1 cup (150 g) confectioners' (icing) sugar
- 1 tablespoon light (single) cream

Right: *Filled cookies, Mantua-style*

Chocolate-filled crescents

Makes: about 15 cookies; Preparation: 25 minutes + 30 minutes to chill; Cooking: 15 minutes; Level of difficulty: 2

Pastry: Sift the flour into a large bowl. • Use your fingertips to rub in the butter until the mixture resembles coarse crumbs. • Add enough water to make a smooth dough. • Wrap in plastic wrap (cling film) and refrigerate for 30 minutes. • Preheat the oven to 350°F/180°C/gas 4. • Butter a large baking sheet. • Roll the dough out on a lightly floured surface to ¼ inch (5 mm) thick. Cut out rounds 3 inches (8 cm) in diameter. • Filling: Mix the ricotta, sugar, and chocolate spread in a large bowl. • Place a teaspoon of the filling in the center of each round. Fold in half and pinch the edges together to seal them. • Arrange them on the prepared baking sheet and brush with the egg yolk. • Bake for 15 minutes. • Let cool slightly. Transfer to a serving dish and dust with the confectioners' sugar. • Serve warm.

■ INGREDIENTS

PASTRY
• 1⅔ cups (250 g) all-purpose (plain) flour
• ½ cup (125 g) butter, cut into pieces
• 2-3 tablespoons water

FILLING
• 6 tablespoons ricotta cheese
• 2 tablespoons sugar
• 6 tablespoons good quality chocolate hazelnut spread
• 1 egg yolk, lightly beaten
• 2 tablespoons confectioners' (icing) sugar

Minty chocolate cookies

Makes: about 12 cookies; Preparation: 40 minutes + 1 hour 30 minutes to chill; Cooking: 8 minutes; Level of difficulty: 2

Sift the flour, cocoa, and salt into a medium bowl. • Beat the butter and sugar in a large bowl with an electric mixer at high speed until creamy. • Add the mint extract and egg, beating until just blended. • Mix in the dry ingredients. • Shape the dough into a ball, wrap in plastic wrap (cling film), and refrigerate for 30 minutes. • Preheat the oven to 350°F/180°C/gas 4. • Butter two cookie sheets. • Roll out the dough on a lightly floured surface to a thickness of ⅛ inch (3 mm). • Use a 2-inch (5-cm) cookie cutter to cut out the cookies. Continue cutting out cookies until all the dough is used. • Transfer the cookies to the prepared cookie sheets, placing them 1 inch (2.5 cm) apart. • Bake for about 8 minutes, or until just golden at the edges. • Transfer to racks and let cool completely. • Mint Chocolate Filling: Bring the cream to a boil in a small saucepan over low heat. • Remove from the heat and stir in the white chocolate. Add the mint extract and transfer to a medium bowl. • Cool for 30 minutes. • Stick the cookies together in pairs with filling. • Glaze: Melt the chocolate and butter in a double boiler over barely simmering water. • Spread over the cookies and refrigerate for 30 minutes.

■ INGREDIENTS

• 1 cup (150 g) all-purpose (plain) flour
• 2 tablespoons cocoa powder
• ⅛ teaspoon salt
• ½ cup (125 g) butter
• ¼ cup (50 g) sugar
• 1 teaspoon mint extract
• 1 large egg

MINT CHOCOLATE FILLING
• ½ cup (125 g) heavy (double) cream
• 7 oz (200 g) white chocolate, coarsely chopped
• 1 teaspoon mint extract

GLAZE
• 5 oz (150 g) bittersweet chocolate, coarsely chopped
• 6 tablespoons butter

Left: *Chocolate-filled crescents*

Chocolate marshmallow cookies

Makes: about 15 cookies; Preparation: 40 minutes + 30 minutes to chill; Cooking: 15 minutes; Level of difficulty: 2

Preheat the oven to 375°F/190°C/gas 5. • Butter three cookie sheets. • Sift the flour, cocoa, baking powder, and salt into a medium bowl. • Use a pastry blender to cut in the butter until the mixture resembles fine crumbs. Stir in the sugar. • Mix in the egg yolk. • Shape the dough into a ball, wrap in plastic wrap (cling film), and refrigerate for 30 minutes. • Roll out the dough out on a lightly floured work surface to a thickness of ¼ inch (5 mm). • Use a 2-inch (5-cm) cookie cutter to cut out the cookies. Cut out the centers from half of the cookies with a 1-inch (2.5-cm) cookie cutter. Gather the dough scraps, re-roll, and continue cutting out cookies until all the dough is used. • Bake, one sheet at a time, for about 15 minutes, or until golden brown. Transfer the cookies with holes to racks. • Place a marshmallow on the top of each whole cookie and bake for 3 minutes, or until the marshmallow has melted. Immediately stick a ring cookie on top of each marshmallow base. • Transfer to racks to cool.

■ INGREDIENTS

- 1½ cups (225 g) all-purpose (plain) flour
- 2 tablespoons unsweetened cocoa powder
- 1 teaspoon baking powder
- ⅛ teaspoon salt
- ½ cup (125 g) butter, cut up
- ½ cup (100 g) sugar
- 1 large egg yolk, lightly beaten
- 20–24 white marshmallows

Lemon curd cookies

Serves: 10-12; Preparation: 45 minutes + 30 minutes to chill; Cooking: 8 minutes; Level of difficulty: 1

Preheat the oven to 350°F/180°C/gas 4. • Butter two cookie sheets. • Sift the flour and salt into a large bowl. • Rub in the butter until the mixture resembles fine crumbs. • Stir in the sugar, lemon zest and juice, and egg yolks to form a stiff dough. • Shape the dough into a ball, wrap in plastic wrap (cling film), and refrigerate for 30 minutes. • Roll out the dough on a lightly floured surface to a thickness of ⅛ inch (3 mm). • Use a 3-inch (8-cm) fluted cookie cutter to cut out the cookies. • Use a 1-inch (2.5-cm) star-shaped cookie cutter to cut out the centers from half the cookies. Gather the dough scraps, re-roll, and continue cutting out cookies until all the dough is used. • Transfer the cookies to the prepared cookie sheets. • Bake for about 8 minutes, or until golden brown. Transfer to racks. • Spread the cooled whole cookies with the lemon curd and place the cookies with holes on top. Dust with the confectioners' sugar.

■ INGREDIENTS

- 1½ cups (225 g) all-purpose (plain) flour
- ⅛ teaspoon salt
- ⅔ cup (180 g) butter
- ⅓ cup (70 g) sugar
- 1 tablespoon finely grated lemon zest
- 2 tablespoons lemon juice
- 2 large egg yolks
- 1 cup (250 ml) lemon curd
- 1 tablespoon confectioners' (icing) sugar

Right: *Chocolate marshmallow cookies*

Drizzled spice cookies

Makes: about 10 cookies; Preparation: 40 minutes + 30 minutes to chill; Cooking: 10 minutes; Level of difficulty: 1

Sift the flour, cornstarch, cocoa, cinnamon, allspice, baking soda, ginger, nutmeg, and salt into a medium bowl. • Beat the butter, sugar, and corn syrup in a large bowl with an electric mixer at high speed until creamy. • Add the eggs, beating until just blended. • Mix in the dry ingredients to form a smooth dough. • Shape the dough into a ball, wrap in plastic wrap (cling film), and refrigerate for 30 minutes. • Preheat the oven to 350°F/180°C/gas 4. • Butter two cookie sheets. • Roll out the dough on a lightly floured work surface to a thickness of ½ inch (1 cm). • Use a 2-inch (5-cm) cutter to cut into rounds. • Transfer the cookies to the prepared cookie sheets, placing them 1 inch (2.5 cm) apart. • Bake for about 10 minutes, or until firm. • Cool completely on the cookie sheets. • Stick the cookies together in pairs with the preserves. • Mix the confectioners' sugar, water, and food coloring to make a soft frosting. Spread the frosting over the tops.

■ INGREDIENTS

- 1 cup (150 g) all-purpose (plain) flour
- ¾ cup (125 g) cornstarch (cornflour)
- 2 teaspoons cocoa
- 1 teaspoon cinnamon
- ½ teaspoon each allspice and baking soda
- ¼ teaspoon each ginger, nutmeg, and salt
- ½ cup (125 g) butter
- ¾ cup (150 g) sugar
- 1 tablespoon corn (golden) syrup
- 2 large eggs
- 6 tablespoons raspberry preserves (jam)
- 4 tablespoons confectioners' (icing) sugar
- 1 tablespoon warm water
- 2 drops red food coloring

Zesty coconut stars

Makes: about 30 cookies; Preparation: 40 minutes + 30 minutes to chill; Cooking: 15 minutes; Level of difficulty: 1

Sift the flour, cornstarch, and salt into a medium bowl. • Use a pastry blender to cut in the butter until the mixture resembles fine crumbs. • Stir in the sugar, coconut, lime zest, and enough milk to form a stiff dough. • Shape the dough into a ball, wrap in plastic wrap (cling film), and refrigerate for 30 minutes. • Preheat the oven to 350°F/180°C/gas 4. • Butter two cookie sheets. • Roll out the dough on a lightly floured work surface to a thickness of ¼ inch (5 mm). • Use a 3-inch (8-cm) star-shaped cookie cutter to cut out the cookies. Gather the dough scraps, re-roll, and continue cutting out cookies until all the dough is used. • Use a spatula to transfer the cookies to the prepared cookie sheets, placing them 1 inch (2.5 cm) apart. • Bake for about 15 minutes, or until pale gold. • Transfer to racks to cool.

■ INGREDIENTS

- 1½ cups (225 g) all-purpose (plain) flour
- ⅓ cup (50 g) cornstarch (cornflour)
- ⅛ teaspoon salt
- ¾ cup (200 g) butter
- ¼ cup (50 g) sugar
- ½ cup (60 g) shredded coconut
- finel grated zest of 1 lime
- 2 tablespoons milk + more as needed

Right: Drizzled spice cookies

Chocolate salami

Makes: about 30 cookies; Preparation: 15 minutes + 3 hours to chill; Level of difficulty: 2

Mix the egg yolks, brandy, and half the sugar in a double boiler over barely simmering water until the mixture lightly coats a wooden spoon or registers 160°F (71°C) on an instant-read thermometer. Plunge the pan into a bowl of ice water and stir until cooled. • Mix in the cookies, cocoa, coffee, and butter. • Stir the egg whites, remaining sugar, and cream of tartar in a double boiler until blended. Cook over low heat, beating constantly with an electric mixer at low speed until the whites register 160°F (71°C) on an instant-read thermometer. Beat at high speed until stiff. • Fold them into the mixture with the hazelnuts. • Transfer the mixture to a sheet of waxed paper. Make a sausage shape with the mixture and wrap in the waxed paper. • Refrigerate for 3 hours. • Cut in slices.

■ INGREDIENTS

- 3 large eggs, separated
- 4 tablespoons brandy
- 1 cup (200 g) sugar
- 3¼ cups (400 g) coarsely crushed cookies
- ⅔ cup (100 g) unsweetened cocoa powder
- 1 tablespoon strong coffee
- ⅔ cup (180 g) butter
- ⅛ teaspoon cream of tartar
- ⅔ cup (100 g) hazelnuts

Marshmallow crunchies

Makes: about 40 cookies; Preparation: 40 minutes + 1 hour to chill; Level of difficulty: 1

Melt the milk and semisweet chocolates with the butter in a double boiler over barely simmering water. • Remove from the heat and let cool for 15 minutes. • Mix in the marshmallows, graham cracker crumbs, and macadamia and Brazil nuts until well mixed. • Set out two large sheets of plastic wrap (cling film) and place a 10-inch (25-cm) square piece of waxed paper on top of each. • Pour half of the mixture onto the center of one piece of waxed paper. • Wrap up tightly in the paper and plastic wrap, squeezing into a log. • Repeat with the remaining mixture. • Refrigerate for 1 hour, or until firm. • Leave at room temperature for 10 minutes. • Cut the mixture into ½-inch (1-cm) thick slices.

■ INGREDIENTS

- 7 oz (200 g) milk chocolate, coarsely chopped
- 3½ oz (100 g) semisweet chocolate, coarsely chopped
- 3 tablespoons butter
- 2½ oz (60 g) mini marshmallows
- ½ cup (60 g) graham cracker (digestive biscuit) crumbs
- 1 cup (100 g) coarsely chopped macadamia nuts
- 1 cup (100 g) coarsely chopped Brazil nuts

Right: *Chocolate salami*

Sprinkle balls

Serve these scrumptious little sweets with tea or coffee or at the end of a meal.

Makes: about 30 cookies; Preparation: 25 minutes + 4 hours to chill; Level of difficulty: 1

Place the hazelnuts in a medium bowl. Bring 1 quart (1 liter) of water to a boil and pour over the hazelnuts. Let stand for 5 minutes, then use a slotted spoon to remove and place on a clean kitchen towel. Fold the towel over the hazelnuts and rub gently until the thin inner skins come away. • Place the hazelnuts and sugar in a food processor and chop finely. • Transfer to a large bowl and stir in the mandarin juice and liqueur. • Sift the cocoa into the bowl and mix until well combined. • Use a teaspoon to scoop out the dough and shape into balls the size of large marbles. • Place the sugar strands or sprinkles in a bowl and roll the balls in them so that they are well-coated. • Refrigerate for at least 4 hours before serving.

> VARIATION
> – To make chocolate almond balls, replace the hazelnuts with the same quantity of finely ground almonds.

■ INGREDIENTS

- 2⅔ cups (400 g) shelled hazelnuts
- 1 cup (200 g) sugar
- 3 tablespoons mandarin or orange juice
- 2 tablespoons orange or lemon liqueur
- ⅔ cup (100 g) unsweetened cocoa powder
- sugar strands or sprinkles, to decorate

Marzipan moons

Makes: about 35 cookies; Preparation: 30 minutes; Level of difficulty: 1

Lightly dust a surface with confectioners' sugar. • Roll the marzipan out to a thickness of about ½ inch (1 cm). • Sprinkle the chopped pistachios and oats evenly over the marzipan and press down lightly with a rolling pin. • Use a 1-inch (2.5-cm) round cutter to stamp out small circles. • Re-roll the leftovers and stamp out more circles until all the marzipan has been used. • Melt the chocolate in a double boiler over barely simmering water. Dip one half of each full moon in the melted chocolate. • Decorate with the almond halves, if liked.

■ INGREDIENTS

- 14 oz (400 g) marzipan
- ⅓ cup (30 g) finely chopped pistachios
- ⅔ cup (100 g) old-fashioned rolled oats
- 7 oz (200 g) bittersweet chocolate, coarsely chopped
- 15 almond or pistachios, halved, toasted (optional)

Right: *Sprinkle balls*

Chocolate hazelnut sweets

Makes: about 35 cookies; Preparation: 20 minutes + 4 hours to chill; Level of difficulty: 1

Process the hazelnuts with the sugar in a food processor until very finely chopped. • Mix in the apple juice, liqueur, and cocoa. • Form the mixture into small balls about ⅔ inch (1.5 cm) in diameter. • Roll in the sugar sprinkles until well coated. • Arrange on a serving dish and refrigerate for 4 hours. • Serve with coffee.

■ INGREDIENTS

- 2⅔ cups (400 g) hazelnuts
- 1 cup (200 g) sugar
- 3 tablespoons apple juice
- 3 tablespoons apple liqueur
- ½ cup (75 g) unsweetened cocoa powder
- ½ cup (75 g) sugar strands or sprinkles

No-bake Halloween cookies

Makes: about 15 cookies; Preparation: 25 minutes; Level of difficulty: 1

Mix the graham cracker crumbs, sugar, cocoa, and almonds in a large bowl. • Stir in the butter and enough milk to form a stiff dough. • Divide the mixture into 15 pieces and form into balls the size of walnuts. • Flatten into 1-inch (2.5-cm) thick rounds. • Colored Butter Icing: Beat the butter, confectioners' sugar, and vanilla in a large bowl with an electric mixer at high speed until creamy. • Divide among three small bowls. Add one shade of food coloring to each bowl. • Spread the icing over the tops of the cookies. • Decorate with candies or candied cherries to resemble eyes and noses. • Cut up the licorice whips into short lengths to resemble smiley mouths, hair, and other decorative details.

■ INGREDIENTS

- 1¾ cups (215 g) graham cracker (digestive biscuit) crumbs
- ¾ cup (150 g) sugar
- 2 tablespoons unsweetened cocoa powder
- ½ cup (75 g) finely ground almonds
- 6 tablespoons butter, melted
- 2 tablespoons milk + more as needed

COLORED BUTTER ICING
- ½ cup (125 g) butter
- 1⅔ cups (250 g) confectioners' (icing) sugar
- ½ teaspoon vanilla extract (optional)
- few drops each blue, yellow, or red food coloring
- small candies, licorice whips, and candied cherries, to decorate

Right: *Chocolate hazelnut sweets*

Louise's peanut bars

INGREDIENTS

- 1 cup (250 g) smooth peanut butter
- ⅔ cup (140 g) firmly packed light brown sugar
- 6 tablespoons corn (golden) syrup
- 1 tablespoon butter
- 4 cups (600 g) lightly crushed corn flakes
- 1¼ cups (125 g) coarsely chopped peanuts
- ½ cup (60 g) shredded (desiccated) coconut
- ½ teaspoon vanilla extract
- 1 cup (180 g) semisweet chocolate chips

Makes: about 40 bars; Preparation: 20 minutes + 30 minutes to chill; Level of difficulty: 1

Butter a 13 x 9-inch (33 x 23-cm) baking pan. • Mix the peanut butter, brown sugar, corn syrup, and butter in a large saucepan. Bring to a boil and boil for 1 minute. • Remove from the heat and stir in the corn flakes, 1 cup (125 g) peanuts, coconut, and vanilla. • Spread the mixture into the prepared pan, smoothing the top. Sprinkle with the chocolate chips and remaining peanuts. • Refrigerate for 30 minutes, or until firmly set. • Use a sharp knife to cut into bars.

Double chocolate truffles

■ INGREDIENTS

- 1 tablespoon sugar
- 2 tablespoons water
- ½ cup (125 ml) heavy (double) cream
- 5 oz (150 g) white chocolate, chopped
- 4 oz (125 g) semisweet chocolate, chopped
- 2 tablespoons candied peel, very finely chopped
- 4 tablespoons confectioners' (icing) sugar

Makes: about 40 truffles; Preparation: 20 minutes + 1 hours 30 minutes to chill; Cooking: 5 minutes; Level of difficulty: 2

Bring the sugar and water to a boil in a large saucepan over low heat. Boil for 2 minutes, or until pale golden. • Transfer to a double boiler and mix in the cream and both types of chocolate. Stir with a wooden spoon until the chocolate has melted completely. • Remove from the heat and let cool completely. • Stir again before putting the mixture in the refrigerator for 30 minutes. • Form the mixture into small balls the size of marbles. Arrange on a sheet of waxed paper and refrigerate for 1 hour. • Mix the candied peel and confectioners' sugar in a small bowl. Roll each truffle in the confectioners' sugar and candied peel and arrange on a serving dish.

White chocolate snowmen

■ INGREDIENTS

- ½ cup (125 g) butter
- 3 cups (150 g) mini marshmallow pieces
- 6 cups (400 g) rice krispies cereal
- 8 oz (250 g) white chocolate, coarsely chopped
- 2 tablespoons snowflake sprinkles (optional)
- black and red licorice, to decorate

Makes: about 10-12 cookies; Preparation: 25 minutes + 1 hour to chill and stand; Level of difficulty: 1

Line a 10½ x 15½-inch (26 x 36-cm) jelly-roll pan with aluminum foil. • Melt the butter with the marshmallows in a small saucepan over low heat. • Remove from the heat and stir in the rice krispies. • Lightly press the mixture into the prepared pan. • Refrigerate for 30 minutes, or until firmly set. • Use a snowman cookie cutter or 2-inch (5-cm) and 3-inch (8-cm) cookie cutters to cut out the cookies. • Press craft sticks into the base of the cookies to form handles. • Melt the white chocolate in a double boiler over barely simmering water. • Spread the chocolate over the tops of the cookies and decorate with the snowflakes, if using, and licorice to form eyes and mouths. • Let stand for 30 minutes until set.

Left: *Double chocolate truffles*

Savory Cookies and Snacks

Versatile savory cookies make great starters, snacks, and party food. Serve them to hungry children with a glass of milk as after-school treats or make several different kinds to fill out a barbecue or buffet spread.

Cheese and herb savory cookies

Makes: 20 savory cookies; Preparation: 30 minutes; Cooking: 10 minutes; Level of difficulty: 2

Savory Cookies: Preheat the oven to 375°F/190°C/gas 5. • Oil a baking sheet. • Sift the flour, baking powder, and salt into a large bowl. • Use your fingertips to rub in the butter until the mixture resembles coarse crumbs. • Mix in the egg, chives, marjoram, and emmental to make a smooth, soft dough. • Roll the dough out on a lightly floured work surface to ⅛ inch (3 mm) thick. Cut into 20 rounds. • Transfer to the prepared baking sheet. • Bake for about 10 minutes, or until golden brown. • Let cool completely. • Topping: Beat the ricotta, emmental, and chopped marjoram in a medium bowl. Spread each savory cookie with this mixture and arrange on a serving dish. Garnish with freshly ground black pepper.

> VARIATIONS
> – Top with slices of fresh tomato.
> – Replace the topping with a mixture of 1 cup (250 g) of soft, fresh goat's cheese and ½ teaspoon of cumin seeds.

■ INGREDIENTS

SAVORY COOKIES
- 1 cup (150 g) all-purpose (plain) flour
- ½ teaspoon baking powder
- ⅛ teaspoon salt
- 6 tablespoons butter
- 1 large egg, lightly beaten
- 1 teaspoon chives
- 1 teaspoon marjoram
- 3 oz (90 g) emmental cheese, grated

TOPPING
- ½ cup (125 g) ricotta cheese
- 3 oz (90 g) emmental cheese, grated
- 1 tablespoon finely chopped fresh marjoram
- freshly ground black pepper to taste

Tomato pinwheels

Makes: 15-20 pinwheels; Preparation: 30 minutes + 2 hour to rise; Cooking: 25 minutes; Level of difficulty: 2

Prepare the bread dough and set aside to rise. • Finely chop the carrot, onion, and celery together. • Sauté the chopped vegetables in the oil in a large frying pan for 5 minutes. • Blanch the tomatoes in boiling water for 1 minute. Drain and slip off the skins. • Chop the tomatoes coarsely and add to the pan with the vegetables. Season with salt and pepper. Partially cover and simmer over low heat for 30 minutes, stirring often. The sauce should be quite dense. • Stir in the basil, capers, and anchovy paste, if using. • Preheat the oven to 350°F/180°C/gas 4. • Oil a large baking sheet. • Punch down the dough and roll out on a lightly floured surface into a rectangle about ¼ inch (5 mm) thick. • Spread evenly with the tomatoes and sprinkle with the oregano. • Roll the rectangle up from the short side. Cut into slices about 1 inch (2.5 cm) thick. • Transfer to the prepared baking sheet. Let rise for 30 minutes. • Bake for about 25 minutes, or until golden brown. • Serve warm.

■ INGREDIENTS

- ½ quantity *Bread Dough* (see page 20)
- 1 medium carrot
- 1 small onion
- 1 stalk celery
- 1 tablespoon extra-virgin olive oil
- 6 large tomatoes
- salt and freshly ground black pepper to taste
- 8 fresh basil leaves, torn
- 1 tablespoon salted capers, rinsed
- anchovy paste (optional)
- ½ teaspoon dried oregano

Right: *Tomato pinwheels*

Parmesan biscuits with salami

Makes: 12 biscuits; Preparation: 15 minutes; Cooking: 10 minutes; Level of difficulty: 2

Preheat the oven to 400°F/200°C/gas 6. • Oil a baking sheet. • Melt the butter in a large saucepan over low heat. Remove from the heat and add the flour, parmesan, water, and pepper. Mix well to make a smooth dough. • Roll the dough out on a lightly floured surface to ¼ inch (5 mm) thick. Cut into 12 squares. • Transfer to the prepared baking sheet. • Bake for about 10 minutes, or until golden brown. • Drape a slice of salami over each biscuit.• Let cool for 10 minutes before transferring to a serving dish.

> VARIATIONS
> – If preferred, omit the salami and serve the biscuits straight from the oven spread with fresh creamy cheese.
> – Top any leftover biscuits with thin slices of bacon and cheese and bake in a preheated oven at 400°F/200°C/gas 6 for 5–10 minutes, or until the bacon is crisp and the cheese is melted.

■ INGREDIENTS

- generous ⅓ cup (100 g) butter
- 1⅓ cups (200 g) all-purpose (plain) flour
- ¾ cup (90 g) freshly grated parmesan cheese
- 6 tablespoons water
- freshly ground black pepper to taste
- 12 large slices salami

Cheese and almond puffs

Makes: 16-20 puffs; Preparation: 30 minutes; Cooking: 20 minutes; Level of difficulty: 3

Preheat the oven to 400°F/200°C/gas 6. • Butter a baking sheet and dust with flour. • Blanch the almonds in boiling water for 1 minute. Drain and slip off the skins. Chop fairly finely with a knife. • Mix the water with 3 tablespoons of butter in a small saucepan. Place over medium heat. When the water starts to boil, remove from the heat. Mix in the flour and salt, stirring constantly with a wooden spoon. • Return the pan to the heat and cook until thick, stirring constantly. • Remove from the heat and stir in the parmesan and paprika. Set aside to cool. • Add the eggs, beating until just blended. • Transfer to a pastry bag fitted with a smooth tip about ¼ inch (5 mm) in diameter. • Pipe marble-size balls of dough onto the prepared baking sheet. Sprinkle with the almonds, making sure they stick to the puffs. • Bake for about 20 minutes, or until puffed and lightly golden. • Serve warm or at room temperature.

■ INGREDIENTS

- ¾ cup (120 g) almonds
- ⅔ cup (180 ml) cold water
- 4 tablespoons butter
- 1 cup (150 g) all-purpose (plain) flour
- salt to taste
- ¾ cup (90 g) freshly grated parmesan cheese
- ⅛ teaspoon paprika
- 2 large eggs

Right: *Parmesan biscuits with salami*

Bacon, cheese, and tomato toasts

Makes: 6 toasts; Preparation: 10 minutes; Cooking: 15 minutes; Level of difficulty: 1

Toast the bread. • Spread with the butter and place a slice of cheese on each one. Top with a slice of tomato and two slices of bacon. Season with salt and pepper. • Cook the bacon in a small frying pan for 5 minutes, or until half-cooked. • Place under a hot broiler (grill) and cook until the cheese has melted and the bacon is crisp. • Serve hot.

■ INGREDIENTS

- 6 large slices firm-textured bread
- 2 tablespoons butter
- 6 large slices of tasty cheddar or other sharp cheese
- 6 slices tomato
- salt and freshly ground black pepper to taste
- 12 slices bacon

Paprika savory cookies

These spicy little cookies are perfect to serve with pre-dinner drinks. Serve them on their own or with accompanied by a tempting platter of creamy fresh cheeses, prosciutto, or other deli meats.

Makes: about 24 savory cookies; Preparation: 20 minutes; Cooking: 10 minutes; Level of difficulty: 1

Preheat the oven to 350°F/180°C/gas 4. • Butter a large baking sheet. • Sift the flour, paprika, and salt into a large bowl. • Use your fingertips to rub in the butter until the mixture resembles coarse crumbs. • Beat the egg and tomato paste in a small bowl and add to the mixture. Mix to make a smooth dough. • Roll the dough out on a lightly floured surface to ⅛ inch (3 mm) thick. Use a cookie cutter to cut into star shapes. Re-roll the offcuts and cut into stars. Transfer to the prepared baking sheet. • Bake for about 10 minutes, or until golden brown. • Remove from the oven and let cool. • Transfer to a serving dish and serve warm or at room temperature.

INGREDIENTS

- 1⅓ cups (200 g) all-purpose (plain) flour
- 1½ teaspoons paprika
- ⅛ teaspoon salt
- 7 tablespoons butter
- 1 large egg
- 1 tablespoon tomato paste

Cheese straws

Serve these moorish little treats with a glass of cool, fruity white wine and a tray of freshly cut crudités.

Makes: about 25 straws; Preparation: 20 minutes; Cooking: 10 minutes; Level of difficulty: 1

Preheat the oven to 400°F/200°C/gas 6. • Butter two large baking sheets. • Sift the flour and baking powder into a large bowl. • Use your fingertips to rub in the butter until the mixture resembles coarse crumbs. Stir in the cheddar and season with salt and pepper. • Mix in enough milk to make a stiff dough. • Roll the dough out on a lightly floured surface to ⅛ inch (3 mm). Cut into long, thin straws. • Place the straws on the prepared baking sheets. • Bake for about 10 minutes, or until crisp and golden brown. • Serve hot or at room temperature.

INGREDIENTS

- ⅔ cup (100 g) all-purpose (plain) flour
- 1 teaspoon baking powder
- 4 tablespoons butter
- ¾ cup (90 g) freshly grated cheddar or emmental cheese
- salt and freshly ground black pepper to taste
- ½ cup (125 ml) milk

Left: *Paprika savory cookies*

Shrimp and gorgonzola crostini

Yet another idea for a tastebud-tempting snack to serve with pre-dinner drinks.

Makes: 32 crostini; Preparation: 10 minutes; Cooking: 10 minutes; Level of difficulty: 1

Preheat the oven to 350°F/180°C/gas 4. • Butter a baking sheet. • Toast the bread and cut each slice into four. • Sauté the shrimp in the butter in a large frying pan over medium heat for 3 minutes. • Add the brandy and let evaporate for 2 minutes. • Beat the cream and gorgonzola cheese in a large bowl. Add to the pan and mix well. • Arrange the toast on the prepared baking sheet. Spoon some of the shrimp sauce onto each piece. • Bake for 5 minutes. • Remove from the oven and transfer to a serving dish. • Serve hot.

VARIATIONS
– Replace the gorgonzola with the same quantity of Danish blue, Roquefort, or Stilton.
– Add 1 tablespoon finely chopped fresh parsley to the mixture to lighten the topping.

■ INGREDIENTS

- 8 slices of bread, crusts removed
- 12 oz (350 g) shrimp (prawns)
- 2 tablespoons butter
- 2 tablespoons brandy
- 4 tablespoons heavy (double) cream
- 4 oz (125 g) gorgonzola cheese, crumbled

Blue cheese bites

Makes: 14-16 savory cookies; Preparation: 15 minutes; Cooking: 15 minutes; Level of difficulty: 2

Preheat the oven to 400°F/200°C/gas 6. • Crumble the blue cheese into a bowl and mix in the cream cheese. Season with pepper. • Roll the pastry out on a lightly floured surface to ⅛ inch (3 mm) thick. Cut out 3-inch (8-cm) rounds. • Transfer half the rounds to a large baking sheet. • Moisten the edges of the pastry rounds with the egg. • Spoon the cheese mixture into the centers of the rounds and cover with the remaining pastry rounds. Ensure that the edges are sealed by pinching them together with your fingers. • Make a small slit in each top to allow the steam to escape and brush with egg. • Bake for about 15 minutes, or until the pastry is golden brown. • Serve hot or at room temperature.

■ INGREDIENTS

- 8 oz (250 g) blue cheese
- ⅔ cup (180 ml) cream cheese
- freshly ground black pepper to taste
- 12 oz (350 g) fresh or frozen puff pastry, thawed if frozen
- 1 large egg, lightly beaten

Right: *Shrimp and gorgonzola crostini*

Brie, walnut, and cumin twists

Makes: about 30 twists; Preparation: 20 minutes + 2 hours to rise; Cooking: 20 minutes; Level of difficulty: 1

Preheat the oven to 350°F/180°C/gas 4. • Oil a large baking sheet. • Roll the dough out on a lightly floured surface to ¼ inch (5 mm) thick. Cut the dough into 3-inch (8-cm) triangles. • Sprinkle one edge with brie, walnuts, and cumin seeds. Roll up the triangles starting with the filled edge. Pull the ends of each twist around slightly, so that they look a little like croissants. • Transfer to the prepared baking sheet. Let rise for about 30 minutes, or until they have doubled in volume. • Bake for about 20 minutes, or until the twists are golden brown. • Serve hot straight from the oven or at room temperature.

VARIATION
– Replace the brie with the same quantity of tangy semi-cured goats' cheese.

■ INGREDIENTS

• 1 quantity *Bread Dough* (see page 20)

• 8 oz (550 g) brie, cut into small cubes

• 1 cup (100 g) chopped walnuts

• 1 tablespoon cumin seeds

Barquettes with mayonnaise and herbs

The little savories call for barquette ("little boat") molds. These can be found in any good kitchen supply store. If you don't have them on hand, substitute with tartlet pans.

Makes: about 20 barquettes; Preparation: 15 minutes + 30 minutes to chill; Cooking: 15 minutes; Level of difficulty: 2

Sift the flour and salt into a large bowl. • Use a pastry blender to cut in the butter until the mixture resembles coarse crumbs. • Mix in enough water to form a smooth dough. • Shape the dough into a ball, wrap in waxed paper, and refrigerate for 30 minutes. • Preheat the oven to 350°F/180°C/gas 4. • Set out about 20 barquette or tartlet molds. • Roll the dough out on a lightly floured surface to ⅛ inch (3 mm) thick. • Line the molds with the dough and prick all over with a fork. Cover with waxed paper and fill with dried beans. • Bake for about 15 minutes, or until golden brown. • Discard the paper and beans. Turn out the pastry cases and let cool. • Place the eggs in a bowl and mix with the parsley, marjoram, and mayonnaise. • Fill the shells with the sauce. • Serve at once (before the pastry becomes soggy).

■ INGREDIENTS

• 2 cups (300 g) all-purpose (plain) flour

• ⅛ teaspoon salt

• ⅔ cup (180 g) butter

• 2–3 tablespoons cold water

• 2 hard-boiled eggs, peeled and chopped

• 2 tablespoons each finely chopped parsley and marjoram

• 1 cup (250 ml) mayonnaise

Right: *Brie, walnut, and cumin twists*

Parmesan biscuits

Makes: about 40 biscuits; Preparation: 20 minutes + 30 minutes to chill the dough; Cooking: 15 minutes; Level of difficulty: 1

Sift the flour into a large bowl. • Use your fingertips to rub in the butter until the mixture resembles coarse crumbs. • Stir in the parmesan. Add 2 egg yolks and the cream and mix to make a soft dough. Cover and refrigerate for 30 minutes. • Preheat the oven to 475°F/250°C/gas 9. • Oil a large baking sheet. • On a lightly floured work surface, shape the dough into a 2-inch (5-cm) thick sausage. Cut into biscuits ½ inch (1 cm) thick and transfer to the prepared baking sheet. • Brush with the remaining egg yolk. • Bake for about 15 minutes, or until golden brown. • Remove from the oven and transfer to a rack. Let cool.

■ INGREDIENTS

- 1⅓ cups (200 g) all-purpose (plain) flour
- generous ⅓ cup (100 g) butter, cut into pieces
- 1½ cups (250 g) freshly grated parmesan cheese
- 3 large egg yolks
- 4 tablespoons heavy (double) cream

Butter and cayenne cheese snacks

These delectable little snacks are impossible to resist and go well with anything from a glass of wine to a bowl of soup. Try them as a midnight snack!

Makes: 30 savory cookies: Preparation: 15 minutes; Cooking: 12 minutes; Level of difficulty: 2

Preheat the oven to 375°F/190°C/gas 5. • Put the first 5 ingredients in a food processor and pulse until combined. • Add the gin and pulse again until the mixture forms a ball. • (Alternatively, beat the butter and cheese and work in the dry ingredients with your fingers, adding the liquid to bind the dough.) • Divide the dough in two. Form into two 2-inch (5-cm) sausages. • Cut into thin rounds and transfer to baking sheets. • Bake for about 12 minutes, or until golden. • Cool on racks.

■ INGREDIENTS

- 1 cup (250 g) butter
- 1¾ cups (215 g) freshly grated cheddar cheese
- 1½ cups (225 g) all-purpose (plain) flour
- ½ teaspoon salt
- ½ teaspoon cayenne pepper
- 1–2 teaspoons gin or water

Right: Parmesan biscuits

Cornmeal bites

■ INGREDIENTS

- 1 cup (150 g) finely ground yellow cornmeal
- ½ cup (75 g) all-purpose (plain) flour
- ½ teaspoon salt
- 1 teaspoon sugar
- 1 teaspoon baking powder
- ⅛ teaspoon paprika
- 1 teaspoon cracked black pepper
- 1 cup (125 g) freshly grated sharp cheddar cheese
- 2 tablespoons butter
- 1 large egg
- ⅔ cup (180 ml) water

Makes: about 45 savory cookies; Preparation: 30 minutes; Cooking: 12 minutes; Level of difficulty: 1

Preheat the oven to 400°F/200°C/gas 6. • Oil two baking sheets. • Place the cornmeal, flour, salt, sugar, baking powder, paprika, and pepper in a medium bowl. • Stir in the cheddar. • Beat the melted butter, egg, and water in a small bowl. • Use a wooden spoon to stir the egg mixture into the cornmeal mixture to form a smooth dough. • Drop rounded teaspoons of the dough onto prepared baking sheets. • Bake for about 12 minutes, or until crisp and golden brown. • Cool on racks.

Ricotta and parmesan balls

Makes: about 40 savory cookies; Preparation: 10 minutes + 30 minutes to chill; Cooking: 15 minutes; Level of difficulty: 1

Place all the ingredients in a large bowl and mix well to make a smooth dough. • Form the dough on a floured surface into a sausage shape, about 1½ inches (4 cm) in diameter. • Wrap in plastic wrap (cling film) and refrigerate for 30 minutes. • Preheat the oven to 400°F/200°C/gas 6. • Oil three baking sheets. Slice the dough ¼ inch (5 mm) thick and transfer to the prepared baking sheets. • Bake for about 15 minutes, or until lightly browned. • Serve warm.

- 1 cup (250 g) ricotta cheese
- ⅔ cup (100 g) whole-wheat (wholemeal) flour
- 2 tablespoons bran, toasted
- 2 cups (300 g) all-purpose (plain) flour
- 4 tablespoons extra-virgin olive oil
- ¾ cup (90 g) freshly grated parmesan cheese
- ⅛ teaspoon salt
- 1½ teaspoons baking powder
- 4 tablespoons milk

Fiery hazelnut shortbread

Makes: about 16 shortbread; Preparation: 30 minutes; Cooking: 15 minutes; Level of difficulty: 1

Preheat the oven to 400°F/200°C/gas 6. • Butter a 12 x 8-inch (20 x 30-cm) jelly roll pan. • Sift the flour, baking powder, red pepper flakes, and salt into a medium bowl. • Use your fingertips to rub in 6 tablespoons of butter until the mixture resembles coarse crumbs. • Stir in the hazelnuts. • Sauté the onion in the remaining butter for 5 minutes, or until transparent. • Stir the onion into the dough. Add enough water and mix to form a firm dough. • Roll the dough out on a lightly floured surface into a rectangle large enough to fit into the prepared pan. • Place in the pan and prick all over with a fork. • Bake for about 10 minutes, or until golden. • Cut into squares. • Cool completely in the pan.

- 1⅓ cups (200 g) whole-wheat (wholemeal) flour
- 2 teaspoons baking powder
- 1 teaspoon red pepper flakes or 1–2 dried red chile peppers, crumbled
- ½ teaspoon salt
- 7 tablespoons butter
- ½ cup (60 g) coarsely chopped hazelnuts
- 1 small onion, finely chopped
- 1–2 tablespoons cold water

Right: *Ricotta and parmesan balls*

Savory bignè

Makes: 30-40 bignè; Preparation: 40 minutes; Cooking: 30 minutes; Level of difficulty: 3

Bignè: Bring the water and butter to a boil in a large saucepan over low heat. • Remove from the heat and add the flour and salt. • Mix quickly to prevent any lumps from forming. • Return the pan to the heat and continue stirring until the mixture comes away from the sides of the pan and forms a ball. • Remove from the heat and let cool slightly. • Add the eggs, beating until just blended. • Preheat the oven to 350°F/ 180°C/gas 4. • Oil a baking sheet. • Use a pastry bag to pipe teaspoonfuls of the mixture onto the prepared baking sheet. • Bake for 15 minutes, or until well risen and golden brown. • Transfer to racks and let cool completely. • Cheese Filling: Beat the mascarpone and gorgonzola in a medium bowl. Add the milk if the mixture is too thick. Season with salt and pepper. • Onion and Egg Filling: Cook the onion in the vegetable stock in a small saucepan over medium heat for 5 minutes. Transfer to a food processor with the goat's cheese and eggs and process until smooth. Season with salt and pepper. • Ham and Ricotta Filling:Mix the chopped ham into the ricotta. Season with salt and pepper. • Make any—or all—of these fillings. Place them in a pastry bag with a plain tip and fill the bigné.

INGREDIENTS

BIGNÈ
- ½ cup (125 ml) water
- 3 tablespoons butter
- 1 cup (150 g) all-purpose (plain) flour
- ⅛ teaspoon salt
- 4 large eggs

CHEESE FILLING
- ½ cup (125 g) mascarpone cheese
- 4 oz (125 g) gorgonzola cheese, crumbled
- 1–2 tablespoons milk (optional)
- salt and freshly ground black pepper to taste

ONION AND EGG FILLING
- 1 large onion, chopped
- 4 tablespoons vegetable stock
- ⅔ cup (180 g) goat's cheese
- 2 large soft-boiled eggs

HAM AND RICOTTA FILLING
- ¾ cup (90 g) chopped ham
- ½ cup (125 g) ricotta cheese

Soda cookies

Makes: about 25 savory cookies; Preparation: 30 minutes; Cooking: 10 minutes; Level of difficulty: 1

Preheat the oven to 450°F/225°C/gas 7. • Butter two large cookie sheets. • Sift the flour, baking soda, cream of tartar, salt, and cayenne pepper in a large bowl. • Stir in the butter and enough milk to make a soft dough. • Drop spoonfuls of the dough 2 inches (5 cm) apart onto the prepared cookie sheets. • Bake for about 10 minutes, or until golden. • Let cool on the sheets for 5 minutes. • Transfer to racks to cool completely.

INGREDIENTS

- 2 cups (300 g) all-purpose (plain) flour
- 1 teaspoon baking soda
- 1 teaspoon cream of tartar
- ½ teaspoon salt
- ¼ teaspoon cayenne pepper
- 6 tablespoons butter, melted
- ¾ cup (200 ml) milk

Right: *Savory bignè*

Quick Breads

Quick breads can be sweet or savory, small and oval like muffins, scones, or rolls, or shaped into traditional round or rectangular loaves. What these "breads" have in common is their bread-like texture and the fact that they are leavened using fast-acting rising agents.

Pumpkin muffins

*Try these muffins at breakfast with plenty of salted butter or
serve them later in the day with fresh creamy cheese.*

Makes: about 12 muffins; Preparation: 20 minutes; Cooking: 20 minutes; Level of difficulty: 1

Preheat the oven to 400°F/200°C/gas 6. • Butter a 12-cup muffin pan. • Sift the flour, baking powder, paprika, and salt into a large bowl. Stir in the sugar. • Beat the egg, milk, carrot juice, and oil in a large bowl until frothy. • Use a wooden spoon to gradually fold in the dry ingredients and pumpkin purée. • Spoon the batter evenly into the prepared cups. • Bake for about 20 minutes, or until a toothpick inserted into the centers comes out clean. • Cool in the pan for 5 minutes. • Serve warm with fresh goat's cheese.

■ INGREDIENTS

- 2 cups (300 g) all-purpose (plain) flour
- 1 tablespoon baking powder
- ½ teaspoon paprika
- ¼ teaspoon salt
- ¼ teaspoon sugar
- 1 large egg
- 1 cup (250 ml) milk
- 2 tablespoons carrot juice
- 1 tablespoon sunflower oil
- ⅔ cup (180 ml) pumpkin purée

Prosciutto and pea muffins

Makes: about 16 muffins; Preparation: 10 minutes; Cooking: 30 minutes; Level of difficulty: 1

Preheat the oven to 350°F/180°C/gas 4. • Arrange about 16 foil baking cups on a baking sheet. • Sift the flour and baking powder into a large bowl. • Beat the eggs and milk in a large bowl. • Mix in the dry ingredients, prosciutto, peas, parmesan, parsley, and butter. Season with salt and pepper. • Spoon the batter evenly into the prepared cups. • Bake for about 25 minutes, or until risen and golden brown. • Serve warm.

■ INGREDIENTS

- 2 cups (300 g) all-purpose (plain) flour
- 2 teaspoons baking powder
- 2 large eggs, lightly beaten
- ¾ cup (200 ml) milk
- 1 cup (120 g) chopped prosciutto (Parma ham)
- 1 cup (125 g) cooked peas
- 2 tablespoons freshly grated parmesan cheese
- 1 tablespoon finely chopped parsley
- 4 tablespoons butter, melted
- salt and freshly ground black pepper to taste

Right: Pumpkin muffins

Scones with chocolate hazelnut filling

■ INGREDIENTS

- 2⅔ cups (400 g) all-purpose (plain) flour
- 2 teaspoons baking powder
- ½ teaspoon salt
- 1 large egg, lightly beaten
- ½ cup (125 g) butter
- ⅓ cup (70 g) sugar
- ½ cup (125 ml) warm milk
- 6 tablespoons good quality chocolate hazelnut spread (Nutella)

Makes: about 18 scones; Preparation: 15 minutes; Cooking: 20 minutes; Level of difficulty: 1

Preheat the oven to 400°F/200°C/gas 6. • Butter a cookie sheet. • Sift the flour, baking powder, and salt into a large bowl. • Beat in the egg, butter, and sugar. Add enough milk to make a soft dough. • Turn out onto a floured surface and roll the dough out to ¾ inch (2 cm) thick. • Use a 2-inch (5-cm) cookie cutter to cut out 18 rounds. • Transfer the scones to the prepared sheet. • Bake for about 20 minutes, or until risen and golden brown. • Remove from the oven and cut in half horizontally. • Stick the halves together with the chocolate spread. • Serve warm.

VARIATION
– These simple scones are also delicious filled with whipped cream and chunky fruit preserves (jam) for a full-fat treat.

Raisin and rosemary scones

■ INGREDIENTS

- 2½ cups (375 g) all-purpose (plain) flour
- 1 teaspoon baking powder
- ⅛ teaspoon salt
- 4 tablespoons sugar
- 4 tablespoons butter
- 2 large eggs + 1 large egg yolk, lightly beaten
- 1 cup (250 ml) heavy (double) cream
- 1 cup (180 g) golden raisins (sultanas)
- 3 tablespoons finely chopped rosemary leaves

Makes: about 18 scones; Preparation: 20 minutes; Cooking: 15 minutes; Level of difficulty: 1

Preheat the oven to 350°F/180°C/gas 4. • Butter a large baking sheet. • Sift the flour, baking powder, and salt into a large bowl. Stir in the sugar. • Use your fingertips to rub in the butter until the mixture resembles coarse crumbs. • Make a well in the center and pour in the eggs, egg yolk, and cream. Add the raisins and rosemary. Mix to form a soft dough. • Drop tablespoons of the dough onto the prepared baking sheet. • Bake for about 15 minutes, or until risen and golden brown. • Serve warm.

Right: *Scones with chocolate hazelnut filling*

Yogurt scones

The yogurt lends these scones a slightly sharp flavor that blends beautifully with butter. Slice in half and serve hot spread with lashings of salted butter. The scones are equally good with or without the golden raisins.

Makes: about 10 scones; Preparation: 15 minutes; Cooking: 15 minutes; Level of difficulty: 1

Preheat the oven to 450°F/230°C/gas 8. • Sift the flour, baking powder, and salt into a large bowl. • Use your fingertips to rub in the butter until the mixture resembles coarse crumbs. • Make a well in the center and add the egg and yogurt. Mix well to form a stiff dough. Add the raisins, if using, and milk, if needed. • Turn the dough out onto a lightly floured work surface and knead for 1 minute. Roll the dough out to about 1 inch (2.5 cm) thick. • Use a 2-inch (5-cm) cookie cutter to cut out rounds. Transfer to a large baking sheet. Brush the top of each scone with milk. • Bake for about 20 minutes, or until golden brown and risen. • Serve warm.

■ INGREDIENTS

- 1⅔ cups (250 g) all-purpose (plain) flour
- 1 teaspoon baking powder
- ⅛ teaspoon salt
- 2 tablespoons butter
- 1 large egg, lightly beaten
- ½ cup (125 ml) plain yogurt
- ⅓ cup (60 g) golden raisins (sultanas) (optional)
- 3 tablespoons milk

Onion and parmesan scones

Makes: about 25 scones; Preparation: 30 minutes; Cooking: 30 minutes; Level of difficulty: 1

Preheat the oven to 375°F/190°C/gas 5. • Sauté the onion in the oil in a large frying pan over medium heat until lightly golden. • Sift the flour, baking powder, and salt into a large bowl. • Stir in the parmesan and onion. • Beat the cream in a large bowl with an electric mixer at high speed until stiff. Gradually fold the cream into the batter and mix to form a soft dough. • Turn the dough out onto a lightly floured work surface and knead for 1 minute. Roll the dough out to a thickness of about ¾ inch (2 cm). Use a 2-inch (5-cm) cookie cutter to cut out rounds. Transfer to a large baking sheet. • Bake for about 20 minutes, or until risen and golden brown. • Serve warm.

■ INGREDIENTS

- 1 onion, finely chopped
- 2 tablespoons extra-virgin olive oil
- 4 cups (600 g) all-purpose (plain) flour
- 1 tablespoon baking powder
- 1 tablespoon salt
- 2 cups (250 g) freshly grated parmesan cheese
- 2 cups (500 ml) heavy (double) cream

Right: *Yogurt scones*

Sun-dried tomato scones

Makes: about 18 scones; Preparation: 20 minutes; Cooking: 15 minutes; Level of difficulty: 1

INGREDIENTS

- 2 cups (300 g) all-purpose (plain) flour
- 1 teaspoon baking soda
- 2 teaspoons cream of tartar
- ⅛ teaspoon salt
- 4 tablespoons butter
- ¾ cup (200 ml) milk
- 2 tablespoons finely chopped sun-dried tomatoes

Preheat the oven to 450°F/230°C/gas 8. • Butter a large baking sheet. • Sift the flour, baking soda, cream of tartar, and salt into a large bowl. • Use your fingertips to rub in the butter until the mixture resembles coarse crumbs. • Make a well in the center and pour in the milk. Add the tomatoes and mix to form a soft dough. • Turn the dough out onto a lightly floured work surface and knead for 1 minute. • Roll the dough out to a thickness of about ¾ inch (2 cm). Use a 2-inch (5-cm) cookie cutter to cut out rounds. Transfer to a large baking sheet. • Bake for about 15 minutes, or until risen and golden brown. • Serve warm.

Irish potato scones

Makes: about 15 scones; Preparation: 20 minutes; Cooking: 35 minutes; Level of difficulty: 2

Cook the potatoes in a large pot of salted, boiling water for 20 minutes, or until tender. • Drain and mash until smooth. • Preheat the oven to 400°F/200°C/gas 6. • Grease a large baking sheet with oil. • Sift the flour, baking powder, and mustard into a large bowl. Stir in the cheddar and season with salt and pepper. • Beat in the butter, garlic, egg, and milk. • Add the potatoes and mix well. • Spoon balls of the mixture onto the prepared sheet. • Bake for 15 minutes, or until risen golden brown. • Serve hot with butter.

■ INGREDIENTS

- 14 oz (400 g) yellow potatoes, peeled
- 1 cup (150 g) all-purpose (plain) flour
- 1 teaspoon baking powder
- 1 teaspoon mustard powder
- 2 tablespoons freshly grated cheddar cheese
- salt and freshly ground black pepper to taste
- 3 tablespoons butter
- 1 clove garlic, finely chopped
- 1 large egg, lightly beaten
- 6 tablespoons milk

Chive and parmesan muffins

Makes: about 12 muffins; Preparation: 15 minutes; Cooking: 30 minutes; Level of difficulty: 1

Preheat the oven to 400°F/200°C/gas 6. • Butter a 12-cup muffin pan. • Sift the flour into a large bowl. • Use your fingertips to rub in the butter until the mixture resembles coarse crumbs. • Stir in the parmesan, chives, poppy seeds, and red pepper flakes. • Mix in the eggs, buttermilk, and oil. • Spoon the batter evenly into the prepared cups. • Bake for about 30 minutes, or until a toothpick inserted into the centers comes out clean. • Serve warm.

■ INGREDIENTS

- 2 cups (300 g) all-purpose (plain) flour
- ½ cup (125 g) butter
- 1 cup (125 g) freshly grated parmesan cheese
- 1 small bunch chives, finely chopped
- 2 tablespoons poppy seeds
- ½ teaspoon red pepper flakes
- 2 large eggs
- 1 cup (250 ml) buttermilk
- 2 tablespoons extra-virgin olive oil

Right: Irish potato scones

Whole-wheat soda bread

■ INGREDIENTS

- 3 cups (450 g) whole-wheat (wholemeal) flour
- 1⅔ cups (250 g) all-purpose (plain) flour
- 1½ teaspoons baking soda
- 1 teaspoon salt
- 2 cups (500 ml) milk
- 2 tablespoons melted butter

Serves: 10-12; Preparation: 20 minutes; Cooking: 40 minutes; Level of difficulty: 1

Preheat the oven to 400°F/200°C/gas 6. • Lightly grease a large baking sheet with oil. Dust with flour. • Sift both flours, baking soda, and salt into a large bowl. • Gradually stir in the milk, a little at a time. Stir in the butter. • Finish adding the milk. Even though the dough should be fairly soft you may not need to add it all. • Turn the dough out onto a lightly floured work surface. Knead for 1 minute, then shape into a large round loaf. • Place on the prepared sheet and flatten slightly. It should be about 2 inches (5 cm) high. • Bake for about 40 minutes, or until the loaf sounds hollow when tapped on the bottom. • Serve slices warm or at room temperature spread with salted butter.

Raisin and yogurt soda bread

■ INGREDIENTS

- 2 cups (300 g) all-purpose (plain) flour
- 2 cups (300 g) whole-wheat (wholemeal) flour
- 2 teaspoons baking soda
- 1 teaspoon salt
- ½ cup (100 g) sugar
- 1 cup (125 g) raisins
- 1½ cups (375 g) plain yogurt
- 4 tablespoons melted butter

Serves: 10-12; Preparation: 20 minutes; Cooking: 50 minutes; Level of difficulty: 1

Preheat the oven to 375°F/190°C/gas 5. • Lightly grease a large baking sheet with oil. Dust with flour. • Sift both flours, baking soda, and salt into a large bowl. Stir in the sugar and raisins. • Gradually stir in the yogurt, a little at a time. Stir in the butter. • Finish adding the yogurt. Even though the dough should be fairly soft you may not need to add it all. The dough should be fairly soft. • Turn the dough out onto a lightly floured work surface. Knead for 1 minute, then shape into a large round loaf. • Place on the prepared baking sheet. Use a large knife to mark a cross on the top of the loaf. • Bake for about 50 minutes, or until the loaf sounds hollow when tapped on the bottom. • Let cool on a rack. • Serve slices warm or at room temperature spread with salted butter.

Left: *Whole-wheat soda bread*

Genovese quick bread

Serves: 6-8; Preparation: 30 minutes; Cooking: 40 minutes; Level of difficulty: 1

Preheat the oven to 350°F/180°C/gas 4. • Butter a 9-inch (23-cm) springform pan. • Chop the almonds with half the sugar in a food processor. • Beat the butter and remaining sugar in a large bowl with an electric mixer at high speed until creamy. • Add the eggs, one at a time, beating until just blended after each addition. • Gradually beat in the cornstarch and salt. • Mix in the almonds and kirsch. • Spoon the batter into the prepared pan, smoothing the top. • Bake for about 40 minutes, or until a toothpick inserted into the center comes out clean. • Turn out onto a rack and let cool completely.

■ INGREDIENTS

- ⅔ cup (100 g) shelled almonds
- ¾ cup (150 g) sugar
- ½ cup (125 g) butter
- 3 large eggs
- ⅓ cup (50 g) cornstarch (cornflour)
- ¼ teaspoon salt
- 2 tablespoons kirsch

Walnut and carrot loaf

Serves: 8–10; Preparation: 20 minutes; Cooking: 50 minutes; Level of difficulty: 1

Preheat the oven to 350°F/180°C/gas 4. • Butter and flour a 9½ x 5½-inch (24 x 14-cm) loaf pan. • Sift both flours, baking powder, cinnamon, and salt into a large bowl. Stir in the walnuts, carrots, both sugars, milk, oil, and egg. • Pour the batter into the prepared pan. • Bake for about 50 minutes, or until a toothpick inserted into the center comes out clean. • Cool in the pan for 10 minutes. Turn out onto a rack to finish cooling.

■ INGREDIENTS

- 1 cup (150 g) all-purpose (plain) flour
- 1 cup (150 g) whole-wheat (wholemeal) flour
- 2 teaspoons baking powder
- 1 teaspoon ground cinnamon
- ½ teaspoon salt
- 1 cup (100 g) chopped walnuts
- 2 cups (200 g) finely grated carrots
- ½ cup (100 g) sugar
- ½ cup (100 g) firmly packed brown sugar
- ½ cup (125 ml) milk
- 6 tablespoons vegetable oil
- 1 large egg, lightly beaten

Right: *Genovese quick bread*

Quick golden raisin buns

Serves: 8-10; Preparation: 10 minutes; Cooking: 20 minutes; Level of difficulty: 1

Preheat the oven to 400°F/200°C/gas 6. • Butter a baking sheet. • Sift the flour, baking powder, and salt into a large bowl. Stir in the sugar and raisins. • Make a well in the center and add the butter, eggs, and enough milk to form a soft, malleable dough. • Divide the dough into 20 balls about the size of golf balls. • Arrange on the prepared sheet and brush with the egg yolk. • Bake for about 20 minutes, or until risen and golden. • Dust with the confectioners' sugar and let cool on racks.

> VARIATIONS
> – Add 1 teaspoon each of ground ginger and cinnamon along with the flour.
> – Add 1–2 tablespoons finely ground orange or lemon zest together with the eggs.

■ INGREDIENTS

- 2 cups (300 g) all-purpose (plain) flour
- 2 teaspoons baking powder
- ½ teaspoon salt
- ½ cup (100 g) sugar
- 1 cup (180 g) golden raisins (sultanas)
- 7 tablespoons butter
- 3 large eggs, lightly beaten
- 4 tablespoons milk
- 1 egg yolk, lightly beaten
- 4 tablespoons confectioners' (icing) sugar, to dust

Sherry raisin loaf

Serves: 8-10; Preparation: 10 minutes; Cooking: 1 hour; Level of difficulty: 1

Preheat the oven to 300°F/150°C/gas 2. • Butter a 9 x 5-inch (23 x 13-cm) loaf pan. Line with waxed paper. • Beat the raisins, flour, brown sugar, butter, eggs, sherry, marmalade, baking powder, and salt in a large bowl with an electric mixer at low speed until well blended. • Spoon the batter into the prepared pan. • Bake for about 1 hour, or until a toothpick inserted into the center comes out clean. • Cool the loaf in the pan for 15 minutes. • Turn out onto a rack to cool completely.

■ INGREDIENTS

- 1 lb (500 g) raisins or golden raisins (sultanas)
- 1 cup (150 g) all-purpose (plain) flour
- ¾ cup (150 g) firmly packed brown sugar
- ½ cup (125 g) butter, melted
- 2 large eggs, lightly beaten
- 4 tablespoons sweet sherry
- 2 tablespoons orange marmalade
- 1 teaspoon baking powder
- ¼ teaspoon salt

Right: *Quick golden raisin buns*

Angela's banana loaf

Serves: 12-15; Preparation: 20 minutes; Cooking: 45 minutes; Level of difficulty: 1

Preheat the oven to 350°F/180°C/gas 4. • Butter two 9 x 5-inch (23 x 13-cm) loaf pans. Line with aluminum foil, letting the edges overhang. Butter the foil. • Sift the whole-wheat flour, baking powder, and salt into a medium bowl. Stir in the bran. • Beat the butter and brown sugar in a large bowl with an electric mixer at medium speed until creamy. • Add the eggs, one at a time, beating until just blended after each addition. • With mixer at low speed, beat in the bananas, dates, and walnuts. Beat in the dry ingredients, alternating with the milk. • Spoon the batter into the prepared pans. • Bake for about 45 minutes, or until a toothpick inserted into the centers comes out clean. • Cool the loaves in the pans for 10 minutes. Using the foil as a lifter, remove the loaves from the pans. Carefully remove the foil and let cool completely on racks.

■ INGREDIENTS

- 1½ cups (225 g) whole-wheat (wholemeal) flour
- 2 teaspoons baking powder
- ¼ teaspoon salt
- ½ cup (75 g) wheat bran
- ½ cup (125 g) butter
- ¾ cup (150 g) firmly packed brown sugar
- 2 large eggs
- 1 cup (250 g) mashed very ripe banana
- 1 cup (180 g) pitted dates, chopped
- ½ cup (50 g) chopped walnuts
- 4 tablespoons milk

Date and carrot loaf

Serves: 10-12; Preparation: 20 minutes; Cooking: 50 minutes; Level of difficulty: 1

Preheat the oven to 350°F/180°C/gas 4. • Butter two 8½ x 4½-inch (22 x 12-cm) loaf pans. Line with aluminum foil, letting the edges overhang. Butter the foil. • Sift the whole-wheat flour, baking powder, baking soda, and salt in a large bowl. Stir in the toasted wheat germ, brown sugar, and dates. • Beat in the milk, butter, eggs, banana, and carrots with an electric mixer at low speed. • Spoon half the batter into each of the prepared pans. Sprinkle with the peanuts. • Bake for about 50 minutes, or until golden brown and a toothpick inserted into the centers comes out clean. • Cool the loaves in the pans for 10 minutes. Using the foil as a lifter, remove the loaves from the pans. Carefully remove the foil and let cool completely on racks.

■ INGREDIENTS

- 1½ cups (225 g) whole-wheat (wholemeal) flour
- 1½ teaspoons baking powder
- ½ teaspoon baking soda
- ¼ teaspoon salt
- 1 cup (150 g) toasted wheat germ
- ¾ cup (150 g) firmly packed dark brown sugar
- 1 cup (180 g) chopped dates
- 1¼ cups (310 ml) milk
- ½ cup (125 g) butter
- 2 large eggs, lightly beaten
- 1 cup (250 g) mashed very ripe banana
- ½ cup (50 g) grated carrots
- ¾ cup (90 g) chopped peanuts

Right: Date and carrot loaf

Hazelnut and almond loaf

INGREDIENTS

- ¾ cup (120 g) raisins
- 1½ cups (225 g) all-purpose (plain) flour
- ½ cup (100 g) sugar
- 1½ teaspoons baking powder
- ¼ teaspoon salt
- ½ cup (125 ml) milk
- 1 large egg, lightly beaten
- 4 tablespoons butter
- ¾ cup (75 g) hazelnuts, finely chopped
- ½ cup (50 g) almonds, finely chopped
- 2 tablespoons mixed nuts, coarsely chopped

Serves: 8-10; Preparation: 15 minutes + 30 minutes to soak the raisins; Cooking: 45 minutes; Level of difficulty: 1

Plump the raisins in warm water for 30 minutes. • Drain well and pat dry with paper towels. • Preheat the oven to 350°F/180°C/gas 4. • Butter an 8½ x 4½-inch (22 x 12-cm) loaf pan. Line with aluminum foil, letting the edges overhang. Butter the foil. • Stir together the flour, sugar, baking powder, and salt into a large bowl. • Beat in the milk, egg, and butter. Stir in the hazelnuts, almonds, and raisins. • Spoon the batter into the prepared pan. • Bake for about 45 minutes, or until a toothpick inserted into the center comes out clean. • Cool the loaf in the pan on a rack for 10 minutes. Using the foil as a lifter, remove the loaf from the pan. Carefully remove the foil and let cool completely. Decorate with the chopped nuts.

Walnut loaf

Serves: 6-8; Preparation: 25 minutes; Cooking: 1 hour; Level of difficulty: 1

Preheat the oven to 350°F/180°C/gas 4. • Butter a 9 x 5-inch (23 x 13-cm) loaf pan. Line with aluminum foil, letting the edges overhang. Butter the foil. • Sift the flour and baking powder into a large bowl. • Beat the butter and sugar in a large bowl with an electric mixer at high speed until creamy. • Add the milk and egg, beating until just blended. Gradually fold in the dry ingredients and walnuts. • Spoon the batter into the prepared pan. • Bake for 1 hour, or until springy to the touch. • • Cool in the pan for 10 minutes. Using the foil as a lifter, remove the loaf from the pan. Carefully remove the foil and place on a rack. Serve warm or at room temperature.

> VARIATION
> – Add 1 teaspoon of vanilla extract to the batter along with the walnuts.

■ INGREDIENTS

- 2 cups (300 g) all-purpose (plain) flour
- 2 teaspoons baking powder
- 7 tablespoons butter
- ¾ cup (150 g) sugar
- 1 cup (250 ml) milk
- 1 large egg, lightly beaten
- 1¾ cups (180 g) chopped walnuts

Caroline's best date loaf

Serves: 6-8; Preparation: 15 minutes; Cooking: 40 minutes; Level of difficulty: 1

Preheat the oven to 350°F/180°C/gas 4. • Butter and flour an 8½ x 4½-inch (22 x 12-cm) loaf pan. Line with aluminum foil, letting the edges overhang. Butter the foil. • Beat the egg yolks, butter, and sugar in a large bowl with an electric mixer at high speed until pale and thick. • With mixer at low speed, gradually beat in the flour and baking powder, alternating with the milk and brandy. Stir in the dates and walnuts. With mixer at high speed, beat the egg whites and salt until stiff peaks form. • Use a large rubber spatula to fold them into the batter. • Spoon the batter into the prepared pan. • Bake for about 40 minutes, or until a toothpick inserted into the center comes out clean. • Cool in the pan for 10 minutes. Using the foil as a lifter, remove the loaf from the pan. Carefully remove the foil and place on a rack. • Turn out onto a rack to cool completely.

■ INGREDIENTS

- 2 large eggs, separated
- ½ cup (125 g) butter
- ½ cup (100 g) sugar
- 1 cup (150 g) all-purpose (plain) flour
- 2 teaspoons baking powder
- 6 tablespoons milk
- 2–3 tablespoons rum or brandy
- 1 cup (180 g) pitted dates, chopped
- ¾ cup (75 g) chopped walnuts
- ¼ teaspoon salt

Right: *Walnut loaf*

Moist apricot loaf

INGREDIENTS

- 1½ cups (225 g) wheat cereal
- 1½ cups (375 ml) milk
- 1 cup (200 g) firmly packed brown sugar
- 1 cup (180 g) dried apricots, coarsely chopped
- 4 tablespoons honey
- 2 cups (300 g) all-purpose (plain) flour
- 1½ teaspoons baking powder
- ½ teaspoon baking soda
- ¼ teaspoon salt

Serves: 8-10; Preparation: 15 minutes + 12 hours to stand; Cooking: 1 hour; Level of difficulty: 1

Stir the cereal, milk, brown sugar, apricots, and honey in a large bowl until well blended. Cover and refrigerate for 12 hours, or overnight. • Preheat the oven to 350°F/180°C/gas 4. • Butter two 9 x 5-inch (23 x 13-cm) loaf pans. Line with aluminum foil, letting the edges overhang. Butter the foil. • Sift the flour, baking powder, baking soda, and salt into the cereal mixture. Mix well. • Spoon the batter into the prepared pans. • Bake for about 1 hour, or until a toothpick inserted into the center comes out clean. • Cool in the pans for 10 minutes. Using the foil as a lifter, remove the loaves from the pans. Carefully remove the foil and let cool completely on racks.

Marsala fruit loaf

INGREDIENTS

- ¾ cup (120 g) raisins
- 3 tablespoons rum
- 1¼ cups (180 g) all-purpose (plain) flour
- 3 large eggs
- ½ cup (100 g) sugar
- 1 teaspoon baking powder
- ¼ teaspoon salt
- ⅔ cup (70 g) mixed candied fruit, chopped
- 6 tablespoons butter, melted
- 3 tablespoons dry Marsala wine
- 2 tablespoons finely grated lemon zest

Serves: 6-8; Preparation: 20 minutes + 30 minutes to soak; Cooking: 50 minutes; Level of difficulty: 1

Plump the raisins in the rum in a small bowl for 30 minutes. Drain well and pat dry with paper towels. Sprinkle with the 2 tablespoons flour. • Preheat the oven to 350°F/180°C/gas 4. • Butter an 8½ x 4½-inch (22 x 12-cm) loaf pan. Line with aluminum foil, letting the edges overhang. Butter the foil. • Beat the eggs and sugar in a large bowl with an electric mixer at high speed until pale and thick. • With mixer at low speed, gradually beat in the remaining flour, baking powder, salt, candied fruit, butter, marsala, raisins, and lemon zest. • Spoon the batter into the prepared pan. • Bake for about 50 minutes, or until a toothpick inserted into the center comes out clean. • Cool the loaf completely in the pan. Using the foil as a lifter, remove the loaf from the pan. Turn out onto a rack. Carefully remove the foil before serving.

Left: *Moist apricot loaf*

Almond and candied peel loaf

Serves: 12-15; Preparation: 25 minutes; Cooking: 1 hour; Level of difficulty: 1

Preheat the oven to 350°F/180°C/gas 4. • Butter two 9 x 5-inch (23 x 13-cm) loaf pans. Line with aluminum foil, letting the edges overhang. Butter the foil. • Sift the flour, baking powder, cinnamon, cloves, and salt into a large bowl. • Beat the eggs and sugar in a large bowl with an electric mixer at high speed until frothy. • Gradually fold in the dry ingredients, milk, almonds, candied peel, and orange zest. • Spoon the batter evenly into the prepared pans. • Bake for about 1 hour, or until a toothpick inserted into the centers comes out clean. • Cool the loaves in the pans for 15 minutes. • Using the foil as a lifter, remove the loaf from the pan. Carefully remove the foil and let cool completely.

■ INGREDIENTS

- 3⅓ cups (500 g) all-purpose (plain) flour
- 1 tablespoon baking powder
- 1 teaspoon ground cinnamon
- ⅛ teaspoon ground cloves
- ⅛ teaspoon salt
- 4 large eggs
- 1¼ cups (250 g) sugar
- 1 cup (250 ml) milk
- 1 cup (100 g) chopped almonds
- 1 cup (100 g) mixed candied peel, diced
- finely grated zest of 1 orange

Scottish loaf

Serves: 6-8; Preparation: 25 minutes + 30 minutes to soak the raisins; Cooking: 50 minutes; Level of difficulty: 1

Plump the raisins in the water in a small bowl for 30 minutes. Drain well and pat dry with paper towels. Return to the bowl and drizzle with 3 tablespoons of whisky. • Preheat the oven to 350°F/180°C/gas 4. • Butter an 8½ x 4½-inch (22 x 12-cm) loaf pan. Line with aluminum foil, letting the edges overhang. Butter the foil. • Beat the egg whites and salt in a medium bowl with an electric mixer at high speed until stiff peaks form. • Sift the flour, sugar, baking powder, and nutmeg into a large bowl. • With mixer at low speed, gradually beat in the egg yolks, butter, and remaining whisky. Stir in the walnuts and raisins. • Use a large rubber spatula to fold the beaten whites into the batter. • Spoon the batter into the prepared pan. • Bake for about 50 minutes, or until a toothpick inserted into the center comes out clean. • Cool the loaf in the pan for 15 minutes. • Using the foil as a lifter, remove the loaf from the pan. Carefully remove the foil and let cool completely.

■ INGREDIENTS

- 1 cup (180 g) raisins
- 1½ cups (375 ml) warm water
- 6 tablespoons Scotch whisky
- 2 large eggs, separated
- ¼ teaspoon salt
- ¾ cup (125 g) all-purpose (plain) flour
- ⅔ cup (140 g) sugar
- 1 teaspoon baking powder
- 1 teaspoon ground nutmeg
- 6 tablespoons butter, melted
- 1 cup (100 g) walnuts, coarsely chopped

Right: Almond and candied peel loaf

Simple orange loaf

INGREDIENTS

- 1½ cups (225 g) all-purpose (plain) flour
- 1 teaspoon baking powder
- ½ teaspoon baking soda
- 4 tablespoons butter
- ½ cup (100 g) sugar
- finely grated zest and juice of 1 orange
- 1 cup (180 g) raisins
- ½ cup (125 ml) milk

Serves: 6-8; Preparation: 20 minutes; Cooking: 50 minutes; Level of difficulty: 1

Preheat the oven to 325°F/170°C/gas 3. • Butter a 9 x 5-inch (23 x 13-cm) loaf pan. Line with aluminum foil, letting the edges overhang. Butter the foil. • Sift the flour, baking powder, and baking soda into a medium bowl. • Use your fingers to rub in the butter until the mixture resembles coarse crumbs. • Stir in the sugar, orange zest, and raisins. • Use a large rubber spatula to mix in the orange juice and milk until well blended. • Pour the batter into the prepared pan. • Bake for about 50 minutes, or until a toothpick inserted into the center comes out clean. • Cool in the pan for 15 minutes. Using the foil as a lifter, remove the loaf from the pan. Carefully remove the foil and let cool completely.

Fig loaf

Serves: 12-15; Preparation: 30 minutes; Cooking: 1 hour; Level of difficulty: 1

Preheat the oven to 350°F/180°C/gas 4. • Butter two 9 x 5-inch (23 x 13-cm) loaf pans. Line with aluminum foil, letting the edges overhang. Butter the foil. • Bring the water to a boil in a medium saucepan over high heat. Add the figs, reduce the heat to low, and simmer, uncovered, for 10 minutes. • Stir in the butter and brown sugar until the butter has melted. • Set aside to cool. • Stir in the eggs, flour, muesli, baking powder, and salt. • Spoon the batter into the prepared pans. • Bake for about 50 minutes, or until a toothpick inserted into the centers comes out clean. • Cool the loaves in the pans for 10 minutes. Using the foil as a lifter, remove the loaves from the pans. Carefully remove the foil and let cool completely on racks.

■ INGREDIENTS

- 1½ cups (375 ml) water
- 1 cup (180 g) dried figs, coarsely chopped
- ½ cup (125 g) cold butter, cut up
- 1 cup (200 g) firmly packed brown sugar
- 2 large eggs, lightly beaten
- 1½ cups (225 g) all-purpose (plain) flour
- ¾ cup (125 g) toasted muesli or granola
- 1½ teaspoons baking powder
- ¼ teaspoon salt

Tropical loaf

Serves: 6-8; Preparation: 30 minutes; Cooking: 50 minutes; Level of difficulty: 1

Preheat the oven to 350°F/180°C/gas 4. • Butter a 9 x 5-inch (23 x 13-cm) loaf pan. Line with aluminum foil, letting the edges overhang. Butter the foil. • Place the pineapple in a large bowl and stir in the egg. Stir in the flour, coconut, brown sugar, milk, baking powder, and salt. Stir in the walnuts. • Spoon the batter into the prepared pan. • Bake for about 45 minutes, or until a toothpick inserted into the center comes out clean. • Cool the loaf in the pan for 10 minutes. Using the foil as a lifter, remove the loaf from the pan. Carefully remove the foil and let cool completely on a rack.

■ INGREDIENTS

- ¾ cup (200 g) well-drained crushed canned pineapple (squeeze out excess liquid)
- 1 large egg, lightly beaten
- 1 cup (150 g) all-purpose (plain) flour
- 1 cup (120 g) shredded (desiccated) coconut
- ½ cup (100 g) firmly packed brown sugar
- ½ cup (125 ml) milk
- 1 teaspoon baking powder
- ¼ teaspoon salt
- 1 cup (100 g) toasted walnuts, finely chopped

Left: *Fig loaf*

Ginger and cinnamon loaf

Serves: 10-12; Preparation: 30 minutes; Cooking: 55 minutes; Level of difficulty: 1

Preheat the oven to 350°F/180°C/gas 4. • Butter two 9 x 5-inch (23 x 13-cm) loaf pans. Line with aluminum foil, letting the edges overhang. Butter the foil. • Melt the butter with the corn syrup in a large saucepan over low heat. • Add the brown sugar and stir until dissolved completely. Sift the flour, ginger, allspice, and cinnamon into a large bowl. • Mix the milk and baking soda in a small bowl. • Use a wooden spoon to stir the milk mixture and butter mixture into the dry ingredients. • Pour the batter into the prepared pan. • Bake for about 55 minutes, or until a toothpick inserted into the center comes out clean. • Cool the loaves in the pans for 10 minutes. Using the foil as a lifter, remove the loaves from the pans. Carefully remove the foil. • Spread lightly with butter and serve warm.

INGREDIENTS

- ½ cup (125 g) butter
- 1 cup (250 ml) light corn (golden) syrup
- 1 cup (200 g) brown sugar
- 2½ cups (375 g) all-purpose (plain) flour
- 1 teaspoon each ground ginger, allspice, and cinnamon
- 1 cup (250 ml) milk
- 1 teaspoon baking soda

Summer loaf

Serves: 6-8; Preparation: 30 minutes; Cooking: 40 minutes; Level of difficulty: 1

Preheat the oven to 350°F/180°C/gas 4. • Butter a 9 x 5-inch (23 x 13-cm) loaf pan. Line with aluminum foil, letting the edges overhang. Butter the foil. • Sift the flour, cornstarch, baking powder, baking soda, and salt into a medium bowl. • Purée the strawberries in a food processor until smooth. • Beat the butter, confectioners' sugar, and vanilla in a medium bowl with an electric mixer at medium speed until creamy. • Add the egg yolks, one at a time, until just blended after each addition. • With mixer at low speed, gradually beat in the dry ingredients, alternating with the puréed strawberries. • With mixer at high speed, beat the egg whites in a medium bowl until stiff peaks form. Use a large rubber spatula to fold them into the mixture. • Spoon the batter into the prepared pan. • Bake for about 40 minutes, or until a toothpick inserted into the center comes out clean. • Cool the loaf in the pan for 10 minutes. Using the foil as a lifter, remove the loaves from the pans. Carefully remove the foil and let cool completely.

INGREDIENTS

- 1⅓ cups (200 g) all-purpose (plain) flour
- ⅓ cup (50 g) cornstarch (cornflour)
- 1 teaspoon baking powder
- ½ teaspoon baking soda
- ¼ teaspoon salt
- 5 oz (150 g) sliced strawberries
- 6 tablespoons butter
- ½ cup (75 g) confectioners' (icing) sugar
- 1 teaspoon vanilla extract
- 2 large eggs, separated

Right: *Ginger and cinnamon loaf*

Quiches

☙

Quiches are a type of savory pie from northeastern France. Use our Never-Fail Crust (see page 16) or about 8 oz (250 g) of store-bought puff pastry as a base. Once you have learned the basic proportions, you will be able to vary the filling to create your own fabulous pies.

Mini quiches

Serves: 4-8; Preparation: 20 minutes + 15 minutes to chill the pastry; Cooking: 20 minutes; Level of difficulty: 1

Roll the pastry out on a floured work surface to ⅛ inch (3 mm) thick. • Butter eight 3-inch (8-cm) tartlet pans and line them with the pastry. • Sprinkle with the gruyère and refrigerate for 15 minutes. • Preheat the oven to 400°F/200°C/gas 6. • Sauté the onion in the butter in a small frying pan over low heat for 2–3 minutes, or until it begins to soften. • Add the bacon and sauté for 3 minutes. • Spoon the bacon and onion mixture evenly into the pastry cases. • Beat the egg, cream, parsley, and nutmeg in a large bowl. Season with pepper. • Pour the egg mixture into the pastry cases. • Bake for about 15 minutes, or until the pastry is golden brown and the filling has set. • Let cool slightly. • Serve warm.

■ INGREDIENTS

- 14 oz (400 g) fresh or frozen puff pastry, thawed if frozen
- ½ cup (60 g) freshly grated gruyère cheese
- 1 large onion, finely chopped
- 1 tablespoon butter
- 1 rasher of bacon, diced
- 1 large egg, lightly beaten
- 6 tablespoons heavy (double) cream
- 1 tablespoon finely chopped parsley
- ¼ teaspoon ground nutmeg
- freshly ground black pepper to taste

Cherry tomato quiche

Serves: 6-8; Preparation: 30 minutes + 30 minutes to chill the dough; Cooking: 45 minutes; Level of difficulty: 2

Prepare the quiche dough. • Shape into a ball and wrap in plastic wrap (cling film). Refrigerate for 30 minutes. • Preheat the oven to 350°F/180°C/gas 4. • Butter a 10-inch (25-cm) springform pan or pie plate. • Filling: Cut the cherry tomatoes in half and gently squeeze out as many seeds as possible. • Beat the eggs, cream, ricotta, and parmesan in a large bowl. Season with salt and pepper. • Stir in the basil and oregano. • Roll the pastry out on a lightly floured work surface to ¼-inch (5 mm) thick. • Line the prepared pan with the pastry. • Pour the egg and cheese mixture into the crust. • Add the tomatoes one by one, cut side down, pressing them into the filling slightly. • Bake for about 45 minutes, or until the pastry is golden brown and the filling has set. • Serve hot or at room temperature.

■ INGREDIENTS

- 1 quantity *Never-Fail Quiche Crust* (see page 16)

FILLING
- 15–20 cherry tomatoes
- 4 large eggs
- ½ cup (125 ml) cream
- ½ cup (125 g) ricotta cheese
- 6 tablespoons freshly grated parmesan cheese
- salt and freshly ground black pepper to taste
- 4–6 leaves fresh basil, finely chopped
- ½ teaspoon dried oregano

Right: *Cherry tomato quiche*

Zucchini flower quiche

- 1 quantity *Never-Fail Quiche Crust* (see page 16)

FILLING
- 25 zucchini (courgette) flowers, stamen and green part removed, and halved
- 2 tablespoons extra-virgin olive oil
- 5 large eggs
- 1 cup (250 ml) cream
- salt and freshly ground black pepper to taste
- 1¼ cups (150 g) freshly grated parmesan cheese
- 1¼ cups (150 g) freshly grated emmental cheese

Serves: 6-8; Preparation: 30 minutes + 30 minutes to chill the dough; Cooking: 30 minutes; Level of difficulty: 2

Prepare the quiche dough. • Shape into a ball and wrap in plastic wrap (cling film). Refrigerate for 30 minutes. • Preheat the oven to 350°F/ 180°C/gas 4. • Butter a 10-inch (25-cm) springform pan or pie plate. • Filling: Sauté the zucchini flowers in the oil in a small frying pan over medium heat for 2 minutes. Drain well on paper towels. • Beat the eggs and cream in a large bowl. Season with salt and pepper. • Roll the dough out on a lightly floured work surface to ¼ inch (5 mm) thick. • Line the prepared pan with the dough. • Sprinkle with the parmesan and emmental. • Add the zucchini flowers and pour the egg mixture over the top. • Bake for about 25 minutes, or until the pastry is golden brown and the filling has set. Let cool slightly. • Serve warm.

Tomato quiche with herbs

- 1 quantity *Never-Fail Quiche Crust* (see page 16)

FILLING
- 4 large tomatoes, peeled, seeded, and cubed
- 4 large eggs
- ⅔ cup (180 ml) milk
- salt and freshly ground black pepper to taste
- ⅔ cup (150 g) heavy (double) cream, whipped
- 1¼ cups (150 g) freshly grated gruyère cheese
- 2 cloves garlic, finely chopped
- 1 tablespoon finely chopped parsley
- 4 leaves basil, torn
- 1 tablespoon finely chopped thyme

Serves: 6-8; Preparation: 15 minutes + 1 hour to drain and chill the dough; Cooking: 40 minutes; Level of difficulty: 2

Prepare the quiche dough. • Shape into a ball and wrap in plastic wrap (cling film). Refrigerate for 30 minutes. • Drain the tomatoes in a colander for 30 minutes. • Preheat the oven to 400°F/200°C/gas 6. • Butter a 10-inch (25-cm) springform pan or pie plate. • Roll the pastry out on a lightly floured work surface to ¼-inch (5 mm) thick. • Line the prepared pan with the dough. • Filling: Beat the eggs and milk in a large bowl. Season with salt and pepper. • Stir in the tomatoes, cream, gruyère, garlic, parsley, basil, and thyme. • Pour the mixture into the crust. • Bake for about 40 minutes, or until the pastry is golden brown and the filling has set. • Serve hot or at room temperature.

Left: *Tomato quiche with herbs*

Borage quiche

Serves: 6-8; Preparation: 30 minutes; Cooking: 40 minutes; Level of difficulty: 1

Preheat the oven to 350°F/180°C/gas 4. • Butter a 10-inch (25-cm) springform pan or pie plate. • Sauté the shallots in the butter in a large frying pan for 2–3 minutes, or until they begin to soften. • Add the borage and sauté for 5 minutes. • Transfer to a food processor and add the ricotta and parmesan. Process until smooth. Season with salt and pepper. • Beat the eggs and egg yolks, milk, and cream in a large bowl. Add the borage purée and mix well. • Roll the pastry out on a lightly floured work surface to ⅛ inch (3 mm) thick. • Line the prepared pan with the pastry. Prick all over with a fork. • Add the pancetta and cover with the borage mixture. • Bake for about 30 minutes, or until the pastry is golden brown and the filling has set. • Serve warm.

INGREDIENTS

- 2 shallots, finely chopped
- 2 tablespoons butter
- 1¾ lb (800 g) borage or spinach leaves
- generous ⅓ cup (100 g) ricotta cheese
- 4 tablespoons freshly grated parmesan cheese
- salt and freshly ground black pepper to taste
- 3 large eggs
- 2 large egg yolks
- ¾ cup (200 ml) milk
- ¾ cup (200 ml) cream
- 1 lb (500 g) fresh or frozen puff pastry, frozen if thawed
- 1⅔ cups (200 g) diced pancetta

Arugula and emmental quiche

Serves: 6-8; Preparation: 30 minutes + 30 minutes to chill the dough; Cooking: 45 minutes; Level of difficulty: 2

Prepare the quiche dough. • Shape into a ball and wrap in plastic wrap (cling film). Refrigerate for 30 minutes. • Preheat the oven to 375°F/190°C/gas 5. • Butter a 10-inch (25-cm) springform pan or pie plate. • Roll the dough out on a lightly floured work surface to ¼ inch (5 mm) thick. • Line the prepared pan with the dough. • Filling: Sauté the onion in the oil in a large frying pan over medium heat until softened. • Add the arugula and sauté for 5–7 minutes, or until tender. • Spread the arugula mixture onto the crust. • Beat the cream, eggs, and emmental in a large bowl. Season with salt and pepper. • Pour the egg mixture into the crust. • Bake for about 35 minutes, or until the pastry is golden brown and the filling has set. • Serve warm.

INGREDIENTS

- 1 quantity *Never-Fail Quiche Crust* (see page 16)

FILLING
- 1 onion, finely chopped
- 1 tablespoon extra-virgin olive oil
- 8 oz (250 g) arugula (rocket)
- 1 cup (250 ml) heavy (double) cream
- 3 large eggs
- 1 cup (125 g) freshly grated emmental cheese
- salt and freshly ground black pepper to taste

Right: *Borage quiche*

Quiche Lorraine

Serves: 6-8; Preparation: 30 minutes + 1 hour to chill the pastry; Cooking: 50 minutes; Level of difficulty: 2

Pastry: Sift the flour and salt into a large bowl. • Use your fingertips to rub in the butter until the mixture resembles coarse crumbs. • Mix in enough water to make a smooth dough. Cover and refrigerate for 1 hour. • Preheat the oven to 350°F/180°C/gas 4. • Butter a 10-inch (25-cm) pie plate. • Sauté the shallots and pancetta in the oil in a small frying pan for 5 minutes. • Beat the eggs and egg yolks, cream, and milk in a large bowl. Season with salt and pepper. • Roll the pastry out on a lightly floured work surface to ¼ inch (5 mm) thick. • Line the prepared pan with the pastry. • Sprinkle with the emmental and the onion mixture. Pour in the egg mixture. • Bake for about 45 minutes, or until the pastry is golden brown and the filling has set. • Serve hot or at room temperature.

PASTRY
- 2 cups (300 g) all-purpose (plain) flour
- ⅛ teaspoon salt
- ¾ cup (200 g) butter, cut into pieces
- 5 tablespoons water

FILLING
- 2 shallots, finely chopped
- ¾ cup (100 g) diced pancetta
- 1 tablespoon extra-virgin olive oil
- 2 large eggs
- 2 large egg yolks
- ¾ cup (200 ml) cream
- ¾ cup (200 ml) milk
- salt and freshly ground black pepper to taste
- ½ cup (60 g) freshly grated emmental cheese

Broccoli and pancetta quiche

Serves: 6-8; Preparation: 40 minutes + 30 minutes to chill the dough; Cooking: 1 hour; Level of difficulty: 2

Prepare the quiche dough. • Shape into a ball and wrap in plastic wrap (cling film). Refrigerate for 30 minutes. • Preheat the oven to 350°F/180°C/gas 4. • Butter a 10-inch (25-cm) springform pan or pie plate. • Roll the dough out on a lightly floured surface to ¼ inch (5 mm) thick. • Line the prepared pan with the dough. • Filling: Cook the broccoli in salted, boiling water for 7–10 minutes, or until crunchy-tender. • Drain and set aside. • Sauté the pancetta in the oil in a large frying pan over medium heat until crispy. • Add the broccoli and sauté for 2 minutes. • Beat the eggs, milk, and emmental in a large bowl. Season with pepper. • Arrange the broccoli mixture in the crust. Pour over the egg mixture. • Bake for about 40 minutes, or until the pastry is golden brown and the filling has set. • Serve warm.

- 1 quantity *Never-Fail Quiche Crust* (see page 16)

FILLING
- 7 oz (200 g) broccoli florets
- 1 cup (120 g) diced pancetta
- 1 tablespoon extra-virgin olive oil
- 4 large eggs
- 1 cup (250 ml) milk
- 1½ cups (180 g) freshly grated emmental cheese
- salt and freshly ground black pepper to taste

Right: Quiche Lorraine

Pear and gorgonzola quiche

Serves: 4-6; Preparation: 15 minutes + 30 minutes to chill the dough; Cooking: 20 minutes; Level of difficulty: 2

Prepare the quiche dough. • Shape into a ball and wrap in plastic wrap (cling film). Refrigerate for 30 minutes. • Preheat the oven to 400°F/ 200°C/gas 6. • Butter an 8-inch (20-cm) springform pan or pie plate. • Roll the dough out on a lightly floured work surface to ¼ inch (5 mm) thick. • Line the prepared pan with the dough. • Filling: Beat the gorgonzola, ricotta, eggs, cream, and tarragon in a large bowl. Season with salt and pepper. • Add the chopped pears and mix well. • Spread the mixture in the crust. • Decorate with the remaining pears and drizzle with the butter. • Bake for about 20 minutes, or until the pastry is golden brown and the filling has set. • Let rest for 20 minutes before serving.

■ INGREDIENTS

- 1 quantity *Never-Fail Quiche Crust* (see page 16)

FILLING
- 2 oz (60 g) gorgonzola cheese, crumbled
- 4 tablespoons ricotta cheese
- 2 large eggs
- ½ cup (125 ml) cream
- 1 tablespoon chopped tarragon
- salt and freshly ground black pepper to taste
- 2 large pears, peeled and cored, 1 chopped and 1 sliced
- 1 tablespoon butter, melted

Easy asparagus quiche

Serves: 4-6; Preparation: 30 minutes + 30 minutes to chill the dough; Cooking: 45 minutes; Level of difficulty: 2

Prepare the quiche dough. • Shape into a ball and wrap in plastic wrap (cling film). Refrigerate for 30 minutes. • Preheat the oven to 375°F/ 190°C/gas 5. • Butter a 9-inch (23-cm) springform pan or pie plate. • Roll the dough out on a lightly floured work surface to ¼ inch (5 mm) thick. • Line the prepared pan with the dough. • Filling: Cook the asparagus in salted, boiling water for 5–7 minutes, or until crunchy-tender. • Drain and set aside. • Arrange the asparagus in the crust and sprinkle with the emmental. • Beat the eggs, sour cream, and milk in a large bowl. Season with salt and pepper. • Pour the egg mixture into the crust. • Bake for about 40 minutes, or until the pastry is golden brown and the filling has set. • Serve warm.

■ INGREDIENTS

- 1 quantity *Never-Fail Quiche Crust* (see page 16)

FILLING
- 8 oz (250 g) asparagus tips, cut into short lengths
- ½ cup (60 g) freshly grated emmental cheese
- 6 large eggs
- ½ cup (125 ml) sour cream
- 1 cup (250 ml) milk
- salt and freshly ground white pepper to taste

Right: *Pear and gorgonzola quiche*

Mushroom and bacon quiche

Serves: 6-8; Preparation: 30 minutes + 30 minutes to chill the dough; Cooking: 50 minutes; Level of difficulty: 2

Prepare the quiche dough. • Shape into a ball and wrap in plastic wrap (cling film). Refrigerate for 30 minutes. • Preheat the oven to 350°F/ 180°C/gas 4. • Butter a 10-inch (25-cm) springform pan or pie plate. • Roll the dough out on a lightly floured work surface to ¼ inch (5 mm) thick. • Line the prepared pan with the dough. • Filling: Sauté the bacon and onion in the oil in a small frying pan over medium heat until crispy. • Add the mushrooms and cook until tender. • Beat the eggs, milk, and emmental in a large bowl. • Arrange the bacon and mushroom mixture in the crust. Pour in the egg mixture. • Bake for about 35 minutes, or until golden brown and set. • Serve warm.

INGREDIENTS

- 1 quantity *Never-Fail Quiche Crust* (see page 16)

FILLING
- 2 cups (250 g) diced bacon
- 1 small onion, finely chopped
- 1 tablespoon olive oil
- 4 oz (125 g) mushrooms, thinly sliced
- 3 large eggs
- 1 cup (250 ml) milk
- 1½ cups (180 g) freshly grated emmental cheese

Potato and tomato quiche

Serves: 6-8; Preparation: 30 minutes; Cooking: 45 minutes; Level of difficulty: 1

Preheat the oven to 400°F/200°C/gas 6. • Butter an 8-inch (20-cm) springform pan or pie plate. • Peel the potatoes and cut into ¼-inch (5-mm) slices. Steam the potato slices for 15 minutes, or until tender. • Beat the eggs, cream, parmesan, and oregano in a large bowl. Season with salt and pepper. • Roll the pastry out on a lightly floured work surface to ⅛ inch (3 mm) thick. • Line the prepared pan with the pastry. Arrange the potatoes and tomato in the pastry base. • Pour in the egg mixture. • Bake for 15 minutes. • Lower the oven temperature to 350°F/180°C/gas 4. • Bake for 15 minutes more, or until the pastry is golden brown and the filling has set. • Let cool completely.

■ INGREDIENTS

- 2 potatoes
- 2 large eggs
- ½ cup (125 ml) heavy (double) cream
- 1 tablespoon freshly grated parmesan cheese
- ½ teaspoon dried oregano
- salt and freshly ground black pepper to taste
- 8 oz (250 g) fresh or frozen puff pastry, thawed if frozen
- 1 large firm-ripe tomato, thinly sliced

Spinach quiche

Serves: 6-8; Preparation: 30 minutes + 30 minutes to chill the pastry; Cooking: 45 minutes; Level of difficulty: 2

Prepare the quiche dough. • Shape into a ball and wrap in plastic wrap (cling film). Refrigerate for 30 minutes. • Preheat the oven to 375°F/190°C/gas 5. • Butter a 10-inch (25-cm) springform pan or pie plate. • Roll the dough out on a lightly floured surface to ¼ inch (5 mm) thick. • Line the prepared pan with the dough. • Filling: Cook the spinach with just the water clinging to the leaves in a large saucepan for 5–7 minutes, or until wilted. • Shred the spinach finely. • Sauté the garlic in the oil in a large frying pan until pale gold. • Add the spinach and sauté for 1 minute. • Beat the eggs, cream, and cheese in a large bowl. Season with salt and pepper. • Arrange the spinach in the crust and pour in the egg mixture. • Bake for about 35 minutes, or until the pastry is golden brown and the filling has set. • Serve warm.

■ INGREDIENTS

- 1 quantity *Never-Fail Quiche Crust* (see page 16)

FILLING
- 7 oz (200 g) spinach, tough stalks removed and washed
- 1 clove garlic, finely chopped
- 2 tablespoons extra-virgin olive oil
- 3 large eggs
- 1½ cups (375 ml) heavy (double) cream
- 6 tablespoons soft creamy cheese
- salt and freshly ground black pepper to taste

Right: *Potato and tomato quiche*

Mustard and ginger quiche

■ INGREDIENTS

- 4 leeks, white parts only, finely chopped
- 2 shallots, finely chopped
- 2 tablespoons extra-virgin olive oil
- 1 teaspoon thinly sliced fresh ginger root
- 1 tablespoon hot mustard
- 1 tablespoon finely chopped parsley
- 12 oz (300 g) fresh or frozen puff pastry, thawed if frozen
- ½ cup (60 g) fine dry bread crumbs
- 6 oz (180 g) emmental cheese, thinly sliced
- 4 large eggs
- salt and freshly ground black pepper to taste
- 2 tablespoons sesame seeds, toasted

Serves: 6-8; Preparation: 30 minutes; Cooking: 45 minutes; Level of difficulty: 1

Butter a 10-inch (25-cm) springform pan or pie plate. • Sauté the leeks and shallots in the oil in a large frying pan until lightly browned. • Add the ginger and cook over low heat for 10 minutes. • Add the mustard and parsley. • Roll the pastry out on a lightly floured work surface to ⅛ inch (3 mm) thick. Line the prepared pan with the pastry. • Sprinkle with the bread crumbs. Spread the sautéed mixture over the pastry case and top with the emmental. • Beat the eggs in a large bowl and season with salt and pepper. Pour into the pastry case. Sprinkle with the sesame seeds. • Bake for about 30 minutes, or until the pastry is golden brown and the filling has set. • Serve warm.

Artichoke and gruyère quiche

■ INGREDIENTS

- 1 quantity *Never-Fail Quiche Crust* (see page 16)

FILLING
- 7 oz (200 g) artichoke hearts
- 1 tablespoon butter
- 6 large eggs
- 2 cups (500 ml) cream
- 1 cup (125 g) freshly grated gruyère cheese
- salt and freshly ground black pepper to taste

Serves: 6-8; Preparation: 30 minutes + 30 minutes to chill the dough; Cooking: 40 minutes; Level of difficulty: 2

Prepare the quiche dough. • Shape into a ball and wrap in plastic wrap (cling film). Refrigerate for 30 minutes. • Preheat the oven to 325°F/170°C/gas 3. • Butter a 10-inch (25-cm) springform pan or pie plate. • Roll the dough out on a lightly floured work surface to ¼ inch (5 mm) thick. • Line the prepared pan with the dough. • Filling: Sauté the artichokes in the butter in a large frying pan over medium heat for about 10 minutes, or until tender. • Beat the eggs, cream, and gruyère in a large bowl. Season with salt and pepper. • Arrange the artichokes in the crust and pour in the egg mixture. • Bake for about 30 minutes, or until the pastry is golden brown and the filling has set. • Serve warm.

Left: *Mustard and ginger quiche*

Zucchini and ham pie

Serves: 4-6; Preparation: 30 minutes; Cooking: 50 minutes; Level of difficulty: 1

Sauté the garlic in the oil in a large frying pan until pale gold. • Discard the garlic. Add the zucchini and crumble in the stock cube. Cook over low heat for 1 minute. • Pour in the milk and cook over medium heat for 5 minutes, or until the zucchini are tender and the milk has been absorbed. • Add the potato and cream. • Preheat the oven to 350°F/180°C/gas 4. • Butter a 9-inch (23-cm) springform pan or pie plate. • Roll the pastry out on a lightly floured work surface to ⅛ inch (3 mm) thick. Line the prepared pan with the pastry. • Arrange the ham in the pastry case and top with the zucchini mixture. Add the asiago. • Cut out decorative shapes from the remaining pastry and arrange them on top of the pie. • Bake for about 35 minutes, or until the pastry is golden brown and the filling has set. • Serve warm.

- 1 clove garlic, lightly crushed but whole
- 2 tablespoons extra-virgin olive oil
- 2 zucchini (courgettes), coarsely grated
- ½ vegetable bouillon cube
- 4 tablespoons milk
- 1 boiled potato, cubed
- 3 tablespoons heavy (double) cream
- 8 oz (250 g) fresh or frozen puff pastry, thawed if frozen
- 4 slices of ham
- 1 oz (30 g) asiago or cheddar cheese, cut in small cubes

Tuna mayonnaise quiche

Serves: 4-6; Preparation: 30 minutes + 30 minutes to chill the dough; Cooking: 45-50 minutes; Level of difficulty: 2

Prepare the quiche dough. • Shape into a ball and wrap in plastic wrap (cling film). Refrigerate for 30 minutes. • Preheat the oven to 375°F/190°C/gas 5. • Butter a 9-inch (23-cm) springform pan. • Roll the dough out on a lightly floured work surface to ¼ inch (5 mm) thick. • Line the prepared pan with the dough. • Filling: Beat the tuna, cheese, eggs, and cream in a large bowl. Season with salt and pepper. • Pour the mixture into the crust. • Bake for about 45 minutes, or until the pastry is golden brown and the filling has set. • Serve at room temperature.

- 1 quantity *Never-Fail Quiche Crust* (see page 16)

FILLING
- 12 oz (300 g) canned tuna, drained and flaked
- 1 cup (250 ml) soft creamy cheese
- 3 large eggs
- 2 cups (500 ml) cream
- salt and freshly ground white pepper to taste

Right: *Zucchini and ham pie*

Onion quiche

Serves: 4-6; Preparation: 30 minutes; Cooking: 35 minutes; Level of difficulty: 1

Preheat the oven to 350°F/180°C/gas 4. • Roll the pastry out on a lightly floured work surface to ⅛ inch (3 mm) thick. • Line a 10-inch (25-cm) springform pan or pie plate with the pastry. • Sauté the onions in the oil in a large frying pan over medium heat until softened. • Beat the eggs, cream, and emmental in a large bowl. Season with salt and pepper. • Add the onions and mix well. • Pour the onion mixture into the pastry case. • Bake for 15 minutes. • Increase the oven temperature to 400°F/ 200°C/gas 6. • Bake for about 15 minutes more, or until the pastry is golden brown and the filling has set. • Serve warm or at room temperature.

■ INGREDIENTS

• 8 oz (250 g) puff pastry, thawed if frozen

• 12 onions, thinly sliced

• 2 tablespoons extra-virgin olive oil

• 5 large eggs

• 1 cup (250 ml) heavy (double) cream

• 1¾ cups (215 g) freshly grated emmental cheese

• salt and freshly ground black pepper to taste

Ligurian pesto quiche

Serves: 4-6; Preparation: 30 minutes + 30 minutes to chill the dough; Cooking: 45 minutes; Level of difficulty: 2

Prepare the quiche dough. • Shape into a ball and wrap in plastic wrap (cling film). Refrigerate for 30 minutes. • Preheat the oven to 375°F/ 190°C/gas 5. • Butter a 9-inch (23-cm) springform pan or pie plate. • Roll the dough out on a lightly floured work surface to ¼ inch (5 mm) thick. • Line the prepared pan with the dough. • Sauté the zucchini in the butter in a large frying pan until golden and slightly softened. • Arrange the zucchini, pesto, and parmesan in the crust. • Beat the eggs and cream in a large bowl. Season with salt and pepper. Pour the egg mixture into the crust. • Bake for about 35 minutes, or until the pastry is golden brown and the filling has set. • Serve hot.

■ INGREDIENTS

• 1 quantity *Never-Fail Quiche Crust* (see page 16)

FILLING
• 3 zucchini (courgettes), thinly sliced

• 2 tablespoons butter

• 2 tablespoons pesto

• 2 cups (250 g) freshly grated parmesan cheese

• 3 large eggs

• 1 cup (250 ml) cream

• salt and freshly ground black pepper to taste

Right: *Onion quiche*

Pizze and Focacce

☙

Quintessentially Italian, pizze and focacce are actually quite similar. They both have leavened, bread-like bases with varying amounts of topping. Most of the recipes in this chapter will make one 12-inch (30-cm) pizza or focaccia; enough for 2 people as a meal or for 4 as a snack.

Focaccine with herbs

Vary the herbs in these little focacce according to taste or season. Serve them at room temperature as a snack (drizzled with a little extra olive oil), or piping hot as a starter to accompany fresh cheeses and salad.

Serves: 3-6; Preparation: 30 minutes + 1 hour 30 minutes to rise; Cooking: 15 minutes; Level of difficulty: 1

Prepare the dough following the instructions on page 20. Knead and set aside in a warm place to rise for 1 hour, or until doubled in bulk. • Oil a large baking sheet. • Place the risen dough on a lightly floured work surface. Knead briefly and shape into a ball. Break into 6 equal size pieces of dough. Shape into small balls and place, well spaced, on the prepared baking sheet. Spread a little with your hands. • Sprinkle each little focaccia with herbs and salt. Drizzle with the oil and let rise for 30 more minutes. • Preheat the oven to 400°F/200°C/gas 6. • Bake for about 15 minutes, or until pale golden brown. • Serve hot or at room temperature.

■ INGREDIENTS

- 1 quantity *Basic Pizza or Focaccia Dough* (see page 20)
- 4 tablespoons finely chopped parsley
- 2 tablespoons finely chopped basil
- 1 tablespoon finely chopped marjoram or thyme
- 1 teaspoon finely chopped rosemary
- 1–2 teaspoons coarse sea salt
- 3–4 tablespoons extra-virgin olive oil

Mediterranean mini focacce

Serves: 2-4; Preparation: 30 minutes + 1 hour 30 minutes to rise; Cooking: 15 minutes; Level of difficulty: 1

Prepare the dough following the instructions on page 20. Knead and set aside in a warm place to rise for 1 hour, or until doubled in bulk. • Oil a large baking sheet. • Place the risen dough on a lightly floured work surface. Knead briefly and shape into a ball. Break into 6 equal size pieces of dough. Shape into small balls and place, well spaced, on the prepared baking sheet. Spread a little with your hands. • Place the tomatoes, capers, garlic, if using, oregano, salt, and pepper in a medium bowl. Mix well. • Spoon a little of the tomato topping over each piece of dough. Drizzle with the oil and let rise for 30 more minutes. • Preheat the oven to 400°F/ 200°C/gas 6. • Bake for about 15 minutes, or until pale golden brown. • Serve hot.

■ INGREDIENTS

- 1 quantity *Basic Pizza or Focaccia Dough* (see page 20)
- 14 oz (400 g) canned tomatoes, drained and chopped
- 1 tablespoon salted capers, rinsed
- 1 clove garlic, finely chopped (optional)
- ½ teaspoon dried oregano
- salt and freshly ground black pepper to taste
- 3–4 tablespoons extra-virgin olive oil

Right: Focaccine with herbs

Onion focaccia with sage

Serves: 2-4; Preparation: 30 minutes + 1 hour to rest the onions + 1 hour 30 minutes to rise; Cooking: 35 minutes; Level of difficulty: 2

Prepare the dough following the instructions on page 20. Knead and set aside in a warm place to rise for 1 hour, or until doubled in bulk. • Spread the onions out on a baking sheet, sprinkle with salt, and let rest for 1 hour. • Rinse and drain well. • Oil a 10 x 15-inch (25 x 38-cm) jelly-roll pan. • Place the risen dough in the pan and use your fingertips to spread it evenly over the bottom. • Top with the onions and sage leaves. Drizzle with the oil and season with salt. • Let rise for 30 minutes more. • Preheat the oven to 400°F/200°C/gas 6. • Bake for about 25 minutes, or until golden brown. • Serve hot.

INGREDIENTS

- 1 quantity *Basic Pizza or Focaccia Dough* (see page 20)
- 3 large white onions, thinly sliced
- ½ teaspoon salt
- 15 leaves fresh sage
- 6 tablespoons extra-virgin olive oil

Quick and easy mini pizzas

Serves: 4-6; Preparation: 30 minutes + 1 hour 30 minutes to rise; Cooking: 15 minutes; Level of difficulty: 2

Prepare the dough following the instructions on page 20. Knead and set aside in a warm place to rise for 1 hour, or until doubled in bulk. • Oil a 10 x 15-inch (25 x 38-cm) jelly-roll pan. • Place the risen dough on a lightly floured work surface. Knead briefly and shape into a ball. Break into about 12 equal size pieces of dough. Shape into small balls and place, well spaced, on the prepared baking sheet. Spread a little with your hands. • Top with a teaspoon of tomato, a piece of mozzarella, capers, garlic, and basil. Season with salt, pepper, and oregano. • Let rise for 30 more minutes. • Preheat the oven to 400°F/200°C/gas 6. • Bake for about 15 minutes, or until golden brown. • Transfer to a serving dish and garnish with the tomato. • Serve hot or at room temperature.

INGREDIENTS

- 1 quantity *Basic Pizza or Focaccia Dough* (see page 20)
- 2 large tomatoes, chopped
- 5 oz (150 g) mozzarella cheese, cubed
- 1 tablespoon salted capers, rinsed and drained
- 2 cloves garlic, finely sliced
- leaves from 2 sprigs of basil, torn
- salt and freshly ground black pepper to taste
- 2 teaspoons chopped oregano
- 1 large tomato, sliced, to garnish

Right: Onion focaccia with sage

Walnut and onion focaccia

Serves: 2-4; Preparation: 30 minutes + 1 hour 30 minutes to rise; Cooking: 35 minutes; Level of difficulty: 2

Prepare the dough following the instructions on page 20. Knead and set aside in a warm place to rise for 1 hour, or until doubled in bulk. • Oil a 10 x 15-inch (25 x 38-cm) jelly-roll pan. • Place the risen dough in the pan and use your fingertips to spread it evenly over the bottom. • Heat the oil with the rosemary in a small saucepan over low heat for 3 minutes. Remove from the heat and let cool. • Sauté the onions in the butter in a large frying pan over medium heat for 5–10 minutes, or until soft and golden. Season with salt and pepper. • Spread the onions over the surface of the dough. Sprinkle with the gorgonzola and walnuts. Drizzle with the rosemary oil and let rise for 30 more minutes. • Preheat the oven to 400°F/200°C/gas 6. • Bake for about 20 minutes, or until golden brown. • Serve hot.

■ INGREDIENTS

• 1 quantity *Basic Pizza or Focaccia Dough* (see page 20)
• 3 tablespoons extra-virgin olive oil
• leaves from 1 sprig rosemary
• 1¾ lb (800 g) onions, thinly sliced
• 4 tablespoons butter
• salt and freshly ground black pepper to taste
• 7 oz (200 g) gorgonzola cheese, crumbled
• ¾ cup (75 g) chopped walnuts, toasted

Bell pepper and pine nut focaccia

Serves: 2-4; Preparation: 30 minutes + 1 hour 30 minutes to rise; Cooking: 45 minutes; Level of difficulty: 2

Prepare the dough following the instructions on page 20. Work in the olive paste. Knead and set aside in a warm place to rise for 1 hour, or until doubled in bulk. • Preheat the oven to 400°F/200°C/gas 6. • Roast the bell peppers on a large baking sheet for 30 minutes, or until blackened all over. Wrap in brown paper for 10 minutes, then peel off the skins. Rinse the flesh, dry well, and cut into thin strips. • Oil a baking sheet. • Place the risen dough on a lightly floured work surface. Divide into four pieces. Use your fingertips to spread each piece out into an oval shape about ½ inch (1 cm) thick. Place, well spaced, on the prepared baking sheet. • Arrange the bell peppers, olives, and pine nuts on top. Drizzle with the oil and season with salt and pepper. • Let rise for 30 more minutes. • Bake for about 15 minutes, or until golden brown. • Serve hot.

■ INGREDIENTS

• 1 quantity *Basic Pizza or Focaccia Dough* (see page 20)
• 2 tablespoons olive paste
• ½ red bell pepper (capsicum), seeded
• ½ yellow bell pepper, seeded
• ½ green bell pepper, seeded
• 12 black olives
• 2 tablespoons pine nuts
• 4 tablespoons extra-virgin olive oil
• salt and freshly ground black pepper to taste

Right: Walnut and onion focaccia

Focaccia with prosciutto, tomatoes, and parmesan

Serves: 2-4; Preparation: 20 minutes + 1 hour 30 minutes to rise; Cooking: 15 minutes; Level of difficulty: 2

Prepare the dough following the instructions on page 20. Knead and set aside in a warm place to rise for 1 hour, or until doubled in bulk. • Oil a 12-inch (30-cm) pizza pan. • Place the risen dough in the pan and use your fingertips to spread it evenly over the bottom. Let rise for 30 more minutes. • Preheat the oven to 400°F/200°C/gas 6. • Bake for about 15 minutes, or until golden brown. • Remove from the oven and top with the prosciutto, arugula, parmesan, and tomatoes. • Cut into wedges and serve hot.

■ INGREDIENTS

- 1 quantity *Basic Pizza or Focaccia Dough* (see page 20)
- 4 oz (125 g) sliced prosciutto (Parma ham)
- 4 oz (125 g) arugula (rocket), coarsely chopped
- 3 oz (90 g) parmesan cheese, cut into flakes
- 12 cherry tomatoes, quartered

Garbanzo bean focaccia with spinach and scallions

Serves: 4-6; Preparation: 30 minutes + 3 hours to rest the batter; Cooking: 40 minutes; Level of difficulty: 2

Sift the flour into a large bowl. • Gradually pour in the water, whisking constantly to prevent any lumps from forming. Season with salt and let the batter rest at room temperature for 3 hours. • Preheat the oven to 425°F/220°C/gas 7. • Oil a 10 x 15-inch (25 x 38-cm) jelly-roll pan. • Pour the batter into the prepared pan. • Top with the scallions and drizzle with ½ cup (125 ml) of oil. Season with pepper. • Bake for about 30 minutes, or until set and golden. • Sauté the onion in the remaining oil in a frying pan until softened. • Add the spinach and cover and cook over medium heat until wilted. Season with salt and pepper. • Top the focaccia with the spinach mixture and serve hot.

■ INGREDIENTS

- 3⅓ cups (500 g) garbanzo bean (chickpea) flour
- 1½ quarts (1.5 liters) water
- salt and freshly ground black pepper to taste
- 5 scallions (spring onions), thinly sliced
- ⅔ cup (180 ml) extra-virgin olive oil
- 2 lb (1 kg) spinach, tough stalks removed and shredded
- ½ onion, finely chopped

Right: Focaccia with prosciutto, tomatoes, and parmesan

Focaccia with tomatoes and olives

Serves: 2-4; Preparation: 20 minutes + 1 hour 30 minutes to rise; Cooking: 20 minutes; Level of difficulty: 2

Prepare the dough following the instructions on page 20. Knead and set aside in a warm place to rise for 1 hour, or until doubled in bulk. • Oil a 12-inch (30-cm) pizza pan. • Place the risen dough in the pan and use your fingertips to spread it evenly over the bottom. • Spread the tomatoes over the surface of the dough. Sprinkle with the olives, capers, and oregano. Let rise for 30 more minutes. • Preheat the oven to 400°F/200°C/gas 6. • Drizzle with the oil and bake for about 20 minutes. • Serve hot.

■ INGREDIENTS

- 1 quantity *Basic Pizza or Focaccia Dough* (see page 20)
- 14 oz (400 g) canned tomatoes, drained and chopped
- 1 cup (100 g) pitted black olives
- 1 tablespoon capers, rinsed and drained
- leaves from 1 sprig oregano, chopped
- 2 tablespoons extra-virgin olive oil

Mozzarella and cherry tomato pizza

Serves: 2-4; Preparation: 30 minutes + 1 hour 30 minutes to rise; Cooking: 20 minutes; Level of difficulty: 2

Prepare the dough following the instructions on page 20. Knead and set aside in a warm place to rise for 1 hour, or until doubled in bulk. • Oil a 12-inch (30-cm) pizza pan. • Place the risen dough in the pan and use your fingertips to spread it evenly over the bottom. • Arrange the cherry tomatoes and basil on top of the dough and season with salt and pepper. Sprinkle with the mozzarella and parmesan. • Drizzle with the oil. Let rise for 30 more minutes. • Preheat the oven to 450°F/225°C/gas 7. • Bake for about 20 minutes, or until golden brown. • Serve hot or at room temperature.

■ INGREDIENTS

- 1 quantity *Basic Pizza or Focaccia Dough* (see page 20)
- 20–25 cherry tomatoes, halved
- 1 small bunch basil, torn
- salt and freshly ground black pepper to taste
- 14 oz (400 g) mozzarella cheese, cut into cubes
- 3 tablespoons freshly grated parmesan cheese
- 4 tablespoons extra-virgin olive oil

Right: *Focaccia with tomatoes and olives*

Focaccia with tomatoes, anchovies, and olives

INGREDIENTS

- 1 quantity *Basic Pizza or Focaccia Dough* (see page 20)
- 2 tablespoons anchovy paste
- 2 lb (1 kg) onions, finely sliced
- 8 salted anchovy fillets, rinsed
- 6-8 cherry tomatoes, thinly sliced
- 1 cup (100 g) pitted black olives
- 6 tablespoons extra-virgin olive oil
- salt to taste

Serves: 2-4; Preparation: 30 minutes + 1 hour 30 minutes to rise; Cooking: 20 minutes; Level of difficulty: 2

Prepare the dough following the instructions on page 20. Knead and set aside in a warm place to rise for 1 hour, or until doubled in bulk. • Oil a 10 x 15-inch (25 x 38-cm) jelly-roll pan. • Place the risen dough in the pan and use your fingertips to spread it evenly over the bottom. • Spread the anchovy paste over the dough. Top with the onions, anchovies, tomatoes, and olives. Drizzle with the oil and season with salt; do not salt too much as the anchovies are already quite salty. • Let rise for 30 more minutes. • Preheat the oven to 400°F/200°C/gas 6. • Bake for about 20 minutes, or until golden brown. • Serve hot or at room temperature.

Sausage and olive pizza

INGREDIENTS

- 1 quantity *Basic Pizza or Focaccia Dough* (see page 20)
- 14 oz (400 g) canned tomatoes, drained and chopped
- ¼ teaspoon dried basil
- 10 oz (300 g) mozzarella cheese
- 5 oz (150 g) Italian sausage meat, crumbled
- 1 cup (100 g) green and black olives, pitted
- ⅛ teaspoon dried oregano
- salt to taste
- 2 tablespoons extra-virgin olive oil

Serves: 2-4; Preparation: 30 minutes + 1 hour 30 minutes to rise; Cooking: 15 minutes; Level of difficulty: 2

Prepare the dough following the instructions on page 20. Knead and set aside in a warm place to rise for 1 hour, or until doubled in bulk. • Oil a 10 x 15-inch (25 x 38-cm) jelly-roll pan. • Place the risen dough in the pan and use your fingertips to spread it evenly over the bottom. • Spread the tomatoes over the dough and season with the basil. Sprinkle with the mozzarella, sausage meat, olives, and oregano. Season with salt and pepper. • Drizzle with the oil and let rise for 30 more minutes. • Preheat the oven to 450°F/225°C/gas 7. • Bake for about 15 minutes, or until golden brown. • Serve hot.

Left: *Focaccia with tomatoes, anchovies, and olives*

Focaccia with green olives, mint, and fennel

Serves: 2-4; Preparation: 10 minutes + 1 hour 30 minutes to rise; Cooking: 25 minutes; Level of difficulty: 1

Prepare the dough following the instructions on page 20. Knead and set aside in a warm place to rise for 1 hour, or until doubled in bulk. • Oil a 10 x 15-inch (25 x 38-cm) jelly-roll pan. • Place the risen dough in the pan and use your fingertips to spread it evenly over the bottom. • Sprinkle with the olives, garlic, mint, fennel seeds, red pepper flakes, and salt. Drizzle with the oil and let rise for 30 more minutes. • Preheat the oven to 400°F/200°C/gas 6. • Bake for about 25 minutes, or until golden brown. • Serve hot.

■ INGREDIENTS

- 1 quantity *Basic Pizza or Focaccia Dough* (see page 20)
- 3 cups (300 g) green olives, pitted and quartered
- 3 cloves garlic, finely sliced
- 3 mint leaves, finely chopped
- 2 tablespoons fennel seeds
- ⅛ teaspoon red pepper flakes
- 1 teaspoon salt
- 3-4 tablespoons extra-virgin olive oil

Cherry tomato and potato focaccia

Serves: 2-4; Preparation: 30 minutes + 90 minutes to prove the dough; Cooking: 30 minutes; Level of difficulty: 2

Boil the potato in salted, boiling water for 10–15 minutes, or until tender. Drain and transfer to a large bowl. Use a fork to mash the potato with 2 tablespoons of oil. • Prepare the dough following the instructions on page 20. Work the potato into the dough. Knead and set aside in a warm place to rise for 1 hour, or until doubled in bulk. • Oil a 12-inch (30-cm) pizza pan. • Place the risen dough in the pan and use your fingertips to spread it evenly over the bottom. • Top with the cherry tomatoes, pushing them into the dough. Sprinkle with the sea salt and oregano. • Drizzle with the remaining oil and let rise for 30 more minutes. • Preheat the oven to 425°F/220°C/gas 7. • Bake for about 30 minutes, or until golden brown. • Serve hot or at room temperature.

■ INGREDIENTS

- 1 large potato, cut into cubes
- 4 tablespoons extra-virgin olive oil
- 1 quantity *Basic Pizza or Focaccia Dough* (see page 20)
- 10 oz (300 g) cherry tomatoes, halved
- 1 tablespoon coarse sea salt
- 2 sprigs fresh oregano

Right: *Focaccia with green olives, mint, and fennel*

Focaccia with summer vegetables

Serves: 2–4; Preparation: 35 minutes + 1 hour 30 minutes to rise; Cooking: 35 minutes; Level of difficulty: 2

Prepare the dough following the instructions on page 20. Knead and set aside in a warm place to rise for 1 hour, or until doubled in bulk. • Oil a 12-inch (30-cm) pizza pan. • Place the risen dough in the pan and use your fingertips to spread it evenly over the bottom. • Let rise for 30 more minutes. • Preheat the oven to 400°F/200°C/gas 4. • Slice the tomatoes, remove the seeds, and sprinkle with salt. Let drain in a colander for 10 minutes to remove any excess water. • Rinse and pat dry with paper towels. • Sauté the garlic and zucchini in 2 tablespoons of oil in a large frying pan for 5 minutes. Season with salt. • Top the dough with the zucchini, garlic, bell peppers, and tomatoes. Season with salt and pepper. Drizzle with the remaining oil. • Bake for about 15 minutes. • Sprinkle with the olives, capers, basil, and parmesan. • Bake for 10 minutes more or until golden brown. • Serve hot.

■ INGREDIENTS

- 1 quantity *Basic Pizza or Focaccia Dough* (see page 20)
- 2 large ripe tomatoes
- salt and freshly ground black pepper to taste
- 1 clove garlic, lightly crushed
- 2 large zucchini/courgettes, sliced
- 6 tablespoons extra-virgin olive oil
- 1 large red bell pepper (capsicum), seeded and sliced
- 1 large yellow bell pepper, seeded and sliced
- ½ cup (50 g) black olives, pitted and halved
- 1 tablespoon capers, rinsed and drained
- leaves from 2 sprigs basil, torn
- 4 oz (125 g) parmesan cheese, cut into flakes

Pizza with mussels and olives

Serves: 2–4; Preparation: 35 minutes + 1 hour 30 minutes to rise + 1 hour to purge the mussels; Cooking: 35 minutes; Level of difficulty: 2

Prepare the dough following the instructions on page 20. Knead and set aside in a warm place to rise for 1 hour, or until doubled in bulk. • Oil a 12-inch (30-cm) pizza pan. • Place the risen dough in the pan and use your fingertips to spread it evenly over the bottom. • Spread the tomatoes over the dough. Season with oregano and salt and pepper. Drizzle with the oil and let rise for 30 more minutes. • Soak the mussels in a bowl of warm water for 1 hour. This will remove any grit. • Preheat the oven to 400°F/200°C/gas 4. • Bake the pizza for 25 minutes. • Drain the mussels and remove any beards or barnacles. • Cook the mussels with the garlic in a large saucepan over high heat for 7–10 minutes, or until they open up. Remove the mollusks from the shells. • Remove the pizza from the oven and top with the mussels and olives. • Bake for 5 minutes more. • Add the basil and serve hot.

■ INGREDIENTS

- 1 quantity *Basic Pizza or Focaccia Dough* (see page 20)
- 10 oz (300 g) canned tomatoes, chopped
- ¼ teaspoon dried oregano
- salt and freshly ground black pepper to taste
- 2 tablespoons extra-virgin olive oil
- 1 lb (500 g) mussels
- 1 clove garlic, lightly crushed but whole
- 12 green olives, pitted
- 1 small bunch basil, torn

Right: *Focaccia with summer vegetables*

Focaccia with bell peppers and eggplant

INGREDIENTS

- 1 quantity *Basic Pizza or Focaccia Dough* (see page 20)
- 1 large eggplant/ aubergine, thinly sliced
- 1 large red bell pepper/ capsicum, thinly sliced
- 1 large yellow bell pepper, thinly sliced
- 1 tablespoon capers, rinsed and drained
- 1 cup (100 g) black olives, pitted and quartered
- 2 anchovy fillets, chopped
- 2 cloves garlic, finely chopped
- 1 fresh red chile pepper, seeded and sliced
- 4 tablespoons extra-virgin olive oil
- salt and freshly ground black pepper to taste
- leaves from 1 sprig basil, torn

Serves: 2-4; Preparation: 15 minutes + 1 hour 30 minutes to rise; Cooking: 30 minutes; Level of difficulty: 1

Prepare the dough following the instructions on page 20. Knead and set aside in a warm place to rise for 1 hour, or until doubled in bulk. • Oil a 12-inch (30-cm) pizza pan. • Place the risen dough in the pan and use your fingertips to spread it evenly on the bottom. • Arrange a layer of the eggplant and bell peppers on top of the dough. Sprinkle with capers, olives, anchovies, garlic, and chile pepper. Drizzle with the oil and season with salt and pepper. • Let rise for 30 more minutes. • Preheat the oven to 400°F/200°C/gas 6. • Bake for about 30 minutes, until browned. • Sprinkle with the basil and serve hot.

Potato and leek focacce

INGREDIENTS

- 1 quantity *Basic Pizza or Focaccia Dough* (see page 20)
- 1 leek, white part only, shredded
- 7 oz (200 g) potatoes, cut into cubes
- 2 tablespoons extra-virgin olive oil
- salt and freshly ground black pepper to taste
- 6 green olives, pitted and finely chopped

Serves: 2-4; Preparation: 30 minutes + 1 hour 30 minutes to rise; Cooking: 25 minutes; Level of difficulty: 2

Prepare the dough following the instructions on page 20. Knead and set aside in a warm place to rise for 1 hour, or until doubled in bulk. • Oil a large baking sheet. • Place the risen dough on a lightly floured work surface. Use your fingertips to spread it out to about ¼ inch (5 mm) thick. Cut into disks using a large cookie cutter or glass. Reroll the remaining dough and cut into disks too. Place, well spaced, on the prepared baking sheet. • Sauté the leek and potatoes in the oil in a large frying pan over medium heat until lightly golden. Season with salt and pepper. • Arrange the leeks and potatoes on top of the focacce. Sprinkle with the olives. Let rise for 30 more minutes. • Preheat the oven to 400°F/200°C/gas 4. • Bake for about 25 minutes, or until golden brown. • Serve hot.

Left: Focaccia with bell peppers and eggplant

Carrot, olive, and mushroom focaccia

Serves: 2-4; Preparation: 30 minutes + 1 hour 30 minutes to rise; Cooking: 40 minutes; Level of difficulty: 2

Prepare the dough following the instructions on page 20. Knead and set aside in a warm place to rise for 1 hour, or until doubled in bulk. • Oil a 10 x 15-inch (25 x 38-cm) jelly-roll pan. • Place the risen dough in the pan and use your fingertips to spread it evenly over the bottom. • Sauté the onion in 2 tablespoons of oil in a large frying pan over medium heat for 2 minutes. • Add the carrots and wine and cook for 10 minutes. • Add the mushrooms and water and cook for 5–10 minutes, or until the liquid has evaporated. • Spoon the carrot and mushroom mixture over the dough. Sprinkle with the mozzarella and olives. Season with salt and drizzle with the remaining oil. Let rise for 30 more minutes. • Preheat the oven to 400°F/200°C/gas 6. • Bake for about 20 minutes, or until golden brown. • Serve hot.

■ INGREDIENTS

• 1 quantity *Basic Pizza or Focaccia Dough* (see page 20)
• 1 medium onion, sliced
• 4 tablespoons extra-virgin olive oil
• 2 large carrots, peeled and sliced
• 4 tablespoons dry white wine
• 7 oz (200 g) mushrooms, sliced
• 6 tablespoons water
• 8 oz (250 g) mozzarella cheese, sliced
• ¾ cup (80 g) black olives, pitted
• salt to taste

Focaccia with tomatoes and mozzarella

Serves: 2-4; Preparation: 40 minutes + 1 hour 30 minutes to rise; Cooking: 25 minutes; Level of difficulty: 2

Prepare the dough following the instructions on page 20. Knead and set aside in a warm place to rise for 1 hour, or until doubled in bulk. • Oil a 12-inch (30-cm) pizza pan. • Place the risen dough in the pan and use your fingertips to spread it evenly over the bottom. • Let rise for 30 more minutes. • Preheat the oven to 400°F/200°C/gas 6. • Bake the focaccia for 20 minutes, or until risen and golden. • Place the tomatoes in a colander and sprinkle with salt. Let drain for 10 minutes. • Arrange the tomatoes and mozzarella on top of the focaccia, overlapping the slices slightly. Season with salt. Sprinkle with the oregano and drizzle with the oil. • Bake for about 5 minutes more, or until golden brown. • Sprinkle with the parmesan and serve warm.

■ INGREDIENTS

• 1 quantity *Basic Pizza or Focaccia Dough* (see page 20)
• 2 firm-ripe tomatoes, thinly sliced
• salt to taste
• 5 oz (150 g) mozzarella cheese, thinly sliced
• ⅛ teaspoon dried oregano
• 3 tablespoons extra-virgin olive oil
• 2 tablespoons freshly grated parmesan cheese

Right: Carrot, olive, and mushroom focaccia

Rustic focaccia

Serves: 2-4; Preparation: 30 minutes + 1 hour 30 minutes to rise; Cooking: 30 minutes; Level of difficulty: 1

Prepare the dough following the instructions on page 20. Knead and set aside in a warm place to rise for 1 hour, or until doubled in bulk. • Oil a 12-inch (30-cm) pizza pan. • Place the risen dough in the pan and use your fingertips to spread it evenly over the bottom. • Boil the eggs for 8–10 minutes. • Drain, shell, and slice them. • Spread the ricotta over the dough with the back of a spoon. Arrange the eggs, sausage meat, and olives over the ricotta. Sprinkle with oregano, salt, and red pepper flakes. Drizzle with the remaining oil and let rise for 30 more minutes. • Preheat the oven to 425°F/220°C/gas 7. • Bake for about 20 minutes, or until golden brown. • Serve hot.

■ INGREDIENTS

- 1 quantity *Basic Pizza or Focaccia Dough* (see page 20)
- 3 large eggs
- generous ¾ cup (200 g) ricotta cheese
- 7 oz (200 g) sausage meat, broken into bite-size pieces
- 10 green olives, pitted and chopped
- 1 teaspoon chopped oregano
- salt to taste
- ⅛ teaspoon red pepper flakes
- 6 tablespoons extra-virgin olive oil

Pizza with mozzarella and capers

Serves: 2-4; Preparation: 30 minutes + 1 hour 30 minutes to rise; Cooking: 15 minutes; Level of difficulty: 2

Prepare the dough following the instructions on page 20. Knead and set aside in a warm place to rise for 1 hour, or until doubled in bulk. • Oil a 10 x 15-inch (25 x 38-cm) jelly-roll pan. • Place the risen dough in the pan and use your fingertips to spread it evenly over the bottom. • Spread the dough with the tomatoes. Sprinkle with the mozzarella and capers. Drizzle with the oil and let rise for 30 more minutes. • Preheat the oven to 450°F/225°C/gas 7. • Bake for about 15 minutes, or until golden brown. • Serve hot.

■ INGREDIENTS

- 1 quantity *Basic Pizza or Focaccia Dough* (see page 20)
- 7 oz (200 g) chopped tomatoes
- 7 oz (200 g) mozzarella cheese, cut into cubes
- 1 tablespoon salted capers, rinsed
- 2 tablespoons extra-virgin olive oil

Right: *Rustic focaccia*

Italian riviera pizza

Serves: 2-4; Preparation: 15 minutes + 1 hour 30 minutes to rise; Cooking: 45 minutes; Level of difficulty: 1

Prepare the dough following the instructions on page 20. Knead and set aside in a warm place to rise for 1 hour, or until doubled in bulk. • Oil a 12-inch (30-cm) pizza pan. • Place the risen dough in the pan and use your fingertips to spread it evenly over the bottom. • Heat half the oil and the milk in a large frying pan over medium heat. Add the onions and cook for about 15 minutes, or until the onions are very soft and the liquid has evaporated. • Season with salt and pepper. Add the cinnamon and sugar. • Arrange the onions on top of the dough. Top with the tomatoes. Sprinkle with the anchovies, olives, garlic, parmesan, and oregano. Drizzle with the remaining oil and let rise for 30 more minutes. • Preheat the oven to 400°F/200°C/gas 6. • Bake for about 30 minutes, or until golden brown. • Serve hot.

■ INGREDIENTS

- 1 quantity *Basic Pizza or Focaccia Dough* (see page 20)
- 6 tablespoons extra-virgin olive oil
- 4 tablespoons milk
- 14 oz (400 g) onions, sliced
- salt and freshly ground black pepper to taste
- ⅛ teaspoon cinnamon
- 1 teaspoon sugar
- 14 oz (400 g) tomatoes, sliced
- 8 anchovy fillets, chopped
- 3 cups (300 g) black olives
- 1 clove garlic, finely sliced
- 2 tablespoons freshly grated parmesan cheese
- 1 tablespoon oregano

Prosciutto focaccia

Serves: 2-4; Preparation: 45 minutes + 2 hours to rise; Cooking: 30 minutes; Level of difficulty: 2

Place the fresh or active dry yeast in a small bowl. If using fresh yeast, crumble it with your fingertips. • Add half the warm water and stir until the yeast has dissolved. • Set the mixture aside for 15 minutes. It will look creamy when ready. Stir well. • Sift the flour onto a work surface and sprinkle with the salt. Make a well in the center and pour in the eggs, yeast mixture, butter, and half the prosciutto. Use a wooden spoon to stir the mixture until the flour has almost all been absorbed. • Knead the dough following the instructions for bread dough on page 20. • Set aside in a warm place to rise for 1 hour, or until doubled in bulk. • Butter a baking sheet. • Place the risen dough on the sheet and use your fingertips to spread it evenly over the bottom. • Sprinkle with the remaining prosciutto and the coarse salt. Let rise for 1 hour more. • Preheat the oven to 400°F/200°C/gas 6. • Bake for about 30 minutes, or until golden brown. • Serve hot or at room temperature.

■ INGREDIENTS

- 1 oz (30 g) fresh yeast or 2 (¼-oz/7-g) packages active dry yeast
- ⅔ cup (180 ml) warm water
- 2 cups (300 g) all-purpose (plain) flour
- ⅛ teaspoon salt
- 2 large eggs, lightly beaten
- 5 tablespoons butter
- 8 oz (250 g) prosciutto (Parma ham), cut into cubes
- 1 tablespoon coarse sea salt

Right: *Italian riviera pizza*

Bread and Rolls

☙

There is nothing more inviting than the odor of freshly baked bread wafting through your kitchen. Bread-making is often seen as time-consuming or difficult. Take a look at our basic instructions for kneading; they simplify the process, encouraging you to make your own bread.

Herb and walnut loaf

Serves: 8-10; Preparation: 40 minutes + 1 hour 30 minutes to rise; Cooking: 45 minutes; Level of difficulty: 2

Place the yeast in a small bowl with the milk. Stir well and let rest for 10 minutes, or until foamy. • Sift the flour and salt into a large bowl. • Beat the egg in a small bowl until frothy. Season with pepper and beat in the sage, rosemary, and butter. • Gradually stir the yeast mixture into the dry ingredients. Add the egg mixture and stir well. Add enough warm water to make a fairly soft dough. • Transfer to a lightly floured surface and knead for 5–10 minutes, or until smooth and elastic. • Shape into a ball and place in an oiled bowl. Cover with a cloth and place in a warm place to rise for 1 hour 30 minutes, or until doubled in bulk. • Preheat the oven to 350°F/180°C/gas 4. • Oil a 9 x 5-inch (23 x 13-cm) loaf pan. Line with waxed paper. • Punch the dough down. Place on a lightly floured surface and knead in the walnuts. • Place the dough in the pan and bake for about 45 minutes, or until well-risen and golden brown.

■ INGREDIENTS

- 1 oz (30 g) fresh yeast or 2 (¼-oz/7-g) packages active dry yeast
- ½ cup (125 ml) warm milk
- 3 cups (450 g) all-purpose (plain) flour
- 1 teaspoon salt
- 1 large egg
- freshly ground black pepper to taste
- 1 tablespoon finely chopped fresh sage
- 1 tablespoon finely chopped fresh rosemary
- 4 tablespoons butter
- about ½ cup (125 ml) warm water
- ½ cup (75 g) finely chopped walnuts

Braided herb loaf

Serves: 8-10; Preparation: 40 minutes; 1 hour 30 minutes to rise; Cooking: 45 minutes; Level of difficulty: 2

Place the yeast and sugar in a small bowl with half the water. Stir well and let rest for 10 minutes, or until foamy. • Sift the flour and salt into a large bowl. • Beat the egg, sage, rosemary, and oil in a small bowl. • Gradually stir the yeast mixture into the flour. Add the egg mixture and stir well. Add enough remaining water to make a fairly soft dough. • Transfer to a lightly floured surface and knead for 10–15 minutes, or until smooth and elastic. • Shape into a ball and place in an oiled bowl. Cover with a cloth and place in a warm place to rise for 1 hour 30 minutes, or until doubled in bulk. • Preheat the oven to 350°F/ 180°C/gas 4. • Oil a baking sheet. • Punch the dough down. Place on a lightly floured surface and knead in the pine nuts. • Divide the dough in three and roll each piece into a rope. Braid the three pieces of dough together, pulling the ends round and joining them. • Place on the prepared sheet and bake for about 45 minutes, or until well-risen and golden brown.

■ INGREDIENTS

- 1 oz (30 g) fresh yeast or 2 (¼-oz/7-g) packages active dry yeast
- 1 teaspoon sugar
- 1 cup (250 ml) warm water
- 3⅓ cups (500 g) all-purpose (plain) flour
- 1 teaspoon salt
- 1 large egg
- 1 tablespoon finely chopped fresh sage
- 1 tablespoon finely chopped fresh rosemary
- 1 tablespoon extra-virgin olive oil
- 6 tablespoons pine nuts

Right: Herb and walnut loaf

Pumpkin herb bread

Serves: 8-10; Preparation: 40 minutes + 1 hour to rise; Cooking: 45 minutes; Level of difficulty: 2

Place the yeast and sugar in a small bowl with the milk. Stir well and let rest for 10 minutes, or until foamy. • Sift the flour and salt into a large bowl. • Beat the egg in a small bowl until frothy. Season with pepper and beat in the sage, rosemary, nutmeg, and butter. • Use a wooden spoon to gradually stir the milk and yeast mixture into the flour. Add the egg mixture and stir well. Stir in the pumpkin. The dough should be fairly soft but kneadable. • Transfer to a lightly floured work surface and knead for 5–10 minutes, or until smooth and elastic. • Shape into a ball and place in an oiled bowl. Cover with a cloth and place in a warm place to rise for 1 hour, or until doubled in bulk. • Preheat the oven to 350°F/180°C/gas 4. • Oil a 9 x 5-inch (23 x 13-cm) loaf pan. • Punch the dough down and knead briefly. • Place the dough in the pan and bake for about 45 minutes, or until well-risen and golden brown.

■ INGREDIENTS

- 1 oz (30 g) fresh yeast or 2 (¼-oz/7-g) packages active dry yeast
- 1 teaspoon sugar
- ½ cup (125 ml) warm milk
- 3 cups (450 g) all-purpose (plain) flour
- 1 teaspoon salt
- 1 large egg
- freshly ground white pepper to taste
- 2 teaspoons finely chopped sage
- 2 teaspoons finely chopped rosemary
- ½ teaspoon ground nutmeg
- 3 tablespoons melted butter
- 1 cup (250 g) canned pumpkin purée

Whole-wheat buttermilk bread

Serves: 6-8; Preparation: 30 minutes + 45 minutes to rise; Cooking: 35 minutes; Level of difficulty: 2

Place the yeast and sugar in a small bowl with the water. Stir well and let rest for 10 minutes, or until foamy. • Sift both flours, salt, and baking soda into a large bowl. • Use a wooden spoon to gradually stir in the yeast mixture, buttermilk, and butter. • Shape into a ball and place in an oiled bowl. Cover with a cloth and place in a warm place to rise for 45 minutes, or until doubled in bulk. • Preheat the oven to 375°F/190°C/gas 5. • Oil a 9-inch (23-cm) round cake pan. • Punch the dough down and knead briefly. • Place the dough in the pan and bake for about 35 minutes, or until well-risen and browned.

■ INGREDIENTS

- ½ oz (15 g) fresh yeast or 1 (¼-oz/7-g) package active dry yeast
- 2 tablespoons sugar
- 4 tablespoons warm water
- 2¼ cups (330 g) whole-wheat (wholemeal) flour
- 1 cup (150 g) all-purpose (plain) flour
- ¾ teaspoon salt
- ½ teaspoon baking soda
- 1 cup (250 ml) buttermilk
- 2 tablespoons butter

Right: Pumpkin herb bread

Spiced pumpkin bread

Serves: 6-8; Preparation: 30 minutes + 1 hour 30 minutes to rise; Cooking: 30 minutes; Level of difficulty: 2

Warm half the milk in a small saucepan. Place the yeast and sugar in a small bowl with the warmed milk. Stir well and let rest for 10 minutes, or until foamy. • Cook the pumpkin in a large pot of boiling water until tender. • Drain and let cool. Chop coarsely. • Sift both flours and salt into a large bowl. • Stir in the yeast mixture, cinnamon, cloves, nutmeg, oil, pumpkin, and the remaining milk. The dough should be fairly soft but kneadable. • Transfer to a lightly floured work surface and knead until smooth and elastic. • Shape into a ball and place in an oiled bowl. Cover with a cloth and place in a warm place to rise for 1 hour, or until doubled in bulk. • Knead for 3 minutes. Divide the dough into 8 balls and arrange just touching one another in a circle on an oiled baking sheet so that they will join to make a ring as the dough expands and rises. Let rise for 30 minutes. • Preheat the oven to 425°F/220°C/gas 7. • Beat the egg yolk and milk in a small bowl and brush over the bread. • Bake for about 30 minutes, or until it sounds hollow when tapped on the bottom.

INGREDIENTS

- generous ⅓ cup (100 ml) milk
- 1 oz (30 g) fresh yeast or 2 (¼-oz/7-g) packages active dry yeast
- ½ teaspoon sugar
- 12 oz (350 g) pumpkin flesh, diced
- 1 cup (150 g) whole-wheat (wholemeal) flour
- 1 cup (150 g) all-purpose (plain) flour
- ½ teaspoon salt
- ½ teaspoon ground cinnamon
- ¼ teaspoon each ground cloves and nutmeg
- 2 tablespoons extra-virgin olive oil
- 1 egg yolk, to glaze
- 2 tablespoons milk, to glaze

Granary bread

Serves: 8-10; Preparation: 30 minutes + 1 hour 30 minutes to rise; Cooking: 35 minutes; Level of difficulty: 2

Place the yeast in a small bowl with the warm water. Stir well and let rest for 10 minutes, or until foamy. • Soak the bulgur in the boiling water for about 10 minutes, or until the grains swell and the water has been absorbed. • Sift both flours and salt into a large bowl. • Use a wooden spoon to gradually stir in the yeast mixture, bulgur, butter, molasses, and honey. Add enough milk to make a soft dough. • Transfer to a lightly floured work surface and knead for 5–10 minutes, or until smooth and elastic. • Shape into a ball and place in an oiled bowl. Cover with a cloth and place in a warm place to rise for 1 hour and 30 minutes, or until doubled in bulk. • Preheat the oven to 375°F/190°C/gas 5. • Oil two 9 x 5-inch (23 x 13-cm) loaf pans. • Punch the dough down and knead briefly. • Place the dough in the pans and bake for about 35 minutes, or until well-risen and browned.

INGREDIENTS

- ½ oz (15 g) fresh yeast or 1 (¼-oz/7-g) package active dry yeast
- 6 tablespoons warm water
- ½ cup (75 g) bulgur (cracked wheat)
- 1½ cups (375 ml) boiling water
- 4 cups (600 g) all-purpose (plain) flour
- 1 cup (150 g) whole-wheat (wholemeal) flour
- 1½ tablespoons salt
- 4 tablespoons butter
- 2 tablespoons molasses (treacle)
- 2 tablespoons clear honey
- 1 cup (250 ml) milk

Right: Spiced pumpkin bread

Whole-wheat herb bread

Serves: 6-12; Preparation: 30 minutes + 2 hours 10 minutes to rise; Cooking: 30 minutes; Level of difficulty: 2

Place the yeast and sugar in a small bowl with 6 tablespoons of water. Stir well and let rest for 10 minutes, or until foamy. • Sift both flours and salt into a large bowl. • Use a wooden spoon to gradually stir in the yeast mixture, oregano, and marjoram. Add enough remaining water to make a fairly soft dough. • Transfer to a lightly floured work surface and knead for 5–10 minutes, or until smooth and elastic. • Shape into a ball and place in an oiled bowl. Cover with a cloth and place in a warm place to rise for 1 hour and 30 minutes, or until doubled in bulk. • Turn the dough out onto a floured surface and knead for 3 minutes. Divide the dough into 6 balls and shape into 12-inch (30-cm) sausages. Let rise for 40 minutes. • Preheat the oven to 425°F/220°C/gas 7. • Bake for about 30 minutes, or until they sound hollow when tapped on the bottom.

INGREDIENTS

- 1 oz (30 g) fresh yeast or 2 (¼-oz/7-g) packages active dry yeast
- 1 teaspoon sugar
- 1 cup (250 ml) warm water
- 2⅔ cups (400 g) whole-wheat (wholemeal) flour
- ¾ cup (125 g) all-purpose (plain) flour
- 1 tablespoon salt
- 1 tablespoon finely chopped oregano
- 1 tablespoon finely chopped marjoram

Mary's mixed seed bread

Serves: 6-8; Preparation: 45 minutes + 1 hour 40 minutes to rise; Cooking: 30 minutes; Level of difficulty: 2

Place the yeast and sugar in a small bowl with 6 tablespoons of the water. Stir well and let rest for 10 minutes, or until foamy. • Sift both flours and salt into a large bowl. • Use a wooden spoon to gradually stir in the yeast mixture, buttermilk, seeds, butter, and honey. Add enough remaining water to make a fairly soft dough. • Transfer to a lightly floured work surface and knead for 5–10 minutes, or until smooth and elastic. • Shape into a ball and place in an oiled bowl. Cover with a cloth and place in a warm place to rise for 1 hour, or until doubled in bulk. • Butter two 9 x 5-inch (23 x 13-cm) loaf pans. • Punch the dough down and knead briefly. • Divide the dough in half and place in the pans. Let rise for 40 minutes. • Preheat the oven to 375°F/190°C/gas 5. • Bake for about 30 minutes, or until well-risen and browned.

INGREDIENTS

- ½ oz (15 g) fresh yeast or 1 (¼-oz/7-g) package active dry yeast
- 1 teaspoon sugar
- ¾ cup (200 ml) warm water
- 4 cups (600 g) all-purpose (plain) flour
- 2 cups (300 g) whole-wheat (wholemeal) flour
- 2 teaspoons salt
- 1½ cups (375 ml) buttermilk
- 2 tablespoons each sesame seeds, poppy seeds, and sunflower seeds
- 2 tablespoons butter
- 3 tablespoons honey

Right: Whole-wheat herb bread

Julia's Bavarian bread

Serves: 10-12; Preparation: 45 minutes + 3 hours to rise; Cooking: 40 minutes; Level of difficulty: 2

Place the yeast and sugar in a small bowl with 6 tablespoons of the water. Stir well and let rest for 10 minutes, or until foamy. • Sift the flour and salt into a large bowl. Stir in the oats. • Use a wooden spoon to gradually stir in the yeast mixture, butter, and molasses. Add enough remaining water to make a fairly soft dough. • Transfer to a lightly floured work surface and knead for 5–10 minutes, or until smooth and elastic. • Shape into a ball and place in an oiled bowl. Cover with a cloth and place in a warm place to rise for 2 hours, or until doubled in bulk. • Turn the dough out onto a floured surface and knead for 3 minutes. • Transfer to a baking sheet and let rise for 1 hour. • Preheat the oven to 350°F/180°C/gas 4. • Bake for about 40 minutes, or until well-risen and golden brown.

■ INGREDIENTS

- ½ oz (15 g) fresh yeast or 1 (¼-oz/7-g) package active dry yeast
- 1 teaspoon sugar
- 1 cup (250 ml) warm water
- 3 cups (450 g) whole-wheat (wholemeal) flour
- ½ teaspoon salt
- 1 cup (150 g) rolled oats
- 2 tablespoons butter, melted
- 6 tablespoons molasses (treacle)

Whole-wheat aniseed bread

Serves: 18-20; Preparation: 45 minutes + 1 hour 40 minutes to rise; Cooking: 50 minutes; Level of difficulty: 2

Place the yeast and 1 teaspoon of sugar in a small bowl with 6 tablespoons of the water. Stir well and let rest for 10 minutes, or until foamy. • Sift the flour, baking powder, and baking soda into a large bowl. • Use a wooden spoon to gradually stir in the yeast mixture, remaining sugar, and the aniseeds. Add enough remaining water to make a fairly soft dough. • Transfer to a lightly floured work surface and knead for 5–10 minutes, or until smooth and elastic. • Shape into a ball and place in an oiled bowl. Cover with a cloth and place in a warm place to rise for 1 hour, or until doubled in bulk. • Butter three 9 x 5-inch (23 x 13-cm) loaf pans. • Punch the dough down and knead briefly. • Divide the dough in three and place in the pans. Let rise for 40 minutes. • Preheat the oven to 400°F/200°C/gas 6. • Brush the loaves with the beaten whites. • Bake for about 50 minutes, or until risen and browned.

■ INGREDIENTS

- ½ oz (15 g) fresh yeast or 1 (¼-oz/7-g) package active dry yeast
- ½ cup (100 g) sugar
- 2½ cups (625 ml) warm water
- 6 cups (900 g) whole-wheat (wholemeal) flour
- 1 tablespoon baking powder
- 2 teaspoons baking soda
- 2 tablespoons aniseeds
- 1 large egg white, lightly beaten, to glaze

Right: *Julia's Bavarian bread*

Whole-wheat walnut bread

■ INGREDIENTS

- ½ oz (15 g) fresh yeast or 1 (¼-oz/7-g) package active dry yeast
- 1 teaspoon sugar
- ⅔ cup (180 ml) warm milk
- 2 cups (300 g) whole-wheat (wholemeal) flour
- ⅛ teaspoon salt
- ½ cup (75 g) walnuts
- 2 tablespoons clear honey (preferably chestnut)
- 1 medium potato, mashed

Serves: 6-8; Preparation: 45 minutes + 3 hours to rise; Cooking: 30 minutes; Level of difficulty: 2

Place the yeast and sugar in a small bowl with 6 tablespoons of milk. Stir well and let rest for 10 minutes, or until foamy. • Sift the flour and salt into a large bowl. • Use a wooden spoon to gradually stir in the yeast mixture, two-thirds of the walnuts, honey, and potato. Add enough remaining milk to make a soft dough. • Transfer to a lightly floured work surface and knead for 5–10 minutes, or until smooth and elastic. • Shape into a ball and place in an oiled bowl. Cover with a cloth and place in a warm place to rise for 2 hours, or until doubled in bulk. • • Turn the dough out onto a floured surface and knead for 3 minutes. • Roll the dough out into a rectangle and sprinkle with the remaining walnuts. Roll up the dough into a fairly flat loaf and make several cuts along the top. Transfer to an oiled baking sheet. Let rise for 1 hour. • Preheat the oven to 400°F/200°C/gas 6. • Bake for 30 minutes, or until well-risen and browned.

Challah bread

■ INGREDIENTS

- 1 oz (30 g) fresh yeast or 2 (¼-oz/7-g) packages active dry yeast
- 2 tablespoons sugar
- ½ cup (125 ml) warm water
- 6½ cups (975 g) all-purpose (plain) flour
- 2 teaspoons salt
- 6 tablespoons butter
- 4 large eggs, separated
- 1 tablespoon poppy seeds

Serves: 14-16; Preparation: 45 minutes + 2 hours 30 minutes rise; Cooking: 45 minutes; Level of difficulty: 3

Place the yeast and sugar in a small bowl with 6 tablespoons of the water. Stir well and let rest for 10 minutes, or until foamy. • Sift the flour and salt into a large bowl. • Use a wooden spoon to gradually stir in the yeast mixture, butter, and 3 egg yolks and all the whites. • Add enough remaining water to make a fairly soft dough. • Transfer to a lightly floured work surface and knead for 10–15 minutes, or until smooth and elastic. • Shape into a ball and place in an oiled bowl. Cover with a cloth and place in a warm place to rise for 1 hour 30 minutes, or until doubled in bulk. • Turn out onto a floured surface and knead for 3 minutes. • Divide into six equal portions and roll each one into 12-inch (30-cm) long sausages. Place three "sausages" on an oiled baking sheet and braid them, tucking under the ends. Repeat with the remaining pieces of dough. Brush with the remaining beaten egg yolk and sprinkle with poppy seeds. • Let rise for 1 hour. • Preheat the oven to 375°F/ 190°C/gas 5. • Bake for about 45 minutes, or until well-risen and golden.

Left: Whole-wheat walnut bread

Cheese twists

Serves: 8-10; Preparation: 45 minutes + 2 hours to rise; Cooking: 30 minutes; Level of difficulty: 2

Place the yeast and sugar in a small bowl with 6 tablespoons of water. Stir well and let rest for 10 minutes, or until foamy. • Sift the flour and salt into a large bowl. Mix in the cheese and pepper. • Use a wooden spoon to gradually stir in the yeast mixture. Add enough of the remaining water to make a fairly soft dough. • Transfer to a lightly floured work surface and knead for 5–10 minutes, or until smooth and elastic. • Shape into a ball and place in an oiled bowl. Cover with a cloth and place in a warm place to rise for 1 hour, or until doubled in bulk. • Turn the dough out onto a floured work surface and knead for 3 minutes. Divide the dough into 4 balls and shape each one into a 16-inch (40-cm) long sausage. Fold each sausage in two and gently twist the dough on itself. Arrange the dough twists, well spaced, on an oiled baking sheet. Brush with the egg and sprinkle with sesame and poppy seeds. • Let rise for 1 hour. • Preheat the oven to 400°F/200°C/gas 6. • Bake for 30 minutes, or until the bread sounds hollow when tapped on the bottom.

■ INGREDIENTS

- 1 oz (30 g) fresh yeast or 2 (¼-oz/7-g) packages active dry yeast
- 1 teaspoon sugar
- generous 1 cup (280 ml) warm water
- 4 cups (600 g) all-purpose (plain) flour
- 2 teaspoons salt
- 2 cups (250 g) freshly grated pecorino or parmesan cheese
- ⅛ teaspoon freshly ground white pepper
- 1 large egg, lightly beaten
- 2 tablespoons sesame seeds
- 2 tablespoons poppy seeds

Lard rolls

Serves: 10; Preparation: 50 minutes + 7 hours to rise; Cooking: 30 minutes; Level of difficulty: 3

Place the yeast and sugar in a small bowl with 4 tablespoons of the water. Stir well and let rest for 10 minutes, or until foamy. • Sift ½ cup (75 g) of flour and salt into a large bowl. • Use a wooden spoon to gradually stir in the yeast mixture to form a stiff dough. • Transfer to a lightly floured work surface and knead for 5–10 minutes, or until smooth. • Shape into a ball, cover with a cloth, and place in a warm place to rise for 5 hours. • Knead in the remaining flour, remaining water, lard, and oil until smooth and elastic. • Cover with a cloth and place in a warm place to rise for 2 hours. • Preheat the oven to 450°F/230°C/gas 8. • Shape the dough into 10 balls and arrange them, well-spaced, on a greased baking sheet. • Bake for about 30 minutes, or until golden brown.

■ INGREDIENTS

- 1 oz (30 g) fresh yeast or 2 (¼-oz/7-g) packages active dry yeast
- 1 teaspoon sugar
- 8 tablespoons warm water
- 5⅓ cups (800 g) all-purpose (plain) flour
- 1 teaspoon salt
- ½ cup (125 g) lard, melted
- ⅔ cup (180 ml) extra-virgin olive oil

Right: *Cheese twists*

Potato bread

■ INGREDIENTS

- 5 oz (150 g) potatoes, peeled
- 1 oz (30 g) fresh yeast or 2 (¼-oz/7-g) packages active dry yeast
- 1 teaspoon sugar
- ¾ cup (200 ml) warm water
- 3⅓ cups (500 g) all-purpose (plain) flour
- 2 teaspoons salt
- 2 tablespoons extra-virgin olive oil

Serves: 6-8; Preparation: 45 minutes + 1 hour 50 minutes to rise; Cooking: 50 minutes; Level of difficulty: 2

Cook the potatoes in a large pot of salted, boiling water for 20 minutes, or until tender. • Drain and mash until puréed. • Place the yeast and sugar in a small bowl with 6 tablespoons of the water. Stir well and let rest for 10 minutes, or until foamy. • Sift the flour and salt into a large bowl. Use a wooden spoon to gradually stir in the yeast mixture, potatoes, and oil. Add enough of the remaining water to make a fairly soft dough. • Transfer to a lightly floured work surface and knead for 5–10 minutes, or until smooth and elastic. • Shape into a ball and place in an oiled bowl. Cover with a cloth and place in a warm place to rise for 1 hour, or until doubled in bulk. • Turn the dough out onto a floured surface and knead for 3 minutes. • Divide the dough into 6-8 balls and arrange, well spaced, on a large oiled baking sheet. Let rise for 50 minutes. • Preheat the oven to 400°F/200°C/gas 6. • Bake for 30 minutes, or until the bread sounds hollow when tapped on the bottom.

Parisian baguette

■ INGREDIENTS

- 1 oz (30 g) fresh yeast or 2 (¼-oz/7-g) packages active dry yeast
- 1 teaspoon sugar
- ⅔ cup (180 ml) warm water
- 4⅔ cups (700 g) all-purpose (plain) flour
- ⅛ teaspoon salt
- 2 tablespoons extra-virgin olive oil

Serves: 8-10; Preparation: 45 minutes + 1 hour to rise; Cooking: 1 hour; Level of difficulty: 2

Place the yeast and sugar in a small bowl with 6 tablespoons of the water. Stir well and let rest for 10 minutes, or until foamy. • Sift the flour and salt into a large bowl. • Use a wooden spoon to gradually stir in the yeast mixture. Add enough of the remaining water to make a soft dough. • Transfer to a lightly floured work surface and knead for 5–10 minutes, or until smooth and elastic. • Shape into a ball and place in an oiled bowl. Cover with a cloth and place in a warm place to rise for 1 hour, or until doubled in bulk. • Preheat the oven to 475°F/250°C/gas 9. • Turn the dough out onto a floured surface and knead for 3 minutes. • Divide the dough into 3 portions and shape into sausages. Arrange them, well-spaced, on greased baking sheets and drizzle with the oil. • Bake for 15 minutes. • Lower the oven temperature to 325°F/170°C/gas 3. Bake for about 45 minutes more, or until well-risen and golden brown.

Right: Potato bread

Whole-wheat oat bread

Serves: 8-10; Preparation: 45 minutes + 2 hours to rise; Cooking: 50 minutes; Level of difficulty: 2

Place the yeast in a small bowl with 6 tablespoons of the water. Stir well and let rest for 10 minutes, or until foamy. • Sift the flour and salt into a large bowl. • Use a wooden spoon to gradually stir in the yeast mixture, oats, milk, butter, and honey. Add enough of the remaining water to make a soft dough. Transfer to a lightly floured work surface and knead for 5–10 minutes, or until smooth and elastic. • Shape into a ball and place in an oiled bowl. Cover with a cloth and place in a warm place to rise for 2 hours, or until doubled in bulk. • Turn the dough out onto a floured work surface and knead for 3 minutes. • Preheat the oven to 425°F/220°C/gas 7. • Oil a 9 x 5-inch (23 x 13-cm) loaf pan. • Punch the dough down and knead briefly. • Place the dough in the pan and bake for about 50 minutes, or until well-risen and golden brown.

■ INGREDIENTS

- 1 oz (30 g) fresh yeast or 2 (¼-oz/7-g) packages active dry yeast
- 1 cup (250 ml) warm water
- 1⅔ cups (250 g) whole-wheat (wholemeal) flour
- 1 tablespoon salt
- 2½ cups (250 g) rolled oats
- 4 tablespoons milk
- 4 tablespoons butter
- 4 tablespoons honey

Mexican cheese bread

Serves: 8-10; Preparation: 45 minutes + 45 minutes to rise; Cooking: 45 minutes; Level of difficulty: 2

Place the yeast and sugar in a small bowl with 6 tablespoons of the water. Stir well and let rest for 10 minutes, or until foamy. • Sift the flour and salt into a large bowl. • Use a wooden spoon to gradually stir in the yeast mixture, jalapeno peppers, cheese, egg, butter, and garlic salt. Add enough of the remaining water to make a soft dough. • Transfer to a lightly floured work surface and knead for 5–10 minutes, or until smooth and elastic. • Shape into a ball and place in an oiled 9 x 5-inch (23 x 13-cm) loaf pan. Cover with a cloth and place in a warm place to rise for 30 minutes, or until doubled in bulk. • Preheat the oven to 400°F/200°C/gas 6. • Bake for about 45 minutes, or until well-risen and golden brown.

■ INGREDIENTS

- ½ oz (15 g) fresh yeast or 1 (¼-oz/7-g) package active dry yeast
- 1 tablespoon sugar
- 1 cup (250 ml) warm water
- 4 cups (600 g) all-purpose (plain) flour
- ¾ teaspoon salt
- 3 small fresh jalapeno peppers
- 1 cup (125 g) freshly grated Monterey Jack cheese
- 1 large egg, lightly beaten
- 2 tablespoons butter
- ¼ teaspoon garlic salt

Right: *Whole-wheat oat bread*

Sesame and poppy rolls

Serves: 6-8; Preparation: 30 minutes + 2 hours 30 minutes to rise; Cooking: 30 minutes; Level of difficulty: 2

Prepare the dough following the instructions on page 20. • Divide the dough into three equal parts. Shape each portion into a sausage and brush two of the portions with milk. Roll one portion in the sesame seeds until well coated and the other in the poppy seeds. Braid the three pieces of dough into a long braid (plait). Cut into 3-inch (10-cm) rolls and arrange, well-spaced, on a large baking sheet. Cover with a cloth and place in a warm place to rise for 1 hour, or until doubled in bulk. • Preheat the oven to 350°F/180°C/gas 4. • Brush all over with milk. Bake for 15 minutes. Lower the oven temperature to 300°F/150°C/gas 2. • Bake for about 15 minutes more, or until well-risen and golden brown.

■ INGREDIENTS

- 1 quantity *Basic Bread Dough* (see page 20)
- 2 teaspoons milk, to glaze
- 2 tablespoons sesame seeds
- 2 tablespoons poppy seeds

Pretzels

Serves: 10-12; Preparation: 45 minutes + 2 hours to rise; Cooking: 15 minutes; Level of difficulty: 2

Place the yeast and sugar in a small bowl with 6 tablespoons of the water. Stir well and let rest for 10 minutes, or until foamy. • Sift the flour and salt into a large bowl. • Use a wooden spoon to gradually stir in the yeast mixture. Add enough of the remaining water to make a soft dough. • Transfer to a lightly floured work surface and knead for 5–10 minutes, or until smooth and elastic. • Shape into a ball and place in an oiled bowl. Cover with a cloth and place in a warm place to rise for 2 hours, or until doubled in bulk. • Preheat the oven to 450°F/230°C/gas 8. • Turn the dough out onto a floured surface and divide into 12 portions. Roll out into long ropes and make each rope into a pretzel shape by twisting the ends around each other. Bring both ends back to the center of the strip. • Arrange the pretzels, well-spaced, on baking sheets. Brush with the egg and sprinkle with the salt. • Bake for about 15 minutes, or until well-risen and golden brown.

■ INGREDIENTS

- 1 oz (30 g) fresh yeast or 2 (¼-oz/7-g) packages active dry yeast
- ½ teaspoon sugar
- ¾ cup (200 ml) warm water
- 2 cups (300 g) all-purpose (plain) flour
- ¼ teaspoon salt
- 1 large egg, lightly beaten
- 2 tablespoons coarse salt

Right: *Sesame and poppy rolls*

Sesame rolls

Serves: 10; Preparation: 30 minutes + 2 hours to rise; Cooking: 30 minutes; Level of difficulty: 2

Place the yeast and sugar in a small bowl with 6 tablespoons of water. Stir well and let rest for 10 minutes, or until foamy. • Sift both flours and salt into a large bowl. Use a wooden spoon to gradually stir in the yeast mixture and half the sesame seeds. Add the remaining water to make a fairly soft dough. • Transfer to a lightly floured work surface and knead for 5–10 minutes, or until smooth and elastic. • Shape into a ball and place in an oiled bowl. Cover with a cloth and place in a warm place to rise for 1 hour, or until doubled in bulk. • Turn the dough out onto a floured surface and knead for 2 minutes. • Divide the dough into 10 balls and arrange them, well spaced, on an oiled baking sheet. Brush with the egg white and sprinkle with the remaining sesame seeds. Let rise for 1 hour. • Preheat the oven to 425°F/220°C/gas 7. • Bake for 30 minutes, or until well risen and golden brown.

INGREDIENTS

- 1 oz (30 g) fresh yeast or 2 (¼-oz/7-g) packages active dry yeast
- 1 teaspoon sugar
- 1 cup (250 ml) warm water
- 2⅔ cups (400 g) all-purpose (plain) flour
- 1⅔ cups (250 g) whole-wheat (wholemeal) flour
- 2 teaspoons salt
- ½ cup (50 g) sesame seeds
- 1 large egg white, lightly beaten

Traditional rye bread

Serves: 6-8; Preparation: 40 minutes + 1 hour to rise; Cooking: 50 minutes; Level of difficulty: 2

Place the yeast in a small bowl with 6 tablespoons of water. Stir well and let rest for 10 minutes, or until foamy. • Sift both flours and salt into a large bowl. Use a wooden spoon to gradually stir in the yeast mixture, oil, and vinegar. Add enough of the remaining water to make a stiff dough. • Transfer to a lightly floured work surface and knead for 5–10 minutes, or until smooth and elastic. • Shape into a ball and place in an oiled 9 x 5-inch (23 x 13-cm) loaf pan. Cover with a cloth and place in a warm place to rise for 1 hour, or until doubled in bulk. • Preheat the oven to 350°F/180°C/gas 4. • Bake for about 50 minutes, or until well-risen and browned on top.

INGREDIENTS

- 1 oz (30 g) fresh yeast or 2 (¼-oz/7-g) packages active dry yeast
- ½ cup (125 ml) warm water
- 2 cups (300 g) rye flour
- ½ cup (75 g) all-purpose (plain) flour
- 1 teaspoon salt
- 2 tablespoons vegetable oil
- 2 tablespoons vinegar

Right: Sesame rolls

Rustic spiced nut loaf

Serves: 6-8; Preparation: 45 minutes + 1 hour 30 minutes to rise; Cooking: 1 hour; Level of difficulty: 2

Place the yeast and 2 tablespoons of sugar in a small bowl with 6 tablespoons of milk. Stir well and let rest for 10 minutes, or until foamy. • Sift both flours and salt into a large bowl. Use a wooden spoon to gradually stir in the yeast mixture, remaining sugar, and butter. Add the remaining milk to make a coarse dough. • Transfer to a lightly floured work surface and knead in the almonds, hazelnuts, and walnuts, reserving 2 tablespoons. Continue kneading for 5–10 minutes, or until smooth and elastic. • Shape into a ball and place in an oiled bowl. Cover with a cloth and place in a warm place to rise for 1 hour, or until doubled in bulk. • Punch the dough down and knead briefly. • Oil two 9 x 5-inch (23 x 13-cm) loaf pans. Line with waxed paper. • Brush with the honey and sprinkle with the remaining nuts. • Place the dough in the pans and let rise for 30 minutes. • Preheat the oven to 425°F/220°C/gas 7. • Bake for about 1 hour, or until well-risen and golden brown. • Serve with preserves.

■ INGREDIENTS

- ⅔ oz (20 g) fresh yeast or 1½ (¼-oz/7-g) packages active dry yeast
- ½ cup (100 g) sugar
- 1 cup (250 ml) warm milk
- 1⅔ cups (250 g) all-purpose (plain) flour
- 1 cup (150 g) fine semolina flour
- ⅛ teaspoon salt
- 3 tablespoons melted butter
- ⅓ cup (50 g) blanched almonds, chopped
- ⅓ cup (50 g) blanched hazelnuts, chopped
- ⅓ cup (50 g) walnuts, chopped
- 1 tablespoon clear honey

Piquant onion pinwheels

Serves: 8-10; Preparation: 45 minutes + 1 hour 30 minutes to rise; Cooking: 20 minutes; Level of difficulty: 2

Place the yeast and sugar in a small bowl with 6 tablespoons of water. Stir well and let rest for 10 minutes, or until foamy. • Sift the flour and salt into a large bowl. • Use a wooden spoon to gradually stir in the yeast mixture, 1 tablespoon butter, and the egg. Add enough of the remaining water to make a soft dough. • Transfer to a lightly floured work surface and knead for 5–10 minutes, or until smooth and elastic. • Cover with a cloth and place in a warm place to rise for 1 hour, or until doubled in bulk. • Sauté the onions in the remaining butter in a large frying pan until softened. Season with the red pepper flakes. • Turn the dough out onto a floured surface and roll into a rectangle. Top with the onions. Roll the dough up tightly and slice thinly. Arrange, well-spaced, on a greased baking sheet and let rise for 30 minutes. • Preheat the oven to 350°F/180°C/gas 4. • Bake for about 20 minutes, or until golden brown.

■ INGREDIENTS

- ⅔ oz (20 g) fresh yeast or 1½ (¼-oz/7-g) packages active dry yeast
- 1 tablespoon sugar
- 1 cup (250 ml) hot water
- 2 cups (300 g) all-purpose (plain) flour
- 1 teaspoon salt
- 5 tablespoons butter
- 1 large egg, lightly beaten
- 4 large onions, finely sliced
- ½ teaspoon red pepper flakes

Right: Rustic spiced nut loaf

Seeded bread spirals

Serves: 10-12; Preparation: 35 minutes + 2 hours 30 minutes to rise; Cooking: 30 minutes; Level of difficulty: 3

Prepare the two doughs following the instructions on page 20. • Roll both doughs out separately into rectangles. Brush one of the rectangles with oil and top with the second rectangle. • Roll up the dough tightly. Slice 1 inch (2.5 cm) thick to form the spirals. Brush the outer edges of the spirals with milk and roll half in the sesame seeds and the other half in the poppy seeds. • Arrange the spirals, well-spaced, on an oiled baking sheet. Cover with a cloth and place in a warm place to rise for 1 hour, or until doubled in bulk. • Preheat the oven to 350°F/180°C/gas 4. • Bake for 15 minutes. Lower the oven temperature to 300°F/150°C/gas 2. • Bake for about 15 minutes more, or until well-risen and golden brown.

■ INGREDIENTS

- ½ quantity *Basic Bread Dough* (see page 20)
- ½ quantity *Basic Bread Dough* (see page 20), made with whole-wheat (wholemeal) flour
- 1 tablespoon extra-virgin olive oil
- 2 teaspoons milk
- 2 tablespoons sesame seeds
- 2 tablespoons poppy seeds

Parsley and onion bread

Serves: 8-10; Preparation: 45 minutes + 1 hour 20 minutes to rise; Cooking: 30 minutes; Level of difficulty: 2

Place the yeast and sugar in a small bowl with 6 tablespoons of water. Stir well and let rest for 10 minutes, or until foamy. • Sift the flour and salt into a large bowl. • Use a wooden spoon to gradually stir in the yeast mixture and 4 tablespoons of butter. Add enough milk to make a fairly soft dough. • Transfer to a lightly floured work surface and knead for 5–10 minutes, or until smooth and elastic. • Shape into a ball and place in an oiled bowl. Cover with a cloth and place in a warm place to rise for 1 hour, or until doubled in bulk. • Preheat the oven to 400°F/200°C/gas 6. • Sauté the onion, garlic, and parsley in the remaining butter in a large frying pan until the onion has softened. • Turn the dough out onto a floured surface and roll into a rectangle. • Spread with the onion mixture and roll up the dough tightly. Let rise for 20 minutes. • Bake for about 30 minutes, or until well-risen and golden brown. • Serve hot.

■ INGREDIENTS

- 1 oz (30 g) fresh yeast or 2 (¼-oz/7-g) packages active dry yeast
- 1 teaspoon sugar
- 4 tablespoons warm water
- 3½ cups (525 g) all-purpose (plain) flour
- 1 teaspoon salt
- 6 tablespoons butter
- 1 cup (250 ml) milk
- 1 small onion, finely chopped
- 1 clove garlic, finely chopped
- 1 tablespoon finely chopped parsley

Right: Seeded bread spirals

Dinner rolls

- ½ oz (15 g) fresh yeast or 1 (¼-oz/7-g) package active dry yeast
- ½ cup (100 g) sugar
- 1 cup (250 ml) warm milk
- 4 cups (600 g) all-purpose (plain) flour
- 1 teaspoon salt
- 2 large eggs, lightly beaten
- ½ cup (125 g) melted butter

Serves: 10-12; Preparation: 45 minutes + overnight to rise; Cooking: 15 minutes; Level of difficulty: 2

Place the yeast and 1 tablespoon sugar in a small bowl with 6 tablespoons of milk. Stir well and let rest for 10 minutes, or until foamy. • Sift the flour and salt into a large bowl. • Use a wooden spoon to gradually stir in the yeast mixture, eggs, and butter. Add enough remaining milk to make a soft dough. • Transfer to a lightly floured work surface and knead for 5–10 minutes, or until smooth and elastic. • Cover with a cloth and place in a warm place to rise overnight, or until doubled in bulk. • Preheat the oven to 375°F/190°C/gas 5. • Divide the dough into balls and arrange, well-spaced, on two greased baking sheets. • Bake for 12–15 minutes, or until well-risen and golden brown.

Raisin rolls

Serves: 8; Preparation: 10 minutes + 2 hours to rise; Cooking: 20 minutes; Level of difficulty: 1

Place the yeast in a small bowl with the milk. Stir well and let rest for 10 minutes, or until foamy. • Sift the flour into a large bowl. Stir in the oats. • Transfer to a lightly floured work surface and knead for 5–10 minutes, or until smooth and elastic. • Shape into a ball and place in an oiled bowl. Cover with a cloth and place in a warm place to rise for 1 hour, or until doubled in bulk. • Knead in the honey and raisins. Let rise for 1 hour. • Preheat the oven to 450°F/230°C/gas 8. • Divide the dough into 8 balls and arrange them, well spaced, on an oiled baking sheet. Brush with the egg yolk. • Bake for 20 minutes, or until well-risen and golden brown.

Thanksgiving favorites

Serves: 10-12; Preparation: 45 minutes + 1 hour 30 minutes to rise; Cooking: 20 minutes; Level of difficulty: 2

Place the yeast and 1 tablespoon sugar in a small bowl with 6 tablespoons of water. Stir well and let rest for 10 minutes, or until foamy. • Sift the flour and salt into a large bowl. • Use a wooden spoon to gradually stir in the yeast mixture, sweet potato purée, eggs, and butter. Add enough remaining water to form a soft dough. • Transfer to a lightly floured work surface and knead for 5–10 minutes, or until smooth and elastic. • Shape into a ball and place in an oiled bowl. Cover with a cloth and place in a warm place to rise for 1 hour, or until doubled in bulk. • Preheat the oven to 375°F/190°C/gas 5. • Punch down the dough and knead briefly. • Divide the dough into 20 balls and arrange, well-spaced, on a greased baking sheet. Let rise for 30 minutes. • Bake for about 20 minutes, or until well-risen and golden.

Left: *Raisin rolls*

Belgian raisin bread

- ⅔ oz (20 g) fresh yeast or 1½ (¼-oz/7-g) packages active dry yeast
- 1 cup (250 ml) warm milk
- 3⅓ cups (500 g) all-purpose (plain) flour
- ½ teaspoon salt
- ⅔ cup (180 g) butter
- ¾ cup (150 g) firmly packed dark brown sugar
- 2 large eggs
- 1⅓ cups (240 g) raisins
- ⅛ teaspoon ground cinnamon

Serves: 10-12; Preparation: 45 minutes + 2 hours to rise; Cooking: 1 hour; Level of difficulty: 2

Place the yeast in a small bowl with 4 tablespoons of the milk. Stir well and let rest for 10 minutes, or until foamy. • Sift the flour and salt into a large bowl. Use a wooden spoon to gradually stir in the yeast mixture, butter, brown sugar, eggs, raisins, and cinnamon. Add enough remaining milk to make a soft dough. • Transfer to a lightly floured work surface and knead for 5–10 minutes, or until smooth and elastic. • Shape into a ball and place in an oiled bowl. Cover with a cloth and place in a warm place to rise for 2 hours, or until doubled in bulk. • Preheat the oven to 400°F/200°C/gas 6. • Transfer the dough to a buttered baking sheet. • Bake for about 1 hour, or until well-risen and golden brown.

Chive rolls

- 1 oz (30 g) fresh yeast or 2 (¼-oz/7-g) packages active dry yeast
- ½ cup (100 g) sugar
- ½ cup (125 ml) warm water
- 4 cups (600 g) all-purpose (plain) flour
- 1 teaspoon salt
- 1 cup (250 ml) sour cream
- ½ cup (125 g) butter, melted
- 2 large eggs, lightly beaten
- 2 tablespoon finely chopped chives

Serves: 10-12; Preparation: 40 minutes + 1 hour to rise; Cooking: 20 minutes; Level of difficulty: 2

Place the yeast and 1 tablespoon sugar in a small bowl with 6 tablespoons of water. Stir well and let rest for 10 minutes, or until foamy. • Sift the flour and salt into a large bowl. Use a wooden spoon to gradually stir in the yeast mixture, sour cream, butter, eggs, and chives. Add enough remaining water to make a fairly soft dough. • Transfer to a lightly floured work surface and knead for 5–10 minutes, or until smooth and elastic. • Shape into a ball and place in an oiled bowl. Cover with a cloth and place in a warm place to rise for 1 hour, or until doubled in bulk. • Preheat the oven to 375°F/190°C/gas 5. • Turn the dough out onto a floured surface and knead for 2 minutes. • Divide the dough into about 25 balls and arrange them, well spaced, on oiled baking sheets. • Bake for about 20 minutes, or until golden brown.

Left: *Belgian raisin bread*

Viennese sweet bread

Serves: 8-10; Preparation: 45 minutes + 3 hours to rise; Cooking: 45 minutes; Level of difficulty: 2

Soak the raisins and candied peel in the rum in a small bowl for 15 minutes. • Drain. • Place the yeast and 1 teaspoon of sugar in a small bowl with 4 tablespoons of the milk. Stir well and let rest for 10 minutes, or until foamy. • Sift the flour and salt into a large bowl. • Use a wooden spoon to gradually stir in the yeast mixture, butter, egg yolks, the remaining sugar, and lemon zest. Add enough remaining milk to make a soft dough. • Transfer to a lightly floured work surface and knead for 5–10 minutes, or until smooth and elastic. • Beat the egg whites in a large bowl with an electric mixer at high speed until stiff peaks form. • Knead the egg whites into the dough with the raisins and candied peel. • Shape into a ball and place in an oiled bowl. Cover with a cloth and place in a warm place to rise for 2 hours, or until doubled in bulk. • Butter a fluted brioche pan. • Place the dough in the pan and let rise for 1 hour. • Preheat the oven to 375°F/190°C/gas 5. • Bake for about 45 minutes, or until well-risen and golden brown.

■ INGREDIENTS

- ½ cup (90 g) raisins
- 1 cup (100 g) diced candied citron peel
- 4 tablespoons dark rum
- ⅔ oz (20 g) fresh yeast or 1½ (¼-oz/7-g) packages active dry yeast
- ¾ cup (150 g) sugar
- 1 cup (250 ml) warm milk
- 3½ cups (500 g) all-purpose (plain) flour
- ⅛ teaspoon salt
- ½ cup (125 g) butter
- 5 large eggs, separated
- grated zest of 1 lemon

Italian ciabatta bread

Serves: 8-10; Preparation: 40 minutes + 19 hours and 30 minutes to rise; Cooking: 50 minutes; Level of difficulty: 3

Place the yeast in a small bowl with 4 tablespoons of the water. Stir well and let rest for 10 minutes, or until foamy. • Sift the flour into a large bowl. Use a wooden spoon to gradually stir in the yeast mixture and enough remaining water to make a dough. • Transfer to a lightly floured work surface and knead until smooth and elastic. • Shape into a ball and place in an oiled bowl. Cover with a cloth and place in a warm place to rise for 18 hours. • Turn the dough out onto a lightly floured surface. Make an indentation in the center. • Mix the honey in the remaining water. Knead the honey mixture into the dough until well blended. Place the dough on a baking sheet. Cover with plastic wrap (cling film) and let rise for 30 minutes. • Cover with a cloth and set aside for 1 hour. • Preheat the oven to 425°F/220°C/gas 7. • Bake for 10 minutes. Lower the oven temperature to 350°F/180°C/gas 4 and bake for 40 minutes more.

■ INGREDIENTS

- 1 oz (30 g) fresh yeast or 2 (¼-oz/7-g) packages active dry yeast
- 1½ cups (375 ml) + 1 tablespoon warm water
- 3⅓ cups (500 g) all-purpose (plain) flour
- ½ teaspoon natural or organic honey
- 1 teaspoon salt
- 4 tablespoons extra-virgin olive oil

Right: Viennese sweet bread

Golden raisin bread

Serves: 10; Preparation: 45 minutes + 1 hour 20 minutes to rise; Cooking: 20 minutes; Level of difficulty: 2

Place the yeast and 1 teaspoon of sugar in a small bowl with 6 tablespoons of the milk. Stir well and let rest for 10 minutes, or until foamy. • Sift the flour and salt into a large bowl. • Use a wooden spoon to gradually stir in the yeast mixture, raisins, remaining sugar, butter, and eggs. Add enough remaining milk to form a soft dough. • Transfer to a lightly floured work surface and knead for 5–10 minutes, or until smooth and elastic. • Drizzle the oil over the dough, wrap in plastic wrap (cling film), and place in a warm place to rise for 1 hour, or until doubled in bulk. • Preheat the oven to 425°F/220°C/gas 7. • Divide the dough into 10 balls and arrange, well-spaced, on a buttered baking sheet. Let rise for 20 minutes. • Bake for about 20 minutes, or until well-risen and browned.

■ INGREDIENTS

- 1 oz (30 g) fresh yeast or 2 (¼-oz/7-g) packages active dry yeast
- ⅓ cup (70 g) sugar
- ¾ cup (200 ml) warm milk
- 3⅓ cups (500 g) all-purpose (plain) flour
- ⅛ teaspoon salt
- 2 cups (360 g) golden raisins (sultanas), soaked in warm water for 1 hour and drained
- 3 tablespoons butter
- 2 large eggs
- 1 tablespoon extra-virgin olive oil

Almond and candied cherry bread

Serves: 12-14; Preparation: 45 minutes + 2 hours to rise; Cooking: 25 minutes; Level of difficulty: 2

Place the yeast and 1 teaspoon of sugar in a small bowl with the water. Stir well and let rest for 10 minutes, or until foamy. • Sift the flour and salt into a large bowl. • Use a wooden spoon to gradually stir in the yeast mixture, the remaining sugar, 4 tablespoons butter, and the eggs. Add enough milk to make a fairly soft dough. • Transfer to a lightly floured work surface and knead for 5–10 minutes, or until smooth and elastic. • Shape into a ball and place in an oiled bowl. Cover with a cloth and place in a warm place to rise for 2 hours, or until doubled in bulk. • Preheat the oven to 350°F/180°C/gas 4. • Beat the remaining butter in a medium bowl until creamy. Stir in the cherries, lemon peel, almonds, and almond extract. • Punch down the dough and turn out onto a floured surface. Roll into a rectangle and sprinkle with the cherry mixture. Roll up the dough tightly and cut in half lengthwise. Braid the two halves and join up the ends to form a ring. Transfer to a greased baking sheet. • Bake for about 25 minutes, or until well-risen and golden.

■ INGREDIENTS

- ½ oz (15 g) fresh yeast or 1 (¼-oz/7-g) package active dry yeast
- 3 tablespoons sugar
- 4 tablespoons warm water
- 3½ cups (525 g) all-purpose (plain) flour
- 1 teaspoon salt
- ½ cup (125 g) butter
- 2 large eggs, lightly beaten
- ½ cup (125 ml) milk
- 1 cup (100 g) chopped red candied cherries
- 1 cup (100 g) chopped green candied cherries
- 2 tablespoons diced lemon peel
- ½ cup (50 g) flaked almonds
- 1 teaspoon almond extract

Right: *Golden raisin bread*

French epiphany bread

Serves: 8-10; Preparation: 45 minutes + 3 hours to rise; Cooking: 1 hour; Level of difficulty: 2

Place the yeast with 1 teaspoon of sugar in a small bowl with the water. Stir well and let rest for 10 minutes, or until foamy. • Sift the flour and salt into a large bowl. • Use a wooden spoon to gradually stir in the yeast mixture, eggs, milk, butter, remaining sugar, and lemon zest. • Shape into a ball and place in an oiled bowl. Cover with a cloth and place in a warm place to rise for 2 hours, or until doubled in bulk. • Turn the dough out onto a floured surface and knead in the candied peel and almonds for 3 minutes. Roll into a large sausage 2½ inches (6 cm) in diameter. Join the ends to make a large ring shape and transfer to a greased baking sheet. Let rise for 1 hour. • Preheat the oven to 425°F/220°C/gas 7. • Bake for 55 minutes. • Remove from the oven and brush with milk. Sprinkle with the sugar and bake for 5 minutes, or until lightly browned and glossy.

INGREDIENTS

- 1 oz (30 g) fresh yeast or 2 (¼-oz/7-g) packages active dry yeast
- 1 cup (200 g) sugar
- 6 tablespoons warm water
- 3⅓ cups (500 g) all-purpose (plain) flour
- ⅛ teaspoon salt
- 3 large eggs, lightly beaten
- 1 cup (250 ml) warm milk
- 4 tablespoons butter
- finely grated zest of 1 lemon
- 1½ cups (150 g) coarsely chopped candied peel
- 1½ cups (150 g) coarsely chopped almonds
- 2 tablespoons milk, to glaze
- 2 tablespoons sugar, to glaze

Bread of the dead

This bread is traditionally served on November 2 in Mexico.

Serves: 10-12; Preparation: 45 minutes + 3 hours to rise; Cooking: 45 minutes; Level of difficulty: 2

Place the yeast with 1 teaspoon of sugar in a small bowl with the water. Stir well and let rest for 10 minutes, or until foamy. • Sift the flour and salt into a large bowl. • Use a wooden spoon to gradually stir in the yeast mixture, remaining sugar, orange juice, butter, milk, eggs, orange zest, and aniseed to make a soft dough. • Transfer to a lightly floured work surface and knead for 5–10 minutes, or until smooth and elastic. • Shape into a ball and place in an oiled bowl. Cover with a cloth and place in a warm place to rise for 2 hours, or until doubled in bulk. • Preheat the oven to 350°F/180°C/gas 4. • Punch down the dough and knead briefly. Transfer to a greased baking sheet and let rise for 1 hour. • Bake for 35–45 minutes, or until well-risen and golden brown.

INGREDIENTS

- 1 oz (30 g) fresh yeast or 2 (¼-oz/7-g) packages active dry yeast
- 4 tablespoons sugar
- 4 tablespoons warm water
- 3 cups (450 g) all-purpose (plain) flour
- ½ teaspoon salt
- 4 tablespoons orange juice
- 4 tablespoons butter
- 4 tablespoons milk
- 2 large eggs, lightly beaten
- 1 tablespoon finely grated orange zest
- 2 teaspoons ground aniseed

Right: French epiphany bread

Easter rolls

Serves 6-8; Preparation: 40 minutes + 2 hours rise; Cooking: 30 minutes; Level of difficulty: 2

Place the yeast in a small bowl with 6 tablespoons of the milk. Stir well and let rest for 10 minutes, or until foamy. • Sift the flour into a large bowl. Use a wooden spoon to gradually stir in the yeast mixture, eggs, sugar, butter, lemon zest, and raisins. Add enough remaining milk to make a soft dough. • Shape into a ball and place in an oiled bowl. Cover with a cloth and place in a warm place to rise for 2 hours, or until doubled in bulk. • Preheat the oven to 325°F/170°C/gas 3. • Turn the dough out onto a floured surface and knead for 3 minutes. • Set aside a small piece of dough. Divide the dough into about 6-8 pieces and roll each one into a roll. Roll out the reserved dough and cut into thin strips. Place two thin strips of dough in a cross on top of each roll. Arrange the rolls, well-spaced, on an oiled baking sheet. • Bake for about 30 minutes, or until well-risen and golden brown.

■ INGREDIENTS

- ⅔ oz (20 g) fresh yeast or 1½ (¼-oz/7-g) packages active dry yeast
- 1¾ cups (400 ml) warm milk
- 1⅔ cups (250 g) fine semolina flour
- 2 large eggs, lightly beaten
- ¼ cup (50 g) sugar
- 1 tablespoon butter
- finely grated zest of ½ lemon
- generous ¼ cup (50 g) golden raisins (sultanas), soaked in warm water for 1 hour and drained

Sesame-topped loaf

Serves: 10-12; Preparation: 40 minutes + 2 hours 30 minutes to rise; Cooking: 45 minutes; Level of difficulty: 2

Place the yeast and sugar in a small bowl with 6 tablespoons of the water. Stir well and let rest for 10 minutes, or until foamy. • Sift the flour into a large bowl. • Use a wooden spoon to gradually stir in the yeast mixture. Add enough remaining water to make a fairly soft dough. • Transfer to a lightly floured work surface and knead for 5–10 minutes, or until smooth and elastic. • Shape into a ball and place in an oiled bowl. Cover with a cloth and place in a warm place to rise for 2 hours, or until doubled in bulk. • Turn the dough out onto a floured surface and knead for 3 minutes. • Transfer to a greased baking sheet and let rise for 30 minutes. • Brush with the water and sprinkle with the sesame seeds. • Bake for about 45 minutes, or until well-risen and golden brown.

■ INGREDIENTS

- ½ oz (15 g) fresh yeast or 1 (¼-oz/7-g) package active dry yeast
- 1 teaspoon sugar
- 1 cup (250 ml) warm water
- 4 cups (600 g) all-purpose (plain) flour
- 1 tablespoon cold water
- 1 tablespoon sesame seeds

Right: *Easter rolls*

Hazelnut and cheese bread

■ INGREDIENTS

- 1 oz (30 g) fresh yeast or 2 (¼-oz/7-g) packages active dry yeast
- 1 teaspoon sugar
- 1 cup (250 ml) warm water
- 3⅓ cups (500 g) all-purpose (plain) flour
- 1½ cups (150 g) chopped hazelnuts
- 5 oz (150 g) pecorino or parmesan cheese, cut into small cubes
- 3 tablespoons extra-virgin olive oil
- 2 teaspoons salt
- freshly ground black pepper to taste

Serves: 6-8; Preparation: 45 minutes + 3 hours to rise; Cooking: 30 minutes; Level of difficulty: 2

Place the yeast and sugar in a small bowl with 6 tablespoons of the water. Stir well and let rest for 10 minutes, or until foamy. • Sift the flour into a large bowl. Use a wooden spoon to gradually stir in the yeast mixture, hazelnuts, cheese, oil, and salt and pepper. Add enough remaining water to make a soft dough. • Transfer to a lightly floured work surface and knead for 5–10 minutes, or until smooth and elastic. • Shape into a ball and place in an oiled bowl. Cover with a cloth and place in a warm place to rise for 2 hours, or until doubled in bulk. • Turn the dough out onto a floured surface and knead for 3 minutes. • Transfer the dough to an oiled 12-inch (30-cm) baking pan and let rise for 1 hour. • Preheat the oven to 450°F/230°C/gas 8. • Bake for 30 minutes, or until it sounds hollow when tapped on the bottom. • Serve warm with cheese.

Black bread

■ INGREDIENTS

- 1 oz (30 g) fresh yeast or 2 (¼-oz/7-g) packages active dry yeast
- 6 tablespoons dark corn (golden) syrup
- 1 cup (250 ml) warm water
- 5 cups (750 g) dark rye flour
- 2 teaspoons salt

Serves: 10-12; Preparation: 45 minutes + 3 hours to rise; Cooking: 35 minutes; Level of difficulty: 2

Place the yeast and corn syrup in a small bowl with 6 tablespoons of the water. Stir well and let rest for 10 minutes, or until foamy. • Sift the flour and salt into a large bowl. Use a wooden spoon to gradually stir in the yeast mixture. Add enough remaining water to make a fairly soft dough. • Transfer to a lightly floured work surface and knead for 5–10 minutes, or until smooth and elastic. • Shape into a ball and place in an oiled bowl. Cover with a cloth and place in a warm place to rise for 2 hours, or until doubled in bulk. • Turn the dough out onto a floured surface and knead for 3 minutes. • Oil a 9 x 5-inch (23 x 13-cm) loaf pan and place the dough in the pan. Let rise for 1 hour. • Preheat the oven to 350°F/180°C/gas 4. • Bake for about 35 minutes, or until well-risen and golden.

Left: Hazelnut and cheese bread

Bagels

Serves: 10-12; Preparation: 45 minutes + 1 hour to rise; Cooking: 30 minutes; Level of difficulty: 3

Place the yeast in a small bowl with the water and oil. Stir well and let rest for 10 minutes, or until foamy. • Sift the flour and salt into a large bowl. • Use a wooden spoon to gradually stir in the yeast mixture and sugar. • Transfer to a lightly floured work surface and knead for 5–10 minutes, or until smooth and elastic. • Shape into a ball and place in an oiled bowl. Cover with a cloth and place in a warm place to rise for 45 minutes, or until doubled in bulk. • Turn the dough out onto a floured surface and knead for 3 minutes. • Line two baking sheets with waxed paper. • Divide the dough into 24 balls. Press your thumb into the center of each ball to form rings. • Arrange the bagels on the baking sheets, cover with a cloth, and place in a warm place to rise for 15 minutes, or until doubled in bulk. • Preheat the oven to 400°F/200°C/gas 6. • Bring a large pot of water to a simmer. Cook the bagels, one at a time, in the water for 1 minute. Remove with a slotted spoon and return to the baking sheets. Cool for 5 minutes. • Brush with the beaten egg. • Bake for 20 minutes, or until golden brown.

INGREDIENTS

- 1 oz (30 g) fresh yeast or 2 (¼-oz/7-g) packages active dry yeast
- 1 cup (250 ml) warm water
- 2 tablespoons oil
- 3⅓ cups (500 g) all-purpose (plain) flour
- 2 teaspoons salt
- ¼ cup (50 g) sugar
- 1 large egg, lightly beaten, to glaze

French herb bread

Serves: 8-10; Preparation: 45 minutes + 1 hour 20 minutes to rise; Cooking: 20 minutes; Level of difficulty: 3

Place the yeast in a small bowl with 4 tablespoons of the water. Stir well and let rest for 10 minutes, or until foamy. • Sift the flour into a large bowl. • Use a wooden spoon to gradually stir in the yeast mixture and mixed herbs. Add enough remaining water to make a stiff dough. • Transfer to a lightly floured work surface and knead for 5–10 minutes, or until smooth and elastic. • Shape into a ball and place in an oiled bowl. Cover with a cloth and place in a warm place to rise for 1 hour, or until doubled in bulk. • Preheat the oven to 450°F/230°C/gas 8. • Punch the dough down and divide the dough in half. Transfer to two greased baking sheets. Brush with the oil and sprinkle with the salt. Let rise for 20 minutes. • Bake for about 20 minutes, or until golden.

INGREDIENTS

- ½ oz (15 g) fresh yeast or 1 (¼-oz/7-g) package active dry yeast
- 1½ cups (375 ml) warm water
- 4 cups (600 g) all-purpose (plain) flour
- 2 teaspoons dried basil
- 2 teaspoons dried thyme
- 2 teaspoons dried oregano
- 2 teaspoons dried rosemary
- 4 tablespoons extra-virgin olive oil
- 1 tablespoon coarse salt

Right: *Bagels*

Italian flatbread

Serve with cheese, tomatoes, and olives.

Serves: 6-8; Preparation: 25 minutes + 30 minutes to rest; Cooking: 15 minutes; Level of difficulty: 2

Sift the flour, baking soda, and salt into a large bowl. Shape into a mound and make a well in the center. Add the lard and 1 tablespoon of water. Gradually mix in the flour, adding enough water to make a firm dough. • Knead the dough on a clean, lightly floured work surface until smooth. Return to the bowl greased with oil and cover with a cloth. Set aside for 30 minutes. • Roll the dough out into a very thin sheet (less than ⅛ inch (3 mm) thick). • Cut out disks 6–8 inches (15–20 cm) in diameter. • Cook on a griddle or dry-fry in a very hot cast-iron frying pan, turning once, until lightly browned. • Serve very hot.

INGREDIENTS

- 3⅓ cups (500 g) all-purpose (plain) flour
- 1 teaspoon baking soda
- ¼ teaspoon salt
- 4 tablespoons lard, melted
- ¼ –½ cup (60–125 ml) warm water

Garbanzo bean bread with ricotta

Serves: 6-8; Preparation: 40 minutes + 2 hours 30 minutes; Cooking: 30 minutes; Level of difficulty: 2

Dough: Dissolve the yeast and sugar in 4 tablespoons of water and let rest for 15 minutes, until foamy. • Sift both flours and the salt into a large bowl. Mix in the yeast mixture, oil, and enough of the remaining water to make a stiff dough. Knead for 5–10 minutes, until smooth and elastic. Set aside to rise for 2 hours. • Oil four baking sheets. • Divide the dough in four and roll out thinly on a lightly floured surface. • Transfer to the prepared baking sheets. • Topping: Spread with the chopped tomatoes and season with salt. Let rise for 30 more minutes. • Preheat the oven to 450°F/220°C/gas 7. • Bake for 25 minutes. • Remove from the oven and spread with the ricotta. Sprinkle with the olives. Drizzle with the oil. • Bake for 5 more minutes. • Serve hot.

INGREDIENTS

DOUGH
- ½ oz (15 g) fresh yeast or 1 (¼-oz/7-g) package active dry yeast
- ½ teaspoon sugar
- 1¼ cups (310 ml) warm water
- 2⅔ cups (400 g) all-purpose (plain) flour
- ¾ cup (125 g) garbanzo bean (chickpea) flour
- ½–1 teaspoon salt
- 1 tablespoon olive oil

TOPPING
- ½ cup (125 ml) chopped tomatoes
- salt to taste
- ½ cup (125 g) ricotta cheese
- 1 cup (100 g) pitted black olives
- 1 tablespoon extra-virgin olive oil

Right: Italian flatbread

Index